O9-BTJ-576

The Gardener's A-Z Guide to Growing flowers from Seed to Bloom

Eileen Powell

Storey Publishing

For Cicely Angleton

With thanks for sharing her garden, her wisdom,
her joyful spirit, and her loving heart

The mission of Storey Publishing is to serve our customers by publishing practical information that encourages personal independence in harmony with the environment.

Edited by Gwen Steege, Marie Salter, and Barbara W. Ellis

Art direction by Cynthia McFarland

Cover design by Kent Lew

Text design by Kent Lew

Text production by Jennifer Jepson Smith

Line illustrations in Part 1 by Elayne Sears

Photography credits appear on pp 369–432. Abbreviations are as follows:

GBP: Global Book Publishing Pty. Ltd., Australia
HA: © Henry W. Art
IBC: International Bloembollen Centrum, Holland
JDS: © Joseph DeSciose
JP: © Jerry Pavia
MC: Macore, Inc.
SC: © Stacey Cyrus
SH: © Saxon Holt
VB: © Valleybrook International Ventures, Inc., Canada

Text copyright © 2004 by Eileen Powell

All rights reserved. No part of this book may be reproduced without written permission from the publisher, except by a reviewer who may quote brief passages or reproduce illustrations in a review with appropriate credits; nor may any part of this book be reproduced, stored in a retrieval system, or transmitted in any form or by any means — electronic, mechanical, photocopying, recording, or other — without written permission from the publisher.

The information in this book is true and complete to the best of our knowledge. All recommendations are made without guarantee on the part of the author or Storey Publishing. The author and publisher disclaim any liability in connection with the use of this information. For additional information please contact Storey Books, 210 MASS MoCA Way, North Adams, MA 01247.

Storey Books are available for special premium and promotional uses and for customized editions. For further information, please call 1-800-793-9396.

Printed in the United States by Von Hoffmann
10 9 8 7 6 5 4 3 2 1

Library of Congress Cataloging-in-Publication Data

Powell, Eileen, 1953–
The gardener's A–Z guide to growing flowers from seed to bloom / by Eileen Powell.
p. cm.
Includes index.
ISBN 1-58017-517-1 (pbk. : alk. paper)
1. Flower gardening. 2. Flowers. I. Title.
SB405 .P688 2004
635.9'03 — dc21

2003012603

Contents

Creating Successful Gardens

NEARLY 400 YEARS AGO, the British philosopher Frances Bacon declared that "knowledge is power." While *power* isn't a word we usually associate with gardening, most of us do long for a degree of control over our gardening activities that will lead to healthier plants and more glorious gardens. In the pages that follow, I hope you'll find the specific information you need to increase your knowledge and give you the power to become a more successful gardener.

My early gardening experience began with grand plans and little real knowledge. My first seed order included the most exotic plants in the catalog: *Eustoma, Rhodochiton, Cerinthe,* and, believe it or not, tree ferns. My seeds finally arrived in the mail. With great excitement, I tore open the envelope and out spilled a dozen small packets of seeds. Immediately I began scanning the packets, eager to find out how to begin growing my treasure. But instead of coming in typical, illustrated packets, with complete growing information, these unusual seeds were contained in generic envelopes, with the briefest of printed instructions: "HHA: Sow indoors in early spring; plant outdoors after all danger of frost has passed." How was that supposed to help me? It was like receiving a longed-for toy at Christmas, only to find that some assembly was required, but instructions were not included.

This book emerged out of the frustration I faced that year and many years after, whenever a new seed order arrived. I developed a ritual that included trips to the library, armfuls of books, seed packets, and catalogs spread around me on the floor, as I hunted down any information essential to tackle my seed starting with confidence. I wanted to know exactly when I should begin sowing the seeds, how deeply to plant them, how long they would take to germinate, and any special treatment they needed to ensure success. I carefully recorded my findings and personal observations on file cards. Fifteen years, and many successes and failures later, this book represents the results of my studies.

As well as having specific seed-starting requirements, every plant also has its own special needs when it comes to ongoing care. The closer you come to providing your plants with exactly the best conditions for their growth, the more successful your garden will be. You'll learn that a little pinching back at the right time makes a favorite plant bloom longer and more lavishly. You'll discover that many exotic plants you thought too cold sensitive for your area actually grow quite happily if you treat them as annuals; often they can be brought indoors for winter, and planted outdoors again as mature plants in spring. You'll learn it's quite easy to save seed of certain plants or take cuttings or divisions in order to expand the numbers of your garden plants at no cost and surprisingly little effort. Whether you start from seed or purchase seedlings, the A–Z of Garden Plants (Part 2) is a valuable resource for caring for your garden.

But caring for your plants properly is only half the challenge in creating a successful garden; equally important is each gardener's vision of the perfect garden. Many of us strive for a garden filled with color throughout the season, but many of our favorite perennial plants bloom for little more than a week. The charts in Part 4 are designed to provide invaluable help. As you struggle to fill gaps in your garden with plants that bloom at just the right time in just the right color — as well as being just the right height — choose the most important feature and run your finger down the appropriate column. In no time at all, you'll have many plants to choose from that fit your aesthetic needs, as well as your garden's environmental conditions. Refer to these charts for at-a-glance data on cold and heat tolerance, light and soil needs, bloom season, height, and flower color of more than 1,200 species of widely available plants. Color photos of many of these plants are shown in Part 3.

The resources, maps, and lists in the Appendix are additional, important partners in your search for knowledge. Most gardeners quickly come to realize the value of using a plant's botanic name in order to be sure they get the plant they want. A friend discovered this first-hand when, wanting a 'Goldenchain' tree, a small, charming tree no more than 15 feet tall, she mistakenly ordered a 'Goldenrain' tree, which is now 30 feet tall and still growing. The Common to Botanic Names list will help you pin down plants whose scientific name you do not already know. But scientific names can also be confusing, as ongoing research has resulted in plants being renamed or moved to a different genus. If you don't find a botanic name you may have seen in an old gardening book, check the Botanic Synonyms list to see if the name has been changed.

With knowledge at your fingertips, may power combine with the gentle art of gardening to help you achieve the garden of your dreams!

1 Starting from Seed

How often have you spotted in a gardening book or magazine a *Campanula* in the precise shade of blue that will transform your summer garden to perfection, only to discover that you simply can't buy the variety you want locally? Or, maybe you are planning an extravagant mass planting of petunias, impatiens, or marigolds, only to realize that the cost is prohibitive. What can you do? You either have to give up the idea or give in to the temptation to buy the greatest number of plants for the least amount of money, even though doing so often results in the purchase of plants of inferior quality.

Starting your own plants from seed can help you overcome these challenges and achieve your goal, whether it is to grow unusual, hard-to-find plants or to have dozens of healthy plants at an affordable price. Indeed, most gardeners are first prompted to venture down the seed-starting road by that great motivator, necessity.

Happily, unusual, exotic, or marginally hardy plants that you can't find at local nurseries are often available in seed form. And although mature plants that are finicky and difficult to grow from seed are generally expensive, buying these plants in seed form can make them affordable, and growing them will provide an interesting challenge. In addition, starting your own plants from seed helps to ensure that the plants in your magnificent display get the healthy start they need.

It Starts with One Little Seed . . .

Whether it makes more sense for you to start seedlings indoors or outdoors depends on the number of plants you want to grow, the amount of suitable space you have in your home, and the feasibility of dedicating space in your garden to seedbeds. Tending seedlings grown outdoors in a single bed that has been prepared specifically for that purpose is certainly simpler than hunting down individual containers scattered about the house. On the other hand, starting seed indoors provides you with hardy plants early in the season that you can move outdoors as soon as weather permits, giving you extra weeks of color in early spring.

You will probably have a significantly higher success rate if you start plants in the controlled environment of your home. The germination rate is markedly higher indoors than outdoors, and of those seeds that sprout outdoors some will likely be lost to extreme weather (torrential rain, unseasonably high or low temperatures) or wildlife (rambunctious dogs are particular culprits). It's also easy to mistake very young seedlings for weeds and to remove them or, conversely, to exercise so much caution that the seedlings are overwhelmed by weeds before you can confidently distinguish one from the other.

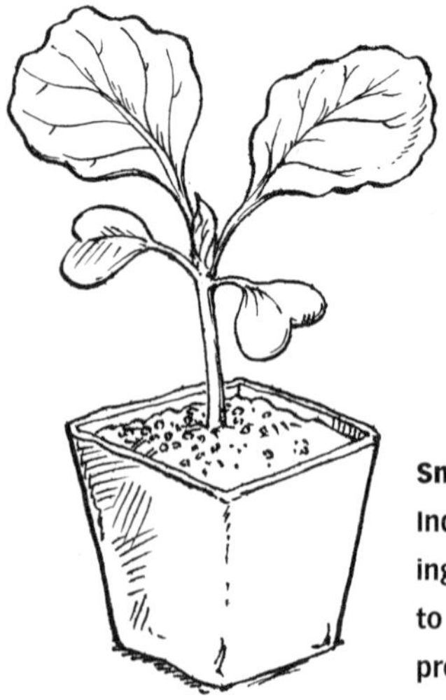

For most people, these reasons are sufficient motivators for filling a living room with trays of pungent black potting mix every winter and starting seeds indoors, but most compelling for me is the almost mystical pleasure this process brings. Why would I miss the wondrous emergence of a seedling by letting it happen outdoors in the garden, when I can watch with pleasure the entire miraculous show inside, in the comfort of my living room?

Small miracles. Indoor seed starting allows you to observe the process close up.

Some Plants May Decide for You

If the case for starting seeds indoors is so strong, you might wonder, why would anyone consider starting them outdoors? Like people, some seedlings can be temperamental, kicking up such a fuss at being transplanted that it is simply more prudent to start them outdoors. Annual poppies are a classic example of the reluctant emigrant: Even if you approach the task of transplanting poppies with the skill and care of a surgeon, these delicate creatures, when lifted from the soil, will promptly respond by wilting and dying. Also, if you don't have sufficient space in your house for numerous seed trays, starting seed outdoors will provide abundant blooms at considerably less cost than buying mature plants, although naturally you will have to wait a bit longer for them to flower.

Keep It Manageable

Before you start seed indoors, it pays to give careful consideration to two gardening essentials: available time and space.

Filling a few flats with growing medium, popping in the seeds, and standing back to watch the garden grow is not inordinately time-consuming and can be fun and rewarding. But the time required to care for even the most obliging seedlings multiplies as the number of seedlings increases, and some varieties require particularly close attention and precise care.

If you can accommodate one or two fussy varieties but feel that an entire crop of prima donnas is more than you want to take on, consider limiting the quantity of plants you start from seed, or perhaps be more discriminating in your choice of plants. If you don't have the time or inclination to coax difficult seeds to life or to coddle delicate young seedlings, you may prefer to grow the easier plants on your list from seed and to purchase the difficult ones from a nursery. (*Note:* In the individual plant entries in this book, seeds that require high maintenance are described as *difficult* in the Germinating/Requirements sections.)

The Mystery and Magic of Seeds

Seeds capable of germinating are termed *viable.* Some seeds are viable for only a short time and should be planted as soon as they are obtained, but most will retain a high degree of viability over long periods if kept chilled and dry. You can keep unused seeds for several years in a sealed container in the refrigerator. Be aware, however, that older seeds should be sown rather more liberally than usual, as the germination rate is likely to be considerably lower.

Dream On!

During the winter, "armchair" gardening can provide pleasures equal to outdoor gardening for enthusiasts who are temporarily unable to get their hands into the soil. It also can help you plan your garden.

Winter does not officially start for me until the first glossy garden catalog arrives at my door. When it does, I lose no time in beginning the long and pleasurable process of studying every entry. I urge you to gather together all of your catalogs, sink into a comfortable chair—preferably one with a view of the sleeping garden—and with bold felt-tip pen in hand circle any plant that strikes your fancy. At the end of this exercise in spontaneity, reason must prevail, of course, but recording everything your heart desires will help you form a clearer image of your dream garden. Your likes and loves can then be analyzed to good purpose and will help make your vision a reality.

A Taste of Reality

Study the plants you've highlighted to determine your overall preferences. Is your dream garden composed of delicate pastels? Vibrant primary colors? Succulents? Large, dramatic plants, or alpine miniatures? Will you need to provide a site for vines, water plants, shade lovers?

Having analyzed your wish list, take some time away from catalogs, then return with your feet firmly planted on the ground and a more deliberate eye, and try to determine which plants you'll actually select. You'll have to reject some plants because of their obvious unsuitability to your geographic location (with all the will in the world, you will never grow flourishing larkspurs in Florida or showstopping freesias in Maine). You may want to prune other plants from the list because your garden does not provide an appropriate habitat (abandon any thought of growing roses if your garden is permanently cloaked in heavy shade) or because, visually, the plant would appear out of place in your existing garden (it is impossible to gracefully incorporate a giant cactus into a cottage garden).

Other plants may need to be crossed off the list because the effort required to grow them from seed is out of proportion to the pleasure they will provide as mature plants. (I finally gave up growing *Eustoma* from seed for this reason.) There should be room in every garden for a few experimental plants, however, despite the unfavorable odds that they will flourish.

Time for Commitment

Having compiled a list of those plants you plan to grow from seed, fill in order forms without delay and send them on their way. The temptation will be great to dash to your local nursery with list in hand, intending to return with all of those precious seed packets so you can begin planting immediately. Resist the urge, as this route often leads to disappointment. Many of the seeds on which your heart is set and around which your grand scheme may revolve won't be available in the variety or color you have chosen. It takes a lot of character not to waver and purchase substitutes at this point, but if you weaken now, the garden will be a diluted version of your dream, one possibly accompanied by diminished enthusiasm.

You Get What You Pay For

Do not be tempted by "bargain" seeds, no matter how low the price. High-quality seed, which often costs more, is essential to successful growing. Seeds sold by a reputable seed dealer have been nurtured and handled in a manner that is conducive to success and will produce healthier plants.

When purchasing plants by mail it is a good idea to buy from nurseries in your geographic region whenever possible. Their stock will be best suited to your climate and soil type, and consequently more likely to thrive in your own garden. There are several useful websites where customers provide feedback on their experiences with specific mail-order nurseries. See page xxx in the Appendix for websites to check before making a purchase through the mail.

Do It Yourself: Collecting and Starting Your Own Seed

Collecting seed by hand can be fun and, if you're careful and lucky, a rewarding undertaking, but it is not a reliable source for many plants. So before investing any time, energy, or emotion attempting to collect and propagate seeds, determine whether your efforts might be successful. If a plant is particularly difficult to grow from seed, that information will be noted in the entries in Part 2, An A–Z of Garden Plants and alternative propagation methods will be suggested, such as dividing clumps or taking cuttings.

If you're still feeling optimistic, your first challenge will be to collect seed at precisely the correct time. For a seed to be viable, it must be completely ripe but not yet released by the plant. As seeds mature, the structures that contain them (e.g., pod, berry, or capsule) expand and change color — usually growing considerably darker, often changing to brown or black — and split open to reveal the seeds inside. Seeds, too, usually darken as they mature.

Once seeds have the appearance of maturity, break open an individual seed and look for the moist, white embryo that is an indication of ripeness. Remove individual seed capsules from plants or cut off entire stems containing seed heads. Spread the stems or capsules on paper-lined trays (white paper is best) and allow the seeds to dry completely in a warm, dry, sunny location. When fully dry, shake or gently rub the seeds onto the paper, removing any chaff or other debris. Store the seeds in the same manner you would store purchased seeds, keeping them in a sealed container in a cool place until sowing time.

Whereas most of the plants mentioned in this book can be propagated by seed, not all will develop into clones of their parents. In fact, if you try starting certain plants from seed, you may actually get some quite surprising results. This element of surprise can be intriguing or disappointing. (See page 12 for a more detailed discussion of how to predict a plant's appearance.) Hybrids are the least likely to resemble their parents, with only a limited range of plants, mainly annuals, coming true from seed.

A Warning about Wildflower Seed

Because many wildflowers are not available through nurseries or seed catalogs, they may seem like obvious targets for seed collection. Before collecting wildflower seed, however, contact your local native plant society, Audubon Society, or Cooperative Extension Service to determine whether the plant is endangered. Removing endangered plants from the wild is prohibited and the collection of seed may be restricted.

A Quick Lesson in Nomenclature

Predicting a plant's appearance is possible only when one understands the difference between a genus, a species, a variety, a cultivar, and a hybrid. Although the subject is a little more complicated than the following discussion suggests, these simple definitions are adequate for determining whether specific plants are likely to grow true from seed. (When a plant grows "true from seed," it bears all of the characteristics of the parent plant.) Of course, this information will be useful only if you have some means of determining the full name of the plant in question — a detailed plant marker in your neighbor's perennial garden, for example.

Genus. A group of species that are linked by common botanical characteristics. A genus may include only a single species or several hundred.

Species. For our purposes, *species* is defined as being equivalent to a person's first name — that is, the name that distinguishes him from his brothers, sisters, and cousins. In the case of plants, though, the names appear in the reverse order: The surname comes first. Rather than being called John Smith, for example, a plant is known as Smith John. In the plant name *Viola cornuta, Viola* is the genus or surname (equivalent of Smith) and *cornuta* the species or first name (equivalent of John).

A straight species—that is, a species that is not a form, variety, or cultivar—can be propagated from collected seed with certainty that the resulting plants will bear a close resemblance to their parents.

GENUS	SPECIES
Viola	*cornuta*

Form or variety. A naturally occurring variation from the straight species is called a *form* or *variety.* Often a variety will have a different flower color from the straight species. Incidentally, the word *variety* is frequently, and incorrectly, used interchangeably with the terms *species, cultivar,* and *hybrid.*

Forms and varieties *probably* will come true from seed.

	GENUS	SPECIES	FORM
	Dicentra	*spectabilis*	f. *alba*
or	*Dicentra*	*spectabilis*	*alba*

	GENUS	SPECIES	VARIETY
	Gentiana	*septemfida*	var. *lagodechiana*
or	*Gentiana*	*septemfida*	*lagodechiana*

Cultivar. When plants of the same species are bred by horticulturists or nurserymen to produce a distinct variation that has specific desirable characteristics (for example, bloom size or color), the resulting plant is called a *cultivar.* In other words, a cultivar is a variety (as defined previously) that has been engineered by humans. The name of the cultivar appears in single quotes after the name of the species. Although the outcome is not guaranteed, there is a good chance that a cultivar will come true (or nearly true) from seed. If you have your heart set on an exact duplicate of the parent, however, you should use an asexual method of reproduction (see pages 33–36).

GENUS	SPECIES	CULTIVAR
Boltonia	*asteroides*	'Pink Beauty'

Hybrid. A man-made cross between different species within a genus or even different *genera* (the plural of genus). A cultivar, by contrast, is bred from within only one species. The hybrid condition is denoted by an ×, either before or in the middle of the plant's name. Hybrids rarely come true from seed.

	GENUS	HYBRID	SPECIES
	Pelargonium	×	*domesticum*

	HYBRID	GENUS	SPECIES
or	×	*Heucherella*	*alba*

Purchasing hybrid seeds from a reputable seed dealer is the only way to ensure that you'll get the plant you want.

When you're ready to propagate seed you've collected, do so with a spirit of experimentation, starting a small number of plants indoors or a more extensive crop in an out-of-the-way corner of the garden, possibly with the vegetables or in a cutting bed. Successful plants can then be transplanted to your main beds and less attractive ones committed to the compost heap. If any particularly successful plants result, propagate them by division or take cuttings to obtain a true clone.

Starting Seed Indoors

Finding suitable space to devote to flats of seedlings for several months can be a challenge, but with a little creative thinking and perhaps some rearranging of furniture, anything is possible. Seedlings can be grown in a sunny window, but the sturdiest plants are grown under artificial lights (see below and pages 20–21). This is good news, because it allows for tremendous flexibility.

Plan Ahead

When considering potential locations for seed flats, keep in mind that few things are more irresistible to a cat than a tray of soil in an out-of-the way corner. In addition, children have been known to harvest unattended crops prematurely and with much less care than adults might use.

Where space is limited, consider purchasing an inexpensive shelving unit, one that can be assembled and dismantled easily and outfitted with fluorescent lights; it might provide sufficient space for all of your flats. When not using it, simply disassemble the unit and store it in an attic, in the garage, or under a bed.

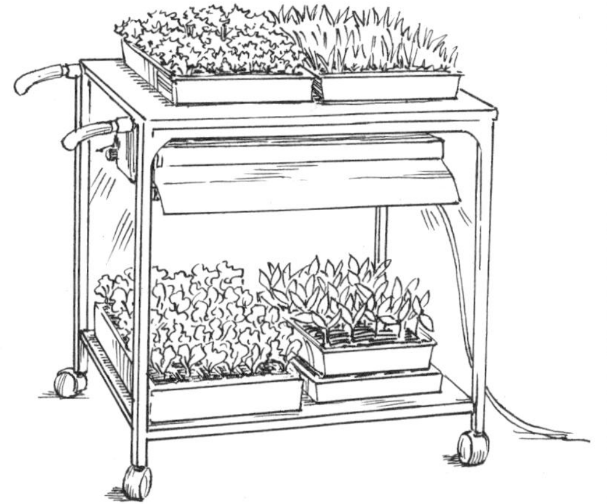

Portable seed starting. A two-tiered trolley, with lighting below, is ideal as a growing platform.

A two-tiered trolley is another good storage option (an old-fashioned drinks trolley works well). It can be loaded with flats, which then become conveniently mobile. Simply move the trolley away from a sunny window during the hottest part of the day and wheel it back when the sun has moved. A fluorescent light will be needed for plants on the lower tier.

Any free space on any shelf could potentially house flats: bookcases, kitchen cabinets, the space above kitchen cabinets, bedroom closets, laundry room counters, workshop tables. If natural light is insufficient, simply hang fluorescent lights above the growing space.

Container Savvy

Suitable planting containers come in all shapes and sizes. The only absolute requirements are that the vessels be scrupulously clean and that they afford proper drainage. The two main styles of container in which seeds can be planted are seed trays and individual seed pots.

Seed trays have a number of advantages over individual pots. They are less expensive, take up less space, and are quicker to use if you are doing mass plantings of a single variety. But if you are growing plants that resent root disturbance, individual pots are the better choice. When it's time to transplant seedlings grown in pots, you can simply lift the plant out of its pot with the root-ball intact, and almost no root disturbance takes place. If peat pots or other porous or degradable containers have been used, the plant goes right in the ground, pot and all.

Seed trays. Known also as *flats,* seed trays allow seedlings to grow communally, sharing growing medium and eventually mingling roots. Acceptable alternatives to store-bought plastic seed trays include:

- *Shallow wooden boxes* with slats spaced at least ⅛ inch apart to allow proper drainage.
- *Clay flower pots.* New clay pots should be soaked in water for several days. Place a layer of broken pottery, small pebbles, or a clean coffee filter in the bottom of the pot to permit free drainage and to prevent the growing medium from spilling out through the drainage holes.
- *The bottom of a plastic 1-gallon milk jug.* Use scissors or a utility knife to cut off the bottom 2 inches of the jug, then punch drainage holes from the inside through the bottom.
- *The bottom of a large plastic bucket.* As for the milk jug, cut off the bottom 2 inches of the bucket, then punch drainage holes from the inside through the bottom. Local delicatessens may be a good source of these buckets.
- *A cardboard milk or juice carton.* Staple the top shut and remove one side panel to form an oblong trough. Punch drainage holes in the bottom.

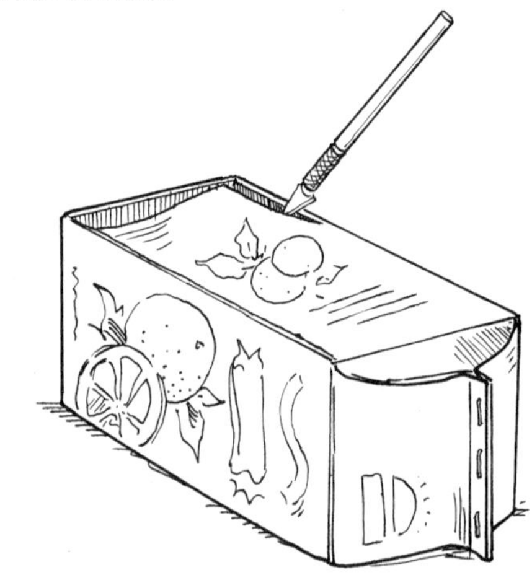

Recycled container. Milk or juice cartons make excellent plant flats.

Individual containers. Separate seed starters provide each seed with its own small ball of soil. The container may be a single, such as an old yogurt tub, or a multiple, like an egg carton. Options include:

- *Plastic "market packs,"* either newly purchased or recycled. Used ones may be available from helpful local garden centers, but these must be thoroughly cleaned before use.

Manufactured peat pots. Although more expensive than homemade containers, these have the advantage of carrying a seedling through its entire life before planting, thereby reducing work for you and transplant shock for the plant.

Two-inch plastic or clay flowerpots. If pots have been used previously, clean them thoroughly with a solution of 9 parts water to 1 part household bleach.

Yogurt or similar-size containers with drainage holes punched in the bottom.

Egg cartons, either cardboard or foam. Punch several holes in the bottom of each compartment and place the lid underneath the container as a drainage tray. Egg cartons should be used only for very small seeds, such as loberias.

Individual pots made from newspaper or paper bags. Put three layers of paper together and cut a 9-inch square. With a pencil, divide the square into thirds, vertically and horizontally, creating a tic-tac-toe grid. Make four cuts as shown in the diagram (below left), fold up flaps, and secure with staples or tape. This creates an individual 3-inch pot that can be planted directly in the ground and so is especially useful for seedlings that prefer not to have their roots disturbed.

Paper pots. With a few snips and folds, you can make a sturdy seed starter from several thicknesses of newspaper.

A paper pot. A less elaborate cylindrical pot can be fashioned from paper. Cut a length of paper the desired height (usually 2 or 3 inches) and about 8 inches long. Form a cylinder and attach the ends with glue or tape; this yields a bottomless container. Stand cylinders upright, side by side, in a tray that has sides high enough to provide support. Fill each cylinder with growing medium, firm the soil lightly, and sow.

Cardboard pots. Make cylindrical pots from the cardboard tubes of paper towels, wrapping paper, or toilet paper by cutting them to 2 or 3 inches tall.

Other options. Many products are easier and usually neater to use than the traditional seed-starting alternatives. For instance, you can buy individual peat pellets that expand when moistened, or Styrofoam cell packs that contain a dry compressed growing medium. These items can be rather expensive but are fun to experiment with.

Preparing the Growing Medium

As with many things in life, the preparation of a growing medium can be as simple or as complicated as you choose to make it. If you like things simple, purchase a bag of ready-mixed growing medium and proceed to sow. If you want to concoct your own surefire super-soil, on the other hand, be prepared to draw on your knowledge of chemistry, alchemy, even sorcery (see below). In my experience, however, the simpler method is usually quite successful.

Seedlings are often started in a soilless, nutrient-free medium, because an overabundance of nutrients is detrimental to plants in the very early stages of life. Seeds started in such a medium (generally labeled *seed-starting mix*) will require either frequent feeding in later life or transplanting to a container with a nutrient-rich, soil-based medium. Seeds started in individual containers should be sowed in a soil-based mixture that will sustain the plant throughout its life indoors. A good commercial potting soil mixed with a lighter substance (such as vermiculite) will suffice for this purpose. These seedlings can remain in the same container until they are ready to be transplanted outdoors.

Preparing the Seeds

Most seeds can be sown straight from the packet, but occasionally the seed casings are so tough that they need to be chipped or soaked before planting to hasten germination. (*Note:* In this book, if chipping or soaking is necessary, it is specified in the Germinating/Requirements section of the individual plant entries.)

Chipping (also called *scarification*) is the process of removing a small sliver from the end of a seed, using a sharp knife.

Soaking seeds in warm water, usually for 24 hours, helps soften seed cases, thereby facilitating speedy germination.

In addition, some seeds require a period of cold, known as *cold stratification,* to germinate. This can be accomplished by refrigerating the seeds for a specified period. Larger seeds can be

So You Want to Make Your Own

The essential qualities of a growing medium are that it drains freely, is disease-free, and is not too high in nutrients. Acceptable home-mixed growing mediums include the following:

- A combination of one-half vermiculite or perlite and one-half sphagnum peat (measure by volume, not weight). Seedlings that are grown on in this medium (that is, seedlings that will *not* be transplanted to a larger container before planting outdoors) will require frequent feeding.
- Equal quantities of good garden soil (if your own soil is less than perfect, purchase a bag of pasteurized potting soil); clean, coarse sand (often called *builders' sand,* it can be purchased at hardware and lumber stores; don't buy the much finer playground sand, which is unsuitable for soil mixes); and peat moss. Sterilize garden soil by spreading it in a shallow pan and baking it at 275°F for at least 30 minutes. (*Warning:* Baking soil smells *bad.*) Purchased soil does not need to be sterilized. If you have any doubts as to whether a growing medium will drain well, put a layer of coarse sand in the bottom of the container. Less frequent feeding will be required using this soil-based mix.

With the addition of nutrients (1 teaspoon ground limestone per quart plus 1 teaspoon bonemeal), both of the above homemade growing mediums will provide a suitable environment for seedlings throughout their indoor life. After three true leaves have appeared, feed regularly with a liquid fertilizer (see page 23, Step 6).

Note: Succulents, orchids, wildflowers, and others may require a specialized soil mixture, which can be purchased ready-mixed.

refrigerated before sowing, but it is usually easiest to sow tiny seeds before they're refrigerated. Sowing methods and refrigeration length are given in the Germinating/Requirements section of the individual plant entries.

Sowing the Seeds

Preparing seed trays for sowing is a most satisfying task, in many ways akin to baking. First assemble the ingredients, then measure and mix, and finally pour the "batter" — that is, the growing medium — into the prepared containers. With a little care, this need not be a messy job.

Step 1: Preparing the Containers To avoid the possibility of exposing seedlings to disease, sanitize all containers with a solution of 9 parts water to 1 part household bleach. Diligently scrub containers that have held plants in the past, as disease can cling to even small particles of soil left in a container. Water must be able to drain freely from containers or the soil will become waterlogged, drowning roots and fostering fungal diseases. Use an ice pick, pencil point, or tapestry needle to punch drainage holes in the container bottom. To prevent the growing medium from slipping through the drainage holes, line the bottom with a layer of newspaper cut to fit it neatly.

Step 2: Preparing the Growing Medium Dry soilless growing mediums are almost impossible to moisten through normal watering and must be dampened thoroughly *before* seeds are sown. Fill a plastic bag halfway with the growing medium and add water at the rate of about 1 part water to 4 parts soil. Squeeze the bag gently until the water is evenly incorporated. The medium should be damp but not wet. Squeeze out any excess water.

Step 3: Filling the Containers If you plan to transplant the seedlings that you start in flats to more spacious quarters before moving them outdoors, sow them in a nutrient-free growing medium. If you prefer to keep seedlings in the same container or flat until they are moved outdoors, use a richer, soil-based medium (for example, potting soil mixed with vermiculite), which will provide nutrients to the seedlings throughout their indoor life. You may also want to add a layer of sand or other porous material, such as pea gravel or perlite, to the bottoms of these containers to ensure perfect drainage.

Fill the containers, distributing soil evenly. Tamp the soil lightly and top up, keeping the final soil level about ½ inch below the rim of large pots and ¼ inch below the rim of small or shallow containers. Use a spoon to fill market packs and tap the packs lightly on a flat surface to settle the soil.

Settling in. Use a flat board to lightly tamp the surface.

Step 4: Sowing the Seeds Eliminate potential confusion by sowing only one variety of seed per container, if possible. If you do sow more than one kind in a container, combine only those that have similar requirements for germination and that will emerge at roughly the same time.

Sowing Depth

- *As a general rule,* seeds should be covered with soil to three times their diameter.
- *Very small seeds* can be mixed in with just a little fine sand to facilitate even distribution on the soil surface.
- *Small to medium seeds* can be sprinkled directly from the packet onto the soil, or you can shake the seeds from the packet onto your palm and sow them individually. If the seeds require covering, scatter a fine layer of growing medium over them.
- *Large seeds* can either be sown individually in rows in a tray or sown one per small pot.
- *Very large seeds* (for example, beans) should be sown in individual pots.
- *Seedlings that object to root disturbance* should be started in biodegradable pots that can be planted directly into the ground (for instance, peat pots). (*Note:* If transplanting is particularly stressful to a plant, this is noted in the individual plant listings.)

Step 5: Labeling the Containers As you sow, label each container with the variety of seed, date planted, and the range of dates when you might expect germination. Also mark the germination dates on a calendar; if you are growing a variety of plants, this will make your life much easier.

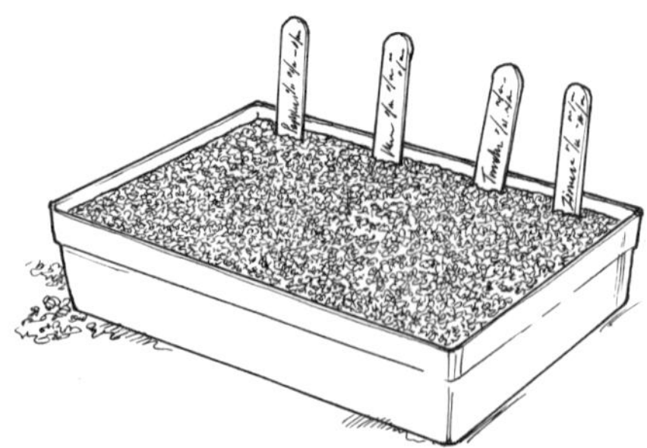

Name recognition. Don't forget to label each container.

Step 6: Watering the Seeds Premoistened growing medium should not need additional watering at this point. If watering is required, however, stand each container in a tray of water, removing it and allowing it to drain when the soil surface appears damp. If you plan to use a fungicide to deter damping-off (see page 20), do so now.

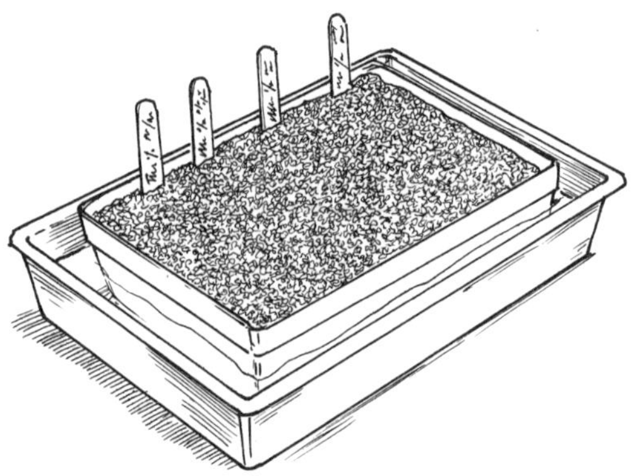

Gentle watering. Place seed-starting container in a pan of water to moisten the soil from below.

Step 7: Covering the Containers Cover containers with a piece of glass or plastic wrap, or place each inside a plastic bag and secure in a manner that will keep out air but will allow for easy access to check the progress of germina-

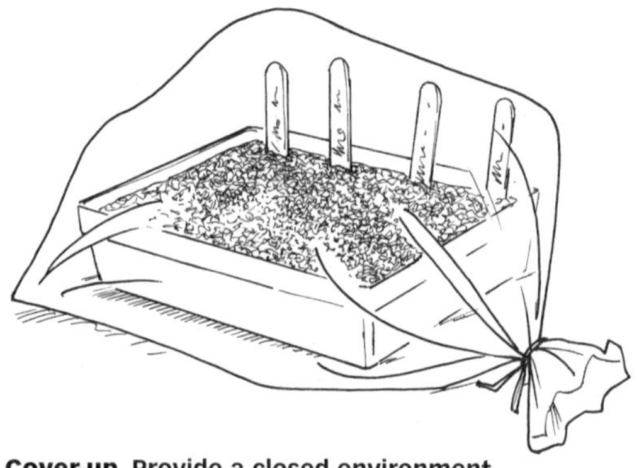

Cover-up. Provide a closed environment by covering containers with plastic or glass.

tion. The plastic bags that newspapers are delivered in on rainy days are ideal for individual pots, but any clear plastic bag will do.

Waiting for Germination

If the seeds require darkness to germinate, drape the containers with an opaque cover such as newspaper, cardboard, or aluminum foil, or simply place them in a closet or in any dark, safe location that can be kept at a suitable temperature. Place those that require light in a bright location that does not receive direct sunlight. A temperature of 65°–70°F suits most seeds; all perform best if the temperature is constant. A moderate amount of bottom heat speeds germination considerably but it is not necessary. (*Note:* Light and temperature requirements of seeds are specified in the individual plant entries in Part 2.)

Getting the Watering Right

If the growing medium was moistened sufficiently before sowing, additional watering probably won't be necessary until the seeds have germinated. But do check the containers regularly for signs of dryness; once either a seed or a seedling has been allowed to dry out completely, it can never be revived.

To moisten, place the entire container in a tray of water, then allow it to drain once the soil surface appears damp. Do not allow containers to stand in water longer than it takes to moisten the soil surface. Alternatively, mist the soil gently from above.

A more modern and efficient method of watering seedlings is through *capillary matting.* Capillary matting is a highly absorbent, relatively inexpensive fabric that, in effect, does your watering for you. Stretch out the fabric and soak it thoroughly or immerse one end in a reservoir of water. Press seed trays or individual pots firmly onto the matting, and *voilà!* The soil will absorb as much water as it needs — no more, no less — which keeps you from overwatering or underwatering. If it is inconvenient to place a reservoir near the matting, simply moisten the fabric periodically, ensuring that it never becomes dry. If algae appear on the mat, remove the mat immediately and soak it for 30 minutes in water and laundry detergent. Rinse repeatedly until the water runs clear, then reposition the trays.

Efficient watering. A capillary mat system ensures even, adequate watering.

Caring for the Babies

When you see the first signs of life — a few green crooks nosing their way out of the soil — it's time to give the seedlings some fresh air.

A breath of fresh air. Expose seedlings to air gradually after they emerge.

Dealing with Damping-Off

If you find seedlings lying prone on the soil with the leaves green but the base of the stems blackened and shriveled, they have probably fallen victim to damping-off. *Damping-off* is a sickening fungal disease, marked by wilting or rotting, that can wipe out every seedling in a flat in less than a day. Damping-off can strike at any stage in a young plant's development and is usually due to excess moisture combined with a lack of ventilation. Just one experience with damping-off will instill in you a lifelong dread of the disease. Extreme caution is a small price to pay to avoid a visit from this grim reaper.

How to Avoid It

- Sterilize all seed containers and any instruments you use for the sowing process (see page 17).
- Use only a sterile growing medium, such as vermiculite or sterilized soil (see pages 15–16).
- Before sowing, thoroughly moisten the growing medium in seed trays with a commercial fungicide, preferably an organic product.
- Sow seeds thinly to promote healthy air circulation among seedlings. Promptly thin overcrowded containers as seedlings emerge.
- Water seed trays from below. When growing plants that are particularly susceptible to damping-off, keep soil on the dry side.
- Damping-off can be stimulated by the presence of nitrogen. Always allow seedlings to develop three true leaves before using fertilizer.

What to Do If You Detect It

- If even one seedling exhibits signs of damping-off, immediately remove it and neighboring seedlings from the container.
- If the soil appears to be too moist, move the containers away from other plants to increase air circulation, and place an absorbent material on the soil surface. Crushed charcoal is most effective for this purpose, but paper towels can also be used in a pinch.
- Once the soil has dried out sufficiently, return the containers to their regular location and resume cautious watering — only from below.

Be careful to expose seedlings to air only gradually, however, for if air is allowed to enter too suddenly, damping-off might occur.

Completely remove any opaque coverings. Next, lift a corner of the plastic or glass to allow a little air to reach the seedlings. If plastic was used, punch a few holes in it to allow controlled amounts of air into the miniature greenhouse. Increase the space of the opening or punch additional holes in the plastic every few hours; the entire process should take about a day.

Light and Temperature

Sturdy plants are produced at moderate temperatures. When seeds have germinated, most will prefer a constant temperature of about 60°F. Sufficient light is also essential for strong, healthy development of seedlings. When seedlings have sprouted, place their containers in a bright location but not in strong sunlight. Although a south-facing window will do, it is not ideal. Plants that have been grown in a sunny window may become spindly because they have received too much heat in relation to light. Also, without added insulation, the nighttime temperature next to windows may drop too drastically for the plants' liking.

If your windows fail to provide ideal light and temperature or adequate sill space for your embryonic garden, consider moving containers elsewhere and installing fluorescent lights. Cool-white 40-watt fluorescent bulbs are sufficient for starting seeds indoors. Grow lights, which are considerably more expensive, are necessary only when plants are intended to flower and fruit indoors.

Fluorescent lights should hang 3 to 4 inches above seedlings and should be left on for about 15 hours a day. Plants grown under fluorescent lights require more frequent watering and feeding than those grown in natural light.

Let there be light. Fluorescent bulbs hung over seed trays get plants off to a healthy start.

As they mature and strengthen, seedlings growing in natural light should gradually be moved into more direct sunlight but should always be protected from direct midday sun.

Water Wisely

Check the soil frequently for signs of dryness. When the soil surface appears dry, stand the seedling pots in a larger container filled with tepid water until the surface of the mixture is moist, then allow the container to drain. Alternatively, you can moisten the soil by misting it well. On an unusually hot spring day, the soil may need moistening more than once a day, but take particular care not to overwater. Always water young plants in the morning rather than in the evening.

Food for Thought

Before true leaves appear on your seedlings, the plants will put out *cotyledons*, usually one pair. These are similar in appearance to true leaves but contain sufficient nutrients to both nourish the seed and sustain the young seedling for a short time. As soon as the plant has developed three true leaves, *you* are the responsible party for providing additional nutrients to the seedling.

Feed seedlings growing in a rich, soil-based medium with a liquid fertilizer at half the rate recommended by the manufacturer. Apply this weak solution twice weekly for the first 3 weeks, then use a full-strength fertilizer about every 10 days.

You will transplant seedlings that have been started in a nutrient-free medium normally before fertilizing becomes necessary (see Care of Young Seedlings, below). If for any reason transplanting is delayed beyond the appearance of the first three true leaves (sometimes the real world interferes, even with gardening), feed the seedlings with a half-strength solution twice weekly until they are transplanted. Feed only *after* watering.

Care of Young Seedlings

As soon as the first pair of true leaves has developed, seedlings should be given more space. Delaying transplanting until the seedling has two pairs of leaves is unwise, for by then the stem will be considerably longer and more prone to breakage or damage. Likewise, seedlings that have been allowed to grow freely before thinning or transplanting will become spindly, weak, and more susceptible to disease.

Seedlings can be thinned or transplanted to individual pots, which is known as *pricking out*. The goal should be to provide each plant with satisfactory air circulation and space sufficient for strong and healthy development.

Thinning

Seedlings grown from very fine seeds that have been scattered on the surface of a flat will probably require thinning before they are large enough to be handled easily. Pulling up unwanted plants by the roots is the butcher's way of performing this operation and will result in disturbance of neighboring plants and possible root damage. The safest way to thin is by carefully snipping off unwanted plants at soil level with small, sharp scissors, thereby leaving all roots undisturbed. Thin to one plant every 1½ to 2 inches.

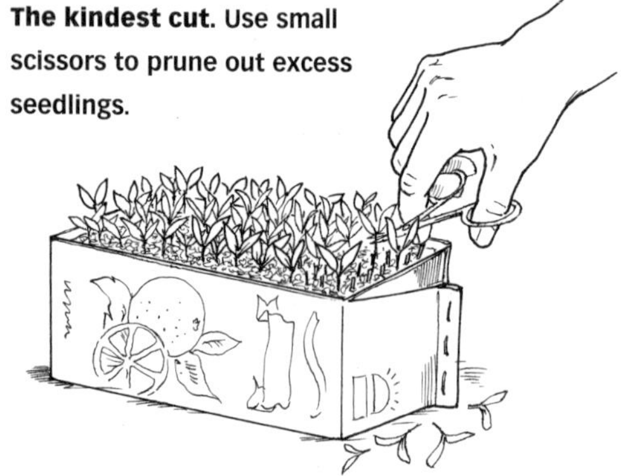

The kindest cut. Use small scissors to prune out excess seedlings.

Pricking Out

Pricking out is a wonderfully delicate operation, similar in many respects to fine needlework, in that it requires nimble fingers, careful attention, and patience. The work should be performed at a table where you have plenty of space and at a time when you will not be rushed.

Step 1: Selecting Containers Choose containers that will hold sufficient soil for the mature seedlings, and prepare containers as for sowing (see page 17). Generally, a plant grown from a large seed, such as a morning glory, will require far more space than that grown from a tiny seed, such as a lobelia. Line containers with a layer of newspaper neatly cut to fit the container. A thin layer of a porous material (e.g., sand or perlite) can be added next to promote drainage. Fill the containers — either flats or individual pots — with a nutrient-rich growing medium to ½ inch below the rim. Tamp the soil, top up, then tamp again.

Step 2: Pricking Out Seedlings Prick out seedlings by gently loosening a small clump of them with a knife, fork, or small stick. Using a pencil as a dibble (hole maker), in the new container make one small planting hole for each seedling. If you are transplanting to flats, space the holes about 1½ to 2 inches apart; if you are trans-

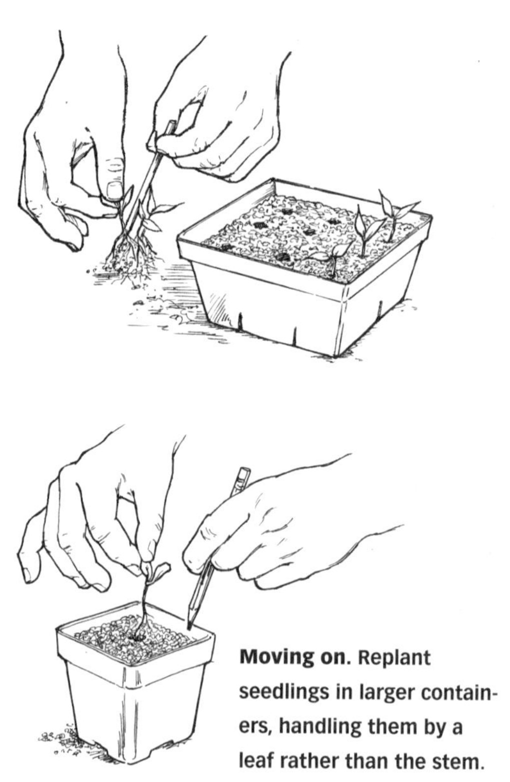

Moving on. Replant seedlings in larger containers, handling them by a leaf rather than the stem.

planting to individual containers, use a separate container for each individual seedling. Carefully separate individual seedlings from the clump and plant one per hole, positioning each so it sits at the same level in the soil as it did before transplanting. With a pencil, tamp lightly around each seedling. Seedlings that have been started in small individual containers should be moved to larger containers with as much of the root-ball intact as possible.

Step 3: Moistening the Soil Moisten the soil by placing the containers in a shallow dish of tepid water and allowing the water to be absorbed slowly, or thoroughly moisten the soil using a mister. Label the containers with the name of the plant variety and the date when seedlings can be safely planted out.

Step 4: Shielding from Light For about 24 hours after transplanting, do not place seedlings in direct sunlight or under fluorescent light. If the plants still show signs of stress (wilting or pale color) after one day, ensure that the soil is moist. Water from below or mist the soil if necessary, and keep containers out of direct light until the seedlings have perked up. Stressed seedlings will not grow vigorously.

Step 5: Water Consistently To water, mist the soil. This is perhaps the most prudent watering method in the early days after transplanting, especially when dealing with tiny seedlings. In warm, sunny locations, the soil may require moistening twice a day, and small containers will require more frequent watering than large ones. Once plants are sturdier, they can be watered carefully from above or by standing containers in water so it can be absorbed from below. At this stage, the soil will probably require moistening no more than once or twice a week, but be vigilant, continuing to check the soil daily, and watering mornings rather than evenings.

Step 6: Feeding the Plants Feed plants only *after* watering. For the first 3 weeks after transplanting seedlings, apply a half-strength fertilizer twice a week. After this, a full-strength fertilizer can be applied every 10 to 14 days. You might like to make a note on the calendar to remind yourself when to fertilize.

Preparing Seedlings for Outdoors

Most annuals and perennials can safely be planted outdoors after the last expected frost date (see map on page 501), and many perennials will not object to being planted out a week or two earlier. But some plants are best kept inside until the soil is thoroughly warm, as chilly weather and cold soil will stunt their growth. (Before planting outdoors, review each plant's transplanting preference, as listed in the individual plant entries in this book.)

Hardening off. Plants grown from seed indoors need to be "hardened off" before being planted in the garden. This process gradually exposes young plants to the harsher, more extreme outdoor environment and is necessary to reduce transplant shock. It also results in plants that are more adaptable and that will resume growth more quickly when planted in the garden. Whether planted outdoors in spring or in autumn, seedlings require hardening off.

About 2 weeks before transplanting time, diminish watering slightly and cease feeding altogether. At this time, plants that are growing in flats may be divided by cutting through the soil with a knife, leaving each plant with its own square root-ball; leave these divided plants in their flats until they are planted out.

Begin acclimatizing plants to the outdoors on a mild, windless day, approximately 1 week before they are due to be transplanted. Place containers outdoors in a sheltered spot in filtered light — the shade of a large tree or porch, or the area against a north-facing wall is ideal. Leave containers outside for about half a day before bringing them back indoors. Each day for a week, leave seedlings outside for progressively longer and in a progressively more exposed location. By week's end, they will be outside all day and all night in conditions similar to those they will experience in their new home.

Getting ready to grow. In preparation for planting outdoors, cut around seedlings started in flats.

Starting Ferns from Spores

Ferns can be reproduced in large quantity from *spores,* the fern's version of a seed. Spores are minuscule and are produced by the million. Propagating from spores is fun and highly satisfying. They do require care, however, as the dustlike spores thrive only in the warm, moist conditions that foster molds, so they are particularly prone to fungal diseases. Also, many will take up to 1 year to germinate, so they require patience and a serious commitment of time.

Collecting the Spores

Spores are stored in small capsules, called *sporangia,* on the undersides of fronds. The sporangia begin to mature from early summer to early autumn, when their appearance changes from flat to noticeably round, and from dull green to a shiny brown or plum. It's at this "pregnant" stage that the fronds should be collected for propagation. If the sporangia are dark brown or black with irregular edges, the spores have already been released.

Pick a frond that is strong and healthy with many mature sporangia. Place the frond inside a small paper bag and set the bag in a warm, dry location. After 1 or 2 days the tiny dustlike spores will have been released.

Sterilize Everything, Then Begin

From this point forward, propagation success depends on how effectively the spores and everything with which they come into contact are sterilized. Don't forget to wash your hands well with soap and water before handling sterilized equipment.

Step 1: Assemble and Sterilize Equipment You will need a large plastic bag; a shallow plastic storage container of roughly shoebox size with a tightly fitting lid; a spoon; a knife; and tweezers. Soak the equipment in a solution of 1 part bleach to 9 parts water (1/4 cup bleach to 2 1/4 cups water).

Step 2: Prepare the Growing Medium Fill the plastic bag with a light seed-starting mix. Pour small amounts of the sterile water into the bag, incorporating it as you go by squeezing the bag with your hands. Continue adding water until the growing medium is just moistened.

Step 3: Sterilize the Spores Boil a kettle of water and set it aside to cool. Mix a solution of 1 part bleach to 19 parts water (about 2 teaspoons bleach to 3/4 cup water). Carefully shake the spores from the bag into the bleach solution and let it stand for about 5 minutes. Line a strainer with a coffee filter or several sheets of paper towel, then pour the bleach solution through it. Last, pour the cooled boiled water over the spores. Set aside to dry completely.

Step 4: Sow the Spores Fill the plastic container with 1 1/2 to 2 inches of the sterilized seed-starting mix, tamping it lightly with the back of the spoon. Using the sterilized knife, shake the spores thinly onto the surface. Remove any large pieces of leaf or stem with the tweezers. Cover the container with the lid and place it in a bright location but not in direct sun. An east-facing window is ideal.

Moisture will accumulate on the inside of the lid, which you can tap down with your fingers to keep the soil moist. If no condensation appears and the soil seems to be drying, remove the lid and mist the soil lightly using a steriziled mister and sterilized water.

Step 5: Caring for Emerging Ferns After 2 or more weeks, the first sign of life — a green film — will appear on the surface of the soil. It will take anywhere from 1 to 6 months for the film to develop into the small, erect, leaflike *prothalli.* Once they've appeared, mist the soil lightly twice a week. New, tiny fern plantlets, called *sporophytes,* will grow out of the prothalli.

Step 6: Prick Out Young Ferns When the sporophytes reach about 3/4 inch and have three frondlets, they will be ready for pricking out into flats or individual 2-inch pots. Transplant them carefully in the same way that you would any tender seedling. Use an ordinary potting soil and space plants about 2 inches apart. Place the containers in a location with filtered light and keep them under plastic or glass for about 2 weeks, or until new growth is visible. Check the soil daily and mist with sterile water when it becomes dry to the touch.

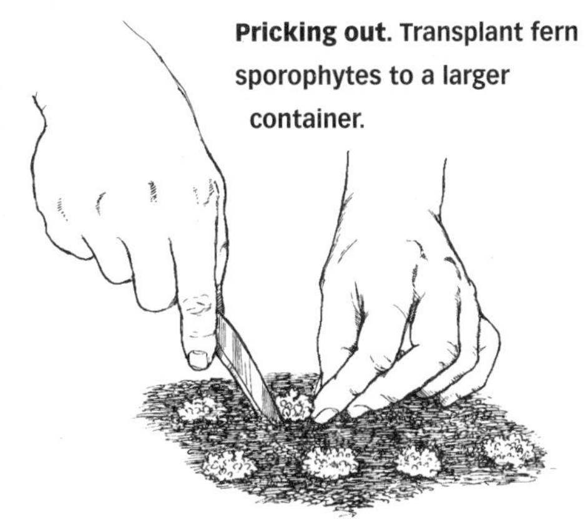

Pricking out. Transplant fern sporophytes to a larger container.

Step 7: Potting the Plantlets The ferns can be transplanted to larger containers or moved to a shaded nursery bed when they reach 3 to 4 inches. They will be ready to transplant to their final homes when they reach 6 to 12 inches.

Starting Seed Outdoors

IDEALLY, SOW SEEDS OUTDOORS in a specially designated seedbed. Having such a seedbed allows you to keep an eye on each plant without having to search for it, and the plants will be immeasurably easier to tend. It actually requires less time to tend seedlings in a seedbed and to later transplant them than it does to care for seedlings that were started *in situ* (see page 27).

Gazing at your flower beds in March, you might see vast stretches of inviting, accessible, bare earth. In fact, the flower beds probably don't look all that different from large seedbeds. And it may seem like unnecessary work to start plants in a seedbed only to move them to a flower bed later, when you could just as easily sow the seed in the exact location where you want the plant to grow. But remember that in another month, much of this empty space will be occupied by young plants, the flower bed becoming more like a jungle by the day. In such a situation, tiny seedlings can easily be lost, crowded, shaded, and overlooked. Starting plants in a seedbed eliminates these challenges.

Locating the Seedbed

Seedbeds are best sited in an out-of-the-way corner that is not a focal point from the house but is still within easy reach of a water supply. Near a vegetable bed or garden shed would be the perfect spot, assuming the area receives plenty of light. Locating beds against a fence or wall provides shelter from drying winds, but be sure that young plants are not shaded excessively; at least 6 hours of sunlight a day is necessary.

Preparing the Soil

It's best to prepare seedbeds in autumn for spring sowing. For new and existing beds, follow the procedure on pages 28–29. Nitrogen should *not* be added at this point, as it will foster weak seedlings. Here are some tips for success:

- Make a smooth, fine-textured soil surface. After breaking down clods as far as possible with a spade, use a short-tined rake and go over the soil surface repeatedly to minimize bumps and crevices in which seeds can be lost.
- Water the bed thoroughly using a fine mist, allowing the soil to drain for at least 24 hours before you begin sowing.

Raised Beds

Although you can prepare a seedbed at grade level, you'll get the best results if you create a raised bed, which provides a deeper, more nutrient-rich growing environment that retains water well without becoming waterlogged. A raised seedbed need be nothing more than an area of about 3 feet by 6 feet and 6 to 12 inches high, edged with timbers, brick, or stone and filled with a good, rich loam. Amend the soil annually as you would for beds at grade level.

Starting Seeds *in Situ*

If a plant is particularly sensitive to root disturbance, sowing it *in situ* is the best approach.

Sowing Seeds Outdoors

One of the first challenges when starting seeds outdoors is to get the timing right. Many seeds will not germinate in cold soil, and seeds sown too early may actually rot before they have a chance to sprout. Also, early sowing exposes seeds to adverse elements unnecessarily. Refer to suggestions about timing for specific plants in Part 2 of this book. When the time is right, follow this procedure:

1. *Fine seeds.* Mix fine seeds with sand; this makes it easier to distribute the seeds evenly over the soil surface. Press the seeds lightly into the soil using a board or the back of a spade or trowel. Seeds that require light for germination can be left as is; those that require darkness should be covered with a porous material, such as sand, perlite, or peat or sphagnum moss, through which the young seedlings can push themselves with ease.

   Large seeds. When planting large seeds, scratch a shallow furrow into the seedbed with a stick. This method is preferable to making individual planting holes, because in a large bed it's easy to lose track of where individual seeds have been planted. Fill in the trenches with a porous material such as vermiculite.
2. Use string or twigs to mark off areas of different plants, and label each with a plant marker or popsicle stick.
3. Use a hand mister to gently water the seedbeds, so the seeds won't wash away or collect into a small clump, which would cause them to become overcrowded and difficult to handle. After the seeds have sprouted, graduate to a fine spray from the hose.

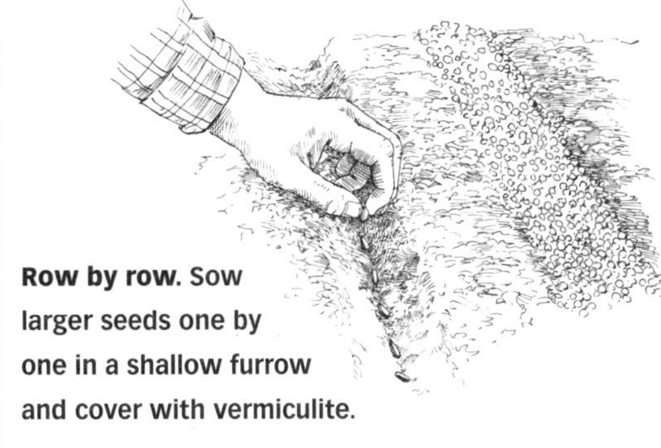

Row by row. Sow larger seeds one by one in a shallow furrow and cover with vermiculite.

Care of Young Seedlings

Keeping seedlings in the nursery bed rather than transplanting them to their final location makes it easier to feed and water them as a group. When the first pair of true leaves appears, thin or transplant the seedlings, just as for seedlings started indoors (see page 22). Begin fertilizing at this time as well. Feed with a half-strength liquid solution twice a week for the first 3 weeks, then increase to a full-strength solution every 10 to 14 days.

Tender young seedlings may require shade from drying winds or unseasonably hot sun. Shade cloth stretched over hoops (available from nurseries and gardening catalogs) is the most convenient method, but you can also fashion a shade using a wooden board propped up on bricks, several sheets of newspaper, or plastic or wire mesh such as a window screen.

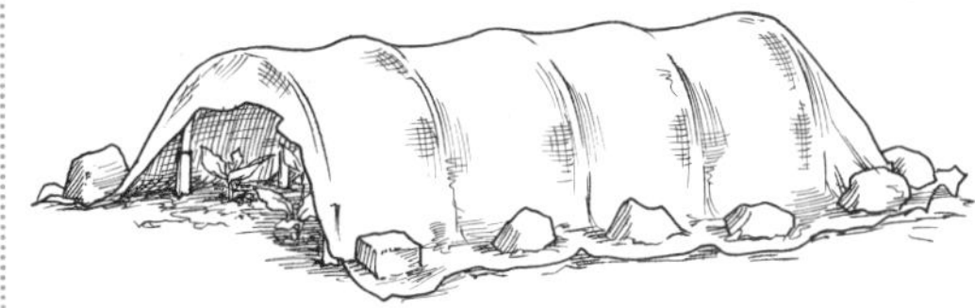

Made in the shade. Protect tender seedlings from too-hot sun with a shade-cloth cover.

Shades should be held several inches above the seedlings and left in place for 3 to 4 days, or a little longer if the sun is very hot.

When seedlings are young and delicate, water carefully with a gentle spray. Water in the morning rather than the evening to allow leaves to dry in the sun, thereby minimizing the risk of fungal diseases.

Plants started outdoors do not require the hardening-off process and can be transplanted to their permanent sites at the same stage you would transplant seedlings started indoors.

Preparing the Garden and Planting

IF YOU MAKE ONE RESOLUTION THIS YEAR, it should be to begin soil preparation in autumn rather than waiting until spring, when so many other jobs are demanding your attention. In addition to saving you time in spring, digging the soil in autumn yields an added benefit: It exposes to predators and freezing temperatures many pests that would otherwise overwinter underground, emerging in spring to feast on your tender young seedlings.

Test the Soil

To ascertain the *pH level* (relative alkalinity/acidity of the soil), have the soil tested professionally several weeks before you are ready to plant. Soil pH levels vary naturally in different geographic locations. They can also be affected by external conditions, such as proximity to building materials, which are often extremely alkaline, or pine trees, whose fallen needles can make the soil very acid. On a scale of 0 to 14, a pH level of 6.0 to 7.5 usually will be satisfactory.

A Note about Plant Choice

If the pH level of your soil is naturally unappealing to a plant, it makes more sense to select a different plant for that location rather than to continually battle the soil's natural inclinations.

Many plants perform happily in a wide range of pH levels, and you need only ensure that your soil measures within this broad range. Others are very particular, and if you are to have any success, the soil may need to be amended drastically to bring it into the favored range.

You can also use a soil test to tell you the nutrient content of the soil. Beds in which annuals and perennials are planted year after year will inevitably become depleted of nutrients, and the soil will need to be enriched annually. A soil test will determine which nutrients are missing from the soil and the precise quantities of supplements required to restore the soil to good health.

You can purchase soil-testing kits at garden centers and hardware stores, and it's possible that some people have success using these. But in my experience, they are expensive and the

pH Numbers Explained

pH	What It Means
5.0–6.0	The soil is acid.
6.0–7.0	The soil is somewhat acid.
7.0	The soil is neutral.
7.0–8.0	The soil is somewhat alkaline
8.0–9.0	The soil is alkaline.

results are unsatisfactory. Commercial testers are another option, but they can also be expensive. In most areas, the simplest and most economical method to test soil is through the local Cooperative Extension Service. Call your Extension agent for details on what you need to do and the cost. Depending on your state's policy, a fee (usually nominal) may be charged for testing, or it may be free.

To ensure that you obtain a sample that accurately reflects the soil throughout the bed, take several samples, mixing the soil well. If you prepare more than one bed, test at least one sample from each bed. To get an accurate sample, use a trowel to dig a hole 6 to 8 inches deep and remove a section of soil from the length of the hole. This way the sample will include more than just the nutrient-rich topsoil.

Amending the Soil

Amending the soil to suit the plants you want to grow is a vital step. Like a baby, a young plant needs specific nutrients and a physical environment that will support its healthy development. It is important, and in the long run simpler, to provide these from the beginning. Not only will you be rewarded with healthier plants that are less susceptible to stress and disease, but their blooms will be bigger and more abundant.

Organic vs. Inorganic Supplements

To continue the human analogy, the difference between feeding a garden with organic versus inorganic supplements is comparable to nourishing the human body with a healthy, balanced diet versus relying on synthetic vitamin supplements. Obviously, a balanced diet is preferable, but there are times when supplements are appropriate—for instance, to provide more rapid treatment in an emergency. Similarly, there is a place in the garden for inorganic fertilizers, but I try to reserve their use for emergency treatment of plants that may not recover without immediate assistance.

Preparing the Beds

If you did not prepare the soil in autumn, try to do it a week or so before transplanting begins, adding the supplements recommended by the soil analysis test.

If, on the other hand, you dug over the beds and amended them with organic supplements and soil conditioners in autumn, they will need only a light digging and leveling before planting in spring. Do this about 1 week before planting out begins, but proceed with caution, working the soil only when it is sufficiently drained to ensure that cultivation will not harm its natural structure.

The best way to determine whether your soil is ready for digging is to roll up your sleeves, plunge in your hands, and collect a fistful. Form the soil into a ball, then drop it from waist height onto the ground. Does it land with a thud and spread out rather than crumbling? If the answer is yes, the soil is still too wet to work and digging now would cause compaction, reducing the soil's capacity to hold air and drain freely. If the soil ball breaks fairly easily when it hits the ground, you can begin soil preparation.

If the soil is dry, water it and let it drain for 24 hours before you begin to dig.

Transplanting into New Beds

If seedlings will be planted in a new bed or in large sections of an existing bed, prepare the entire area simultaneously. In large beds, spread an inch of manure, compost, peat moss, or other organic matter over the entire planting area. To this, add soil amendments as recommended in the soil analysis. Dig over the soil to a depth of 6 to 8 inches, mixing it well to ensure even distribution of all additives. Using a fine spray, water the beds thoroughly 24 hours before transplanting begins.

When working in large beds, take care not to walk through and compact the soil you've so carefully prepared. To minimize compaction, place a wide board on the soil, which will help to distribute your weight. For a more permanent solution, incorporate stepping-stones in the bed. Choose the stepping-stones with their year-round appeal in mind. They can add visual interest to your winter garden as well as providing a framework around which you can group your plantings.

Step lightly.
Strategically placed stones provide access to your beds without compacting the soil.

Transplanting into Existing Beds

If seedlings will be scattered throughout existing beds, prepare the soil in each area separately. Sprinkle over the soil a handful of organic matter and individual amendments (bonemeal, blood meal, or wood ash, for example) or a commercial complete fertilizer (preferably organic), following the directions on the package. Using a trowel or border spade, dig over the soil well. About 24 hours before you start transplanting, deeply water all areas to be planted.

Transplanting Seedlings into Outdoor Beds

A mild, overcast day is perfect for planting out seedlings. If a perfect day does not coincide with the need to transplant, leave the job until late afternoon, to avoid planting during the hottest part of the day. You will use slightly different transplanting techniques (described below) depending on how you grew the seedlings: in individual containers, in biodegradable containers, or in flats. Most critical of all, though, is to immediately water newly planted seedlings with a gentle sprinkler. Try not to drench the leaves if you are watering late in the day.

From Individual Containers

Water plants an hour or two before transplanting. Loosen the soil from the edges of the pot by tapping it lightly on the ground or by gently rolling flexible containers between your palms. Carefully ease the plant and root-ball from the container. Set the plant in the hole at the same level at which it grew in the container, gently firming the soil around it. Water immediately.

From Biodegradable Containers

These seedlings can be planted in the ground

container and all. Before planting, cut off any edges that might protrude above the soil level, as they can act like a wick, drawing water away from the plant. Use a utility knife or scissors to slit the sides in two or three places to allow roots to grow through more easily. Set the plant in the ground, taking care to keep the soil level of the transplant even with the surrounding soil. Check to be sure no edge of the container protrudes. Gently firm the soil around the plant. Water immediately and thoroughly.

From Flats

About 2 weeks before it's time to transplant your seedlings into the garden, cut the soil into blocks containing one plant each (see illustration on page 23). Water plants an hour or two before transplanting. Tap flats gently on the ground to loosen the soil mix around them, and with a trowel carefully loosen one plant from the flat (Step 1).

Dig a hole in the bed large enough to accommodate one plant. Keeping as much soil mixture around the root-ball as possible, place the plant in the hole at the same level at which it grew in the flat, then gently firm the soil around it (Step 2).

Continue transplanting, spacing the seedlings at the distance recommended in the individual plant listings (see Part 2). Water immediately, using a gentle spray so as not to damage the plants (Step 3).

Nurturing New Transplants

Newly transplanted seedlings are more susceptible than mature plants to environmental stress and attack from garden pests and will require special attention for the first few weeks after transplanting.

Planting Out Seedlings

Step 1: Remove plant from flat or container.

Step 2: Set the plant so that it is growing at the same level as it was in the container.

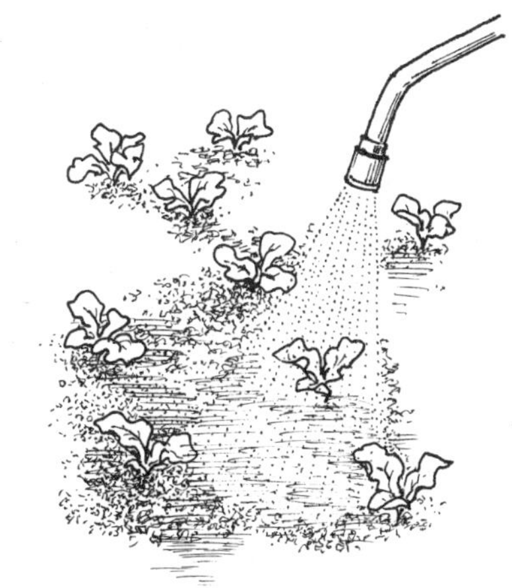

Step 3: Use a gentle sprinkler to water well.

Monitor Them for Stress

Like people, plants display visible signs of stress when deprived of basic needs (such as water) or subjected to sudden changes (such as transplanting). New transplants should be monitored frequently for signs of wilting or distress, especially during the first few days. If plants look pale or begin to droop as the sun rises in the sky, ensure that the soil is moist. If desiccation is not the problem, heat may be causing the stress. Protect despondent seedlings with a sunshade fashioned from newspaper, fine plastic, or wire mesh or, better yet, shade cloth through which filtered light can penetrate. Hold covers in place with skewers, sod pins, or sturdy twigs. Remove the cover gradually, allowing more direct sunlight to reach the plants over several days. In addition, be sure to allow for healthy air circulation.

Foil Cutworms and Slugs

Young plants are irresistible to many garden pests, most notably slugs and cutworms, which can decapitate an entire bed of new transplants overnight.

A good defense against these loathsome creatures is a protective collar encircling each plant. These can be made from paper cups, cardboard rolls, milk cartons, or lightweight card stock (such as an index card). Because the cutworm does its damage by encircling the plant's stem, allow 1 inch of space between the stem and the collar.

To fashion a collar from a paper cup, remove the bottom, make a slit down one side, and carefully encircle the seedling, overlapping the edges to create an unbroken barrier. Push the cup gently into the soil, deeply enough to anchor it well. Slit cardboard rolls down the side, cut into 2-inch sections, and set in position with ends overlapping. Flexible card stock can easily be wrapped around plant stems and pushed into the ground; secure the ends with tape, if necessary. Collars can be removed once plants are well established, as older, tougher stems are unappealing to cutworms.

Defensive tactics. Protect new transplants against cutworms and slugs by encircling the stem about 1 inch above and below ground with a paper collar.

Always remain vigilant, as slugs may be only temporarily dissuaded, retreating to the moist undersides of your stepping-stones or decorative rocks to lie in wait for a chance to devour your hostas and other tasty treats.

Keep Plants Cool, Moist, and Weed-Free

Mulching beds will save you time and energy as well as make your plants healthier and happier by keeping the soil cool, moist, and weed-free. When young plants are tall and stems are sturdy enough to tolerate it, apply a 2-inch layer of shredded hardwood, leaf mold, compost, cocoa shells, or any other organic mulch you prefer. To help them through their first winter, newly planted perennials — whether propagated by seed, division, or cuttings, homegrown or store-bought — will benefit from a second application of mulch after an initial hard freeze.

Asexual Propagation

Growing new plants from seed is usually quite easy, but it is not always appropriate. Why can't all plants be propagated by seed? Simply put, some plants are too difficult to grow from seed: The seed may be viable for only a short time, germination time too long, or seedlings too delicate. In addition, many plants do not "grow true" from seed—that is, they do not bear all the characteristics of the parent plant. Artificially bred hybrids, for example, generally do not grow true from seed.

The most common methods of asexual propagation are described below. Some plants are highly accommodating, accepting several methods; others are less obliging. It's rarely possible to successfully divide perennials that have a long taproot, for instance. (*Note:* The propagation preferences of individual plants are listed in their respective entries in Part 2, as well as the frequency with which plants may be—or should be—renewed, where appropriate.)

New Plants from Cuttings

Depending on the plant, one of three cuttings methods may be appropriate: leaf cuttings, root cuttings, or stem cuttings.

Leaf Cuttings

Remove individual leaves (still attached to their stems) from the parent plant and insert them in a growing medium (occasionally this can be water) until roots have grown. In some cases, the leaf may be laid on the soil surface and slits made across the veins of the leaf, from which new plants will grow. Leaf cuttings growing in soil will develop roots more quickly if they are first dipped in a commercial rooting hormone.

Begin with a leaf. Pull leaves from the stem, dip in rooting hormone, and then insert in growing medium.

Root Cuttings

Cut long pieces of root from the parent plant; this can be done with a spade below the soil surface, without uprooting the parent. Next, cut these pieces into 1- to 2-inch-long sections and dip them in rooting hormone. Plant thick roots standing upright, either in individual pots or directly in the garden; lay thin roots on the soil surface and cover them shallowly with soil.

Stem Cuttings

Using a sharp knife, cut the tip of a side shoot —not the plant's main stem—that contains at least three leaf joints. Remove the leaves from the bottommost leaf joint, dip stem into rooting hormone, and insert the cutting in a growing medium, burying the bottom leaf joint. Roots will grow from the buried portion.

Start with a stem. A side shoot cutting is an easy way to start many kinds of plants.

Propagation by Division

You can usually divide plants that grow from roots and tubers, depending on the plant.

Dividing Roots

This is the simplest and most common form of perennial propagation. Dig up the plant, roots and all, and use one of the following methods to divide the clumps, depending on the size and fragility of the plant:

- Use your hands to carefully tease out substantial clumps.
- Divide the clump with two garden forks inserted back to back.
- Cut right through the clump with a sharp instrument such as a pruning saw or spade.

When plants have been divided successfully, replant them.

Dare to divide. It's easy to divide many plants, such as Shasta daisies, by simply digging them up and pulling them apart.

Some perennials die back in the center as they become older. If this has occurred to one of your plants, discard the deteriorating part and replant only the vigorous outer clumps.

Dividing Tubers

A tuber is a thick, fleshy root found on some perennials. Tubers are divided either by carefully untangling them from each other or by cutting them apart. Each piece that is to be replanted must contain at least one growth bud, also called an "eye," as well as a piece of the old stem. Tubers are usually replanted with the eye an inch or two below the surface.

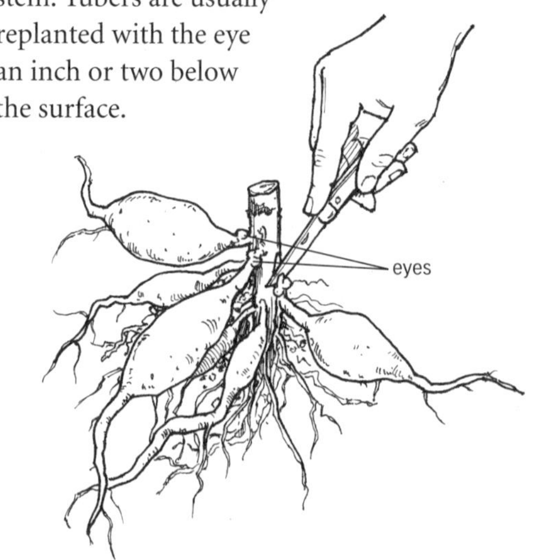

The kindest cut. Cut pieces with at least one eye from plants that grow tubers.

Propagation by Layering

Choose a stem that is long enough to touch the soil surface while it is still attached to the parent plant and either pin it to the soil with a U-shaped piece of wire or bury it lightly with soil. Before long, roots will develop where the stem is in contact with the soil. When this happens, cut the stem from the parent and either leave it growing in that spot until it is well established or dig it up and replant it in another location.

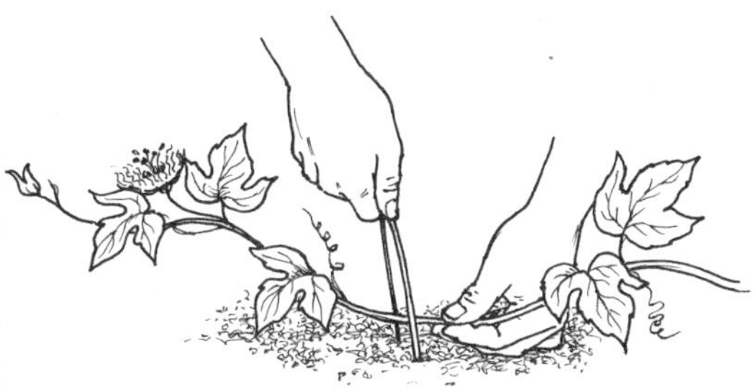

The layered look. Fasten a long stem against the soil until it develops roots where it touches the soil.

New Plants from Offsets

An offset is a miniature version of the parent plant that can be detached and cultivated to create a new plant. Rosettes and runners are offsets, as are bulblets and cormels.

Rosettes

A rosette is a cluster of leaves, all of which radiate from the same point. Many rosettes grow at ground level, such as primroses. They can easily be cut or scooped out of the crown of the plant using a sharp knife, and replanted.

Runners

Many ground-cover plants grow long, flexible stems that reach out along the ground, usually sprouting tiny roots at intervals. When detached from the parent and planted with the roots held firmly in the soil, these runners will quickly develop into strong plants.

Catch the runaway. If roots form on a long stem, cut away that portion and replant.

Bulbs and Corms

Most bulbs can be divided every year or two if a rapid increase of stock is desired, but many can be left almost indefinitely without any need for division. Bulbs and corms are usually propagated by separating small, newly developed bulbs from the parent plant. The following terms are commonly used to describe these young bulbs and corms.

Bulbil. A bulbil is a very small bulb that is produced above ground. Bulbils usually form at the base of a leaf, one bulbil per leaf, all the way up the stem. These can be detached,

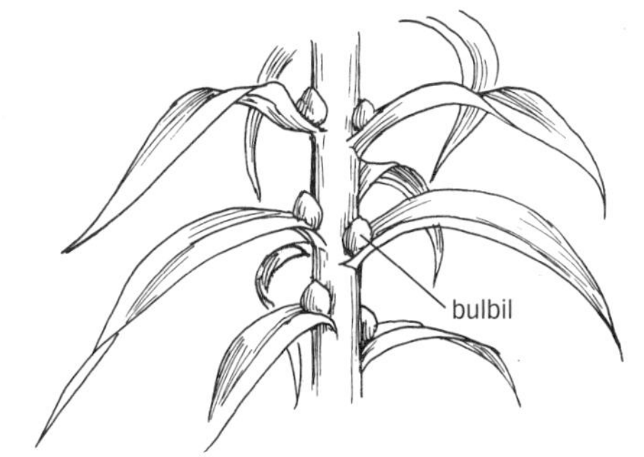

Bulbils. Detach the small bulbils and plant them to create young plants.

planted, and grown on to flower, usually in 2 or 3 years. Bulbils are most often found on lilies.

Bulblet. A small bulb that forms from the base of the parent bulb is a bulblet. This develops fairly quickly until it is large enough to sustain itself. Bulblets are relatively large and easily detached from the parent bulb. Normally they will bloom 1 or 2 years after division.

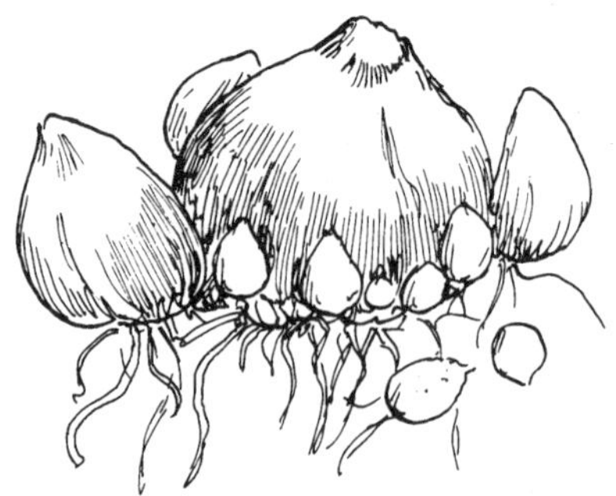

Bulblets. Detach bulblets that develop at the base of some mature bulbs.

Corm. A corm lives for only one season, but during that season it grows replacements in the form of one large new corm plus several tiny cormels (see above right). Discard the old corm and plant the new one, which will flower the following year.

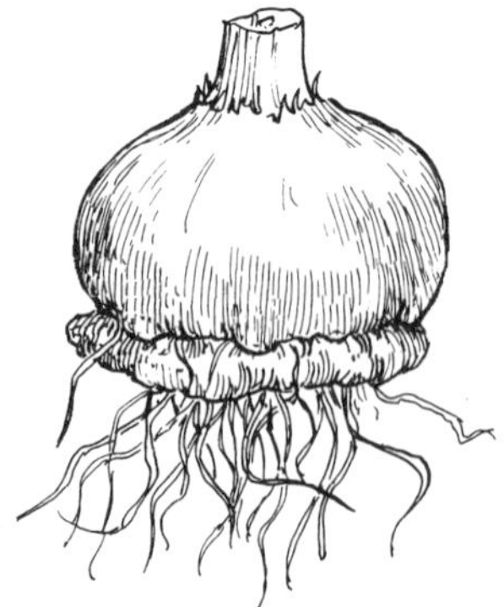

Corm. A corm lives for only one season.

Cormels. Many corms produce a crop of miniature corms, known as cormels, which grow along the base of the old corm. Detach these and grow them in a nursery bed for several years until they are of flowering size.

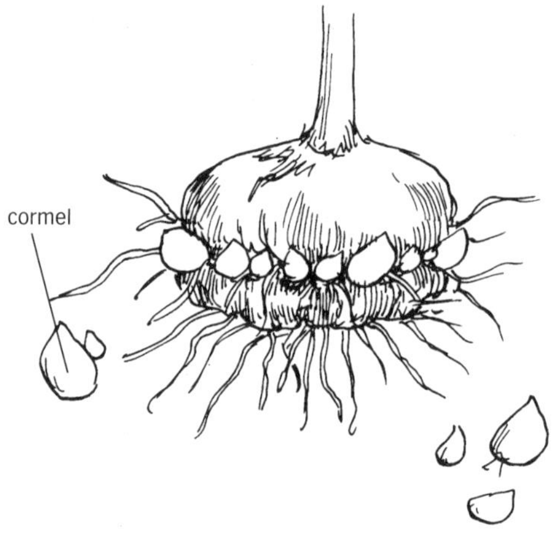

Cormels. Detach cormels from the base of an old corm.

Scales. Some bulbs are made up of large, fleshy, overlapping segments known as scales. These can be detached and planted and will usually flower 1 or 2 years after planting.

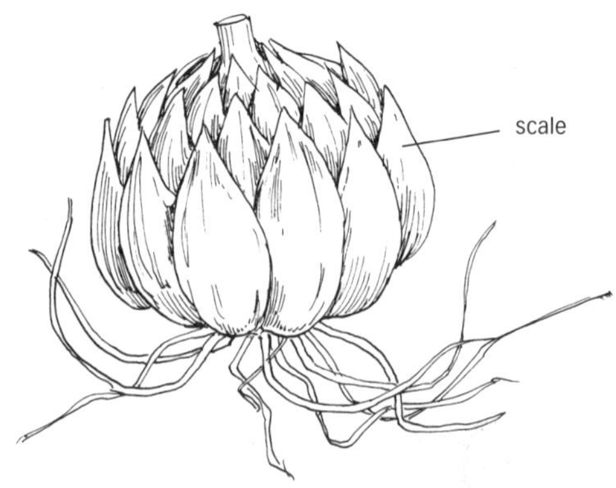

Scales. Detach scales from the parent bulb.

Enjoy Your Garden!

At last, your protégés are in the ground, enthusiastically pushing their roots deep into the rich and welcoming soil that you've so carefully prepared for them, their heads reaching skyward in anticipation of the day they will break into glorious bloom. But remember that this is just the beginning: The work doesn't stop here. In addition to watering and weeding, plants may need pinching, staking, deadheading, and frequent inspection for signs of pests and diseases. Don't forget to make time throughout the season, however, to pat yourself on the back, and take every opportunity to admire your garden.

To make your life easier, create a calendar of gardening jobs you need to perform throughout the year, tailored to the specific needs of the plants you are growing. (Consult the Caring for Plants section of the individual plant listings for this information.) This way you'll be reminded to pinch back the salvia before it's lying flat across the candytuft, to feed the petunias and not to feed the nasturtiums. Preparing the calendar will be a time-consuming job initially, but after years of consistently proving to myself that I really won't remember to pinch back the mums or stake the young asters unless it's written down, I don't begrudge the time I spend on the task each spring. In the end, you're doing your plants a favor by making sure they get the attention they need when they need it, and they will repay you with healthy growth and glorious blooms.

2 An A–Z of Garden Plants

THE FOLLOWING PLANT GUIDE — the heart of this book — is much more than an ordinary encyclopedic listing of information. I like to think of it as a collection of really good seed packets. And like any compact reference, you'll get more out of the information as you become familiar with the way it is organized and with the terminology that is used. As an introduction, let's look at the entry for *Gladiolus* (at right):

A. Botanic name. Plants in this book are alphabetized by botanic name. See A Quick Lesson in Nomenclature (page 12) for an explanation of plant names. The synonyms that follow some botanic names refer to outdated names for the genus. For a complete list of synonyms of plants in this book, see pages 523–526.

B. Common names. Any one genus may have several common names, often regional in origin, and some common names refer to plants from different genera: "daisy," "bluebell," and "bachelor button" are three typical examples. In addition, some common names describe a whole genus, whereas others apply to only one or two species. The common names shown here refer to the genus as a whole. Sometimes the genus name is the accepted common name; in these cases, no common name is given. For common names of individual species, see pages 504–522.

C. [camera icon] Refers to the page number for a color photo or photos of plants in this entry.

D. Description. A short paragraph introduces the plants in each genus, with general information about their appearance, size, color, and best use in the garden.

E. Type. Plants in this book are divided as follows to describe their life cycle and their cold hardiness:

A (Annual): A plant that grows from seed, flowers, produces seed, and dies, all in one year.

Bi (Biennial): A plant that lives two years, germinating and making top growth the first year, flowering, producing seed, and dying the second.

TP (Tender Perennial): In this book, "TP" indicates a plant that naturally lives for more than two years, but is cold hardy only south of Zone 8 (see Zone, below). Many plants designated as TP are grown for a season in colder regions and then either discarded or brought indoors. These plants are noted with an asterisk.

HP (Hardy Perennial): Perennials are plants that live for more than two years. In this book, we classify hardy perennials as those plants that can be successfully grown in regions where temperatures regularly fall below freezing, or in Zones 8 or colder (see Zone, below).

TB (Tender Bulb) and **HB** (Hardy Bulb): A bulb is an underground bud that contains food stores and produces leaves and flowers above ground. The criteria for designating a bulb as "tender" or "hardy" is the same as that used for perennials.

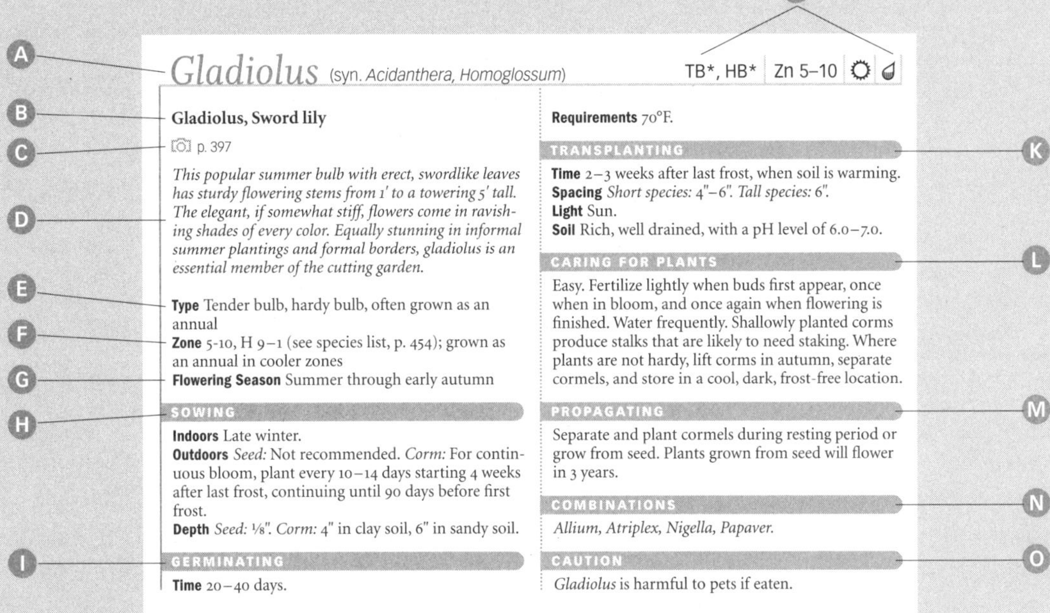

Gladiolus (syn. *Acidanthera, Homoglossum*) TB*, HB* | Zn 5–10

Gladiolus, Sword lily

p. 397

This popular summer bulb with erect, swordlike leaves has sturdy flowering stems from 1' to a towering 5' tall. The elegant, if somewhat stiff, flowers come in ravishing shades of every color. Equally stunning in informal summer plantings and formal borders, gladiolus is an essential member of the cutting garden.

Type Tender bulb, hardy bulb, often grown as an annual
Zone 5-10, H 9–1 (see species list, p. 454); grown as an annual in cooler zones
Flowering Season Summer through early autumn

SOWING

Indoors Late winter.
Outdoors *Seed:* Not recommended. *Corm:* For continuous bloom, plant every 10–14 days starting 4 weeks after last frost, continuing until 90 days before first frost.
Depth *Seed:* 1/8". *Corm:* 4" in clay soil, 6" in sandy soil.

GERMINATING

Time 20–40 days.
Requirements 70°F.

TRANSPLANTING

Time 2–3 weeks after last frost, when soil is warming.
Spacing *Short species:* 4"–6". *Tall species:* 6".
Light Sun.
Soil Rich, well drained, with a pH level of 6.0–7.0.

CARING FOR PLANTS

Easy. Fertilize lightly when buds first appear, once when in bloom, and once again when flowering is finished. Water frequently. Shallowly planted corms produce stalks that are likely to need staking. Where plants are not hardy, lift corms in autumn, separate cormels, and store in a cool, dark, frost-free location.

PROPAGATING

Separate and plant cormels during resting period or grow from seed. Plants grown from seed will flower in 3 years.

COMBINATIONS

Allium, Atriplex, Nigella, Papaver.

CAUTION

Gladiolus is harmful to pets if eaten.

F. Zone. The range of hardiness and heat ("H") zones in which this genus can be grown. The range given here is for the entire genus, but individual species may be suited to a narrower range of zones; see Part 4 for this information. To learn about your hardiness and heat zones, see pages 499–500.

G. Flowering season. The full range of bloom times for the genus is given here, although individual species may bloom for a shorter period. Consult Part 4 for information on individual species.

H. Sowing. The timing is given for sowing the seed both indoors and out, with a recommendation for planting depth and preferred location.

I. Germinating. Consult here for data about how long it may take these seeds to germinate, the optimal temperature for germination, and advice on how easy or hard these seeds are to germinate.

J. Quick reference. The symbols and abbreviations on this line offer a quick-look overview at the genus's plant type or types, hardiness zone range, and light and soil needs (see key at the bottom of each page). For more detailed information, refer to the entry itself, as well as to the charts in Part 4.

K. Transplanting. For seeds you've started or purchased seedlings, this section advises on when and how far apart to plant seedlings, as well as light and soil preferences, including acidity, textural quality, and nutritional needs. Transplanting times are often expressed in relation to the last frost date. To determine the approximate time of your last spring frost, see page 501.

L. Caring for plants. Advice about watering, staking, mulching, and pruning during the season is augmented by suggestions about how to prepare plants for winter and whether or not they may be successfully transplanted.

M. Propagating. For gardeners who wish to propagate more plants, here is advice about which methods work best for each plant. Refer to pages 33–36 for guidance on how to carry out these methods.

N. Combinations. To help you plan a more attractive garden, this section offers combinations with contrasting or complementary colors and textures.

O. Caution. Plants with toxic parts, as well as those that may be invasive in some regions, are indicated here. For advice about invasives, see pages 494–498.

Abelmoschus (syn. *Hibiscus*)

TP* | Zn 9–10

These charming heat-loving plants are covered over a long period with many small, hibiscuslike flowers, from pale yellow and pink to fiery orange-red and scarlet. Size ranges from 1' (in cooler climates) to 6'.

Type Tender perennial; often grown as an annual
Zone 9–10 (see species list, p. 435); grown as an annual in Zones 3–8
Flowering Season Summer to frost; blooms most profusely where summers are long

SOWING

Indoors 8 weeks before planting out.
Outdoors Only in Zones 9–10: early spring when the temperature reaches 45°F.
Depth 1/16".

GERMINATING

Time 10–30 days.
Requirements Use fresh seed. Chip or file seed and soak overnight in warm water before sowing in peat pots. Provide temperature of 70°F, reducing to 60°F after germination.

TRANSPLANTING

Time 2–3 weeks after last frost.
Spacing *Small species:* 12"–18". *Large species:* 24"–36".
Light Prefers full sun, with shade from hot afternoon sun; tolerates part shade, but flowers will diminish.
Soil Rich, very moist but well drained.

CARING FOR PLANTS

Water frequently during dry spells, keeping water off leaves; feed periodically with a balanced fertilizer. Mulch well in autumn in Zones 9–10. Susceptible to powdery mildew, rust, slugs, and whiteflies.

PROPAGATING

Root cuttings of woody stems in water or soil (easy) or grow from seed. Plants self-seed freely where warm. Plants from seed flower in about 100 days.

Abutilon

HP | Zn 8–10

Flowering maple

p. 369

The solitary 2"–3", bell-shaped, pendulous blossoms of flowering maple are often veined, and range from vibrant orange, red, and yellow, to pink, lavender, or white. On some, attractive maple-shaped leaves are variegated. Container-grown as annuals, they remain 12"–18"; plants reach 6' or more where perennial.

Type Hardy perennial; often grown as an annual
Zone 8–10. Grown as an annual in cooler zones. Prefers warm weather.
Flowering Season Most species bloom from spring to autumn as annuals, or year-round where perennial.

SOWING

Indoors 8–10 weeks before last frost.
Outdoors Start seeds indoors only.
Depth Just cover.

GERMINATING

Time 20–90 days.
Requirements Chip seeds or soak for 24 hours. Provide a temperature of 60°–70°F.

TRANSPLANTING

Time After last frost.
Spacing *Annual bedding plants:* 12"–14". *Larger plants:* 24"–48" or grow singly as specimens.
Light Full sun where summers are cool; afternoon shade is beneficial in warmer climates.
Soil Rich, moist, well drained. Plant deeply.

CARING FOR PLANTS

Pinch young tips to stimulate bushiness. Water well during dry spells; feed several times in season. Move containers indoors to a bright, cool location for winter; keep soil fairly dry. Prune as needed in late winter or early spring. Older plants flower less. Plants attract whiteflies and spidermites, especially indoors.

PROPAGATING

Take cuttings in spring, summer, or fall, or grow plants from seed. Most species flower from seed in their first year; cultivars do not come true from seed.

COMBINATIONS

In shade, pair with tuberous begonias, *Browallia, Coleus, Lobelia, or Torenia.* In cool, Northern sun, use *Alyssum, Lysimachia nummularia,* or petunias.

Acaena

HP | Zn 6–8

Bidi-bidi, New Zealand burr

p. 369

Evergreen, mat-forming perennials and subshrubs, Acaena *are native to South America, Australia, and New Zealand. Flowers are inconspicuous, but leaves and brightly colored burrs make this vigorous little plant useful as a ground cover or in the rock garden.*

Type Hardy perennial
Zone 6–8, H 9–6
Flowering Season Summer

SOWING

Indoors At least 12 weeks before planting out.
Outdoors Spring or autumn.
Depth ¼".

GERMINATING

Time 30–100 days.
Requirements Very difficult. 50°–60°F.

TRANSPLANTING

Time After last spring frost or in early autumn.
Spacing 3"–5".
Light Full sun to part shade.
Soil Sandy or gritty. Will not tolerate standing water.

CARING FOR PLANTS

Difficult. Do not water from above.

PROPAGATING

Divide in early spring, take cuttings, or grow from seed.

Acantholimon

HP | Zn 7–9

Prickly thrift

A fine-textured, cushiony perennial, prickly thrift bears abundant star-shaped flowers and needlelike leaves. Usually evergreen, these little plants are native to desert regions and are most at home in rock gardens or tucked into the crevices of walls.

Type Hardy perennial
Zone 7–9, H 9–7; must have dry winters and summers
Flowering Season Late spring to late summer, depending on species

SOWING

Growing from seed not recommended; seed is hard to obtain and germination is unreliable.

TRANSPLANTING

Time Set out purchased plants after last spring frost or in early autumn.
Spacing 3"–5".
Light Full sun.
Soil Alkaline; sandy or gritty. Ideal for dry stone walls.

CARING FOR PLANTS

Plants are slow to establish and almost impossible to move. Mulch with straw in winter.

PROPAGATING

Difficult. Take cuttings in early spring or late summer and overwinter in a cold frame.

Acanthus

HP | Zn 6–10

Bear's breeches

p. 369

Large, rather stiff perennials of 1'–4', bear's breeches are used in the border for dramatic effect. Flowers, usually white or shades of purple, appear in bottle-brushes above deeply cut, spiky leaves. This Mediterranean native may be evergreen or deciduous.

Type Hardy perennial
Zone 6–10, H 12–5 (see species list, p. 435); does not tolerate high heat and humidity
Flowering Season Late spring through summer

Acanthus (cont'd)

SOWING

Indoors Late winter to early spring in peat pots.
Outdoors Early spring, when soil is still cool.
Depth ¼".

GERMINATING

Time 21–25 days.
Requirements Easy. 50°–60°F.

TRANSPLANTING

Time After last spring frost or in early autumn.
Spacing 36"–48".
Light Full sun to part shade. Flowers best in sun but needs some shade where the afternoon sun is very hot.
Soil Deep, rich, well drained, with a pH level of 6.0–7.0. Highly drought tolerant and suitable for xeriscaping; will not survive in wet sites.

CARING FOR PLANTS

Easy. Water regularly during growing season but allow plants to become somewhat dry after flowering. Do not disturb roots. In the South, cut back hard after flowering. In northern climates, mulch with salt hay in winter. Cut back stems to ground level in spring.

PROPAGATING

Take root cuttings, divide in autumn, or grow from seed.

COMBINATIONS

Alcea, Crocosmia, Erigeron, Phlox.

Achillea

HP | Zn 3–10

Achillea, Milfoil, Yarrow

p. 369

Easy and useful perennials, 6"–48" tall, achilleas are grown in meadows or to lend a carefree or naturalistic look to a border; small species are attractive in rock gardens. Leaves are usually soft and feathery, with tiny flowers borne in dense clusters on flat heads. Beguiling shades of pink are a welcome change from the ubiquitous yellow.

Type Hardy perennial
Zone 3–10, H 9–1 (see species list, p. 435). Most species are very tolerant of hot, humid summers.
Flowering Season Late spring to early autumn

SOWING

Indoors 8–10 weeks before planting out.
Outdoors Early spring or early autumn, depending on species.
Depth Surface.

GERMINATING

Time 10–100 days.
Requirements Easy. Light and 60°–65°F.

TRANSPLANTING

Time Early spring, when soil is cool and a light frost is still possible, or early autumn.
Spacing 12"–24".
Light Full sun.
Soil Will grow in poor, dry soil but performs best in a good loam with a pH level of 5.5–7.0. Suitable for xeriscaping.

CARING FOR PLANTS

Easy. Divide every 3–4 years to maintain vigor. Very tall or floppy species may need support. Cut plants to ground level in autumn. *A. millefolium* can be invasive. To dry for indoor displays, cut flowers at their peak and hang upside down in a dry, shady place.

PROPAGATING

Divide after flowering in spring (in autumn south of Zone 6), take basal cuttings in spring, or grow from seed. Plants grown from seed will usually bloom in their first year.

COMBINATIONS

Achillea mix well with many plants, including *Artemisia, Crocosmia, Geranium, Helianthus, Heuchera, Perilla, Platycodon, Salvia, Santolina, Stachys,* and *Stokesia.*

CAUTION

Achillea millefolium is listed as an invasive in many areas, including California and Missouri. See pp. 494–495 for advice.

Achimenes

TP* | Zn 10  

Achimenes, Cupid's bower, Hot water plant

Small, elegant plants, achimenes grow from scaly rhizomes. They bear abundant, trumpetlike flowers that emerge through clean, dark green foliage with vibrantly colored petals in reds, purples, pinks, and purest white. Most effective in pots, window boxes, and hanging baskets.

Type Tender perennial
Zone 10, H 12–1; grown as annual in Zones 3–9; performs well in high humidity
Flowering Season Late summer to late autumn.

SOWING

Indoors *Seed:* 8 weeks before planting out. *Rhizome:* Late winter to spring. For a succession of blooms, start rhizomes indoors at intervals from February to May.
Outdoors *Seed:* In Zone 10 only, 2–3 weeks after last frost dates.
Rhizome: Late winter to spring, when temperatures will remain above 60°F.
Depth *Seed:* Surface. *Rhizome:* ½".

GERMINATING

Time 15–30 days.
Requirements *Seed:* Easy. Provide temperature of 65°–75°F. *Rhizome:* Plant 1" apart in a moist seed-starting mix and place trays in a temperature of 65°–70°F. Provide more room and nourishment when plants reach 2" and grow on at 60°–65°F. Pinch out tips when plants are 3"–4".

TRANSPLANTING

Time When nighttime temperatures will remain above 50°F.
Spacing *Small species:* 12". *Large species:* 18"–24".
Light Bright shade; shade from hot afternoon sun is essential.
Soil Moist, humusy, well drained.

CARING FOR PLANTS

Pinch back young plants to encourage bushy growth. Plants will hang gracefully over the edge of a container but will require staking if upright growth is desired. Water regularly during dry spells, and feed periodically throughout the growing season. Reduce watering in autumn. To store plants over winter in their pots, reduce watering in autumn to induce dormancy; turn pots on their sides, stop watering altogether for winter, and leave in a dry location at 50°–55°F. Or lift rhizomes before the first frost and store in peat moss or vermiculite in a cool, dry location at 50°–55°F.

PROPAGATING

Divide clumps of rhizomes in late winter to spring in Zone 10 (in late winter before starting plants indoors farther north) or grow from seed. Plants grown from seed will bloom in 2 years.

Achnantherum See *Stipa*

Acidanthera See *Gladiolus*

Aconitum

HP | Zn 3–8

Aconite, Monkshood

p. 369

Aconites are much neglected, curiously old-fashioned perennials with mysterious, hooded purple, white, or yellow flowers borne majestically on stems of up to 8'. The impressive size limits the usefulness of these somewhat fussy plants to the back of the border.

Type Hardy perennial
Zone 3–8, H 8–4 (see species list, p. 435); does not tolerate high heat and humidity
Flowering Season Mid summer to early autumn, depending on species

SOWING

Indoors Start seed outdoors.
Outdoors Autumn.
Depth Surface.

Aconitum *(cont'd)*

GERMINATING

Time 5–270 days.
Requirements Sow seed in flats and sink these into the ground against a north-facing wall, covering with glass. Moisten soil as necessary. Bring flats indoors in spring. Transplant seedlings to individual pots after 8 weeks and to the garden in autumn.

TRANSPLANTING

Time Autumn.
Spacing *Small species:* 8"–10". *Tall species:* 24"–36".
Light Prefers part shade but withstands full sun if soil is kept moist. In the South, provide shade from hot midday sun.
Soil Cool, moist, humus-rich, with a pH level of 5.0–6.0. Add well-rotted manure at planting time.

CARING FOR PLANTS

Mulch and water frequently in summer. Stake tall species in windy sites and cut back to ground level in autumn. Divide carefully every 3–4 years.

PROPAGATING

Divide carefully in spring (in autumn south of Zone 6) or grow from seed.

COMBINATIONS

Astilbe, Chelone, Hosta, Lobelia, Sanguisorba. In cooler climates where it can withstand more sun, combine with *Euphorbia, Helenium, Rudbeckia, Sedum,* or *Stachys.*

CAUTION

All parts of the plant are toxic if eaten.

Acroclinium See *Rhodanthe*

Aconogonon See *Persicaria*

Actinidia

HP | Zn 4–9

p. 369

These mainly deciduous, woody climbers are native to China and Japan. The most popular species, Actinidia kolomikta, *has striking and unusual foliage: Young leaves emerge with a purple hue, then change to a variegation of pink and white. Vines grow to 12'–15' on a wall or fence.*

Type Hardy perennial
Zone 4–9, H 9–7 (see species list, p. 435 and 479); fruiting and general performance will be most successful in warmer climates
Flowering Season Spring or summer, depending on species

SOWING

Indoors October to November.
Outdoors Early spring, when soil is cool and a light frost is still possible, or late autumn.
Depth 1/8".

GERMINATING

Time 60–90 days.
Requirements Easy. 50°F.

TRANSPLANTING

Time Spring or autumn.
Spacing Plant vines singly, or 2' apart if fruiting is desired.
Light Sun or shade. Variegated leaves will have better color in full sun.
Soil Well drained, fertile, humus-rich, and moist.

CARING FOR PLANTS

Except for *A. polygama,* you must have both male and female plants for pollination and fruiting; to ensure pollination, grow three or four plants in one group. Prune in early spring, cutting back as necessary and thinning out stems to retain neat appearance. Water plants well during dry periods and provide a trellis for support. Plants flower on 2-year-old wood.

PROPAGATING

Take cuttings in summer or grow from seed.

Actinotus

TP* | Zn 9–10 

Flannel flower

p. 369

Flannel flower is a sturdy 2' plant whose small, white, daisylike flowers have an unusual woolly texture. Although useful for drying, this difficult Australian native would probably be best left to the connoisseur looking for a new challenge.

Type Tender perennial; often grown as an annual
Zone 9–10, grown as an annual in Zones 3–8; tolerant of considerable heat but only in dry climates
Flowering Season Late spring to summer

SOWING

Indoors 8–10 weeks before planting out.
Outdoors In Zones 9–10 only: after last frost.
Depth ¼".

GERMINATING

Time 7–42 days.
Requirements Store fresh seed for 4–6 months, then sow at 60°–65°F.

TRANSPLANTING

Time 2–3 weeks after last frost.
Spacing *Small species:* 8"–10". *Large species:* 18–24".
Light Sun to part shade.
Soil Sandy, well-drained soil that is not too rich; prefers a pH of 5.0–6.0. *A. helianthi* is suitable for xeriscaping.

CARING FOR PLANTS

Difficult. Mulch lightly to protect the shallow roots, and do not move established plants. Where plants are perennial, cut back to the ground after flowering to increase the next year's flowering and to prevent legginess; mulch well before winter.

PROPAGATING

Take stem cuttings, divide, or grow from seed. Plants may self-seed. Propagation from seed is erratic and not dependable; oddly, older seed appears to be more reliable.

Adenophora

HP | Zn 3–9

Ladybells, Gland bellflower

p. 370

Summer-flowering perennials bearing a strong resemblance to campanulas. These attractive 18"–4' tall plants bear pale blue bell-shaped flowers and are most often used in the border.

Type Hardy perennial
Zone 3–9, H 8–1
Flowering Season Summer

SOWING

Indoors 8–10 weeks before planting out, in peat pots.
Outdoors Early spring, when soil is cool and a light frost is still possible, or early autumn.
Depth Surface.

GERMINATING

Time 30–90 days.
Requirements Easy. 50°–55°F.

TRANSPLANTING

Time Early spring, when soil is cool and a light frost is still possible, or early autumn.
Spacing 12"–24".
Light Full sun or part shade.
Soil Moist, rich, well-drained loam.

CARING FOR PLANTS

Water and deadhead regularly. Do not transplant.

PROPAGATING

Take cuttings in spring or grow from seed.

COMBINATIONS

Delphinium, Geranium, Hemerocallis, Stachys.

Adiantum

HP | Zn 4–10

Maidenhair fern

p. 370

A large genus, these graceful, airy ferns with showy dark, wiry stems bear either a froth of short, rounded leaves or longer segments of a more traditionally fern-like appearance. The shape of the fronds often gives the appearance of a cluster of miniature beach umbrellas. A charming addition to any woodland garden.

Type Hardy perennial
Zone 4–10, H 9–1
Flowering Season N/A

SOWING

Indoor When spores are ripe, in August to October.
Outdoor Not recommended.
Depth *Spores:* Surface. *Rhizome:* 1".

GERMINATING

Time 10–365 days.
Requirements Difficult. 59°F for hardy species, 70°F for tender species. See pp. 24–25 for instructions on starting ferns from spores.

TRANSPLANTING

Time After last frost.
Spacing *Small species:* 12"–18". *Large species:* 24"–36". Space plants to allow for healthy air circulation.
Light Morning sun is acceptable, but fronds will scorch in hot sun; bright shade is most desirable.
Soil Moist.

CARING FOR PLANTS

Very easy. Water regularly as needed to keep the soil moist. Remove fading fronds periodically to maintain a neat appearance. Divide plants when stands become congested.

PROPAGATING

Carefully divide rhizomes in early spring north of Zone 7 (in early autumn in warmer zones) or grow from spores.

COMBINATIONS

Spring fiddleheads are attractive with early bulbs and wildflowers. Mature plants combine nicely with *Asarum, Helleborus, Hosta, Mimulus, Polygonatum, Phlox divaricata,* and *Pulmonaria.*

CAUTION

A. hispidulum is invasive.

Adlumia

Bi | Zn 5–9

This dainty climber looks very much like a large, white-flowered bleeding heart. A charming plant, it reaches 15' and is native to the woods of the eastern United States; it is most at home in a naturalistic garden.

Type Hardy biennial
Zone 5–9, H 8–1; favors the climate of New England and will not thrive in extreme heat or drought
Flowering Season June through August

SOWING

Indoors 6–8 weeks before planting out, in peat pots.
Outdoors After last frost.
Depth ¼".

GERMINATING

Time 14–42 days.
Requirements Easy. 55°–65°F.

TRANSPLANTING

Time Early summer.
Spacing Grow vines singly.
Light Part to full shade.
Soil Cool, moist, sandy, humus-rich, and not too acid.

CARING FOR PLANTS

Easy. Requires a trellis for support and protection from wind. Mulch with organic matter to keep soil cool and moist; water regularly during dry spells. Vines grow very slowly their first year but will take off in their second.

PROPAGATING

Grow from seed only. Plants may self-seed once established.

Adonis

A, HP | Zn 3–9

Adonis

These low-growing, clump-forming annuals and perennials bear buttercup-like flowers of yellow, blue, red, or white; perennials are useful for their very early flowering. Plants are most effective when situated along a path, in the rock garden, or massed among early bulbs.

Type Annual, hardy perennial
Zone *Annual:* 3–9. *Perennial:* 4–9; H 9–1. (See species list, p. 436.) Will grow well only in cool weather with a nighttime temperature below 65°F.
Flowering Season *Annual:* Summer. *Perennial:* Spring.

SOWING

Indoors Start seed outdoors.
Outdoors *Annual:* After last frost. *Perennial:* Spring or autumn.
Depth Just cover.

GERMINATING

Time *Annual:* 14 days. *Perennial:* 30–120 days.
Requirements 60°–65°F. Annuals are easy to start from seed; perennials require more care.

TRANSPLANTING

Time *Annual:* After last frost. *Perennial:* Autumn or very early spring, when soil is cool and a light frost is still possible.
Spacing *Small species:* 5"–8". *Larger species:* 12".
Light Sun or part shade.
Soil Prefers moist, sandy soil with a pH of 6.0–8.0 but will tolerate dry conditions.

CARING FOR PLANTS

Cultivation varies from easy to difficult, depending on species. Plants are sometimes troubled by slugs. Apply fertilizer to perennials immediately after flowering. Plants disappear altogether in midsummer; mark their locations to avoid disturbing the roots. Apply a thick winter mulch in Zones 3–5.

PROPAGATING

Grow both annuals and perennials from seed. Annuals self-seed freely. Carefully divide perennials after flowering in spring, although plants prefer not to be disturbed. Perennials propagated by division produce more blooms than those grown from seed.

CAUTION

Harmful if eaten.

Aegopodium

HP | Zn 3–10

Bishop's weed, Goutweed

p. 370

Easy care and low growing, these rhizomatous perennials are inclined to become weedy, as the common names imply. Most bear clean, attractive, if unexceptional, foliage and are useful as ground covers. White flowers, which are held on tall stalks high above the foliage, are considered a drawback by some.

Type Hardy perennial
Zone 3–10, H 12–1
Flowering Season June

SOWING

Not grown from seed.

TRANSPLANTING

Time Set out purchased plants in spring or autumn.
Spacing 6"–8" for ground cover or edging, otherwise 10"–12".
Light Prefers part shade but will tolerate full sun.
Soil Ordinary; withstands wet, dry, or poor soil. Suitable for xeriscaping.

CARING FOR PLANTS

Very easy, thriving almost anywhere, even in poor soil and shade where little else will grow. Once established, plants may be difficult to eradicate. If colonies show signs of taking over your garden, mow to the ground periodically. When growing variegated species, pull up any plants that revert to green.

PROPAGATING

Divide in spring north of Zone 7 (in autumn in the South).

CAUTION

Aegopodium podagraria is listed as invasive in many areas, including Connecticut, Pennsylvania, Vermont, and Wisconsin. See pp. 494–495 for advice.

Aethionema (syn. *Eunomia*)

HP | Zn 5–9

Stone cress

p. 370

Short-lived perennials and subshrubs native to the Mediterranean region, stone cresses are evergreen or semievergreen. They bear clusters of tiny pink, white, or lilac flowers in profusion. Use low-growers in stone walls or rock gardens and tall ones at the border front.

Type Short-lived hardy perennial; often grown as an annual or a biennial
Zone 5–9, H 9–7 (see species list, p. 436); moderately tolerant of high heat but not humidity (except *A.* × *warleyense,* which thrives in both)
Flowering Season Early spring to late summer, depending on species

SOWING

Indoors 10–12 weeks before planting out.
Outdoors After last frost.
Depth Just cover.

GERMINATING

Time 30–90 days.
Requirements 60°–65°F.

TRANSPLANTING

Time Spring or autumn.
Spacing 4"–7".
Light Full sun.
Soil Well drained, sandy. Suitable for xeriscaping. Add 1 teaspoon lime to each planting hole.

CARING FOR PLANTS

Water regularly and feed occasionally. Trim lightly after flowering. Plants are short lived and may die out after 1–2 years but will survive longer in a dry, sunny location.

PROPAGATING

Divide or take softwood cuttings after flowering, or grow from seed. Plants self-seed.

Agapanthus

HP, TP* | Zn 7–10

Agapanthus, African blue lily

p. 370

Sophisticated, refined, and irresistible plants, agapanthus bear clumps of funnel-shaped blue or white flowers held on strong 1'–4' stalks. The gently arching leaves are thick and straplike. Pots of these elegant plants are essential on any sunny patio.

Type Hardy perennial, tender perennial; often grown as an annual
Zone 7–10, H 12–1 (see species list, p. 436). Although *A.* × Headbourne Hybrids and *A. inapertus* are hardy only in Zones 9–10, they may survive farther north if heavy winter mulch is provided
Flowering Season Summer to early autumn

SOWING

Indoors Any time.
Outdoors Spring.
Depth *Seed:* Just cover. *Roots:* 2"–4".

GERMINATING

Time 20–90 days.
Requirements Rarely grown from seed; 60°–70°F.

TRANSPLANTING

Time After last frost.
Spacing 18"–24".
Light Full sun to light shade.
Soil Moist, well drained. *A. africanus* is drought tolerant and suitable for xeriscaping.

CARING FOR PLANTS

Easy. Fertilize every 2 weeks during the growing season and water frequently. Deadhead regularly. Blooms most profusely when roots are somewhat crowded. Where plants are not frost hardy, dig roots in autumn and store in sand in a cool, frost-free location, replanting in spring. Where plants are grown in containers, simply move pots indoors for the winter.

PROPAGATING

Every 4–5 years, divide evergreen forms in spring or autumn and deciduous species only in autumn. Soak roots in water for several hours to ease division. Or grow from seed. Plants grown from seed will bloom in 3–4 years.

COMBINATIONS

Stunning alone, or mix with *Achillea, Allium, Helenium, Hemerocallis, Lilium, Phygelius, Romneya.*

Agastache (syn. *Brittonastrum*)

HP, TP | Zn 4–10

Agastache, Giant hyssop, Mexican hyssop

p. 370

Summer-blooming plants of 2'–6' bear spikes of purple, blue, pink, yellow, or green flowers above anise-scented leaves. The coarse texture of these perennials makes them most useful in a wildflower garden. Most species are native to North America and Mexico.

Type Hardy perennial, tender perennial
Zone 4–10, H 12–7 (see species list, p. 436); all prefer cool temperatures
Flowering Season Summer to early autumn

SOWING

Indoors 6–8 weeks before planting out.
Outdoors Autumn.
Depth Just cover.

GERMINATING

Time 30–90 days.
Requirements 55°F.

TRANSPLANTING

Time After last frost.
Spacing 12".
Light Sun or very light shade.
Soil Well drained, fairly rich.

CARING FOR PLANTS

Feed annually in spring and renew every year or two to maintain vigor by dividing, allowing volunteers to mature, or setting out new plants; discard old clumps. Transplant only before plants bloom.

PROPAGATING

Divide plants in spring in Zones 4–6 (in early autumn in the South), take cuttings in late summer, or grow from seed. Plants self-seed. Plants grown from seed will bloom in 2 years.

COMBINATIONS

Clarkia, Platycodon, Verbena bonariensis.

Ageratum

A | Zn 1–10

Ageratum, Floss flower

p. 370

Attractive annuals and biennials with downy flowers of pink, white, or palest blue to deepest violet. Plants may form compact mounds suitable for edging or stand erect up to 24". All are useful in the border; tall species are also at home in naturalized gardens.

Type Annual
Zone 1–10; H 12–1; prefers warm summers
Flowering Season Spring to frost

SOWING

Indoors 6–8 weeks before planting out.
Outdoors 2 to 3 weeks after last frost, when soil is quite warm. Where winters are mild, sow seed again in late summer for autumn bloom.
Depth Surface.

GERMINATING

Time 5–14 days.
Requirements Light and 70°–75°F.

TRANSPLANTING

Time 2 to 3 weeks after last frost.
Spacing *Dwarf species:* 6". *Medium species:* 6"–10". *Tall species:* 12"–24".
Light Full sun, with light shade where summers are hot.
Soil Very adaptable. Prefers a pH level of 5.0–6.0.

CARING FOR PLANTS

Easy. Deadhead regularly, feed monthly, and water during hot, dry weather. Pinch out tall species to encourage a bushy habit. Susceptible to root rot when weather is cool and wet.

PROPAGATING

Grow from seed. Some species self-seed to the point of being invasive.

COMBINATIONS

Ageratums combine well with many plants, including *Salpiglossis, Salvia, Tagetes,* and *Tanacetum.*

A

Agrostemma

A | Zn 1–9

Corn cockle

p. 371

These dainty, easy annuals are 2'–4' tall. Covered in tiny, deep pink, trumpet-shaped blooms, they are at home in cottage gardens and borders.

Type Annual
Zone 1–9; H 9–1; prefers cool temperatures
Flowering Season Summer

SOWING

Indoors 6–8 weeks before planting out.
Outdoors Early spring, when soil is cool and a light frost is still possible, or early autumn where winters are mild.
Depth 1/8".

GERMINATING

Time 14–21 days.
Requirements 55°–65°F.

TRANSPLANTING

Time After last frost.
Spacing 9"–12".
Light Sun.
Soil Tolerates most soils, but rich, well-drained loam will give the best results.

CARING FOR PLANTS

Easy. Deadhead regularly to prolong flowering and prevent self-seeding. Water during dry spells. Support with stakes or twiggy branches pushed into the ground.

PROPAGATING

Grow from seed. Self-seeds freely.

CAUTION

All parts of the plant are toxic if eaten. *Agrostemma* is listed as invasive in many areas. See pp. 494–495 for advice.

Agrostis

A | Zn 3–9

Bent grass

This annual grass grows 18" tall, with flat green leaves. One species, Agrostis nebulosa, *gets its common name, cloud grass, from its haze of fragile flowers.*

Type Annual
Zone 3–9. Prefers warm temperatures
Flowering Season Mid to late summer

SOWING

Indoors 4–6 weeks before planting out.
Outdoors Early spring, when soil is cool and a light frost is still possible, or late autumn.
Depth Surface.

GERMINATING

Time 21–25 days.
Requirements 50°–55°F.

TRANSPLANTING

Time After last frost.
Spacing 6"–8".
Light Sun or light shade.
Soil Very adaptable but prefers good drainage. *A. nebulosa* is suitable for xeriscaping.

CARING FOR PLANTS

Easy. Feed regularly and do not allow soil to dry out. Pick all flowers before seed sets to prevent self-seeding. To dry for flower arrangements, cut stems just before flower spikes open and hang upside down in a dark place.

PROPAGATING

Grow from seed only.

COMBINATIONS

Echium, Viola.

Ajania

HP | Zn 5–9

p. 371

A genus of perennials until recently classified as Chrysanthemum, *most are 1′–2′ tall with very attractive, deeply lobed, light green leaves. Some have leaves edged in silver or bearing silky white hairs. Flowers are yellow and either button- or daisylike. Although plants may not bloom in colder regions, they are often grown simply for their handsome foliage.*

Type Hardy perennial
Zone 5–9, H 9–1
Flowering Season Mid- to late autumn

SOWING

Indoors 6–8 weeks before planting out.
Outdoors Early spring when soil is cool and a light frost is still possible, or early autumn.
Depth Surface.

GERMINATING

Time 7–28 days.
Requirements Light and a temperature between 60°–75°F.

TRANSPLANTING

Time After last frost or in autumn.
Spacing 15″–18″.
Light Full sun, with shade from the hot afternoon sun in the South.
Soil Tolerates a wide range of soil types, from average to poor or dry, but is happiest where soil is humusy and moist, with very good drainage and a pH of 6.1–7.8; will not survive where soil stays wet in winter.

CARING FOR PLANTS

Easy. Pinch back tips regularly from early spring until 6 weeks before flowering to increase number of blooms. Water during dry spells, and mulch well in the North in late autumn. Plants may be troubled by aphids.

PROPAGATING

Divide in spring, take cuttings in spring or summer, or grow from seed.

COMBINATIONS

Hemerocallis, Salvia, Veronica.

Ajuga

HP | Zn 3–10

Ajuga, Bugleweed

p. 371

Vigorous, mat-forming plants, usually perennial and evergreen, ajugas are useful both for their attractive foliage of deep green, bronze-purple, or variegated pink and cream and for the impressive forest of upright blue- or purple-flowering stems borne in spring. This European native may be used as a ground cover or in a small shady planting.

Type Hardy perennial
Zone 3–10, H 9–1 (see species list, p. 436); *A. genevensis* and *A. reptans* do not like hot, humid locations
Flowering Season Late spring to midsummer

SOWING

Indoors Start seed outdoors only.
Outdoors Early spring, when soil is cool and light frost is still possible.
Depth Just cover.

GERMINATING

Time 21–28 days.
Requirements 50°–55°F.

TRANSPLANTING

Time Set out purchased plants in spring or autumn.
Spacing 6″–12″, depending on how quickly you want to cover the ground.
Light Sun or shade.
Soil Thrives in quite dry soil with a pH level of 5.5–7.0. Must have very good drainage to prevent root rot. Tolerates poor soil. *A. reptans* is suitable for xeriscaping.

CARING FOR PLANTS

Easy, although careful attention produces a more handsome ground cover. Feed once in spring and water regularly. Diligently weed new ground-cover plantings, deadhead after flowering, and remove fallen leaves from beds in autumn to obtain the look you see in garden books. Do not plant near lawns, as *Ajuga* will quickly and ineradicably make itself at home in lawn grass.

Ajuga (cont'd)

PROPAGATING

Root stolons in spring or autumn or start from seed.

COMBINATIONS

Use for contrasting foliage color with *Artemisia, Camellia, Daphne odora, Helleborus,* or *Hosta,* or combine with other spring-flowering plants like *Crocus, Lamium, Mahonia* and *Primula.*

CAUTION

A. reptans is listed as invasive in many areas, including Florida and Maryland. See pp. 494–495 for advice.

Alcea (syn. *Althaea*)

HP | Zn 2–9

Hollyhock

p. 371

These charming upright plants evoke old-fashioned cottage gardens and Impressionist paintings. New species are often double-flowered and confined to a modest 2'–3', while old-timers tower over the border at 5'–9'. They are available in almost every color, including a sumptuous black.

Type Short-lived hardy perennial; often treated as an annual
Zone 2–9, H 9–1 (see species list, p. 436); likes warm temperatures but not excessive heat and humidity
Flowering Season Summer to early autumn

SOWING

Indoors 6–8 weeks before planting out, in peat pots.
Outdoors *Perennial:* After last frost; 1 week before last frost in warmer climates. *Biennial:* July.
Depth Surface.

GERMINATING

Time 10–14 days.
Requirements Easy. Light and 60°–70°F.

TRANSPLANTING

Time *Perennial:* After last frost. *Biennial:* Early autumn.
Spacing 18"–36".
Light Full sun or light shade.
Soil Rich, moist, well drained, with a pH level of 6.0–7.5. Will tolerate dry soil.

CARING FOR PLANTS

Easy. Unrestricted air circulation is essential. Stake tall plants and feed and water regularly during growing season. Cutting back stalks immediately after flowering may produce a second blooming. Mulch well in autumn. Do not move mature plants. May be troubled by powdery mildew, rust, leaf spot, Japanese beetles, or slugs. Rust is more common on older plants and can often be avoided by replacing plants every 1 or 2 years.

PROPAGATING

Grow from seed. Plants self-seed, but resulting flowers may differ in color from those of the parent.

COMBINATIONS

Allium, Linaria, Paeonia, climbing roses.

Alchemilla

HP | Zn 3–9

Lady's mantle

p. 371

Gardeners value members of this large genus of low-growing perennials for their attractive and unusual crimped, pale green foliage and sprays of green or pale yellow flowers. Plants make good edgings, ground covers, or rock garden inhabitants. They are incomparable as a foil for plants of strongly contrasting color.

Type Hardy perennial
Zone 3–9, H 7–1; does not like excessive heat and humidity
Flowering Season Summer

SOWING

Indoors 6–8 weeks before last frost.
Outdoors Early spring, when soil is still cool, or late autumn.
Depth ⅛".

GERMINATING

Time 21–30 days.
Requirements 60°–70°F.

TRANSPLANTING

Time Spring or autumn.
Spacing *Small species:* 12". *Large species:* 12"–18".
Light Full sun or part shade. Prefers shade where sun is very hot.
Soil Moist, well drained. Enrich with humus in hot, dry climates.

CARING FOR PLANTS

Easy. Deadhead to prevent self-seeding. Top-dress with compost in autumn. Harvest flowers at their peak and hang upside down in a dark room to dry for winter arrangements.

PROPAGATING

Divide in early spring in Zones 3–6 (in early autumn in the South) or grow from seed. Plants also self-seed.

COMBINATIONS

Arenaria, Bellis, Digitalis, ferns, *Myosotis, Scilla.*

Allium

HB | Zn 3–9 | ☼ ◐ | dry soil, ordinary soil

Allium, Onion

p. 371

This large genus of spring- and summer-flowering bulbs includes species that range in height from 6"–5'. They are best known for their dramatic balls of blue, purple, yellow, or pink flowers held above stiff, upright stems, although many other forms exist. Uses are as varied as forms.

Type Hardy bulb
Zone 3–9, H9–1 (see species list, p. 437)
Flowering Season Spring or summer, depending on species

SOWING

Indoors Any time.
Outdoors *Seed:* Spring or autumn. *Bulb:* Autumn.
Depth *Seed:* Surface. *Bulb:* Small, 3"–5". Large, 6"–8". Rule of thumb: Cover bulb with twice its diameter of soil.

GERMINATING

Time 14–365 days.
Requirements Difficult. Place seed in a plastic bag together with moist growing medium and refrigerate for 30 days. Provide light and 55°–65°F thereafter. Grow in flats for 1 year, then pot up singly and sink pots in the ground outdoors in spring. Move to the garden in autumn.

TRANSPLANTING

Time Autumn. Set out purchased chive plants in spring; where summers are very hot, plant in late summer or autumn for winter harvest.
Spacing *Small species:* 3"–4". *Medium species:* 4"–6". *Large species:* 12". Chives: 5"–6".
Light Full sun to light shade.
Soil Very well drained, not too rich. Chives prefer soil amended with plenty of manure or compost and a pH level of 6.0–7.0.

CARING FOR PLANTS

Easy. Feed once in spring and remove faded blooms after flowering to prevent prolific self-seeding. *A. giganteum* may need staking. Chives will be edible in 1 year when grown from seed. Feed with 5-10-5 and divide every 2–3 years to maintain vigorous plants. May be potted up and brought indoors for winter use. *Allium* bulbs are susceptible to bulb rot, which will cause dieback of the leaves.

PROPAGATING

Divide spring-flowering bulbs in late summer, summer-flowering bulbs in spring; or grow from seed. Many species will self-seed and become invasive. Bulbs grown from seed will flower in 2–4 years.

COMBINATIONS

Combines well with many other perennials: *Achillea, Hosta, Lilium, Lupinus, Papaver, Polygonum, Salvia, Stachys,* or *Veronica.* Mixed with *Tradescantia,* the fading leaves of *Allium* will be neatly hidden by the *Tradescantia* foliage.

Alonsoa

TP* | Zn 9–10

Mask flower

Branching, upright plants create a rather untidy tangle of stems, leaves, and flowers. Blossoms are flat with wavy or reflexed petals and prominent yellow stamens; petals are red, orange, pink, or white. 12"–36" tall. They may be grown in the border or cutting bed.

Type Tender perennial; often grown as an annual
Zone 9 –10, H 12–10; grown as an annual in Zones 1–8. Prefers the climate of the Pacific Northwest and will not flower well in hot, humid weather. Requires night temperatures below 65°F
Flowering Season Late spring through first frost

SOWING

Indoors 6–8 weeks before planting out.
Outdoors After last frost.
Depth Just cover.

GERMINATING

Time 14–21 days.
Requirements 60°F.

TRANSPLANTING

Time After last frost.
Spacing 10"–12".
Light Full sun.
Soil Light, well drained, fertile.

CARING FOR PLANTS

Pinch back seedlings when 2"–3" tall to promote bushiness. Staking may be necessary on windy sites. In the autumn, mulch plants well in Zones 9–10. Much loved by aphids.

PROPAGATING

Take cuttings or grow from seed.

COMBINATIONS

Antirrhinum, Aster, Chrysanthemum, Coreopsis, Hemerocallis.

Alstroemeria

HP | Zn 7–10

Lily of Peru, Lily-of-the-Incas, Peruvian lily

p. 372

Prized for their extraordinarily lovely trumpet-shaped flowers borne on tall, erect stems, these South American natives should be given their own bed due to their invasive tendencies. They make exquisite cut flowers.

Type Hardy perennial
Zone 7–10, H 10–7 (see species list, p. 437); prefer cool, damp winters and sunny, warm summers
Flowering Season Mainly summer, though some species bloom in spring or autumn

SOWING

Indoors 8–10 weeks before planting out, in peat pots.
Outdoors Early spring in cool soil, or early autumn.
Depth *Seed:* Just cover. *Roots:* 6"–8".

GERMINATING

Time 15–365 days.
Requirements Difficult. Soak seed in warm water for 12 hours before sowing. Provide 65°–70°F thereafter.

TRANSPLANTING

Time After last frost.
Spacing 15"–18".
Light Full sun; sun or part shade in hot summers
Soil Well drained, humus-rich. Cultivate to a depth of 15" to avoid root rot, to which *Alstroemeria* is highly susceptible.

CARING FOR PLANTS

Most species require one annual feeding in late winter, although *A. aurantiaca* prefers light monthly feeds. Plants disappear altogether after blooming; mark locations to avoid unintentional root damage. Mulch in early winter and do not disturb roots. Staking may be necessary. Once established, *A. ligtu* develops deep, invasive roots and can be difficult to eradicate.

PROPAGATING

Very carefully divide in autumn (successful division is difficult) or grow from seed.

COMBINATIONS

Delphinium, Geranium, Helenium, Lilium, Papaver, annual *Phlox, Salvia.*

CAUTION

Contact with plants may cause skin irritation.

Alyssum (syn. *Aurinia, Lobularia*)

HP | Zn 3–10 | ☼ | Ordinary soil

Alyssum

p. 372

Shrubby, low-growing perennials (sometimes evergreen), alyssums are grown for their clusters of tiny yellow, orange, or white flowers. Use them in rock gardens or as an edging. They are stunning in full bloom cascading over a stone wall.

Type Hardy perennial
Zone 3–10, H 9–1 (see species list, 437)
Flowering Season Spring or summer, depending on species

SOWING

Indoors 8–10 weeks before planting out.
Outdoors Early spring or early autumn.
Depth Surface.

GERMINATING

Time 5 days.
Requirements Cool temperatures and light.

TRANSPLANTING

Time Early spring, when soil is cool and a light frost is still possible, or early autumn.
Spacing 12".
Light Full sun.
Soil Tolerant of many soils but must have perfect drainage; very rich soil produces weak, leggy plants. Prefers a pH level of 5.5–7.5.

CARING FOR PLANTS

Easy. Water only during droughts. After flowering, cut back stems by one third.

PROPAGATING

Take cuttings in summer or grow from seed.

COMBINATIONS

Cerastium, Erysimum, Iberis, Sedum, tulips.

Amaranthus

A | Zn 3–10 | Full sun, Partial shade | Dry soil, Ordinary soil

Amaranth

p. 372

Amaranthus are bushy, 3'–4' tall annuals grown for their extraordinary (some might say alarming) tassels of deep red or green flowers. Some species have erect flowering stems or interesting yellow and red foliage. Use them in containers or as an accent in the border.

Type Annual
Zone 3–10, H 12–5; does best in warm temperatures
Flowering Season Summer through early autumn

SOWING

Indoors 6–8 weeks before last frost, in peat pots.
Outdoors 2 to 3 weeks after last frost, when soil is warm.
Depth Just cover.

GERMINATING

Time 10–15 days.
Requirements Easy. 70°–75°F.

TRANSPLANTING

Time After last frost.
Spacing *Small species:* 9"–12". *Tall species:* 18".
Light Full sun to half shade.
Soil Tolerant of most soils; prefers a pH level of 6.0–7.0. Rich soil produces larger but less brightly colored leaves.

CARING FOR PLANTS

Easy. Water frequently and feed occasionally during the summer. Watch for aphids.

PROPAGATING

Grow from seed only.

COMBINATIONS

Antirrhinum, Solenostemon, Nicotiana, Salvia.

CAUTION

A. spinosus and *A. viridis* may be invasive. (See pp. 494–495 for advice.)

A

Amaryllis

TB*, HB* | Zn 7–10

Belladonna lily, Naked ladies, Jersey lily

p. 372

These autumn-flowering bulbs bear large, trumpet-shaped flowers on sturdy 18" stalks. South African natives, they are difficult to incorporate successfully in the border, but they are attractive in pots or might make an interesting display massed on their own.

Type Tender bulb, hardy bulb
Zone 7–10, H 12–7 (see species list, p. 437); prefers hot, dry summers
Flowering Season Late summer to autumn

SOWING

Indoors Late winter, in individual pots.
Outdoors *Seed:* After last frost. *Bulb:* Late summer.
Depth *Seed:* Just cover. *Bulb:* Zones 5–6, 10", ideally against a south-facing wall. Zones 7–8, 6"–8". Zones 9–10, just cover.

GERMINATING

Time 21–120 days.
Requirements 65°–75°F.

TRANSPLANTING

Time Late spring to early summer.
Spacing 9"–12".
Light Full sun.
Soil Average or rich, moist, and well drained.

CARING FOR PLANTS

As soon as flowers open, pinch off anthers to prolong blooming. Move with care, retaining a large root-ball, and do not divide frequently as plants may not flower for several years after division or moving. Provide a thick winter mulch in Zones 7–8. Bulbs may be lifted after flowering and stored indoors where winters are severe. Bulbs planted against a south-facing wall and deeply mulched in autumn may survive north of Zone 7.

PROPAGATING

Divide bulbs after blooming or grow from seed. Plants grown from seeds may take up to 8 years to flower.

CAUTION

All parts of the plant are toxic to humans and pets if eaten.

Ammi

A | Zn 3–9

Bishop's weed

These naturalistic-looking annuals bear stiff, upright stems topped by 6" wide flower heads smothered in tiny white blooms. Although not a native wildflower, Ammi *is at home in a wildflower garden or informal planting. It is useful for cut flower arrangements.*

Type Annual
Zone 3–9. Prefers cool weather
Flowering Season Mid summer to mid autumn

SOWING

Indoors 6–8 weeks before last frost.
Outdoors Early spring, when soil is cool and a light frost is still possible, or late autumn.
Depth Just cover.

GERMINATING

Time 7–25 days.
Requirements Chill in the refrigerator for 1–2 weeks, then grow at 55°–65°F.

TRANSPLANTING

Time After last frost.
Spacing 12".
Light Full sun to light shade.
Soil Prefers soil that is fertile and quite moist.

CARING FOR PLANTS

Water regularly until plants are established, then only during dry spells.

PROPAGATING

Grow from seed only.

COMBINATIONS

Digitalis, roses, *Stachys*

CAUTION

Contact with sap may cause skin irritation.

Ammobium

A | Zn 2–10 | ☼ | dry soil, ordinary soil

Winged everlasting

p. 372

Somewhat coarse everlasting annuals, Ammobium *feature showy white flowers on upright, 2'–3' tall stems. Use in the border or cutting bed.*

Type Annual; sometimes treated as a biennial
Zone 2–10; needs warm, dry days and cool nights to thrive
Flowering Season Summer to early autumn

SOWING

Indoors 6–8 weeks before planting out.
Outdoors Early spring or early autumn.
Depth Just cover.

GERMINATING

Time 10–15 days.
Requirements 60°F.

TRANSPLANTING

Time Spring, when night temperatures will stay above 50°F.
Spacing 10"–15".
Light Full sun.
Soil Grows well in average, well-drained soil; will tolerate dry soil.

CARING FOR PLANTS

Easy. Water only during dry periods. To dry for flower arrangements, cut just before flowers are fully opened and hang upside down to dry.

PROPAGATING

Grow from seed. Plants self-seed.

Amsonia (syn. *Rhazya*)

HP | Zn 4–9 | full sun, partial shade | ordinary soil, moist soil

Amsonia, Blue star

p. 372

Neat, attractive, clump-forming perennials, 2'–3' tall, amsonias bear dainty blue, star-shaped flowers atop long, supple stems. Use these North American natives in naturalistic plantings, along woodland edges, or in informal beds.

Type Hardy perennial
Zone 4–9, H 9–1 (see species list, p. 437)
Flowering Season Mid-spring–summer

SOWING

Indoors 8–10 weeks before planting out, in peat pots.
Outdoors Mid-spring or autumn.
Depth Just cover.

GERMINATING

Time 28–42 days.
Requirements 55°–60°F.

TRANSPLANTING

Time Late spring.
Spacing 18"–36".
Light Light shade; full sun where soil is moist and summers are relatively cool.
Soil Cool, moist.

CARING FOR PLANTS

Easy. Prune lightly to maintain neat appearance. Water occasionally during dry spells. Feed in early autumn. Divide periodically to keep plants healthy and blooming, but otherwise avoid root disturbance.

PROPAGATING

Divide in early spring, early autumn in Zones 7–8, take cuttings in summer, or grow from seed. May self-seed.

COMBINATIONS

Athyrium nipponicum, Ceratostigma, Digitalis, Penstemon, Phlox divaricata, Stachys.

Anacyclus

HP | Zn 6–9

p. 372

These prostrate alpine perennials are native to the rocky soils of North Africa. They feature white — or, less frequently, yellow — daisylike flowers and dense gray foliage. Grow them in rock gardens or in the cracks of stone walls.

Type Hardy perennial
Zone 6–9, H 8–6; does not like excessively hot and humid summers or very wet winters
Flowering Season Spring to midsummer

SOWING

Indoors Prechilled seed 8 weeks before planting out.
Outdoors Autumn.
Depth Just cover.

GERMINATING

Time Usually 30–60 days but may take up to 3 years.
Requirements Easy. Place seed in a plastic bag together with moist growing medium and refrigerate for 48 hours. Provide light and 55°–60°F thereafter.

TRANSPLANTING

Time After last spring frost or early autumn.
Spacing 12"–18".
Light Full sun.
Soil Dry, rather gritty; excellent choice for xeriscaping, even in the driest regions. Doesn't tolerate alkaline soils.

CARING FOR PLANTS

Easy. Where summers are very hot, cut back plants hard after blooming. Surround with stone chips to ensure good drainage and to protect from winter wetness.

PROPAGATING

Take cuttings in summer, divide in spring, or grow from seed.

COMBINATIONS

Dianthus, Pulsatilla, Salvia.

Anagallis

A, HP, TP* | Zn 2–10

Pimpernel

p. 373

Low-growing, bushy plants are smothered in small, star-shaped blooms, usually of deep blue or red. The flowers smell distinctly of honey. Use them at the front of the border or in rock gardens.

Type Annual, hardy perennial, tender perennial often grown as an annual
Zone *Annual:* 2–10. *Perennial:* 5–10, H 7–5 (see species list, p. 437). *A. arvensis* is short lived and often grown as an annual; *A. monelli* is often grown as an annual in Zones 3–7
Flowering Season Early summer to early autumn

SOWING

Indoors Not recommended due to difficulty in transplanting. If attempting, sow seed in peat pots 6 weeks before planting out.
Outdoors After last frost.
Depth 1/8".

GERMINATING

Time 30–42 days.
Requirements 50°–65°F.

TRANSPLANTING

Time After last frost.
Spacing 5"–9".
Light Full sun.
Soil Tolerates most soils.

CARING FOR PLANTS

Easy. Mulch after planting. Do not move.

PROPAGATING

Divide perennials in autumn (in spring in Zones 5 and 6), take cuttings, or grow from seed. Annuals self-seed.

Anaphalis

HP | Zn 3–9

Pearly everlasting

p. 373

Upright perennials with small, white, everlasting flowers, Anaphalis *is often used in dried arrangements. Flowers are borne in clusters above 8"–36" stems. Leaves are lance-shaped, silver, and slightly woolly. Grow pearly everlasting in cutting beds or borders.*

Type Hardy perennial
Zone 3–9, H 8–1 (see species list, p. 438)
Flowering Season Summer

SOWING

Indoors 6–8 weeks before planting out.
Outdoors Early spring, when soil is cool and a light frost is possible, or late autumn.
Depth Just cover.

GERMINATING

Time 10–60 days.
Requirements 55°–65°F.

TRANSPLANTING

Time After last frost.
Spacing 9"–12".
Light Full sun or light shade.
Soil Prefers good drainage. With the exception of *A. triplinervis,* these plants are very drought tolerant and suitable for xeriscaping.

CARING FOR PLANTS

Easy. Cut back after flowering to encourage a second bloom. Provide winter mulch in northern zones.

PROPAGATING

Divide in spring in the North (in autumn south of Zone 6), take cuttings in spring, or start from seed.

COMBINATIONS

Echinacea, Schizostylis, Veronica.

Anchusa

A, HP | Zn 1–10

Anchusa, Alkanet

p. 373

A diverse genus of plants, Anchusa *includes upright and mat-forming, evergreen and deciduous forms. Most are grown for their small, intensely blue, usually tubular flowers. Use tall species at the border rear, and small ones in rock gardens or beside stepping-stones.*

Type Annual, hardy perennial
Zone *Annual:* 1–10. *Perennial:* 3–8, H 8–1 (see species list, p. 438). Prefers cool weather
Flowering Season Spring to late summer, depending on species

SOWING

Indoors 6–8 weeks before planting out.
Outdoors *Annual:* Early spring, when soil is cool and a light frost is still possible, or late autumn. *Perennial:* After last frost. In the South, seed may be started in early spring or late autumn.
Depth Just cover.

GERMINATING

Time 7–30 days.
Requirements 70°F.

TRANSPLANTING

Time After last frost.
Spacing *Small species:* 10"–12". *Large species:* 18"–30".
Light *Annual:* Full sun. *Perennial:* Full sun to light shade.
Soil Most require moist, with a pH level of 6.0–7.5; *A. cespitosa* prefers dry.

CARING FOR PLANTS

Easy. Keep well watered. Feed once in spring and again during the growing season. Plants may require staking. Cut back stems by half after flowering to stimulate a second bloom. Cut back to ground level in autumn. Transplant with care. Watch for cucumber mosaic, which causes yellow spotting on the leaves.

PROPAGATING

Divide, take root cuttings of perennials in spring, or grow from seed. Annuals self-seed and may become a nuisance.

COMBINATIONS

Achillea, Anthemis, Consolida, Dianthus barbatus, Eschscholzia, Trachelium.

Androsace (syn. Douglasia)

HP | Zn 3–8

Rock jasmine

p. 373

Very low-growing (1"–6"), short-lived plants, rock jasmines are often evergreen, with small, pointed, needlelike or woolly leaves. They bear small cup-shaped or flat pink, white, or red flowers. These mountain natives are happiest in rock gardens.

Type Hardy perennial; often grown as an annual
Zone 3–8, H 7–1 (see species list, p. 438); plants do not like extreme heat or drought
Flowering Season Spring, summer, or autumn, depending on species

SOWING

Indoors Any time.
Outdoors Early spring, when a light frost may still occur, or autumn.
Depth Surface.

GERMINATING

Time 30–365 days.
Requirements Difficult. *Indoors:* Place seed and moistened growing medium in a plastic bag and refrigerate for 2 weeks. Provide light and 50°–55°F thereafter. *Outdoors:* Prepare ground well, press seed lightly into the soil, then cover with a glass jar pushed firmly into the ground.

TRANSPLANTING

Time Early spring or autumn.
Spacing 6".
Light Full sun but appreciates some afternoon shade where summers are very hot.
Soil Gritty or sandy. Add stone chips to improve drainage, if necessary. Prefers a slightly alkaline soil.

CARING FOR PLANTS

Can be difficult. Water during dry spells, taking care to keep water off rosettes. Plants may require protection from heavy rains. Apply a light mulch of stone chips in winter.

PROPAGATING

Detach rosettes from the parent plant in summer. Pot up and grow indoors, then plant out rooted rosettes the following spring.

Anemone

TP*, HP | Zn 3–10

Anemone, Windflower

p. 373

Large, incredibly diverse group of perennials ranging from 6" to 4' tall and bearing blossoms of every color, except yellow, at any time from spring through autumn. Most species are more effective when planted in large clumps, in either the border or woodland garden.

Type Tender perennial, hardy perennial; less hardy species are sometimes grown as annuals in cooler zones
Zone 3–10, H 12–1 (see species list, p. 438). *A. coronaria* does not tolerate high heat and humidity
Flowering Season Any time from early spring through late autumn, depending on species

SOWING

Indoors See Germinating, Requirements.
Outdoors *Seed:* See Germinating, Requirements. *Tuber:* Most can be planted in mid-autumn, but tender species should be planted in spring in cold northern areas.
Depth *Seed:* Just cover. *Tuber:* 3"–5", with the fuzzy side facing up. If in doubt, plant tubers on their sides.

GERMINATING

Time 15–180 days.
Requirements *Autumn sowing:* Sow seed in market packs, sink in the ground against a north-facing wall, and cover with glass. Moisten soil occasionally, if necessary. Bring indoors in spring to 60°–70°F. *Spring sowing:* Sow seed in moistened medium, secure in a plastic bag, and refrigerate for 2–3 weeks. Sink containers in the ground in a shady location and cover with glass. Transplant seedlings as they appear.

TRANSPLANTING

Time Early spring, when soil is cool and a light frost is possible, or early autumn.
Spacing *Small species:* 5"–8". *Large species:* 12"–15".
Light Most species prefer part shade but will tolerate full sun with plenty of moisture.

Anemone (cont'd)

Soil Average, with humus or well-rotted manure added and a pH level of 6.0–7.5. *A. coronaria* must have cool, moist, well-drained soil. *A. blanda* tolerates dry soil and is suitable for xeriscaping.

CARING FOR PLANTS

Easy. Water regularly, mulch in summer to keep soil cool, and leave roots undisturbed. Provide mulch where winters are severe, or lift plants after foliage dies and store in a cool, frost-free location, replanting in spring. If leaf miners are present, pick off and destroy any infested leaves.

PROPAGATING

Take root cuttings in spring or summer, divide in spring, or grow from seed. Plants grown from seed will flower in 2 years.

COMBINATIONS

Early bloomers: *Dicentra, Digitalis, Galium, Impatiens, Mertensia, Muscari, Narcissus, Papaver, Phlox stolonifera, Podophyllum.* Late bloomers: *Aconitum, Bergenia, Hosta, Lilium, Nerine.*

CAUTION

Harmful if eaten.

Anemonella

HP | Zn 4–7

p. 373

These charming, low-growing (4"–8") woodland perennials are grown for their delicately tinted pink or white cup-shaped flowers and fine, fernlike foliage. They are best suited to a naturalistic setting or rock garden.

Type Hardy perennial
Zone 4–7, H 7–1
Flowering Season Spring to early summer

SOWING

Indoors Not grown from seed.
Outdoors *Tuber:* Late summer to early autumn.
Depth *Tuber:* 1".

TRANSPLANTING

Spacing 5"–7".
Light Part shade.
Soil Rich, moist, well drained, woodland, with plenty of organic matter added; prefers a pH level of 5.0–7.0.

CARING FOR PLANTS

Keep soil moist while plants are in bloom. Shelter plants from winds. Mulch well in autumn. Do not disturb roots except when dividing, which should be done infrequently in early spring, but no more than once every 3–5 years.

PROPAGATING

Plants are most easily propagated by division. Divide tubers in very early spring or after foliage has died back in autumn.

Anethum (syn. *Peucedanum*)

A | Zn 3–10

Dill

This 2'–3' herb bears feathery blue-green leaves and flat clusters of minute yellow flowers. Because the habit is somewhat ungainly, plants are best grown in the herb garden.

Type Annual
Zone 3–10
Flowering Season June through October, with successive sowings

SOWING

Indoors 6–8 weeks before planting out.
Outdoors Sow seed every 2 weeks for a continuous supply of leaves. In Zones 3–8, sow from early spring through midsummer; in Zones 9–10, from late summer through midwinter.
Depth Surface.

Anethum (cont'd)

GERMINATING

Time 21–25 days.
Requirements Start seed in vermiculite at 60°–75°F.

TRANSPLANTING

Time As soon as seedlings develop true leaves and are large enough to handle.
Spacing 10"–12".
Light Full sun.
Soil Rich, well drained, with a pH level of 5.5–6.5. Add compost or manure at planting time.

CARING FOR PLANTS

Feed in early spring with 5-10-5 fertilizer. To keep plants growing vigorously all summer, water abundantly, especially during hot, dry spells. Shelter from strong winds and do not plant near fennel, as these two herbs will cross-pollinate freely with unpredictable results. Before first frost, harvest leaves and freeze, either whole or chopped. Dill can be potted up and grown indoors if given 5 hours of sunlight a day.

PROPAGATING

Grow from seed. Plants self-seed.

Angelica

HP | Zn 4–9

Angelica

p. 373

Large, imposing, somewhat cumbersome plants are more striking than conventionally attractive. Massive clumps are 5'–6' tall, with large, deeply lobed leaves and white or purple flowers of the Queen Anne's lace variety. They are best used for their dramatic effect with other bold plants that can hold their own against this giant.

Type Short-lived hardy perennial often grown as a biennial, although it may be perennial in effect through self-seeding
Zone 4–7 (to Zone 9 in the West), H 8–2 (see species list, p. 438)
Flowering Season Midsummer to early autumn

SOWING

Indoors 4–6 weeks before planting out.
Outdoors As soon as seed is ripe, in late summer to early autumn.
Depth Surface.

GERMINATING

Time 20–60 days.
Requirements *A. archangelica:* Sow seed in moistened growing medium in peat pots, seal pots loosely in plastic bags, and refrigerate for 2 weeks. Provide light and a temperature of 60°–65°F thereafter. *All other species:* Easy, although the germination rate may be low. Sow in peat pots, provide light, and 60°–65°F.

TRANSPLANTING

Time 20–60 days.
Spacing 24"–48".
Light Full sun in the North, light shade in the South. Plants will tolerate more southern sun if the soil is quite moist.
Soil Will tolerate ordinary, even dry, soil, but for larger, more robust plants, provide rich, deep, well-drained soil with plenty of moisture.

CARING FOR PLANTS

Plants are short lived and will need to be replaced every 2–3 years. Deadheading will extend their lives, but will also limit self-seeding, which may be desired to produce a regular supply of new plants. Plants do not transplant well. Stems of *A. archangelica* may be harvested before flowering in spring and crystallized in sugar syrup for use in cooking.

PROPAGATING

Grow from seed. Where plants are happy, they will self-seed with abandon. Plants grown from seed will bloom in 2 years.

COMBINATIONS

Smaller plants are easily overwhelmed by the bold architectural form of angelica. Pair with other substantial plants such as giant *Allium,* large dahlias, and ornamental grasses.

Angelonia

TP* | Zn 9–10

These sublimely lovely, shrubby, 2'–3' tall annuals have the appearance of being delicate and finicky, but they are actually amazingly tough and tolerant of even extreme heat. They bear racemes of small, lipped, orchidlike flowers in abundance from early summer to frost. Flowers are solid white, blue, purple, or attractively striped. Angelonia *makes a charming border plant or cut flower.*

Type Tender perennial, often grown as an annual
Zone 9–10; grown as an annual in cooler zones; performs most successfully where summers are hot. Apparently oblivious to heat and humidity
Flowering Season Summer to late autumn

SOWING

Seed, which sets only in very warm climates, is rarely available.
Indoors 6–8 weeks before last frost.
Outdoors After all danger of frost, in Zones 9–10 only.
Depth Just cover.

GERMINATING

Time 10–14 days.
Requirements 70°–75°F. When seedlings reach 4", pinch back to encourage branching.

TRANSPLANTING

Time 2–3 weeks after last frost, when warm weather is assured.
Spacing 12" in cool climates, 18"–24" in warmer regions.
Light Full sun to light shade.
Soil Damp soil is their natural habitat but plants are tolerant of dry soil; pH of 6.1–7.8.

CARING FOR PLANTS

Very easy. Pinch back young plants to increase branching. Supplementary watering will be required only during very dry weather. If plants begin to outgrow their site, cut back hard in summer. May be troubled by aphids or powdery mildew.

PROPAGATING

Take stem tip cuttings. Because plants may be plagued by viruses that will be perpetuated through cuttings, however, starting with newly purchased plants every year is advisable.

COMBINATIONS

For a soft, romantic look, combine with silvery plants like dusty miller, *Plectranthus,* or *Stachys.* The blues and purples combine well with yellow flowers like *Lantana* and *Tagetes* which, along with *Angelonia,* thrive in the hot days of late summer.

Anoda

TP* | Zn 9–10

Anoda

*These upright plants are similar in appearance to hardy geraniums (*Geranium *species). Anodas' leaves may be lobed or entire. They bear pretty, veined, cup-shaped flowers, usually solitary, in blue, yellow, purple, or white. Plants are 12"–30" tall.*

Type Tender perennial, often grown as an annual
Zone 9–10; grown as an annual in Zones 3–8; prefers cool climates
Flowering Season Summer through first frost

SOWING

Indoors 6–8 weeks before planting out.
Outdoors After last frost.
Depth ¼".

GERMINATING

Time 14–21 days.
Requirements 55°–60°F.

TRANSPLANTING

Time After last frost.
Spacing 12".
Light Sun, with light afternoon shade where summers are hot.
Soil Ordinary, well drained.

CARING FOR PLANTS

Easy. Deadhead regularly and water only during very dry spells. Plants may require staking. Flowers much less in wet summer weather. A heavy autumn mulch may bring plants through winter north of Zone 9.

PROPAGATING

Grow from seed only.

Anomatheca (syn. *Lapeirousia*)

HB* | Zn 7–10

These bulbs produce small (6"–12"), upright plants with narrow, sword-shaped leaves and spikes of red, white, or pink tubular flowers, some spotted. Flowers are followed by egg-shaped seedpods. Use these bulbs in the rock garden or border.

Type Hardy bulb; often grown as an annual
Zone 7–10. Grown as an annual in Zones 3–6
Flowering Season Summer

SOWING

Indoors 8–10 weeks before planting out.
Outdoors *Seed:* Early spring, when soil is cool and a light frost is still possible, or late autumn in Zones 9–10. *Corm:* Early autumn.
Depth *Seed:* 1/8". *Corm:* 2"–4".

GERMINATING

Time 30–90 days.
Requirements 55°–60°F.

TRANSPLANTING

Time Early spring.
Spacing 3"–5".
Light Sun; part shade where summers are very hot.
Soil Well drained, acid.

CARING FOR PLANTS

Do not allow soil to dry out during spring and summer. Divide every few years to maintain vigor. North of Zone 7, dig up corms and store in trays in a cool, frost-free location over the winter.

PROPAGATING

Divide cormels in spring. Allow to self-seed in the South.

Anredera (syn. *Boussingaultia*)

TP* | Zn 9–10

These twining climbers are grown for their thick, lush foliage and clusters of tiny white flowers. Vines can grow to 20' tall. Grow them on a trellis near a patio or open window where its sweet scent can be enjoyed.

Type Tender perennial sometimes grown as annual
Zone 9–10, H 12–1; may survive in Zone 8 with a heavy mulch, or may be grown as an annual
Flowering Season Late summer to early autumn

SOWING

Indoors 6–8 weeks before planting out.
Outdoors *Seed:* Early spring, when soil is cool and a light frost is still possible, or late autumn. *Tuber:* After last frost.
Depth *Seed:* Just cover. *Tuber:* 2".

GERMINATING

Time 30 days.
Requirements 60°–65°F.

TRANSPLANTING

Time After last frost, when temperatures remain above 45°F.
Spacing 24"–36".
Light Full sun.
Soil Light, sandy, well drained, humus-rich.

CARING FOR PLANTS

Soil must be quite dry in autumn and winter but fairly moist throughout the growing season. Vines require a trellis for support. Cut back by half in spring, or to ground level if plants have suffered frost damage. North of Zone 9, lift tubers in autumn and store in a frost-free place over winter, replanting after last spring frost.

PROPAGATING

Root the small tubers that form at leaf bases in moist sand in spring, take softwood cuttings in early winter, or grow from seed.

Antennaria

HP | Zn 3–8

Everlasting, Pussy-toes, Cat's ears, Ladies' tobacco

p. 373

These mat-forming evergreen or semievergreen perennials are native to North and South America. Leaves are small and woolly, sometimes gray-green. The tubular flowers, usually borne in clusters, may be white, pink, or red. Plants are usually under 6". Use them in rock gardens, around paving stones, or as ground cover.

Type Hardy perennial
Zone 3–8, H 9–4
Flowering Season Spring through early summer

SOWING

Indoors Late winter to early spring.
Outdoors Early spring, when soil is cool and a light frost is still possible, or autumn.
Depth Just cover.

GERMINATING

Time 30–60 days.
Requirements 55°–60°F.

TRANSPLANTING

Time Autumn or spring.
Spacing 12".
Light Full sun.
Soil Poor, somewhat dry; suitable for xeriscaping.

CARING FOR PLANTS

Easy. Use judiciously, as plants may become invasive. Deadhead regularly.

PROPAGATING

Divide in late summer or autumn, take cuttings in summer, or grow from seed.

Anthemis

HP | Zn 4–9

Dog fennel

p. 374

This genus of upright or mounding perennials, 6"–36" tall, includes plants with white or yellow daisylike flowers. Foliage may be green or silvery, sometimes aromatic and sometimes evergreen. Use Anthemis *in borders, rock gardens, or dry stone walls.*

Type Hardy perennial
Zone 4–9, H 8–1; all species object to high heat and humidity; *A. marschalliana* is most tolerant of high temperatures
Flowering Season Summer to autumn

SOWING

Indoors 8–10 weeks before planting out.
Outdoors Early spring or early autumn.
Depth Surface.

GERMINATING

Time 8–14 days.
Requirements Light and 70°F.

TRANSPLANTING

Time Early spring, when soil is cool and a light frost is still possible, or early autumn.
Spacing *Small species:* 6". *Large species:* 12"–24".
Light Prefers full sun but will tolerate part shade.
Soil Average to poor, well drained, and slightly alkaline. Very tolerant of dry soil; useful plants for xeriscaping.

CARING FOR PLANTS

Easy. Susceptible to mildew and should be sited in an open location where air can circulate freely. Plants may require staking where heavy rain and wind are frequent. Divide every 3–4 years if plants show signs of deteriorating.

PROPAGATING

Divide in spring, take cuttings in autumn, or grow from seed. Some species will self-seed. Most species will bloom from seed in their first year.

COMBINATIONS

Anchusa, Coreopsis, Lavandula, Malva, Phlomis, and *Santolina.*

Anthericum

HP | Zn 3–9

p. 374

Airy, upright perennials bear grassy leaves and racemes of delicate white, trumpet-shaped flowers on 18"–36" stems. Use in borders and naturalistic gardens.

Type Hardy perennial
Zone 3–9, H 9–5 (see species list, p. 439); does not like hot, dry weather
Flowering Season Summer

SOWING

Indoors 8–10 weeks before planting out.
Outdoors Early spring, when soil is cool and a light frost is still possible, or early autumn.
Depth 1/8".

GERMINATING

Time 30–90 days.
Requirements Soak seed in warm water for 12 hours; provide 50°F thereafter.

TRANSPLANTING

Time Spring or autumn.
Spacing 6"–8".
Light Part shade.
Soil Moist, with plenty of organic matter added.

CARING FOR PLANTS

Easy. Feed in spring, water regularly in summer, and mulch to keep soil cool and moist. Where summers are hot, cut back plants hard after blooming.

PROPAGATING

Divide in autumn (in Zones 7 and 8, divide after flowering) or grow from seed. Plants grown from seed will bloom in 2–3 years.

Anthriscus

A | Zn 3–10

p. 374

An upright herb with flat, green, indented leaves similar to parsley, Anthriscus *bears flat clusters of tiny white flowers atop sturdy 18"–36" stems. Most species are suitable only for the herb garden, although several new cultivars have showy, colored foliage.*

Type Annual
Zone 3–10; does not perform well in high heat and humidity
Flowering Season Late spring to early summer

SOWING

Indoors 6–8 weeks before planting out, in peat pots.
Outdoors Every 3–4 weeks from early spring through late autumn. Where summers are very hot, sow from late summer through autumn only.
Depth Surface.

GERMINATING

Time 14 days.
Requirements Light and 50°–60°F.

TRANSPLANTING

Time After last frost.
Spacing 9"–12".
Light Part shade.
Soil Light, moist, with a pH level of 6.0–7.0.

CARING FOR PLANTS

Water regularly during dry spells. Where summers are very hot, cut back plants hard midseason. Mulch lightly in autumn to protect seeds. Leaves are tastiest early in the season. Harvest for cooking before flowers open, immediately freezing any that are not used. Carefully dig and pot up plants to grow indoors over winter, giving 4–5 hours of sunlight and a cool location. Chervil does not transplant well.

PROPAGATING

Grow from seed. Plants self-seed.

CAUTION

Anthriscus sylvestris is invasive in some areas. See pp. 494–495 for advice.

Anthyllis

HP | Zn 3–8

These low-growing, spreading perennials have unusual erect, fernlike leaves. Plants are covered with masses of attractively contrasting pink or red cloverlike flowers. Use in rock gardens and wall plantings, between pavers, or as an edging in a well-drained border.

Type Hardy perennial
Zone 3–8, H 8–6
Flowering Season Late spring to early summer

SOWING

Indoors Late winter to early summer. *A. tetraphylla* is best started *in situ.*
Outdoors Autumn.
Depth 1/8".

GERMINATING

Time 30–60 days.
Requirements Difficult. Soak seed in warm water overnight; sow seed and leave undisturbed at 50°F.

TRANSPLANTING

Time Spring or autumn.
Spacing 12"–24".
Light Full sun to part shade.
Soil Poor, dry, with good drainage and a pH level of 5.0–6.0.

CARING FOR PLANTS

Easy once established, but this may take some time.

PROPAGATING

Take cuttings in summer or grow from seed.

Antirrhinum

HP* | Zn 5–10

Snapdragon

p. 374

Actually a subshrub, though usually grown as an annual, these obliging plants are the backbone of many public gardens, providing months of color ranging from pale pastels to vibrant reds and oranges. Dwarf plants of 6" may be rather floppy; taller (3') species are sturdier. Natives of southern Europe.

Type Hardy perennial; often grown as an annual
Zone 5–10, H 12–1; grown as an annual in Zones 1–10. Snapdragons must have a cool spring and will not flourish where temperatures are high for long periods
Flowering Season Late spring through late autumn, resting during the summer where temperatures are high

SOWING

Indoors 8–10 weeks before planting out.
Outdoors Not recommended, except in cold frames, where seeds may be sown in late summer to early autumn.
Depth Surface.

GERMINATING

Time 10–21 days.
Requirements Light and 55°F. Sow in vermiculite to avoid damping-off, and water only from below.

TRANSPLANTING

Time After last frost in the North; autumn in Zones 8–10.
Spacing *Dwarf species:* 6". *Tall species:* 12".
Light Full sun or very light shade.
Soil Tolerant of all but very heavy soils; prefers rich, neutral soil.

CARING FOR PLANTS

Easy. Pinch back young plants after four to six leaves have appeared to encourage a bushy habit. Feed lightly twice before first flowers appear. Stake tall species when young, removing stakes when plants fill out. Deadhead often. If blooms become scarce, cut back plants drastically, then feed and water generously. Susceptible to fungal diseases, so be sure to buy resistant plants or seeds of resistant cultivars. Young plants may suffer from mildew, and aphids are always a possibility.

PROPAGATING

Take tip cuttings in summer or grow from seed.

COMBINATIONS

Snapdragons obligingly fit in with many other plants, including *Amaranthus, Chrysanthemum, Dianthus, Geranium, Heliotropium, Linaria, Nicotiana, Salpiglossis.*

Aquilegia

HP | Zn 3–9

Columbine, Granny's bonnet

p. 374

These lovely perennials feature dainty, intricate flowers, often of more than one color. Blooms are held high, 4"–36", on thin stalks above delicate, toothed leaves. Grow in any shaded location where their subtle beauty will not be overlooked; they are essential to any woodland planting.

Type Hardy perennial
Zone 3–9, H 8–1
Flowering Season Mid-spring to early summer

SOWING

Indoors See Germinating, Requirements.
Outdoors See Germinating, Requirements.
Depth Surface.

GERMINATING

Time 30–90 days.
Requirements *Spring sowing:* Sow seed in flats of moistened medium, place flats in plastic bags, and refrigerate. After 2–3 weeks, remove and sink flats in the ground in a shady location, covering with glass. Transplant seedlings as they appear. *Summer sowing:* Sow seed in flats, sink flats in the ground against a north-facing wall, and cover with glass. Moisten soil occasionally, if necessary. Leave outdoors from summer to spring. Bring indoors in spring to a light location at 65°–75°F.

TRANSPLANTING

Time After last frost.
Spacing *Small species:* 6"–12". *Large species:* 15"–20".
Light Part shade is usually preferred but plants will tolerate full sun where summers are relatively cool.
Soil Humus-rich, moist but well drained, with a pH level of 5.5–7.0. *A. canadensis* is suitable for xeriscaping.

CARING FOR PLANTS

Seedlings are delicate; keep out of strong sunlight and water gently and often. Deadhead regularly to encourage continuous blooming and prolong the plant's life. Tall species may require support. If leaf miners are present, remove affected leaves immediately. Short lived; replant every 3–4 years. Provide winter mulch in northern zones.

PROPAGATING

Divide plants in spring (although this does not produce strong specimens) or grow from seed. Plants often self-seed. Different species grown close together may result in hybridized offspring, which may be fun—or annoying. Seedlings are easy to move.

COMBINATIONS

Azaleas, *Caltha, Iris cristata, Phlox stolonifera, Pulmonaria, Trillium, Viola.*

CAUTION

Harmful if eaten.

Arabis

HP | Zn 3–10

Rock cress

p. 374

Diminutive, dainty, mat-forming perennials, Arabis *species are useful in rock gardens or wall plantings, or as edgings. Clusters of small, scented white, or pink flowers are borne above evergreen leaves in early spring.*

Type Hardy perennial
Zone 3–10, H 8–1 (see species list, p. 439); hot, humid summers may cause plants to rot
Flowering Season Spring to early summer

SOWING

Indoors 6–8 weeks before planting out, in peat pots.
Outdoors Early spring, when soil is cool and a light frost is still possible, or late autumn.
Depth Surface.

GERMINATING

Time 14–25 days.
Requirements Light and 70°F.

TRANSPLANTING

Time After last spring frost, or early autumn.
Spacing *Small species:* 5"–9". *Tall species:* 12".
Light Most species require full sun, but some will take light shade.
Soil Average, well drained, with a pH level of 5.5–7.0; tolerant of poor soil. Many species are suitable for xeriscaping.

CARING FOR PLANTS

Easy. Cut plants back after blooming to maintain a neat habit and to limit self-seeding. Do not disturb roots.

PROPAGATING

Divide in spring in Zones 3–6 (in autumn south of Zone 6), take stem cuttings in late summer, or grow from seed. Plants self-seed freely.

COMBINATIONS

Armeria, Dianthus, Euphorbia.

Arctotis (syn. × *Venidioarctotis, Venidium*)

TP* | Zn 9–10 | Full sun | Dry soil, Ordinary soil

African daisy

p. 374

Short-lived though long-blooming perennials, African daisies are grown for their abundant daisylike flowers, which range in color from a cool, sophisticated silver to a hot and gaudy orange. Plant tall species (up to 48") at the back of the border; shorter species (12") are ideal for rock gardens. Arctotis *is native to South Africa.*

Type Tender perennial; often grown as an annual
Zone 9–10, H 12–10; grown as an annual in Zones 3–10. Performs most successfully in coastal regions and areas where summer nights are cool. Tolerant of heat and drought but does not like humid heat
Flowering Season Summer through late autumn

SOWING

Indoors 6–8 weeks before planting out.
Outdoors Early spring, when soil is cool and a light frost is still possible, or late autumn.
Depth Just cover.

GERMINATING

Time 7–35 days.
Requirements Easy. 60°–70°F.

TRANSPLANTING

Time After last frost, when temperature remains above 40°F; in autumn where winters are mild.
Spacing 9"–12".
Light Full sun.
Soil Sandy, well-drained soil; 6.0–7.0 pH. Tolerate most soils. *A. venusta* suitable for xeriscaping.

CARING FOR PLANTS

Easy. Pinch out young plants to stimulate bushy growth. Water regularly in early spring, but keep fairly dry during summer months. Deadhead regularly. Blooming rapidly diminishes after the first year. Aphids are attracted to new growth, and fungal diseases can be a problem during wet weather.

PROPAGATING

Take stem cuttings or grow from seed. *Arctotis* will self-seed in the South.

Arenaria

HP | Zn 3–8 | Full sun, Partial shade | Dry soil, Ordinary soil

Sandwort

p. 375

These modest, low-growing perennials (under 12") bear masses of white or pink flowers hovering above evergreen cushions. They are used most often in rock gardens and wall plantings or between paving stones.

Type Hardy perennial
Zone 3–8, H 7–1 (see species list, p. 439); does not like humid summers
Flowering Season Late spring to early summer

SOWING

Indoors 6–8 weeks before last frost.
Outdoors Early spring, when soil is cool and a light frost is still possible, or late autumn.
Depth Surface.

GERMINATING

Time 8–30 days.
Requirements 55°–65°F.

TRANSPLANTING

Time After last frost.
Spacing 3"–5".

Arenaria (cont'd)

Light Full sun; will tolerate part shade where summers are hot.
Soil Well drained, gritty or sandy, with a pH level of 6.0–8.0.

CARING FOR PLANTS

Easy. Plants grown in full sun will require occasional watering; give an occasional light feeding.

PROPAGATING

Divide in early spring, take cuttings in summer, or (most successful) grow from seed.

COMBINATIONS

Alchemilla, Aquilegia, Bellis, Dianthus.

Argemone

A, HP | Zn 3–10

Argemony, Prickly poppy

p. 375

Upright, short-lived perennials, prickly poppies are rather coarse in appearance. They are grown for their continuous stock of fragrant, poppylike flowers, which are usually white or yellow. Their foliage is spiky and dangerous-looking. Use these plants in the midsection of the border.

Type Annual or short-lived perennial; usually grown as an annual
Zone 3–10, H 12–7; prefers the warm, dry climate of the Southwest
Flowering Season Early to late summer

SOWING

Indoors Not often successful; if attempted, start in peat pots 6 weeks before planting out.
Outdoors After last frost.
Depth ⅛".

GERMINATING

Time 14 days.
Requirements 55°–60°F.

TRANSPLANTING

Time After last frost.
Spacing *Small species:* 9"–12". *Large species:* 24"–36".
Light Full sun.
Soil Prefers slightly alkaline soil that is poor and sandy; rich soil produces lush foliage but few flowers. Well adapted for hot, dry spots; a good choice for xeriscaping.

CARING FOR PLANTS

Easy. Deadhead regularly to prolong flowering. Stems are easily damaged and should not be tied to supports. Difficult to transplant.

PROPAGATING

Grow from seed. Plants self-seed.

COMBINATIONS

Looks most attractive mixed in with ornamental grasses, particularly *Calamagrostis* and *Miscanthus.*

Arisaema

TP, HP | Zn 3–9

Arisaema

p. 375

These curious-looking woodland plants are grown for their mysterious, hooded flowers, which are erect and tubular, in shades of green and palest cream with dark contrasting stripes. Plants are 12"–36". Arisaema *is native to woodlands around the globe.*

Type Hardy perennial, tender perennial
Zone 3–9, H 9–1 (see species list, p. 440)
Flowering Season Late spring to early summer

SOWING

Indoors Any time.
Outdoors Late summer or early autumn.
Depth Just cover.

GERMINATING

Time 30–180 days.
Requirements Difficult. Place seed in a plastic bag with moistened growing medium and refrigerate for 6 weeks. Provide 55°–60°F thereafter.

TRANSPLANTING

Time Spring or autumn.
Spacing 8"–10".
Light Part shade.
Soil Moist, humus-rich, nearly neutral pH.

CARING FOR PLANTS

Easy, if conditions are favorable. Arisaemas require plenty of moisture between spring and mid-autumn, but otherwise prefer to be on the dry side. Apply a mulch of compost in autumn. Attractive to slugs.

PROPAGATING

Divide in autumn south of Zone 6 (in spring north of Zone 7) or grow from seed.

COMBINATIONS

Aquilegia, Bletilla, Primula.

Armeria

HP | Zn 3–10 | ☼ | dry soil, ordinary soil

Sea pink, Thrift

p. 375

Dwarf evergreen perennials and subshrubs, Armeria *species are native to temperate seaside regions and alpine meadows. They bear small globes of pink or white flowers above mounds or rosettes. Use them in rock gardens or mass them at the front of the border. They are remarkably tolerant of seaside conditions.*

Type Hardy perennial
Zone 3–10, H 9–1 (see species list, p. 440)
Flowering Season Spring through early summer

SOWING

Indoors 8–10 weeks before planting out.
Outdoors Early spring or early autumn.
Depth Just cover.

GERMINATING

Time 10–21 days.
Requirements Easy. Soak seed for 6–8 hours in warm water before sowing. Provide darkness and 60°–70°F thereafter.

TRANSPLANTING

Time Early spring, when soil is cool and a light frost is still possible, or early autumn.
Spacing *Small species:* 6". *Large species:* 12".
Light Full sun.
Soil Ordinary, well drained, fairly sandy, not too rich, with a pH level of 5.5–7.5. *A. maritima* is suitable for xeriscaping.

CARING FOR PLANTS

Easy. Deadhead after flowering, water during dry spells, and mulch lightly with straw in winter.

PROPAGATING

Divide clumps, take cuttings in spring, or grow from seed.

COMBINATIONS

Anthericum, Campanula, Geranium, Salvia, Scabiosa, Sedum, Thymus, Veronica.

Arnica

HP | Zn 6–9 | full sun, partial shade | moist soil

p. 375

Grown for their large, daisylike, orange or yellow flowers with prominent eyes, Arnica *species are perennials, with narrow, aromatic, sometimes gray leaves. Use low, cushion-forming species at the front of the border or in rock gardens; use larger species for cutting.*

Type Hardy perennial
Zone 6–9, H 8–5
Flowering Season Summer

SOWING

Indoors Usually sown outdoors, but may be started indoors at any time in individual pots; grow for one season before moving outdoors.

Outdoors As soon as fresh seed is available, usually late summer.
Depth Just cover.

GERMINATING

Time 25–30 days.
Requirements Easy. 55°F.

TRANSPLANTING

Time After last frost.
Spacing 12"–15".

Light Full sun in the North but prefers shade from afternoon sun where summers are hot.
Soil Moist, well drained, acid (pH level of 5.0–6.5) soil that's not too high in nitrogen.

CARING FOR PLANTS

Easy. Do not use high-nitrogen fertilizer, as it fosters leggy, ungainly plants.

PROPAGATING

Divide in spring or early autumn, take cuttings in summer, or grow from seed.

Artemisia

A, TP, HP | Zn 2–10

Artemisia, Mugwort, Sagebrush, Wormwood

p. 375

A large and diverse genus of perennials and subshrubs, artemisias are grown mainly for their foliage, which may be gray or green and is often feathery and strongly scented. Large species make excellent specimen plants, or position one in the border as a foil for plants of contrasting color or texture. Depending on species, they range from less than 1'–6' tall. Artemisias are native to Asia, Europe, and North America.

Type Annual, tender perennial, hardy perennial
Zone *Annual:* 2–10. *Perennial:* 4–10, H 12–1 (see species list, p. 479)
Flowering Season Late summer

SOWING

Indoors 10–12 weeks before planting out.
Outdoors *Annual:* Spring or autumn. *Perennial:* Autumn.
Depth *Annual:* 1/8". *Perennial:* Surface.

GERMINATING

Time 14–60 days.
Requirements 55°–65°F. Seed of perennial species requires light. *Outdoor sowing:* Sow seed in flats, sink in the ground against a north-facing wall, and cover with glass. Moisten soil occasionally, if necessary. Remove glass when seeds begin to germinate.

TRANSPLANTING

Time After last frost.
Spacing *Small species:* 12". *Large species:* 12"–24".

Light Sun or light shade.
Soil Most species will be happy in average, well-drained soil that is not too rich and prefer a pH level of 5.5–7.0. Many species are suitable for xeriscaping.

CARING FOR PLANTS

Easy. Cut back plants to ground level in autumn or spring and pinch back new growth to maintain a neat habit. Mulch in winter. If clumps spread beyond their desired size, dig up and discard unwanted plants. Tarragon *(A. dracunculus)* does not grow true from seed and should be bought as a young plant. Grow tarragon in very well-drained soil, apply a 5-10-5 fertilizer in early spring, and mulch in winter after the ground has frozen. Divide it in spring every 3–4 years. Harvest tarragon leaves at any time for culinary use. To dry, hang in bunches in a dark place, then crush the dried leaves and store in an airtight container. To grow tarragon indoors, pot up plants in midsummer and give 5 hours of sunlight a day.

PROPAGATING

Divide in spring in the North (in autumn south of Zone 6), take cuttings in spring, or grow from seed.

COMBINATIONS

Aster, Digitalis, Geum, purple-leaved *Heuchera, Lupinus, Perilla, Salvia argentia, Stachys.*

CAUTION

A. absinthium, A. annua, and *A. vulgaris* are listed as invasives in some areas. See pp. 494–495 for advice.

Arum

TP, HP | Zn 5–10

Arum, Lords and ladies

p. 375

Upright perennials, arums are grown for their distinctive arrow-shaped leaves and unusual pitcherlike flowers, which range in appearance from elegant to otherworldly. Flowers are followed in late summer to fall by spikes of showy red or orange berries. Use near streams or in other naturalistic settings.

Type Tender perennial, hardy perennial
Zone 5–10, H 10–3 (see species list, p. 440); does not like humid heat
Flowering Season Early to late spring, depending on species

SOWING

Indoors 10–12 weeks before planting out.
Outdoors Autumn.
Depth *Seed:* ⅛". *Tuber:* 3".

GERMINATING

Time 30–180 days.
Requirements Easy. 55°–65°F.

TRANSPLANTING

Time Spring or autumn.
Spacing *Compact species:* 6"–12". *Larger species:* 12"–18".
Light Sun or part shade. Provide shade from afternoon sun where summers are hot.
Soil Cool, moist, humus-rich soil that does not remain wet in winter.

CARING FOR PLANTS

Water regularly, especially during growing season. Mulch to keep soil cool and moist; give a balanced fertilizer occasionally. Leaves attract slugs. *Arum* leaves die back shortly after flowering; mark locations so plants will not be inadvertently disturbed.

PROPAGATING

Divide tubers in autumn or grow from seed. Plants may self-seed.

COMBINATIONS

Astilbe, ferns, *Galanthus*, *Hosta*, *Liriope*.

CAUTION

May be harmful if eaten; plant sap may cause a rash.

Aruncus

HP | Zn 3–8  

Goat's beard

p. 375

These bushy perennials feature feathery plumes of white flowers borne on long, gracefully arching stalks and resembling a shower of tiny white fireworks. Large species (3'–7' tall) belong at the border rear; all are useful in naturalistic plantings and wildflower gardens or near streams. Aruncus *is native to Central Europe.*

Type Hardy perennial
Zone 3–8, H 9–1
Flowering Season Early to mid summer

SOWING

Indoors Late winter to spring.
Outdoors 2–3 weeks after last frost, when soil has warmed.
Depth Surface.

GERMINATING

Time 30–90 days.
Requirements 55°–65°F.

TRANSPLANTING

Time Spring or autumn.
Spacing 2'–5'.
Light Part shade; can be grown in full sun where the summer sun is not intensely hot.
Soil Moist and rich.

CARING FOR PLANTS

Easy. Feed in spring and keep soil moist throughout the growing season. Cut stems to ground level in autumn. Plants will not flower in poor, dry soil.

PROPAGATING

Divide in spring (in autumn in Zones 7–8) or grow from seed. Allow plants to become well established before dividing.

COMBINATIONS

Aconitum, *Baptisia*, *Bergenia*, *Heuchera*, *Hosta*, *Iris siberica*, *Ligularia*.

A

Asarina (syn. *Maurandya*)

TP, HP | Zn 7–10

Twining snapdragon

p. 376

Unusual climbers and trailing plants, Asarina *species are grown for their attractive, rather old-fashioned, trumpet-shaped flowers in yellow, blue, white, red, purple, or pink. Their heart-shaped leaves are often scented. Trailing species are lovely in containers.*

Type Tender perennial or hardy perennial; often grown as an annual
Zone 7–10, H 9–6 (see species list, p. 440); grown as an annual in Zones 3–8; prefers warm temperatures
Flowering Season Late spring through late autumn, depending on species

SOWING

Indoors 10–12 weeks before planting out, in peat pots.
Outdoors Late winter through early spring.
Depth Surface.

GERMINATING

Time 9–21 days.
Requirements Light and 60°–75°F.

TRANSPLANTING

Time Early spring, when temperatures remain above 40°F.
Spacing 12".
Light Sun. *A. scandens* will take part shade.
Soil Cool, moist, fertile, well drained, near neutral.

CARING FOR PLANTS

Easy. Water frequently and feed occasionally; mulch to keep roots cool. Climbers require a trellis or other support. Plants can be lifted before the first frost, potted up, and grown indoors for the winter.

PROPAGATING

Take cuttings in summer or grow from seed.

Asarum (syn. *Heterotropa, Hexastylis*)

HP | Zn 2–9  

Asarabacca, Wild ginger

p. 376

This genus of diminutive, low-growing perennials includes some that are evergreen. Plants are grown for their attractive deep green or variegated, heart-shaped leaves; the flowers are inconspicuous. Use as a ground cover for small spaces or in woodland plantings.

Type Hardy perennial
Zone 2–9, H 9–1 (see species list, p. 479)
Flowering Season Early spring, but flowers, which are generally inconspicuous, sometimes persist for several months

SOWING

Indoors As soon as ripe seed is available.
Outdoors As soon as seed is ripe, usually in early summer.
Depth Just cover.

GERMINATING

Time 7–18 days.
Requirements Easy. Place seed in a plastic bag together with moist growing medium and refrigerate for 3 weeks. Provide 60°–65°F after chilling.

TRANSPLANTING

Time After last frost.
Spacing 12–16 plants per square yard.
Light Light to full shade.
Soil Slightly moist, humus-rich, nearly neutral.

CARING FOR PLANTS

Easy. Water during dry spells. Feed once in spring, then top-dress with peat moss or compost in autumn. Slugs and snails love to feed on these leafy plants.

PROPAGATING

Divide creeping rootstock in the North in the spring (in late autumn south of Zone 6), take cuttings in summer, or grow from seed. Plants may self-seed.

COMBINATIONS

Astilbe, Athyrium, Convallaria, Helleborus, Hosta, Polygonatum.

Asclepias

TP*, HP* | Zn 3–10

Milkweed, Silkweed

p. 376

A large genus of rather coarse, resilient perennials and subshrubs, Asclepias *includes species ranging from 1' to 6' tall. Their clusters of sturdy, usually hot-colored blooms often attract butterflies. Use with restraint in borders or freely in wildflower plantings.*

Type Tender perennial, hardy perennial; often grown as an annual
Zone 3–10, H 9–1; *A. curassavica* and *A. physocarpa* are often grown as annuals in Zones 5–7. Prefers warm summers
Flowering Season Summer

SOWING

Indoors *Hardy perennial:* Remove prechilled seed from refrigerator 8–10 weeks before planting. *Tender perennial:* 8–10 weeks before last frost.
Outdoors *Hardy perennial:* Early spring or early autumn. *Tender perennial:* Early spring
Depth Just cover.

GERMINATING

Time *Hardy perennial:* 30–90 days. *Tender perennial:* 7–35 days.
Requirements *Hardy perennial:* Sow seed in peat pots, secure in plastic bags, and refrigerate for 21 days. Provide light and 50°–75°F thereafter. *Tender perennial:* 50°–75°F.

TRANSPLANTING

Time *Hardy perennial:* Early spring, when soil is cool and light frost is still possible, or early autumn. *Tender perennial:* After last frost.
Spacing 12"–24".
Light Full sun to light shade.
Soil Prefers average, sandy soil; most tolerate dry soil but not heavy clay or chalky conditions. *A. speciosa* and *A. tuberosa* are excellent choices for xeriscaping.

CARING FOR PLANTS

Easy. Pinch back young plants when 4"–6" tall. Do not move or disturb roots.

PROPAGATING

Take root cuttings in spring, carefully divide clumps in spring (but plants are often lost during division if the delicate taproot is damaged), or grow from seed. Plants grown from seed bloom in their first year.

COMBINATIONS

Echinacea, Helliopsis, Liatris, Miscanthus, and *Thalictrum.*

CAUTION

All parts of the plant are harmful if eaten.

Asperula (syn. *Galium*)

A, HP | Zn 3–9

Woodruff

p. 376

These modest but charming spreading plants bear often fragrant, tiny white, pink, or blue, fading to lavender, flowers. They make delightful ground cover or rock garden plants.

Type Annual, hardy perennial
Zone *Annual:* 4–8. Prefers warm climates. *Perennial:* 3–9
Flowering Season *Annual:* Midsummer; *Perennial:* Late spring

SOWING

Indoors Remove prechilled seed from refrigerator 8–10 weeks before planting out.
Outdoors *Annual:* Spring. *Perennial:* Spring through early summer.
Depth Surface.

GERMINATING

Time 21–42 days.
Requirements Easy, although seed must be fresh for guaranteed success. Sow seed in containers, secure in a plastic bag, and refrigerate for 2 weeks. Provide light and 50°F thereafter.

TRANSPLANTING

Time After last frost.
Spacing *Small species:* 3"–4". *Large species:* 6"–9".
Light Flowers most profusely in full sun but will perform quite well in light shade if the soil is kept moist.
Soil Average; very well drained, especially in winter.

Asperula (cont'd)

CARING FOR PLANTS

Easy. Dislikes a wet crown: Locate away from dripping overhangs.

PROPAGATING

Grow annuals from seed only. Divide perennials in spring or autumn, take stem cuttings, or grow from seed. Plants may self-seed.

Asphodeline

HP | Zn 6–8

Jacob's rod

p. 376

This genus of clump-forming perennials displays sturdy, upright 1'–3' stems that bear terminal clusters of fragrant, bright yellow, star-shaped flowers. Mass for best effect.

Type Hardy perennial
Zone 6–8, H 9–6
Flowering Season Late spring and summer

SOWING

Indoors Late winter to early spring.
Outdoors *Seed:* Spring through summer. *Root:* Spring or autumn.
Depth *Seed:* Just cover. *Root:* 3"–4".

GERMINATING

Time 30 days.
Requirements 70°–75°F.

TRANSPLANTING

Time After last spring frost or in early autumn.
Spacing *Small species:* 6"–12". *Large species:* 15"–18".
Light Sun or part shade but will flower more freely in sun.
Soil Ordinary, well drained, with a pH level of 6.0–8.0.

CARING FOR PLANTS

Easy. Remove flowering stems after last spring frost. Feed once in spring and water during very dry spells. Provide a winter mulch in the North.

PROPAGATING

Divide in early autumn or grow from seed.

COMBINATIONS

Aster, Caryopteris, Hemerocallis, Platycodon.

Asplenium (syn. *Ceterach, Phyllitis*)

HP | Zn 2–9

Spleenwort

p. 376

Mainly evergreen or semievergreen ferns, some of which have uncut fronds that resemble straplike leaves, some with more traditional-looking featherlike fronds. These are handsome plants for use in a moist, shady garden.

Type Hardy perennial
Zone 2–9, H 8–3 (see species list, p. 479)
Flowering Season N/A

SOWING

Indoors When spores are ripe, in midsummer to late summer.
Outdoors Not recommended.
Depth *Spores:* Surface. *Rhizomes:* 1".

GERMINATING

Time 10–365 days.
Requirements Difficult. Hardy species require a temperature of 59°F, tender species 70°F. See pp. 24–25 for information on starting ferns from spores.

TRANSPLANTING

Time Spring or autumn. Plants grown from spores will generally be ready to plant out in 2–3 years.
Spacing *Small species:* 6"–12". *Large species:* 12"–18".

Light Part to full shade; most species require shade from the hot afternoon sun. *A. scolopendrium* and *A. trichomanes* tolerate full sun; *A. rhizophyllum* tolerates deep shade.
Soil Soil that is moist during the growing season but dry over the winter is best. *A. platyneuron* tolerates dry, acid soil. Most terrestrial species prefer soil with an acid pH, but *A. rhizophyllum, A. scolopendrium,* and *A. trichomanes* prefer alkaline conditions.

CARING FOR PLANTS

Feed with a weak liquid fertilizer twice monthly throughout the growing season and remove ragged fronds periodically to improve appearance. Slugs and snails may be a problem.

PROPAGATING

Divide in spring, grow from spores, or remove bulbils from species that produce them (e.g., *A. bulbiferum*) in late summer. Plants will self-sow where they are happy.

COMBINATIONS

Arum, Lilium, Lithodora, Ramonda.

Aster

HP | Zn 2–9 | Full sun; Partial shade | Dry soil; Ordinary soil

Aster

p. 377

This very large group of perennials includes plants that vary in size from 6" to more than 5'. They are grown for their daisylike flowers of white or shades of blue, purple, or pink. It is an indispensable late bloomer in the border; small species are useful for edging or rock gardens.

Type Hardy perennial
Zone 2–9, H 8–1 (see species list, pp. 440–441)
Flowering Season Spring through late autumn, depending on species

SOWING

Indoors Remove prechilled seed from refrigerator 6–8 weeks before planting out.
Outdoors Early spring, when soil is cool and a light frost is still possible, or late autumn.
Depth Just cover.

GERMINATING

Time 14–36 days.
Requirements Easy. Sow seed in flats, secure in plastic bags, and refrigerate for 2 weeks. Provide 70°–75°F thereafter.

TRANSPLANTING

Time After last frost.
Spacing *Small species:* 9"–12". *Tall species:* 24".

Light Most species require full sun; *A. divaricatus* and *A.* × *frikartii* tolerate part shade.
Soil Light, average, with humus added and a pH level of 5.5–7.5. Performs best where soil is neither dry in the summer nor wet in the winter. Several species are suitable for xeriscaping.

CARING FOR PLANTS

Easy. Pinch back young plants to stimulate bushy growth. Encourage larger blooms by thinning out young shoots in spring, leaving six to eight shoots per plant to develop. Feed lightly twice during summer. Tall species may require staking. Divide every 3 years to maintain vigor. Minimize the risk of powdery mildew by siting in full sun where air circulation is good; keep water off leaves. Hybrids often are more prone to mildew than are species.

PROPAGATING

Divide in spring or grow from seed. Asters will self-sow but, especially with cultivars, resulting plants will not have predictable characteristics. Species grown in isolation will produce seedlings that match their parents.

COMBINATIONS

Achillea, autumn-blooming *Anemone, Chrysanthemum, Delosperma, Kniphofia, Leucanthemum, Nerine, Ratibida, Rudbeckia, Saponaria, Schizostylis,* or *Solidago.*

Astilbe

HP | Zn 4–8

Astilbe, Spiraea

p. 377

These neat, airy perennials have deeply cut leaves and attractive plumelike flowers in soft pinks and white; newer cultivars include some intense pinks, salmons, and corals. They range in size 6" to 4' tall. Mass them in a cool or shady border; they are of unrivaled beauty in a woodland planting.

Type Hardy perennial
Zone 4–8, H 8–1 (see species list, p. 441); plants lose their vigor in persistently hot weather
Flowering Season Late spring to late summer, depending on species

SOWING

Indoors 6–8 weeks before planting out.
Outdoors Early spring, when soil is cool and a light frost is still possible, or late autumn.
Depth Surface.

GERMINATING

Time 25–60 days.
Requirements Diffused light and 65°F. Seedlings are very susceptible to damping-off; sow in vermiculite and water only from below.

TRANSPLANTING

Time After last frost.
Spacing *Small species:* 12". *Large species:* 20"–30".
Light Shade, or sun where summers are not hot.
Soil Moist, humus-rich, well drained, with a 5.5–7.0 pH . *A. chinensis* var. *taquetii* thrives in dry soil.

CARING FOR PLANTS

Easy. Water during dry spells and feed once during the summer. Where summers are very hot, cut back plants hard after blooming. Divide every 3 years.

PROPAGATING

Divide in spring where summers are cool (in autumn in the South) or grow from seed.

COMBINATIONS

Mix with *Aconitum, Anemone, Asarum, Athyrium, Convallaria,* ferns, *Hosta, Iris siberica* or *I. ensata, Polygonatum, Pulmonaria, Tiarella.*

Astilboides

HP | Zn 4–7

Formerly classified as Rodgersia tabularis, Astilboides *has the massive leaves of* Gunnera *and the feathery plumes of* Astilbe. *The size of a small shrub, this dramatic plant performs best where summers are temperate and where its size will not pose a problem.*

Type Hardy perennial
Zone 4–7, H 7–1 in the East or to Zone 9 in coastal California
Flowering Season Early to midsummer

SOWING

Indoors 6 weeks before last frost.
Outdoors Autumn.
Depth Surface.

GERMINATING

Time 12–60 days.
Requirements *Indoors:* Sow seed at 68°F and provide light. If seeds have not germinated in 3–4 weeks, refrigerate for 2–3 weeks. *Outdoors:* Sow seed in peat pots, sink pots in the ground against a north-facing wall, and cover with glass. Check periodically to see if soil needs to be moistened. Remove glass when germination begins.

TRANSPLANTING

Time Spring or autumn, after 2 years' growth.
Spacing 36"
Light Full sun to part shade.
Soil Moist, rich.

CARING FOR PLANTS

Mulch plants in spring to keep soil cool and moist and water regularly during dry spells. When plants are happy, rhizomes may spread beyond their desirable bounds and require periodic removal. Leaves may be scorched by strong sun or eaten by slugs.

PROPAGATING

Divide in spring or grow from seed.

COMBINATIONS

Provides dramatic textural contrast when planted with *Astilbe,* ferns, or *Hosta.* Also attractive with *Acorus, Aruncus, Mecanopsis,* or candelabra *Primula.*

Astrantia

HP | Zn 4–8

Hattie's pincushion, Masterwort

p. 377

These unusual, long-blooming perennials bear pink or white cloverlike blooms surrounded by a spiky collar. Plants are 6"–24" tall. Use these European or Asian natives in cottage gardens, borders, or cutting beds.

Type Hardy perennial
Zone 4–8, H 8–1; will not tolerate excessive heat and humidity
Flowering Season Summer through autumn

SOWING

Indoors Late winter.
Outdoors Spring or early autumn.
Depth Surface.

GERMINATING

Time 30–180 days.
Requirements Sow seed in flats, secure in a plastic bag, and refrigerate for 4 weeks. Provide light and 55°–65°F thereafter.

TRANSPLANTING

Time After last spring frost or in autumn.
Spacing 12"–15".
Light Sun or part shade.
Soil Moist, rich.

CARING FOR PLANTS

Easy. Keep soil moist in summer.

PROPAGATING

Divide in autumn in the South (in spring north of Zone 7) or grow from seed.

COMBINATIONS

Campanula, Chelone, Hosta, Tricyrtis.

Atholyza See *Crocosmia*

Athyrium

HP | Zn 2–9

p. 377

Like many ferns Athyrium *has long, lacy pinna on sturdy fronds of mid-green, forming nicely compact clumps that are 1'–3' high. A useful ground cover for shade or for textural contrast with other shade lovers.*

Type Hardy perennial
Zone 2–9, H 9–1 (see species list, p. 479)
Flowering Season N/A

SOWING

Indoors When spores are ripe, from June to October.
Outdoors Not recommended.
Depth Surface.

GERMINATING

Time 10–365 days.
Requirements Difficult. See pp. 24–25 for information on starting ferns from spores.

TRANSPLANTING

Time After last spring frost or early autumn. Will reach planting-out size in 1–2 years.
Spacing *Small species:* 12". *Large species:* 18"–24".
Light Part to full shade. *A. filix-femina* will grow in full sun if the soil is very moist.
Soil Moist, acid. *A. filix-femina* will tolerate wet soil; *A. niponicum* 'Ghost' tolerates dry conditions.

CARING FOR PLANTS

Easy. Mulch in spring to keep soil moist and water regularly during dry spells. Ragged-looking plants can be renewed at any time by cutting back to the ground. Divide when clumps become overgrown.

PROPAGATING

Divide in spring or autumn or grow from spores. Division is the only ensurance that new plants share a particularly desirable feature, such as coloring.

COMBINATIONS

Combine with many flowering shade lovers, such as *Chelone, Cimicifuga, Ligularia, Iris ensata, Polygonatum, Pulmonaria.* Use for textural contrast with hostas; *A. niponicum* and *A. niponicum* var. *pictum* add a bright, frilly hem around dark evergreens.

A

Atragene See *Clematis*

Atriplex

A | Zn 5–9

Orach, Salt bush

These large, imposing plants (4′–6′ tall) are grown for their striking red, green, or silver-gray foliage. Use leaves in dried arrangements or cooking. Plants make an unusual background for plants of contrasting color.

Type Annual
Zone 5–9, H 9–7. Prefers warm climates
Flowering Season Summer

SOWING

Indoors 6 weeks before planting out, in peat pots.
Outdoors Early spring, when soil is cool and a light frost is still possible.
Depth Just cover.

GERMINATING

Time 9–21 days.
Requirements 50°–55°F.

TRANSPLANTING

Time After last frost.
Spacing 12″.
Light Sun.
Soil Withstands any conditions, even dry soil, though leaves have best flavor when soil is kept moist. Suitable for xeriscaping.

CARING FOR PLANTS

Shear to maintain shape and neat appearance. May become invasive. Does not like to be moved.

PROPAGATING

Take cuttings or grow from seed. May self-seed.

COMBINATIONS

Dahlia, Monarda, Nicotiana, Rudbeckia, Solidago, and silver-leaved plants such as *Artemisia* or *Senecio.*

CAUTION

Atriplex rosea, A. semibaccata, and *A. suberecta* are listed as invasives in many parts of the United States. See pp. 494–495 for advice.

Aubrieta

HP | Zn 4–9

Aubrieta

p. 377

Native to southern Europe and Asia, these mat-forming alpines are covered at blooming time in a cloak of purple, deepest pink, or blue. Use in rock gardens or to edge borders or paths; they are essential wall plants.

Type Hardy perennial
Zone 4–9, H 7–5; does not like hot, dry conditions
Flowering Season Early spring, sometimes reblooming in late summer

SOWING

Indoors 6–8 weeks before last frost.
Outdoors Early spring, when soil is cool and a light frost is still possible, or late autumn.
Depth Surface.

GERMINATING

Time 14–21 days.
Requirements Light; 65°–70°F. Highly susceptible to damping-off; sow in vermiculite; water from below.

TRANSPLANTING

Time After last frost.
Spacing 12″.
Light Full sun where cool; part shade in the South.
Soil Average, well drained, with a pH level of 6.0–7.5.

CARING FOR PLANTS

Easy. Spring: Use compost to mulch. After flowering: deadhead; feed lightly; if very hot, cut back hard.

PROPAGATING

Take cuttings in summer or grow from seed.

COMBINATIONS

Muscari, Myosotis, Scilla, Tulipa.

Aurinia (syn. *Alyssum*)

HP | Zn 4–10

Basket of gold

p. 377

Aurinia saxatilis is an easy, well-behaved perennial, no more than 6"–12" tall. In spring, it is completely cloaked in a mass of tiny, vibrant yellow blooms, making a strong statement at the border edge, on a dry hillside, or cascading over a wall. When not blooming, narrow gray-green leaves form an attractive mound.*

Type Hardy perennial
Zone 4–10, H 9–1
Flowering Season Spring to early summer

SOWING

Indoors 8–10 weeks before planting out.
Outdoors Early spring or early autumn.
Depth Surface

GERMINATING

Time 5–14 days.
Requirements Light and 50°–55°F.

TRANSPLANTING

Time Early spring when soil is cool and a light frost is still possible, or early autumn.
Spacing 12".
Light Full sun.
Soil Well-drained soil; becomes leggy in rich soil.

CARING FOR PLANTS

Easy. Water during very dry weather. Cut plants back hard after flowering to prevent self-seeding.

PROPAGATING

Divide in spring, take cuttings in summer, or grow from seed.

COMBINATIONS

Erysimum, Myosotis, Omphalodes, pansies, tulips.

Azorina

TP* | Zn 10

These 1'–2' tall, shrubby plants bear elongated, plump, bell-shaped flowers with turned-up hems, atop whorls of shiny green leaves that resemble Euphorbia. *The charming pink or white waxy flowers appear in spring or summer. Use them in pots or near a patio.*

Type Tender perennial, often grown as an annual
Zone 10, H 12–10; grown as an annual in Zones 3–9
Flowering Season Spring to summer

SOWING

Indoors 8 weeks before last frost.
Outdoors After last frost, but only in Zone 10.
Depth Surface.

GERMINATING

Time 14–30 days.
Requirements Requires light and about 60°F.

TRANSPLANTING

Time After last frost.
Spacing 24"–36".
Light Full sun to part shade, with shade from the hot afternoon sun in the South.
Soil Well drained, average to dry.

CARING FOR PLANTS

Easy; tolerates considerable neglect. Cut back individual stalks after flowering.

PROPAGATING

Take softwood cuttings of nonflowering shoots in spring or summer or start from seed.

COMBINATIONS

Use with other romantic plants: *Delphinium, Digitalis, Fuchsia,* roses.

Babiana

HB* | Zn 8–10

Baboon flower, Monkeyroot

p. 378

Diminutive, long-blooming, and sweet-smelling, Babiana *is a bulb that produces lance-shaped leaves and brightly colored blooms reminiscent of freesias. Flowers may be pink, red, violet, or, more rarely, yellow or white. The intensity of the colors gives them more impact than one would expect from such a delicate-looking plant.*

Type Hardy bulb
Zone 8–10, H 12–10; grown as an annual in cooler zones. May survive as far north as Zone 6 with a heavy winter mulch. Prefers dry, mild summers
Flowering Season Where *Babiana* is perennial, it will bloom in late winter or spring, but corms sold through catalogs are usually manipulated to bloom in summer

SOWING

Indoors As soon as seed is ripe, usually in autumn.
Outdoors *Seed:* Not recommended. *Corm:* Zones 8–10, autumn; north of Zone 8, after last frost.
Depth *Seed:* Just cover. *Corm:* 2"–3".

GERMINATING

Time 10–56 days.
Requirements Sow seed thinly in trays at 60°–70°F. After germination, grow seedlings in their trays for 1 year, feeding occasionally with a dilute liquid fertilizer. Pot up 1-year-old bulbs in winter, two or three per pot. Grow these for 1 year more before planting corms in the garden.

TRANSPLANTING

Time Zones 8–10, autumn; north of Zone 8, after last frost.
Spacing 4"–6".
Light Sun to light shade.
Soil Moist, well drained, with a pH of 6.1–7.8.

CARING FOR PLANTS

Water freely during spring and early summer, then allow the soil to become dryer. Plants may be susceptible to spider mites. North of Zone 8, dig corms in autumn and store in peat or vermiculite in a dry, frost-free location, then replant after the last spring frost.

PROPAGATING

Divide corms in autumn or start from seed.

Bacopa (syn. *Sutera cordata*)

TP* | Zn 9–10

Water hyssop

p. 378

Bacopa *seems to have come out of nowhere to become a prominent player in containers and baskets everywhere. And why not? Two or three plants will happily fill a basket and spill over the sides to a length of 18" producing small white (more rarely blue) flowers from spring to autumn.*

Type Tender perennial; often grown as an annual
Zone 9–10, H 12–10; grown as an annual in Zones 3–8
Flowering Season Spring to autumn, but with a break in the hottest part of summer in the South

SOWING

The desirable cultivars available in the trade do not come true from seed.

TRANSPLANTING

Time Set out purchased plants in spring.
Spacing 12".
Light Full sun, with protection from the hot afternoon sun in the South.
Soil Most species are aquatic, but those generally grown in the garden are happy in average, moist, well-drained soil.

CARING FOR PLANTS

Pinch back young plants to improve their shape. Do not allow soil to dry out, watering faithfully during dry spells. Feed periodically with a balanced fertilizer. Can be brought inside in autumn and overwintered as a houseplant.

PROPAGATING

Cuttings taken in spring or early summer will root easily in water.

COMBINATIONS

Ageratum, Pelargonium, Petunia, annual *Phlox.*

Balsamita See *Tanacetum*

Baptisia

HP | Zn 4–9

False indigo, Wild indigo

p. 378

Upright, branching perennials esteemed for their white, yellow, or blue sweet pea-like flowers arranged along slender, 2'–6' stalks. Plant at the back of the border. Native to North America.

Type Hardy perennial
Zone 4–9, H 9–1 (see species list, pp. 441–442)
Flowering Season Late spring to early summer, depending on species

SOWING

Indoors 6–8 weeks before last frost, in peat pots.
Outdoors Early spring or late autumn.
Depth ¼".

GERMINATING

Time 5–36 days.
Requirements Soak seed in warm water for 24 hours, then chip with a knife. Provide 70°–75°F thereafter.

TRANSPLANTING

Time After last spring frost or in early autumn.
Spacing 2'–3'.
Light Full sun or light shade.
Soil Well drained, with a pH level of 5.5–7.0. *B. australis* and *B. perfoliata* are suitable for xeriscaping.

CARING FOR PLANTS

Plants grown from seed will take a year or two to become well established. Stake tall plants. Do not disturb roots.

PROPAGATING

Divide with care in spring in Zones 4–6 (in autumn in Zones 7–9) or grow from seed.

COMBINATIONS

Allium, Aruncus, Gaura, Hosta, Iris, Miscanthus, Paeonia, Penstemon, Salvia.

Bassia (syn. *Kochia*)

A | Zn 2–10

p. 378

A genus of upright, shrubby annuals and perennials, one of which, B. scoparia *f.* tricophylla, *is grown for its fine, lance-shaped leaves, which are intense green in summer, turning to deep red in autumn. These 30"–36" plants are most often used to form temporary hedges, but also make unusual container plants.*

Type Annual
Zone 2–10, H 9–2; prefers warm temperatures and will perform well in very hot weather
Flowering Season Summer

SOWING

Indoors 6–8 weeks before planting out, in peat pots.
Outdoors 1–2 weeks before last frost.
Depth Surface.

GERMINATING

Time 10–15 days.
Requirements Soak seed for 24 hours; provide light and 70°–75°F thereafter.

TRANSPLANTING

Time Late spring.
Spacing 8" for hedging, otherwise 18"–24".
Light Full sun.
Soil Average, with a pH level of 6.0–7.0; tolerant of dry soil. *B. scoparia* f. *tricophylla* is suitable for xeriscaping.

CARING FOR PLANTS

Easy. Water during dry spells and feed with a high-nitrogen fertilizer several times during the summer.

PROPAGATING

Often self-seeds and may become invasive.

COMBINATIONS

Bidens, Coreopsis, Nigella, Sanvitalia.

Begonia

TP*, HP | Zn 6–10

Begonia

p. 378

These tropical plants are grown for both foliage and flowers. Commonly used in borders and containers, it is also striking in formal and informal masses. Crisp, glossy leaves come in strong greens or reds, or attractively striped or variegated. Blooms are pink, white, apricot, yellow, orange, or red. It grows 6"–30" tall.

Type Tender perennial or hardy perennial; often grown as an annual
Zone 6–10, H 12–1 (see species list, p. 442); grown as annual in Zones 3–10, H 12–1. Most thrive in warm summers; tuberous ones prefer cool climates
Flowering Season Summer through autumn

SOWING

Indoors *Seed:* 3–4 months before planting out. *Tuber:* North of Zone 10, start tubers indoors in early spring at 65°F in peat moss.
Outdoors *Annual:* Start seed indoors only. *Perennial:* Early spring, when soil is cool and a light frost is still possible, or late autumn.
Depth Surface.

GERMINATING

Time 15–60 days.
Requirements 65°–75°F.

TRANSPLANTING

Time After last frost.
Spacing *Small species:* 9"–12". *Large species:* 10"–15".

Light Sun where summers are cool, otherwise part or full shade. *B. semperflorens* and *B.* × *tuberhybrida* will tolerate full shade. Plants grown in sun will require more moisture.
Soil Rich, moist, slightly acid, with a pH level of 6.0–7.0.

CARING FOR PLANTS

Water regularly, keeping leaves as dry as possible. Feed lightly every month, avoiding fertilizer contact with leaves. In northern zones, cover hardy species thickly with mulch. Where tuberous begonias are not hardy, decrease watering when leaves start to yellow in autumn, lift tubers when leaves drop, carefully remove soil from roots, dry tubers, and store in a cool, frost-free location. Replant in spring. Occasionally, powdery mildew may be a problem.

PROPAGATING

Take stem or leaf cutting or grow from seed. Some species self-seed freely. Plants grown from seed will bloom in their first year. Tuberous begonias can be divided. Some, including *B. grandis* ssp. *evansiana* and some other species (including *B. sutherlandii*) produce bulblets in the leaf axils. These can be picked and planted, much like seeds, and they develop more quickly.

COMBINATIONS

Heliotropium, Lobelia, Salvia, Viola.

CAUTION

B. cucullata is listed as invasive in many areas, including Florida. See pg. 494–495 for advice.

Belamcanda

HP | Zn 5–10

p. 378

These charming, unobtrusive, old-fashioned perennials have sparse, swordlike leaves and flattish, brightly colored, freckled flowers atop sturdy stalks, 18"–36" tall. They are now available in a wide range of colors beyond the original orange, including shades of purple, pink, and yellow.

Type Hardy perennial
Zone 5–10, H 9–5
Flowering Season Summer

SOWING

Indoors 8–10 weeks before planting out.
Outdoors Early spring or early autumn.
Depth *Seed:* Just cover. *Roots:* 2"–3".

GERMINATING

Time 14–60 days.
Requirements Easy. Place seed and moistened growing medium in a plastic bag and refrigerate for 7 days. Provide 65°–85°F thereafter.

TRANSPLANTING

Time Early spring, when soil is cool and a light frost is still possible, or early autumn.

Spacing 6"–8".
Light Full sun to part shade.
Soil Prefers moist, rich, well-drained soil with a pH level of 5.0–7.0, but is tolerant of a wide variety of conditions.

CARING FOR PLANTS

Easy. Water during dry spells. Cut leaves and flower stalks to the ground in autumn.

PROPAGATING

Divide roots in spring or grow from seed. Plants grown from seed will bloom in their first year.

COMBINATIONS

Asiatic lilies, *Campanula*, ornamental grasses, *Heliopsis, Nepeta, Scabiosa.*

Bellis

HP | Zn 3–9 | Full sun, Partial shade | Ordinary soil, Moist soil

Daisy

p. 378

Dwarf carpeting plants of just 6"–8", these daisies are grown for their cheerful solitary white, red, or pink pompom flowers. They are useful in the rock garden or as an edging.

Type Hardy perennial grown as a biennial in Zones 3–7, as an annual in Zones 8–9
Zone 3–9, H 9–6 (see species list, p. 442); plants will not flourish in intense heat and will perform best in cool climates
Flowering Season Late spring through early summer

SOWING

Indoors 8–10 weeks before planting out.
Outdoors *Zones 3–7:* Midsummer through early autumn for flowering the following year. *Zones 8–9:* Early spring, when soil is cool and a light frost is still possible, or autumn.
Depth Surface.

GERMINATING

Time 10–25 days.
Requirements Light and 70°F.

TRANSPLANTING

Time *Zones 3–7:* October. *Zones 8–9:* After last frost.
Spacing 6"–8".
Light Sun or part shade.
Soil Rich, moist loam.

CARING FOR PLANTS

Easy. Feed early in the growing season and water frequently. Deadhead to curtail self-seeding. Where summers are hot, cut back plants hard after flowering. In northern zones, mulch seedlings lightly before the first frost in autumn.

PROPAGATING

Divide after flowering or grow from seed.

COMBINATIONS

Arenaria, Muscari, Myosotis, dwarf tulips, *Veronica.*

Bergenia (syn. *Megasea*)

HP | Zn 2–8 | Full sun, Partial shade, Full shade | Dry soil, Ordinary soil, Moist soil

Bergenia, Elephant's ears, Pigsqueak

p. 379

Imposing perennials of strong character, bergenias are grown for their large, glossy, rounded leaves of green or bronze. Plants are generally 12"–18" tall, with thick, fleshy flowering stems. The ungainly clusters of small pink or white, trumpet-shaped flowers are often removed before blooming. Use judiciously as edging plants or as a foil for fine-textured plants.

Type Hardy perennial
Zone 2–8, H 9–1 (see species list, p. 442 and 480); dislikes hot, dry summers
Flowering Season Early spring to early summer, depending on species, sometimes reblooming in autumn

SOWING

Indoors Prechilled seed 6–8 weeks before last frost.
Outdoors Early spring when soil is cool and a light frost is still possible, or late autumn.

Depth Surface.

GERMINATING

Time 15–180 days.
Requirements Place seed and moistened growing medium in a plastic bag and refrigerate for 2 weeks. Provide 60°–70°F thereafter.

TRANSPLANTING

Time After last frost.
Spacing 12"–18".
Light Full sun where summers are mild, part to full shade elsewhere. Must have moist soil in full sun.
Soil Performs most successfully in deep, moist, fertile soil with a pH level of 6.0–7.5. *B. cordifolia* and *B. crassifolia* tolerate poor, dry soil and are suitable for xeriscaping where summers are mild.

CARING FOR PLANTS

Water regularly and remove dead flowers and leaves to maintain a tidy appearance. Feed once in spring with a low-nitrogen fertilizer. Division is required only when clumps begin to die off in the center. Slugs will come from miles away to feast on the leaves, especially where soil is damp.

PROPAGATING

Divide clumps after flowering as needed, perhaps every 3–4 years. Take cuttings of sections of rhizome in spring or start from seed.

COMBINATIONS

Geranium, ornamental grasses, *Iris, Kniphofia,* dwarf *Narcissus, Stachys.* Makes a magnificent edging to a rose bed. Contrasts dramatically with tiny-leaved shrubs: *Berberis, Buxus, Cotoneaster, Ilex crenata.*

Betonica See *Stachys*

Bidens

HP* | Zn 8–10

Beggar's tick, Bur-marigold, Pitchforks, Spanish needles, Stick-tight, Tickseed

p. 379

This large genus of primarily weedy plants is found most often in the garden as annuals or short-lived perennials, less than 1'–2' tall. They are useful for the profusion of star-shaped yellow flowers they bear from summer to frost. They are equally at home in borders and containers.

Type Hardy perennial
Zone 8–10, H 12–8; grown as annual in Zones 3–7. Plants become very leggy in high heat and humidity, except for *B. ferulifolia,* which tolerates both cool, wet summers and the heat of the South
Flowering Season Midsummer to frost

SOWING

Indoors 6–8 weeks before last frost.
Outdoors After last frost, or autumn.
Depth Just cover.

GERMINATING

Time 5–21 days.
Requirements Easy. 65°–70°F.

TRANSPLANTING

Time After last frost.
Spacing *Small species:* 12". *Medium species:* 18"–24". *Large species:* 25"–36".
Light Sun to light shade.
Soil Moist, well drained. Roots spread quickly, and established plants require regular watering. *B. ferulifolia* is drought tolerant.

CARING FOR PLANTS

Easy. Cut back hard if plants spread beyond their desired size.

PROPAGATING

Take stem cuttings, divide in spring or late summer to early fall, or grow from seed. Some species self-seed. Plants grown from seed will flower in 3 months.

COMBINATIONS

Chrysanthemum, Gazania, Bassia, Lobelia, Nigella.

Billardiera

HP | Zn 8–9

Billardiera is an interesting and unusual Australian vine that grows 8′–10′ tall. Its unremarkable pale green flowers are followed in autumn by stunning eggplant-colored fruits. A real conversation piece for a sunny wall.

Type Hardy perennial
Zone 8–9, H 9–8
Flowering Season Summer

SOWING

Indoors January.
Outdoors As soon as fruit is ripe in autumn, or in spring.
Depth Surface.

GERMINATING

Time 30–300 days.
Requirements Requires light and 55°–60°F.

TRANSPLANTING

Time After last frost.
Spacing Grow singly.
Light Sun, with shade from the hot afternoon sun in the South.
Soil Cool, deep, moist, fertile, and slightly acid.

CARING FOR PLANTS

Provide trellis or other structure for twining. Keep soil relatively moist. Prune after fruiting to remove any unruly branches. Young plants grow slowly.

PROPAGATING

Take softwood cuttings in early summer or grow from seed.

Bistorta See *Persicaria*

Blechnum

TP, HP | Zn 6–10

Hard fern

p. 379

Blechnum *is a very large genus of ferns most of which are tropical. They have sturdy, classic upright, dark green fronds that form substantial clumps.*

Type Tender perennial, hardy perennial
Zone 6–10 (see species list, p. 480)
Flowering Season N/A

SOWING

Indoors Late summer.
Outdoors Not recommended.
Depth Surface.

GERMINATING

Time 10–365 days.
Requirements See pp. 24–25 for information on starting ferns from spores.

TRANSPLANTING

Time After last frost in spring, or early autumn. Seedlings will be ready to plant out in 2–3 years.
Spacing 12″–24″.
Light Full to part shade. All species need shelter from the hot afternoon sun. *B. spicant* tolerates deep shade.
Soil Humusy, moist, neutral to acid. *B. penna-marina* will tolerate dry soil.

CARING FOR PLANTS

Do not let soil dry out completely. Remove faded fronds regularly to improve the appearance of plants. Susceptible to leaf spot, mealybugs, and scale.

PROPAGATING

Divide in spring or grow from spores. Division is rarely necessary, and plants take some time to reestablish.

COMBINATIONS

Asarum, Gallium, Tiarella, Trillium.

CAUTION

B. indicum (syn. *B. serrulatum*) is invasive in some areas. See pp. 494–495 for advice.

Bletilla

TP, HP | Zn 5–10

Orchid

p. 379

Grown for their exotic purplish pink or white flowers, these orchids have erect flower stems , 1′–2′ tall. Leaves are lance-shaped. Use in containers or near a patio.

Type Tender perennial, hardy perennial
Zone 5–10, H 9–5 (see species list, 442); some tender species may survive outdoors in Zones 7–8 with a heavy mulch
Flowering Season Early summer

SOWING

Indoors As soon as seed is available.
Outdoors *Seed:* Early spring to midsummer. *Root:* Late winter to early spring.
Depth *Seed:* Surface. *Root:* Just cover.

GERMINATING

Time 30–365 days.
Requirements Difficult. Sow seed in a saucer on the surface of a damp paper towel, covering with glass or plastic wrap. Keep soil moist; transplant to individual pots as seeds germinate, giving light and 65°–70°F.

TRANSPLANTING

Time After last frost.
Spacing 6″–12″.
Light Part to full shade, with shade from afternoon sun where summers are hot.
Soil Well drained, a bit acid; add peat and leaf mold.

CARING FOR PLANTS

Feed and water regularly during growing season. May require staking and may attract slugs. Cut back to ground in late fall. Transplant only in late winter, when dormant. Where not hardy, lift plants in fall, and store in sawdust in a frost-free location over winter; or grow in tubs that can be moved indoors.

PROPAGATING

Divide large clumps only infrequently immediately after flowering or grow from seed.

COMBINATIONS

Cyclamen, Hosta, Primula, Tiarella.

Bocconia See *Macleays*

Boltonia

HP | Zn 3–8

Boltonia, False chamomile

p. 379

These 2′–6′, unassuming, upright perennials bear a profusion of late-season, daisylike flowers in white, soft pink, or lavender with yellow centers. Boltonia is ideal for the perennial border or cottage garden.

Type Hardy perennial
Zone 3–8, H 9–1; gratifyingly resistant to humid heat.
Flowering Season Late summer through autumn

SOWING

Indoors 6–8 weeks before planting out.
Outdoors Early spring, when soil is cool and a light frost is still possible.
Depth Just cover.

GERMINATING

Time 14–21 days.
Requirements 60°F.

TRANSPLANTING

Time After last frost.
Spacing 18″–36″.
Light Full sun or light shade.
Soil Any with a pH level of 5.5–7.0.

CARING FOR PLANTS

Easy. May require staking in windy or shady sites. Short-lived plant; will require renewal by division every 2–4 years.

PROPAGATING

Divide in spring or after blooming in autumn or grow from seed.

COMBINATIONS

Aster, ornamental grasses, *Nepeta, Sedum, Solidago.*

CAUTION

Boltonia self-seeds and is listed as invasive in many areas. See pp. 494–495 for advice.

Brachychilum See *Hedychium*

Brachyscome (syn. *Brachycome*)

A | Zn 1–10 | Full sun, Partial shade | Dry soil, Ordinary soil

Swan River daisy

p. 379

These delightful airy, sprawling perennials bear masses of dainty daisylike flowers, usually deep blue with black or yellow eyes. Sited near the front door, a display of these 8"–18" tall charmers will revive your spirits after a long day at work.

Type Annual
Zone 1–10, H 12–1 (see species list, p. 442); prefers cool temperatures and will perform poorly, or disappear altogether, during a prolonged hot spell
Flowering Season Summer through autumn, although blooming will cease during very hot weather

SOWING

Indoors 6–8 weeks before last frost.
Outdoors After last frost. Where summers are cool, sow every 3–4 weeks for continuous blooms.
Depth Just cover.

GERMINATING

Time 10–21 days.
Requirements Easy. 65°–75°F.

TRANSPLANTING

Time After last frost.
Spacing 9", or 6" for edging.
Light Sun or light shade.
Soil Deep, rich, well drained, with a pH level of 6.0–7.0; tolerates dry soil. *B. iberidifolia* is suitable for xeriscaping in cool climates.

CARING FOR PLANTS

Easy. Deadhead regularly to prolong blooming. Support with twiggy branches pushed into the ground when plants are young.

PROPAGATING

Grow from seed only.

COMBINATIONS

Ageratum, Heliotropium, Nemesia, Salvia, Senecio.

Brimeura

HB | Zn 3–8 | Full sun, Partial shade | Ordinary soil

p. 379

Subtle and charming, these spring-blooming bulbs bear narrow, lance-shaped leaves and 6"–10" tall stalks of china blue, bell-shaped flowers. An unusual addition to the rock garden, or naturalize in the lawn or woodland. They are native to northern Spain.

Type Hardy bulb
Zone 3–8, H 8–4
Flowering Season Late spring

SOWING

Indoors Late winter to early spring.
Outdoors *Seed:* Early to midspring. *Bulb:* Autumn.
Depth *Seed:* Just cover. *Bulb:* 3" where soil is heavy, 5" in light soil.

GERMINATING

Time 30–60 days.
Requirements Easy. *Indoor sowing:* 60°–65°F. *Outdoor sowing:* Sow seed in flats or individual containers. Lift and overwinter indoors the first year; plant out the following spring.

TRANSPLANTING

Time After last frost, 1 year after sowing.
Spacing 3"–5".
Light Full sun to part shade.
Soil Well drained, humus-rich, alkaline.

CARING FOR PLANTS

Easy. Water throughout the growing season if weather is dry. Apply a complete fertilizer in spring and mulch with well-rotted manure in autumn. Allow leaves to die back completely before removing. Divide every 3–4 years, if necessary.

PROPAGATING

Divide bulbs in late summer or grow from seed.

Brittonastrum See *Agastache*

Briza

A, HP | Zn 4–8

Quaking grass

p. 379

Although quaking grass is not a showy plant, a display of these airy grasses is beautiful and restful. Plants reach 12"–30" tall with fine stalks bearing drooping, silvery spearheads or tiny, sparsely scattered seed heads. It is used mainly in naturalistic plantings.

Type Annual, hardy perennial
Zone *Annual:* 5–8, H 12–1. *Perennial:* 4–8, H 12–1 (see species list, p. 442). Prefers cool temperatures
Flowering Season Late spring to early autumn, depending on species

SOWING

Indoors 6–8 weeks before last frost. Sow annuals in peat pots.
Outdoors After last spring frost or in late summer.
Depth ⅛".

GERMINATING

Time 10–21 days.
Requirements Easy. 55°F.

TRANSPLANTING

Time After last frost.
Spacing 12".
Light Full sun to light shade.
Soil Light, well drained, rather poor. Most species are drought tolerant, but *B. minor* will die in hot, dry conditions. *B. maxima* and *B. media* are suitable for xeriscaping.

CARING FOR PLANTS

Easy. Water plants regularly for best results. Cut back to the ground when plants start to look ragged in midsummer. Do not move annuals.

PROPAGATING

Propagate annuals by seed only. Divide perennials in early spring or grow from seed. Plant may self-seed.

Brodiaea

HB | Zn 6–10

These lovely bulbs are native to the Americas and grown for their dazzling star- or funnel-shaped blooms of white or violet-blue. They grow 12"–36" tall with narrow, grassy leaves. Plant them in masses under shrubs. Several species once included in Brodiaea *are now classified as* Dichelostemma *or* Triteleia *species. All are grown in a similar fashion and are treated here.*

Type Hardy bulb
Zone 6–10, H 10–8. Prefers the Pacific Coast and will not thrive where summers are hot and humid
Flowering Season Spring to early summer

SOWING

Indoors Early spring.
Outdoors *Seed:* Autumn. *Bulb:* Early autumn.
Depth *Seed:* ⅛". *Bulb:* 3"–4".

GERMINATING

Time 30–90 days.
Requirements 55°–60°F. Seeds are highly susceptible to damping-off; sow in vermiculite and water only from below.

TRANSPLANTING

Time Autumn.
Spacing 3"–6".
Light Full sun.
Soil Loose, gritty, with very good drainage.

CARING FOR PLANTS

Water regularly during growing season but cease altogether after flowering. Where summers are wet or hot, lift bulbs after flowering and store in a cool, dry place, replanting in the autumn.

PROPAGATING

Plant cormels in autumn or grow from seed. Plants grown from seed will flower in about 2 years.

COMBINATIONS

Dwarf iris, *Pulsatilla, Tulipa,* as well as many spring-blooming alpines.

Browallia

TP* | Zn 9–10

Amethyst violet, Bush violet

p. 380

Browallia's *lush green foliage sets off pretty, trumpet-shaped purple or white flowers. Use the upright, somewhat bushy plants as an edging for shady borders, or in naturalistic plantings or containers. They grow to 24".*

Type Tender perennial, usually grown as annual
Zone 9–10, H 8–1; grown as annual in Zones 3–8; prefers warm days with cool nights
Flowering Season Spring through autumn

SOWING

Indoors 6–8 weeks before last frost.
Outdoors After last frost, but only where summers are very long.
Depth Surface.

GERMINATING

Time 6–21 days.
Requirements Light and 65°–75°F.

TRANSPLANTING

Time Spring, when temperatures remain above 40°F.
Spacing *Small species:* 6"–10". *Large species:* 12"–18".
Light Sun or part shade.
Soil Moist, with a pH level of 6.0–7.0.

CARING FOR PLANTS

Regularly mulch plants that are growing in full sun and water often. Pinch back young plants when 6" high to encourage bushiness. Feed only lightly.

PROPAGATING

Grow from seed. Plant may self-seed in the South.

COMBINATIONS

Mixes well in beds with *Coreopsis* or *Salvia,* or in containers with tall marigolds or dwarf *Cosmos.*

Brugmansia (syn. *Datura*)

TP*, HP* | Zn 8–10

Angels' trumpets

p. 380

These heavenly tropical shrubs, 4'–15' tall, bear large (up to 12" long), showy, pendulous, trumpet-shaped yellow, white, orange-red, or peach flowers. Grow them near patios where their stunning blooms and delicious fragrance can be appreciated. Several species, including B. suaveolens, *are especially fragrant at night.*

Type Tender perennial, hardy perennial
Zone 8–10, H 12–1 (see species list, p. 442). Grown as annual north of Zone 8. If growing as an annual, purchase only established plants, as young plants will not bloom for several years. Consider overwintering plants indoors
Flowering Season Summer to early autumn

SOWING

Indoors 12 weeks before planting out.
Outdoors 6 weeks before last frost, only in Zones 8–10.
Depth ⅛".

GERMINATING

Time 21–60 days.
Requirements Easy. 68°–86°F.

TRANSPLANTING

Time When weather has warmed in spring and temperatures remain above 40°F.
Spacing 3'–5'.
Light Sun to part shade.
Soil Rich, well drained.

CARING FOR PLANTS

Easy. Prune plants heavily in spring; feed every 2–3 weeks; water regularly throughout growing season. North of Zone 8, cut back slightly before first autumn frost; store indoors in a cool, bright location, keeping soil almost dry. Most leaves will drop; plants may be attacked by whitefly or spider mites. In early spring, cut back to 12" and begin watering and feeding. If container-grown, repot every spring.

PROPAGATING

Take softwood cuttings in spring or summer or grow from seed. Plants from seed flower in 2–5 years.

COMBINATIONS

Most effective when grown singly but could combine with *Canna, Dahlia,* or ornamental grasses.

CAUTION

All parts of the plant are extremely toxic.

Brunnera

HP | Zn 3–8

p. 380

This small genus comprises low-growing perennials that bear attractive green or variegated heart-shaped leaves and dainty white or blue forget-me-not-like flowers. The plants are stunning when used sensitively in combination with others of contrasting color or texture in shady, naturalistic settings.

Type Hardy perennial
Zone 3–8, H 7–1
Flowering Season Mid to late spring

SOWING

Indoors Prechilled seed 8–10 weeks before planting out.
Outdoors Late summer or early autumn.
Depth Just cover.

GERMINATING

Time 30–90 days.
Requirements Place seed and moistened growing medium in a plastic bag, seal, and refrigerate for 4 weeks. Provide 55°–60°F thereafter.

TRANSPLANTING

Time After last frost or in autumn.
Spacing 10"–15"; allow more space in rich soils.
Light Sun or part shade.
Soil Not fussy, but performs best in moist, rich soil with a pH level of 5.5–7.0.

CARING FOR PLANTS

Keep soil quite moist. *Brunnera* is short lived and should be divided in autumn or early spring when plants show signs of deteriorating.

PROPAGATING

Divide in early autumn in the South and in spring north of Zone 7, take root cuttings in autumn, or grow from seed. Plant may self-seed. Propagate cultivars by division only.

COMBINATIONS

Astilbe, azaleas, *Erysimum*, ferns, *Hepatica*, *Hosta*.

Bulbinella

TP, HP | Zn 7–10

These bright, early-blooming bulbs bear terminal spikes of small, yellow, star-shaped flowers on erect stalks, 1' to 2' tall. The leaves are grasslike. Mix Bulbinella *with other early-blooming bulbs or mass it in front of evergreen shrubs.*

Type Tender perennial, hardy perennial
Zone 7–10 (see species list, p. 442). Does not like high heat and humidity.
Flowering Season Late winter to summer, depending on species

SOWING

Indoors Spring.
Outdoors Autumn.
Depth *Seed:* just cover. *Roots:* just below soil level.

GERMINATING

Time 10–90 days.
Requirements 55°F. Grow seedlings indoors for two full seasons.

TRANSPLANTING

Time *Seedlings:* In spring, when nighttime temperatures remain above 50°F.
Spacing 18".
Light Sun or part shade.
Soil Cool, rich, moist, acid.

CARING FOR PLANTS

Water only occasionally during summer, keeping soil quite moist the rest of the year. Remove dead foliage when plant goes dormant (after flowering); mark location to avoid accidentally disturbing roots. Divide when plants become crowded.

PROPAGATING

Divide in spring or grow from seed.

Bulbocodium

HB | Zn 5–10

This genus of bulbs is grown for its stemless purple flowers, which resemble large, open crocuses. Growing only 1"–2", these little bulbs are at home in the rock garden or massed under shrubs.

Type Hardy bulb
Zone 5–10, H 9–7; will not thrive where winters are wet
Flowering Season Early spring

SOWING

Indoors Start seeds outdoors.
Outdoors *Seed or bulb:* Autumn.
Depth *Seed:* Surface. *Bulb:* 3".

GERMINATING

Requirements Since division is the most common method of propagation and little is known about growing this bulb from seed, the information given here is only a general guideline. Sow seeds in flats, covering first with compost, then a thin layer of fine gravel. Plunge flats into the ground outdoors and cover with glass. Twelve months after germination, transplant corms to a nursery bed, spacing 12" apart.

TRANSPLANTING

Time Autumn.
Spacing 3"–4".
Light Full sun to very light shade.
Soil Moist, very well drained, acid, with plenty of organic matter added.

CARING FOR PLANTS

Keep soil moist until after flowering. Feed only if soil is poor. Allow leaves to wither naturally after flowering. Divide every 2–3 years.

PROPAGATING

Divide after flowers and foliage have died back or, less reliably, grow from seed.

Buphthalmum

HP | Zn 3–8

Ox eye

Ox eye is a summer-blooming perennial grown for its yellow, daisylike flowers, some of which bear unusually fine and delicate petals. It is native to Europe and Asia. Ox eyes are useful in a sunny border.

Type Hardy perennial
Zone 3–8, H 8–4
Flowering Season Summer

SOWING

Indoors Spring.
Outdoors Spring or autumn.
Depth Surface.

GERMINATING

Time 14–30 days.
Requirements Light and 70°–75°F.

TRANSPLANTING

Time After last frost.
Spacing 8"–12".
Light Full sun or light shade.
Soil Moist, well drained, rather infertile, with a pH level of 6.0–8.0.

CARING FOR PLANTS

Easy. Water during dry spells. Plants may require staking. Divide frequently and withhold fertilizer so that plants don't take over your beds.

PROPAGATING

Divide in spring or early autumn or grow from seed. Plant may self-seed.

COMBINATIONS

Lychnis, Salvia, Verbena, Veronica.

Bupleurum

A, HP | Zn 3–9

B

Thorow-wax

These rather shrubby plants are useful in dry or rocky locations. Plants are 6"–36" tall, with greeny yellow flowers similar to Euphorbia.

Type Annual or hardy perennial
Zone *Annual:* 3–9. *Perennial:* 5–9, H 9–5
Flowering Season Summer

SOWING

Indoors 6–8 weeks before last frost, in peat pots.
Outdoors 2 weeks before last frost.
Depth Just cover.

GERMINATING

Time 7–30 days.
Requirements Prechill seed in the refrigerator for 1 week, then provide 60°–70°F.

TRANSPLANTING

Time After last frost.
Spacing *Small species:* 12". *Large species:* 24".
Light Sun to part shade.
Soil Prefers sweet, fertile, well drained; will tolerate poor, dry, rocky.

CARING FOR PLANTS

Easy and tolerant of much neglect, but slow growing. Prune perennials after flowering to form an attractive hedge. *B. falcatum* is short lived but self-seeds freely.

PROPAGATING

Divide in spring, take semi-ripe cuttings in summer, or grow from seed.

COMBINATIONS

Aster, Leontopodium, Lilium, Saxifraga.

Cacalia See *Emilia*

Caladium

TP* | Zn 9–10

Caladium, Angel wings, Elephant's ears

p. 380

Heat-lovers, caladiums are unsurpassed for large, colorful, showy foliage that is mottled, freckled, or striped in shades of pink, green, silver, or red. Growing 1'–3' tall, plants should be massed or planted in containers.

Types Tender perennial, usually grown as an annual
Zone 9–10, H 12–4; grown as annual in Zones 4–8. Performs well only where summers are very warm.
Flowering Season N/A

SOWING

Indoors Short-lived seed should be sown as soon as available. Where summers are short, start tubers indoors in late winter.
Outdoors In Zones 9–10 only, as soon as ripe seed is available.
Depth *Seed:* Just cover. *Tuber:* 2".

GERMINATING

Time 30–90 days.
Requirements 75°–85°F.

TRANSPLANTING

Time When temperatures will not drop below 60°F.
Spacing 8"–10".
Light Leaf colors most striking if grown in full sun, but in hot-summer areas, provide afternoon shade.
Soil Rich, moist, well drained, acid. Amend with well-rotted cow manure at planting time.

CARING FOR PLANTS

Water and feed frequently throughout growing season. North of Zone 9, ease off watering in fall; lift tubers before first frost. Store, frost-free, in dry sand over winter. In Zones 9–10, do not water in winter.

PROPAGATING

Divide tubers in spring, with each section containing at least two eyes, or grow from seed.

COMBINATIONS

Begonia, Solenostemon, Impatiens.

CAUTION

All parts of the plant may be harmful to humans and pets if eaten.

Calamagrostis

HP | Zn 5–9

Reed grass, Smallweed

p. 380

Neat and clump-forming, these grasses have dramatic upright plumes of 4′–6′, but usually a spread of no more than 18″–24″. Useful for massing or architectural interest.

Type Hardy perennial
Zone 5–9, H 9–6; tolerant of heat and humidity
Flowering Season Early to late summer, with plumes remaining quite showy all winter unless flattened by snow

SOWING

Indoors 3 weeks before last frost.
Outdoors As soon as fresh seed is available, in midsummer to late summer.
Depth Just cover.

GERMINATING

Time 14–100 days
Requirements Sow at 68°F. If seeds have not germinated in 28 days, refrigerate for 14–28 days, then return to 68°F.

TRANSPLANTING

Time Spring or autumn.
Spacing 18″–24″.
Light Full sun to part shade, with protection from afternoon sun in hot climates.
Soil Tolerant of a wide range of soils, including wet and dry. May become invasive in sandy soil. *C. epigens* and *C. canadensis* are suitable for xeriscaping.

CARING FOR PLANTS

Easy. Cut back to ground level in early spring. Plants are susceptible to powdery mildew, rust, and root rot.

PROPAGATING

Divide in spring or grow from seed.

COMBINATIONS

Alchemilla, Argemone, Eupatorium, Iris, Lilium.

Calamintha

HP | Zn 5–10

Calamint

p. 380

Bushy herbs with small, aromatic leaves, calamint produces an abundance of tiny, tubular, lipped flowers of pink, blue, or purple. Growing 9″–18″ tall, these long-blooming plants are useful in flower beds.

Type Hardy perennial
Zone 5–7 in the East or to Zone 10 in the West
Flowering Season Summer through autumn

SOWING

Indoors 12 weeks before last frost.
Outdoors Spring, or in a cold frame in autumn.
Depth Just cover.

GERMINATING

Time 7–28 days.
Requirements Easy. 60°–85°F.

TRANSPLANTING

Time Spring or autumn.
Spacing 12″–18″.
Light Sun to part shade.
Soil Prefers moist, well-drained soil with a pH of 6.6–8.5 but will tolerate drought and poor soil. Set plants high in the soil where summers are wet.

CARING FOR PLANTS

Easy. Cut back hard after flowering to keep plants looking tidy. If older plants become woody, cut back hard in spring to regenerate.

PROPAGATING

Divide in early spring, take stem cuttings in summer, or grow from seed. Plant may self-seed.

COMBINATIONS

Aster, Hemerocallis, Iris, Platycodon.

Calandrinia

HP* | Zn 8–10

These mainly low-growing plants are valued for their brightly colored blooms, usually in shades of pink or purple. They make a stunning edging display or liven up a humdrum rock garden. They are native to North, Central, and South America.

Type Short-lived perennial, often grown as an annual
Zone 8–10 (see species list, p. 443); grown as annual in Zones 3–10. Of about 150 known species, some prefer hot, dry climates; others are at home in milder regions.
Flowering Season Midsummer to late autumn, depending on species

SOWING

Indoors 6–8 weeks before last frost.
Outdoors After last frost.
Depth 1/8".

GERMINATING

Time 5–14 days.
Requirements Easy. 55°–60°F.

TRANSPLANTING

Time After last frost.
Spacing *Short species:* 6". *Tall species:* 10".
Light Full sun.
Soil Sandy or gritty. Withstands dry conditions. *C. umbellata* is suitable for xeriscaping.

CARING FOR PLANTS

Requires no feeding but appreciates protection from winter wetness. Plants are short lived and must be replaced frequently.

PROPAGATING

Take cuttings or grow from seed. Plant may self-seed.

Calceolaria

A, TP, HP, Bi | Zn 6–10

Pocketbook flower, Pouch flower, Slipper flower, Slipperwort

p. 380

A large genus of old-fashioned plants, the best known of which are diminutive, (6"–8") often used as houseplants. They bear brightly colored, heavily pouched flowers, often freckled or blotched, and have an irresistibly animated look. Attractive in containers or in more formal plantings where summers are cool.

Type Annual, tender perennial, hardy perennial, or biennial
Zone 6–10, H 6–1 (see species list, p. 443); prefers mild winters and cool summers and will perform poorly where summers are hot
Flowering Season Late spring to autumn, depending on species

SOWING

Indoors 10–12 weeks before planting out. Start in spring or summer to plant out in autumn; start in winter to plant out for summer bloom.
Outdoors *Annual:* Spring. *Biennial:* Autumn. *Perennial:* In a cold frame in autumn or early spring.
Depth Surface.

GERMINATING

Time 14–21 days.
Requirements Seed requires light to germinate. Sow indoors at 55°–75°F or (for biennial or perennial) sow in containers, plunge in the ground in a sheltered location in June, and plant in the garden in autumn.

TRANSPLANTING

Time Late spring after the soil has warmed.
Spacing 10"–12".
Light Sun to part shade, with afternoon shade in warm weather.
Soil Moist, well drained, humus-rich.

CARING FOR PLANTS

Difficult. Deadhead regularly and water regularly once flower buds have formed; protect from winter wetness. Mulch lightly in spring to keep soil cool. Stake tall species. Discard annuals after flowering. Can be troubled by aphids and slugs.

PROPAGATING

Divide in spring, take softwood cuttings in spring to early summer, or grow from seed. Plants grown from seed will bloom in their first year.

COMBINATIONS

This old-fashioned plant mixes most successfully with other old-fashioned favorites, including *Heliotropium, Pelargonium, Petunia, Verbena.*

Calendula

A | Zn 2–10 | ☼ ◐ | Ordinary soil, Moist soil

English marigold

p. 380

Unsophisticated but cheerful, these bushy 12"–30" tall annuals are grown for their sturdy orange and yellow, daisylike flowers. Use them in the border or cottage garden.

Type Annual
Zone 2–10, H 6–1; prefers cool temperatures, particularly during early growth stages
Flowering Season Spring through first frost; in Zones 8–10, winter blooming is possible from an autumn sowing

SOWING

Indoors 6–8 weeks before last frost.
Outdoors Early spring, when soil is cool and a light frost is still possible, or late autumn. Where summers are mild, sow in early summer for autumn flowering. In Zones 8–10, early autumn sowing is best.
Depth ¼".

GERMINATING

Time 6–14 days.
Requirements Darkness and 70°F.

TRANSPLANTING

Time After last frost.
Spacing *Dwarf cultivars:* 6"–12". *Tall cultivars:* 18"–24".
Light Full sun; plants will also grow in light shade where summers are very hot.
Soil Ordinary, with a pH level of 5.5–7.0; tolerates damp soils.

CARING FOR PLANTS

Easy. Pinch back young plants to stimulate bushy growth. Feed occasionally and deadhead and water often, keeping leaves as dry as possible because plants are susceptible to mildew. Fresh or dried flower petals of *C. officinalis* can be used in cooking as a substitute for saffron. Dig and pot up plants in midsummer to grow indoors over winter.

PROPAGATING

Take cuttings in summer or grow from seed.

COMBINATIONS

Alchemilla, Anchusa, Echium, Eschscholzia, Nepeta.

Calibrachoa

TP* | Zn 9–10 | ☼ | Dry soil, Ordinary soil, Moist soil

Million Bells, Trailing petunia

p. 380

Like trailing miniature petunias (6" high, 20"spread) that never need deadheading, these perfect plants are exceptional in containers and hanging baskets. Flowers are pretty shades of red, pale pink, deep cerise, yellow, or white.

Type Tender perennial often grown as an annual
Zone 9–10; grown as an annual farther north. Tolerates heat and humidity, as well as cold spring and autumn weather
Flowering Season Spring to frost, although flowering is reduced in cooler weather.

SOWING

Plants produce few seeds and should be propagated vegetatively, although most hybrid cultivars are patented and therefore cannot be propagated.

TRANSPLANTING

Time After last frost.
Spacing 12"–14".
Light Full sun.
Soil Moist, rich, well drained, with a pH of 5.6–6.0. Plants are more tolerent of dry soil when grown in the ground than in containers.

CARING FOR PLANTS

Very easy, requiring little more than regular watering.

PROPAGATING

Take stem cuttings or divide plants.

COMBINATIONS

Centaurea, Diascia, Ipomoea, Scaevola.

Calliopsis See *Coreopsis*

Callirhoe

A, HP | Zn 3–9

Poppy mallow

p. 381

These long-blooming plants have showy cup-shaped flowers of purple, pink, or magenta. From 6"–2' tall and impervious to heat and drought, they are attractive in rock gardens or cascading over a wall.

Type Annual, hardy perennial
Zone 3–9, H 9–1 (see species list, p. 443); evergreen in Zones 8–9; tolerant of extreme heat
Flowering Season Late spring to late summer, depending on species

SOWING

Indoors Spring.
Outdoors Spring, in cold frame or where plants grow.
Depth Surface.

GERMINATING

Time 15–180 days.
Requirements Sow at 25°–50°F for 4 months, then move to 68°F. Seeds need light to germinate.

TRANSPLANTING

Time Spring or autumn.
Spacing 24".
Light Full sun, with afternoon shade where summers are very hot.
Soil Tolerates hot, dry soil. Must have very good drainage. *C. involucrata* is an excellent choice for xeriscaping.

CARING FOR PLANTS

Very easy, requiring almost no attention. Watering is necessary only where summers are very hot. Difficult to transplant established plants.

PROPAGATING

Take stem cuttings in early summer or grow from seed. Most plants grown from seed bloom their first year. Division is possible, but because of a long taproot, it is usually successful only with young plants.

COMBINATIONS

Cerastium, Echinacea, Limonium, Lupinus, Perovskia, Stachys.

Callistephus

A | Zn 1–10

Annual aster, China aster

p. 381

Upright and bushy, these 8"–24" tall plants bear chrysanthemum-like blooms in almost every color but yellow. Long bloomers for borders; excellent cut flowers.

Type Annual
Zone 1–10, H 10–1; prefers cool weather, particularly in spring
Flowering Season Summer

SOWING

Indoors 6–8 weeks before planting out, in peat pots.
Outdoors After last frost.
Depth Just cover.

GERMINATING

Time 6–14 days.
Requirements 65°–70°F. Very susceptible to damping-off; grow in vermiculite and water only from below.

TRANSPLANTING

Time After last frost.
Spacing *Dwarf cultivars:* 6"–12". *Medium cutivars:* 12"–18". *Tall cultivars:* 18"–24".
Light Sun or light shade.
Soil Rich, well drained, with a pH level of 6.0–7.0.

CARING FOR PLANTS

Difficult. Do not pinch back young plants. Feed once or twice during the growing season and water regularly but carefully during droughts. (*Callistephus* is particularly sensitive to overwatering.) Keep roots cool with mulch in summer. Weed and deadhead frequently, and stake tall species. For greatest success, grow species that are resistant to aster yellows, and change location in the garden every year; do not use high-nitrogen fertilizer, which may encourage disease. Destroy any unhealthy plants immediately before others are infected. Will not flourish if overcrowded, poorly ventilated, or situated close to a heat-reflecting surface. Aphids and leafhoppers are attracted to *Callistephus,* and because both can spread aster yellows, it is essential to patrol for these pests regularly and control them.

PROPAGATING

Grow from seed only. Plants grown from seed will bloom in 4 months.

Calochortus

HB | Zn 5–10 | ☼ ◐ | Ordinary soil

Calochortus, Butterfly tulip, Cat's ear, Fairy lantern, Globe tulip, Mariposa tulip, Sego lily, Star tulip

p. 381

These unusual bulbous plants, native to western North America, feature wispy stems and leaves and showy, tuliplike blooms. Flowers are generally cup shaped, pretty, and delicate-looking, blooming on stems of 6"–36". Some blooms are nodding, some have backward-curling petals, others are balloon shaped. Petals may be white, purple, red, pink, or yellow.

Type Hardy bulb
Zone 5–10, H 10–6; performs best in the warm, dry summers and mild winters of the West Coast; particularly dislikes frequent cycles of freezing and thawing in winter and moist soil when dormant
Flowering Season Spring to early summer

SOWING

Indoors Late summer or early spring.
Outdoors *Seed or bulb:* Autumn.
Depth *Seed:* Just cover. *Bulb:* 3"–4".

GERMINATING

Time 30–180 days.
Requirements 55°–65°F. Seedlings started indoors should be left undisturbed for 2 years; pot up and leave for another 2 years before planting outdoors.

TRANSPLANTING

Time *Seed-grown bulbs:* After last frost.
Spacing 4".
Light Sun or part shade.
Soil Sandy, well-drained, slightly acid loam. Do not add manure.

CARING FOR PLANTS

Water in winter and spring, leaving ground quite dry in summer. Do not feed with manure. Mulch in winter in colder zones; north of Zone 7, bulbs may require lifting in autumn and storing over winter in a cool, frost-free location. In the East, these lilies are often grown in a potting mixture in containers plunged into the ground, as heavy Eastern soils do not yield strong bulbs. Bulbs grown this way should rest in a cool, dry place over the summer *outside* their pots. Repot in autumn and return to the ground; mulch after the ground freezes.

PROPAGATING

Divide corms in autumn or grow from seed. Plants grown from seed will flower in 5–6 years.

Caltha

HP | Zn 4–10 | ☼ ◐ ● | Ordinary soil, Moist soil

Kingcup, Marsh marigold

p. 381

Mainly low-growing perennials (under 12") thriving near water, grown for their cheerful, buttercuplike blooms; flowers are usually yellow, less often white or pink.

Type Hardy perennial
Zone 4–10, H 7–1 (see species list, p. 443)
Flowering Season Spring

SOWING

Indoors Start seeds outdoors only.
Outdoors Sow in peat pots as soon as ripe seed is available (usually early summer).
Depth Just cover.

GERMINATING

Time 30–90 days.
Requirements Seed must be fresh—old seed is unlikely to germinate. Stand peat pots in a saucer of shallow water and keep soil constantly moist until planted in the garden.

C

TRANSPLANTING

Time Transplant peat pots to their permanent location in midsummer.
Spacing *Small species:* 8"–12". *Medium species:* 18". *Large species:* 24"–36".
Light Prefers part to full shade, but tolerates full sun in very moist soil.
Soil Rich, clay soil that is moist or even wet, with a pH level of 5.0–7.0.

CARING FOR PLANTS

Easy. Keep soil moist at all times. Mark plant locations, as foliage dies back altogether after flowering.

PROPAGATING

Divide after flowering in Zones 4–6 (in early autumn elsewhere) or grow from seed.

COMBINATIONS

Aquilegia, Lysichiton, Primula, Skimmia.

CAUTION

May be harmful if eaten.

Camassia

HB | Zn 4–9

Camassia, Camass, Quamash

p. 381

This small genus of spring-blooming bulbs produces blue or white star-shaped flowers along leafless stalks of 1'–6'. Use these dramatic plants as an accent or in a naturalistic setting.

Type Hardy bulb
Zone 4–9, H 10–1
Flowering Season Summer

SOWING

Indoors Start seeds outdoors only.
Outdoors *Seed:* As soon as ripe seed is available (usually in summer). *Bulb:* Autumn.
Depth *Seed:* Just cover. *Bulb:* 4"–5".

GERMINATING

Time 30–180 days.
Requirements Easy. Sow seed in flats, sink flats in the ground against a north-facing wall, and cover with glass. Moisten soil occasionally, if necessary.

TRANSPLANTING

Time Transplant to the garden in autumn after two full growing seasons.
Spacing 6"–8".
Light Full sun or light shade.
Soil Moist, well drained, fertile, slightly acid.

CARING FOR PLANTS

Easy. Water frequently and feed once in early spring. After blooming, cut back flowering stems to ground. Mulch with compost in winter. Plants resent disturbance and should be divided only when they are overcrowded. Replant bulbs immediately or store them in a cool, dry place until early autumn.

PROPAGATING

Divide clumps and separate bulbs and bulblets in early autumn or grow from seed. Plants grown from seed will take up to 5 years to flower.

COMBINATIONS

Allium, Campanula, early *Gladiolus.*

Campanula (syn. *Azorina*)

A, Bi, HP | Zn 3–10

Campanula, Bellflower

p. 381

This very large genus includes plants of widely differing appearance, but usually bearing bell-shaped flowers of blue, white, or, less commonly, pink. Use small species to edge borders or paths or in rock gardens; larger species are at home anywhere, from a formal border to a cottage garden.

Type Hardy perennial, biennial, or, rarely, annual
Zone *Perennial:* 3–8. *Annual:* 3–10, H 9–1 (see species list, pp. 443–444)
Flowering Season Spring through autumn, depending on species

SOWING

Indoors 8–10 weeks before planting out.
Outdoors Early spring or, where winters are mild, early autumn. *Biennial:* Late spring to early summer.
Depth Surface.

GERMINATING

Time 14–28 days.
Requirements Difficult. Light and 60°–70°F. Keep out of strong sunlight.

TRANSPLANTING

Time Early spring, when soil is cool and a light frost is still possible, or early autumn. *Biennial:* Autumn.
Spacing *Small species:* 5"–10". *Tall species:* 15"–20".
Light Most campanulas like full sun, but part shade is preferable where summers are very hot.
Soil Ordinary, with a pH level of 7.0–7.5. Rock garden species need cool, gritty soil. *C. poscharskyana* is suitable for xeriscaping.

CARING FOR PLANTS

Easy. Feed in early spring, water during dry spells, deadhead regularly, and you will be repaid with abundant blooms. Watch for slugs throughout the growing season and top-dress with well-rotted manure in winter. Tall species may need staking.

PROPAGATING

Propagate annuals by seed. Take cuttings or divide perennials in autumn (in spring north of Zone 7) or grow from seed.

COMBINATIONS

Allium, Delphinium, Digitalis, Geranium, Lilium, Rodgersia, roses, *Stachys,* to name but a few. Campanulas combine well with practically every other plant in the garden.

Canna

HP* | Zn 8–10

Canna, Indian shot

p. 382

These tall, stately, substantial plants demand a large space and dominate the landscape. They bear big, complex blossoms in shades of pink, red, and yellow borne in terminal spikes on stiff stalks of 3'–5'. New dwarf plants (2'–3') are suitable for containers. Selections with handsomely colored foliage are also available.

Type Hardy perennial, usually grown as an annual
Zone 8–10, H 12–1; grown as annual in Zones 3–7
Flowering Season Summer through early autumn

SOWING

Indoors 2–3 weeks before last frost.
Outdoors Several weeks after last frost, when soil is warm.
Depth *Seed:* ¼". *Rhizome:* 4"–5".

GERMINATING

Time 21–365 days.
Requirements Germination is erratic. Take a small chip from seed with a sharp knife and soak in warm water for 48 hours; provide 70°–75°F thereafter.

TRANSPLANTING

Time Several weeks after last frost, when soil is warm and temperatures remain above 50°F.
Spacing 18"–24".
Light Full sun.
Soil Moist, fertile, well drained, with a pH level of 6.0–8.0.

CARING FOR PLANTS

Easy. Feed monthly and provide adequate water during dry spells. Watch for slugs and beetles, which enjoy munching on the succulent leaves. In Zones 4–7, cut back to 6" in autumn, lift clumps of rhizomes, dry, and store in peat moss or vermiculite in a cool, frost-free place. Provide winter mulch for plants left in the ground over winter.

PROPAGATING

Divide rhizomes in spring; each new section should contain at least two buds. You can also grow from seed. Selections with colored foliage must be propagated by division.

COMBINATIONS

Achillea, Crocosmia, Dahlia, ornamental grasses, *Hemerocallis.*

Cardamine (syn. *Dentaria*)

A, Bi, HP | Zn 3–9 

Bittercress

These delicate-looking plants have erect, 1'–2' stems bearing charming flat or cup-shaped flowers of white, purple, or pink. Use them in rock gardens, at streamside, or in borders in cool regions.

Type Annual, biennial, or hardy perennial
Zone 3–9: H 8–5 (see species list, p. 444); none is tolerant of hot, humid conditions; performs best where summers are cool
Flowering Season Late spring to early summer

SOWING

Indoors When seed is ripe, around midsummer
Outdoors Early spring or autumn.
Depth 1/8".

GERMINATING

Time 20–60 days.
Requirements Sow at 55°–65°F. If seed does not germinate in 3–4 weeks, refrigerate for 2–4 weeks. Grow seedlings in containers for 1 year before planting out.

TRANSPLANTING

Time Early spring or midautumn.
Spacing *Small species:* 6"–12". *Large species:* 18"–24".
Light Part shade in the North, with more shade farther south, particularly in the afternoon.
Soil Rich, moist, well drained, with a pH of 6.1–7.8.

CARING FOR PLANTS

Water faithfully during dry spells; deciduous species will go dormant in summer if the soil is too dry. Powdery or downy mildew and rust may be a problem.

PROPAGATING

Divide carefully in spring or after flowering, take leaf cuttings, or grow from seed. *C. pratensis* self-seeds rampantly.

COMBINATIONS

Lathyrus, Narcissus, Omphalodes, Tulipa.

Cardiocrinum

HB | Zn 7–9

Large, lovely, fragrant white trumpets adorn the sturdy 4'–10' stems of these gracious plants. Impossible to misuse, these stunning bulbs work well individually or in masses, in formal settings or informally.

Type Hardy bulb
Zone 7–9, H 9–7; may survive in Zones 5–6 with a heavy winter mulch. Grows best in the Pacific Northwest, where summers are cool and humid and winters are mild
Flowering Season Summer

SOWING

Indoors Start seed outdoors only.
Outdoors *Seed:* As soon as fresh seed is available in autumn. *Bulb:* Autumn.
Depth *Seed:* Just cover. *Bulb:* Plant with tip at soil level.

GERMINATING

Time 90 days–2 years.
Requirements Difficult. Sow seed in flats, cover with a sheet of glass, and place containers outdoors against a north-facing wall. Water if necessary to keep growing medium moist but not wet. In spring, bring flats indoors where seeds will germinate at 50°F.

TRANSPLANTING

Time After last frost.
Spacing 24"–36".
Light Part shade.
Soil Deep, moist loam with abundant organic matter added.

CARING FOR PLANTS

Difficult. Apply bulb food in spring and feed monthly thereafter with a weak fertilizer solution. Water during dry spells in summer. Plants go dormant in dry weather. Mulch with compost to keep soil cool and moist. Parent bulbs die after blooming, and their offsets do not bloom for 3–5 years more. Plant annually for the first few years to ensure that you will have some plants in flower each summer.

PROPAGATING

Divide bulbs in October, discarding the exhausted parent bulb, or grow from seed. Plants grown from seed will flower in 5–7 years.

COMBINATIONS

Gunnera, Iris ensata, Matteuccia, Rodgersia.

Cardiospermum

TP* | Zn 9–10 | Full sun | Ordinary soil

Balloon vine, Heart seed

A shrubby climber, Cardiospermum *has lush, feathery foliage, inconspicuous white flowers, and an abundance of showy, balloonlike green fruits. Plants grow to 10', making an excellent cover for a trellis, fence, or pergola.*

Type Tender perennial usually grown as an annual
Zone 9–10, H 12–1 (see species list, p. 444); grown as an annual in Zones 3–8
Flowering Season Summer

SOWING

Indoors 6–8 weeks before last frost.
Outdoors After last frost, but only where the growing season is long.
Depth ½".

GERMINATING

Time 21–30 days.
Requirements Easy. 65°–70°F.

TRANSPLANTING

Time In spring, when temperatures remain above 40°F.
Spacing 12"–24" for rapid cover, otherwise 24"–48".
Light Full sun.
Soil Ordinary, well drained.

CARING FOR PLANTS

Requires a trellis or other support. Water regularly.

PROPAGATING

Take cuttings in summer or grow from seed. Plants may self-seed where winters are mild.

CAUTION

C. halicacabum is listed as invasive in some areas, including Virginia. See pp. 494–495 for advice.

Carex

HP | Zn 3–9 | Full sun, Partial shade | Moist soil

Sedge

p. 382

A large genus of handsome, grasslike plants, Carex *includes many species that are evergreen. Generally neater and less pushy than many ornamental grasses, sedges make an attractive addition to shade gardens, containers, and waterside plantings.*

Type Hardy perennial
Zone 3–9, H 9–1 (see species list, p. 480)
Flowering Season Summer

SOWING

Indoors 8–12 weeks before last frost.
Outdoors Autumn.
Depth Just cover.

GERMINATING

Time Up to several months.
Requirements Provide 65°–70°F for 2–4 weeks. If there is no germination, move to 25°–40°F for 4–6 weeks, then to 40°–50°F.

TRANSPLANTING

Time After last frost.
Spacing *Small species:* 8"–12". *Larger species:* 18".
Light Sun to part shade, with more shade in hotter climates.
Soil Rich, moist, well drained. *C. muskingumensis* and *C. siderosticha* tolerate wet soil.

CARING FOR PLANTS

Easy. Cut back deciduous species in early spring. Plants may go dormant in summer if soil is too dry.

PROPAGATING

Divide in spring or early summer or grow from seed. Propogate variegated cultivars by division.

COMBINATIONS

Campanula, Dryopteris, Iris, Pulmonaria, Tagetes, Verbena.

CAUTION

Species of *Carex* are listed as invasive in some areas (for example, *C. kobomugi* in Virginia and all species in Florida). See pp. 494–495 for advice.

Carpanthea

HP* | Zn 7–10

This low-growing succulent, highly drought-tolerant plant produces cheerful yellow, dandelion-like flowers. It is useful for planting on dry slopes and makes an attractive addition to containers or borders.

Type Hardy perennial; usually grown as an annual
Zone 7–10; grown as an annual in Zones 3–10; prefers cool nights and low humidity
Flowering Season Spring to summer; flowers most profusely during cool weather

SOWING

Indoors 10–12 weeks before last frost.
Outdoors Spring.
Depth Just cover.

GERMINATING

Time 7–30 days.
Requirements 70°–75°F. Keep seedlings on the dry side.

TRANSPLANTING

Time After last frost.
Spacing 8"–10".
Light Full sun.
Soil Well drained; very drought tolerant.

CARING FOR PLANTS

Easy, requiring little care.

PROPAGATING

Grow from seed.

CAUTION

C. pomeridiana is listed as invasive in some areas. See pp. 494–495 for advice.

Carthamus

A | Zn 3–9

Safflower

p. 382

Upright, stiff, rather prickly looking annuals, Carthamus *are grown for use in cooking and dried flower arrangements. Plants grow to 3'; blossoms are tubular, orange or yellow.*

Type Annual
Zone 3–9, H 12–1; prefers cool, dry climates and will not tolerate wet summers
Flowering Season Midsummer

SOWING

Indoors 6–8 weeks before last frost, in peat pots.
Outdoors Early spring, when soil is cool and a light frost is still possible, or late autumn.
Depth ¼".

GERMINATING

Time 10–24 days.
Requirements 60°–70°F.

TRANSPLANTING

Time After last frost.
Spacing 6"–8".
Light Full sun.
Soil Poor, light, dry, with a pH level of 6.0–7.0.

 Type: A = Annual; Bi = Biennial; HP = Hardy Perennial; TP = Tender Perennial; HB = Hardy Bulb; TB = Tender Bulb; * = May be grown as annual where colder

CARING FOR PLANTS

Young plants are attractive to rabbits; screening may be required as protection. Difficult to transplant. Cut flower heads in late summer and dry indoors to use as a substitute for saffron in cooking. For dried flower arrangements, cut stems when flower heads contain both blooms and buds.

PROPAGATING

Grow from seed. Plant may self-seed.

COMBINATIONS

Centaurea, Gypsophila, Lupinus.

Carum

Bi | Zn 3–8 | ☼ | Ordinary soil

Caraway

p. 382

Grown for its distinctively flavored seed, this upright herb grows 2'–4' tall. It has fernlike leaves and flat clusters of tiny white flowers.

Type Biennial
Zone 3–8
Flowering Season Spring to early summer of its second year

SOWING

Indoors Sow seed outdoors only.
Outdoors 2–3 weeks before last spring frost or early autumn.
Depth ⅛".

GERMINATING

Time Fresh seed will germinate in 14 days; old seed will take considerably longer.
Requirements 70°F.

TRANSPLANTING

Time Set out purchased plants after last frost.
Spacing 6"–12".
Light Full sun.
Soil Light, fertile, well drained, with a pH level of 6.0–7.0.

CARING FOR PLANTS

Do not move. Feed at planting time and again when rapid growth begins; watering is not necessary. To harvest seeds for cooking, cut flower heads in midsummer when seeds are just turning brown. Hang upside down in a paper bag to collect. Immerse seeds in boiling water to destroy any insects, then dry in the sun for several days. Store in an airtight container.

PROPAGATING

Grow from seed. Plant may self-seed.

Cassia

A, HP | Zn 4–9 | Full sun, Partial shade | Good for xeriscaping, Ordinary soil

Senna

The Cassia *genus features unusual, shrubby perennials, many of which are native to North America. They have the habit and appearance of a small tree. Leaves are compound; flowers are bright yellow and pealike. This 2'–4' curiosity should be used judiciously, probably in the wild garden.*

Type Hardy perennial or annual
Zone *Perennial:* 4–9, H 12–9 (see species list, p. 444)
Flowering Season Summer

SOWING

Indoors 6–8 weeks before planting out.
Outdoors Summer through autumn for flowering the following year.
Depth ⅛".

GERMINATING

Time 5–90 days.
Requirements Chip seed with a sharp knife and soak in warm water for 2–3 hours. Keep at 70°–75°F thereafter.

C

TRANSPLANTING

Time After last spring frost or in autumn.
Spacing 24"–36".
Light Full sun to light shade.
Soil Will grow in most well-drained soils. All species are tolerant of dry soil and are useful for xeriscaping.

CARING FOR PLANTS

Easy. Water and feed regularly for best results. Thinning plants in autumn will improve flowering the following year.

PROPAGATING

Take cuttings, divide in spring, or grow from seed.

Catananche

HP | Zn 4–9

Cupid's dart, Blue cupidone

p. 382

Rather stiff, upright plants, 24" tall, Catananche *plants bear silvery leaves and upward-pointing flower buds; flowers are lavender and daisylike. When used in combination with plants of strongly contrasting shape and harmonizing color, these unimposing perennials can be stunning.* Catanache *are excellent cut flowers, either fresh or dried.*

Type Hardy perennial, often grown as an annual
Zone 4–9, H 8–1; does not like intense heat and humidity
Flowering Season Summer to early autumn

SOWING

Indoors 6–8 weeks before last frost.
Outdoors Early spring, when soil is cool and a light frost is still possible; where winters are mild, late autumn.
Depth Just cover.

GERMINATING

Time 20–25 days.
Requirements 65°–75°F.

TRANSPLANTING

Time After last frost.
Spacing 9"–12".
Light Full sun.
Soil Average, well drained. Drought tolerant. *C. caerulea* is suitable for xeriscaping.

CARING FOR PLANTS

Easy. Requires little care. Cut back to the ground in autumn and mulch for winter. Where summers are hot, cut back plants hard after flowering. Plants are short lived, especially in clay soil, and must be renewed regularly.

PROPAGATING

Divide in early spring in the North (early autumn in the South), take root cuttings in late winter, or grow from seed. Plant may self-seed.

COMBINATIONS

Dianthus, dusty miller, *Heliopsis, Hemerocallis, Layia, Veronica.*

Catharanthus

TP* | Zn 9–10

Annual vinca, Madagascar periwinkle, Periwinkle vinca

p. 382

Bushy, 6"–24" annuals, with neat, glossy green leaves, Catharanthus *provides a constant display of simple, flattish flowers in white or shades of pink, sometimes with a deeply stained center. A dependable plant for massing, borders, or containers.*

Type Tender perennial, usually grown as an annual
Zone 9–10, H 12–1; grown as an annual in Zones 1–8; thrives where summers are hot and humid
Flowering Season Summer through first frost

SOWING

Indoors 12–16 weeks before planting out.
Outdoors Late winter, only in Zones 9–10.
Depth 1/4".

GERMINATING

Time 15–20 days.
Requirements Darkness and 70°–75°F.

TRANSPLANTING

Time Spring, when temperatures remain above 40°F.
Spacing 8″–10″.
Light Full sun or very light shade.
Soil Moist, with a pH level of 6.0–7.0.

CARING FOR PLANTS

Easy. Feed lightly in spring and water regularly throughout the year. In Zones 9–10, cut back plants occasionally to stimulate new growth.

PROPAGATING

Take cuttings or grow from seed. Plant may self-seed.

Caulophyllum

HP | Zn 4–7

Caulophyllum *includes two species of erect perennials, one of which is native to eastern North America. Grown in woodlands and wild gardens, it has compound, lobed leaves that are bluish green in spring, then turn green with maturity. Inconspicuous flowers are followed by attractive blue fruit. Plants grow 18″–36″ tall.*

Type Hardy perennial
Zone 4–7
Flowering Season May

SOWING

Plants are most successfully propagated by division or cuttings.
Depth *Roots:* 1″.

TRANSPLANTING

Time Set out purchased plants in autumn.
Spacing 12″–15″.
Light Part to full shade.
Soil Deep, moist, rich woods soil with a pH level of 4.5–7.0.

CARING FOR PLANTS

Mulch with oak leaves and do not allow soil to dry out. Do not disturb established plants.

PROPAGATING

Divide in spring or early autumn or take cuttings from rhizomes.

Celmisia

HP | Zn 5–9

Mountain daisy, New Zealand daisy

p. 382

This genus of perennials is native to Australia and New Zealand. It has widely varying foliage that may be green or gray, small and lance-shaped or bold and swordlike. Its flowers are white and daisylike, borne singly on upright stems of 4″–3′. Grow it in rock gardens and borders.

Type Hardy perennial
Zone 5–9, H 8–7 (see species list, p. 444); requires mild winters and humid, mild summers
Flowering Season Early summer to midsummer

SOWING

Indoors As soon as ripe seed is available.
Outdoors Starting seed outdoors is not recommended.
Depth Surface.

GERMINATING

Time 30–180 days.
Requirements Difficult to start from seed and difficult to obtain seed. Because of its brief viability, seed must be sown as soon as ripe. Provide light and 60°–65°F.

C

TRANSPLANTING

Time After last frost, but only after a strong root system is established.
Spacing *Small species:* 4"–8". *Medium species:* 12"–24". *Spreading species:* 4'–6'.
Light Full sun to light shade.
Soil Acid, peaty, well-drained soil that does not dry out in summer.

CARING FOR PLANTS

Do not allow soil to dry out in summer. Protect furry-leaved species from overhead water, especially in winter. Place stone chippings around plants to improve drainage.

PROPAGATING

Divide, root individual rosettes in the same manner as cuttings in early summer, or grow from seed.

Celosia

A | Zn 2–10

Cockscomb, Woolflower

p. 382

These upright, 6"–36" tall plants bear blossoms in bold —almost unnatural—shades of pink, red, orange, or yellow. Some flower heads are soft, erect plumes, while others resemble intricately worked chenille. Celosia *is very heat tolerant and can make a striking display when planted en masse.*

Type Annual
Zone 2–10, H 9–2; prefers warm temperatures
Flowering Season Summer through early autumn

SOWING

Indoors 6–8 weeks before last frost, in peat pots.
Outdoors After last frost.
Depth Just cover.

GERMINATING

Time 6–14 days.
Requirements Easy. 70°–75°F.

TRANSPLANTING

Time After last frost.
Spacing *Dwarf species:* 12". *Tall species:* 18".
Light Full sun to light shade.
Soil Ordinary, moist, with a pH level of 6.0–7.0.

CARING FOR PLANTS

Easy. Keep soil moist and fertilize lightly during the growing season. Plants are susceptible to fungal diseases, which will cause wilting.

PROPAGATING

Grow from seed. Plant may self-seed.

COMBINATIONS

Because of their bold colors, furry texture, and sometimes eccentric shape, many cultivars are difficult to use successfully in combination with other plants and may be most attractive grown alone. For the gardener who likes a challenge, careful selection of plants in contrasting or complementary colors can result in pleasing combinations: Try *Catharanthus, Salvia, Petunia,* or dusty miller for a sunny location, or Begonia or *Solenstemon* for lightly shaded beds or containers.

Celsia See *Verbascum*

Centaurea

A, Bi, HP | Zn 1–10

Centaurea, Hardheads, Knapweed, Star thistle

p. 383

A large genus of charming upright plants, Centaurea *species bear deeply colored, fine-petaled pom-poms, evocative of country meadows and carefree summers. Use these 12"–36" plants in borders, wildflower plantings, or cottage gardens.*

Type Annual, biennial, or hardy perennial
Zone *Annual:* 1–10, H 8–1. *Perennial:* 3–9, H 8–1 (see species list, pp. 445 and 480). Most species prefer cool temperatures
Flowering Season *Annual:* Late spring through late summer. *Perennial:* Spring or summer, depending on species

SOWING

Indoors 6–8 weeks before planting out.
Outdoors Just before last frost, or in autumn where winters are mild. Successive sowing will ensure continuous bloom.
Depth Just cover.

GERMINATING

Time 7–30 days.
Requirements Provide darkness and 60°–70°F.

TRANSPLANTING

Time *Annual:* Late spring. *Biennial or perennial:* Late spring or early autumn.
Spacing *Dwarf species:* 6". *Tall species:* 12".
Light Full sun.
Soil Ordinary, well drained, with a pH level of 5.5–7.0. *C. macrocephala* is very tolerant of dry soil and is a useful plant for xeriscaping.

CARING FOR PLANTS

Easy. Water regularly and feed once in spring. Deadhead frequently to prolong blooming. Where summers are very hot, cut back perennials hard after blooming. Plants may require staking. Divide perennials every 2–3 years. Generally pest-free, but fungal diseases can be a problem.

PROPAGATING

Divide perennials in spring in Zones 3–6 (in autumn in Zones 7–10), or grow both annuals and perennials from seed. Annuals may self-seed.

COMBINATIONS

Artemisia, Bergenia, Colchicum, Echium, Geranium, Nerine, Phacelia, Salvia.

Centaurium (syn. *Erythraea*)

A | Zn 1–9

Canchalagua, Mountain pink

These very low-growing plants, up to 8", display clusters of red or pink blooms. They are an attractive edging, or use them in rock gardens or borders.

Type Annual
Zone 1–9; performs best where summers are cool
Flowering Season Summer

SOWING

Indoors Seed should be sown *in situ.*
Outdoors Very early spring or autumn where winters are mild; after last frost elsewhere.
Depth Just cover.

GERMINATING

Time 21–60 days.
Requirements 65°–75°F.

TRANSPLANTING

Time After last frost.
Spacing *Small species:* 6"–8". *Large species:* 12".
Light Full sun or part shade; shade from very hot afternoon sun is desirable.
Soil Light, sandy, very well drained. *C. erythraea* is suitable for xeriscaping.

CARING FOR PLANTS

Easy. Requires no special care.

PROPAGATING

Grow from seed. Plant may self-seed.

Centranthus

HP | Zn 4–9

Valerian

p. 383

A shrubby perennial, usually 2′–3′, Centranthus *bears white or deep pink blooms on upright stems. These Mediterranean natives are grown in rock gardens and borders or cascading over dry stone walls.*

Type Hardy perennial
Zone 4–9, H 8–5; does not tolerate excessive heat and humidity
Flowering Season Late spring through frost

SOWING

Indoors 8 weeks before planting out, in peat pots.
Outdoors Early spring when soil is cool and a light frost is still possible.
Depth Just cover.

GERMINATING

Time 21–30 days.
Requirements Easy. 60°–70°F.

TRANSPLANTING

Time After last frost.
Spacing 12″–18″.
Light Full sun.
Soil Well drained, slightly alkaline. Rich soil will produce large plants, poor soil more compact ones. *C. ruber* is well suited to xeriscaping in California.

CARING FOR PLANTS

Easy. Feed plants in spring and cut back after flowering to encourage a second bloom. Although *Centranthus* is drought tolerant, more attractive plants will result from regular watering during dry spells. Cut back flowering stems to the ground in winter. Plants are short lived and require frequent renewal. Do not transplant.

PROPAGATING

Take basal cuttings in early summer or grow from seed. Plant self-seeds quite freely. Plants grown from seed will bloom in their first year.

COMBINATIONS

Allium, Aster, Campanula, Coreopsis, Kniphofia, Nepeta, roses, *Salvia.*

Cephalaphora

TP* | Zn 9–10

An interesting Chilean native, Cephalaphora *grows 12″ tall with bright green foliage. Its cheerful yellow pom-pom flowers emit an applelike fragrance. Use it in borders and containers.*

Type Tender perennial; often grown as an annual
Zone 9–10; grown as an annual farther north; will not thrive where summers are very hot
Flowering Season Summer

SOWING

Indoors 8 weeks before last frost.
Outdoors After last frost, only in Zones 9–10
Depth Surface.

GERMINATING

Time 14–30 days.
Requirements Provide 60°–70°F for 3–4 weeks; if germination does not take place, move to 40°F for 6 weeks, then back to 60°–70°F. Requires light to germinate.

TRANSPLANTING

Time After last frost.
Spacing 12″.
Light Full sun to part shade.
Soil Light, rich, well drained.

CARING FOR PLANTS

No special care required.

PROPAGATING

Divide in spring or grow from seed.

Cephalaria

HP | Zn 3–9

Scabious

Large, coarse, clump-forming perennials, Cephalaria *can grow up to 6' tall. It bears cheerful, cup-shaped yellow flowers in summer. Allow plenty of room for it at the back of the border, or set it loose in a wild garden. The flowers are useful for cutting.*

Type Hardy perennial
Zone 3–9, H 8–1
Flowering Season Summer

SOWING

Indoors Late winter to early spring.
Outdoors Spring.
Depth ¼".

GERMINATING

Time 21–60 days.
Requirements Easy. 55°–65°F. If seeds have not sprouted in 60 days, chill for 3 weeks.

TRANSPLANTING

Time After last frost.
Spacing 24"–36".
Light Sun or part shade.
Soil Adaptable, but prefers moist soil.

CARING FOR PLANTS

Easy. Pinch back in late spring to restrict size. Water regularly and cut back after flowering. Plants may require staking. Divide every 2–3 years to keep plants vigorous.

PROPAGATING

Divide in early spring or grow from seed.

COMBINATIONS

Galega, Thalictrum, Valerian.

Cephalipterum

A | Zn 1–10

Silver-flowered everlasting

Grow these annual plants for their yellow or white everlasting flowers, which are small, round, and papery, held on wiry 12" stems. They can be used in the border or a cutting bed.

Type Annual
Zone 1–10; flowering will be reduced in hot, dry weather
Flowering Season Summer

SOWING

Indoors 6–8 weeks before planting out.
Outdoors After last frost.
Depth Just cover.

GERMINATING

Time 14–21 days.
Requirements 65°–75°F.

TRANSPLANTING

Time After last frost.
Spacing 12".
Light Full sun or light shade.
Soil Flowers best in poor soil that is cool and moist, but plants are fairly drought tolerant.

CARING FOR PLANTS

Mulch to keep soil cool. Water regularly for best results. Watch out for slugs in wet spring weather. For use in dried arrangements, cut stems before flowers are fully open; hang upside down in a cool, shady spot.

PROPAGATING

Grow from seed only.

Cerastium

HP | Zn 3–9

Mouse-ear chickweed

p. 383

Delightful, dwarf, mat-forming perennials, mouse-ear chickweed is a useful ground cover, edging, or rock garden plant. Its downy leaves are often gray; the small, star-shaped flowers are white.

Type Hardy perennial
Zone 3–9, H 7–1; does not thrive in humid heat
Flowering Season Early spring to summer, depending on species

SOWING

Indoors 6–8 weeks before planting out.
Outdoors Early spring, when soil is cool and a light frost is still possible, or late autumn.
Depth Just cover.

GERMINATING

Time 5–15 days.
Requirements 65°–75°F.

TRANSPLANTING

Time After last spring frost or autumn.
Spacing *Small species:* 4"–6". *Spreading species:* 12"–18".
Light Full sun to light shade.
Soil Prefers moist, well-drained soil with a pH level of 6.0–7.0, but will tolerate dry. *C. tomentosum* is suitable for xeriscaping.

CARING FOR PLANTS

Easy. Cut back plants after flowering to maintain a tidy appearance. Divide every 2–3 years.

PROPAGATING

Take cuttings in early summer, divide in spring in the North or in autumn south of Zone 6, or grow from seed.

COMBINATIONS

Armeria, Campanula, Nepeta, Penstemon.

Ceratostigma

HP | Zn 5–9

Plumbago

p. 383

Low-growing, spreading, and shrubby, these perennials are invaluable for their late-summer blooms of intense blue, as well as for their clean foliage, which turns a showy bronze in autumn. Use them as a ground cover or edging plant, or in rock gardens or stone walls. They are vital players on the autumn garden team.

Type Hardy perennial
Zone 5–9, H 9–6 (see species list, p. 445)
Flowering Season Summer to autumn

SOWING

Indoors Prechilled seed 10–12 weeks before planting out.
Outdoors Early spring, when soil is cool and a light frost is still possible, or late autumn.
Depth Just cover.

GERMINATING

Time 30–90 days.
Requirements Place seed together with moistened sand in a plastic bag, seal lightly, and refrigerate for 4–6 weeks. Provide 60°F thereafter.

TRANSPLANTING

Time Zones 7–9, Early spring or early autumn. Zones 5–6, Spring, when temperatures remain above 50°F.
Spacing 12"–18".
Light Full sun or part shade.
Soil Tolerant of many soils, including poor, stony, or heavy, but prefers a rich, well-drained soil with plenty of organic matter. *C. plumbagoides* is suitable for xeriscaping.

CARING FOR PLANTS

Water regularly, but do not allow soil to become soggy. Cut back to ground level in autumn.

PROPAGATING

Divide clumps in autumn or late winter (after last spring frost in Zones 5–6), or grow from seed.

COMBINATIONS

Liriope, Pachysandra, Sedum, Solidago.

Cerinthe

HP | Zn 6–9

p. 383

Unusual and elegant 1'–2' plants, Cerinthe *have remarkable tubular blue or yellow flowers that, clustered with their petal-like bracts, resemble a small chain of bells. This is a stunning plant for the temperate border.*

Type Short-lived hardy perennial where winters are mild; usually grown as an annual
Zone 6–9, H 12–8; prefers the cool, moist summers of the Northeast and the Northwest
Flowering Season Early summer to autumn, fading quickly during hot weather

SOWING

Indoors 6–8 weeks before last frost.
Outdoors Only where summer are cool, in early to late spring.
Depth 1⁄16".

GERMINATING

Time 5–21 days.
Requirements Sow seed and provide 65°–70°F. If germination does not begin in 3–4 weeks, move to 25°–40°F for 2–4 weeks, then return to 65°–70°F.

TRANSPLANTING

Time After last frost.
Spacing *Short species:* 6"–12". *Tall species:* 18".
Light Part shade to full sun, with protection from hot afternoon sun.
Soil Moist, humus-rich, well drained, slightly alkaline.

CARING FOR PLANTS

Easy. Water regularly during dry spells and mulch in spring to keep soil cool and moist.

PROPAGATING

Divide in spring or grow from seed. Plant self-seeds politely, without being invasive. Plants grown from seed will bloom in about 3 months.

COMBINATIONS

Agapanthus, Cirsium, Echinops, annual *Gypsophila, Iris.*

Ceterach See *Asplenium*

Chaenorhinum

HP* | Zn 8–10  

Dwarf snapdragon

Once a member of the Linaria *genus, the one species of* Chaenorhinum *commonly grown more closely resembles* Aubrieta. *It bears masses of small purple flowers with cheerful white centers, and is an excellent plant for walls or containers or for edging a bed or path.*

Type Hardy perennial; often grown as an annual
Zone 8–10; grown as an annual in cooler climates; tolerant of both heat and humidity
Flowering Season Early summer

SOWING

Indoors January–February.
Outdoors Early spring.
Depth 1⁄4".

GERMINATING

Time 14–30 days.
Requirements Sow seed and provide 65°–70°F for 2 weeks, then refrigerate for 4–6 weeks. Prick out seedlings as they germinate and provide 65°–70°F. After 4–6 weeks, remove flats from refrigerator.

TRANSPLANTING

Time After last frost.
Spacing 6"–8".
Light Full sun to part shade.
Soil Ordinary, well drained, with a pH of 6.6–7.5.

CARING FOR PLANTS

Water regularly during dry spells and protect young plants from slugs and snails. In Zones 8–10, mulch well before winter.

PROPAGATING

Take cuttings in summer, divide in spring or autumn, or grow from seed. Plants grown from seed will bloom in 10–12 weeks.

Chamaenerian See *Epilobium*

Charieis See *Felicia*

Cheiranthus See *Erysimum*

Chelidonium

HP, Bi | Zn 4–8

p. 383

This small genus includes rather weedy plants that bear bright green leaves and cheerful yellow blooms. It has an upright habit, and grows 2'–4' tall. Use in wild gardens and areas where its propensity to overrun will not cause problems.

Type Hardy perennial or biennial
Zone 4–8, H 8–5
Flowering Season Spring to summer, depending on species

SOWING

Indoors Start seed outdoors only.
Outdoors Early spring or autumn.
Depth Surface.

GERMINATING

Time 30–365 days.
Requirements Sow seed in flats of moistened growing medium, sink flats in the ground against a north-facing wall, and cover with glass. Transplant seedlings as they appear.

TRANSPLANTING

Spacing 12".
Light Sun or shade.
Soil Any that is moist but not wet.

CARING FOR PLANTS

Easy. This wildflower thrives with no care.

PROPAGATING

Divide in spring (autumn in Zones 7 and 8) or grow from seed. Plant self-seeds freely.

COMBINATIONS

Anemone, ferns, *Hosta*

Chelone

HP | Zn 3–9

Shellflower, Turtlehead

p. 383

North American native perennials, Chelone *species bear curiously shaped pink or white flowers at the tips of stiff, upright stems. Plants are 3'–6'. Grow them at the back of the border or near water.*

Type Hardy perennial
Zone 3–9, H 8–1; *C. lyonii* will not thrive in high heat and humidity
Flowering Season Late summer

SOWING

Indoors 6–8 weeks before planting out.
Outdoors After last frost.
Depth Just cover.

GERMINATING

Time 14–48 days.
Requirements 55°–65°F.

TRANSPLANTING

Time After last spring frost or in autumn.
Spacing 7"–12".
Light Sun or light shade.
Soil Moist, rich, with a pH level of 5.0–7.0.

CARING FOR PLANTS

Requires little care beyond regular watering. Mulch lightly in spring and autumn with leaf mold. Cut back to ground level after flowering. Susceptible to mildew if air circulation is poor and soil is allowed to remain dry.

PROPAGATING

Divide in early spring where winters are harsh (early autumn in milder climates), take cuttings in spring or summer, or grow from seed.

COMBINATIONS

Aconitum, Aster, Astilbe, Dicentra, Tricycrtis

Chenopodium

A | Zn 6–10

Goosefoot, Pigweed

p. 383

These annuals are sometimes grown for their colorful leaves or interesting fruit rather than for their insignificant flowers. Ranging from 18" to 5' tall, these rather graceless plants might be used in containers or at the back of the border.

Type Annual
Zone 6–10
Flowering Season Midsummer to mid-autumn

SOWING

Indoors 4–5 weeks before last frost, in peat pots.
Outdoors Late spring to early summer.
Depth Just cover.

GERMINATING

Time 5–30 days.
Requirements Easy. 70°–75°F.

TRANSPLANTING

Time After last frost.
Spacing *Small species:* 8"–12". *Large species:* 24"–36".
Light Full sun to part shade.
Soil Deep, rich, well drained, dry.

CARING FOR PLANTS

Easy. Feed once during the growing season; water during prolonged dry spells. A long taproot makes transplanting difficult.

PROPAGATING

Grow from seed.

Chiastophyllum

HP | Zn 4–8

p. 383

An evergreen, succulent perennial, Chiastophyllum *is a small green mound throughout most of the year but comes to life in summer, when arching wands appear, bearing drooping sprays of tiny yellow flowers. Use it in rock gardens, dry stone walls, and rock crevices.*

Type Hardy perennial
Zone 4–8, H 9–6
Flowering Season Late spring to summer

SOWING

Indoors Prechilled seed 8–10 weeks before planting out.
Outdoors Early spring or late autumn.
Depth Surface.

GERMINATING

Time 15–60 days.
Requirements Place seed and moist growing medium in a plastic bag and refrigerate for 2 weeks. Provide 70°–75°F thereafter.

TRANSPLANTING

Time After last spring frost or in autumn.
Spacing 6".
Light Full sun or part shade.
Soil Tolerant of dry soil but prefers some moisture and light, well-drained soil.

CARING FOR PLANTS

Water well during the growing season, but keep plants fairly dry otherwise.

PROPAGATING

Take cuttings in mid- to late summer, divide in spring (autumn in Zones 7–8), or grow from seed.

COMBINATIONS

Astrantia, Campanula, Omphalodes.

Chionodoxa

HB | Zn 4–8

Glory of the snow

p. 384

A genus of small (3"–8"), pretty, very early-blooming bulbs, plants bear star-shaped, usually blue flowers; less commonly flowers may be pink or white. Use them in rock gardens or naturalize them in the lawn or around shrubs. Plant thickly to give the effect of a blue carpet.

Type Hardy bulb
Zone 4–8, H 9–1
Flowering Season Late winter to early spring

SOWING

Indoors There is little need to start plants indoors as *Chionadoxa* species self-seed so readily, but for those who wish to, start seed at any time.
Outdoors *Seed:* Midsummer to late summer. *Bulb:* Autumn.
Depth *Seed:* ¼". *Bulb:* 3".

GERMINATING

Time 30–90 days.
Requirements 55°F.

TRANSPLANTING

Time Early autumn, after 1 year of growth.
Spacing 3"–6".
Light Sun or part shade.
Soil Moist, rather fertile, well drained, with a pH level of 6.0–7.0.

CARING FOR PLANTS

These easy bulbs require little maintenance. Water regularly during dry spells, feed every 2 years in early spring, and leave bulbs undisturbed except for division every 4–5 years.

PROPAGATING

After flowering, dig bulbs, then detatch plant bulblets or grow from seed. Plant may self-seed.

COMBINATIONS

Azaleas, *Eranthis, Galanthus, Narcissus.*

Chlorogalum

HB | Zn 8–10

Amole, Soap plant

This bulb, native to western North America, is something of a botanical curiosity. Growing 2'–8' tall, the plant has rosettes of long, thin, gray-green leaves with wavy margins. Its spidery-looking white, pink, or blue flowers with narrow, deeply reflexed petals and long, prominent stamens are borne terminally and bloom only in the afternoon. Use judiciously, possibly as a focal point.

Type Hardy bulb
Zone 8–10; performs well only on the Pacific Coast
Flowering Season Summer

SOWING

Indoors See Germinating, Requirements.
Outdoors *Seed:* See Germinating, Requirements. *Bulb:* Autumn.
Depth *Seed:* ⅛". *Bulb:* Cover with twice its diameter of soil.

GERMINATING

Time 30–90 days.
Requirements *Autumn sowing:* Sow seed in flats, sink in the ground against a north-facing wall, and cover with glass. Moisten soil occasionally, if necessary. Bring indoors in spring to 55°–60°F. *Spring sowing:* Sow seed in moistened medium, place containers in plastic bags, and refrigerate for 2–3 weeks. Remove and sink in the ground to the rim in a shady location, covering with glass. Transplant seedlings as they appear.

TRANSPLANTING

Time Autumn.
Spacing 3"–4".
Light Sun or light shade.
Soil Moist, fertile, and well drained, especially in winter.

CARING FOR PLANTS

Water frequently and leave bulbs undisturbed, dividing only when they exhibit signs of overcrowding. Cut back flowering stems after blooming. Mulch with compost in winter.

PROPAGATING

Plant offsets in spring or autumn or grow from seed.

 Type: A = Annual; Bi = Biennial; HP = Hardy Perennial; TP = Tender Perennial; HB = Hardy Bulb; TB = Tender Bulb; * = May be grown as annual where colder

Chrysanthemum (syn. *Coleostephus*)

ANNUAL

A | Zn 3–10

Chrysanthemum

These long-blooming, easy-care annuals bear masses of pretty, daisylike flowers in every shade of yellow, red, pink, and white; many have two-toned petals or contrasting eyes. Plants are upright and branching, 12"–36" tall, with feathery or lance-shaped leaves, often gray-green. These are dependable in the border or cottage garden. Small species make attractive edging; taller species are excellent cut flowers. Plants deteriorate quickly in hot weather.

Type Annual
Zone 3–10, H 9–1 (see species list, pp. 445–446)
Flowering Season Spring through frost where summers are relatively cool.

SOWING

Indoors 6–8 weeks before last frost.
Outdoors Just before last frost.
Depth 1/8".

GERMINATING

Time 10–13 days.
Requirements 60°–70°F.

TRANSPLANTING

Time After last frost. In warmer climates, plant in spring for early blooming, discarding plants when flowering diminishes, or plant when cooler weather returns in autumn.
Spacing *Small cultivars: 6". Medium/tall cultivars: 12"–18".*
Light Sun.
Soil Ordinary, well drained, with a pH level of 6.0–7.0.

CARING FOR PLANTS

Pinch out seedling stem tips to encourage a bushy habit; deadhead regularly. Tall plants may require staking in windy sites. Susceptible to mildew and aphids, although neither is likely to be fatal.

PROPAGATING

Grow from seed. Some species may self-seed.

COMBINATIONS

Antirrhinum, Bidens, Pelargonium, Rudbeckia, Salpiglossis.

CAUTION

Contact may cause skin irritation.

PERENNIAL

HP | Zn 5–9

Chrysanthemum

p. 384

These shrubby perennials are grown for the masses of blooms that cover plants in late summer and autumn. Plants are 1'–5' tall, with daisylike flowers, often double, in shades of red, yellow, orange, lavender, and white. They are an essential part of the autumn garden and also useful as container plants. As with all the chrysanthemums, species are frequently being reclassified by botanists, causing much confusion.

Type Hardy perennial
Zone 5–9; most chrysanthemums prefer a cool growing season and low humidity
Flowering Season Summer through late autumn, depending on species

SOWING

Indoors 6–8 weeks before planting out.
Outdoors Early spring, when soil is cool and a light frost is still possible, or late autumn.
Depth Surface.

GERMINATING

Time 7–28 days.
Requirements Light and 60°–75°F.

TRANSPLANTING

Time After last spring frost or in autumn.
Spacing *Small species:* 12"–15". *Large species:* 18"–24".
Light Plants must receive at least 6 hours of sunlight per day to bloom.
Soil Rich, deep, well drained, with a pH level of 5.5–7.0. *C.* × *morifolium* tolerates dry soil and is suitable for xeriscaping.

C

CARING FOR PLANTS

Feed with a balanced fertilizer 2 weeks after planting and again when plants are 12" tall. Pinch tips when plants are 6" and again after every additional 6" of new growth until 6 weeks before flowering begins. Water and deadhead regularly. After blooming, cut back to ground level and mulch lightly. Some species may require division every 1–2 years to maintain strong blooming.

PROPAGATING

Take cuttings, divide after flowering in autumn south of Zone 6 (elsewhere in early spring), or grow from seed. Chrysanthemums may bloom from seed in their first year.

COMBINATIONS

Aster, Lavandula, Salvia, Solidago, Stachys.

Chrysogonum

HP | Zn 5–9

Golden knee, Green-and-gold

p. 384

This low-growing American native is valued for its bright yellow, daisylike flowers borne over a long period. Plant in the rock garden or near a woodland path; useful as a ground cover for small areas.

Type Hardy perennial
Zone 5–9, H 9–5
Flowering Season Spring to early summer, then sporadically until autumn

SOWING

Indoors As soon as fresh seed is available.
Outdoors As soon as fresh seed is available.
Depth ¼".

GERMINATING

Time 21 days.
Requirements 70°–75°F. Propagation by division or runners is easier and more successful than by seed.

TRANSPLANTING

Time Early spring or autumn.
Spacing 6"–8".
Light Part shade; full sun in northern zones or in moist soil in the South.
Soil Moist, sandy, well-drained soil that is never very wet or very dry; prefers a pH level of 6.0–7.5.

CARING FOR PLANTS

Mulch to retain soil moisture and water during dry spells. Keep soil on the poor side to maintain compact growth. Flowering is curtailed by very hot weather.

PROPAGATING

Divide in early spring in Zones 5 and 6 (in early autumn elsewhere), propagate by root runners, or grow from seed. Plants will self-seed.

COMBINATIONS

Cerastium, Phlox, Sedum.

Cimicifuga

HP | Zn 3–9

Bugbane, Cohosh, Rattletop, Snakeroot

p. 384

Intriguing woodland perennials, these plants are upright, usually 4' high and wide with handsome, deeply cut, green or dark purple leaves. Deceptively undistinguished when not in bloom, these plants become magical when their long bottlebrushes of tiny white flowers appear on 2'–8' tall stems. Most effective when blooming alone or in subtle combination with other woodland plants.

Type Hardy perennial
Zone 3–9, H 8–1
Flowering Season Midsummer to mid autumn, depending on species

SOWING

Indoors Autumn, as soon as seed is ripe.
Outdoors Sow fresh seed in autumn.
Depth Just cover.

GERMINATING

Time 30–365 days.
Requirements Leave seed (unsown) at 55°–60°F for a period of 6–8 weeks, then place in a plastic bag and refrigerate for 8 weeks. Sow seed and provide 60°F.

TRANSPLANTING

Time After last spring frost or in autumn.
Spacing *Small species:* 24". *Large species:* 36".
Light Flowers most profusely in part shade but will grow quite happily in full shade.
Soil Moist, humus-rich, with a pH level of 5.0–6.0.

CARING FOR PLANTS

Feed once in spring and water regularly during dry periods. Mulch with leaf mold or compost. Do not disturb established plants.

PROPAGATING

Divide roots in spring where winters are very cold (in the South, divide in autumn) or grow from seed.

COMBINATIONS

Brunnera, Geranium, Heuchera, Hosta, Lilium, Phlox, Thalictrum.

Cirsium

Bi, HP | Zn 3–9 | Full sun, Partial shade | Ordinary soil, Moist soil

Plume thistle

p. 384

These erect, spiny, dangerous-looking plants are tolerated only for their decorative thistle heads of purple, pink, red, white, or yellow at heights of 3'–4'. Use them at the back of the border or in the wild garden.

Type Hardy perennial, or biennial grown as an annual
Zone 3–9, H 8–1 (see species list, p. 446); prefers cool temperatures
Flowering Season Late summer to early autumn

SOWING

Indoors 4–6 weeks before last frost.
Outdoors After last spring frost or in autumn.
Depth ⅛".

GERMINATING

Time 15–18 days.
Requirements 70°–75°F.

TRANSPLANTING

Time After last frost.
Spacing 24".
Light Full sun or part shade.
Soil Moist, well drained.

CARING FOR PLANTS

Easy. Requires little maintenance. In congenial surroundings, *Cirsium* can become very weedy and will effect a hostile takeover of your garden. To control, cut down plants and destroy them before seed matures.

PROPAGATING

Grow from seed only.

COMBINATIONS

Not easily used in anything less than a grand mixed border, but can be paired with some success with *Gladiolus, Kniphofia, Nautia,* or *Rudbeckia.*

CAUTION

Cirsium species can be very invasive. *C. arvense* is listed as invasive in several areas, including Arizona, Indiana, Maryland, and Tennessee; *C. vulgare* is listed as invasive in several areas, including Virginia, Tennessee, and Maryland. See pp. 494–495 for advice.

Cladanthus

A | Zn 1–9

A genus of one species of mound-forming annual, Cladanthus *plants grow 24" tall. Golden daisylike flowers peek through a mass of feathery green leaves; both flowers and foliage are fragrant. It is an extremely attractive border plant.*

Type Annual
Zone 1–9, H 12–1; flowers best where summers are cool
Flowering Season Summer through first frost

SOWING

Indoors 6–8 weeks before planting out.
Outdoors Early spring to mid-spring.
Depth Just cover.

GERMINATING

Time 30–35 days.
Requirements Easy. 70°–75°F.

TRANSPLANTING

Time After last frost.
Spacing 12".
Light Sun.
Soil Tolerates dry but prefers moist, well-drained soil.

CARING FOR PLANTS

Easy. Feed in spring and water during dry spells. Deadhead to prolong flowering.

PROPAGATING

Grow from seed. Plant may self-seed.

Clarkia (syn. *Eucharidium, Godetia*)

A | Zn 2–10

Farewell to spring, Godetia, Rocky Mountain garland

p. 384–385

A genus of bushy, upright annuals, 12"–48" tall, Clarkia *bears funnel-shaped flowers, often double or semi-double, with satiny petals. Even single blooms wave and ripple, almost like a full skirt. Flowers are usually white or shades of pink or purple. It makes a lovely border plant.*

Type Annual
Zone 2–10, H 7–1; prefers the cool, damp climate of the Pacific Coast; blooming will be reduced where summers are very hot
Flowering Season Summer through early autumn

SOWING

Indoors Stronger plants result when seed is started outdoors; if indoor sowing is necessary, start 6–8 weeks before last frost, in peat pots.
Outdoors After last frost, then twice more at 2-week intervals to extend the blooming period. In Zones 8–10, seed may be sown in autumn.
Depth Surface.

GERMINATING

Time 5–21 days.
Requirements Light and 55°–70°F. Seedlings are very susceptible to damping-off; grow seedlings in vermiculite, and water only from below.

TRANSPLANTING

Time After last frost.
Spacing *Small species:* 6"–9". *Tall species:* 9"–12".
Light Full sun in cool climates, otherwise part shade.
Soil Cool, moist, well drained, with a pH level of 6.0–7.0. Prefers soil with a low nitrogen content.

CARING FOR PLANTS

Easy. Water regularly and feed lightly in spring. Support with twiggy branches pushed into the ground when plants are young; tall species may require staking. For better blooming, keep plants slightly crowded and do not overfeed. Flowering will be greatly diminished in hot weather. Do not move plants. Older plants are susceptible to fungal diseases.

PROPAGATING

Grow from seed. Some species may self-seed. Plants grown from seed will bloom in 3–6 months.

COMBINATIONS

Antirrhinum, Campanula, Geranium, annual *Phlox, Salvia.*

Claytonia

HP | Zn 5–8  

Purslane, Spring beauty

p. 385

The evergreen, rosette-forming perennials of this genus exhibit succulent leaves and small pink or white flowers. It usually grows 3"–6" tall. Use these American natives in a wildflower, rock, or woodland garden.

Type Hardy perennial
Zone 5–8, H 6–1; prefers cool summers
Flowering Season Early spring

SOWING

Indoors Seed is best started outdoors.
Outdoors As soon as ripe seed is available, in summer.
Depth 1/8".

GERMINATING

Time 14–21 days.
Requirements Seed is difficult to collect and rarely available. Sow in flats, sink in the ground against a north-facing wall, and cover with glass. Moisten soil occasionally, if necessary.

TRANSPLANTING

Time Set out purchased plants in spring or autumn.
Spacing 4"–6".
Light Shade.
Soil Moist, gritty, rich, with a pH level of 5.0–7.0.

CARING FOR PLANTS

Easy if situated correctly, otherwise difficult. Water regularly; plants will not survive in dry soil. Foliage dies back to ground after blooming.

PROPAGATING

Divide carefully in autumn or grow both from seed. Plant may self-seed.

COMBINATIONS

Lovely as a carpet under *Rhododendron, Gunnera,* or *Ligularia,* or mixed with ferns.

Clematis (syn. *Atragene*)

HP | Zn 3–9

Clematis, Leather flower, Old man's beard, Traveler's joy, Vase vine, Virgin's bower

p. 385

A large genus of climbing vines and some herbaceous perennials, prized for its eye-catching flowers. Most commonly grown species flaunt large, flat flower heads of great beauty. Lesser-known species bear smaller blooms of simpler colors, upright or pendulous, some of which resemble tulips, hellebores, and campanulas. Flowers are pink, purple, white, blue, yellow, or cream, sometimes with a contrasting stripe.

Type Hardy perennial
Zone 3–9, H 9–1 (see species list, p. 446)
Flowering Season Spring, summer, or autumn, depending on species

SOWING

Indoors See Germinating, Requirements.
Outdoors See Germinating, Requirements.
Depth *Seed:* 1/8". *Roots:* 2"–3".

GERMINATING

Time Usually 30–365 days but may take up to 3 years.
Requirements *Autumn sowing:* Sow seed in flats, sink in the ground next to a north-facing wall, and cover with glass. Moisten soil occasionally, if necessary. Bring indoors in spring to 70°–75°F. *Spring sowing:* Sow seed in containers and freeze for 3 weeks. Remove containers and sink in the ground in a shady location, covering with glass. Transplant seedlings as they appear.

TRANSPLANTING

Time Plant purchased vines in spring or autumn.
Spacing 36"–48".
Light Most species prefer full sun, although many will tolerate part shade in winter climates. All *Clematis* must have shaded roots.
Soil A cool, rich, sandy loam with a pH level of 6.0–7.5, liberally enriched with organic matter, will produce strong, healthy vines. Prepare planting holes to a depth of 18"–24", adding gravel to the bottom to improve drainage. Many species will tolerate dry soil, especially *C. ligusticifolia,* which is useful for xeriscaping.

CARING FOR PLANTS

Easy. Begin feeding 2-year-old plants with a weak 5-10-5 fertilizer in early spring and again every 6 weeks throughout the growing season. Water frequently and mulch liberally. The roots and base of stem are fragile and should be protected from accidental injury. Provide support, preferably one that encourages branching, thus exposing all parts of the vine to sunlight. To prune vines that flower in spring or early summer (i.e., on old wood), remove only dead or weak stems before flowering, carefully cutting back overgrown crowns. After flowering, vines may be pruned to maintain a desirable size and shape and to stimulate new growth, which will bear flowers the following season. Late-blooming vines (which flower on new growth) should be cut back to 12"–18" in late winter or early spring, *before* new growth begins.

PROPAGATING

Take cuttings in early summer. Cultivars do not come true from seed, but some species can be propagated by seed.

COMBINATIONS

A beautiful backdrop to *Delphinium, Paeonia,* shrub or tea roses, or twining through climbing roses or *Wisteria.*

CAUTION

All *Clematis* species can be harmful to pets if eaten.

Cleome

A | Zn 2–10

Spider flower

p. 385

These fast-growing, carefree 18"–4' tall annuals are a haze of open, rounded, spiky flower heads from early summer through frost. Mass at the back of the border or in a neglected corner. New dwarf cultivars may be grown in containers or at the front of the border. Blooms are pink, white, or an unusual shade of purple. Native to South America.

Type Annual
Zone 2–10, H 12–1 (see species list, p. 446); prefers warm temperatures
Flowering Season Summer through late autumn

SOWING

Indoors 6–8 weeks before last frost.
Outdoors After last frost.
Depth Surface.

GERMINATING

Time 10–14 days.
Requirements Place seed and moistened growing medium in a plastic bag and refrigerate for 2 weeks. Seed requires 70°–75°F thereafter.

TRANSPLANTING

Time 2–3 weeks after last frost, when temperatures remain above 40°F.
Spacing 18"–24".
Light Full sun or very light shade.
Soil Average, with a pH level of 6.0–7.0. All species are tolerant of dry soil, especially *C. hassleriana,* which is suitable for xeriscaping.

CARING FOR PLANTS

Easy. Feed and water during the growing season. To avoid self-seeding, cut off flower heads before seeds open. Generally remarkably trouble-free, but plants may be attractive to aphids. Self-seeds wantonly.

PROPAGATING

Grow from seed. Plant self-seeds with enthusiasm.

COMBINATIONS

Aster, Chrysanthemum, Cosmos, Sedum.

Clintonia

HP | Zn 3–9

p. 385

These spreading, clump-forming woodland plants grow 8"–24" tall. Species native to North America are grown for their attractive leaves, which resemble long green tongues. Its petite, bell-shaped flowers of pink, yellow, or white have an elfin quality.

Type Hardy perennial
Zone 3–9, H 8–1; prefers cool climates
Flowering Season Late spring to early summer

SOWING

Indoors Late winter to early spring.
Outdoors As soon as fresh seed is available (usually midsummer to late summer).
Depth Just cover.

GERMINATING

Time 30–90 days.
Requirements *Indoor sowing:* Seed requires 55°–60°F. *Outdoor sowing:* Sow seed in flats, sink in the ground against a north-facing wall, and cover with glass. Moisten soil occasionally, if necessary.

TRANSPLANTING

Time *Indoors:* Can be moved to garden in fall. *Outdoors:* Move to garden after two growing seasons.
Spacing 6"–8".
Light Shade.
Soil Rich, acid, moist, well-drained soil or sphagnum moss.

CARING FOR PLANTS

Easy. Cover roots with a mulch of leaf mold and keep plants well watered during summer. Do not disturb established plants.

PROPAGATING

Divide in spring or grow from seed.

Clivia

TP* | Zn 9–10

Kaffir lily

p. 385

Showy, exotic-looking plants from Africa, Clivia *have thick, fleshy leaves and stems that carry large umbels of deep orange, red, or yellow trumpet-shaped flowers. The plants are impressive in pots on the patio or tucked into shady plantings.*

Type Tender perennial; often grown as a houseplant in the North
Zone 9–10, H 12–1; grown as a houseplant in cooler zones
Flowering Season Late winter to early summer, depending on species

SOWING

Indoors Winter or early spring.
Outdoors Not recommended.
Depth ¼".

GERMINATING

Time 7–30 days.
Requirements Use fresh seed harvested from ripe berries. Requires darkness and a temperature of 70°–75°F.

TRANSPLANTING

Time When night temperature remains above 50°F.
Spacing 18"–24".
Light Part to full shade, with shade from the hot afternoon sun.
Soil Light and moist, with plenty of organic material.

CARING FOR PLANTS

Grow in pots north of Zone 9. Water regularly while plants are growing; reduce watering in fall and winter. Fertilize before and during flowering. Bring pots indoors when night temperatures fall to 50°F; keep at 40°–60°F over winter. When flower spikes begin to grow in late winter, give more light, water, and heat. Patrol regularly for slugs and snails, and for mealybugs over winter. Container-grown plants prefer to be pot-bound; divide only when flowering declines.

PROPAGATING

Divide carefully as new growth begins in spring from offsets after flowering, or grow from seed. Plants grown from seed bloom in 4–5 years but may not come true.

COMBINATIONS

Most successful combinations include other tropicals or foliage plants such as *Colocasia*, ferns, or *Hosta*.

Cobaea

TP* | Zn 9–10

p. 385

A sturdy climbing vine, Cobaea *is grown for its large, showy, bell-shaped flowers of purple, white, or cream. The flowers of one species intriguingly start off yellow, then change to purple. Vines grow 12'–20' long.*

Type Tender perennial often grown as an annual
Zone 9–10, H 12–10; grown as an annual in Zones 1–8; prefers warm temperatures
Flowering Season Summer through autumn

SOWING

Indoors 6–8 weeks before last frost, in peat pots.
Outdoors Only in Zones 9–10, after last frost date.
Depth Just cover.

GERMINATING

Time 10–30 days.
Requirements Easy. Nick seed with a sharp knife before sowing and provide 70°–75°F.

TRANSPLANTING

Time 2–3 weeks after last frost, when temperatures remain above 40°F.
Spacing 24"–36".
Light Full sun, with shade from afternoon sun where summers are hot.
Soil Ordinary, amended with well-rotted manure. *C. scandens* tolerates dry soil and can be used for xeriscaping.

CARING FOR PLANTS

Easy. Pinch out tips of young plants to encourage branching and provide a trellis for support. Water regularly and feed occasionally. Prune perennials in early spring. Aphids may be a problem.

PROPAGATING

Propagate from seed only.

COMBINATIONS

Eccremocarpus, Quamoclit, Tropaeolum.

Codonopsis

HP | Zn 5–8

Bonnet bellflower

These unusual perennial climbers are grown for their profuse blooms, which may be pretty blue stars or odd, bell-shaped curiosities of green, yellow, or blue. Grow this vine on a trellis or allow it to ramble artistically through shrubs.

Type Hardy perennial
Zone 5–8, H 9–7
Flowering Season Summer

SOWING

Indoors Sow seed in late winter to early spring, in peat pots.
Outdoors Late spring, when soil is cool and a light frost is still possible, or late autumn.
Depth Surface.

GERMINATING

Time 7–24 days.
Requirements Light and 60°–70°F.

TRANSPLANTING

Time After last frost.
Spacing 12"–24".
Light Full sun or part shade; plants will be stronger when grown in full sun.
Soil Acid, well drained, on the dry side.

CARING FOR PLANTS

Easy. Provide a trellis or other support. Mulch heavily in winter. Do not attempt to move established plants.

PROPAGATING

Divide in spring, take cuttings in spring or autumn, or grow from seed.

Coix

TP* | Zn 9–10

p. 386

Stiff, coarse, upright grasses, 3' tall, Coix *display sword-shaped, randomly drooping leaves, somewhat unkempt looking. Highly decorative, beadlike fruit is green and hard . Use in natural or meadow plantings.*

Type Tender perennial; grown as an annual
Zone 9–10, H 12–1; grown as an annual in Zones 1–8 although it may not set fruit where summers are short; prefers cool temperatures
Flowering Season Summer; fruit, which is more ornamental, is set in autumn

SOWING

Indoors 6–8 weeks before last frost, in peat pots.
Outdoors After last frost, but attempt this only where the growing season is long.
Depth ½".

GERMINATING

Time 15–28 days.
Requirements Soak seed in warm water overnight and provide 60°–70°F thereafter.

TRANSPLANTING

Time After last frost, when temperatures remain above 45°F.
Spacing 18".
Light Full sun or light shade.
Soil Rich, well drained.

CARING FOR PLANTS

Easy. Requires nothing more than watering during dry weather; keep leaves dry to discourage mildew.

PROPAGATING

Grow from seed. Plant may self-seed.

Colchicum

HB | Zn 4–9

Autumn crocus, Fall crocus, Meadow saffron, Naked ladies

p. 386

These autumn-blooming corms are grown for their large, pink, crocuslike flowers that appear when leaves are dormant. (The leaves appear in spring and die back in summer.) A stunning water lily-flowered variety should not be missed. Successful use requires some thought: Try growing these plants through ground covers or peeking out from under spreading shrubs.

Type Hardy bulb
Zone 4–9, H 9–1
Flowering Season Late summer or autumn, depending on species

SOWING

Indoors Start seed outdoors.
Outdoors *Seed or corm:* Late summer to early autumn.
Depth *Seed corms:* ⅛". *Small corms:* 3"–4". *Large bulb:* 4"–5".

GERMINATING

Time 30–365 days.
Requirements Sow seed in flats, covering first with compost, then with a thin layer of fine gravel. Plunge flats into the ground outdoors and cover with glass. Twelve months after germination, transplant corms to a nursery bed, spacing 12" apart. After 2 years, move to their final location.

TRANSPLANTING

Time Late summer to early autumn.
Spacing *Small species:* 4"–6". *Large species:* 6"–9".
Light Full sun or part shade.
Soil Light, rich, well drained, with a pH level of 5.5–6.5.

CARING FOR PLANTS

Easy. Plants grown from seed bloom in 4–6 years. Foliage dies back in late spring, reappearing after flowering or following spring. Allow leaves to wither completely before removal. Water during dry spells, even when foliage is not visible. Do not disturb.

PROPAGATING

Divide cormels in summer. *C. autumnale* will self-seed.

COMBINATIONS

Centaurea, ferns, *Helichrysum*, *Nepeta*, *Rhododendron*.

CAUTION

All plant parts are toxic to humans and pets if eaten.

Coleostephus See *Chrysanthemum*

Coleus See *Solenostemon*

C

Collinsia

A | Zn 3–10

p. 386

Graceful, delicate, and small, Collinsia *are annuals native to western North America. Willowy stalks hold clusters of small flowers that resemble parted lips. Blooms may be white, purple, pink, or blue. Plants are 12"–24" tall. Grow them in borders or containers.*

Type Annual
Zone 3–10, H 11–1; prefers mild days and cool nights and will not tolerate intense heat
Flowering Season Spring to midsummer

SOWING

Indoors Seed is best started *in situ.*
Outdoors *Where summers are cool:* Early spring, when soil is cool and a light frost is still possible; make successive plantings for continuous blooming. *Where winters are mild:* Autumn.
Depth ¼".

GERMINATING

Time 14–21 days.
Requirements 65°–70°F.

TRANSPLANTING

Time Set out purchased plants after last frost.
Spacing 6"–12".
Light Full sun where summers are mild, elsewhere provide afternoon shade.
Soil Prefers moist, fertile, well-drained soil with a pH level of 5.0–8.0; tolerates dry soil. *C. ambigua, C. grandiflora,* and *C. heterophylla* grow well in dry soil and are suitable for xeriscaping.

CARING FOR PLANTS

Easy. Deadhead regularly. Weak stems may necessitate staking. High summer temperatures will reduce blooming considerably.

PROPAGATING

Grow from seed. Plant may self-seed.

Colocasia

HP* | Zn 8–10

Cocoyam, Dasheen, Taro

p. 386

Impressive tropicals, Colocasia *exhibit 1'–2' long heart-shaped leaves of deep green elegantly striped with white or deep red veins or dramatic pure black. These are imposing plants suitable for containers or patio plantings.*

Type Hardy perennial
Zone 8–10, possibly Zone 7 with winter protection, H 12–8; grown as an annual north of Zone 8
Flowering Season Late spring to early summer, although plants seldom bloom north of Zone 10

SOWING

Starting plants from seed is not recommended.
Indoors *Tubers:* 8–10 weeks before planting out.
Outdoors *Tubers:* 2–3 weeks after last frost.
Depth *Tubers:* 4–6".

GERMINATING

Requirements *Tubers:* Humid conditions and 70°–75°F.

TRANSPLANTING

Time 2–3 weeks after last frost.
Spacing *Small species:* 18". *Large species:* 4"–5".
Light Part to full shade, although leaf color will be deeper with more sun.
Soil Deeply dug, fertile soil enriched with organic matter; moist or even wet; will tolerate up to 6" of standing water.

CARING FOR PLANTS

Shelter from winds to avoid damage to leaves. Mulch to keep the soil moist and water regularly during dry weather. Feed periodically throughout the growing season. Cut back tops and dig tubers together with a large root-ball in autumn. Pack root-ball in dry peat or sand and store in a cool, frost-free place over winter. Replant in spring.

PROPAGATING

Remove offsets from tubers before planting in spring, divide, or take basal cuttings in spring.

COMBINATIONS

Dicentra, Dryopteris, tree ferns, *Impatiens, Iris ensata, I. siberica, Lobelia cardinalis, Matteuccia.*

CAUTION

Leaves are harmful if eaten raw; sap may cause skin irritation. *C. esculenta* is listed as invasive in some regions, including Florida. See pp. 494–495 for advice.

Comarum See *Potentilla*

Consolida

A | Zn 3–9 | Full sun | Dry soil; Ordinary soil

Larkspur

p. 386

Narrow and upright, these annuals feature feathery leaves and tall spires of blossoms that pack a punch all summer. Flowers are pink, purple, blue, or white; height is 12"–48". Exquisite when planted in clumps and seen towering at the back of the border.

Type Annual
Zone 3–9, H 9–1; must have cool temperatures and may fail altogether where summers are too hot
Flowering Season Early spring to early summer

SOWING

Indoors Prechilled seed 6–8 weeks before planting out, in peat pots, but outdoor sowing is preferable.
Outdoors 2 weeks before last frost or in late autumn.
Depth Just cover.

GERMINATING

Time 14–21 days.
Requirements Place seed and moistened growing medium in a plastic bag and refrigerate for 2 weeks. Provide darkness and 50°–55°F thereafter.

TRANSPLANTING

Time After last spring frost.
Spacing 18"–24".
Light Full sun.
Soil Rich, amended with well-rotted cow manure. *C. ajacis* is tolerant of dry soil and can be used in xeriscaping.

CARING FOR PLANTS

Feed once or twice during the growing season. Stake tall species and deadhead to avoid self-seeding. Do not transplant.

PROPAGATING

Grow from seed. Plant may self-seed.

COMBINATIONS

Anchusa, Antirrhinum, Clarkia, Dianthus, Trachelium.

CAUTION

All parts of the plant are harmful if eaten; seeds are particularly toxic.

Convallaria

HP | Zn 2–9

C

Lily-of-the-valley

p. 386

Grow these much loved, deeply scented, spring-blooming perennials for their tiny white bell-shaped flowers. The rich green, broadly lance-shaped leaves, 6"–8" tall, contribute to making Convallaria *a marvelous ground cover for shady spots.*

Type Hardy perennial
Zone 2–9, H 8–1; leaves will turn brown and die back during prolonged hot weather
Flowering Season Late spring to early summer

SOWING

Indoors Autumn.
Outdoors *Seed or rhizome:* Late winter or early spring.
Depth *Seed:* Just cover. *Rhizome:* 2"–3".

GERMINATING

Time 60–365 days.
Requirements Sow seed in flats and cover with compost, then a layer of fine gravel. Plunge flats in the ground outdoors and cover with glass. Transplant seedlings to individual pots when they are big enough to handle. When plants are sufficiently strong, move to a nursery bed for 2 years before planting in a permanent location.

TRANSPLANTING

Time Early spring or autumn.
Spacing 4"–6".
Light Part to full shade, although flowering will be diminished in full shade.
Soil Fertile, moist, well drained, enriched with plenty of organic matter.

CARING FOR PLANTS

Water deeply during dry spells to avoid scorched leaves. Top-dress with 2" of leaf mold in autumn or apply a complete fertilizer in early spring, taking care to wash residual fertilizer from leaves. Regular applications of liquid seaweed during the growing season will greatly improve the look of plants in summer. Divide after flowering every 4–6 years to maintain good blooming. Plants are tough, vigorous spreaders in rich soil and in areas with cool summers.

PROPAGATING

Divide in autumn in the South (in early spring north of Zone 7) or grow from seed.

COMBINATIONS

Asarum, Astilbe, Athyrum, Hosta, Polygonatum.

CAUTION

All parts of the plant are harmful to humans if eaten and may be lethal to pets.

Convolvulus

A, TP*, HP | Zn 3–10

Bindweed, Morning glory

p. 386

Scourge or boon? That depends on the species. The best are twining vines with large, heart-shaped leaves and showy, trumpet-shaped flowers that bloom for just one day, or mounding annuals or tender perennials with showy blooms. The worst — C. arvensis *— is a pernicious weed that's nearly impossible to eradicate. Flowers are shades of blue, purple, pink, or white. Grow climbers on trellises; dwarf varieties make excellent edging plants.*

Type Annual, tender perennial, hardy perennial
Zone *Annual:* 3–9, H 10–8; *Perennial:* 6–10, H 10–8 (see species list, p. 447). Likes warm weather, but does not thrive where summers are very hot and humid
Flowering Season Late spring to frost, depending on species.

SOWING

Indoors 5–6 weeks before last frost, in peat pots.
Outdoors In spring, when soil is warm and nighttime temperatures remain above 50°F, but only where summers are long.
Depth 1/8".

GERMINATING

Time 5–14 days.
Requirements Chip seed or soak in warm water for 24 hours before sowing. Leave flats where temperature is a constant 70°–80°F.

TRANSPLANTING

Time After last frost.
Spacing *Small species:* 6"–12". *Large species:* 12"–24".
Light Full sun; some species will grow in part shade.
Soil Tolerant of most, but prefers well-drained soil with a pH level of 6.0–8.0. Suitable for xeriscaping.

CARING FOR PLANTS

Easy. Prefers regular watering but tolerates considerable neglect. Do not move.

PROPAGATING

Take cuttings in late spring or summer or grow from seed. Plant may self-seed.

COMBINATIONS

Eschscholzia, Lobelia, Petunia, Salpiglossis, Salvia.

CAUTION

Harmful if eaten. *C. arvensis* is the loathsome, highly invasive weed known as bindweed.

Cooperia See *Zephyranthes*

Coreopsis (syn. *Calliopsis*)

A, TP*, HP | Zn 2–10 | Full sun, Partial shade | Dry soil, Ordinary soil

Coreopsis, Tickseed

p. 386–387

Versatile, carefree plants, coreopsis are grown for their reliable abundance of yellow orange, or rust-colored daisylike blooms borne over a long period. They grow 8"–36" tall. Use small species in the rock garden; mix different species in the border for spots of lively color.

Type Annual, tender perennial, hardy perennial
Zone *Annual:* 2–10; *Perennial:* 3–10, H 9–1 (see species list, p. 447); all except *C. maritima* are highly tolerant of hot, humid weather
Flowering Season Late spring through early autumn, depending on species

SOWING

Indoors *Annual:* 6–8 weeks before last frost. *Perennial:* 8–10 weeks before planting out.
Outdoors After last frost or, where winters are mild, in late autumn.
Depth Surface.

GERMINATING

Time 5–25 days.
Requirements Light and 55°–70°F.

TRANSPLANTING

Time *Annual:* After last frost. *Perennial:* After last frost or in autumn.
Spacing *Dwarf species:* 6". *Tall species:* 12"–18".
Light Full sun, *C. auriculata* and *C. rosea* will tolerate part shade.
Soil Withstands a wide range of conditions but prefers rich, well-drained soil with a pH level of 5.5–7.0. Many species are well suited to xeriscaping.

CARING FOR PLANTS

Easy. Deadhead often and feed only lightly, as excessive fertilizing decreases flowering. Tall species may need support.

PROPAGATING

Divide hardy perennial species after blooming in Zones 3–6 (in autumn in the South), divide tender perennials in spring, or grow from seed. Annuals may self-seed.

COMBINATIONS

Hemerocallis, Heuchera, purple *Petunia, Sedum, Sidalcea.*

Coriandrum

A | Zn 2–9

C

Cilantro, Coriander

p. 387

A culinary herb of 1′–2′, coriander bears tiny white, pink, or lavender flowers in lacy umbels. Its leaves are toothed and fernlike.

Type Annual
Zone 2–9; prefers cooler temperatures
Flowering Season Early summer

SOWING

Indoors 6–8 weeks before planting out, in peat pots.
Outdoors After last frost and at 2-week intervals for a constant supply of fresh leaves; autumn in southern states.
Depth ½″.

GERMINATING

Time 10 days.
Requirements Darkness and 55°–65°F.

TRANSPLANTING

Time Early spring.
Spacing 8″–10″.
Light Full sun or light shade.
Soil Rich, very well drained, with a pH level of 6.0–7.0.

CARING FOR PLANTS

Shelter plants from winds and do not move. Feed only with low-nitrogen fertilizer for most flavorful leaves. Sow seed in pots or put up seedlings to bring indoors for winter use. Cut fresh leaves for cooking; leaves freeze with only moderate success. To harvest seeds, cut flowering stalks when seeds are light brown, then hang upside down in a paper bag in a warm spot to dry. When dry, rub fruit gently to release seeds, and store in an airtight container. One plant will produce ¼ cup of seeds in 2 months.

PROPAGATING

Grow from seed. Plant may self-seed.

Coronilla

HP | Zn 3–10

Crown vetch

Somewhat weedy and sprawling, these shrubby perennials are used as a low-maintenance ground cover in difficult sites. Yellow, pink, purple, or white pealike flowers cover plants over a long period.

Type Hardy perennial
Zone 3–10 (see species list, p. 447)
Flowering Season Late spring to summer

SOWING

Indoors More practical to start *in situ.*
Outdoors Mid-spring. Sow at the rate of 1 pound per 1,000 square feet.
Depth ⅛″.

GERMINATING

Time 30 days.
Requirements Chip or soak seed to hasten germination.

TRANSPLANTING

Time Set out purchased plants in late spring or autumn.
Spacing 8″–12″.
Light Full sun or very light shade.
Soil Well drained, with a pH level of 6.5–7.5. Tolerant of dry conditions and suitable for xeriscaping.

CARING FOR PLANTS

Easy. Feed with a low-nitrogen fertilizer and water only during droughts. Cut back hardy species to ground level in late autumn.

PROPAGATING

Divide in spring where winters are very cold (in autumn in the South), take cuttings in autumn, or grow from seed.

CAUTION

C. varia is a very vigorous spreader and is listed as invasive in some areas, including Indiana, Kentucky, Maryland, and Tennessee.

Cortaderia

HP* | Zn 7–10

C

Pampas grass, Tussock grass

These ornamental grasses produce dramatic 8'–12' tall clumps, topped by spires of cream or pink plumes. An excellent specimen, it is also effective planted in groups in a large garden. Female plants have showier plumes.

Type Hardy perennial
Zone 8–10, H 12–7 (see species list, pp. 447 and 480); can be grown as an annual or tender perennial north of Zone 8
Flowering Season Late summer through early autumn

SOWING

Indoors 8–10 weeks before planting out.
Outdoors Early spring or early autumn.
Depth Surface.

GERMINATING

Time 14–21 days.
Requirements Light; prefers 60°–75°F. Highly susceptible to damping-off; grow seedlings in vermiculite, and water only from below.

TRANSPLANTING

Time Early spring, when soil is cool and a light frost is still possible, or early autumn.
Spacing Allow 4'–5' between plants, although this enormous grass is most effective when grown singly.
Light Full sun.
Soil Rich, well drained. Drought tolerant and suitable for xeriscaping.

CARING FOR PLANTS

Easy. Trim off dead leaves occasionally to keep plants looking tidy. North of Zone 8, dig roots in autumn and store in a cool, dry, frost-free location.

PROPAGATING

Divide in early spring or grow from seed. Cultivars are propagated only by division.

COMBINATIONS

Best grown alone as a dramatic accent.

CAUTION

Cortaderia is listed as invasive in some regions, including California. See pp. 494–495 for advice.

Corydalis (syn. *Pseudofumaria*)

A, Bi, HP | Zn 3–8

Corydalis, Fumitory

p. 387

These delicate, low-growing plants exhibit fernlike leaves and small clusters of tubular flowers, most commonly yellow but also blue or deep pink. Plants are 6"–24" tall. They are useful in stone walls, rock gardens, or borders.

Type Annual, biennial, or hardy perennial
Zone *Annual:* 3–7; *Perennial:* 3–8, H 8–3 (see species list, p. 447). Plants are severely weakened by excessive heat and humidity
Flowering Season Early spring to autumn, depending on species

SOWING

Indoors Seed is best started *in situ.*
Outdoors *Annual:* Early spring; spring or autumn, where winters are mild. *Biennial:* Early summer. *Perennial:* As soon as ripe seed is available.
Depth *Seed:* Surface. *Tuber:* 3".

GERMINATING

Time 30–365 days.
Requirements Difficult. Keep seed at 60°–65°F for 6–8 weeks, then chill for 2 weeks, and finally sow and keep at 60°–65°F. Seed requires light for germination.

TRANSPLANTING

Time Set out purchased plants after last frost or in autumn.
Spacing *Small species:* 4"–6". *Large species:* 10"–15".
Light Part shade, or full sun where summers are not hot.
Soil Prefers moist, rich, well drained, with a pH level of 6.0–8.0 but will tolerate poor soil. *C. lutea* is drought tolerant and useful for xeriscaping.

CARING FOR PLANTS

Easy. Survives considerable neglect. Water regularly and mulch with leaf mold. Trim plants after flowering to keep tidy and curtail self-seeding. Do not disturb established plants.

Corydalis (cont'd)

PROPAGATING

Divide after flowering or grow from seed. Some species may self-seed.

COMBINATIONS

Carex, ferns, *Hosta, Polemonium, Polystichum, Pulmonaria, Tanacetum, Tiarella.*

C

Cosmidium See *Thelesperma*

Cosmos

A, HP* | Zn 2–10

Cosmos, Cosmea

p. 387

Useful in any garden, these cheerful, carefree, airy plants add lightness and color to borders and wildflower plantings. Flowering stems of 12"–48" and feathery foliage are topped with good-sized, daisylike flowers in pinks, reds, oranges, yellow, and white.

Type Annual or hardy perennial
Zone *Annual:* 2–10 H 12–8. *Perennial:* 7–10 H 12–8. Grown as an annual north of Zone 7 (*C. atrosanguineus* is the only commonly available perennial form); prefers warm temperatures
Flowering Season Late spring through mid autumn

SOWING

Indoors 4–5 weeks before last frost.
Outdoors After last frost.
Depth 1/8".

GERMINATING

Time 3–10 days.
Requirements Easy. 70°–75°F.

TRANSPLANTING

Time After last frost.
Spacing *Small species:* 8"–10". *Tall species:* 18"–36".
Light Full sun.
Soil Plants will flower more abundantly in poor soil than in rich. Prefers a pH level of 5.0–7.0. *C. bipinnatus* and *C. sulfureus* are very tolerant of dry soil and may be used for xeriscaping.

CARING FOR PLANTS

Easy. Pinch out stem tips when plants are 18" high; stake tall species. Water during very dry spells. Provide winter mulch in Zones 7–8. Perennials can be lifted, stored over winter, and replanted after the last frost in the North.

PROPAGATING

Grow annuals from seed only. *C. atrosanguineus* can be grown from basal cuttings taken in spring.

COMBINATIONS

Cleome, Dianthus, Lythrum, Papaver, Verbena bonariensis.

Cotula

A, TP, HP | Zn 1–10

Brass buttons

Annuals and perennials are usually grown for their fragrant, long-lasting, bright orange, buttonlike flowers. Plants are 6"–2' tall and grown in rock gardens and cutting beds.

Type Annual, tender perennial, hardy perennial
Zone *Annual:* 1–9; *Perennial:* 7–10, H 9–7 (see species list, p. 447); prefers cool, dry summers and mild winters
Flowering Season Summer to early autumn

SOWING

Indoors 6–8 weeks before planting out.
Outdoors After last frost.
Depth Just cover.

GERMINATING

Time 14–21 days.
Requirements Easy. 50°F.

TRANSPLANTING

Time After last frost.
Spacing 4"–6".
Light Full sun or part shade, except *C. coronopifolia,* which will grow only in full sun.
Soil Most species require moist soil; some, including *C. coronopifolia,* will grow in boggy soil or standing water. May become invasive if grown in rich soil.

CARING FOR PLANTS

Water regularly. May become invasive.

PROPAGATING

Divide perennials in spring or grow annuals and perennials from seed.

Crambe

A, Bi, HP | Zn 5–9  

p. 387

Enormous (3'–7' tall) perennials, Crambe *feature large, ruffled leaves and tall, woody flowering stems that bear a profusion of surprisingly airy and delicate white blooms that resemble clouds of smoke. Carefully placed, these giants are stunning in the border.*

Type Annual, biennial, hardy perennial
Zone 5–9, H 9–6
Flowering Season Summer

SOWING

Indoors Most successfully started *in situ.* Indoor sowing may be attempted 8–10 weeks before last frost, in peat pots.
Outdoors *Annual:* After last spring frost. *Biennial:* Late summer. *Perennial:* Early spring, when soil is cool and a light frost is still possible, or in autumn.
Depth ½".

GERMINATING

Time 21–180 days.
Requirements Seed started indoors must be kept cool and moist at 60°–65°F.

TRANSPLANTING

Time *Annual:* After last frost. *Biennial:* Autumn. *Perennial:* Autumn, or after last spring frost.
Spacing 24"–36".
Light Sun to light shade.
Soil Fertile, well drained, slightly alkaline.

CARING FOR PLANTS

Crambe is susceptible to many insect pests and may require frequent spraying with insecticidal soap. Tall species will need staking. Cut back plants to ground level in autumn and mulch where winters are cold. Do not move plants unnecessarily.

PROPAGATING

Divide or take root cuttings in spring or grow from seed. Plant may self-seed. Plants grown from seed will not bloom well until their third year.

COMBINATIONS

Campanula, Linaria, Paeonia, Scabiosa.

Craspedia

TP*, HP | Zn 7–10

Bachelor's buttons, Billy buttons

These jolly plants have flower heads that are tightly packed balls of dull yellow florets. Blooms resemble a super-sized Santolina *flower on a tall (1'–3') stalk. It is a useful cut or dried flower.*

Type Tender perennial, hardy perennial
Zone 7–10, H 10–9 (see species list, p. 447); grown as an annual in cooler zones
Flowering Season Early spring to late summer, depending on species

SOWING

Indoors 6–8 weeks before last frost.
Outdoors 6 weeks before last frost.
Depth ⅛".

Craspedia (cont'd)

GERMINATING

Time 10–30 days.
Requirements Easy. 65°–85°F.

TRANSPLANTING

Time After last frost.
Spacing *Small species:* 12–18". *Large species:* 18–24".
Light Full sun to part shade.
Soil Well drained with a pH of 6.1–7.8. Where perennial, plants must have perfect drainage in winter.

CARING FOR PLANTS

Easy. Water regularly during dry spells. Tall species are easily flattened by wind; grow through a peony ring or site in a sheltered location.

PROPAGATING

Divide in spring, take stem cuttings, or grow from seed.

COMBINATIONS

Achillea, Geum, Iris, Lupinus.

Crepis

A, Bi, HP | Zn 3–9

Hawk's beard

Despite blooms that resemble dandelions, this plant is in fact a member of the Aster Family. Plants are 12"–18" tall, with lance-shaped leaves and an abundance of solitary flowers in pink, red, orange, or white. They are pretty plants for the rock garden or front of the border.

Type Annual, biennial, hardy perennial
Zone *Annual:* 3–9, H 7–4 (see species list, p. 447). *Perennial:* 4–9, H 7–4. Blooming will be greatly diminished in hot, humid weather
Flowering Season Midsummer to late summer

SOWING

Indoors 6–8 weeks before last frost.
Outdoors *Annual:* Early spring; where winters are mild, seeds may be sown in autumn. *Perennial:* Early spring, when soil is cool and a light frost is still possible.
Depth Just cover.

GERMINATING

Time 5–14 days.
Requirements 70°–80°F.

TRANSPLANTING

Time After last frost.
Spacing 4"–6".
Light Full sun.
Soil Well drained.

CARING FOR PLANTS

Easy. Support with twiggy branches pushed into the ground when plants are young; deadhead regularly to prolong blooming.

PROPAGATING

Take root cuttings of perennials in late winter, or grow from seed. Plants may self-seed.

Crinum

HB* | Zn 7–10

Crinum lily, Milk-and-wine lily, Spider lily

The bulbs in this genus are grown for their funnel-shaped, lilylike flowers, borne in terminal whorls on stiff, leafless, upright stems, 18"–36" tall. Blooms may be pink, red, or white and are often fragrant. They are best grown on their own in front of walls and shrubs.

Type Hardy bulb; often grown as an annual
Zone 7–10, H 12–8 (see species list, pp. 447–448); grown as an annual in cooler zones 3–7
Flowering Season Mid summer to autumn, depending on species

SOWING

Indoors As soon as seed is ripe.
Outdoors *Seed:* As soon as seed is ripe. *Bulb:* Late spring, when the temperatures remain above 60°F.
Depth *Seed:* ¼". *Bulb:* 8".

GERMINATING

Time 7–21 days.
Requirements Easy. 60°–70°F.

TRANSPLANTING

Time Late spring.
Spacing *Small species:* 12"–24". *Large species:* 24"–36".
Light Full sun, with afternoon shade where summers are very hot.
Soil Moist, humus-rich, with excellent drainage.

CARING FOR PLANTS

Water frequently during dry weather and feed 2 or 3 times per year. Remove faded blooms and dead leaves to keep plants tidy. In Zones 3–6, bulbs are often grown in containers. Lift bulbs or bring containers indoors in autumn and store over winter in a cool, frost-free location; provide a winter mulch in Zones 7 and 8. Disturb as little as possible and divide only very rarely.

PROPAGATING

Plant offsets or start from seed. Plants grown from seed flower in 4–5 years.

COMBINATIONS

Not an easy plant to use successfully in combinations. Try with *Cistus, Nicotiana,* darker-colored roses, or opt for a showy mass planting.

Crocosmia (syn. *Antholyza, Curtonus, Montbretia*)

HB* | Zn 6–10 | 

Montbretia

p. 387

The plants in this small genus from Africa grow from corms and form clumps of sword-shaped leaves. Stiff, arching branches of 2'–5' emerge above the foliage and bear bright red or orange, funnel-shaped flowers. Interesting foliage and flowers make these plants useful in the border.

Type Hardy bulb; often grown as an annual
Zone 6–10, H 9–2; grown as an annual in Zones 3–5
Flowering Season Summer

SOWING

Indoors 6–8 weeks before planting out.
Outdoors *Seed:* In Zones 9–10, sow as soon as ripe in early autumn; early spring is preferable in Zones 7–8. *Corm:* Autumn in Zones 9–10; well after last frost in Zones 3–8.
Depth *Seed:* Just cover. *Corm:* Plant 6" deep in Zones 7–10, 3" in Zones 3–6.

GERMINATING

Time 30–90 days.
Requirements Easy. 55°–60°F.

TRANSPLANTING

Time After last frost.
Spacing 4"–8".
Light Sun or light shade.
Soil Average, well drained. Tolerant of dry conditions but prefers adequate moisture.

CARING FOR PLANTS

Easy. Plants grown from seed will flower in 2–3 years. Water and feed regularly in summer; mulch in winter. Divide every 3 years. Provide a heavy winter mulch north of Zone 8. In Zones 3–5, lift corms and store in a cool, frost-free place, replanting in spring.

PROPAGATING

Plant offsets in spring or grow from seed.

COMBINATIONS

Canna, Cynoglossum, Echinops, Helenium, Helianthus, Perovskia, Salvia.

Crocus

HB | Zn 3–10

C

Crocus, Spring crocus

p. 387–388

Much-loved harbingers of spring, these little bulbs, have grassy leaves and purple, yellow, or white upturned, funnel-shaped flowers. They are ideal for filling naked beds in late winter and early spring, naturalizing in the lawn, or using under shrubs. While most crocuses are spring bloomers, there also are fall-blooming species.

Type Hardy bulb
Zone 3–10, H 9–1 (see species list, p. 448)
Flowering Season Late winter, spring, or autumn, depending on species

SOWING

Indoors Not recommended.
Outdoors *Seed:* Early spring, preferably in a cold frame. Leave undisturbed for two growing seasons. *Corm:* Plant spring-blooming corms in autumn, autumn-bloomers in July or August.
Depth *Seed:* ⅛". *Corm:* 2"–3".

GERMINATING

Time 30–180 days.
Requirements 55°–65°F.

TRANSPLANTING

Spacing 2"–4".
Light Leaves must receive full sun during spring to early-summer growing season, but can take light shade throughout the rest of the year, when they are dormant.
Soil Rich, light, well drained, with a pH level of 6.0–8.0. *Crocus* spp. are suitable for xeriscaping.

CARING FOR PLANTS

Easy. Feed annually in early spring; use manure only sparingly. Allow leaves to wither before removing or mowing. Where rodents are a problem, plant corms in wire cages.

PROPAGATING

Divide clumps of corms in autumn or grow from seed. Some crocuses may self-seed. Bulbs grown from seed will flower in 3–4 years.

COMBINATIONS

Cyclamen, Ionopsidium, Iris reticulata, Primula. Grow in front of an evergreen backdrop for the strongest impact.

Crucianella See *Phuopsis*

Cuminum

A | Zn 5–10

Low-growing (4"–6") and feathery-leaved, this annual herb is grown for its piquant seeds. Tiny white or pink flowers are held in umbels. Plants make an attractive edging for the herb bed.

Type Annual
Zone 5–10; needs 3–4 months of hot weather to mature
Flowering Season Midsummer

SOWING

Indoors 6–8 weeks before planting out, in peat pots.
Outdoors South of Zone 6 only, 2–3 weeks after last frost, when soil has warmed.
Depth ¼".

GERMINATING

Time 10–14 days.
Requirements Easy. 70°F.

TRANSPLANTING

Time When nighttime temperatures remain above 55°F.
Spacing 4"–6"; plants grown close together will support each other.
Light Full sun.
Soil Well drained, fertile.

CARING FOR PLANTS

Feed once at planting time; water regularly in hot, dry weather to ensure a good seed crop. Harvest pods when they turn brown. Dry thoroughly, then rub pods gently to release seed. Store airtight.

PROPAGATING

Grow from seed only.

Cuphea

TP* | Zn 10

p. 388

This genus of widely varying plants that bear tubular flowers is native to the Americas. Flowers may be deep purple and orchidlike, and feature long, deep red tubes or look like bright pink pinwheels. Use in containers or borders.

Type Tender perennial; grown as an annual
Zone 10, H 12–6; grown as an annual in Zones 6–9; requires long, hot growing season
Flowering Season Early summer to frost

SOWING

Indoors 10–12 weeks before planting out.
Outdoors Not recommended, as flowering takes 4–5 months from sowing.
Depth Surface.

GERMINATING

Time 8–10 days.
Requirements Light and 70°–75°F.

TRANSPLANTING

Time Late spring, when soil is warm and temperatures remain above 40°F.
Spacing 9"–12".
Light Sun or part shade.
Soil Somewhat heavy, humus-rich. *C. micropetala* is suitable for xeriscaping.

CARING FOR PLANTS

Very easy. Pinch out stem tips to induce branching. Water regularly. Plants may be potted up in autumn and overwintered indoors.

PROPAGATING

Take stem or root cuttings in spring or autumn or grow from seed.

Curtonus See *Crocosmia*

Cyclamen

HP | Zn 5–9  

Cyclamen, Alpine violet, Persian violet, Sowbread

p. 388

This genus of low-growing perennials, 3"–6", has plants with heart-shaped leaves, often patterned with white or silver. Graceful flowers with reflexed petals have the appearance of hovering butterflies. Plant near a woodland path or use as a ground cover.

Type Hardy perennial; cultural information for tender or florist's *Cyclamen* species is not included here
Zone 5–9, H 9–5 (see species list, p. 448); will not flourish where summer temperatures are hot
Flowering Season Any time from late winter through autumn, depending on species

SOWING

Indoors See Germinating, Requirements.
Outdoors See Germinating, Requirements.
Depth *Seed:* ¼". *Tuber:* 1"–2".

GERMINATING

Time 21–380 days.
Requirements Difficult. Soak seed in hot water for 24 hours before sowing. *Autumn sowing:* Sow seed in flats, plunge in the ground against a north-facing wall, and cover with glass. Moisten soil occasionally, if necessary. Bring indoors in spring to 55°–60°F. *Spring sowing:* Sow seed in flats, place in a plastic bag, and refrigerate. Remove after 2–3 weeks and sink flats in the ground in a shady location, covering with glass. Transplant seedlings as they emerge.

TRANSPLANTING

Time After last frost.
Spacing 6"–8".
Light Part shade.
Soil Cool, well drained, very rich, slightly alkaline.

CARING FOR PLANTS

Very easy. Water regularly only during growing period. Top-dress with leaf mold in late summer. In cold climates, provide a winter mulch. Do not disturb established plants.

PROPAGATING

Divide tubers in late summer or grow from seed. Plant may self-seed.

COMBINATIONS

Acer japonica, Ajuga, Bletilla, Crocus, ferns, *Galanthus, Helleborus,* dwarf *Iris, Senecio, Skimmia.*

CAUTION

Cyclamen spp. can be lethal to pets if eaten.

Cymbalaria

HP | Zn 4–9 

p. 388

Cymbalaria *are creeping plants grown for their neat, ivylike leaves and masses of tiny purple, yellow-throated, tubular flowers that resemble snapdragons. They are useful as a ground cover or a container plant.*

Type Short-lived hardy perennial; usually grown as an annual
Zone 4–9, H 8–1 (see species list, p. 448)
Flowering Season Midsummer

SOWING

Indoors 8–10 weeks before planting out.
Outdoors After last frost.
Depth Surface.

GERMINATING

Time 14–30 days.
Requirements Easy. Light and 60°–65°F.

TRANSPLANTING

Time After last frost.
Spacing 5"–7".
Light *C. pilosa* prefers full sun, but all other species must have shade where afternoon sun is very hot.
Soil Moist, gritty, slightly alkaline, not too rich.

CARING FOR PLANTS

Water frequently but feed only sparingly. May become invasive.

PROPAGATING

Divide in autumn, take cuttings, or grow from seed. In the South, it self seeds and may be a nuisance.

COMBINATIONS

Low-growing *Campanula, Corydalis, Sempervivum.*

Cymbopogon

TP* | Zn 9–10

p. 388

Lemongrass (Cymbopogon citratus) *is an attractive and tasty herb mainly grown for culinary use in Asian dishes. A tropical grass that grows rapidly to 2'–6', its leaves exude a lemony fragrance and flavor.*

Type Tender perennial; often grown as an annual
Zone 9–10; grown as an annual farther north
Flowering Season N/A

SOWING

Indoors 12 weeks before last frost.
Outdoors May or September/October, only in Zones 9–10.
Depth Surface.

GERMINATING

Time 7–40 days.
Requirements Requires light to germinate and 70°F.

TRANSPLANTING

Time 2–3 weeks after last frost when soil has warmed.
Spacing *Small species:* 18". *Large species:* 2'–3'.
Light Sun.
Soil Moist but well drained.

CARING FOR PLANTS

Easy. Water regularly and feed periodically. Harvest leaves from the base and use fresh or dried for cooking or tea. To overwinter indoors, cut back leaves (which can be frozen) to 6" and pot up in early autumn or grow in containers year-round. Place plants in a bright location and keep soil barely moist; watch for spider mites.

PROPAGATING

Divide, take root cuttings, or grow from seed, although seed is difficult to obtain. Stalks can be purchased in Asian markets and rooted in water.

Cynara

HP* | Zn 8–10

p. 388

*This small group of coarse, prickly plants includes species grown for the architectural form of its members and for its purple, thistlelike flowers. Its foliage is silvery green; flower stalks grow up to 8'. (*Cynara scolymus *is the edible artichoke.)*

Type Hardy perennial; often grown as an annual
Zone 8–10, H 9–7; grown as an annual in Zones 6–7
Flowering Season Summer through autumn

SOWING

Indoors Very early spring.
Outdoors In Zones 9–10 only, after last frost date.
Depth 1/8".

GERMINATING

Time 14–30 days.
Requirements 50°–55°F.

TRANSPLANTING

Time Just before last frost.
Spacing 2'–3'.
Light Full sun, with some protection from afternoon sun in very hot locations.
Soil Rich, moist, well drained. Add plenty of manure or compost if growing for food.

CARING FOR PLANTS

Water regularly and deeply. Plants grown for food will respond well to a topdressing of 5-10-10 fertilizer every 3–4 weeks. Harvest artichokes when fruit is green but still unopened. Cut plants back to ground level in autumn and mulch.

PROPAGATING

Propagation by seed is most successful, but plants also can be increased by dividing them in early spring.

COMBINATIONS

Acanthus, Delphinium, summer-blooming *Phlox, Salvia, Stachys.*

Cynoglossum

Bi | Zn 2–10

Hound's tongue

This genus of long-blooming, rather weedy plants is grown for its dainty blue, purple, or white forget-me-not flowers. Leaves are small and lance-shaped, sometimes grayish green. Plants grow 18"–36". Use with care in the border as plants self-seed rampantly.

Type Biennial; usually grown as an annual
Zone 2–10, H 8–5; requires cool temperatures
Flowering Season Spring through late autumn, declining in summer where temperatures are high for long periods

SOWING

Indoors 6–8 weeks before planting out.
Outdoors Several weeks before last frost, or in autumn where winters are mild.
Depth 1/4".

GERMINATING

Time 5–10 days.
Requirements Darkness and 65°–75°F.

TRANSPLANTING

Time Late spring.
Spacing 10"–12".
Light Full sun or light shade.
Soil Ordinary, well drained, with a pH level of 6.0–7.0. Tolerant of both wet and dry conditions; *C. amabile* is suitable for xeriscaping. Rich soil produces weak plants.

CARING FOR PLANTS

Easy. Support with twiggy branches pushed into ground when young. Prevent self-seeding by removing flowers before seed sets. Cut back to ground level in autumn. Tobacco mosaic virus may be a problem.

PROPAGATING

Divide in spring, take root cuttings in autumn, or grow from seed. Plants may self-seed.

COMBINATIONS

Achillea, Crocosmia, Petunia.

CAUTION

Some species are listed as invasive in some areas, including Utah. See pp. 494–495 for advice.

Cyperus

TP*, HP* | Zn 8–10 

p. 388

This large genus includes grasslike plants with thick, erect stems, 18"–60". Stems are topped with an umbrella of leaves and tiny green or cream-colored flowers. Grow in or near water.

Type Tender perennial, hardy perennial
Zone 8–10, H 12–1 (see species list, p. 448); may survive in Zone 7 with a heavy winter mulch
Flowering Season Summer or autumn

SOWING

Indoors 6–8 weeks before planting out.
Outdoors Spring or early autumn.
Depth Just cover.

GERMINATING

Time 25–30 days.
Requirements 70°–75°F.

TRANSPLANTING

Time Late spring, when temperatures remain above 45°F, or early autumn.
Spacing *Dwarf species:* 12". Medium species: 24"–36". *Large species:* 48".
Light Full sun, with light shade from afternoon sun where summers are hot.
Soil Rich, moist. Some species prefer to grow in shallow water that is a constant 65°–70°F.

CARING FOR PLANTS

Potted plants can be submerged in outdoor pools in summer, then brought indoors in autumn when temperatures fall below about 50°F.

PROPAGATING

Divide in early spring or grow from seed.

CAUTION

C. involucratus is listed as invasive in some areas, including Florida. See pp. 494–495 for advice.

Cypripedium

HP | Zn 3–9

Lady's slipper orchid, Moccasin flower, Slipper orchid

p. 388

A genus of wild orchids native to North America, flowers are usually bicolored: The pouched lower lip (the "slipper") is one color and the petals another. Pink, white, yellow, brown, and purple are the most common colors. Plants grow 12"–30" and are best suited to the woodland garden. These beautiful plants are closely protected and neither plants nor seed may be collected in the wild. It is important to ascertain that purchased plants have been nursery propagated and not wild-collected. See p. 11 for further information on approved sources for restricted wildflowers.

Type Hardy perennial
Zone 3–9; H 7–1 (see species list, p. 448)
Flowering Season Late spring to early summer

SOWING

Indoors Spring or autumn.
Outdoors Do not attempt outdoors.
Depth Surface.

GERMINATING

Time 30–365 days.
Requirements At the risk of sounding defeatist, it must be stated that propagation from seed is virtually impossible. For the determined: Sterilize a margarine tub with boiling water and half-fill with crumpled paper towels; soak towels with cooled boiled water. Cut five or six pieces of paper towel to fit the tub, place over the crumpled towels, and moisten. Sterilize seed by placing in a jar filled with 1 cup water and ¾ teaspoon vinegar; shake well and drain. With a sterilized instrument, place seed on the damp towels in the tub. Cover with a clear plastic lid that has been sterilized, place tub in plastic bag, and seal with a rubber band. Leave in a light location at 65°–75°F. Transplant seedlings to peat pots after they germinate.

Cypripedium (cont'd)

TRANSPLANTING

Time After last spring frost, or autumn.
Spacing 12"–18".
Light Part to full shade.
Soil Cool, rich, moist, acid, forest soil with plenty of humus.

CARING FOR PLANTS

Difficult to establish but fairly easy thereafter. Keep soil very moist even during dormancy; this is especially important the first season after planting. Mulch with leaf mold in early spring. Do not disturb roots. If moving is necessary, do so with a large rootball.

PROPAGATING

Divide in autumn where winters are mild (in early spring north of Zone 7). Keep at least one bud per new plant and set this just below the soil surface.

COMBINATIONS

Ferns, *Phlox divaricata, Podphylum, Pulmonaria.*

Cyrtomium (syn. *Phanerophlebia*)

HP | Zn 7–9 |  

p. 389

The shiny, leathery fronds of this small genus of handsome ferns are distinguished by prickly pinnae that strongly resemble holly leaves. Plants are seldom more than 12" tall but can reach 2'. They are either semi-evergreen or fully evergreen, which, combined with their striking appearance, makes them a most useful plant, either massed or grown singly.

Type Hardy perennial
Zone 7–9, H 8–1
Flowering Season N/A

SOWING

Indoors When spores are fresh in late summer.
Outdoors Not recommended.
Depth Surface.

GERMINATING

Time 10–365 days.
Requirements Difficult. Requires a temperature of 61°F. See pp 24–25 for instructions on starting ferns from spores.

TRANSPLANTING

Time After last frost.
Spacing 18"–24".
Light Part to full shade. *C. falcatum* tolerates deep shade.
Soil Moist, acid, humus-rich, and well drained, especially in winter.

CARING FOR PLANTS

Mulch in spring to keep soil moist, and water regularly during dry weather. Remove faded fronds periodically to improve appearance. Plants can be dug in autumn north of Zone 7 and overwintered indoors in a warm location with bright shade or grown in containers year-round. Watch for scale.

PROPAGATING

Divide in spring or summer or grow from spores.

COMBINATIONS

Azalea, Hosta, fine-textured ferns, tree ferns, small palms.

Dactylorhiza (syn. *Orchis*)

HP | Zn 5–8

Marsh orchid, Spotted orchid

p. 389

These tuberous orchids are native to woods and swamps. Flowers, which grow in terminal spikes, are small, intricate, lipped, purple, pink, or white, often spotted. Plants grow 1' to 2'.

Type Hardy perennial
Zone 5–8, H 8–6 (see species list, p. 448); prefers warm temperatures
Flowering Season Late spring to summer, depending on species

SOWING

Indoors Any time.
Outdoors *Seed:* Start seed indoors. *Tuber:* Early April.
Depth *Seed:* Surface. *Tuber:* 3"–4".

GERMINATING

Time 3–12 months.
Requirements Light and 65°–75°F.

TRANSPLANTING

Time After last frost.
Spacing 4"–6".
Light Part shade.
Soil Rich, peaty, slightly acid.

CARING FOR PLANTS

Do not allow soil to dry out in summer and do not disturb plants. Beyond this, each species has its own requirements and is unlikely to thrive if these are not met. Serious growers should consult texts devoted to orchid care.

PROPAGATING

Divide in late autumn; mark locations of plants to be divided before they die back in summer.

Dahlia

HP* | Zn 8–10

Dahlia

p. 389

These bold plants are often the showpiece of the summer border. Plants are sturdy, branched, and erect, 1'–7' tall. Dahlias are grown for their showy, often huge, usually double flowers. Flower colors range from demure pastels to deep unnatural neons. They are the Ethel Mermans of the perennial bed: Though they often lack subtlety, you can't help but love them. Easy, reliable, and versatile, dahlias are eye-catching in borders and containers.

Type Hardy perennial; often grown as an annual
Zone 8–10, H 12–1 (see species list, p. 449); grown as an annual in Zones 3–7, H 12–1; prefers warm summers
Flowering Season Early summer to frost, depending on species

SOWING

Indoors 8–10 weeks before planting out.
Outdoors *Seed:* 1–2 weeks before last frost. *Tuberous roots:* After last frost.
Depth *Seed:* Just cover. *Tuberous roots:* 6", with eye pointing upward.

GERMINATING

Time 5–20 days.
Requirements 65°–70°F. Sow in individual pots, not in flats.

TRANSPLANTING

Time 4 weeks after last frost, when soil and air temperatures are consistently warm.
Spacing *Dwarf species:* 12"–15". *Medium species:* 18"–24". *Tall species:* Up to 36".
Light Full sun.
Soil Deeply prepared, enriched with humus and bonemeal, with a pH level of 6.0–7.5. Excessive nitrogen will produce leggy plants with few blooms.

CARING FOR PLANTS

Easy. Site plants where air circulation is unrestricted. Pinch out dwarf cultivars to increase branching; stake tall cultivars occasionally as plants grow taller. Feed with bonemeal in June and early August. Water only during very dry weather until flowering begins; give ground a good soaking once a week while plants are in bloom. Mildews may take hold during wet summers; watch for aphids. Deadhead regularly. Cut back to ground level in autumn; north of Zone 9, lift tubers. Store over winter in a cool, frost-free location.

PROPAGATING

Divide clumps in autumn or before planting in spring, take cuttings from new shoots in late winter, or grow from seed.

COMBINATIONS

Canna, Helenium, Hemerocallis, Sedum.

Dalechampia

TP* | Zn 9–10

A tropical vine, Dalechampia dioscoreifolia, *commonly known as bow tie plant, grows about 4' tall with insignificant flowers but unusual and showy rose or white bracts that are configured, as its common name suggests, like a bow tie. A conversation piece to grow up a trellis in a container.*

Type Tender perennial; often grown as an annual
Zone 9–10; grown as an annual farther north
Flowering Season Showy bracts appear from early summer though late autumn

SOWING

Not grown from seed.

TRANSPLANTING

Time After last frost.
Spacing 2'–3'.
Light Full sun to part shade, with shade from hot afternoon sun.
Soil Fertile, quite moist but well drained.

CARING FOR PLANTS

Water regularly during dry weather.

PROPAGATING

Easily propagated from hardwood cuttings.

Darmera (syn. *Peltiphyllum*)

HP | Zn 5–9

p. 389

This striking perennial bears clusters of pale pink flowers similar to Bergenia. *They appear on thick, hairy stems before the leaves, which are large (up to 2' wide) and dramatic, atop 4' stems. Leaves are brilliant red in fall. For moist soil and large spaces only.*

Type Hardy perennial
Zone 5–7, to Zone 9 in the west; H 9–4; will not thrive in heat and humidity
Flowering Season Early to mid-spring, before the foliage appears

SOWING

Indoors Spring or autumn.
Outdoors Early spring.
Depth Surface.

GERMINATING

Time 30–90 days.
Requirements Difficult. Soak seed for 24 hours, then sow and leave at 60°F, keeping soil fairly moist. If seeds do not germinate in 90 days, move to 25°–39°F for 6–8 weeks, then back to 60°F. Keep seedlings indoors over their first winter.

TRANSPLANTING

Time 1–2 weeks after last frost.
Spacing 24"–36".
Light Sun in really wet soil, otherwise part shade.
Soil Moist to wet. Drier soil will produce smaller plants. *Darmera* is a good bog plant.

CARING FOR PLANTS

Easy. Keep well watered throughout growing season, although size and spread can be controlled to some extent by keeping soil drier. Leaf scorch will occur if soil is too dry. Curtail spread by periodically digging up clumps of rhizomes.

PROPAGATING

Divide after flowering in spring or grow from seed.

COMBINATIONS

Acer palmatum, Iris ensata, Iris siberica, Ligularia, Mimulus, Primula.

Datura

TP* | Zn 9–10

Thorn apple, Angel's trumpet

p. 389

Bushy plants of 3'–5' with bluish foliage feature large, exquisite flowers. Blooms are 4"–8" long white trumpets, some delicately edged in palest lavender, some lightly scented. A stunning container or border plant.

Type Tender perennial; often grown as an annual
Zone 9–10, H 12–1; grown as an annual in Zones 3–8; prefers warm temperatures
Flowering Season Summer

SOWING

Indoors 2–3 months before planting out.
Outdoors Start seed outdoors only in Zones 9–10, after last frost date.
Depth 1/8".

GERMINATING

Time 21–42 days.
Requirements Easy. 65°–70°F.

TRANSPLANTING

Time 2–3 weeks after last frost, when temperatures remain above 45°F.
Spacing 3'–4'.
Light Sun.
Soil Prefers rich and moist; will tolerate poor soil.

CARING FOR PLANTS

Easy. Water well during dry spells in summer and throughout the winter. Deadhead regularly.

PROPAGATING

Take cuttings of side shoots when temperature is above 60°F or grow from seed. Plants may self-seed. Plants grown from seed will flower in 14 weeks in ideal conditions.

CAUTION

All parts of these plants are extremely toxic if eaten.

Delosperma

TP, HP | Zn 4–10

Ice plant

p. 389

The most commonly grown of this large group of succulents is 1"–5" tall with short, fleshy leaves. It bears an abundance of pink, bright purple, or yellow daisylike flowers over a long period. It is a useful ground cover for hot, dry areas or in containers.

Type Tender perennial, hardy perennial
Zone 4–10, H 9–6 (see species list, p. 449); very heat tolerant; performs best where autumns and winters are dry
Flowering Season Spring to autumn, depending on species

SOWING

Indoors 6 weeks before last frost.
Outdoors Autumn.
Depth Surface.

GERMINATING

Time 10–40 days.
Requirements Easy. Require light and temperature of 65°–85°F. Seedlings prefer relatively dry soil.

TRANSPLANTING

Time After last frost.
Spacing 12"–18".
Light Sun, with part shade in the afternoon tolerated in very hot climates. *Delosperma* is suitable for xeriscaping, but should not be used in areas where it is invasive (see Caution below).
Soil Withstands poor and dry; must have perfect drainage, especially in winter.

CARING FOR PLANTS

Easy. Tender species can be potted up before first frost and overwintered indoors.

PROPAGATING

Take cuttings in mid-spring to late spring or summer to early autumn or grow from seed.

COMBINATIONS

Coreopsis, Lavandula, Salvia, Sedum, Sempervivum.

CAUTION

Some species of *Delosperma* may be invasive in Florida. See pp. 494–495 for advice.

Delphinium

HP* | Zn 3–9

Delphinium

p. 390

Statuesque perennial of unequaled beauty, evocative of medieval gardens. Delphiniums display tall spires cloaked in spurred blooms of blue, white, purple, pink, or yellow. Their green foliage resembles that of cut-leaf maples. Growing from a dwarf 6" to a towering 7', these plants will add grace to any border.

Type Hardy perennial; usually short-lived
Zone 3–9, H 8–1 (see species list, p. 449); prefer cool, moist summers; often grown as a cool-season annual where summers are hot; *D. grandiflorum* and *D.* Belladona Group are most heat tolerant
Flowering Season Late spring through autumn, depending on species

SOWING

Indoors 8–10 weeks before planting out.
Outdoors Early spring or early autumn.
Depth Just cover.

GERMINATING

Time 14–28 days.
Requirements Place seed and moistened growing medium in a plastic bag and refrigerate for 2 weeks. Provide darkness and 50°–55°F thereafter.

TRANSPLANTING

Time Early spring, when soil is cool and a light frost is still possible, or early autumn. Autumn planting is especially useful where summers are hot.
Spacing *Small species:* 12"–18". *Large species:* 24"–36".
Light Full sun to light shade.
Soil Deep, rich, well drained, with a pH level of 5.5–7.0.

CARING FOR PLANTS

Easy to grow in deep, rich soil in temperate climates, more challenging where summers are hot and humid or soil is less than perfect. Fertilize in early spring. Water well throughout the growing season. Remove faded blooms immediately after first flowering and feed again. When new, secondary growth reaches 9", cut off old growth completely. Plants over 18" tall will require staking. May be affected by powdery mildew or slugs. Delphiniums are short lived and should be replaced regularly.

PROPAGATING

Divide in spring or grow from seed. May self-seed.

COMBINATIONS

It would almost be easier to list plants that don't combine well with *Delphinium.* Among its good companions are *Achillea, Campanula, Lilium, Linum, Papaver, Polygonum,* and roses.

CAUTION

Harmful if eaten, and contact with foliage may cause a skin rash.

Dennstaedtia

HP | Zn 3–8

Cup fern

p. 390

These soft, feathery, bright green plants have the advantage of being less fussy than most ferns about moisture, but they do have the disadvantage of being invasive. They are useful plants for colonizing great sweeps of difficult woodland.

Type Hardy perennial
Zone 3–8
Flowering Season N/A

SOWING

Indoors July through September.
Outdoors Not recommended.
Depth Surface.

GERMINATING

Time 10–365 days.
Requirements Difficult. Requires 59°F. See pp. 24–25 for instructions on starting ferns from spores.

D

TRANSPLANTING

Time After last frost or early autumn, when plants are 2 years old.
Spacing 12".
Light Sun to shade, even deep shade; more tolerant of sun in cooler climates and moist soil.
Soil Moist or dry, acid, humus-rich.

CARING FOR PLANTS

Remove fading fronds periodically to keep plants tidy. Water regularly during dry spells; plants may go dormant during prolonged drought. Can be invasive, especially *D. punctiloba.* Watch for slugs and snails.

PROPAGATING

Divide in spring in Zone 8 (in autumn farther south) or grow from spores.

COMBINATIONS

Hydrangea, Phlox divaricata, Rhododendron, Tradescantia. Easily overwhelms less aggressive plants.

Dentaria See *Cardamine*

DiANTHUS

ANNUAL, TENDER PERENNIAL

TP* | Zn 9–10  

Including *D. chinensis*

China pink, Indian pink

p. 390

Some tender perennial Dianthus *species, including* D. chinensis, *are often grown as annuals. These neat, fine-textured, shrubby plants bear an abundance of saucer-shaped flowers throughout the season. Blooms are red, white, or pink, often bicolored, with pink edges. At 6"–12" tall, they make excellent edging plants, useful in both formal and informal plantings.*

Type Tender perennial; often grown as an annual
Zone 9–10, H 12–1; grown as an annual in Zones 2–10, H 12–1; flowers most freely in cool weather and will burn out quickly where summers are hot
Flowering Season Late spring through early summer

SOWING

Indoors 8–10 weeks before last frost.
Outdoors Early spring, when soil is cool and a light frost is still possible, or late autumn.
Depth Just cover.

GERMINATING

Time 5–21 days.
Requirements 60°–70°F.

TRANSPLANTING

Time After last frost.
Spacing 8"–10".
Light Full sun; part shade where summers are hot.
Soil Rich, moist, well drained, with a pH level of 6.0–7.5.

CARING FOR PLANTS

Easy. Pinch back young plants to stimulate bushy growth and deadhead frequently to prolong blooming. Where summers are very hot, cut back hard after blooming. A good mulch may bring plants through winter, but those that survive should be discarded after their second year of blooming.

PROPAGATING

Take cuttings in summer or grow from seed.

COMBINATIONS

Cosmos, Dahlia, Dimorphotheca, Laurentia, Solenostemon.

BIENNIAL Including *D. armeria, D. barbatus, D. superbus*

HB | Zn 2–10

Sweet William

p. 390

Biennial Dianthus *species are bushy plants, 6"–20" tall, with cushiony tufts of lance-shaped leaves and tightly packed bouquets of blooms borne on rather floppy stems. Flowers are red, white, violet, or pink, bicolored or tricolored, flat or double, often with prettily serrated edges. Mass in the border for best effect.*

Type Hardy perennial or perennial; often grown as a biennial
Zone 2–10, H 9–1 (see species list, p. 449); performs best where summers are mild
Flowering Season Mid-spring to frost, depending on species

SOWING

Indoors 6–8 weeks before planting out.
Outdoors Any time from April to July for blooms the following year.
Depth ¼".

GERMINATING

Time 10 days.
Requirements 70°F.

TRANSPLANTING

Time After last spring frost, or in autumn.
Spacing 9".
Light Sun; *D. barbatus* will grow in light shade.
Soil Deep, rich, well drained, with a pH level of 6.0–7.5. *D. armeria* and *D. barbatus* are drought tolerant and would be suitable for xeriscaping.

CARING FOR PLANTS

Easy. Water regularly and feed once or twice during the growing season. Shear back after flowering to prolong the life of the plant. Mulch in winter.

PROPAGATING

Start from seed or take root cuttings.

COMBINATIONS

Anchusa, Artemisia, Papaver, roses, *Senecio.*

PERENNIAL

HP | Zn 2–10

Pinks, Carnation

True carnations flower in every shade of pink, red, yellow, and white. Blooms are held on slender stems, 6"–24" tall. The distinctive lance-shaped leaves are mid-green or silvery blue. Use different species with abandon in rock gardens, borders, or along stone walls.

Type Hardy perennial
Zone 2–10, H 9–1 (see species list, p. 449); most of the named cultivars will grow in Zones 5–9
Flowering Season Late spring or summer, depending on species

SOWING

Indoors 8–10 weeks before planting out.
Outdoors Early spring or early autumn.
Depth Just cover.

GERMINATING

Time 14–21 days.
Requirements 60°–70°F.

TRANSPLANTING

Time Early spring, when soil is cool and a light frost is still possible, or early autumn.
Spacing *Small species:* 6". *Tall species:* 9".
Light Full sun; light shade in the afternoon where summers are hot.
Soil Rich, well drained, with a pH level of 6.0–7.5. *D. plumarius* is tolerant of dry soil and may be used for xeriscaping.

CARING FOR PLANTS

Easy. Water only during very dry spells. Cut back stems after flowering. Mulch in winter in coldest zones. Renew plants every 2–3 years.

PROPAGATING

Divide in early spring in Zones 3–6 (in autumn in Zones 7–10), take stem cuttings in summer, or grow from seed.

COMBINATIONS

Tall *Anemone, Campanula,* low irises, *Lavandula,* roses, *Scabiosa, Viola,* and silver-leaved plants such as *Perovskia, Senecio,* and *Stachys.*

Diascia

A, HP | Zn 2–10

p. 390

These pretty, unusual, low-growing plants resemble a diminutive foxglove. Pale to deep pink flowers are borne on 9"–12" stems all summer. Suitable for borders, rock gardens, or containers. Native to southern Africa.

Type Annual, hardy perennial
Zone *Annual:* 2–8; *Perennial:* 8–10, H 9–7 (see species list, p. 449). Will not tolerate very hot, humid weather, though *D. barberae* 'Ruby Field' is somewhat resistant to heat and humidity
Flowering Season Summer

SOWING

Indoors 6–8 weeks before last frost.
Outdoors Early spring to mid-spring.
Depth Just cover.

GERMINATING

Time 14–30 days.
Requirements Easy. 60°F.

TRANSPLANTING

Time After last frost.
Spacing *Low species:* 5"–8". *Spreading species:* 12"–14".
Light Full sun, with protection from very hot afternoon sun.
Soil Humus-rich, well drained, but not too dry.

CARING FOR PLANTS

Pinch tips of young plants to establish a bushy habit. Mulch plants with rock chips to ensure excellent drainage, but do not allow soil to dry out. Cut back after first blooms fade to stimulate further flowering. *D. spectabilis* goes dormant in summer after blooming.

PROPAGATING

Take cuttings in late spring or start from seed.

COMBINATIONS

Lobelia, Nemesia, Tanacetum.

Dicentra

HP | Zn 3–9

Bleeding heart

p. 390

Shrubby perennials, 3"–24" tall, bleeding hearts bear dainty flowers of white, pink, or sometimes yellow. Some resemble Lilliputian britches hanging out to dry; others look like a string of tiny hearts. Foliage is deeply cut and fernlike. These are indispensable for any shady garden.

Type Hardy perennial
Zone 3–9, H 9–1; prefers moderate summer temperatures
Flowering Season Early spring through mid autumn, depending on species

SOWING

Indoors Midsummer.
Outdoors Late autumn or early winter.
Depth *Seed:* Just cover. *Roots:* 2"–3".

GERMINATING

Time 30–365 days.
Requirements Place seed together with moistened growing medium in a plastic bag and freeze for 6 weeks. Provide 55°–60°F thereafter.

TRANSPLANTING

Time Spring or autumn.
Spacing *Small species:* 12"–15". *Large species:* 24".
Light Full sun to part shade. More shade is required where summers are very hot.
Soil Light, rich, moist, with a pH level of 5.0–6.0.

CARING FOR PLANTS

Easy. Feed lightly during the growing season and water regularly. Do not move established plants. Where summers are very hot, cut back to ground level after flowering and divide every 3–4 years.

PROPAGATING

Take root cuttings at any time, divide carefully in early spring, or grow from seed.

COMBINATIONS

Astilbe, Digitalis, Doronicum, Epimedium, Heucherella, Hosta, Myosotis, woodland *Phlox.*

Dictamnus

HP | Zn 3–8

Dittany, Burning bush, Fraxinella

p. 390

This upright perennial bears pink, purple, or white star-shaped flowers in stiff terminal spikes; foliage is fragrant and glossy green, 3' tall. Use mid border.

Type Hardy perennial
Zone 3–8, H 8–1. Dislikes extreme heat and humidity.
Flowering Season Late spring to summer

SOWING

Indoors Late autumn.
Outdoors Autumn.
Depth Just cover.

GERMINATING

Time 30–180 days.
Requirements Difficult. Sow seed in flats, seal in plastic bag, and leave at 60°–65°F for 2 weeks. Refrigerate for 3–6 weeks, then return to 60°–65°F. If seed hasn't germinated in 6–10 weeks, chill again for 5–6 weeks. Remove from refrigerator when germination begins.

TRANSPLANTING

Time After last spring frost, or autumn.
Spacing 24"–36".
Light Full sun or part shade.
Soil Tolerates dry soil that is very rich; poor soil must be kept moist. Prefers a pH level of 5.5–7.0.

CARING FOR PLANTS

Easy. Plants grown from seed flower in 3–4 years. Prepare planting hole deeply, adding plenty of compost, and *Dictamnus* almost takes care of itself. Where summers are very hot, prune severely after blooming. Cut back stems in fall; mulch for winter.

PROPAGATING

Division may be successful, although growing from seed is preferable as plants resent disturbance.

COMBINATIONS

Coreopsis, Geranium, Hemerocallis, Penstemon.

Didiscus See *Trachymene*

Dierama

HB | Zn 7–9

African hairbell, Angel's fishingrod, Wand flower

p. 390

Native to eastern and southern Africa, this unusual, clump-forming plant has grassy foliage and drooping, funnel- or bell-shaped flowers in shades of pink. Blossoms are borne loosely on long, arching stems, 3'–5' tall.

Type Hardy bulb
Zone 7–9, H 9–7; will not thrive under hot, humid conditions
Flowering Season Summer

SOWING

Indoors Spring.
Outdoors Autumn or spring.
Depth *Seed:* Surface. *Corm:* 4"–6".

GERMINATING

Time 30–180 days.
Requirements Light and 60°–65°F.

TRANSPLANTING

Time Spring or autumn.
Spacing *Small species:* 6"–8". *Large species:* 12"–20".
Light Full sun. Plant in a location that will be warm and sheltered in winter.
Soil Rich, moist, well drained.

CARING FOR PLANTS

Easy. Keep soil moist in growing season; mulch in winter in Zones 7–8. Unless absolutely necessary, do not lift corms, as they take 2–3 years to recover.

PROPAGATING

Plant offsets or grow from seed. Plants grown from seed will flower in 3 years.

COMBINATIONS

Most effective alone, or surround by lower-growing plants like *Alyssum, Helianthemum,* and *Thymus.*

Digitalis

Bi, HP | Zn 3–9

D

Foxglove

p. 391

Majestic yet unpretentious, this Old World standard adds a touch of class, whether used in the border, in a woodland planting, or allowed to self-seed at random. From a demure 2' to a towering 6', spires carry tubular flowers in subtle shades of pink, salmon, orange, yellow, and cream, often attractively freckled.

Type Biennial or hardy perennial; perennials often grown as an annual or biennial
Zone 3–9, H 8–1 (see species list, p. 450); happiest in cool, moist climates
Flowering Season Late spring to late summer, depending on species

SOWING

Indoors 8–10 weeks before planting out for blooms first year.
Outdoors After last spring frost for flowering the following year. Where winters are mild, late summer or autumn.
Depth Surface.

GERMINATING

Time 14–21 days.
Requirements Light and 60°–65°F.

TRANSPLANTING

Time 2–3 weeks before last frost.
Spacing 18"–24".
Light Full sun to part shade; afternoon shade is necessary in hot climates. *D. lutea* will thrive in full shade.
Soil Cool, moist, rich, with well-rotted manure added at planting time; pH level of 6.0–7.5.

CARING FOR PLANTS

Easy. Water plants deeply and often. Cut flowering stems to ground after blooming if self-seeding is not desired. Mulch after the ground freezes to minimize the chance of crown rot. Foxgloves do not like heat or drought and will languish in unfavorable conditions; where summers are very hot, early-blooming species stand a better chance of surviving. Even under ideal conditions, foxgloves may require renewal by either dividing or replacing every 2–3 years. Much loved by slugs.

PROPAGATING

Divide in early spring in the North (in autumn in the South) or grow from seed. May self-seed.

COMBINATIONS

Dicentra, Geranium, Hosta, Mecanopsis, Paeonia, Polygonatum, roses.

CAUTION

All parts of the plant are toxic to humans and pets if eaten.

Dimorphotheca

TP* | Zn 9–10

African daisy, Cape marigold, Sun marigold

p. 391

Long-blooming Dimorphotheca *plants are covered in delightful, daisylike flowers in every color but blue, with strongly contrasting eyes. They grow 12"–18" tall. Use them in containers or borders. They are native to tropical and South Africa.*

Type Tender perennial; often grown as an annual
Zone 9–10, H 10–1; grown as an annual in cooler zones; requires a long, dry, mild summer with cool nights; will not perform well in humid heat
Flowering Season Winter and spring in Zones 9–10, summer elsewhere

SOWING

Indoors 6–8 weeks before planting out.
Outdoors Early autumn for winter flowering, winter for spring blooms, but only in Zones 9–10.
Depth Just cover.

GERMINATING

Time 10–15 days.
Requirements Difficult. 60°–70°F.

TRANSPLANTING

Time Late spring, when soil is warm.
Spacing 8"–12".
Light Full sun.
Soil Prefers rich, well-drained soil; will tolerate dry soil. *Dimorphotheca* species are suitable for xeriscaping in the Southwest.

CARING FOR PLANTS

Water frequently early in the day, keeping water off leaves, as plants are susceptible to fungal diseases in wet or humid conditions. Cut stems to ground after flowering. Do not move.

PROPAGATING

Take cuttings in late summer or grow from seed.

Dioscorea

TP*, HP | Zn 6–10 | Full sun, Partial shade | Ordinary soil

Plants of this genus of mainly tropical climbers are sometimes grown on porches or pergolas for their handsome, shiny, heart-shaped leaves, some with an attractive mosaic pattern of dark green, pale green, and white. They feature clusters of small, white, cinnamon-scented flowers.

Type Tender perennial, hardy perennial; often grown as an annual in the North
Zone 6–10 (see species list, p. 450); grown as an annual in Zones 4–8
Flowering Season Spring to autumn, depending on species

SOWING

Indoors Late winter to early spring.
Outdoors *Seed:* September to October. *Tuber:* After last frost date.
Depth *Seed:* 1/8". *Tuber:* 3".

GERMINATING

Time 21–36 days.
Requirements 70°–75°F.

TRANSPLANTING

Time When temperatures remain above 45°F.
Spacing *Climbers:* 12". *Others:* 24"–36".
Light Full sun to light shade.
Soil Deep, well drained.

CARING FOR PLANTS

Water well during the growing season. Provide a trellis for climbers. North of Zone 9, lift tubers in autumn and store in a cool, frost-free location; replant in spring.

PROPAGATING

Take cuttings or divide in spring or autumn.

CAUTION

D. alata and *D. bulbifera* are listed as invasive in some areas, including Florida; *D. oppositifolia* is listed as invasive in some areas, including Kentucky, Maryland, Tennessee, and Virginia. See pp. 494–495 for advice.

Diosphaera See *Trachelium*

Diplacus See *Mimulus*

Dipteracanthus See *Ruellia*

Disporopsis

HP | Zn 5–9

Evergreen Solomon's seal

Closely related to Polygonatum, *our native Solomon's seals, these 1' tall plants have the same pendulous, creamy, bell-like flowers but thicker, glossy, evergreen leaves. They make an attractive woodland ground cover.*

Type Hardy perennial
Zone 5–9 (see species list, p. 450)
Flowering Season Late spring or early summer

SOWING

Growing from seed is not recommended.

TRANSPLANTING

Time Late spring.
Spacing 12–15".
Light Full to part shade.
Soil Moist, well drained, humus-rich.

CARING FOR PLANTS

Do not allow soil to dry out completely. Cut back any ragged old stems in spring. Slugs are attracted to new growth in spring.

PROPAGATING

Divide in early spring.

COMBINATIONS

Asarum, Bergenia, Convallaria, Epimedium, Hosta.

Dodecatheon

HP | Zn 3–10

Shooting star, American cowslip

p. 391

Small woodland perennials, most Dodecatheon *plants are no more than 6"–24" tall. Pink, green, or purple star-shaped flowers appear on stalks above a mound of leaves. With their reflexed petals on leafless stalks, the blooms look as though they are battling a strong wind, petals streaming behind them. Use this North American native in the woodland garden.*

Type Hardy perennial
Zone 3–10, H 8–1 (see species list, p. 450)
Flowering Season Spring to early summer

SOWING

Indoors Spring.
Outdoors Late autumn to early winter.
Depth Surface.

GERMINATING

Time 90–365 days.
Requirements Difficult. *Autumn sowing:* Sow seed in flats, sink these in the ground outdoors, and cover with glass. Transplant seedlings to beds when they are large enough to handle. *Spring sowing:* Place seed in a plastic bag together with moist growing medium and refrigerate for 3 weeks. Provide light and 60°–70°F thereafter.

TRANSPLANTING

Time After last spring frost, or in autumn.
Spacing *Small species:* 6"–8". *Large species:* 18"–20".
Light Part to full shade.
Soil Rich, moist, woodland soil, with a pH level of 5.0–7.0.

CARING FOR PLANTS

Easy, when planted in a suitable location. Apply mulch in spring and do not allow soil to dry out during the growing season. Plants go dormant and foliage dies back in summer. Do not move established plants.

PROPAGATING

Divide in spring or fall or grow from seed.

COMBINATIONS

Carex, Narcissus, Pulmonaria.

Dolichos See *Lablab*

Dondia See *Hacquetia*

Doronicum

HP | Zn 4–8

Leopard's bane

Leopard's bane are cheerful perennials, grown for their showy, yellow, daisylike flowers. They grow 12"–36" tall and are useful in the border and for cutting.

Type Hardy perennial
Zone 4–8, H 7–1; prefers cool summers
Flowering Season Spring to early summer, depending on species

SOWING

Indoors 8–10 weeks before planting out.
Outdoors Early spring or early autumn.
Depth Surface.

GERMINATING

Time 15–20 days.
Requirements Light and 70°F.

TRANSPLANTING

Time Early spring, when soil is cool and a light frost is still possible, or early autumn.
Spacing *Small species:* 9"–12". *Large species:* 12"–18".
Light Full sun where summers are cool; elsewhere plant in part shade.
Soil Moist, humus-rich. Plants do not respond well to drought.

CARING FOR PLANTS

Water plants frequently in summer and cut back to ground level in autumn (where summers are hot, this will not be necessary, as leaves will die back naturally). Mulch in spring and again in winter to protect shallow roots. Plants are short lived and require dividing every 2–4 years.

PROPAGATING

Divide in late summer or autumn or grow from seed.

COMBINATIONS

Alchemilla or *Iberis* in cool climates, *Brunnera* or *Myosotis* where it's warmer.

Dorotheanthus (syn. *Mesembryanthemum*)

TP* | Zn 9–10

Ice plant, Livingstone daisy

Of this very large genus of rarely used succulents, the more attractive species are grown for the cheery mass of blooms that cover plants over a long period. Flowers are daisylike, with numerous fine petals in pink, yellow, white, or red. The 4"–12" plants are useful in rock gardens, sunny borders, and dry stone walls, or as edging.

Type Tender perennial; often grown as an annual
Zone 9–10, H 10–1; grown as an annual in Zones 3–8; prefers warm, dry climates
Flowering Season Spring through late summer, depending on species and time of sowing

SOWING

Indoors 10–12 weeks before last frost.
Outdoors After last frost, and at intervals until late May for a longer blooming period.
Depth Just cover.

GERMINATING

Time 15–20 days.
Requirements Darkness and 65°–75°F.

TRANSPLANTING

Time After last frost.
Spacing *Small species:* 4"–8". *Large species:* 6"–12".
Light Full sun.
Soil Poor, dry, sandy or gritty, and very well drained.

CARING FOR PLANTS

Water moderately during the growing season but only sparingly otherwise. Feed with a liquid fertilizer after first flowering.

PROPAGATING

Take cuttings in spring or grow from seed.

Douglasia See **Androsace, Vitaliana**

Draba

HP | Zn 3–8

Draba

p. 391

Compact and mounding, these are good plants for the rock garden. They grow 1"–8" tall, with flowers like diminutive stars of yellow, white, pink, or purple borne in terminal clusters on leafless stems.

Type Hardy perennial
Zone 3–8, H 6–1 (see species list, p. 450)
Flowering Season Early spring to mid spring

SOWING

Indoors 8–10 weeks before planting out.
Outdoors After last frost.
Depth Just cover.

GERMINATING

Time 30–90 days.
Requirements 60°–70°F. For *D. rigida* var. *bryoides*, refrigerate seed for 4–6 weeks.

TRANSPLANTING

Time After last frost.
Spacing 3"–5".
Light Prefers full sun but will tolerate light shade.
Soil Gritty or sandy. Add a little lime to acid soil to raise pH.

CARING FOR PLANTS

Protect plants from overhead water in winter. Mulch in autumn where winters are very cold.

PROPAGATING

Divide in spring or grow from seed.

Dracocephalum See *Physostegia*

Dracunculus

HP | Zn 7–10

Dragon arum

These exotic-looking perennials bear large, blood-red, arum-type flowers of alien appearance and noxious odor. They range from 18" to 36" tall. They are usually grown as a curiosity.

Type Hardy perennial
Zone 7–10, H 10–8; requires warm temperatures
Flowering Season Early summer.

SOWING

Indoors Late winter to early spring.
Outdoors Autumn.
Depth *Seed:* Just cover. *Tuber:* 3".

GERMINATING

Time 30–180 days.
Requirements 55°–65°F.

TRANSPLANTING

Time After last frost.
Spacing 10"–12".
Light Part to full shade.
Soil Rich, well drained, with an abundance of organic matter.

CARING FOR PLANTS

Mulch in spring. Keep soil moist during growing season, fairly dry at all other times.

PROPAGATING

Divide in autumn or grow from seed.

COMBINATIONS

Because of their dramatic appearance, these bulbs are most effective grown alone or massed with other bold shade-lovers, such as ferns and *Hosta*.

Dryas

HP | Zn 2–6  

Mountain avens

p. 391

Creeping evergreen perennials, Dryas *have small, dark green leaves and cup-shaped flowers of white or palest yellow, followed by ornamental, feathery seeds. Use them in the rock garden or as a ground cover for small spaces.*

Type Hardy perennial
Zone 2–6, H 6–1
Flowering Season Late spring to summer

SOWING

Indoors See Germinating, Requirements.
Outdoors See Germinating, Requirements.
Depth Just cover.

GERMINATING

Time 50–365 days.
Requirements *Autumn sowing:* Sow seed in flats, sink in the ground against a north-facing wall, and cover with glass. Moisten soil occasionally, if necessary. Bring indoors in spring to 60°–70°F. *Spring sowing:* Place seeds in a plastic bag together with moist growing medium and refrigerate for 2–3 weeks. Sow seed in flats, plunge in the ground in a shady location, and cover with glass. Transplant seedlings as they emerge.

TRANSPLANTING

Time Spring or autumn.
Spacing 12"–15".
Light Sun or part shade.
Soil Moist, peaty, sandy or gritty, slightly alkaline.

CARING FOR PLANTS

Difficult. Mulch in spring with a mixture of half leaf mold and half rock chips. Cut back creeping stems as they emerge — these do not flower as well as the parent plant.

PROPAGATING

Divide in spring, take cuttings in late summer, or grow from seed.

COMBINATIONS

Lobularia, Nemophila, creeping *Phlox.*

Dryopteris

HP | Zn 2–9

Buckler fern, Male fern, Shield fern, Wood fern

p. 391

In this large species of ferns, the majority have the typical fern look, with broad, sturdy, and impressive fronds that create handsome and substantial clumps. Dryopteris *species are all useful plants for either naturalistic or more formal plantings.*

Type Hardy perennial
Zone 2–9, H 12–1 (see species list, p. 481)
Flowering Season N/A

SOWING

Indoors July through October.
Outdoors Not recommended.
Depth Just cover.

GERMINATING

Time 10–365 days.
Requirements Difficult. Keep temperature at 59°F. See pp. 24–25 for instructions on starting ferns from spores.

TRANSPLANTING

Time After last frost after 2–3 years.
Spacing *Small species:* 18"–24". *Medium species:* 2'–3'. *Large species:* 4'–6'.
Light Part to full shade. Evergreen species will take full shade. *D. filix-mas* and *D. ludoviciana* tolerate sun.
Soil Moist to wet, humusy. *D. intermedia,* and *D. marginalis* tolerate dry; *D. filix-mas* is suitable for xeriscaping.

CARING FOR PLANTS

Easy. Remove faded fronds periodically throughout the growing season to keep plants tidy; cut back to ground level in autumn.

PROPAGATING

Divide in spring or grow from spores.

COMBINATIONS

Dicentra, Digitalis, Heuchera, Hosta, Polygonatum, Pulmonaria, Rhododendron.

Eccremocarpus

HP* | Zn 8–10

Chilean glory flower, Glory flower

p. 391

These shrubby climbers are grown for their decorative, tubular flowers of bright orange, yellow, or scarlet. Growing up to 12', they are native to Chile and Peru.

E

Type Hardy perennial; often grown as an annual
Zone 8–10, H 12–10; grown as an annual in cooler zones, but performs best in areas with warm summers
Flowering Season Mid summer to frost

SOWING

Indoors 4–6 weeks before planting out.
Outdoors Early spring, when soil has warmed.
Depth Just cover.

GERMINATING

Time 14–60 days.
Requirements 60°–70°F.

TRANSPLANTING

Time 2–3 weeks after last frost.
Spacing 12"; most effective when grown singly.
Light Sun.
Soil Prefers light, rich, moist, well drained; will tolerate poor soil.

CARING FOR PLANTS

Requires a trellis or other form of support. Lightly prune perennials in early spring.

PROPAGATING

Self-seeds. Plants grown from seed will flower in their first year.

COMBINATIONS

Ceanothus, purple *Clematis*, *Cobaea*.

Echinacea

HP | Zn 3–9

Coneflower

p. 391

These rugged but beautiful upright perennials bear white or raspberry-colored, daisylike flowers with large pincushion-like centers throughout summer. They are 2'–4' tall, and essential in any border or wildflower garden.

Type Hardy perennial
Zone 3–9, H 8–1
Flowering Season Summer through early autumn

SOWING

Indoors 8–10 weeks before planting out.
Outdoors Early spring or early autumn.
Depth 1/8".

GERMINATING

Time 10–21 days.
Requirements Darkness and 70°–75°F.

TRANSPLANTING

Time Early spring, when soil is cool and a light frost is still possible, or early autumn.
Spacing *Small species:* 12"–15". *Large species:* 18"–24".
Light Full sun or very light shade.
Soil Prefers average, well drained, with a pH level of 5.5–7.0; will tolerate poor, dry soil. *E. purpurea* can be used successfully in xeriscaping.

CARING FOR PLANTS

Easy. For best results, water plants regularly and leave undisturbed once established. Susceptible to powdery mildew, which can be minimized by regular watering during dry spells, keeping leaves as dry as possible. Cut flowering stems to the ground in late autumn or leave seed heads standing for winter interest and to feed birds.

PROPAGATING

Divide in spring north of Zone 7 (in early autumn in the South), take root cuttings in spring, or grow from seed. Plants self-seed.

COMBINATIONS

Hemerocallis, *Liatris*, *Monarda*, *Platycodon*.

Echinops

HP | Zn 3–9

Globe thistle

p. 392

*These unusual-looking perennials are grown for their display of spiky blue or white globes borne atop fleshy white wands. Their leaves are coarse and spiny. Plants are 3′–5′ tall and useful at the back of the border, where their flowers provide an interesting contrast to those of many other plants. (*E. ritro *is smaller: to 2′.)*

Type Hardy perennial
Zone 3–9, H 9–1
Flowering Season Summer to late autumn, depending on species

SOWING

Indoors 2–3 weeks before last frost.
Outdoors After last frost.
Depth Just cover.

GERMINATING

Time 15–60 days.
Requirements 65°–75°F.

TRANSPLANTING

Time After last frost.
Spacing 24″–36″.
Light Full sun or part shade.
Soil Tolerant of almost any soil but must have good drainage. A pH level of 5.5–7.0 is preferred. *E. exaltatus* is very drought tolerant and a good choice for xeriscaping.

CARING FOR PLANTS

Easy. Water during very dry weather and cut back to ground level in autumn. Tall species and plants grown in very rich soil will require staking. Replace every 3–4 years, when plants begin to deteriorate.

PROPAGATING

Divide in spring (in autumn in Zones 7–9), take root cuttings in spring, or grow from seed. Plants self-seed.

COMBINATIONS

Crocosmia, Malva, Monarda, Perovskia, Verbena bonariensis.

Echium

Bi, TP* | Zn 3–10

p. 392

These shrublike plants grow 1′–8′ tall, the best species having narrow, gray-green leaves that create an interesting, spiky texture. Flowers may be stunning bottlebrushes of deepest blue or pretty cups in shades of purple or pink. Use them as an edging or in the border.

Type Biennial or tender perennial; often grown as an annual
Zone *Perennial:* 9–10; *Biennial:* 3–8 (see species list, p. 451); grown as an annual in Zones 1–8; prefers mild, dry climates
Flowering Season Spring to early summer

SOWING

Indoors 6–8 weeks before planting out, in peat pots.
Outdoors Autumn in Zones 9–10, elsewhere in spring.
Depth 1/4″.

GERMINATING

Time 7–21 days.
Requirements 60°–70°F.

TRANSPLANTING

Time Spring, when temperatures remain above 40°F.
Spacing *Small species:* 8″–10″. *Large species:* 18″–24″.
Light Full sun to part shade.
Soil Tolerant of wet or dry soil but prefers good drainage and a pH level of 6.5–7.0. Rich soil produces lush foliage with few flowers. *E. lycopsis* is suitable for xeriscaping.

CARING FOR PLANTS

Water during very dry spells. *Echium* is short lived and needs to be replaced regularly, but it may become invasive if allowed to self-seed. Do not move established plants.

PROPAGATING

Take cuttings or grow from seed. Plants self-seed.

COMBINATIONS

Agrostis, Antirrhinum, Artemisia, Calendula, Centaurea, Dimorphotheca, Lavandula, Linum, Phacelia.

CAUTION

Contact may cause skin irritation; harmful if eaten.

Emilia (syn. *Cacalia*)

A | Zn 3–10

Tassel flower

p. 392

Wiry, unkempt annuals, these 18"–24" tall plants are grown for the small scarlet balls that bloom all summer on long thin stems. They are colorful plants for the border and ideal cut flowers.

E

Type Annual
Zone 3–10, H 9–1; prefers cool temperatures
Flowering Season Summer to early autumn

SOWING

Indoors 6–8 weeks before planting out, in peat pots.
Outdoors *Zones 3–7:* 2–3 weeks before last frost. *Zones 8–10:* Autumn.
Depth Just cover.

GERMINATING

Time 8–15 days.
Requirements Darkness and 60°–70°F.

TRANSPLANTING

Time 2–3 weeks after last frost.
Spacing 8"–10".
Light Full sun.
Soil Average to dry, well drained. *E. coccinea* is suitable for xeriscaping.

CARING FOR PLANTS

Easy. For more abundant blooms, keep plants somewhat crowded and deadhead often. Do not move.

PROPAGATING

Grow from seed only.

Endymion See *Hyacinthoides*

Epigaea (syn. *Orphanidesia*)

HP | Zn 3–9

The Epigaea *genus comprises two species of prostrate, evergreen subshrubs, one of which,* E. repens, *is native to the eastern United States. Commonly known as ground laurel, mayflower, or trailing arbutus, plants have large, dark, oval leaves that make an elegant backdrop for their clusters of cup-shaped white or shell pink flowers. These are charming plants for the woodland garden. Because they are endangered or rare in many areas, it is important to ascertain that you are purchasing nursery-propagated plants or seeds. See p. 11 for information on purchasing endangered plants.*

Type Hardy perennial
Zone 3–9, H 9–1
Flowering Season Spring

SOWING

Indoors Start seed outdoors.
Outdoors As soon as ripe seed is available, usually in July.
Depth ¼".

GERMINATING

Time 30+ days.
Requirements Extremely difficult. It is essential to use a sterile growing medium.

TRANSPLANTING

Time Set out purchased plants in early spring or early autumn.
Spacing 8"–12".
Light Part to full shade.
Soil Slightly sandy or gritty, very acid (pH level of 4.0–5.0). *E. repens* is a good choice for xeriscaping in its native northern and Mid Atlantic states.

CARING FOR PLANTS

Difficult to establish but easy to maintain once this is done. Provide a permanent mulch of pine needles or oak leaves. Do not allow young plants to dry out, and do not disturb or cultivate around roots.

PROPAGATING

Take softwood cuttings in late summer, divide in spring in the North (in autumn south of Zone 6), or grow from seed. Division may be less successful. Plants grown from seed will bloom in 3 years.

Epilobium (syn. *Chamaenerion*)

HP | Zn 2–9 | Full sun, Partial shade | Dry soil, Ordinary soil

Willow herb

p. 392

Epilobium *is a large genus of perennials, many of which are too weedy for the garden. Desirable species are either erect clumps, 4"–8" high, with neat, attractive leaves and white or red funnel-shaped flowers, or large upright plants of 3'–6' bearing terminal spikes of tiny pink or white blooms. Use small species for edging rock gardens and tall species for borders or wildflower gardens.*

Type Hardy perennial
Zone 2–9, H 8–1 (see species list, p. 451)
Flowering Season Summer to fall, depending on species

SOWING

Indoors Start seed outdoors only.
Outdoors Autumn, as soon as ripe seed is available.
Depth ⅛".

GERMINATING

Time 14–30 days.
Requirements Sow seed in flats, sink in the ground against a north-facing wall, and cover with glass. Moisten soil occasionally, if necessary. Transplant seedlings 6 weeks after germinating.

TRANSPLANTING

Time Spring.
Spacing 12"–24".
Light Sun or part shade.
Soil Dry, stony, with a pH level of 6.0–7.0. Plants grown in moist soil develop a weedy appearance.

CARING FOR PLANTS

Easy. Deadhead diligently to avoid unwanted self-seeding; ungroomed plants will take over the garden.

PROPAGATING

Divide in early spring, take softwood cuttings in spring, or grow from seed. Many species self-seed.

COMBINATIONS

Alcea, Heucherella, Linaria.

Epimedium

HP | Zn 4–9 | Partial shade, Full shade | Dry soil, Ordinary soil, Moist soil

Barrenwort, Bishop's hat, Bishop's mitre

p. 392

Shy and lovely, these modest perennials bear handsome deciduous or evergreen leaves, which are divided into heart-shaped leaflets. These leaflets, along with clusters of complex flowers, are held on the slenderest of stems; 6"–18" tall. Blooms may be white, pink, red, or yellow. The mid-green leaves often are marked with maroon in spring. Use these plants as a ground cover in shady spots, rock gardens, or mixed shade plantings.

Type Hardy perennial
Zone 4–9, H 8–1
Flowering Season Spring

SOWING

Indoors Start seed outdoors.
Outdoors Collect seed just before it is dispersed, when it is still green.
Depth ¼".

GERMINATING

Requirements Seed requires cool temperatures (about 50°F) to germinate. Sow seed in a cold frame, pricking out to individual containers as soon as seedlings are big enough to handle. Grow seedlings on in the cold frame or indoors over their first winter.

TRANSPLANTING

Time Set out purchased plants after last frost in spring or early autumn. Plants grown from seed should be moved to their final position in the garden in mid- to late summer where summers are mild; in early autumn in warmer areas.
Spacing 6"–12".
Light Part to full shade. Tolerates sun if soil is rich, moist, and acid.
Soil Prefers moist, well drained, with a pH level of 5.5–7.0; once plants are established, they will tolerate dry soil. Add generous amounts of organic matter.

CARING FOR PLANTS

Where cultural conditions are met, these are good spreaders without being invasive. Where conditions are not to their liking, it will be many years before your plants resemble the photographs in nursery catalogs. Cut back scraggly leaves in late winter before flower buds appear. Water during dry spells.

PROPAGATING

Divide in spring north of Zone 7 (in autumn in the South) or grow from seed. Plants grown from seed will usually bloom in their first year.

COMBINATIONS

Bergenia, Dicentra, Helleborus, Hosta, woodland *Phlox.*

Eragrostis

A, HP | Zn 3–10

Love grass

p. 392

Here's a graceful ornamental grass with fine, arching leaves of pale green and airy flower spikes. It grows 3'–4' tall. Use it in plantings of mixed grasses or in contrast with coarse-textured plants.

Type Annual, hardy perennial
Zone *Annual:* 3–10. *Perennial:* 5–10 (see species list, pp. 451 and 481)
Flowering Season Late spring to autumn, depending on species

SOWING

Indoors 6–8 weeks before planting out.
Outdoors After last frost.
Depth Surface.

GERMINATING

Time 21 days.
Requirements Light and 60°–75°F.

TRANSPLANTING

Time After last frost.
Spacing 24". Allow very large species more room or plant singly.
Light Full sun.
Soil Fertile, well drained. *E. spectabilis* and *E. trichodes* are suitable selections for xeriscaping.

CARING FOR PLANTS

Easy. Site plants in a sheltered location to avoid damage to the delicate flowers from wind and rain. Water regularly for best results; keep direct spray off plants. In late winter, cut back perennials to no less than 8"–12"—more than this will weaken plants. Cut flowers for drying before seed is fully ripe.

PROPAGATING

Annual: Grow from seed. Plants self-seed. *Perennial:* Divide in spring or grow from seed.

Eranthis

HP | Zn 4–9

Winter aconite

p. 392

A low-growing, mat-forming perennial, Eranthis *bears solitary, stalkless, cup-shaped, bright yellow flowers on a whorl of green, leaflike bracts. Mass them under shrubs or throughout a woodland garden.*

Type Hardy perennial
Zone 4–9, H 9–1
Flowering Season Late winter to early spring

SOWING

Indoors See Germinating, Requirements.
Outdoors See Germinating, Requirements.
Depth *Seed:* Just cover. *Tuber:* Soak for 24 hours and plant at a depth of 3"–5".

GERMINATING

Time 30–365 days.
Requirements *Autumn sowing:* Sow seed in flats, sink in the ground against a north-facing wall, and cover with glass. Moisten soil occasionally, if necessary. Bring indoors in spring to 60°–70°F. *Spring sowing:* Sow seed in flats with moistened medium, secure in plastic bags, and refrigerate for 2–3 weeks. Sink flats in the ground in a shady location, covering with glass. Transplant seedlings as they appear.

TRANSPLANTING

Time Late summer to early autumn.
Spacing 3"–4".
Light Likes full sun in winter and early spring when plants are growing and blooming, but light shade is fine the rest of the year.
Soil Ordinary, humus-rich, slightly moist.

CARING FOR PLANTS

Keep soil moist during the growing season. Mark plant locations, as aconites die back completely in summer. Do not disturb.

PROPAGATING

Divide clumps immediately after flowering, or grow from seed. Plants self-seed. Plants grown from seed will not flower for 3–4 years.

COMBINATIONS

Chionadoxa, Galanthus, Hamamelis.

Eremurus

HP | Zn 5–9 | Full sun; Dry soil; Ordinary soil

Desert candle, Foxtail lily, King's spear

These interesting perennials have tufts of narrow, straplike leaves and 2'–6' stalks that bear thick, showy racemes of tiny white, pink, or yellow flowers. They contrast nicely in the border with more horizontal plants.

Type Hardy perennial
Zone 5–9, H 9–5 (see species list, p. 451)
Flowering Season Late spring to early summer

SOWING

Indoors Late winter to early spring.
Outdoors Autumn.
Depth *Seed:* Just cover. *Roots:* 4"–6".

GERMINATING

Time 30–365 days.
Requirements Difficult. *Indoor sowing:* Sow seed in peat pots, secure in plastic bags, and refrigerate for 2–3 weeks. Provide 55°–60°F thereafter. *Outdoor sowing:* Sow seed in flats, sink in the ground against a north-facing wall, and cover with glass. Remove glass when seeds sprout.

TRANSPLANTING

Time Autumn. Handle roots carefully, as they are brittle and break easily.
Spacing *Small species:* 12"–18". *Large species:* 36".
Light Full sun.
Soil Prepare an 18" planting hole for each plant and backfill with one-third good soil, one-third well-rotted cow manure, and one-third peat, well mixed. Set roots 4"–6" deep.

CARING FOR PLANTS

Site plants away from damaging winds. Water well during the growing season, then cease during dormancy. Top-dress in spring with well-rotted manure. Mark location of plants after flowering, as foliage dies back completely. Divide carefully every 5 years to rejuvenate, but otherwise disturb roots as little as possible.

PROPAGATING

Carefully divide in late summer or grow from seed. Plants grown from seed take up to 6 years to flower.

COMBINATIONS

Berberis atropurpurea, Lychnis, Papaver, Pelargonium.

Erigeron

HP | Zn 2–9

Fleabane

p. 393

This genus of North American native plants resembles the Aster *in appearance. It has neat foliage and fine-petaled, daisylike flowers of pink, purple, white, yellow, or orange, with yellow eyes. It grows 4"–36" tall and makes an excellent edging or border plant.*

Type Hardy perennial
Zone 2–9, H 8–5 (see species list, p. 451)
Flowering Season Early summer to early autumn, depending on species

SOWING

Indoors 8–10 weeks before planting out.
Outdoors Early spring or early autumn.
Depth Surface.

GERMINATING

Time 15–50 days.
Requirements 55°F.

TRANSPLANTING

Time Early spring, when soil is cool and a light frost is still possible, or early autumn.
Spacing *Dwarf species:* 9". *Larger species:* 12"–18".
Light Full sun or very light shade.
Soil Ordinary, well drained. Plants are quite drought tolerant and suitable for xeriscaping.

CARING FOR PLANTS

Easy. Feed lightly, deadhead regularly, and cut back stems to ground in autumn. Divide every 3 years.

PROPAGATING

Divide in spring in Zones 2–6 (in early autumn in Zones 7–9) or grow from seed.

COMBINATIONS

Echinacea, ornamental grasses, *Leucanthemum, Oenothera, Phlox, Santolina.*

Erinus

HP | Zn 4–9

Fairy foxglove

p. 393

Erinus *is a small genus containing low-growing, tufted perennials with tiny leaves and masses of small, flat flowers in pink, white, red, or purple. The flowers add color to rock gardens or dry stone walls.*

Type Short-lived hardy perennial
Zone 4–9, H 7–1; not tolerant of high heat and humidity
Flowering Season Late winter to summer, depending on species

SOWING

Indoors 6–8 weeks before planting out.
Outdoors Early spring.
Depth Surface.

GERMINATING

Time 20–25 days.
Requirements Easy. 65°–75°F.

TRANSPLANTING

Time After last frost.
Spacing *Small species:* 3"–4". *Large species:* 6"–8".
Light Sun, but with some shade in the afternoon where summers are hot.
Soil Well drained, sandy, or gritty. Poor drainage is often the cause of plants failing in winter.

CARING FOR PLANTS

Easy. Improve drainage by mulching with fine gravel or rock chips. Grow early-blooming species where summers are hot. These short-lived plants require frequent replacing.

PROPAGATING

Divide in autumn in the South (in spring north of Zone 7), take cuttings in early summer, or grow from seed. Plants self-seed, although rampant cross-fertilization results in unpredictable offspring.

COMBINATIONS

Bellis, Iberis, Lunaria, Tulipa.

Eriophorum

HP | Zn 2–10 |  

Cotton grass

These ornamental grasses are grown for their long-lasting, cottony white flowers held on stiff stems. The grasses are 1'–3' tall. Use them in bog or waterside plantings.

Type Hardy perennial
Zone 2–10 (see species list, p. 451)
Flowering Season Summer

SOWING

Indoors Best started *in situ.*
Outdoors Early spring to mid-spring.
Depth Surface.

GERMINATING

Time 21 days.
Requirements Light and 60°–75°F.

TRANSPLANTING

Time Early spring.
Spacing 12"–18".
Light Full sun or part shade.
Soil Acid and always moist. Will grow in shallow water.

CARING FOR PLANTS

Keep soil moist at all times. Cut back severely in early spring.

PROPAGATING

Divide in spring or start from seed.

Erodium

HP | Zn 6–10

Heron's bill, Stork's bill

p. 393

These low-growing perennials (3"–18" tall) are similar in appearance to Geranium. Erodium *leaves are finely dissected, sometimes with a silver or bluish cast. Flowers are cup-shaped and pink, white, or yellow, often veined. Use them as rock garden and border plants.*

Type Hardy perennial
Zone 6–10, H 9–6 (see species list, p. 451)
Flowering Season Early to mid summer

SOWING

Indoors Start seed outdoors.
Outdoors Autumn, as soon as seed is ripe.
Depth ⅛".

GERMINATING

Time 14–21 days.
Requirements Easy. 55°F.

TRANSPLANTING

Time After last frost.
Spacing *Small species:* 6"–8". *Large species:* 12"–18".
Light Sun or light shade.
Soil Sandy or gritty, slightly sweet. *E. cicutarium* is a suitable plant for xeriscaping.

CARING FOR PLANTS

Improve drainage by mulching with fine gravel; provide additional organic mulch in autumn where winters are cold. Protect hairy-leaved species from overhead water. *Erodium* species can become weedy.

PROPAGATING

Divide in spring, take cuttings in summer, or grow from seed.

COMBINATIONS

Achillea, Bergenia, Dictamnus.

Erpetin See *Viola (perennial)*

Eryngium

Bi, HP | Zn 3–8

Eryngo, Sea holly

p. 393

This large genus of prickly perennials is recognized by its spiny leaves, which are sometimes silver or blue. It has spiky blue or white blooms, made up of a small cone-shaped flower head, surrounded by decorative, pointy bracts. Plants are 1'–4' tall and add an unusual texture to the border.

Type Biennial, hardy perennial
Zone 3–10, H 9–4 (see species list, pp. 451–452)
Flowering Season Midsummer to late summer

SOWING

Indoors See Germinating, Requirements.
Outdoors See Germinating, Requirements.
Depth Surface.

GERMINATING

Time 5–90 days.
Requirements *Autumn sowing:* Sow seed in flats, sink in the ground against a north-facing wall, and cover with glass. Moisten soil occasionally, if necessary. Bring indoors in spring to 65°–75°F. *Spring sowing:* Sow seed in flats with moistened medium, place in a plastic bag, and refrigerate. After 2–3 weeks, remove and sink in the ground in a shady location, covering with glass. Transplant seedlings as they appear.

TRANSPLANTING

Time After last frost.
Spacing *Small species:* 12"–18". *Large species:* 24"–36".
Light Full sun.
Soil Light, very well drained, rather poor, with a pH level between 5.0 and 7.0. *E.* × *zabelii* and *E. bourgatii* are suitable for xeriscaping.

CARING FOR PLANTS

Easy, needing very little care. Water only during very dry spells. Large species grown in rich soil may require staking. Carefully mulch around crowns with fine gravel to keep plants dry over winter. Long taproots make transplanting difficult.

PROPAGATING

Take root cuttings in spring or start from seed.

COMBINATIONS

Helenium, Knautia, Leucanthemum, Rudbeckia, Sidalcea.

Erysimum (syn. *Cheiranthus*)

A, Bi, HP | Zn 3–9

Wallflower

p. 393

Plants in this genus range from 6" to 3' tall. They have lance-shaped leaves and fragrant, four-petaled flowers in almost every color. The most commonly grown is E. cheiri *(syn.* Cheiranthus cheiri*), an upright, bushy plant of 6"–30". It is grown for the tangle of blossoms that cover each stalk for weeks.* Erysimum *is a satisfying plant for the rock garden or for borders.*

Type Annual, biennial, hardy perennial
Zone 3–9, H 8–1 (see species list, p. 452); flowering inhibited by hot weather. *E. cheiri* is often grown as an annual or biennial in Zones 3–7
Flowering Season Spring or summer, depending on species

SOWING

Indoors *Annual and biennial:* 4–8 weeks before planting out. *Perennial:* 8–10 weeks before planting out.
Outdoors *Annual:* Early spring when soil is cool and a light frost is still possible. In Zones 8–10, seeds also may be started in early autumn. *Biennial and perennial:* Early spring or early autumn.
Depth ¼".

GERMINATING

Time 5–30 days.
Requirements 65°–75°F. Very susceptible to damping-off; sow seeds in vermiculite, and water only from below.

TRANSPLANTING

Time *Annual:* North of Zone 9, after last frost (autumn in Zones 9–10). *Biennial and perennial:* Early spring when soil is cool and a light frost is still possible, or early autumn.
Spacing *Dwarf species:* 4"–10". *Medium or tall species:* 12"–18".
Light Full sun to light shade.
Soil Ordinary, well drained, with a pH level of 5.0–8.0; *E. cheiri* requires neutral or slightly alkaline soil. Withstands dry soil. *E. linifolium* and *E. perofskianum* are well suited to xeriscaping.

CARING FOR PLANTS

Easy. Pinch out tips to encourage bushiness and deadhead regularly. *E. cheiri* may be uprooted and discarded when blooming is finished. Mulch in autumn.

PROPAGATING

Take cuttings in mid-spring or grow from seed. Plants self-seed.

COMBINATIONS

Achillea, Aquilegia, Delphinium, annual *Dianthus,* purple *Heuchera, Linum, Myosotis, Stachys, Tulipa.*

Erythaea See *Centaurium*

Erythronium

HP | Zn 4–9 | Partial shade, Full shade | Moist soil

Adder's tongue, Dog's-tooth, Dog's-tooth violet, Fawn lily, Trout lily

Lovely woodland wildflowers, including several North American natives. They boast handsome, mottled basal leaves and dainty, pendant, pink, white, purple, or yellow lilylike flowers with reflexed petals. They grow 6"–12" tall, and are stunning in the wild garden or rock garden.

Type Hardy perennial
Zone 4–9, H 9–1 (see species list, p. 452)
Flowering Season Early spring to mid summer

SOWING

Indoors See Germinating, Requirements.
Outdoors *Seed:* See Germinating, Requirements. *Bulb:* Autumn.
Depth *Seed:* ⅛". *Tuber:* 3"–4".

GERMINATING

Time 1–18 months.
Requirements Difficult. *Autumn sowing:* Sow seed in flats, sink in the ground against a north-facing wall, and cover with glass. Check soil moisture occasionally. Bring indoors in spring to 50°–60°F. *Spring sowing:* Sow seed in containers, secure in plastic bags, and refrigerate. After 2–3 weeks, remove flats and sink in the ground in a shady location, covering with glass. Transplant seedlings as they appear.

TRANSPLANTING

Time After last frost.
Spacing 3"–6".
Light Part to full shade.
Soil Moist, rich, woodland soil that is not too acid.

CARING FOR PLANTS

Easy. Do not allow roots to dry out in summer or winter. Plants disappear shortly after blooming and their locations should be marked to avoid unintentional disturbance. Top-dress in late summer with leaf mold. Divide every 3–4 years, but otherwise leave undisturbed.

PROPAGATING

Dig and replant offsets in early autumn or grow from seed.

COMBINATIONS

Anemone, Dicentra, ferns, *Fritillaria, Trillium, Viola.*

Eschscholzia

HP* | Zn 8–10

California poppy

p. 393

Native to the western U. S., Eschscholzia *is known for its feathery foliage and slim stalks bearing cup-shaped flowers, most commonly orange, yellow, or white. These cheerful, 8"–24" tall plants exude optimism. Grow them in the border or wildflower meadow.*

Type Short-lived hardy perennial; usually grown as an annual
Zone 8–10, H 9–1; most species are grown as annuals in Zones 1–10; performs most successfully in the moderate temperatures of the Pacific Coast
Flowering Season Mid-spring to mid-autumn, depending on species

SOWING

Indoors 2–3 weeks before last frost, in peat pots. Most successful when started outdoors.
Outdoors After last frost, or autumn through early spring where winters are mild.
Depth ¼".

GERMINATING

Time 14–21 days.
Requirements 60°–65°F.

TRANSPLANTING

Time After last frost.
Spacing 8"–10".
Light Full sun.
Soil Ordinary, well drained; tolerant of dry soil. The species *E. californica* may be successfully used when xeriscaping.

CARING FOR PLANTS

Easy. Water and deadhead regularly to prolong blooming. Difficult to transplant.

PROPAGATING

Grow from seed. Plants self-seed.

COMBINATIONS

Allium, Anchusa, Convolvulus, Veronica.

Eucharidium See *Clarkia*

Eucomis

HB* | Zn 8–10

Pineapple flower, Pineapple lily

p. 393

Genus of bulbs, most of which have wide, sword-shaped leaves and thick, erect stems bearing bottlebrush-shaped flower heads packed with small, star-shaped flowers of green or white; 2'–3' tall. Use Eucomis *in the border or in containers.*

Type Hardy bulb
Zone 8–10, H 10–1; grown as an annual in Zones 3–7
Flowering Season Summer

SOWING

Indoors Early spring.
Outdoors *Seed:* Spring. *Bulb:* Spring.
Depth *Seed:* Just cover. *Bulb:* 4"–6".

GERMINATING

Time 20–25 days.
Requirements Easy. 70°–75°F.

TRANSPLANTING

Time Spring.
Spacing 10"–12".
Light Sun.
Soil Average, well drained.

CARING FOR PLANTS

Easy. During growing season, keep soil moist; feed occasionally with weak fertilizer. Watch for slugs and snails (they like the fleshy leaves). Water less during dormancy, but do not allow soil to dry out completely. Alternate periods of wet and dry may induce repeat blooming. North of Zone 8, lift bulbs and store over winter in vermiculite in a cool, dry place.

PROPAGATING

Divide in spring or grow from seed. Plants grown from seed will flower in 5–6 years.

COMBINATIONS

Effective in drifts underplanted with low annuals.

Eunomia See *Aethionema*

Eupatorium

HP | Zn 3–10

Hemp agrimony

p. 394

Grow these late-flowering perennials for their purple, pink, red, or white flowers, carried in fuzzy, rounded, or flat-topped clusters above dense, mid-green foliage; 2'–10' tall. Use them in borders or wildflower gardens.

Type Hardy perennial
Zone 3–10, H 9–1 (see species list, p. 452)
Flowering Season Summer to autumn

SOWING

Indoors 8–10 weeks before planting out.
Outdoors Autumn, as soon as ripe seed is available.
Depth Just cover.

GERMINATING

Time 30–90 days.
Requirements 55°F.

TRANSPLANTING

Time After last spring frost or in early autumn.
Spacing *Small species:* 12"–24". *Large species:* 24"–48".
Light Sun or light shade.
Soil Prefer ordinary, somewhat moist, with a pH level of 5.0–6.0.

CARING FOR PLANTS

Easy. Keep plants mulched in summer. Cut back to ground in autumn. Divide every 3 years.

PROPAGATING

Divide in spring (in autumn in Zones 7–10) or grow from seed. Plants self-seed. Plants grown from seed will flower in their first year.

COMBINATIONS

Aster, Campanula, Heliopsis, Lobelia, Thalictrum.

Euphorbia

ANNUAL, BIENNIAL

A, Bi | Zn 3–10

Spurge

p. 394

Euphorbia cyathophora, E. lathyris, *and* E. marginata *are some of the annuals and biennials in this genus. Grown for their distinctive green-and-red or green-and-white foliage, these shrubby, 18"– 36" plants make good foils for contrasting colors and textures.*

Type Annual or biennial; often grown as an annual
Zone 3–10, H 12–1; prefers warm temperatures
Flowering Season Midsummer

SOWING

Indoors 6–8 weeks before last frost.
Outdoors After last frost, but only where summers are long and hot.
Depth 1/4".

GERMINATING

Time 10–28 days.
Requirements 70°–75°F.

TRANSPLANTING

Time After last frost; usually best to wait until the temperatures remain above 50°F.
Spacing 12"–18".
Light Full sun.
Soil Tolerant of many conditions, but most require well-drained soil; *E. marginata* is useful for xeriscaping. See species list p. 452 for individual preferences.

CARING FOR PLANTS

Easy. Water well during the growing season. Do not plant near ponds, as the juice of *Euphorbia* may be poisonous to fish.

PROPAGATING

Grow from seed. Plants self-seed.

COMBINATIONS

Coreopsis, Nigella, Primula.

CAUTION

Contact with sap may cause skin irritation.

PERENNIAL HP | Zn 3–10

Spurge

p. 394

The Euphorbia *genus includes a great number of perennial species, many of which are useful for their strongly horizontal foliage and the brightly colored bracts that surround insignificant flowers. Plants are 6"–36" tall and useful as edging, in borders, and in rock gardens.*

Type Hardy perennial
Zone 3–10, H 12–1 (see species list, p. 452); the following species do not like hot, humid climates: *E.* × *martinii, E. myrsinites, E. palustris, E. polychroma, E. rigida, E. seguieriana* spp. *niciciana.*
Flowering Season Spring, summer, or autumn, depending on species

SOWING

Indoors Prechilled seed 6–8 weeks before last frost, in peat pots.
Outdoors After last frost.
Depth ⅛".

GERMINATING

Time 10–28 days.
Requirements Chill seed in refrigerator for 7 days, soak in warm water for 2 hours, then sow and place where temperatures remain a constant 65°–70°F.

TRANSPLANTING

Time After last frost.
Spacing *Small species:* 12". *Large species:* 12"–24".
Light Full sun to part shade. *E. amygdaloides* grows in full shade.
Soil Most will do well in average to poor soil with a pH level of 6.0–7.0. *E. palustris* requires moist soil. *E. myrsinites* is happy in dry soils and can be used in xeriscaping.

CARING FOR PLANTS

Easy. Water well during growing season, but allow soil to remain fairly dry otherwise. Some species may become invasive. Do not plant near ponds, as the plant's sap may be poisonous to fish.

PROPAGATING

Carefully divide in spring in the North (in autumn south of Zone 6), take cuttings after flowering, or grow from seed. Plants self-seed.

COMBINATIONS

Aconitum, Bergenia, Geranium, Iris, Limnanthes, Phlox subulata, Phormium; in front of *Clematis* or climbing roses.

CAUTION

Harmful to humans and pets if eaten; contact with sap may cause skin irritation.

Eustoma (syn. *Lisianthus*)

Bi, TP* | Zn 9–10

A North American native, Eustoma *has upright stems holding bell-shaped flowers, often double, in shades of purple, pink, and cream. They make extraordinary cut flowers and are also lovely in the border or as container plants. They grow 6"–24" tall.*

Type Biennial, short-lived tender perennial, usually grown as an annual; performs most successfully where summers are hot
Zone 9–10, H 12–1; grown as an annual in Zones 5–10
Flowering Season Summer

SOWING

Indoors 10–12 weeks before planting out, in peat pots.
Outdoors Early spring, only where growing season is very long.
Depth Surface.

GERMINATING

Time 10–21 days.
Requirements Difficult. Light and 65°–75°F.

TRANSPLANTING

Time Transplant 6" seedlings in spring when temperatures remain above 40°F.
Spacing 12".
Light Full sun.
Soil Moist, well drained.

CARING FOR PLANTS

Pinch out young plants to increase flower production. Water sparingly, keeping blossoms dry; plants will not flourish where summer rainfall is heavy. Dislikes transplanting.

PROPAGATING

Grow from seed.

Evolvulus

HP | Zn 8–10

p. 394

The one commonly available member of this genus, E. pilosus, *is a charming prostrate plant with silvery green leaves and 1" blue flowers, miniatures of their cousins, the morning glories. Lovely in hanging baskets or containers, or edging a path or patio.*

Type Hardy perennial; often grown as an annual
Zone 8–10; grown as an annual in Zones 4–7; likes extreme heat
Flowering Season Late spring to early autumn

TRANSPLANTING

Time After last frost.
Spacing 12"–18"
Light Sun to light shade.
Soil Tolerates poor and dry, but prefers moist, well drained with a pH of 5.6–6.5.

CARING FOR PLANTS

Tough, easy-to-grow plants, *Evolvulus* require little care. Plants can be dug in autumn, potted up, and overwintered indoors.

PROPAGATING

Take stem cuttings in spring to early summer and root in water or moist soil (easy) or grow from seed.

COMBINATIONS

Yellow *Lantana, Lobularia, Ophiopogon nigrescens,* or around the base of low azaleas, dwarf boxwood, dwarf *Deutzia,* or other low shrubs.

Farfugium

HP | Zn 7–9

p. 394

Until recently this small genus of two evergreen perennials belonged to the genus Ligularia. *Leaves are handsome, thick, round, and glossy, some with creamy freckles, 4"–15" across. Tall stalks bear bright yellow daisylike flowers late in the season.*

Type Hardy perennial
Zone 7–10, H 9–7
Flowering Season Late summer to autumn

SOWING

Indoors 6–8 weeks before planting out.
Outdoors Early spring, when soil is cool and a light frost is still possible, or early autumn.
Depth Surface.

GERMINATING

Time 14–42 days.
Requirements 55°–65°F.

TRANSPLANTING

Time Spring.
Spacing 18"–24".
Light Light shade in the North; full shade where summers are hot.
Soil Fertile, well drained, very moist.

CARING FOR PLANTS

Mulch in spring and water regularly during dry spells. Shelter from strong winds. North of Zone 7, plants can be dug in autumn, potted up, and grown indoors in a bright location, away from direct sunlight.

PROPAGATING

Divide in spring or grow from seed.

COMBINATIONS

Small species combine well with other foliage plants such as *Caladium, Hosta,* and *Solenostemon.* Mix larger species with *Lythrum, Phormium, Tradescantia.*

Felicia (syn. *Charieis*)

TP* | Zn 9–10

Blue daisy, Blue marguerite, Kingfisher daisy

Blue, daisylike flowers with yellow eyes cover these pretty 6"–18" plants all summer long, making them useful for containers, edging or borders.

Type Tender perennial; often grown as an annual
Zone 9–10, H 12–1. Grown as an annual in cooler zones. Must have mild temperatures and performs most successfully on the West Coast and in the northern states
Flowering Season Summer through autumn

SOWING

Indoors Prechilled seed 6–8 weeks before last frost.
Outdoors After last frost.
Depth Just cover.

GERMINATING

Time 30 days.
Requirements Place seed together with moistened growing medium in a plastic bag, seal lightly, and refrigerate for 3 weeks. Provide 60°–70°F thereafter.

TRANSPLANTING

Time 2–3 weeks after last frost, when temperatures remain above 40°F.
Spacing *Small species:* 6". *Large species:* 12"–18".
Light Full sun.
Soil Ordinary, well drained; withstands dry soil and is useful for xeriscaping.

CARING FOR PLANTS

Easy. Water often during dry weather and protect from harsh winds.

PROPAGATING

Take cuttings in summer or early autumn or grow from seed.

COMBINATIONS

Helichrysum, Lilium, Lobularia.

Festuca

HP | Zn 4–9

Fescue

p. 394

Tufted ornamental grasses, many fescues display airy blue or gray foliage. Mass these 6"–18" tall grasses for best effect.

Type Hardy perennial
Zone 4–9, H 9–5; will not thrive where summers are hot and humid
Flowering Season Late spring to midsummer

SOWING

Indoors Not recommended.
Outdoors Early to mid-spring.
Depth Surface.

GERMINATING

Time 21 days.

TRANSPLANTING

Time Set out purchased plants in spring or autumn.
Spacing *Small species:* 8"–12". *Large species:* 18"–24".
Light Sun or part shade. Blue-leaved species will be a deeper blue when grown in full sun with dry soil.
Soil Rather dry, infertile soil will produce neater plants, although fescues are highly adaptive as long as they have good drainage. Most commercially available species can be used successfully in xeriscaping.

CARING FOR PLANTS

Easy. Water regularly for best results. Divide every 2–3 years. Where soil is heavy, plants will die back in the center and require more frequent division. Susceptible to rust.

PROPAGATING

Divide in spring or start from seed.

COMBINATIONS

Dianthus, Prunella, Sempervivum, Sisyrinchium.

Filipendula

Hp | Zn 3–9 | ☼ ◐ | dry, ordinary, moist soil

Meadowsweet, Dropwort

p. 394–395

This small genus of lovely and unique perennials is valued for its highly decorative foliage and flowers. Pink or white plumes are held above fernlike leaves; plants grow from 2' to a towering 10'. Use them in any moist situation, from borders to woodlands.

Type Hardy perennial
Zone 3–9, H 9–1
Flowering Season Summer

SOWING

Indoors 8–10 weeks before planting out.
Outdoors Autumn, as soon as seed is ripe.
Depth Just cover.

GERMINATING

Time 30–90 days.
Requirements *Indoor sowing:* 55°–60°F. *Outdoor sowing:* Sow seed in flats, sink in ground against a north-facing wall, and cover with glass. Moisten soil occasionally, if necessary. Transplant seedlings to pots as they germinate; plant out in the garden in autumn.

TRANSPLANTING

Time After last frost.
Spacing 12"–24".
Light Sun or part shade. *F. ulmaria* must have part shade; *F. palmata* and *F. purpurea* should be planted in full sun only where soil is very moist.
Soil Moist, slightly alkaline, enriched with compost or manure. *F. vulgaris* will tolerate dry soil and can be used in xeriscaping.

CARING FOR PLANTS

Easy. Mulch with organic matter in spring to keep soil moist and again in autumn to protect roots. Support with twiggy branches pushed into the ground when spring growth begins; cut back to the ground in autumn.

PROPAGATING

Divide in early spring in the North (in autumn south of Zone 7) or grow from seed. Plants grown from seed will take 2 years to flower.

COMBINATIONS

Astilbe, Eupatorium, Geranium, Monarda, Papaver.

Foeniculum

HP | Zn 4–10 | ☼ ◐ | dry, ordinary soil

Fennel

p. 395

One of the many herbs with blooms that resemble Queen Anne's lace, fennel features feathery leaves and clusters of tiny yellow flowers in umbels atop 3'–5' stalks.

Type Hardy perennial; often grown as an annual
Zone 4–10, H 9–6; prefers cool climates
Flowering Season Late summer to mid-autumn

SOWING

Indoors 4–6 weeks before last frost, in peat pots. May not survive transplanting.
Outdoors Early spring, when soil is cool and a light frost is still possible.
Depth 1/8".

GERMINATING

Time 10–14 days.
Requirements Darkness and 65°F.

TRANSPLANTING

Time Spring or autumn.
Spacing 18".
Light Prefers full sun but will accept light shade.
Soil Well drained, somewhat dry, with a pH level between 6.0 and 8.0.

CARING FOR PLANTS

Easy. Remove flower heads after blooming to stimulate leaf production and curtail self-seeding; cut back stems in autumn. Use either fresh or dried leaves in cooking, cutting anytime after flower heads form. Or, harvest ripe seed in autumn, dry thoroughly, and store in an airtight container. Do not grow near dill, as cross-pollination will result.

PROPAGATING

Divide in early spring or grow from seed. Plants self-seed.

COMBINATIONS

Digitalis, Hosta, summer *Phlox, Sedum.*

Francoa

HP | Zn 7–10

Bridal wreath

p. 395

Rarely seen, clump-forming perennials, Francoa *bear wiry stalks with bottlebrush-shaped blooms packed with tiny pink or white flowers. Foliage hugs the ground, but flowering stems are 2′–3′ tall. Useful in borders.*

Type Hardy perennial
Zone 7–10, H 9–7; requires a temperate climate and is best suited to the West Coast
Flowering Season Summer

SOWING

Indoors See Germinating, Requirements.
Outdoors See Germinating, Requirements.
Depth Surface.

GERMINATING

Time 14–30 days.
Requirements *Autumn sowing:* Sow seed in flats, sink flats in ground against a north-facing wall, and cover with glass. Moisten soil occasionally, if necessary. Bring indoors in spring to 50°–55°F. *Spring sowing:* Sow seed in flats of moistened medium, place in plastic bags, and refrigerate. Remove after 2–3 weeks and sink in the ground in a shady location, covering with glass. Transplant seedlings as they appear.

TRANSPLANTING

Time After last frost.
Spacing 12″.
Light Full sun to light shade.
Soil Average, moist, with good drainage.

CARING FOR PLANTS

Easy. Mulch in spring to keep soil cool and moist.

PROPAGATING

Divide in spring or grow from seed.

Freesia

TB | Zn 9–10

Freesia

p. 395

Freesias' tender corms produce deliciously fragrant funnel-shaped flowers held in clusters on slender stalks. Plants are 12″–18″ high, flowers bright or subtle shades of yellow, orange, pink, red, purple, blue, or white. They are usually grown in containers.

Type Tender bulb
Zone 9–10, H 12–6; requires dry summers and cool, moist winters
Flowering Season Winter and spring

SOWING

Indoors Early spring.
Outdoors Start seed or corms outdoors *only* in Zones 9–10. *Seed:* After last frost. *Corm:* Autumn.
Depth *Seed:* ¼″. *Corm:* 1″–2″.

GERMINATING

Time 25–30 days.
Requirements Easy. Soak seed for 24 hours in warm water; provide 65°–75°F thereafter.

TRANSPLANTING

Time Early autumn.
Spacing 4″–6″.
Light Sun.
Soil Moist, well drained, amended with manure.

CARING FOR PLANTS

Easy. Water well before flowering begins, decrease watering significantly while plants are in bloom, and discontinue altogether after flowering. Plant freesias close together to support each other, or support with twiggy branches pushed into the ground when plants are young.

PROPAGATING

Plant offsets in autumn or grow from seed.

Fritillaria

HB | Zn 3–9

Fritillary

p. 395

This large genus of unusual and enchanting bulbs includes both small (4"–12") and large (2'–4') species, All sport delicate, downward-facing, bell-shaped flowers, giving an effect of shyness and begging for subtle placement in the garden. The orange, yellow, white, green, or deep plum flowers sometimes are marked with contrasting Some are suited to borders; others are most effective massed near the woodland edge.

Type Hardy bulb
Zone 3–9, H 9–1 (see species list, p. 453); most species do not like cold, wet winters
Flowering Season Spring

SOWING

Indoors See Germinating, Requirements.
Outdoors *Seed:* See Germinating, Requirements. *Bulb:* Late summer to early autumn.
Depth *Seed:* Just cover. *Small bulb:* 3"–4". *Large bulb:* 6"–8".

GERMINATING

Time 11–18 months.
Requirements Difficult. *Autumn sowing:* Sow seed in flats, sink in the ground against a north-facing wall, and cover with glass. Moisten soil occasionally, if necessary. Bring indoors in spring to 55°–60°F. *Spring sowing:* Sow seed in moistened medium, place in a plastic bag, and refrigerate. After 2–3 weeks, remove and sink in the ground in a shady location, covering with glass. Transplant seedlings as they appear.

TRANSPLANTING

Time Late summer to early autumn.
Spacing *Small species:* 4"–6". *Large species:* 9"–12".
Light Sun to light shade.
Soil Prefers rich, well-drained soil; F. meleagris is happier in damp soil. Surround bulb with coarse sand when planting.

CARING FOR PLANTS

Difficult. Mark location as plants die down after flowering. Mulch in winter. Divide every 3–5 years when crowding necessitates it.

PROPAGATING

Plant bulblets in autumn or grow from seed. Plants grown from seed will flower in 4–5 years.

COMBINATIONS

Combine tall species with ferns, *Hemerocallis, Iris, Myosotis, Scilla.* Short species make a magnificent display massed on their own.

Fuchsia

TP* | Zn 9–10

Fuchsia

p. 395

One of the loveliest flowers in the garden, fuchsias are prized for their abundant ballerina flowers with layered skirts, often bicolored, in intense shades of pink, purple, or red, or delicate pastel pinks and long, decorative stamens. Use in hanging baskets and containers.

Type Tender perennial ; often grown as an annual
Zone 9–10, H 12–9 (see species list, p. 453); grown as an annual in cooler zones. Most species do not do well in the heat of the South and Southwest, although single-flowered varieties are most heat tolerant, including *F. triphylla, F. boliviana, F. splendens, F.* 'Gartenmeister Bonstedt', *F.* 'Mrs. J. D. Fredericks', and the Angel Earrings series.
Flowering Season Summer through autumn

SOWING

Cultivars will not come true from seed.
Indoors 14–18 weeks before planting out.
Outdoors Spring.
Depth Surface.

GERMINATING

Time 21–120 days.
Requirements Soak seed for 3–4 days, then give light and 65°–85°F.

TRANSPLANTING

Time Early summer.
Spacing *Small species:* 12". *Medium species:* 2'–3'. *Tall species:* 4'–5'.
Light Full sun in cool summers, with more shade in warmer regions, especially in the afternoon.
Soil Moist, fertile, well drained.

CARING FOR PLANTS

Easy. Water regularly and deeply during dry spells and feed regularly throughout summer. Where plants are perennial, prune after flowering. Unhappy plants are highly susceptible to spider mites, mealybugs, whiteflies, and mildew; buds will drop if soil is too dry. Plants can be dug in autumn and grown as houseplants for winter in a cool, frost-free, humid location; prune in late winter. Or induce dormancy by bringing plants indoors before last frost, cutting back to just a few inches, and placing in a dark location at 40°F; keep soil almost dry.

PROPAGATING

Take softwood cuttings in spring, take stem cuttings in late summer, divide in spring or autumn, or grow from seed.

COMBINATIONS

Begonia, low *Campanula, Ipomoea batatas, Lobelia, Solenostemon.*

Gaillardia

A, HP | Zn 1–10 |  

Blanket flower

p. 395–396

Long-blooming plants with cheerful, daisylike flowers, bright yellow and/or orange blossoms with large, colorful eyes; perennial species are also available in red. Annuals are 6"–30"; perennials are 15"–36". Use either as edging, in borders, or in wildflower gardens.

Type Annual or short-lived hardy perennial
Zone *Annual:* 1–10, H 12–1. *Perennial:* 3–9, H 8–1. (See species list, p. 453.) Annuals perform well in dry heat but not humid heat. The perennial *G.* × *grandiflora* will not tolerate hot, humid summers
Flowering Season Summer through early autumn

SOWING

Indoors *Annual:* 4–6 weeks before last frost. *Perennial:* 6–8 weeks before planting out.
Outdoors *Annual:* After last frost; in autumn where winters are mild. *Perennial:* Spring.
Depth Surface.

GERMINATING

Time *Annual:* 7–20 days. *Perennial:* 15–20 days.
Requirements Light and 70°F.

TRANSPLANTING

Time *Annual:* After last frost. *Perennial:* Late spring, when soil is warm.
Spacing *Annual:* 12". *Perennial:* 12"–18".

Light Full sun.
Soil *Annual:* Ordinary, with a pH level of 6.0–7.0. *Perennial:* Prefers a moist, well-drained loam. Both tolerate poor, dry soil. Perennials are short lived in heavy soil. All perennial species are suitable for xeriscaping.

CARING FOR PLANTS

Annual: Feed when flowering begins; top-dress with manure once in summer. Deadhead regularly. Plants are susceptible to mildew, which can be avoided by watering regularly during dry spells, keeping leaves as dry as possible. *Perennial:* Easy. Feed just once in spring with manure; overfertilizing will weaken plants. Deadhead often and cut back completely in late summer to stimulate a second blooming. Provide support for tall species. Divide regularly to maintain vigor.

PROPAGATING

Annual: Grow from seed. Plants self-seed. *Perennial:* Divide in autumn in the South (in spring north of Zone 7), take root cuttings in spring, or grow from seed. Plants self-seed. Plants grown from seed will bloom in their first year.

COMBINATIONS

Annual: aster, coreopsis, *Hemerocallis, Rudbeckia, Salvia.* Perennial: *Linum, Salvia, Tagetes, Zinnia.*

Galanthus

HB | Zn 2–8

Snowdrop

p. 396

Bulbs in this genus are grown for their very early, nodding white flowers. Leaves are narrow and straplike; plants grow 2"–10" tall. Use them in abundance in the lawn, under shrubs, or in the woodland.

Type Hardy bulb
Zone 2–9, H 9–1 (see species list, p. 453)
Flowering Season Midwinter to late winter

SOWING

Indoors As soon as seed is ripe in spring.
Outdoors *Seed:* As soon as ripe seed is available in spring. *Bulb:* Late summer.
Depth *Seed:* ¼". *Bulb:* 3".

GERMINATING

Time Seed should germinate within 4 weeks.
Requirements 60°–65°F.

TRANSPLANTING

Time Summer, 1 year after sowing seed.
Spacing 3"–4".
Light Sun in winter, light shade throughout the rest of the year.
Soil Cool, moist, rich, somewhat heavy, with a pH level of 6.0–8.0.

CARING FOR PLANTS

Easy. Feed with bonemeal in early spring and water regularly, particularly while plants are in bloom. Allow leaves to wither before removing. Revitalize old plants by dividing in early autumn, but do not disturb otherwise.

PROPAGATING

Divide bulbs immediately after flowering (in early autumn south of Zone 6) or grow from seed. Plants self-seed. Bulbs grown from seed will flower in 3–4 years.

COMBINATIONS

Bergenia, Crocus, Cyclamen, Iris reticulata, early *Scilla, Skimmia.*

CAUTION

Bulbs are toxic if eaten.

G

Galega

HP | Zn 3–8

Goat's rue

An unusual, vigorous, upright perennial, goat's rue is rather untidy in overall appearance, with its compound leaves growing at awkward angles along 3'–4' stems. The sprays of lilac, pink, blue, or white flowers are pretty, however; use with discretion at the back of the border.

Type Hardy perennial
Zone 3–9, H 8–5; does not like the intense heat and humidity of the South
Flowering Season Summer

SOWING

Indoors Seed is best started outdoors.
Outdoors Early spring, when soil is cool and a light frost is still possible, or late autumn.
Depth ¼".

GERMINATING

Time 14–60 days.

TRANSPLANTING

Time Set out purchased plants in spring or autumn.
Spacing 8"–36".
Light Full sun to light shade.
Soil Ordinary, not too rich.

CARING FOR PLANTS

Easy. Be sparing with fertilizer to avoid lanky plants that require staking. Cut back flowering stems after blooming. Divide every 2–3 years.

PROPAGATING

Divide in spring (in autumn in Zones 7–9) or grow from seed.

COMBINATIONS

Campanula, Cephalaria, Phlox, Thalictrum.

CAUTION

G. officinalis is listed as invasive in some areas, including Utah. See pp. 494–495 for advice.

Galium (syn. *Asperula*)

HP | Zn 4–9

Bedstraw, Cleavers, False baby's breath, Sweet woodruff

p. 396

More fragile-looking than it really is, this spreading, herb makes an excellent ground cover in cool, shady locations. Bright green whorled leaves grow on slender 6" stems; tiny, white, star-shape flowers are abundant.

Type Hardy perennial
Zone 4–7 in the South to Zone 9 in the West, H 8–5; doesn't perform well in high heat and humidity
Flowering Season Late spring to early summer.

SOWING

Indoors Seed does not store well and should be sown as soon as ripe, around July.
Outdoors Start fresh seed in cold frames.
Depth Just cover.

GERMINATING

Time 14 days.
Requirements 65°–70°F.

TRANSPLANTING

Time After last frost.
Spacing 18"–24" for ground cover; 8"–12" for smaller plantings or quicker cover.
Light Part to full shade; more shade where warm.
Soil Moist, well drained, slightly acid; tolerates dry.

CARING FOR PLANTS

Water regularly during dry weather. Plants are fast growing and durable where they're happy and may become invasive.

PROPAGATING

Divide in early spring or autumn or grow from seed. May self-seed where conditions are favorable.

COMBINATIONS

Garden: *Astilbe, Heuchera, Hosta, Muscari, Myosotis, Narcissus, Podophylum.* Herb garden: *Achillea, Artemisia, Perilla, Salvia argentia, Santolina, Stachys.*

Galtonia

HB | Zn 6–9

p. 396

Dazzlingly white, bell-shaped flowers adorn these summer-blooming bulbs for 3 months. Leaves are straplike, with 2'–4' flower stalks towering above. Use in borders or massed in front of shrubs.

Type Hardy bulb; sometimes grown as an annual
Zone 6–9, H 10–8; grown as an annual where bulbs are not hardy
Flowering Season Midsummer to autumn

SOWING

Indoors 6–8 weeks before planting out.
Outdoors *Seed:* Early spring through summer. *Bulb:* Early spring.
Depth *Seed:* Just cover. *Bulb:* 5"–6".

GERMINATING

Time 15–20 days.
Requirements 70°F.

TRANSPLANTING

Time Early spring or autumn.
Spacing *Small species:* 6"–8". *Tall species:* 15"–18".
Light Sun.
Soil Prefers moist, well-drained soil.

CARING FOR PLANTS

Easy. Water well during dry spells. Provide mulch where winters are cold; north of Zone 6, lift plants, store in a cool, dry place in winter; replant in spring.

PROPAGATING

Plant offsets in early spring or late autumn or grow from seed. Plants grown from seed will flower in 4–5 years.

COMBINATIONS

Hemerocallis, Hosta, Lilium, Lychnis, Phlox.

Gaura

A, HP | Zn 3–10

Gaura

p. 396

This native of the southern United States is useful in hot, dry regions. Plants are shrubby, 18"–5' tall, with white or pink flowers on coarse spikes. Use in informal borders, cutting beds, or wildflower gardens; new dwarf cultivars make excellent container plants.

Type Annual, hardy perennial
Zone *Annual:* 3–10, H 9–6. *Perennial:* 6–9, H 9–6. Prefers warm climates and is well suited to hot, humid conditions
Flowering Season Summer through autumn

SOWING

Indoors *Annual:* 4–6 weeks before last frost. *Perennial:* 8–10 weeks before planting out.
Outdoors *Annual:* After last frost. *Perennial:* Early spring or early autumn.
Depth Just cover.

GERMINATING

Time 14–30 days.
Requirements 65°–75°F.

TRANSPLANTING

Time *Annual:* After last frost. *Perennial:* Early spring, when soil is cool and a light frost is still possible, or autumn.
Spacing 24"–36".
Light Sun.
Soil Ordinary, very well drained. *Gaura* is a useful plant for xeriscaping.

CARING FOR PLANTS

Easy. Drought tolerant once established. Water only during very dry weather. Deadhead to prolong flowering. Perennials take 2–3 years to become established. Midseason of their second year, cut back plants to 8" to encourage bushiness. Provide winter mulch north of Zone 7.

PROPAGATING

Divide perennials in autumn (in spring in Zone 6). Grow annuals and perennials from seed. Plants grown from seed will bloom in their first year.

COMBINATIONS

Echinacea, ornamental grasses, *Hemerocallis, Monarda, Petunia.*

Gazania

TP* | Zn 9–10

Gazania, Treasure flower

p. 396

Compact plants (6"–18"), gazanias bear daisylike flowers in hot yellows, oranges, reds, and dusky pinks, often striped. For edgings, or in borders or containers .

Type Tender perennial; often grown as an annual
Zone 9–10, H 12–3; grown as an annual in Zones 5–8. Likes hot, dry weather; does not do well where the growing season is short and nights are cool
Flowering Season Summer to early autumn.

SOWING

Indoors 6–8 weeks before planting out.
Outdoors After last frost.
Depth 1/8".

GERMINATING

Time 8–21 days.
Requirements Darkness and 60°–65°F.

TRANSPLANTING

Time 2 weeks after last frost, when soil is beginning to warm.
Spacing Plant at intervals equal to the ultimate height of the plant.
Light Full sun.
Soil Light, sandy, with a pH level of 5.5–7.0. Withstands dry soil and can be used for xeriscaping.

CARING FOR PLANTS

Easy. Once plants are established, water only during very dry spells. Do not overfertilize. Deadhead regularly to maintain a tidy appearance. Botrytis can be fatal during very wet periods.

PROPAGATING

In late summer, take basal cuttings, which can be used for overwintering, or grow from seed.

COMBINATIONS

Bidens, Gaura, Oenothera, Veronica.

Gentiana

HP | Zn 3–9

Gentian

p. 396

Gentians are mostly low-growing, mat-forming plants. Some are evergreen, bearing clusters of flowers that are usually an intense blue, but may be white, pink, purple, or yellow.

Type Hardy perennial
Zone 3–9, H 9–5 (see species list, p. 453); prefers the temperate climate of the Pacific Northwest
Flowering Season Summer through autumn, depending on species

SOWING

Indoors Spring.
Outdoors Autumn.
Depth Just cover.

GERMINATING

Time 14–180 days.
Requirements Difficult. *Autumn sowing:* Sow seed in flats, sinking these in the ground against a north-facing wall, and cover with glass. Moisten soil, as necessary. Transplant to peat pots after the first growing season, to the garden after the second. *Spring sowing:* Sow seed in moistened medium in flats. Cover with plastic and refrigerate for 8 weeks. Provide darkness and 70°–75°F thereafter to stimulate germination. Transplant seedlings to pots as they appear.

TRANSPLANTING

Time Spring or autumn.
Spacing *Small species:* 6"–9". *Medium species:* 12"–15". *Tall species:* 18"–24".
Light Full sun or part shade, except *G. lutea*, which must have full sun.
Soil Cool, moist, humus-rich, with a pH level of 5.0–7.5.

CARING FOR PLANTS

Difficult. Must have cultural requirements met precisely in order to flower, and it is often difficult to analyze the reason for poor flowering. Keep soil moist but not wet; plants growing in full sun must be watered regularly. Do not disturb roots.

PROPAGATING

Divide roots after flowering (early spring is preferable in Zones 3–6) or grow from seed.

COMBINATIONS

Anemone, Geranium, ornamental grasses, *Lycoris.*

Geranium

TP, HP | Zn 4–10

Cranesbill, Hardy geranium

p. 396–397

Carefree but underused in American gardens, these perennials have a place in any border and make wonderful ground covers—either deciduous or, in warmer climates, evergreen. Size ranges from 4" to 4'. Leaves are lobed and often deeply cut; flowers are saucer-shaped and plentiful, usually in purples, pinks or white.

Type Tender perennial, hardy perennial
Zone 4–10, H 9–1 (see species list, p. 454); not tolerant of extreme heat and humidity
Flowering Season Spring through autumn, depending on species

SOWING

Indoors Spring.
Outdoors Late autumn.
Depth Just cover.

GERMINATING

Time 3–90 days.
Requirements Easy. *Autumn sowing:* Sow seed in flats, sink flats in the ground against a north-facing wall, and cover with glass. Moisten soil occasionally, if necessary. Bring indoors in spring to 70°–75°F. *Spring sowing:* Sow seed in flats of moistened medium, secure in plastic bags, and refrigerate for 2–3 weeks. Then sink flats in the ground in a shady location, covering with glass. Transplant seedlings as they appear.

TRANSPLANTING

Time After last frost.
Spacing 8"–12".
Light *G. sanguineum, G. oinereum,* and *G. incanum* must be sited in full sun; *G. phaeum* and *G. sylvaticum* perform best in part to full shade; other species will take full sun or part shade but appreciate some shade where summers are very hot.
Soil Average, well drained, with a pH level of 5.5–7.0. Where summers are hot, soil must be moist. Plants grown in rich soil will spread rapidly.

CARING FOR PLANTS

Easy. Cut back hard after blooming to encourage further flowering. Tall species may require the support of twiggy branches pushed into the ground when plants are young. Provide a good winter mulch in northern zones.

PROPAGATING

Divide in spring in Zones 4–6 (in autumn in the South) or grow from seed.

COMBINATIONS

Wonderfully versatile. Combines well with almost anything: *Bergenia, Campanula, Centaurea, Dictamnus, Digitalis,* purple-leafed *Heuchera, Hosta, Paeonia, Stachys,* or use as a ground cover around *Rhododendron* or roses.

Gerbera

TP* | Zn 10 | Full sun; Partial shade | Ordinary soil; Moist soil

Gerbera, Barberton daisy, Gerber daisy, Transvaal daisy

p. 397

Gerberas are elegant plants, 8"–24" tall, grown for their many-petaled, daisylike flowers. In some species these are borne singly on long stems; others form mounds of blooms. Coloring ranges from simple pinks, yellows, and reds to sophisticated mustard, ocher, and burnt umber. Use gerberas in borders, cutting beds, or containers.

Type Tender perennial; often grown as an annual
Zone 10; grown as an annual in cooler zones; performs most successfully where days are warm and nights are cool
Flowering Season Summer to autumn

SOWING

Indoors 12 weeks before planting out, in peat pots.
Outdoors Not recommended.
Depth Surface.

GERMINATING

Time 15–30 days.
Requirements Difficult. Always start with fresh seed; provide light and 70°–75°F.

TRANSPLANTING

Time Late spring, when soil is warm.
Spacing 12"–18".
Light Full sun; part shade where summers are very hot.
Soil Prefers a rich, moist, fertile, and slightly acid soil.

CARING FOR PLANTS

Easy. Water regularly, particularly during hot weather. Fertilize lightly every 6 weeks during the growing season. Deadhead to keep plants tidy.

PROPAGATING

Divide in summer or autumn, take cuttings in summer, or grow from seed. Plants grown from seed will bloom in their first year if they are started early enough.

COMBINATIONS

It is not so easily used in a mixed bed, but *Gerbera* looks wonderful in a pot with a mass of other plants with contrasting textures and habits, such as *Alyssum, Callistephus, Gypsophila,* small-leaved ivies, and *Lobelia.*

Geum

HP | Zn 2–9

Geum, Avens

p. 397

This genus of rather delicate perennials bears long, slender stems topped with red or yellow saucer-shaped flowers. Plants are 6"–36" tall. Plant geums in groups and site them carefully, as they are easily lost in a crowd.

Type Hardy perennial
Zone 2–9, H 8–1 (see species list, p. 454)
Flowering Season Summer

SOWING

Indoors 8–10 weeks before planting out.
Outdoors Early spring or early autumn.
Depth Just cover.

GERMINATING

Time 21–28 days.
Requirements 65°–70°F.

TRANSPLANTING

Time Early spring, when soil is cool and a light frost is still possible, or early autumn.
Spacing 12"–18".
Light Full sun; light shade where summers are very hot.
Soil Rich, well drained, with a pH level of 5.5–7.0. Geums are drought tolerant and are useful for xeriscaping.

CARING FOR PLANTS

Easy. Deadhead regularly. Mulch in winter north of Zone 7. Divide every 3–4 years to maintain vigor.

PROPAGATING

Divide in autumn or grow from seed.

COMBINATIONS

Allium, Geranium, ornamental grasses, *Lychnis, Veronica.*

Gilia

A | Zn 6–10

p. 397

A genus of little-used, rather untidy-looking annuals, Gilia *bears globe- or funnel-shaped blossoms of pink, white, blue, or yellow. Flowers close up on cloudy days. Plants are 6"–30" tall, and are useful in borders or cutting beds.*

Type Annual
Zone 6–10, H 12–1; prefers the temperate climate of the West Coast
Flowering Season Summer to autumn, depending on species

SOWING

Indoors 6–8 weeks before last frost. Most successful started outdoors.
Outdoors 2–3 weeks before last frost; autumn in mild climates.
Depth 1/8".

GERMINATING

Time 17–21 days.
Requirements 55°–65°F.

TRANSPLANTING

Time After last frost.
Spacing *Small species:* 9"–15". *Large species:* 24"–36".
Light Full sun.
Soil Average, well drained. Will grow in very sandy soil. *G. tricolor* is suitable for xeriscaping.

CARING FOR PLANTS

Easy. Support tall species with twiggy branches pushed into the ground when plants are young.

PROPAGATING

Grow from seed. Plants self-seed.

Gillenia (syn. *Porteranthus*)

HP | Zn 4–8 

p. 397

These loose, shrubby, 2'–4' perennials are scattered with white, star-shaped flowers. A native North American, in woodlands or mixed with shade-loving shrubs.

Type Hardy perennial
Zone 4–8, H 9–5; tolerates hot, humid weather
Flowering Season Summer

SOWING

Indoors When ripe seed is available, in autumn.
Outdoors As soon as seed is ripe, in autumn.
Depth ¼".

GERMINATING

Time 14–21 days.
Requirements Difficult. *Indoor:* Refrigerate seed for 3 months before sowing. *Outdoor:* Sow seed in flats, sink in ground in a sheltered location, and cover with glass. Remove glass when seeds sprout.

TRANSPLANTING

Time Autumn.
Spacing 18"–24".
Light Sun or partial shade. *G. trifoliata* requires partial shade where summers are very hot.
Soil Rich, moist, well-drained woods soils, with a pH of 5.0–6.0.

CARING FOR PLANTS

Easy. Mulch well and keep soil moist throughout the growing season. Do not disturb roots. Plants may require staking. Cut back flowering stems after blooming.

PROPAGATING

Divide in early spring in Zones 4–6 (in autumn in Zones 7 and 8) or grow from seed.

COMBINATIONS

Artemisia, Gaultheria, ornamental grasses, summer-blooming *Phlox.*

Gladiolus (syn. *Acidanthera, Homoglossum*)

TB*, HB* | Zn 5–10  

Gladiolus, Sword lily

p. 397

This popular summer bulb with erect, swordlike leaves has sturdy flowering stems from 1' to a towering 5' tall. The elegant, if somewhat stiff, flowers come in ravishing shades of every color. Equally stunning in informal summer plantings and formal borders, gladiolus is an essential member of the cutting garden.

Type Tender bulb, hardy bulb, often grown as an annual
Zone 5–10, H 9–1 (see species list, p. 454); grown as an annual in cooler zones
Flowering Season Summer through early autumn

SOWING

Indoors Late winter.
Outdoors *Seed:* Not recommended. *Corm:* For continuous bloom, plant every 10–14 days starting 4 weeks after last frost, continuing until 90 days before first frost.
Depth *Seed:* ⅛". *Corm:* 4" in clay soil, 6" in sandy soil.

GERMINATING

Time 20–40 days.
Requirements 70°F.

TRANSPLANTING

Time 2–3 weeks after last frost, when soil is warming.
Spacing *Short species:* 4"–6". *Tall species:* 6".
Light Sun.
Soil Rich, well drained, with a pH level of 6.0–7.0.

CARING FOR PLANTS

Easy. Fertilize lightly when buds first appear, once when in bloom, and once again when flowering is finished. Water frequently. Shallowly planted corms produce stalks that are likely to need staking. Where plants are not hardy, lift corms in autumn, separate cormels, and store in a cool, dark, frost-free location.

PROPAGATING

Separate and plant cormels during resting period or grow from seed. Plants grown from seed will flower in 3 years.

COMBINATIONS

Allium, Atriplex, Nigella, Papaver.

CAUTION

Gladiolus is harmful to pets if eaten.

Glaucidium

HP | Zn 5–9

p. 397

The genus Glaucidium *contains one species,* G. palmatum, *a charming 2'–4'-tall woodland plant with large, papery, lavender flowers, similar in appearance to poppies; leaves are bold and maple-shaped.* Glaucidium *thrives in a cool climate.*

Type Hardy perennial
Zone 5–8; to zone 9 in the West
Flowering Season Late spring to early summer

SOWING

Indoors As soon as fresh seed is available.
Outdoors Autumn
Depth Just cover

GERMINATING

Time 30–90 days
Requirements Darkness and 50°–55°F. Sow seeds as soon as possible, as viability is very short.

TRANSPLANTING

Time After last frost.
Spacing 20"–24".
Light Part to full shade.
Soil Cool, moist, slightly acid. Amend with organic matter.

CARING FOR PLANTS

Difficult. Mulch with organic matter in spring and keep soil moist at all times. Do not disturb established plants.

PROPAGATING

Careful division after flowering.

Glaucium

A, Bi, HP | Zn 3–9

Horned poppy, Sea poppy

p. 397

The upright plants of Glaucium *are grown for their papery, poppylike flowers of golden yellow or orange and their ornamental seedpods. Foliage may be an attractive silvery green.* Glaucium *species grow 12"–36" tall. Use them in borders and cutting beds.*

Type Annual, biennial, hardy perennial; often grown as an annual
Zone 3–9, H 9–6
Flowering Season All summer

SOWING

Indoors Most successful when started outdoors. If sown indoors, use peat pots. *Annual or perennial:* 6–8 weeks before planting out. *Biennial:* Late spring to early summer.
Outdoors *Annual or perennial:* After last frost, or in autumn where winters are mild. *Biennial:* Late spring to early summer.
Depth Just cover.

GERMINATING

Time 14–21 days, possibly up to 365 days.
Requirements Darkness and 60°–65°F.

TRANSPLANTING

Time Several weeks after last frost, when soil has warmed.
Spacing 12"–24".
Light Sun.
Soil Tolerates hot, dry soil but must have good drainage.

CARING FOR PLANTS

Fertilize only lightly; overfeeding stimulates lush foliage but fewer flowers. Do not move.

PROPAGATING

Grow from seed. Plants self-seed.

Globba

TP* | Zn 9–10

Dancing girl ginger

Of this large genus of gingers, only a handful are grown, mainly in very warm climates. Plants are 2'–3' tall, with long (up to 15"), lance-shaped leaves and extremely showy blooms. These blooms consist of large bracts surrounding small flowers on pendulous racemes. Bracts are often deep cerise, with sharply contrasting yellow flowers. When in bloom they add a tropical feel to the garden, but are not reliable bloomers north of Zone 9.

Type Tender perennial, sometimes grown as an annual in cooler climates.
Zone 9–10, H 12–8; grown as an annual in cooler zones; roots might survive in Zone 8 with winter protection; performs best in hot, humid climates and goes dormant when night temperatures drop below 65°F.
Flowering Season Late summer to autumn

SOWING

Indoors 6–8 weeks before planting out.
Outdoors After last frost.
Depth ¼".

GERMINATING

Time 21 days.
Requirements 65–72°F. Sow seeds in a mixture of 1 part peat to 1 part sand.

TRANSPLANTING

Time Several weeks after last frost when soil has warmed.
Spacing Grow singly or space 1' apart.
Light Filtered sun or morning sun is best; the more sun plants receive, the more moisture they require.
Soil Rich, very moist, but well drained. Add copious amounts of organic matter when planting.

CARING FOR PLANTS

Easy. Keep soil moist during the growing season, but dry in winter. Feed plants regularly with a low-nitrogen fertilizer. Where plants are not hardy, lift rhizomes and store in dry peat moss in a frost-free location over winter. Or grow plants in containers, bringing indoors in autumn. Keep soil dry over winter, gradually increasing watering in the spring. Divide plants every 3–5 years.

PROPAGATING

Divide in spring, or grow from seed or bulbils.

COMBINATIONS

Colocasia, Hedychium, Impatiens, Musa.

Globularia

HP | Zn 5–9

Globe daisy

p. 397

The plants in this small group of mounding perennials are often evergreen and bear small, round, fluffy blue flowers. Most are edging or rock garden plants of just 4"–8" tall, although larger 2' tall species are grown in the border.

Type Hardy perennial
Zone 5–9, H 7–5
Flowering Season Late spring to early summer; some may bloom again sparsely in autumn

SOWING

Indoors Prechilled seed 6–8 weeks before last frost.
Outdoors Late autumn or early spring.
Depth Surface.

GERMINATING

Time 10–50 days.
Requirements Place seed together with moistened growing medium in a plastic bag and refrigerate for 3 weeks. Provide light and 55°F thereafter.

TRANSPLANTING

Time After last frost.
Spacing *Small species:* 5"–8". *Tall species:* 12".
Light Full sun or part shade.
Soil Moist, well drained, with a pH level of 5.5–7.0.

CARING FOR PLANTS

Easy. Feed occasionally, water regularly, and trim lightly after blooming to maintain shape.

PROPAGATING

Divide in spring in Zones 5–7 (in early autumn in the South) or grow from seed.

Gloriosa

TP* | Zn 9–10

Climbing lily, Creeping lily, Glory lily

p. 398

Compact climbers (4′–6′), Gloriosa *lilies are grown for their exotic lilylike flowers, which are crimson and yellow, wavy-edged, and deeply reflexed. Site them near an entrance or patio where their beauty can be appreciated.*

Type Tender perennial; often grown as an annual
Zone 9–10, H 12–7; grown as an annual in Zones 6–8. Prefers high humidity and a daytime temperature of at least 75°F, with a night temperature of 60°–70°F, although they will survive where the night temperature drops as low as 50°F
Flowering Season Summer to early autumn

SOWING

Indoors Late winter, in peat pots.
Outdoors *Seed:* Spring, in Zones 9–10 only. *Tuber:* Spring, when the temperatures remain above 50°F.
Depth *Seed:* Just cover. *Tuber:* 2″.

GERMINATING

Time 30 days.
Requirements Easy. Soak seed overnight and provide 70°–75°F.

TRANSPLANTING

Time When spring temperatures remain above 50°F.
Spacing 12″.
Light Sun.
Soil Well drained, humus-rich.

CARING FOR PLANTS

Easy. Provide a trellis or other support for vines. Handle very carefully, as stems are brittle. Feed with a liquid fertilizer every 2 weeks in summer. Gradually taper off watering after blooming has finished. North of Zone 9, dig and store tuberous roots at 55°–60°F or keep plants in containers.

PROPAGATING

Divide tubers after last spring frost or grow from seed.

CAUTION

Toxic to humans and pets if eaten.

Godetia See *Clarkia*

Gomphrena

A | Zn 3–10

p. 398

Gomphrena *are compact, upright bedding plants, 8″–18″ tall, with dense foliage. They display masses of bright little everlasting balls of violet, white, pink, orange, or red. Use dwarf species as edging or in containers; taller species are welcome in the border.*

Type Annual
Zone 3–10, H 12–1
Flowering Season Summer to early autumn

SOWING

Indoors 6–8 weeks before last frost.
Outdoors After last frost.
Depth Just cover.

GERMINATING

Time 6–15 days.
Requirements Easy. Soak seed in warm water for 24 hours; leave flats in a dark location at 70°–75°F.

TRANSPLANTING

Time After last frost.
Spacing 9″–12″.
Light Full sun.
Soil Average, well drained, not too rich, with a pH level of 6.0–7.0; tolerant of dry soil.

CARING FOR PLANTS

Easy. Pinch out young plants to increase bushiness; feed lightly when first flowers appear.

PROPAGATING

Grow from seed only.

COMBINATIONS

Callistephus, annual *Rudbeckia, Sanvitalia.*

Gunnera

HP | Zn 7–9

Gunnera

p. 398

These weird and wonderful herbaceous or evergreen perennials are grown for their enormous, exotic-looking foliage. Lobed and toothed leaves up to 6' wide are held on prickly stems up to 6' tall. Small yellow, red, or green blooms form thick cones 3' tall. A 1" dwarf species, G. nagellanica, *is a miniature version of its giant cousins. Use gunnera in large waterside plantings or wild gardens.*

Type Hardy perennial
Zone 7–9, H 12–7
Flowering Season Midsummer through early autumn

SOWING

Indoors 6–8 weeks before planting out.
Outdoors After last frost.
Depth Just cover.

GERMINATING

Time 14–60 days.
Requirements 60°–70°F.

TRANSPLANTING

Time Late spring, when soil has warmed.
Spacing *Dwarf species:* 12". *Large species:* 4'–6'. *Gigantic species:* 8'–10'.
Light Sun or part shade.
Soil Rich, constantly moist, deeply prepared.

CARING FOR PLANTS

Water well during dry weather and feed regularly with liquid fertilizer throughout the growing season. Cut back leaves to the ground in autumn and cover crowns with leaf mold, especially where plants are only marginally hardy.

PROPAGATING

Divide in spring or start from seed.

COMBINATIONS

Iris pseudacorus, Ligularia, candelabra *Primula, Scilla.*

Gypsophila

A, HP | Zn 2–10

p. 398

This large genus of erect, bushy plants with thin, wiry stems includes both annual and perennial species. They have inconspicuous, lance-shaped leaves and are known for their haze of tiny white flowers on branching stems. The overall effect is airy and dainty. Annuals grow 1'–2' tall; perennials are 6"–3'. Use them to soften the border or rock garden or as cutting flowers.

Type Annual, hardy perennial
Zone *Annual:* 2–10, H 9–1; *Perennial:* 3–9, H 9–1; (See species list, p. 455); annuals are most successful where summers are not extremely hot
Flowering Season Late spring through summer, depending on species.

SOWING

Indoors *Annual:* 6–8 weeks before last frost. Seed is normally started outdoors as plants bloom quickly from seed. *Perennial:* 8–10 weeks before planting out, in peat pots.
Outdoors *Annual:* Early spring, when soil is cool and a light frost is still possible. Sow every 3–4 weeks until July for continuous blooms. Sow in late autumn where winters are mild. *Perennial:* Early spring or early autumn.
Depth Just cover.

GERMINATING

Time 10–20 days.
Requirements 70°F.

TRANSPLANTING

Time *Annual:* After last frost. *Perennial:* Early spring, when soil is cool and a light frost is still possible, or early autumn.
Spacing *Annual:* 8"–12". *Perennial, small species:* 15"–24"; *large species:* 24"–48".
Light Full sun; annuals prefer afternoon shade where summers are hot.
Soil *Annual:* Ordinary, not too rich, with a pH level close to 7.0. *G. elegans* is drought tolerant and can be used for xeriscaping. *Perennial:* Average, well drained, with a pH level of 6.5–7.5.

CARING FOR PLANTS

Easy. For best blooming, keep perennials well watered, but do not overwater or overfertilize annuals. Keep annuals slightly crowded. Cut both back after flowering to encourage a second bloom. Support tall species with wire frames or twiggy branches pushed into the ground when plants are young. Cut back perennials to ground level in autumn. Do not disturb roots.

PROPAGATING

Annual: Grow from seed only. *Perennial:* Take cuttings in early summer or grow from seed.

COMBINATIONS

Annuals: *Cerinthe, Leucanthemum, Phlox.* Perennials: *Centaurea, Dianthus, Echinacea, Echinops, Heuchera, Stachys, Stokesia.*

Hacquetia (syn. Dondia)

HP | Zn 4–9 

p. 398

A genus of just one perennial species (H. epipactis), *this little plant is only 2"–8" tall. It bears umbels of yellow blooms that appear before leaves and are surrounded by showy, bright green bracts. This is an unusual rock garden plant.*

Type Hardy perennial
Zone 4–9, H 7–5
Flowering Season Late winter to early spring

SOWING

Indoors Prechilled seed 10–12 weeks before planting out.
Outdoors When seed is fresh in autumn.
Depth Surface.

GERMINATING

Time 30–180 days.
Requirements Place seed and moistened growing medium in a plastic bag, seal loosely, and refrigerate for 2–3 weeks. Sow in flats and maintain at 55°F.

TRANSPLANTING

Time Early spring, when soil is cool and a light frost is still possible.
Spacing 8"–10".
Light Sun or shade.
Soil Moist, well drained.

CARING FOR PLANTS

Mulch in spring to keep roots cool. Do not move established plants.

PROPAGATING

Divide in spring or grow from seed.

Haemanthus

TB* | Zn 10  

African blood lily, Blood lily

p. 398

Unusual-looking bulbs with strong, thick stems. Some Haemanthus *have brightly colored bracts that surround a vast cluster of tiny flowers with prominent stamens. Others carry huge (up to 8"), fluffy red balls on sturdy 12" stems. A real eye-catcher for pots or patios.*

Type Tender bulb
Zone 10; H 12–10 (see species list, p. 455); grown as an annual farther north; may survive in cooler zones with winter protection
Flowering Season Summer

SOWING

Indoors Early spring. Seed does not store well; use as soon as available.
Outdoors *Seed:* As soon as ripe. *Bulb:* After last frost.
Depth *Seed:* Just cover. *Bulb:* With tip exposed.

GERMINATING

Time 7–24 days.
Requirements 60°–65°F.

TRANSPLANTING

Time When night temperature will remain above 50°F.
Spacing 12".
Light Sun, with shade during the hottest part of the afternoon.
Soil Well drained, humus-rich, with a pH of 5.6–8.5; moist during the growing season, dry in autumn and winter.

CARING FOR PLANTS

Feed and water regularly during the growing season; allow soil to dry out between waterings. Bulbs grown in pots prefer to be somewhat pot-bound. Mealybugs may be a problem. Plants go dormant after flowering; taper off watering when foliage begins to die back. Dig bulbs and store in dry peat at 50°–60°F over winter or store bulbs dry in their pots. *H. albiflos,* which is evergreen, requires periodic light watering throughout winter.

PROPAGATING

Remove offsets when active growth is just beginning, divide in early spring, or grow from seed. Plant may self-seed; established plants multiply happily on their own. Plants grown from seed will bloom in 3 years.

CAUTION

Contact with skin may cause irritation.

Hakonechloa

HP | Zn 4–10 | Full sun, Partial shade | Moist soil

Hakone grass, Urahagusa

p. 398

A Japanese ornamental grass, Hakonechloa *has an unusual mounding habit that gives plants a rather eccentric look. These handsome green-and-cream-striped leaves are long, tapering, and arched. Their autumn color is reddish brown. Clumps are a modest 12" tall.* Hakonechloa *makes an interesting specimen plant, edger, ground cover, or container plant.*

Type Hardy perennial
Zone 4–8 in the East, to Zone 10 in the West, H 9–5; prefers cool weather
Flowering Season Late summer to early autumn, although flowers are not showy

SOWING

Indoors Spring. Use seed that has ripened on the plant for 1 year. Variegated cultivars must be propagated by division.
Outdoors Spring or autumn.
Depth Just cover.

GERMINATING

Time 21–28 days.
Requirements 60°F.

TRANSPLANTING

Time After last frost.
Spacing 18"–24".
Light Part shade; full sun is tolerated where summers are cool.
Soil Moist, well drained, with a pH level of 5.1–7.5

CARING FOR PLANTS

Keep well watered, especially when plants are young. Cut back foliage in spring.

PROPAGATING

Divide in spring or grow from seed.

COMBINATIONS

Alchemilla, Astrantia, Geranium, Hosta, Miscanthus, Nepeta, Rodgersia. Effective with an evergreen backdrop or among plants with an Asian flavor, such as junipers and red-leaved Japanese maples.

Hardenbergia

TP | Zn 9–10

Coral pea

p. 398

These evergreen climbers are grown for their dense foliage and racemes of purple or white pealike flowers. An Australian native, Hardenbergia *grows to 10'.*

Type Tender perennial
Zone 9–10, H 12–6; prefers the climate of California and the Southwest
Flowering Season Spring

SOWING

Indoors 8–10 weeks before planting out.
Outdoors After last frost.
Depth ⅛".

GERMINATING

Time 30–90 days.
Requirements Soak seed in warm water for 24 hours; provide 55°–65°F thereafter.

TRANSPLANTING

Time After last frost, when temperatures remain above 45°F.
Spacing Plant singly.
Light Sun or shade.
Soil Prefers moist, peaty, well-drained, and lime-free soil.

CARING FOR PLANTS

Easy. Feed monthly with a weak liquid fertilizer and water regularly during dry spells.

PROPAGATING

Take stem cuttings in summer or autumn or grow from seed.

Hedychium (syn. *Brachychilum*)

TP*, HP | Zn 7–10

Garland lily, Ginger lily

p. 398

Ginger lilies sport broad, lance-shaped leaves and abundant spikes of fragrant white, yellow, orange, red, or bicolored flowers. In some species the foliage is highly ornamental. Plants grow 2'–12'. Use these plants in the border or in containers on patios and decks where their fragrance can be appreciated.

Type Tender perennial, hardy perennial; often grown as an annual
Zone 7–10, H 12–6 (see species list, p. 455); grown as an annual in cooler zones
Flowering Season Summer to early autumn

SOWING

Indoors 6–8 weeks before last frost.
Outdoors Early spring, when soil is cool and light frost is still possible, or late autumn.
Depth Just cover.

GERMINATING

Time 20–25 days.
Requirements Soak seed for 2 hours in warm water; provide 70°–75°F thereafter.

TRANSPLANTING

Time 2–3 weeks after last frost, when temperatures remain above 40°F.
Spacing 24"–36".
Light Sun; part shade where summers are hot.
Soil Humus-rich, very moist (or even wet), and well drained.

CARING FOR PLANTS

Easy. Water well during the growing season and cut back stems after flowers fade. Mulch well in autumn where plants are perennial. To overwinter indoors, dig rhizomes and store in a cool (50°–55°F), dry location over winter.

PROPAGATING

Divide rhizomes, each containing one eye, in late winter, or grow from seed.

Hedyotis (syn. *Houstonia*)

Bluets

p. 399

These native perennials are grown for their tiny, bright green leaves and blue, white, or purple star-shaped flowers. The most commonly used species are 4"–6" tall and are grown mainly in rock gardens. Taller species of up to 18" are useful in shady plantings or wildflower gardens.

Type Hardy perennial
Zone 3–8, H 8–1; not tolerant of arid heat
Flowering Season Late spring to early summer

SOWING

Indoors Seed is best started outdoors.
Outdoors As soon as fresh seed is available, usually in late summer.
Depth Just cover.

GERMINATING

Time 15–20 days.
Requirements Sow seed thinly in vermiculite, sink containers in the ground against a north-facing wall, and cover with glass. Moisten soil occasionally, if necessary. Allow one season of growth before transplanting to the garden.

TRANSPLANTING

Time Spring or autumn.
Spacing 12"–18".
Light Partial to full shade, or morning sun with shade from the afternoon sun where summers are very hot. Will grow in full sun in cool, northern climates.
Soil Moist but well drained, with a pH level of 5.0–6.0.

CARING FOR PLANTS

Water throughout the growing season. Allow foliage to die back naturally before cutting it back. Plants are short lived and require regular division.

PROPAGATING

Divide in early spring (autumn in Zones 7–8) or grow from seed.

Hedysarum

HP | Zn 4–9

Hedysarum is a genus of perennials grown for their fragrant, pealike flowers of crimson, violet, yellow, or purple. Plants are somewhat shrubby, 24"–48" tall. Use them in borders or cutting beds.*

Type Hardy perennial; often grown as an annual or biennial
Zone 4–9, H 9–1; prefers the temperate climate of the Pacific Northwest
Flowering Season All summer

SOWING

Indoors 6–8 weeks before last frost.
Outdoors Early spring, when soil is cool and a light frost is still possible, or late autumn.
Depth Just cover.

GERMINATING

Time 14–90 days.
Requirements Easy. 55°–65°F.

TRANSPLANTING

Time Spring or autumn.
Spacing 24"–36".
Light Sun or light shade.
Soil Tolerates poor soil but prefers a rich loam; soil must be well drained.

CARING FOR PLANTS

Easy. Cut plants to ground level in autumn; the leaves are attractive to slugs.

PROPAGATING

In spring, take root cuttings or divide in Zones 4–6 (in autumn in Zones 7–9) or grow from seed.

Helenium

HP | Zn 3–9

Helenium, Sneezeweed

p. 399

Dependable, late-summer-blooming perennials, heleniums are native to North and Central America. They grow 2'–5', with abundant daisylike flowers with prominent pincushion centers. The blossoms are autumn colors: golden yellow, flame red, orange, russet. Mass heleniums in the border for the greatest impact.

Type Hardy perennial
Zone 3–9, H 8–1 (see species list, p. 455)
Flowering Season Summer to frost, depending on species

SOWING

Indoors 8–10 weeks before planting out.
Outdoors Early spring or early autumn.
Depth Just cover.

GERMINATING

Time 7–10 days.
Requirements 70°F.

TRANSPLANTING

Time Early spring, when soil is cool and a light frost is still possible, or early autumn.
Spacing *Small species:* 12"–18". *Tall species:* 24"–36".
Light Sun.
Soil Will tolerate any soil but is happiest in rich soil, with a pH level of 5.5–7.0.

CARING FOR PLANTS

Pinch back tall species in spring to inhibit growth (this will delay flowering). Support unruly plants with twiggy branches pushed into the ground when plants are young. Deadhead regularly, and do not allow soil to dry out during the growing season. Cut back to the ground in autumn. Divide every 3–4 years to maintain vigor.

PROPAGATING

Divide in spring north of Zone 7 (in autumn in the South) or grow from seed.

COMBINATIONS

Agapanthus, Crocosmia, Eryngium, Helianthus, Hemerocallis, Inula, Nepeta, Salvia.

Helianthemum

TP, HP | Zn 6–9

Rock rose, Sun rose

p. 399

Low (to 18") evergreen subshrubs, Helianthemum *bear showy flowers over a long season. Foliage is silver or green and flowers are orange, yellow, bronze, or scarlet. Plant in rock gardens or dry stone walls, or between paving stones.*

Type Tender perennial, hardy perennial
Zone 6–9, H 8–6; not tolerant of extreme heat and humidity
Flowering Season Spring to autumn, depending on species

SOWING

Indoors 6–8 weeks before last frost.
Outdoors Early spring, when soil is cool and a light frost is still possible, or late autumn.
Depth Surface.

GERMINATING

Time 15–20 days.
Requirements 70°–75°F.

TRANSPLANTING

Time After last frost.
Spacing *Small species:* 5"–8". *Large species:* 12"–18".
Light Full sun.
Soil Tolerant of poor, dry soil; *H. nummularium* is suitable for xeriscaping. Will not stand wet feet in winter and must have excellent drainage.

CARING FOR PLANTS

Difficult. Remove faded blossoms, if desired, which open for just one day. After flowering, cut back lanky growth by one third to maintain size and shape and to encourage a second blooming.

PROPAGATING

Take cuttings in late summer or grow from seed.

COMBINATIONS

Achillea, Aster, purple-leaved *Heuchera, Lavandula, Lysimachia, Saponaria.*

Helianthus

A, HP | Zn 1–10

Sunflower

p. 399

A large genus of coarse, erect plants native to North America, Helianthus *are grown for their showy, daisy-like flowers in yellows, oranges, and creams, usually with very large, flat eyes. Although there are dwarf species (18"), most* Helianthus *tower between 5' and 10' tall. Grow in drifts at the back of the border or in wildflower gardens, or feature them individually as a curiosity plant.*

Type Annual, hardy perennial
Zone *Annual:* 1–10. *Perennial:* 3–10 H 9–1 (see species list, p. 455)
Flowering Season Summer to mid-autumn, depending on species

SOWING

Indoors Seed may be started indoors in peat pots 2–3 weeks before planting out, but little time is gained, as sunflowers grow very quickly outdoors.
Outdoors After last frost.
Depth ¼".

GERMINATING

Time 10–14 days.
Requirements 70°–85°F.

TRANSPLANTING

Time After last frost.
Spacing *Dwarf species:* 12". *Large species:* 36".
Light Full sun to light shade.
Soil Tolerant of both wet and dry soils, but stronger plants will be produced in deep, rich, well-drained soil with a pH level of 5.0–7.0. *H. maximiliani* and *H. salicifolius* are suitable choices for xeriscaping.

CARING FOR PLANTS

Easy. Pinch back small species when young to produce bushier plants; stake tall species. Water regularly and fertilize lightly several times during summer; overfertilization will increase leaf production but reduce flowering. During wet spells, plants are susceptible to botrytis, which causes flowers to rot. If seed is to be harvested, cover flower heads with cheesecloth to protect from birds. Cut back perennials to ground level in autumn.

PROPAGATING

Annual sunflowers are propagated by seed. Divide perennials in spring north of Zone 7 (in autumn elsewhere) or grow from seed.

COMBINATIONS

Shorter species and cultivars can be mixed attractively with *Achillea, Aster, Boltonia, Gaillardia,* or *Hemerocallis,* but the tallest species require their own space or could be dotted throughout a wildflower planting.

CAUTION

Neighboring plants may be harmed by a substance emitted by sunflower roots.

Helichrysum

A, TP, HP | Zn 2–10

Everlasting flower

p. 399

Plants in this genus of mainly upright, branching annuals and perennials are grown for their papery, everlasting flowers or the interesting colors and textures of their foliage. Plants are 1'–4' tall. Use them in rock gardens, borders, cutting beds, and containers.

Type Annual, tender perennial, hardy perennial
Zone *Annual:* 2–10; *Perennial:* 5–10, H 12–1 (see species list, pp. 455 and 481); *Helichrysum* are particularly intolerant of wet winters
Flowering Season Summer to frost; flowers on foliage types (*H. italicum* ssp. *serotinum, H. petiolare*) are often removed.

SOWING

Indoors 6–8 weeks before planting out.
Outdoors After last frost, only where summers are long.
Depth Surface.

GERMINATING

Time 5–20 days.
Requirements Easy. Light and 65°–75°F.

Helichrysum (cont'd)

TRANSPLANTING

Time 2–3 weeks after last frost, when temperatures remain above 40°F.
Spacing *Small species:* 8"–10". *Tall species:* 15"–18".
Light Full sun.
Soil Average, sandy, with a pH level of 6.0–7.0; tolerant of poor, dry soils. *Helichrysum* × 'Sulfur Light' is suitable for xeriscaping.

CARING FOR PLANTS

Easy. Water sparingly. To dry for arrangements, cut stems before flowers are fully open and hang upside down to dry in a shady place; remove leaves.

PROPAGATING

Take cuttings in summer or grow from seed. Plant may self-seed.

COMBINATIONS

Felicia, Impatiens 'New Guinea', *Pelargonium, Petunia, Tagetes.*

H

Helictotrichon (syn. *Avena*)

HP | Zn 4–8

Oat grass

p. 399

These European perennial grasses have very stiff, arching leaves, 12"–36" long. H. sempervirens *is grown for its handsome blue color. Use oat grass in groupings or as an accent plant.*

Type Hardy perennial
Zone 4–8, H 9–1; does not like hot, humid summers
Flowering Season Midsummer

SOWING

Indoors Start seed outdoors only.
Outdoors Early spring to mid-spring.
Depth 1/4".

GERMINATING

Time 5–21 days.
Requirements Easy. 60°–70°F.

TRANSPLANTING

Time Set out purchased plants in early spring or autumn.
Spacing 18"–24".
Light Full sun.
Soil Dry, well drained, poor to average, with a pH level of 6.0–7.5. This grass is drought tolerant but will not do well in clay soil.

CARING FOR PLANTS

Easy. Water regularly for best results. Foliage may be left year-round or cut when seeds are fully developed, then dried for indoor decoration. Dry with stalks upright for a natural drooping effect.

PROPAGATING

Divide clumps in spring or grow from seed. Plants may self-seed.

COMBINATIONS

Aquilegia, Stachys, Tiarella.

Heliophila

A | Zn 3–9

Cape stock

Heliophila *annuals are native to South America and are grown for their racemes of bright blue, pink, white, or yellow (often bicolored) flowers. Plants are 12"–36". Small species make attractive container plants; larger species suit the border.*

Type Annual
Zone 3–9; will bloom only in cool temperatures
Flowering Season Late spring through early summer, or into early autumn with successive plantings. Flowering will be diminished in hot weather.

SOWING

Indoors 6–8 weeks before last frost.
Outdoors Early spring, when soil is cool and a light frost still possible, or late autumn. Make successive plantings for a longer display of blooms.
Depth Just cover.

GERMINATING

Time 14–21 days.
Requirements 60°–65°F.

TRANSPLANTING

Time After last frost.
Spacing *Small species:* 6"–10". *Medium species:* 12"–18". *Large species:* 24"–36".
Light Full sun.
Soil Well drained.

CARING FOR PLANTS

Support plants with twiggy branches pushed into the ground in spring. Water during dry spells.

PROPAGATING

Grow from seed only.

Heliopsis

HP | Zn 4–9 | Full sun | Dry soil, Ordinary soil, Moist soil

Heliopsis, False sunflower, Ox eye

p. 400

Tall, upright, long-blooming native perennials, Heliopsis *includes many rather coarse and weedy plants, but they are appreciated for their cheerful yellow or orange daisylike flowers. Selected varieties are more desirable than the species. At 3'–5', they should be used judiciously in the border, but with abandon in the wildflower garden.*

Type Hardy perennial
Zone 4–9, H 9–1; not tolerant of humid heat
Flowering Season Summer through early autumn

SOWING

Indoors 8–10 weeks before planting out.
Outdoors Early spring or early autumn.
Depth Just cover.

GERMINATING

Time 10–15 days.
Requirements 70°F.

TRANSPLANTING

Time Early spring, when soil is cool and a light frost is still possible, or early autumn.
Spacing 24"–36".
Light Full sun.
Soil Prefers a rich, moist loam with a pH level of 5.5–7.0; will tolerate poor, dry soil.

CARING FOR PLANTS

Easy. Plants appreciate water during dry spells and a light feeding midseason. Cut back to ground level in autumn.

PROPAGATING

Divide in spring, take stem cuttings in summer, or grow from seed. Plants grown from seed will bloom in their first year.

COMBINATIONS

Aster, Catananche, Hemerocallis, Lobelia, Rudbeckia.

Heliotropium

TP* | Zn 9–10 | Full sun, Partial shade | Ordinary soil

Heliotrope, Turnsole

p. 400

Heliotropes are grown for their fragrant deep blue, purple, or white flowers. Individual blossoms are tiny and trumpet-shaped, and are carried in large clusters. Plants grow from 8" to 4'. Use small species in containers or for edging, larger cultivars in the border.

Type Tender perennial; usually grown as an annual
Zone 9–10, H 12–1; grown as an annual in Zones 3–10

Flowering Season Late spring to late autumn, depending on species

SOWING

Indoors 10–12 weeks before planting out.
Outdoors Start seed indoors.
Depth Just cover.

GERMINATING

Time 2–42 days.
Requirements 70°–75°F.

TRANSPLANTING

Time 2–3 weeks after last frost, when temperatures remain above 40°F.
Spacing 12"–24".
Light Full sun, with afternoon shade where summers are hot.
Soil Rich, well drained.

CARING FOR PLANTS

Keep soil evenly moist and feed once a month. Pinch back young plants to encourage bushiness, and deadhead regularly to prolong blooming. Grow plants indoors with 4 hours of sunlight a day; feed lightly every 2 weeks.

PROPAGATING

Take root or stem cuttings in autumn or grow from seed.

COMBINATIONS

Antirrhinum, Brachyscome, Fuchsia, Helichrysum, Phlox drummondii, Rudbeckia, Salvia, Verbena, or gray plants such as *Centaurea* and *Senecio.*

CAUTION

Plants may be toxic if eaten.

Helipterum See *Rhodanthe*

Helleborus

HP | Zn 3–9 | 

Hellebore

p. 400

Striking but subtle perennials, hellebores are grown for their handsome, often evergreen foliage and unusual anemone-like flowers in moody shades of plum, puce, dusky rose, and green, sometimes with attractive stippling, or purest white or cream. Winter bloomers are stunning in a snowy landscape. Plants are a compact 1–2'. Best suited to woodland plantings and shady borders. These beautiful and easy plants are underused in North America mainly because they are at their showiest during the winter, when many nurseries are closed.

Type Hardy perennial
Zone 3–9, H 9–1 (see species list, p. 455); does not like excessive heat
Flowering Season Winter to late spring, depending on species

SOWING

Indoors See Germinating, Requirements.
Outdoors *Seed:* See Germinating, Requirements. *Roots:* Early spring or early autumn.
Depth *Seed:* 1/8". *Roots:* 3".

GERMINATING

Time 1–18 months.
Requirements Difficult. *Autumn sowing:* Sow seed in peat pots, sink in the ground against a north-facing wall, and cover with glass. Moisten soil occasionally, if necessary. Bring indoors in spring to 60°–75°F. *Spring sowing:* Sow seed in peat pots, place in plastic bags, and refrigerate for 3 weeks. Sink pots in the ground in a shady location, covering with glass; remove glass when seedlings emerge.

TRANSPLANTING

Time Spring or autumn, when plants are at least 1 year old.
Spacing *Small species:* 6"–12". *Large species:* 12"–18".
Light Can take a little sun in winter but must have shade in summer.
Soil Prefers rich, moist, well-drained soil, with a pH level of 6.0–7.5, although some species are remarkably tolerant of dry soil. *H. foetidus* and *H. lividus* can be used in xeriscaping.

CARING FOR PLANTS

Easy. Water regularly and feed lightly twice a year. Remove faded flowers in early summer, and dead leaves in autumn. Avoid disturbing established plants. If you must dig them, take a large root-ball.

PROPAGATING

Divide carefully after flowering to retain a large root-ball; give extra attention to newly divided plants, which may take several years to begin blooming again; or grow from seed. Plant may self-seed.

COMBINATIONS

Asarum, Camellia, Crocus, Daphne odora, Fritillaria, Hepatica, Hosta, Hymenocallis, Iris reticulata, Myosotis, Primula, Pulmonaria, Soldanella.

CAUTION

All parts of the plant are toxic if eaten.

Hemerocallis

HP | Zn 3–9

Daylily

p. 400

These irresistible, long-stemmed perennials bear strap-like leaves and large, trumpet-shaped flowers. Daylily growers are producing cultivars and hybrids in an ever-increasing range of colors, including a wide array of reds, pinks, and cream, as well as the more usual yellows, oranges, and apricots. Flower stems are 12"–5'. Individual blooms last only 1 day, but each flower stalk produces flowers for several weeks. Use in the border, massed in a separate bed, or singly in naturalistic plantings. No summer is complete without these carefree charmers.

Type Hardy perennial
Zone 3–9, H 9–1 (see species list, p. 456)
Flowering Season Mid-spring to early autumn, depending on species

SOWING

Indoors 8–10 weeks before planting out.
Outdoors Early spring, when soil is cool and a light frost is still possible; late summer, where winters are mild.
Depth *Seed:* ⅛". *Roots:* 4"–6".

GERMINATING

Time 15–49 days.
Requirements Place seed together with moistened growing medium in a plastic bag and refrigerate for 6 weeks; provide 60°–70°F thereafter.

TRANSPLANTING

Time After last frost.
Spacing 12" for quick cover, 24" if you prefer not to divide plants frequently.
Light Full sun in the North, part shade where summers are very hot. Pastels will retain their color best in light shade, but blooming will probably be sparser.
Soil Prefers rich, moist, with a pH level of 5.5–7.0, but they are famously tolerant of a wide range of conditions, and can be used successfully in xeriscaping.

CARING FOR PLANTS

Very easy. Fertilize in early spring with 5-10-10. Water well during dry spells to maintain flowering. Cut flower stems to the ground after blooming to keep plants looking neat.

PROPAGATING

Divide at any time or grow from seed.

COMBINATIONS

Daylilies fit into almost any planting: *Berberis atropurpurea, Dahlia, Geranium, Helenium, Iris siberica, Lavandula, Nasturtium, Platycodon, Santolina, Veronica.*

CAUTION

Although often assumed to be a native plant because of its widespread appearance along roadsides, *H. fulva* is actually a garden escapee and is listed as invasive in many states, including Maryland. See pp. 494–495 for advice. *H. dumortieri* and *H. graminea* are toxic to cats if eaten.

Hepatica

HP | Zn 4–8

Hepatica

p. 400

These diminutive (2"–9"), slow-growing perennials produce a mass of charming anemone-like blooms in blue, white, or pink on sturdy stems. Attractive leaves are heart-shaped with three lobes. Grow them in shady rock gardens or woodland settings.

Type Hardy perennial
Zone 4–8, H 8–4; happiest in cool climates
Flowering Season Late winter to spring

SOWING

Indoors Prechill seeds 12–14 weeks before planting out, in peat pots. Starting seed outdoors is usually more successful.
Outdoors When seed is fresh, usually May or June.
Depth ¼".

GERMINATING

Time 30–360 days.
Requirements Place seed in a plastic bag together with a moist growing medium, and refrigerate for 3 weeks. Provide 50°–55°F thereafter.

TRANSPLANTING

Time Autumn.
Spacing 6"–12".
Light Part to full shade.
Soil Moist, humus-rich, and well drained. *H. acutiloba* needs a pH over 7.0.

CARING FOR PLANTS

Easy. Feed occasionally for better flowering, and do not allow soil to dry out in summer. Mulch with oak leaves in autumn. Leave plants undisturbed.

PROPAGATING

Carefully divide in spring (autumn in Zones 7 and 8) or grow from seed. Plant may self-seed.

COMBINATIONS

Daphne odora, Helleborus, Leucojum, Primula.

Heracleum

HP | Zn 3–9  

Cow-parsnip

Cow-parsnip is a towering, coarse perennial, 9'–12' tall, resembling enormous Queen Anne's lace. White or pink flowers are held in umbels on thick, fleshy stems. Grow Heracleum *near water, at the woodland's edge, or in a wildflower garden, allowing them plenty of room to spread.*

Type Hardy perennial
Zone 3–9, H 9–1
Flowering Season Midsummer

SOWING

Indoors See Germinating, Requirements.
Outdoors See Germinating, Requirements.
Depth ¼".

GERMINATING

Time 30–90 days.
Requirements *Autumn sowing:* Sow seed in peat pots, sink pots in the ground against a north-facing wall, and cover with glass. Moisten soil occasionally, if necessary. Bring indoors in spring. *Spring sowing:* Sow seed in moistened medium in peat pots, seal loosely in plastic bags, and refrigerate for 2–3 weeks. Sink pots in the ground outdoors against a north-facing wall and cover with glass; remove glass when seedlings emerge. Transplant to the garden in fall.

TRANSPLANTING

Time Autumn.
Spacing 36"–48".
Light Sun or light shade.
Soil Rich, moist.

CARING FOR PLANTS

Remove flowering stems as soon as they appear; this will result in healthier foliage and will prevent a complete takeover of your flower beds by this invasive plant, which self-sows with abandon. Do not disturb roots.

PROPAGATING

Divide very carefully in spring or autumn or grow from seed. Plant will self-seed.

CAUTION

Contact with foliage may cause skin rash. *Heracleum* may be invasive. See pp. 494–495 for advice.

Herniaria

HP | Zn 3–9

Rupture-wort

These diminutive, trailing, mat-forming perennials are grown for their finely textured, durable, evergreen foliage. Plants grow 4"–18" tall. The tiny flowers are green. Herniaria *is a useful rock garden plant or ground cover for difficult areas.*

Type Hardy perennial
Zone 3–9
Flowering Season Summer

SOWING

Indoors 6–8 weeks before last frost.
Outdoors Early spring, when soil is cool and a light frost is still possible, or late autumn.
Depth Just cover.

GERMINATING

Time 10–12 days.
Requirements 70°F.

TRANSPLANTING

Time After last frost.
Spacing *Small species:* 4"–6". *Large species:* 12"–18".
Light Full sun or part shade.
Soil Average to dry, well drained.

CARING FOR PLANTS

No special care is required.

PROPAGATING

Divide in spring north of Zone 7 (in autumn elsewhere) or grow from seed.

Hesperis

HP | Zn 3–9

p. 400

Upright perennials bearing a hazy mass of white, lilac, or purple blossoms, Hesperis species are valued for their heavenly nocturnal fragrance. Plants grow 1'–4' tall. Mass them in the shady border or near a patio where their scent can be enjoyed.

Type Short-lived hardy perennial; often grown as a biennial
Zone 3–9, H 9–1
Flowering Season Late spring to summer

SOWING

Indoors 8–10 weeks before planting out.
Outdoors Midsummer; cover seedbeds in winter with a mulch of straw.
Depth Surface.

GERMINATING

Time 20–25 days.
Requirements Light and 70°–85°F.

TRANSPLANTING

Time After last frost.
Spacing 12"–20".
Light Full sun or part shade; full shade where summers are hot.
Soil Rich, moist, well drained, with a pH level of 5.0–8.0; tolerates poor soil.

CARING FOR PLANTS

Easy. Water regularly during dry weather, feed periodically, and cut back stems after flowering to prolong blooming. Plants are short lived and require regular replacement.

PROPAGATING

Take cuttings or grow from seed. May self-seed.

COMBINATIONS

Digitalis, Hosta, Iris, Matteuccia, Papaver.

CAUTION

H. matronalis is listed as invasive in some areas, including Indiana and Tennessee. See pp. 494–495 for advice.

Hesperoyucca See *Yucca*

Heterotropa See *Asarum*

Heuchera

TP, HP | Zn 3–10

Heuchera, Alum root, Coral bells, Coral flower

p. 401

Heucheras are compact, clump-forming, evergreen or semievergreen perennials. They have attractive toothed or scalloped green, bronze, or silvery leaves and delicate sprays of flowers on long, wiry stems. Commonly grown species are 6"–12" tall; larger species grow to 3'. They make attractive edging plants and ground covers, and are lovely in woodland gardens.

Type Tender perennial, hardy perennial
Zone 3–10, H 8–1 (see species list, p. 456)
Flowering Season Late spring to early autumn, depending on species

SOWING

Indoors 8–10 weeks before planting out.
Outdoors Early spring or late autumn.
Depth Surface.

GERMINATING

Time 10–60 days.
Requirements Light and 60°–70°F.

TRANSPLANTING

Time After last frost.
Spacing 9"–12".
Light Sun where summers are cool, otherwise part shade.
Soil Light, fertile, moist but well drained, with a pH level of 6.0–7.0; intolerant of constantly wet soil.

CARING FOR PLANTS

Mulch well in early spring and water regularly. Remove flowering stems after blooming to maintain neat appearance. Divide every 3–4 years, enriching the soil with organic matter at that time.

PROPAGATING

Divide in spring north of Zone 7 (in autumn farther south) or grow from seed.

COMBINATIONS

Campanula, Erysimum, Impatiens, Iris, Lamium, Liatris, Oenothera, Sedum, Solidago.

× Heucherella

HP | Zn 4–9

Foamy bells

p. 401

A cross between Heuchera *and* Tiarella, *this hybrid has the flowers of the former and the leaves of the latter; generally it is more compact and delicate-looking than* Heuchera.

Type Hardy perennial
Zone 4–9, H 8–5
Flowering Season Spring to summer

SOWING

Plants do not set seed.

TRANSPLANTING

Time After last frost.
Spacing 12"–18".
Light Exhibits best foliage color in full sun but prefers at least afternoon shade where summers are hot.
Soil Moist, well drained, high in organic matter.

CARING FOR PLANTS

Water regularly to maintain a healthy appearance; leaves will scorch and plants decline when soil is too dry. Deadhead to increase blooming. Mulch well after the ground freezes to prevent heaving. Divide when blooming diminishes, about every 3–4 years; in hot, humid climates plants are short lived.

PROPAGATING

Take basal cuttings in spring or divide in spring or autumn.

COMBINATIONS

Digitalis, Hosta, Trollius.

Hexastylis See *Asarum*

Hibiscus

A, TP*, HP | Zn 3–10

Hibiscus, Giant mallow, Mallow, Rose mallow

p. 401

Hibiscus are tall, upright perennials and annuals prized for their large, showy, trumpet-shaped flowers with a decidedly tropical look. Plants grow from 18" to 8' tall. Blooms are hot pink, fiery red, violet, or white. Mass them in borders or use them in containers; large-flowered cultivars make an unusual hedge.

Type Annual, tender perennial, hardy perennial; tender species are often grown as annuals.
Zone *Annual:* 3–10; *Perennial:* 4–10, H 9–1 (see species list, p. 456)
Flowering Season Summer to frost, depending on species

SOWING

Indoors *Annual or tender perennial:* Best started *in situ*, but where summers are shorter, sow seed in peat pots and transplant carefully. Start seed 8 weeks before last frost. *Perennial:* 12 weeks before last frost.
Outdoors After last frost.
Depth Surface.

GERMINATING

Time 10–30 days.
Requirements Chip seed and soak in hot water for 1 hour before sowing. Provide 70°–80°F thereafter.

TRANSPLANTING

Time After last frost, when temperatures remain above 45°F.
Spacing *Small species:* 12"–18". *Large species:* 24"–48".
Light Full sun to light shade.
Soil Prefers rich, moist soil, but will tolerate dry. *H. rosa-sinensis* can be used in xeriscaping.

CARING FOR PLANTS

Water frequently. Prune lightly after flowering. Do not transplant.

PROPAGATING

Divide in spring or grow from seed. Plants grown from seed will bloom in their first year. May self-seed.

COMBINATIONS

Calendula, Chrysanthemum, Phlox drummondii, Platycodon, Salpiglossis.

Homoglossum See *Acidanthera*

Hordeum

HP | Zn 3–8

Barley

H. jubatum *is the only species in this genus of grasses that has ornamental value. This seemingly unremarkable grass comes into its own in summer when it displays a mass of beautiful, silky, silver-gray inflorescences on 2' stems. It is useful in mixed grass plantings or in naturalistic gardens.*

Type Short-lived hardy perennial; usually grown as an annual
Zone 3–10, H 8–1; prefers warm temperatures
Flowering Season Late spring to early summer

SOWING

Indoors Most successfully started outdoors.
Outdoors Early spring, when soil is cool and a light frost is still possible, or late autumn.
Depth 1/8".

GERMINATING

Time 21–50 days.
Requirements 70°F.

TRANSPLANTING

Spacing 12".
Light Sun.
Soil Well drained, somewhat dry, and alkaline. Suitable for xeriscaping.

CARING FOR PLANTS

Site carefully, as grass is easily damaged by wind and rain. May become invasive.

PROPAGATING

Grow from seed. Plant may self-seed.

Hosta

HP | Zn 3–9

Hosta, Plantain lily

p. 401

Surely one of the most widely grown plants in North America, these useful and elegant shade-lovers come in all sizes, from a dainty 3"–4" to an imposing 3'. Leaf color ranges from acid green to true blue, with numerous gradations in between, plus countless variegated forms. Leaves may be lance-shaped or heart-shaped, from 1" to 9" wide, their texture ribbed or puckered. Plants also feature tall stalks of trumpet-shaped blooms in shades from white to purple. Hostas make a stunning shady ground cover; use them as an edging or in the border, in containers, or in a woodland garden.

Type Hardy perennial
Zone 3–9, H 9–1
Flowering Season Summer

SOWING

Indoors 6–8 weeks before planting out.
Outdoors Spring or summer.
Depth *Seed:* Just cover. *Roots:* 3"–5".

GERMINATING

Time 15–90 days.
Requirements Difficult. 50°F.

TRANSPLANTING

Time Early spring.
Spacing *Dwarf species:* 12". *Medium species:* 18"–24". *Large species:* 36"–48".
Light Most prefer light to heavy shade but some will tolerate sun.
Soil Moist, with a pH level of 5.5–7.0. Will tolerate dry soil but will languish if allowed to dry out completely.

CARING FOR PLANTS

Easy. Water regularly and feed twice a year. Very attractive to slugs, which will leave plants with a Swiss cheese look if not controlled. Divide no more than every 2 years.

PROPAGATING

Divide in early spring or autumn or grow from seed. Variegated forms do not come true from seed.

COMBINATIONS

Because of the bold textural characteristic of hostas, most shade-loving plants are enhanced by them: *Aruncus, Asarum, Astilbe, Convallaria,* ferns, *Iris cristata* or *I. siberica, Ophiopogon, Polygonatum, Primula, Pulmonaria, Zantedeschia.*

Houstonia See *Hedyotis*

Houttuynia

HP | Zn 5–9

p. 401

This attractive but highly invasive ground cover features heart-shaped leaves blotched with green, cream, and red. It is best grown where it will be securely restrained by a barrier such as a driveway, a walkway, or walls of buildings.

Type Hardy perennial
Zone 5–9, H 8–1
Flowering Season Spring to summer

SOWING

Not recommended.

TRANSPLANTING

Time After last frost.
Spacing 18".
Light Will grow in full sun to full shade, but variegated leaves tend to revert to green in deep shade.
Soil Prefers moist or even wet but will perform well in any soil and will be less invasive in poor, dry soil.

CARING FOR PLANTS

Very easy; spreads quickly and can consume a small plot. Very difficult to eradicate once established. Restrict growth by withholding water and fertilizer.

PROPAGATING

Take stem cuttings or divide in late spring or summer.

COMBINATIONS

Ferns, *Iris ensata* or *I. pseudacorus, Liriope.*

CAUTION

A very invasive plant that will spread widely.

Humulus

HP | Zn 3–9

Hops

p. 401

Humulus *is an unusual rampant climber with deeply lobed foliage that may be green, golden yellow, or variegated. It bears conelike flower clusters, or "hops," which are highly decorative when dried. Quickly covers unsightly structures, growing up to 25' in one season.*

Type Hardy perennial
Zone 3–9, H 8–3 (see species list, p. 482)
Flowering Season Late spring through autumn, depending on sowing time

SOWING

Indoors 6–8 weeks before planting out.
Outdoors Sow in spring, when a light frost is still possible. Very often grown for dried flowers. Golden hops (*H. lupulus* 'Aureus') does not come true from seed; *H. japonicus* 'Variegata' does come true.
Depth ¼".

GERMINATING

Time 25–30 days.
Requirements 70°–75°F.

TRANSPLANTING

Time After last frost.
Spacing 24"–36".
Light Full sun or light shade.
Soil Prefers moist, rich, well drained; will tolerate dry soil.

CARING FOR PLANTS

Water well during dry weather and provide a sturdy support. Train stems regularly to direct their growth on the support.

PROPAGATING

Take tip cuttings in spring or early summer, divide in spring, or grow from seed.

Hunnemannia

TP* | Zn 9–10

Golden cup, Mexican tulip poppy

p. 401

Golden cup is a fast-growing Mexican native bearing yellow, poppylike blooms on 2' tall stems. Its fernlike foliage has a gray cast. Use it in borders and wildflower plantings.

Type Tender perennial; usually grown as an annual
Zone 9–10, H 12–9 (see species list, p. 457); grown as an annual in Zones 6–8; prefers warm climates
Flowering Season Summer to early autumn

SOWING

Indoors 6–8 weeks before last frost, in peat pots.
Outdoors When nighttime temperatures reach 50°F; where winters are mild, seed also may be sown in late autumn.
Depth Just cover.

GERMINATING

Time 15–20 days.
Requirements 70°–75°F.

TRANSPLANTING

Time After last frost.
Spacing 8"–12".
Light Full sun.
Soil Average, well drained, neutral to slightly alkaline; tolerant of dry soil. *H. fumariifolia* may be used for xeriscaping.

CARING FOR PLANTS

Easy. Do not overwater or attempt to transplant.

PROPAGATING

Grow from seed. Plant may self-seed.

Hutchinsia See Pritzelago

Hyacinthoides (syn. *Endymion, Scilla*)

HB | Zn 4–9 

Bluebell

p. 401–402

Bluebells produce a cluster of thick, straplike leaves from which 12" flower stalks emerge. The charming, downward-facing, bell-shaped flowers are blue, purple, white, or pink; some are fragrant. Massed in a woodland, they create an ethereal, fairyland effect.

Type Hardy bulb
Zone 4–9, H 9–1
Flowering Season Spring

SOWING

Indoors See Germinating, Requirements.
Outdoors *Seed:* See Germinating, Requirements. *Bulb:* Autumn
Depth *Seed:* Just cover. *Bulb:* 4"–6".

GERMINATING

Time 14–180 days.
Requirements Easy. *Autumn sowing:* Sow seed in flats, sink these in the ground against a north-facing wall, and cover with glass. Moisten the soil occasionally, if necessary. Bring flats indoors in spring to 50°F. *Spring sowing:* Sow seed in moistened medium, secure in a plastic bag, and refrigerate for 2–3 weeks. Remove flats and sink in the ground in a shady location, covering with glass. Transplant seedlings as they appear.

TRANSPLANTING

Spacing 4"–6".
Light Part shade.
Soil Moist, well drained, humusy, and fairly rich.

CARING FOR PLANTS

Easy. Apply a complete fertilizer in early spring or top-dress with manure in autumn. Deadhead to prevent self-seeding, unless naturalizing is desired.

PROPAGATING

Divide or plant offsets in late summer or grow from seed. Plant may self-seed. Plants grown from seed will bloom after 1 year.

COMBINATIONS

Azaleas, *Dicentra,* ferns, *Hosta, Rhododendron.*

Hyacinthus

HB | Zn 5–8

Hyacinth

p. 402

A genus of bulbs grown for their showy, highly fragrant blooms, hyacinths have strong, upright flower stalks, 6"–12" tall, covered in trumpets of blue, purple, white, red, yellow, or pink. Mass them for a striking color effect, or use them in mixed bulb plantings or containers.

Type Hardy bulb
Zone 5–8, H 9–5
Flowering Season Mid-spring

SOWING

Indoors Start seed outdoors only.
Outdoors *Seed:* Late summer to early autumn. *Bulb:* Early autumn.
Depth *Seed:* ½". *Bulb:* Plant tip of bulb 3" deep where soil is heavy, 5" in light soil.

GERMINATING

Time 30–365 days.
Requirements Because of the difficulty of propagating hyacinths from seed, starting with purchased bulbs is more practical. But for the adventurous: Sow seed in flats, plunge flats to the rims against a north-facing wall, and cover with glass. Moisten soil occasionally, if necessary. Cultivars may not come true from seed.

TRANSPLANTING

Time Transplant seed-grown bulbs in the autumn of their second year.
Spacing 8"–10".
Light Full sun to light shade.
Soil Rich, very well drained, with a pH level of 6.0–7.0. Bulbs are drought tolerant and may be used for xeriscaping.

CARING FOR PLANTS

Easy. Feed in early spring and again in autumn. Water during dry spells until flowering has ended, then discontinue. Remove flowers after blooming, allowing leaves to die back naturally. Mulch the first winter after planting and annually in cold climates. Old plants will produce smaller flowers in subsequent years. Bulbs may be discarded after 3–4 years, but many gardeners prefer the smaller, more natural-looking clusters that are produced from older bulbs.

PROPAGATING

Hyacinths can be propagated with limited success by offsets, but starting with purchased bulbs is recommended.Plants grown from seed will flower in 3–6 years.

COMBINATIONS

Anemone, Erica, variegated *Liriope, Viola.* In shadier spots: ferns and *Hosta.*

CAUTION

H. orientalis is harmful to pets if eaten.

Hylomecon

HP | Zn 5–8

Hylomecon japonicum, *the only species in this genus, is a compact (1') but vigorous perennial with large, yellow, poppylike flowers and attractive toothed and pinnate leaves. Plants go dormant in summer, but make a beautiful and unusual addition to an informal woodland planting or a moist, shady spring garden.*

Type Hardy perennial
Zone 5–8, H 8–5
Flowering Season Late spring

SOWING

Indoors As soon as fresh seed is available.
Outdoors As soon as fresh seed is available.
Depth Just cover.

GERMINATING

Time 60–80 days.
Requirements Seed remains viable for only a short time and should be sown as soon as available. Add leaf mold to the starting mix. Sow at 65°–70°F for 2–4 weeks, then move to 25°–40°F for 4–6 weeks, gradually increasing the temperature to 40–55° for germination.

TRANSPLANTING

Time Autumn.
Spacing 8"–12".
Light Part shade.
Soil Moist soil, supplemented with well-rotted manure or leaf mold.

CARING FOR PLANTS

Mulch in spring with leaf mold and keep soil moist throughout the growing season. Although these plants may be invasive in the cool, moist, peaty conditions where they thrive, they are easily kept in bounds by removing unwanted clumps. Plants go dormant in summer.

PROPAGATING

Divide in spring, or grow from seed.

COMBINATIONS

Meconopsis, Sanguinarea, Stylophorum.

Hymenocallis (syn. *Ismene*)

TB*, HB* | Zn 8–10

Basket flower, Peruvian daffodil, Spider lily

Though similar in looks to Narcissus, these scented, eye-catching bulbs belong to the Amaryllis family. White or yellow flowers are borne on 2'–3' stems; the cups of many species are surrounded by long, narrow, curved petals, giving them a spidery look, hence their common name. Grow these unusual conversation pieces near the patio, deck, or front door.

Type Tender bulb, hardy bulb, often grown as an annual
Zone 8–10, H 12–8 (see species list, p. 457); grown as an annual in cooler zones.
Flowering Season Spring, summer, or winter, depending on species.

SOWING

Indoors Not grown from seed.
Depth *Bulb:* Plant with tip 1" below the soil surface.

TRANSPLANTING

Time *Where bulbs are perennial:* Late autumn to early winter. *Elsewhere:* When nighttime temperatures reach 60°F.
Spacing 12–18"
Light Full sun to part shade.
Soil Rich, well drained. Will not survive winter wetness.

CARING FOR PLANTS

Easy. Water well during growth and bloom period. Where bulbs are not hardy, dig them before the first frost in autumn, allow leaves to wither before removing, and store bulbs loose in a warm (65°–70°F) location. If growing in containers year-round, bring containers indoors before the first frost to a bright location, watering just enough to prevent leaves from wilting.

PROPAGATING

Plant offsets in spring or early summer.

COMBINATIONS

Crinum, Lycoris, Zantedeschia.

CAUTION

All parts of the plant are toxic if eaten.

Hypericum

HP | Zn 5–9

Hypericum, St. John's wort

p. 402

Hypericum is grown for its large, saucer-shaped, bright yellow flowers, with many fluffy stamens; some are evergreen. Of the perennial and low-growing shrub species, use small ones (6"–12") in rock gardens or as ground cover, and larger ones (24"–36") in borders.

Type Hardy perennial
Zone 5–9, H 7–5; (see species list, p. 457) prefers cool weather
Flowering Season Summer or fall, depending on species

SOWING

Indoors 8–10 weeks before planting out.
Outdoors Early spring or early autumn.
Depth Just cover.

GERMINATING

Time 20–90 days.
Requirements 50°–55°F.

TRANSPLANTING

Time 2–3 weeks before last spring frost, or early autumn.
Spacing *Small species:* 6"–9". *Medium species:* 18"–24". *Large species:* 24"–36".
Light Full sun to part shade.
Soil Highly adaptable. Prefers well-drained soil with a pH level of 5.5–7.0.

CARING FOR PLANTS

Easy. Generally trouble-free, except for a susceptibility to rust. Prune hard in early spring.

PROPAGATING

Divide in autumn after blooming, take cuttings in spring or summer, or grow from seed.

COMBINATIONS

Linum, Oenothera, Penstemon, Veronica.

Hypoestes

TP* | Zn 10

Polka-dot plant

p. 402

A genus of 40 species of shrubs, one of which, H. phyllostachya, *commonly called freckle face, is grown as an annual for its comically spotted foliage. Leaves may be marked with pink, red, green, or white. Small leaves and tidy habit make this a popular addition to containers. Its magenta flowers, which are tiny and borne in loose racemes, are insignificant.*

Type Tender perennial usually grown as an annual or houseplant
Zone 10, H 12–1; grown as annual in Zones 3–9
Flowering Season Inconspicuous flowers appear sporadically throughout the summer

SOWING

Indoors 8–10 weeks before last frost.
Outdoors Spring; spring or autumn in Zone 10.
Depth Just cover.

GERMINATING

Time 7–21 days.
Requirements Easy. 65°–75°F. Pinch back seedlings twice to create well-branched, compact plants.

TRANSPLANTING

Time After last frost.
Spacing *Small species:* 8"–10". *Large species:* 24".
Light Full sun where summers are cool, part shade elsewhere, with shade from hot afternoon sun.
Soil Light, fertile, evenly moist but well drained.

CARING FOR PLANTS

Easy. Pinch new growth to create a bushy habit, and water during dry summer weather. In Zone 10, cut back plants hard in spring. Farther north, plants can be brought inside for the winter, where they make attractive houseplants.

PROPAGATING

Take root, stem, or tip cuttings in spring or summer or grow from seed.

COMBINATIONS

Bacopa, Helichyrsum, Lobelia.

Hyssopus

HP | Zn 3–10

Hyssop

Hyssop is a shrubby perennial herb of 18"–24", grown singly as a specimen or massed to form an unusual hedge. Its flowers are tiny, fragrant tubes of pink, white, or blue carried on slender stalks amid lance-shaped leaves.

Type Hardy perennial
Zone 3–10, H 9–6; does not like extreme heat and humidity
Flowering Season Late summer

SOWING

Indoors 8–10 weeks before planting out.
Outdoors Early spring, when soil is cool and a light frost is still possible.
Depth Just cover.

GERMINATING

Time 14–42 days.
Requirements 60°–70°F.

TRANSPLANTING

Time Spring.
Spacing 18"–36".
Light Full sun to part shade.
Soil Light, somewhat dry.

CARING FOR PLANTS

Easy. Cut back to the ground in autumn or spring and divide every 3–4 years to maintain vigorous growth.

PROPAGATING

Take cuttings in summer, divide carefully in spring in the North (in autumn in the South), or grow from seed.

Iberis

ANNUAL Including *I. amara, I. crenata, I. odorata, I. umbellata*

A | Zn 1–10

Candytuft, Globe candytuft, Hyacinth-flowered candytuft, Rocket candytuft

p. 402

Annual candytuft is upright, about 9"–16" tall, with sometimes fragrant, white, pink, purple, or red flowers, borne in rounded clusters; leaves are lance-shaped. Use in rock gardens, at front of border, or in containers.

Type Annual
Zone 1–10, H 12–1; prefers cool weather
Flowering Season Early summer to frost

SOWING

Indoors 6–8 weeks before last frost, in peat pots.
Outdoors For continuous bloom, sow every 10 days from last frost date to mid-July. In Zones 8–10, seed may also be sown in late summer.
Depth 1/8".

GERMINATING

Time 10–20 days.
Requirements Easy. 70°–85°F.

TRANSPLANTING

Time After last frost.
Spacing 6"–12".
Light Full sun, with some afternoon shade where summers are hot.
Soil Ordinary, well drained, with a pH level of 6.0–7.0.

CARING FOR PLANTS

Easy. Water plants regularly, allowing soil to dry out between waterings. After flowering, trim plants lightly to extend blooming period; discard plants as they decline. Do not move established plants.

PROPAGATING

Grow from seed. Plant may self-seed.

COMBINATIONS

Mimulus, Salpiglossis, Silene.

PERENNIAL

HP | Zn 3–9

Candytuft

Low-growing and evergreen, these spreading perennials are covered in tiny white flowers in spring; they make a neat green mound of 6"–12" the rest of the year. Use in rock gardens, cascading over walls, or as edging.

Type Hardy perennial
Zone 3–9 H 9–7 (see species list, p. 457)
Flowering Season Spring to early summer, depending on species

SOWING

Indoors 6–8 weeks before last frost.
Outdoors Early spring, when soil is cool and a light frost is still possible, or late autumn.
Depth 1/4".

GERMINATING

Time 10–60 days.
Requirements Easy. 55°–65°F.

TRANSPLANTING

Time After last frost.
Spacing *Small species:* 12". *Large species:* 24".
Light Sun or part shade.
Soil Rich, well drained, with a pH level of 6.0–7.5. Plants are quite drought tolerant, although flowering may be diminished in these conditions, and *I. sempervirens* is suitable for xeriscaping.

CARING FOR PLANTS

Easy. Trim lightly after blooming for tidiness.

PROPAGATING

Divide after flowering where summers are mild (in autumn south of Zone 6), take cuttings after flowering, or grow from seed.

COMBINATIONS

Armeria, Campanula, Iris, Nepeta, Papaver, Tulipa, Viola.

Iliama See *Sphaeralcea*

Impatiens

A, TP* | Zn 3–10

Impatiens, Balsam, Busy Lizzie, Patience plant, Sultana

p. 402

These vibrant-colored flowers bloom even in deep shade. Most are 12″–24″, with mid green leaves and flat, open blossoms in rich pinks, oranges, reds, purples, and white; some species have hooded, lipped flowers. Mass under trees, or in woodlands or containers.

Type Annual; tender perennial; often grown as an annual
Zone 10, H 12–1; grown as an annual in Zones 3–8.
Flowering Season Late spring through first frost

SOWING

Indoors 8–10 weeks before last frost.
Outdoors After last frost.
Depth Surface.

GERMINATING

Time 7–30 days.
Requirements Light, high humidity, and 70°–75°F. Highly susceptible to damping-off; sow seed in vermiculite, and water only from below.

TRANSPLANTING

Time Several weeks after last frost, when temperatures remain above 50°F.
Spacing 8″–12″.
Light Most species prefer full shade, but all are more sun tolerant where cool. The New Guinea impatiens need some sun to bloom well, but still need afternoon shade where summers are hot.
Soil Rich, moist, 6.0–7.0 pH; add rotted manure.

CARING FOR PLANTS

Easy. Pinch back young plants once or twice to increase branching; fertilize twice during season; keep watered. Occasionally attacked by aphids.

PROPAGATING

Take cuttings in spring or autumn or grow from seed. Some species may self-seed.

COMBINATIONS

Use with ferns, *Hosta, Lobelia,* and *Viola,* or as an edging to massed azaleas, rhododendrons, and yews.

Incarvillea (syn. *Amphicome*)

HP | Zn 4–9

Clump-forming (1′–4′), with fernlike foliage and strong flower-bearing stems, these Asian perennials have exotic, red, pink, or yellow, trumpet-shaped flowers. Because they grow from a fleshy taproot, they're often sold as bulbs. Use in rock gardens and borders.

Type Hardy perennial
Zone 4–9, H 8–1 (see species list, p. 458); will not thrive in humid heat
Flowering Season Late spring to summer

SOWING

Indoors 8–10 weeks before last frost.
Outdoors Early spring, when soil is cool and a light frost is still possible, or early autumn.
Depth Surface.

GERMINATING

Time 25–60 days.
Requirements 60°–70°F.

TRANSPLANTING

Time After last frost.
Spacing *Small species:* 8″–12″. *Tall species:* 18″–24″.
Light Full sun, with afternoon shade where summers are very hot.
Soil Rich, moist sandy, slightly acid. Wet soil in winter is fatal.

CARING FOR PLANTS

While growing, keep soil moist and deadhead regularly. Mulch heavily in winter at northern extreme of hardiness zone. May attract slugs.

PROPAGATING

Best if undisturbed; can be divided in spring if care is taken not to damage taproot. Take basal stem cuttings in spring, or grow from seed.

Inula

HP | Zn 3–9

Inula

p. 402

Inula *is a large genus of coarse, upright perennials, 1'–7' tall. Plants bear showy, daisylike flowers in yellow or orange with large eyes surrounded by thin, spidery ray florets. They are useful in wildflower gardens; some are suitable for sunny borders.*

Type Hardy perennial
Zone 3–9, H 8–1 (see species list, p. 458)
Flowering Season Summer

SOWING

Indoors 6–8 weeks before last frost.
Outdoors Early spring, when soil is cool and a light frost is still possible, or early autumn.
Depth Just cover.

GERMINATING

Time 14–42 days.
Requirements 55°–65°F.

TRANSPLANTING

Time After last frost.
Spacing *Small species:* 6"–12". *Medium species:* 18"–24". *Large species:* 24"–48".
Light Full sun; *I. ensifolia* can also be planted in part shade.
Soil Ordinary, well drained.

CARING FOR PLANTS

Easy. Top-dress with well-rotted manure in early spring. Keep soil moist in summer. Cut back flowering stems in autumn. Divide every 3 years to maintain healthy plants.

PROPAGATING

Divide in spring in Zones 3–6 (early autumn in Zones 7–9) or grow from seed.

Ionopsidium

A | Zn 1–10

Only one species of these annual plants is sometimes grown, I. acaule. *These fast-growing 2"–3" plants bear a profusion of lilac or white blooms over a long period. Use them in rock gardens and dry stone walls, between pavers, or as edging.*

Type Annual
Zone 1–10; prefers cool climates
Flowering Season Spring through autumn, depending on sowing time

SOWING

Indoors Start seed outdoors only.
Outdoors Early spring for midsummer blooms, summer for autumn blooms, autumn for spring blooms. Or sow at intervals from early spring to early summer, then again in autumn for continuous flowering.
Depth Just cover.

GERMINATING

Time 14–21 days.
Requirements 55°–60°F.

TRANSPLANTING

Spacing 4"–5".
Light Sun to part shade, with shade from hot afternoon sun.
Soil Prefers cool, moist soil, but will tolerate dry.

CARING FOR PLANTS

Mulch to keep soil cool and moist, and water during dry spells. Plants will languish in hot weather.

PROPAGATING

Grow from seed. Plant may self-seed.

COMBINATIONS

Crocus, Iris reticulata, Scilla.

Ipomoea (syn. *Mina, Pharbitis*)

A, TP* | Zn 3–10

Morning glory

p. 403

These climbing plants are grown for their charming trumpet-shaped flowers. The pink, white, blue, purple, red, or bicolored blooms may be small and dainty or large and exotic; some are fragrant. Grow them on a trellis or post, through shrubs, or in containers. Sadly, Ipomoea *species are often avoided by gardeners who confuse them with* Convolvulus arvensis, *a weed of alarming tenacity.*

Type Annual or tender perennial; usually grown as an annual
Zone *Annual:* 3–8; *Perennial:* 9–10, H 12–1 (see species list, p. 458); performs most successfully where temperatures are warm
Flowering Season Summer through early autumn

SOWING

Indoors Starting seed *in situ* is usually more successful but indoor sowing may be attempted in peat pots 3–4 weeks before last frost.
Outdoors 1–2 weeks after last frost.
Depth ¼".

GERMINATING

Time 5–21 days.
Requirements Easy. Chip seed and soak in warm water for 24 hours; provide 70°–85°F thereafter.

TRANSPLANTING

Time 3–4 weeks after last frost, when temperatures remain above 45°F.
Spacing 12"–18".
Light Full sun.
Soil Moist, loose soil that is not too high in nitrogen, with a pH level of 6.0–7.5; tolerates dry soil.

CARING FOR PLANTS

Easy. Provide a trellis for support and pinch tips once as plants begin to climb. Do not fertilize. Aphids may infest young plants but are rarely found on mature vines.

PROPAGATING

Grow from seed only.

CAUTION

Harmful if eaten. Some species of *Ipomoea* are listed as invasive in particular states, but they may be considered invasive in other areas as well. Some examples are: *I. aquatica* and *I. indica* in Florida; all except *I. arborescens* and *I. carnea* in Nevada; *I. hederacea* and *I. purpurea* in Kentucky. See pp. 494–495 for advice.

Iris (for *Iris ensata* see next entry)

HP, HB | Zn 2–10

p. 403

Large genus of justly popular, bulbous or rhizomatous perennials, usually with swordlike leaves and intricate, exquisite flowers. Plants grow from a dwarf 4" to a stately 6'; flower color ranges from pure pastels in every shade to deepest purple, maroon, and even brown. Uses are limitless: in borders, formal or naturalistic plantings, massed, or singly.

Type Hardy perennial, hardy bulb
Zone 2–10, H 12–1 (see species list, pp. 458–459); *I. douglasiana, I. germanica, I. pallida,* and *I. unguicularis* will not thrive in very hot, humid climates
Flowering Season Spring through winter, depending on species

SOWING

Indoors See Germinating, Requirements.
Outdoors *Seed:* See Germinating, Requirements. *Bulb:* Early autumn.
Depth *Seed:* ¼". *Bulb:* 3"–4". *I. germanica:* Plant rhizome level with soil surface.

GERMINATING

Time 1–18 months.
Requirements Difficult. Soak seed for 24 hours in warm water. *Autumn to winter sowing:* Sow in flats, sink these in the ground against a north-facing wall, and cover with glass. Moisten soil occasionally, if necessary. Bring indoors in spring to 60°–70°F.

Spring to summer sowing: Sow seed in moistened medium in flats, place flats in plastic bags, and refrigerate for 2–3 weeks. Then remove and sink in the ground in a shady location; cover with glass. Remove glass when seeds germinate. Grow for 2 seasons before transplanting to the garden.

TRANSPLANTING

Time *Bulb:* Early autumn. *Purchased rhizome:* Spring.
Spacing *Dwarf species:* 4"–8". *Medium species:* 12". *Large species:* 15"–18".
Light See list on pp. 458–459 for indidvidual species' requirements.
Soil I. germanica and *I. laevigata* require a pH level of 7.0–8.0. *I. siberica* requires a pH level of 5.5–7.0.

CARING FOR PLANTS

Easy. Feed in spring with a low-nitrogen fertilizer; add a little lime around *I. germanica* and *I. laevigata.* Water during dry spells. Deadhead regularly. Tall species may require staking. Divide *I. germanica* every 3–4 years. Watch for aphids, slugs, snails, and borers.

PROPAGATING

Divide rhizomes just after flowering ceases, divide bulbs in autumn, or grow from seed.

COMBINATIONS

Purple-leaved *Heuchera, Leucanthemum, Lupinus, Paeonia, Papaver,* roses, *Weigela. I. siberica:* Ferns, *Hemerocallis. I. reticulata: Crocus, Ionopsidium.*

CAUTION

All irises may be harmful to pets if eaten. *I. pseudacorus* is invasive in Florida, Maryland, and Virginia. See pp. 494–495 for advice.

Iris ensata (syn. *I. kaempferi*)

HP | Zn 5–9 |  

Japanese iris, Oriental iris

This native of eastern Asia is a beardless iris with swordlike leaves and beautiful, flat white, purple, or blue flowers with gracefully curved bulbs on 2'–3' stems; flowers often have contrasting centers.

Type Hardy perennial
Zone 5–9, H 8–4
Flowering Season Summer

SOWING

Indoors Anytime.
Outdoors Autumn or winter.
Depth ¼".

GERMINATING

Time 1–18 months.
Requirements *Indoor sowing:* Place seed in a plastic bag together with moist growing medium. Refrigerate for 5 weeks, then provide 60°–70°F. *Outdoor sowing:* Sow seed in flats and sink into the ground against a north-facing wall. Bring inside after 4–5 weeks, then return to the ground in early spring. Feed regularly. Move to a permanent location in late spring or early autumn.

TRANSPLANTING

Time Spring or autumn.
Spacing 9"–12".
Light Full sun to part shade.
Soil Prefers rich soil with a pH level of 5.5–7.0. Moist — or even wet — soil produces best results.

CARING FOR PLANTS

Feed with liquid manure during the growing season. Divide every 3–4 years in autumn to maintain good flowering. Watch for aphids, slugs, snails, and borers.

PROPAGATING

Divide rhizomes after flowering or grow from seed. Japanese iris must be hand-pollinated to produce seed.

COMBINATIONS

Alchemilla, Astilbe, Geranium, Lysimachia, Trollius.

Isatis

Bi, HP | Zn 3–10

Woad

p. 403

Isatis *are vigorous, summer-blooming plants with an upright, branching growth habit. Small yellow flowers are carried in terminal panicles; plants grow 1'–4' tall. Gardeners usually restrict them to cutting beds. This is the plant from which the famous Celtic war paint* woad *was made, but its common use today is in the more peaceful art of flower arranging.*

Type Biennial, hardy perennial
Zone 3–10, H 8–1
Flowering Season Summer

SOWING

Indoors Start seed outdoors only.
Outdoors Late summer.
Depth Just cover.

GERMINATING

Time 14–42 days.
Requirements 50°F.

TRANSPLANTING

Spacing 6"–12".
Light Sun or part shade.
Soil Rich; can be either moist or dry as long as it is well drained.

CARING FOR PLANTS

No special care required. Transplant only in early spring.

PROPAGATING

Grow from seed. Plant may self-seed.

Ismene See *Hymerocallis*

Isotoma See *Solenopsis*

Ixia

HB* | Zn 8–10

African corn lily, Corn lily

p. 403

These South African natives grow from corms. They have grassy leaves and spikes of star-shaped flowers held on wiry, 1'–3' stems. The light blue, red, purple, or white flowers open only in the afternoon and evening.

Type Hardy bulb, often grown as an annual
Zone 8–10, H 12–1; grown as an annual in Zones 3–7
Flowering Season Spring to summer, depending on planting time

SOWING

Indoors Autumn.
Outdoors *Seed:* After last frost. *Corm:* In Zones 3–6, plant in spring for late-summer bloom. In Zones 7–10, plant in late November for spring to early-summer bloom.
Depth *Seed:* Just cover. *Corm:* 4", on a cushion of sand.

GERMINATING

Requirements Not often grown from seed, and little literature exists; information given here is only a general guideline. Bulb seed usually requires 60°–65°F for germination.

TRANSPLANTING

Time After two seasons of growth: spring in the North, autumn in the South.
Spacing 4".
Light Sun or part shade, but the flowers close up in full sun.
Soil Rich, well drained.

CARING FOR PLANTS

Water regularly from early spring until blooming has ceased. Provide a good winter mulch in Zones 8. North of Zone 8, lift corms when leaves die back in autumn and store in a dry, frost-free location over winter; replant in spring.

PROPAGATING

Divide cormels at planting time or grow from seed. Allow to self-seed in areas where no rain falls during the summer. Plants grown from seed will flower in 3 years.

Ixiolirion

HB* | Zn 7–10

Lily-of-the-Altai

These bulbous Asian plants grow 12"–16", with clusters of blue funnel-shaped flowers and grassy leaves. They make dainty plants for rock gardens and filling the crevices of dry stone walls.

Type Hardy bulb; sometimes grown as an annual
Zone 7–10, H 12–7; grown as an annual in Zones 3–6
Flowering Season Late spring to summer

SOWING

Indoors 8–10 weeks before planting out.
Outdoors *Seed:* Early spring, when soil is cool and a light frost is still possible. *Bulb:* Spring.
Depth *Seed:* Just cover. *Bulb:* 2"–3".

GERMINATING

Time 30–90 days.
Requirements 50°F.

TRANSPLANTING

Time After last frost.
Spacing 4".
Light Sun.
Soil Hot, dry, sandy.

CARING FOR PLANTS

Top-dress with well-rotted cow manure in spring. North of Zone 7, lift bulbs after leaves die back and store over winter in a cool, frost-free place.

PROPAGATING

Plant offsets in autumn or grow from seed.

Jasione

A, Bi, HP | Zn 5–9

Sheep's bit

These little-known summer-flowering plants, usually 9"–12", bear blue or white pompon flowers in summer. They are useful in rock gardens and borders.

Type Annual, biennial, hardy perennial
Zone 5–9, H 8–6
Flowering Season Summer

SOWING

Indoors 8–10 weeks before planting out, in peat pots.
Outdoors Early spring, when soil is cool and a light frost is still possible, or early autumn.
Depth Just cover.

GERMINATING

Time 10–25 days.
Requirements Easy. 70°F.

TRANSPLANTING

Time Early spring, when soil is cool and a light frost is still possible, or early autumn.
Spacing 8"–12".
Light Full sun or light shade.
Soil Well drained, acid, not overly rich.

CARING FOR PLANTS

Easy. Mulch lightly in spring to keep the soil moist and remove flowering stems in autumn. Feed only sparingly, as overfertilizing results in lanky growth. Do not move established plants.

PROPAGATING

Divide in spring or grow from seed. Plants may self-seed.

Jeffersonia (syn. *Plagiorhegma*)

HP | Zn 5–8

Twinleaf

This genus of unusual and enchanting small woodland plants was named for Thomas Jefferson, who was at the time secretary of state, to honor his extensive knowledge of natural history. Plants bear distinctive two-lobed leaves and white, yellow, or purple cup-shaped flowers held singly on rigid stems. Use in shady borders or mixed woodland plantings.

Type Hardy perennial
Zone 5–8, H 8–5; prefers cool temperatures
Flowering Season Spring

SOWING

Indoors Start seed outdoors only.
Outdoors As soon as fresh seed is available in late summer/early autumn.
Depth Just cover.

GERMINATING

Time Up to 2 years.
Requirements Sow seed sparsely in flats, sink in the ground against a north-facing wall, and cover with glass. Moisten soil occasionally, if necessary. Transplant seedlings in the autumn of their second growing season.

TRANSPLANTING

Time Autumn.
Spacing 6"–10".
Light Part to full shade.
Soil Moist, rich, peaty, lime-free woods soil.

CARING FOR PLANTS

Mulch with compost to keep soil cool and moist; water during dry spells. Do not disturb. Will not tolerate hot, dry conditions.

PROPAGATING

Divide in spring in Zones 5–6 (autumn in Zones 7–8) or grow from seed.

Justicia

HP* | Zn 8–10

Brazilian plume, King's crown, Shrimp plant

These unusual, evergreen, tender perennials, subshrubs, and shrubs arouse curiosity wherever they are grown. Two species are commonly grown as annuals: J. brandegeana *(shrimp plant) and* J. carnea *(king's crown). Shrimp plant has drooping, white flowers surrounded by pink, red, or pale green bracts that appear to be jointed like a shrimp; it is most effective in hanging baskets and containers. The deep pink, white, or yellow flowers of king's crown are erect and resemble blossoming pinecones; king's crown is useful in containers and borders. Both can reach 5' as perennials, but seldom more than 2'–3' as annuals.*

Type Hardy perennial; often grown as an annual.
Zone 8–10, H 12–9. Grown as an annual in cooler zones. Very tolerant of hot, humid summer weather
Flowering Season Spring through autumn, depending on species

SOWING

Indoors Not grown from seed.

TRANSPLANTING

Time 2 weeks after last frost.
Spacing *Where plants are perennial:* 24"–36". *Elsewhere:* 18"–24".
Light Part shade.
Soil Fertile, moist but well-drained.

CARING FOR PLANTS

Pinch back young plants to establish a compact, mounded habit. Water regularly throughout the growing season. Plants may be troubled by whiteflies. North of Zone 10 *Justicia* may be lifted before the first frost and overwintered indoors in a warm, bright location that is not in direct sunlight; water sparingly throughout winter.

PROPAGATING

Take cuttings in spring or early summer.

Kaulfussia See *Charieis*

Kalimeris

HP | Zn 5–8

A neat plant with chrysanthemum-like flowers, Kalimeris *is long blooming and carefree. The single or semidouble blossoms are mauve or white with yellow centers; plants grow 12"–36" tall. They are attractive in borders and make good cut flowers.*

Type Hardy perennial
Zone 5–8, H 8–1
Flowering Season Summer to autumn

SOWING

Indoors 4–6 weeks before last frost.
Outdoors Autumn, as soon as seed is ripe.
Depth Just cover.

GERMINATING

Time 10–14 days.
Requirements 65°–70°F.

TRANSPLANTING

Time After last frost.
Spacing *Small species:* 12"–18". *Large species:* 24"–36".
Light Full sun in the North; in the South, sun to part shade, with protection from the hot afternoon sun.
Soil Moist, well drained, fairly fertile.

CARING FOR PLANTS

Very easy. Water regularly and divide periodically to maintain strong growth. Tall varieties may require staking, especially in windy sites.

PROPAGATING

Divide in spring or summer or grow from seed.

COMBINATIONS

Coreopsis, Echinacea, Hemerocallis, Platycodon.

K

Kirengeshoma

HP | Zn 5–8

p. 403

These charming late-blooming perennials have attractive, lobed, maplelike leaves and loose clusters of cream, funnel-shaped flowers held on slim purple stems, 3'–4' tall. Subtle but stunning in the woodland garden.

Type Hardy perennial
Zone 5–8, H 8–5; does not like hot and humid summers
Flowering Season Late summer to autumn

SOWING

Indoors Anytime.
Outdoors After last frost.
Depth Just cover.

GERMINATING

Time 30–300 days.
Requirements 55°–65°F.

TRANSPLANTING

Time After last frost.
Spacing 24"–36".
Light Part shade.
Soil Cool, moist, rich, acid, and well drained. Amend with organic matter at planting time.

CARING FOR PLANTS

Performs admirably when given the soil conditions it prefers. Allow plants to become established for 3–4 years before moving or dividing.

PROPAGATING

Divide in spring in Zones 5–6 (in autumn in Zones 7–8) or grow from seed.

COMBINATIONS

Heuchera, Hosta, Lamium, Matteuccia, Tricyrtis.

Knautia

HP | Zn 5–9

Knautia

Imagine buttonlike Scabiosa *flowers colored maroon, blue, pink, and salmon but on 3'–4' stems — there you have* Knautia, *a cheerful, summery plant that looks at home in a wildflower garden or in a border. It is also excellent for cutting.*

Type Hardy perennial; plants are stronger where summers are cool

Zone 5–9, H 9–5
Flowering Season Spring to autumn, depending on species; long blooming

SOWING

Indoors Most successfully started *in situ* but may be started indoors 4–6 weeks before last frost, if necessary.
Outdoors Spring or autumn.
Depth Surface.

GERMINATING

Time 10–30 days. *K. arvensis* and *K. macedonica* are erratic and may take several months.
Requirements Easy. Light and 65°–85°F. *K. arvensis* and *K. macedonica* require cooler temperatures, 59°F for the former, 41°F for the latter.

TRANSPLANTING

Time After last frost.
Spacing 18"–24".
Light Full sun.
Soil Well drained, slightly alkaline, fairly fertile.

CARING FOR PLANTS

Trouble-free. Cut back in spring to encourage stronger growth and again after flowering to stimulate a second bloom in autumn. May require staking or shelter from winds. At best they are short lived and require division every few years to maintain vigor.

PROPAGATING

Take basal cuttings in spring or early autumn, divide, or grow from seed.

COMBINATIONS

Combines well with many summer plants: *Allium, Coreposis, Erygium, Geranium, Heliopsis, Leucanthemum, Linaria, Miscanthus, Scabiosa.*

K

Kniphofia (syn. *Tritoma*)

HP | Zn 5–9 | Full sun, Partial shade | Dry soil, Ordinary soil

Red-hot poker, Torch flower

p. 404

These perennials, with their coarse, rather messy grasslike leaves, bear showy flowers that offer a light-hearted, almost insolent touch to the garden. Held on sturdy 2'–4' stems, the flower heads consist of a dense cluster of tiny downward-drooping tubes of yellow, orange, or green, with sometimes more than one color appearing on each flowering head. Use in the border for dramatic interest.

Type Hardy perennial
Zone 5–9, H 9–1 (see species list, p. 459)
Flowering Season Summer through autumn, depending on species

SOWING

Indoors 6–8 weeks before planting out, in peat pots.
Outdoors *Seed:* Early spring, when soil is cool and a light frost is still possible, or late autumn. *Roots:* Spring or autumn.
Depth *Seed:* ¼". *Roots:* 2"–3".

GERMINATING

Time 10–30 days.
Requirements 70°–75°F.

TRANSPLANTING

Time After last spring frost or in autumn.
Spacing *Small species:* 12"–15". *Large species:* 18"–24".
Light Sun, or part shade where summers are very hot.
Soil Rich, deep, moist, well drained, with a pH level of 6.0–7.5. Regular watering is required while plants are in bloom, but otherwise, they are tolerant of quite dry soil.

CARING FOR PLANTS

Easy. Water well while buds are setting in spring. Cut back flower stems to base after blooming. Plants resent root disturbance; divide very carefully no more than every 4–5 years.

PROPAGATING

Divide in spring or grow from seed. Propagate cultivars by division rather than seed. Some species will flower from seed in their first year.

COMBINATIONS

Aster, Bergenia, Centranthus, Hemerocallis, Salvia, Verbena bonariensis.

Koeleria

HP | Zn 4–9

Hair grass

Only a few of these annual and perennial grasses are of ornamental interest. A particularly useful one is K. glauca, *blue hair grass. Flat leaves are 6"–18" long, mid-green or deep blue; neat, close-cropped inflorescences are held on long stems above the foliage. Use hair grass in mixed-grass plantings.*

Type Short-lived hardy perennial
Zone 4–9; does not like hot climates
Flowering Season Spring to early summer

K

SOWING

Indoors Start seed outdoors.
Outdoors Early spring to mid-spring.
Depth *Seed:* Surface. *Roots:* 2".

GERMINATING

Time 4–21 days.
Requirements 60°–75°F.

TRANSPLANTING

Spacing 6"–12".
Light Full sun.
Soil Sandy, well drained, neither too acid nor too fertile. *K. cristata* and *K. glauca* are useful grasses for xeriscaping.

CARING FOR PLANTS

Water occasionally during dry spells. Plants are short lived and will need replacing every 1–2 years.

PROPAGATING

Divide in spring in Zones 4–6 (autumn in Zones 7–9) or grow from seed.

Lablab (syn. *Dolichos*)

TP* | Zn 9–10

p. 404

These woody-stemmed, rather shrubby climbers have purple or white pealike flowers, followed by shiny, ornamental purple pods. Foliage may be mid green or a handsome purple. Plants grow to 30' tall.

Type Tender perennial; grown as an annual
Zone 9–10; grown as an annual in Zones 3–8, 12–7; performs most successfully where there is a long, warm growing season
Flowering Season Summer through frost

SOWING

Indoors 6–8 weeks before last frost, in peat pots.
Outdoors After last frost.
Depth 1".

GERMINATING

Time 3–30 days.
Requirements Soak seed in warm water for 24 hours and provide 70°F thereafter.

TRANSPLANTING

Time Several weeks after last frost, when temperatures remain above 45°F.
Spacing 24"–36".
Light Full sun.
Soil Rich, moist, warm.

CARING FOR PLANTS

Easy. Provide a trellis for support and do not attempt to transplant.

PROPAGATING

Grow from seed only.

Lagerstroemia

HP | Zn 7–10

Although normally grown as trees, these tender plants are sometimes grown as small shrubs or even perennials, especially where marginally hardy. Plants sold as crape myrtlettes are cultivars developed for this use. They form 12"–18" mounds that are covered from summer through frost in panicles of ruffled blossoms in shades of pink, purple, or white. They make excellent container or specimen plants.

Type Hardy perennial
Zone 7–10, H 9–7
Flowering Season July through frost

SOWING

Indoors 6–8 weeks before planting out.
Outdoors After last frost.
Depth Surface.

GERMINATING

Time 14–21 days.
Requirements Easy. Light and 70°–75°F.

TRANSPLANTING

Time 2–3 weeks after last frost, when temperatures remain above 40°F.
Spacing 12"–24".
Light Full sun.
Soil Fertile, moist.

CARING FOR PLANTS

Easy. Keep soil moist and feed monthly during the growing season. Prune in spring.

PROPAGATING

Take hardwood cuttings in autumn or grow from seed.

L

Lagurus

A | Zn 3–10

Hare's tail, Hare's tail grass, Rabbit-tail grass

This annual ornamental grass bears short, 4" leaves and masses of slender, 1' long stems tipped with silky inflorescences. A Mediterranean native, it is sufficiently compact to be used in the border.

Type Annual
Zone 3–10, H 12–1; prefers warm climates
Flowering Season Summer

SOWING

Indoors 6–8 weeks before last frost.
Outdoors 3 weeks before last spring frost, or early autumn.
Depth ¼".

GERMINATING

Time 15–21 days.
Requirements 55°F.

TRANSPLANTING

Time After last frost.
Spacing *Small species:* 4"–6". *Large species:* 12".
Light Sun.
Soil Light, well drained; tolerates dry conditions.

CARING FOR PLANTS

Water regularly for best results.

PROPAGATING

Grow from seed, Plant may self-seed.

Lamiastrum See *Lamium*

Lamium (syn. *Galeobdolon, Lamiastrum*)

HP | Zn 3–9

Lamium, Deadnettle

p. 404

This large genus of plants is mainly weedy, although the commonly used garden plants are quite beautiful. Low-growing, trailing, or mounding plants have attractive foliage (sometimes silver or variegated) and short spikes of white, yellow, or purple flowers reminiscent of snapdragons. It makes a handsome ground cover or member of a mixed shady planting.

Type Hardy perennial
Zone 3–9, H 9–1 (see species list, pp. 459 and 482)
Flowering Season Spring through summer, depending on species

SOWING

Indoors 8–10 weeks before planting out.
Outdoors *L. armenum, L. maculatum, L. orvala* in spring or in pots in a cold frame in fall; *L. galeobdolon* after last frost in spring or in fall.
Depth Just cover.

GERMINATING

Time 30–60 days.
Requirements Easy. 65°–70°F. *L. galeobdolon* is more difficult. Sow it at 65°–70°F for 2–4 weeks, move to 25°–40°F for 4–6 months, then move to 40°–55°F.

TRANSPLANTING

Time Spring or autumn.
Spacing 12"–18"; *L. galeobdolon* to 24".
Light Full sun or part shade where summers are mild; part to full shade in hot climates.
Soil Prefers fairly poor soil that is well drained, especially in winter. *L. galeobolon* tolerates dry soil and is suitable for xeriscaping.

CARING FOR PLANTS

Easy. Feed once in spring; shear back after flowering for tidiness. Leaves attractive slugs. A vigorous spreader, *L. galeobdolon* is invasive in rich soil.

PROPAGATING

Take root cuttings in spring, divide in spring (autumn in Zones 7–9), or grow from seed.

COMBINATIONS

Ajuga, Astilbe, Crocus, Delphinium, ferns, *Filipendula,* purple-leaf *Heuchera, Hosta, Liriope, Ophiopogon.*

Lampranthus

TP* | Zn 9–10

Lampranthus *are low-growing, succulent perennials prized for the stunning, brightly colored, daisylike flowers that clothe them in spring. Blooms may be orange, purple, white, or pink. Use* Lampranthus *in containers or in dry, sunny beds.*

Type Tender perennial; sometimes grown as an annual
Zone 9–10, H 12–1; grown as an annual in Zones 3–8; not tolerant of high heat combined with humidity
Flowering Season Spring

SOWING

Indoors 6–8 weeks before planting out.
Outdoors After last frost.
Depth Just cover.

GERMINATING

Time 15–30 days.
Requirements Darkness and 65°–75°F.

TRANSPLANTING

Time Spring, when temperatures remain steadily above 40°F.
Spacing *Small species:* 6"–8". *Large species:* 18"–24".
Light Full sun.
Soil Dry, stony, very well drained, and amended with well-rotted manure; well suited to xeriscaping.

CARING FOR PLANTS

Easy. Water only during prolonged dry spells. When growing as a perennial, remove dead stems in autumn. Renew every few years when plants become woody.

PROPAGATING

Take cuttings in spring or grow from seed.

COMBINATIONS

Lavandula, Sedum, Sempervivum.

Lantana

HP* | Zn 8–10

Lantana, Shrub verbena

p. 404

Widely grown as annuals or tender perennials, lantanas are valued for their neat clusters of red, yellow, pink, lilac, white, or orange blooms. As annuals, they grow 12"–24" tall, but will reach 6' where they are perennial. Plants are evergreen in frost-free regions. Grow them in containers or warm, sunny beds.

Type Perennial; usually grown as an annual
Zone 8–10; grown as an annual in Zones 3–7; must have warm temperatures
Flowering Season Early summer through autumn

SOWING

Indoors 6–8 weeks before planting out.
Outdoors Start seed outdoors in the South only, in late winter or early spring.
Depth ⅛".

GERMINATING

Time 30–90 days.
Requirements Soak seed for 24 hours in warm water and provide a constant 70°–75°F thereafter.

TRANSPLANTING

Time In spring, when temperatures remain above 50°F.
Spacing 12"–18".
Light Full sun or light shade.
Soil Rich, well drained. *L. montevidensis* is suitable for xeriscaping in many areas.

CARING FOR PLANTS

Easy. Pinch back young plants to encourage bushiness. Water deeply but infrequently in summer—constantly moist soil produces lush foliage but few flowers. Plants can be potted up in autumn and overwintered indoors or grown in containers year-round. Susceptible to spider mites and whiteflies.

PROPAGATING

Take cuttings in spring or summer or grow from seed.

COMBINATIONS

Ageratum, Evolvulus, Petunia.

CAUTION

Toxic if eaten. *Lantana* is listed as invasive in some areas, including the Gulf States.

Lapageria

HP | Zn 8–10

Chilean bell flower, Chile bells, Copihue

This genus of one species (L. rosea) *of exotic vine bears long, luscious, deep pink trumpets. The leaves are leathery and sharply pointed. A native of Chile, it is suitable only for warm outdoor locations.*

Type Hardy perennial
Zone 8–10, H 12–9 (see species list, p. 459)
Flowering Season Midsummer to autumn

SOWING

Indoors As soon as ripe seed is available, usually early autumn.
Outdoors Start seed indoors only.
Depth ⅛".

GERMINATING

Time 30–90 days.
Requirements Difficult. 65°–75°F.

TRANSPLANTING

Time Grow indoors for 2 years, planting out after last spring frost.
Spacing Grow singly.
Light Prefers full shade; at the very least, must be shaded from hot afternoon sun.
Soil Humus-rich, very well drained.

CARING FOR PLANTS

Water well during dry spells. Mulch lightly with straw in winter.

PROPAGATING

Take cuttings in spring or autumn or grow from seed.

Lapeirousia See *Anomatheca*

Lathyrus

ANNUAL Including *L. chloranthus, L. odoratus, L. tingitanus*

A | Zn 1–10

Sweet pea

p. 404

These erect or climbing plants reach 2'–10'. They are grown for their prolific butterfly-like flowers in both intense reds, blues, and purples as well as pastel pinks, lavenders, and whites. Some are gloriously fragrant. Allow plants to sprawl along the ground or climb a fence or trellis; small species are attractive in the border or cottage garden.

Type Annual
Zone 1–10, H 8–1; prefers long, cool summers
Flowering Season Early spring to autumn, depending on species

SOWING

Indoors 6–8 weeks before last frost.
Outdoors Early spring, when soil is cool and a light frost is still possible. Where winters are mild, a second sowing in late autumn will produce winter blooms. More-robust plants result when started indoors.
Depth ½".

GERMINATING

Time 10–20 days.
Requirements Chip seed or soak in warm water for 24 hours. Inoculate with nitrogen-fixing bacteria. Provide 55°–65°F.

TRANSPLANTING

Time After last frost.
Spacing *Vine:* 6". *Bush:* 12".
Light Full sun.
Soil Prepare ground in autumn to a depth of 12"–18", adding plenty of compost and bonemeal. Prefers a pH level of 6.0–7.0.

CARING FOR PLANTS

Water during dry spells and mulch to keep soil cool. Fertilize with a weak solution several times during the growing season and deadhead often to prolong blooming. Provide a trellis for large species or stake plants when 4" tall. Change location every year to avoid disease problems. Aphids can sometimes be a problem.

PROPAGATING

Grow from seed only.

COMBINATIONS

Clematis, Delphinium, Lavatera.

CAUTION

The seeds are poisonous.

PERENNIAL

HP | Zn 3–9

Everlasting pea, Perennial pea, Spring vetch, Perennial sweet pea

p. 404

Like their annual relatives, the perennial sweet peas are erect or climbing plants reaching 2'–10'. Their butterfly-like flowers are purple, pink, white, often bicolored; some are gloriously fragrant. Allow plants to sprawl along the ground, grow on a fence or trellis, or twine among shrubs. They are attractive in the border or cottage garden.

Type Hardy perennial
Zone 3–9, H 10–1 (see species list, p. 459)
Flowering Season Early spring to late summer, depending on species

SOWING

Indoors 6–8 weeks before planting out, in peat pots.
Outdoors Early spring, when soil is cool and a light frost is still possible, or late summer to early autumn where winters are mild. Seed can be sown earlier in spring if soil is heated by stretching black landscaping plastic over beds in late winter. To sow seed, make slits in the plastic. When seedlings reach 4"–6", apply mulch over the plastic to keep plants cool.
Depth ¼".

GERMINATING

Time 20–30 days.
Requirements Chip seed or soak for 24 hours in warm water. Inoculate with nitrogen-fixing bacteria. Provide a constant 55°–65°F.

TRANSPLANTING

Time After last frost.
Spacing 6"–10".
Light Full sun to light shade.
Soil Prepare beds deeply, adding well-rotted manure and bonemeal. A pH level of 6.0–7.5 is preferred.

L. latifolius will tolerate considerable drought and may be used for xeriscaping.

CARING FOR PLANTS

Easy. Water and deadhead regularly while plants are in bloom. Mulch to keep soil cool.

PROPAGATING

Most successfully propagated by seed.

CAUTION

The seeds are poisonous.

Laurentia See *Solenopsis*

Lavandula

HP* | Zn 5–9

Lavender

p. 404–405

Widely used in borders and herb gardens, lavender is a 1'–3' tall evergreen shrub with narrow, somewhat fleshy, often fragrant leaves. Its tiny, tubular flowers in blue or shades of purple, as well as pink and white, are clustered at the ends of long, slim stems. Attractive hedge-type plants for formal or informal gardens, lavenders can also be grown in containers or in the border.

Type Hardy perennial, sometimes grown as an annual
Zone 5–9, H 9–3 (see species list, p. 460)
Flowering Season Late spring through summer, depending to species

SOWING

Indoors 6–8 weeks before planting out.
Outdoors Early spring, when soil is cool and a light frost is still possible, or early autumn.
Depth Just cover.

GERMINATING

Time 15–90 days.
Requirements Place seed together with moistened growing medium in a plastic bag and refrigerate for 4–6 weeks. Requires 55°–65°F thereafter.

TRANSPLANTING

Time After last frost.
Spacing 15"–18".
Light Full sun. *L. vera* will tolerate part shade.
Soil Ordinary, well drained, somewhat poor, with a pH level of 6.5–7.5. Lavenders are drought tolerant and a good choice for xeriscaping.

CARING FOR PLANTS

Easy. Prune back hard in early spring and cut off all dead flower stalks after blooming to maintain a tidy appearance. Fertilizing plants will decrease flowers' fragrance. Harvest flowers when buds are barely open and dry them in a warm place for several weeks; remove flowers from stems before storing. Try growing *L. dentata* or *L. stoechas* indoors: Add lime to commercial potting soil, feed occasionally with half-strength fertilizer, water sparingly, and give at least 4 hours of sunlight a day.

PROPAGATING

Take cuttings in spring or summer or grow from seed.

COMBINATIONS

Anthemis, Chrysanthemum, Dianthus, Paeonia, roses, *Salvia, Santolina.*

Lavatera

A, Bi, HP* | Zn 2–10

Lavatera, Mallow, Tree mallow

p. 405

Erect, somewhat shrubby plants, lavateras are grown for their charming cup- or trumpet-shaped flowers in shades of pink, purple, or white, blooming over a long period. Leaves are handsome, often maple-shaped; plants grow from 2'–6'. They are at home in cottage gardens and borders.

Type Annual, biennial, hardy perennial; usually grown as an annual
Zone *Annual:* 2–10, H 12–1. *Perennial:* 4–10, H 9–1 (see species list, p. 460); prefers the mild West Coast climates
Flowering Season *Perennial:* Summer. *Annual:* Summer to frost, especially if sown continuously

SOWING

Indoors 6–8 weeks before last frost, in peat pots.
Outdoors Early spring, when soil is cool and a light frost is still possible. For continuous blooming, sow annuals at intervals throughout the spring until nighttime temperatures become warm. Seed may also be sown in early autumn in the South.
Depth Just cover.

GERMINATING

Time 15–20 days.
Requirements Easy. 70°F.

TRANSPLANTING

Time After last frost.
Spacing *Small species:* 12"–18". *Large species:* 24"–36".
Light Full sun.
Soil Moist, well drained. Soil that is too rich will produce lush foliage but few flowers.

CARING FOR PLANTS

Easy. Water and deadhead regularly. Feed monthly with a low-nitrogen fertilizer. Leave plants undisturbed, as they resent transplanting.

PROPAGATING

Take cuttings in early summer or grow from seed. Plant may self-seed.

COMBINATIONS

Clarkia, Delphinium, Lathyrus, Salvia.

Layia

A | Zn 3–10

Native to western North America, Layia *is fast growing and long blooming. Gray-green foliage is smothered in yellow daisylike flowers with white, serrated edges; less commonly, flowers are pure white. Plants are bushy, 18"–24" tall.*

Type Annual
Zone 3–10, H 12–6; prefers cool temperatures
Flowering Season Late spring to autumn

SOWING

Indoors 6–8 weeks before planting out.
Outdoors After last frost, or late summer where winters are mild.
Depth 1/8".

GERMINATING

Time 8–36 days.
Requirements 70°–75°F.

TRANSPLANTING

Time After last frost.
Spacing *Small species:* 4"–8". *Large species:* 12"–15".
Light Full sun or part shade.
Soil Light, well drained, with a pH level of 5.0–8.0.

CARING FOR PLANTS

Easy. Water regularly and feed monthly.

PROPAGATING

Grow from seed only; *Layia* will self-seed in its native habitat.

COMBINATIONS

Catananche, Lobelia, Veronica.

Leonotis

TP* | Zn 9–10

Leonotis, Lion's ear, Lion's tail

p. 405

An unusual tender shrub, Leonotis *is native to South Africa. It is noticeable for its eccentric whorls of bright orange to red, tightly rolled, tubular flowers spaced along 3'–6' stems. It is a delightful curiosity for the border and a fine container plant.*

Type Tender perennial; usually grown as an annual
Zone 9–10 H 12–6; grown as an annual farther north
Flowering Season Newly sown plants bloom in autumn; overwintered plants bloom late spring to summer

SOWING

Indoors 8–10 weeks before last frost.
Outdoors 1 month before last frost.
Depth Surface.

GERMINATING

Time 10–21 days.
Requirements Easy. Provide 55°–70°F; pinch back seedlings twice.

TRANSPLANTING

Time In late spring, when soil has warmed to 50°F.
Spacing 24"–36".
Light Sun; part shade where summers are hot.
Soil Well drained, fertile.

CARING FOR PLANTS

Difficult. Plant in a sheltered location. Feed once in spring and water regularly during dry periods. Pinch back young plants to induce branching; plants may require staking. In Zones 9–10, mulch well in autumn and cut back to 6" in February. North of Zone 9, grow in containers or as bedding plants. To overwinter plants that have flowered in autumn, bring containers into a bright, sunny location, where flowering will continue all winter. For plants that have not flowered late in the year, bring into a cool, bright location for winter and reduce watering; take containers outside again after the last frost. Flowering will begin in late spring.

PROPAGATING

Take stem cuttings in late spring to midsummer, divide in autumn, or grow from seed.

Leontopodium

HP | Zn 4–7

Edelweiss

p. 405

Compact 12" perennials, edelweiss bear bright white, star-shaped flowers above woolly, lance-shaped leaves. Native primarily to the mountains of Asia and Europe, these short-lived plants are suited only to rock gardens.

Type Short-lived hardy perennial
Zone 4–7, H 6–1; all edelweiss prefer cool temperatures, although *L. leontopodioides* is somewhat heat tolerant
Flowering Season Late spring to summer

SOWING

Indoors 8–10 weeks before last frost.
Outdoors Early spring, when soil is cool and a light frost is still possible.
Depth Surface.

GERMINATING

Time 10–42 days.
Requirements Easy. Place seed and moistened growing medium in a lightly sealed plastic bag and refrigerate for 3 weeks. Provide light and 50°F thereafter.

TRANSPLANTING

Time After last frost.
Spacing *Small species:* 3"–6". *Large species:* 6"–12".
Light Sun to part shade.
Soil Gritty, loose soil, with a pH level of 6.5–7.5. *L. alpinum* may be used for xeriscaping in the cool, mountainous regions where it thrives.

CARING FOR PLANTS

Plants prefer a winter mulch of snow; where there is no constant snow cover, mulch lightly with fine gravel, removing mulch in early spring. Shield from winter rains. Edelweiss is short lived, requiring division every 2 years.

PROPAGATING

Carefully divide plants in spring or grow from seed.

Leucanthemella

HP | Zn 4–9

Leucanthemella is a genus of late-blooming daisylike perennials, the most popular of which is *Leucanthemella serotina*. This is a lovely plant with white ray flowers and yellow centers, not unlike many other daisies, but the surprise is that it grows on stiff 4–6' tall stems that look like they were designed to hold lilies; and unlike many plants of this height, they do not need staking. They are charming plants for the back of the border, and they make excellent cut flowers.

Type Hardy perennial
Zone 4–9, H 9–1
Flowering season Autumn

SOWING

Indoors 6–8 weeks before planting out.
Outdoors Early spring when soil is cool and a light frost is still possible, or late autumn.
Depth Surface.

GERMINATING

Time 7–28 days.
Requirements Light and 60–75°F.

TRANSPLANTING

Time After last frost or in early autumn.
Spacing 2–3'.
Light Prefers full sun, but tolerates part shade.
Soil Most at home in moist, but also performs well in average soil.

CARING FOR PLANTS

Easy. Mulch in spring to keep soil moist, and water regularly during dry spells. Feed in the spring; cut back to ground level in late autumn after flowering. Plants spread at a moderate rate, but are easily kept in bounds by digging unwanted clumps. *Leucanthemella* species are hosts of chrysanthemum white rust disease.

PROPAGATING

Division or basal cuttings in spring.

COMBINATIONS

Aconitum charmichaelii, Aster, Bassia, or in front of climbing roses, where they will hide any naked canes.

Leucanthemum

A, HP | Zn 3–9

p. 405

Until recently classified as a species of Chrysanthemum, *these plants are the backbone of many perennial beds. Plants are 10"–36" tall. Flowers are daisylike, white, pink, or yellow. They are usually prolific bloomers.*

Type Annual, hardy perennial
Zone *Annual:* 3–10. *Perennial:* 4–9, H 9–1 (see species list, p. 460). Many varieties are short lived in warmer zones, but *L.* × *superbum* 'Becky' is very heat tolerant; *L. paludosum* is very tolerant of hot, humid weather
Flowering Season Late spring to autumn, depending on species; some rest in midsummer

SOWING

Indoors 6–8 weeks before last frost.
Outdoors *Annual:* After last frost. *Perennial:* Spring or autumn, in a cold frame.
Depth Surface.

GERMINATING

Time 10–14 days.
Requirements Light and 65°–70°F. Start *L. paludosum* in peat pots.

TRANSPLANTING

Time *Annual:* After last spring frost. *Perennial:* Spring or autumn.
Spacing *Small species:* 8"–10". *Taller species:* 18"–24".
Light Sun or light shade; where summers are hot, double varieties prefer light shade.
Soil Rich, well drained, evenly moist; good drainage in winter is vital. Mature plants of *L. paludosum* are quite drought tolerant and suitable for xeriscaping.

CARING FOR PLANTS

Easy. Pinch back young plants to make sturdier. *L. paludosum* flower stalks may droop in very hot weather. All species need staking. Feed in spring and again while plants are in bloom to stimulate larger flowers. Deadhead regularly to extend the blooming season and to prevent self-seeding (*L. paludosum* never requires deadheading). Cut back *L. vulgare* to ground after flowering to encourage repeat blooming. Divide every other year to maintain vigor. Plants are attractive to slugs, snails, aphids, leaf spot, and chrysanthemum nematode. To prevent powdery mildew, keep soil evenly moist in dry weather.

PROPAGATING

Take cuttings from *L. paludosum* in mid- to late summer or grow from seed. *Perennial species:* Divide in spring or autumn, take basal cuttings in spring, or grow from seed. *Cultivars:* Divide in spring or autumn, take basal cuttings in spring, or grow from seed. Plants grown from seed will bloom in about 5 months.

COMBINATIONS

Astilbe, Echinacea, Eryngium, Hemerocallis, Iris, Knautia, Lupinus. Combine the more diminutive *L. poludosum* with lower-growing plants such as *Ageratum, Alyssum, Gomphrena, Petunia.*

CAUTION

L. vulgare is listed as invasive in some areas, including Kentucky. See pp. 494–495 for advice.

Leucojum

HB | Zn 4–9 | Full sun, Partial shade | Dry soil, Ordinary soil, Moist soil

Snowflake

p. 405

These spring- and autumn-blooming bulbs are grown for their dainty white flowers, which resemble clusters of tiny bells. Leaves are grassy or strap-shaped; plants grow from 4" to 3' tall. They are effective when massed under shrubs; woodland species brighten up shady plantings.

Type Hardy bulb
Zone 4–9, H 9–1 (see species list, p. 460)
Flowering Season Late winter, late spring, or late summer to autumn, depending on species

SOWING

Growing from seed not recommended.
Outdoors *Bulb:* October to early November.
Depth *Bulb:* 3"–4".

TRANSPLANTING

Spacing 6".
Light Full sun to part shade.
Soil Woodsy, rather moist but well drained. Tolerant of summer drought.

CARING FOR PLANTS

Easy. Allow leaves to wither naturally before removing. Do not disturb except to divide every 5–8 years.

PROPAGATING

Plant bulblets in autumn.

COMBINATIONS

Cyclamen, Fritillaria, Hepatica, Silene.

Levisticum

HP | Zn 4–8 

p. 405

Levisticum *is an imposing herb, growing 3'–7' tall. The dark green foliage resembles flat parsley. The tiny yellow flowers growing in umbels are similar to those of Queen Anne's lace. Allow it plenty of room in the herb garden.*

Type Hardy perennial
Zone 4–8
Flowering Season Midsummer

SOWING

Indoors 6–8 weeks before planting out, in peat pots.
Outdoors As soon as seed is ripe (late summer to early autumn).
Depth 1/4".

GERMINATING

Time 10–20 days.
Requirements Sow seed thickly, as the germination rate is poor; provide 60°–70°F.

TRANSPLANTING

Time After last frost.
Spacing 24"–36"; one or two plants will be sufficient for a household.
Light Full sun to light shade.
Soil Rich, moist, well drained, with a pH level of 6.0–7.0. Amend with compost or well-rotted cow manure at planting time.

CARING FOR PLANTS

Feed once in spring with compost, well-rotted manure, or 5-10-5. Discard any leaves infested with leaf miner. If growing to use leaves, cut back flowering stems before blooms form. Harvest leaves of 2-year-old plants three times throughout the season. Leaves can be used either fresh, dried, or frozen (blanch before freezing). Harvest seed when fruit begins to open. Cut seed head and hang in a cool, dark place to dry.

PROPAGATING

Divide in early spring or grow from seed.

Lewisia

HP | Zn 4–8

Lewisia

p. 405

Low-growing, rosette-forming perennials, lewisias have succulent leaves that in some species are evergreen. Cup-shaped flowers of white, red, pink, or purple are held on stiff stems. Lewisia is best suited to rock gardens or moist dry stone walls.

Type Hardy perennial
Zone 4–8, H 8–1 (see species list, p. 460); does not perform well where summers are hot and humid
Flowering Season Spring through early summer

SOWING

Indoors 10–12 weeks before planting out.
Outdoors As soon as seed is ripe, in late autumn or early winter.
Depth Surface.

GERMINATING

Time 1–2 years.
Requirements Difficult. Place seed together with moistened growing medium in a plastic bag and refrigerate for 5 weeks. Provide light and 50°–60°F thereafter.

TRANSPLANTING

Time Plant out in spring after 1 year of growth.
Spacing *Small species:* 2"–4". *Larger species:* 6"–8".
Light Full sun or light shade.
Soil Prefers moist, rich, rather gritty, with a pH level of 5.0–8.0; tolerant of dry soil.

CARING FOR PLANTS

Difficult. To avoid crown rot, set crowns 1" above the soil level and surround with stone chips. Keep soil moist during flowering but protect plants from overhead water.

PROPAGATING

Root detached rosettes in summer or grow from seed.

COMBINATIONS

Armeria, Geranium, Iberis, Sedum.

Liatris

HP | Zn 3–10

Liatris, Button snakeroot, Blazing star, Gayfeather, Snakeroot

p. 405

These cheerful native perennials lift the spirit with their mass of purple- or white-tipped flowering stems that erupt from a base of hairy leaves like fireworks shooting skyward. Plants grow from 2' to 6' and are invaluable in the summer border or wildflower garden.

Type Hardy perennial
Zone 3–10, H 9–1 (see species list, p. 460)
Flowering Season Summer to early autumn

SOWING

Indoors 6–8 weeks before last frost.
Outdoors Early spring, when soil is cool and a light frost is still possible, or early autumn.
Depth Just cover.

GERMINATING

Time 20–25 days.
Requirements 55°–75°F.

TRANSPLANTING

Time After last frost.
Spacing 12"–15".
Light Full sun to light shade.
Soil Prefers a sandy, rich loam with a pH level of 5.5–7.5; will tolerate poor, dry soil, and *L. spicata* may be used for xeriscaping. Excellent winter drainage is essential.

CARING FOR PLANTS

Easy. Water during dry spells. Remove flowering stems after blooming. Mulch with well-rotted manure in spring; surround plants with fine gravel where soil is wet.

PROPAGATING

Divide in spring or grow from seed.

COMBINATIONS

Achillea, Heliopsis, Hemerocallis, Heuchera, Monarda, summer *Phlox, Sidalcea.*

L

Libertia

HP | Zn 8–10

A clump-forming perennial, Libertia *features grassy foliage out of which emerge stiff spikes topped with clusters of dainty white flowers. Blooms are followed by showy orange seedpods. Plants are 1'–3' tall. They are useful in the border.*

Type Hardy perennial
Zone 8–10, H 12–8; grows successfully only on the Pacific Coast
Flowering Season Summer

SOWING

Indoors See Germinating, Requirements.
Outdoors See Germinating, Requirements.
Depth 1/8".

GERMINATING

Time 1–6 months.
Requirements *Autumn sowing:* Sow seed in flats, sink in the ground against a north-facing wall, and cover with glass. Moisten soil occasionally, if necessary. Bring flats indoors in spring to 50°F. *Spring sowing:* Sow seed in flats of moistened medium, place in plastic bags, and refrigerate for 2–3 weeks. Sink flats in the ground in a shady location, covering with glass. Transplant seedlings as they appear.

TRANSPLANTING

Time After last frost.
Spacing 18"–24".
Light Sun to part shade.
Soil Sandy, moist, well-drained loam.

CARING FOR PLANTS

Shelter plants from wind and keep soil moist to prevent leaf tips from browning. Leaves become ragged with age; remove unkempt plants to make room for volunteers.

PROPAGATING

Divide in spring or grow from seed. Plants may self-seed.

Ligularia

HP | Zn 4–8

Ligularia, Leopard plant

p. 406

These coarse but intriguing perennials grow 2'–6' tall. Yellow or orange daisylike flowers held on tall stalks may grow in rounded clusters or in long, dramatic racemes. Leaves are generally large and leathery. They are most effective when massed near water or in shady beds. They contrast well with fine-textured plants.

Type Hardy perennial
Zone 4–8, H 8–1
Flowering Season Summer

SOWING

Indoors 6–8 weeks before planting out.
Outdoors Early spring, when soil is cool and a light frost is still possible, or early autumn.
Depth Surface.

GERMINATING

Time 14–42 days.
Requirements 55°–65°F.

TRANSPLANTING

Time Spring.
Spacing 24"–36".
Light Full sun; sun or part shade where summers are hot. Shade during the hottest part of the day, coupled with wet soil, helps prevent plants from wilting in the heat.
Soil Ordinary, moist.

CARING FOR PLANTS

Easy. Water well during dry weather and feed occasionally in spring and summer. Remove flower stalks after blooming to maintain a neat appearance, and cut back to ground level in autumn. Divide every 3 years.

PROPAGATING

Divide in spring or grow from seed.

COMBINATIONS

Astilbe, Gunnera, Hosta, Iris ensata, Lysimachia, Monarda, Phormium, candelabra primroses, *Tradescantia.*

Lilium

HB | Zn 4–9

Lily

p. 406

These bulbs are prized for their exquisite trumpet-shaped blooms. Stems are strong, upright, and unbranched, 1'–6' tall. They usually bear whorled, lance-shaped leaves. Flowers are large, beautifully colored in both bold and pastel shades, and often fragrant. Mass lilies or grow them individually in formal or naturalistic plantings. Small species make excellent container plants, and all are a perfect addition to any border.

Type Hardy bulb
Zone 4–9, H 9–1 (see species list, pp. 460–461); most lilies perform poorly in extreme heat
Flowering Season Late spring through early autumn, depending on species

SOWING

Indoors Anytime.
Outdoors *Seed:* Early spring, when soil is cool and a light frost is still possible, or early autumn. *Bulb:* Early spring or autumn.
Depth *Seed:* ¼". *Bulb: L. candidum,* 2"–3"; *L. auratum,* 6"; *L. regale,* 8"–9". A good rule of thumb is to plant bulbs with their bottoms resting at a depth three times the diameter of the bulb.

GERMINATING

Time 1–8 months.
Requirements Soak seed for 24 hours, then place in a bag together with moist growing medium and seal tightly. Leave at around 70°F. After 4 weeks, begin to check for growth. Move the bag to the refrigerator when first bulblets appear and chill for 2–3 months. Plant bulblets in individual pots.

TRANSPLANTING

Time Plant out seed-grown bulbs in their second spring, after last frost.
Spacing *Small species:* 9"–12". *Large species:* 12"–24".
Light Full sun to light shade, depending on species. Plant *L. hansonii, L. japonicum,* and *L. martagon* in a partly shady location only.
Soil Most lilies require moist, well-drained, slightly acid soil. *L. canadense* requires moist to wet soil; *L. henryi* and *L. monadelphum* prefer alkaline soil.

CARING FOR PLANTS

Mulch soil in spring and water well during the growing season, tapering off toward winter. Feed in early spring and again after flowering. Stake tall species individually. Deadhead regularly to maintain a neat appearance and cut back stems to soil line after first frost. Many lilies do not bloom well in extreme heat; some are short lived and require regular replacing.

PROPAGATING

Plant bulblets or bulb scales in late summer or early autumn or grow from seed. Plants grown from seed will bloom in 2–4 years.

COMBINATIONS

Lilies add elegance and romance to any planting. Combine with *Agapanthus, Allium, Campanula, Delphinium, Papaver.* Shade-tolerant lilies add drama to a primeval planting of *Gunnera, Hosta, Matteuccia,* and *Rodgersia.*

CAUTION

All lilies are highly toxic to cats if eaten.

Limnanthes

A | Zn 1–9 | Full sun, Partial shade | Moist soil

Meadow foam, Poached-egg plant

p. 406

In this genus of annuals, only one, L. douglasii, *is commonly grown. This is a spreading plant, 1' tall, covered in fragrant, cup-shaped flowers that are yellow, deeply edged with white. Use* Limnanthes *in rock gardens, at the front of the border, or edging a path.*

Type Annual
Zone 1–9, H 9–1; prefers the cool temperatures of the Pacific Northwest
Flowering Season Spring through late summer, depending on sowing time

SOWING

Indoors Best started outdoors.
Outdoors For summer blooms, sow in early spring, when soil is cool and a light frost is still possible. Sow in late autumn for early-spring flowers.
Depth Just cover.

GERMINATING

Time 14–21 days.
Requirements 50°–60°F.

TRANSPLANTING

Time After last frost.
Spacing 4".
Light Sun or part shade.
Soil Cool, moist, well drained. Tolerates wet soil. Maintain pH level of 5.5–6.5.

CARING FOR PLANTS

Easy. Water regularly during dry spells. After first heavy spring flowering, allow seed to mature and disperse, then remove plants and replace with summer bloomers. New seedlings will bloom in autumn.

PROPAGATING

Grow from seed. Plant may self-seed.

COMBINATIONS

Acer palmatum 'Dissectum Atropurpureum', *Euphorbia, Hosta, Lobularia, Nemesia, Nemophila.*

Limonium (syn. *Statice*)

TP*, HP* | Zn 4–9

Marsh rosemary, Sea lavender, Statice

p. 406

The plants in this large genus are grown for their flowers, which vary considerably among species. Plants grow from 8"–36", often with coarse woody stems. Small flowers grow in showy clusters; many resemble tiny papery trumpets. Blooms come in pastel lavenders and pinks along with brilliant carmine, red, yellow, and white. The most commonly grown species are everlasting. More refined specimens are attractive in the front of the border; mass coarser plants in a distant border or cutting bed.

Type Tender perennial, hardy perennial; often grown as annuals
Zone 4–9 H 12–1 (see species list, p. 461); tender species grown as annuals in cooler zones
Flowering Season Late spring to autumn, depending on species

SOWING

Indoors 6–8 weeks before last frost.
Outdoors *Tender species:* After last frost. *Hardy species:* Early spring, when soil is cool and a light frost is still possible.
Depth Just cover.

GERMINATING

Time 10–20 days.
Requirements 65°–75°F.

TRANSPLANTING

Time After last frost, plant out half-hardy species when the temperatures remain above 45°F.
Spacing *Small species:* 12"–15". *Large species:* 12"–24".
Light Full sun.
Soil Light, sandy. Tolerant of very dry soil.

CARING FOR PLANTS

Easy. Water only when soil is dry and feed once annually. Plants grown in fertile soil may require staking. Cut back plants to ground level in autumn. Do not move. May be susceptible to nematodes, aster yellows, and fungal leaf spot.

PROPAGATING

Divide spring-blooming perennials in autumn (divide autumn-blooming species in early spring) or grow from seed.

COMBINATIONS

Callirhoe, Cleome, Echinacea, Eupatorium, Iris, Lobelia, Malva, Stachys.

Linaria

A, HP | Zn 2–10

Baby snapdragon, Spurred snapdragon, Toadflax

p. 406

Upright plants with lance-shaped leaves from which shoot stiff spikes bearing small, snapdragon-like flowers in violet, orange, yellow, white, purple, pink, maroon, gold, and more; 6"–4'. Use small species in rock gardens, in dry stone walls, or between paving stones; larger species, in the spring border.

Type Annual, hardy perennial
Zone *Annual:* 2–10, H 9–1; *Perennial:* 4–10 H 9–1 (see species list, p. 461). Prefers cool temperatures and will stop bloomiing in hot weather
Flowering Season Late spring to summer; midsummer where climate is cool

SOWING

Indoors Prechilled seed 6–8 weeks before planting.
Outdoors 2–3 weeks before last frost, at intervals to extend bloom time; in mild-winter areas, sow in early fall.
Depth Just cover.

GERMINATING

Time 10–15 days.
Requirements Easy. Place seed in plastic bag with moist growing mix. Refrigerate 3 weeks. Provide light and a constant temperature of 55°–60°F.

TRANSPLANTING

Time After last frost.
Spacing *Small species:* 8"–10". *Large species:* 24"–36".
Light Full sun.
Soil Any.

CARING FOR PLANTS

Easy. Water during dry spells. Cut back annuals after blooming to stimulate a more abundant second bloom. Perennials bloom more successfully if thinned occasionally, but intense summer heat will stop blooming altogether. Some species are invasive.

PROPAGATING

Take cuttings of perennials in early summer, divide in spring, or grow from seed; may also self-seed. Plants grown from seed will bloom in their first year.

COMBINATIONS

Althaea, Antirrhinum, Atriplex, Cosmos, Dianthus, Knautia, Matthiola.

CAUTION

Toxic if eaten; *L. dalmatica* and *L. vulgaris* are listed as invasive in some areas, including Utah. See pp. 494–495 for advice.

Linnaea

HP | Zn 1–5 | Partial shade, Full shade | Ordinary soil

Twinflower

These delightful little mat-forming woodland subshrubs have diminutive proportions that give them a fairyland quality. Leaves are small, rounded, and evergreen. Flowers are bell-shaped, fragrant, and pink or white. They are borne in pairs on thin, wiry stems high above the foliage. Use twinflower as a shady ground cover for small areas or in rock gardens.

Type Hardy perennial
Zone 1–5, H 6–1
Flowering Season Late spring to early summer

SOWING

Indoors Sow seed outdoors only.
Outdoors As soon as ripe seed is available.
Depth Just cover.

GERMINATING

Time Very slow.
Requirements Difficult; seed is rarely available commercially. Sow in flats, sink in the ground against a north-facing wall, and cover with glass. Moisten soil occasionally, if necessary. Transplant seedlings as they appear.

TRANSPLANTING

Time Set out purchased plants in spring or autumn.
Spacing 12".
Light Part to full shade.
Soil Moist, peaty woods soil with a pH level of 4.0–5.0.

CARING FOR PLANTS

Keep soil very moist and do not disturb roots. Plants will not survive in hot weather but otherwise will spread rapidly when their cultural needs are satisfied.

PROPAGATING

Divide in early spring, root cuttings under glass, or grow from seed.

Linum

A, HP | Zn 2–10 | Full sun | Good for xeriscaping, Ordinary soil

Flax

p. 407

This very large genus includes annuals and perennials that are grown for their cheerful, abundant, funnel- or cup-shaped flowers. Fine, deep green foliage provides a strong foil for their clear blue, red, yellow, or white blooms. Plants are 2"–4' tall. Use flax in borders and rock gardens.

Type Annual, short-lived hardy perennial
Zone *Annual:* 2–10, H 8–1. *Perennial:* 5–9, H 9–3 (see species list, p. 461); flowers most profusely in cool weather
Flowering Season *Annual:* Summer. *Perennial:* Late spring, summer, or autumn, depending on species

SOWING

Indoors Starting seed outdoors is recommended, but seed may be sown indoors 6–8 weeks before last frost, in peat pots.

Outdoors Early spring, when soil is cool and a light frost is still possible. Make successive plantings of annuals every 2–3 weeks for continuous blooming. Sow in early autumn where winters are mild.
Depth 1/8".

GERMINATING

Time 20–25 days.
Requirements 65°–70°F.

TRANSPLANTING

Time After last frost.
Spacing *Small species:* 4"–6". *Medium species:* 6"–12". *Large species:* 12"–18".
Light Full sun.
Soil Ordinary, well drained, not too rich, with a pH level of 5.0–7.0. *L. perenne* is a suitable choice for xeriscaping.

CARING FOR PLANTS

Easy. Cut back half of the flowering stalks early in the growing season to extend the blooming period. Trim perennials to the ground in autumn. Plants resent root disturbance and are short lived.

PROPAGATING

Take cuttings of perennials in early summer, divide in spring in Zones 5–6 (autumn in Zones 7–9), or grow from seed. Annuals and some perennials may self-seed. Plants grown from seed will bloom their first year.

COMBINATIONS

Achillea, Coreopsis, Delphinium, Gaillardia, roses, *Senecio.*

CAUTION

Harmful if eaten.

L

Liriope

HP | Zn 4-9

Lilyturf

p. 407

Liriope *are useful but overused evergreen perennials, 8"–18". They are grown for their resilient, grasslike foliage and pretty spikes of purple or white flowers. They make an attractive ground cover or path edging, or may be used as border plants.*

Type Hardy perennial
Zone 4–9, H 12–1 (see species list, pp. 461 and 482)
Flowering Season Late summer to early autumn

SOWING

Indoors 6–8 weeks before planting out.
Outdoors Early spring, when soil is cool and a light frost is still possible, or late autumn.
Depth 1/4".

GERMINATING

Time 30 days.
Requirements Soak seed in warm water for 24 hours before planting; provide a constant 65°–70°F thereafter.

TRANSPLANTING

Time After last frost.
Spacing 12"–18".
Light Part to full shade; full sun where soil is sufficiently moist.
Soil Prefers moist, fertile, and well-drained soil but will perform quite well in dry. *L. spicata* is suitable for xeriscaping.

CARING FOR PLANTS

Easy. A most obliging plant with almost no faults, which is why they're used so extensively. Water during dry spells. Remove flowering stems after blooming to keep plants looking neat and prevent self-seeding. Tidy throughout winter by removing dead leaves. Cut back plants to 3"–6" in late winter.

PROPAGATING

Divide at any time or grow from seed. Many species will self-seed.

COMBINATIONS

Ferns, *Hosta, Lamium, Muscari, Sedum, Viola.*

CAUTION

L. spicata is invasive in some areas and is listed as such in Maryland. See pp. 494–495 for advice.

Lisianthus See *Eustoma*

Lithodora (syn. *Lithospermum*)

HP | Zn 6–9

Gromwell, Puccoon

p. 407

Shrubs and subshrubs grown as perennials, Lithodora *feature charming blue, purple, white, or yellow funnel-shaped flowers and strong, tidy evergreen foliage. Plants grow from 6" to 4'. Useful in rock gardens and borders.*

Type Hardy perennial
Zone 6–9, H 8–6 (see species list, p. 461)
Flowering Season *L. diffusa* blooms in late spring to midsummer; other species bloom in spring and again in autumn, others still in summer, then sporadically into autumn

GERMINATING

Requirements Not successfully grown from seed.

TRANSPLANTING

Spacing *Small species:* 6"–8". *Medium species:* 12". *Large species:* 18".
Light Full sun to part shade.
Soil Grows in a wide range of conditions but produces more flowers in poor soil. Most species prefer moist, well-drained soil. *L. diffusa* requires acid soil.

CARING FOR PLANTS

Water frequently during hot weather, trim back after flowering, and mulch with straw in winter. Do not disturb.

PROPAGATING

Take cuttings in midsummer.

COMBINATIONS

Alyssum, Asplenium, Campanula, Helianthemum, Iberis, Lobularia, Sedum. The electric blue flowers of *L. diffusa* 'Grace Ward' are stunning in front of crimson or deep pink azaleas.

L

Lithospermum See *Lithodora*

Lobelia

A, TP*, HP | Zn 1–10  

Lobelia

p. 407

Annual and perennial plants grown for their intensely colored flowers. Perennials are usually tall (3'–4') and erect, bearing tiny scarlet, blue, or yellow flowers in terminal spikes; annuals are low (4"–12") with frothy green foliage and masses of tiny blooms in strong shades of purple, blue, purple-red, pink, and white. Grow perennials in borders and wild gardens; use annuals in baskets, containers, or rock gardens or for edging borders and paths.

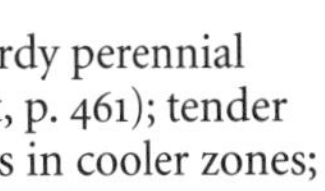

Type Annual, tender perennial, hardy perennial
Zone 1–10, H 10–1 (see species list, p. 461); tender species are often grown as annuals in cooler zones; annuals perform most successfully where summers are not too hot
Flowering Season Spring to fall, depending on species

SOWING

Indoors *Annual:* 6–8 weeks before planting out. *Perennial:* Prechilled seed 8–10 weeks before last frost.
Outdoors Most successful when started indoors.
Depth Surface.

GERMINATING

Time 15–21 days.
Requirements Light and 65°–75°F. Highly susceptible to damping-off; sow in vermiculite, and water only from below. *Perennial:* Place seed in a plastic bag together with moist growing medium and refrigerate for 3 months.

TRANSPLANTING

Time 2–3 weeks after last frost, when temperatures remain above 40°F.
Spacing *Small species:* 4"–6". *Medium species:* 9"–12". *Large species:* 18"–25".
Light Full sun or part shade, with shade from hot afternoon sun in the South.
Soil Moist, humus-rich, with a pH level of 6.0–7.5. Plants are susceptible to root rot where drainage is poor.

CARING FOR PLANTS

Easy. For best results, water frequently during dry periods and keep mulched all year. Deadhead regularly. Plants will survive hot summers if given good drainage, afternoon shade, and abundant water.

PROPAGATING

Take cuttings of perennials, divide in spring in Zones 2–6 (autumn in Zones 7–10), or grow from seed. Both annuals and perennials may self-seed. Plants grown from seed will bloom in their first year.

COMBINATIONS

Combine deep blue and purple species with *Begonia, Impatiens, Nasturtium, Pelargonium,* silver-leaved *Senecio* and *Solenostemon.* Tall species mix well with *Aconitum,* autumn-blooming *Amemone,* and *Gampanula.*

CAUTION

Harmful if eaten.

Lobularia

A | Zn 3–10

Sweet alyssum

p. 407

Fast growing, compact, and carefree, these annuals are grown for the clusters of tiny, scented, deep pink, purple, or white flowers that adorn them in summer. Plants are 3"–12" high. Leaves are small, lance-shaped, and tidy. Useful as edging or container plants.

Type Annual
Zone 3–10, H 12–1; requires cool weather to flower effectively
Flowering Season Late spring through autumn

SOWING

Indoors 6–8 weeks before last frost.
Outdoors Early spring, when soil is cool and a light frost is still possible, or early autumn.
Depth Surface.

GERMINATING

Time 5–14 days.
Requirements Easy. Light and 55°–70°F.

TRANSPLANTING

Time After last frost.
Spacing *Small cultivars:* 6"–8". *Large cultivars:* 8"–12".
Light Full sun or light shade.
Soil Prefers a moist loam with a pH level of 6.0–7.0; tolerates dry soil and may be used for xeriscaping.

CARING FOR PLANTS

Easy. Protect young plants from slugs. Water regularly. If flowering is lessened due to hot weather, cut back plants by half to rejuvenate; shear plants after first flowering to encourage stronger second bloom.

PROPAGATING

Grow from seed. Plant may self-seed.

COMBINATIONS

Campanula, Felicia, Lithodora, Nemophila, and *Ranunculus.*

Lonas

A | Zn 3–9

African daisy, Golden ageratum, Yellow ageratum

A Mediterranean native, African daisy is grown for its yellow, buttonlike, everlasting flowers borne in clusters above feathery, deep green foliage. It grows 12" tall. Site it in a sunny border or cutting bed.

Type Annual
Zone 3–9; prefers cool temperatures
Flowering Season Summer through autumn

SOWING

Indoors 6–8 weeks before last frost.
Outdoors After last frost.
Depth Just cover.

GERMINATING

Time 5–7 days.
Requirements Darkness and 70°F. Sow seed in peat pots.

TRANSPLANTING

Time After last frost.
Spacing 6"–12".
Light Sun.
Soil Light, well drained, not too rich.

CARING FOR PLANTS

Easy. Deadhead regularly and feed only sparingly. For use in dried flower arrangements, cut and dry flowering stems when heads are fully open.

PROPAGATING

Grow from seed only.

COMBINATIONS

Hemerocallis, Salvia, Stachys, Tagetes, Zinnia.

L

Lopezia

A | Zn 3–10

Lopezia *is a small genus of South American herbs and subshrubs, the most commonly available of which is* L. racemosa. *This sturdy 6"–10" plant bears abundant flowers that look remarkably like comical wasps in pink, red, lilac, white, or purple. They make a charming addition to borders, baskets, and containers.*

Type Annual
Zone 3–10; prefers warm weather
Flowering Season Begins flowering 6–8 weeks from sowing and continues through autumn

SOWING

Indoors 4 weeks before last frost.
Outdoors March through May.
Depth Just cover.

GERMINATING

Time 7–30 days.
Requirements Easy. Provide temperature of 65°–85°F.

TRANSPLANTING

Time After last frost.
Spacing 8"–12".
Light Sun to light shade.
Soil Well drained, fairly fertile.

CARING FOR PLANTS

Very easy. Pinch out young plants to encourage a neat, bushy habit, and water during dry spells. Plants attract bees.

PROPAGATING

Take cuttings in spring or grow from seed. Plant self-seeds where happy.

Luffa

A | Zn 5–10

Luffa, Loofah, Dishcloth gourd, Rag gourd, Sponge gourd, Strainer vine, Vegetable sponge

Genus of annual runners, one of which is grown for its fruit, which may be either eaten or dried and used as a sponge. 12'–15' vines are quite handsome, with large, tropical-looking leaves. Lemon-yellow flowers resemble their cousins, the cucumber, and are edible. This is a fun plant to grow, as well as making an attractive climber.

Type Annual
Zone 5–10; must have hot weather and a long growing season to produce satisfactory fruit
Flowering Season Summer

SOWING

Indoors 3–4 weeks before planting out, in peat pots.
Outdoors 2 weeks after last frost.
Depth ½".

GERMINATING

Time 8–28 days.
Requirements Soak seed in warm water for 24 hours and sow where temperature is 70°–80°F.

TRANSPLANTING

Time Several weeks after last frost, when soil is warm.
Spacing 24".
Light Full sun.
Soil Rich, well drained, with a pH level of 6.0–7.0.

CARING FOR PLANTS

Easy. Water regularly and do not move. Vines require support, and fruit must be kept off the ground to avoid rot. Harvest gourds when they are 4"–6" long to eat. Allow fruit to grow to 12" to make sponges. To make luffa sponges, soak ripe luffa gourds in warm water for 2–3 days, after which skins should come away easily. Wash well to remove all seeds and loose pulp. Allow to dry for 1 week before using.

PROPAGATING

Grow from seed only.

Lunaria

Bi, HP | Zn 3–10

Honesty, Moonwort, Satin flower

p. 407

Upright, bushy plants of 18"–36", Lunaria *species bear purple or white flowers followed by showy, silver, papery seedpods. Simple but charming plants, they are most effective when scattered through woodland plantings. Use seedpods in dried flower arrangements.*

Type Hardy perennial, biennial grown as an annual
Zone *Biennial:* 3–10, H 9–1. *Perennial:* 6–9, H 9–6; prefers cool temperatures
Flowering Season Spring or early summer

SOWING

Indoors 6–8 weeks before last frost, but best started *in situ.*
Outdoors Early spring, when soil is cool and a light frost is still possible, or early autumn where winters are mild.
Depth ⅛".

GERMINATING

Time 10–14 days.
Requirements Easy. 70°F.

TRANSPLANTING

Time After last frost.
Spacing 12"–18".
Light Full sun or part shade.
Soil Plants thrive in reasonably good soil but will tolerate dry conditions.

CARING FOR PLANTS

Easy. Mulch well before first winter and do not transplant. Remove plants after blooming if self-seeding is not desired. *L. annua* dies after setting seed.

PROPAGATING

Grow from seed. Plant may self-seed.

COMBINATIONS

Ferns, *Iris, Myosotis, Phlox divaricata, Scilla, Symphytum, Tulipa.*

Lupinus

A, HP | Zn 1–9

Lupin, Lupine

p. 407

Stunning if not subtle, these brightly colored garden favorites usher in summer. Strongly architectural plants have stiff, erect flower spikes of 1'–5' that emerge from horizontal foliage. Flowers are similar to those of peas and sweet peas, and grow in large, crowded racemes of deep blue, purple, yellow, pink, or white; some are fragrant. Mass lupines in the border or scatter them through the cottage garden or wildflower meadow.

Type Annual or hardy perennial
Zone 1–9, H 9–1 (see species list, p. 462). Prefers cool, rather humid summers, and may stop blooming altogether in extreme heat; performs most gratifyingly in the cool zones of the East Coast and the warm zones of the West Coast
Flowering Season *Annual:* Flower from seed in 2 months, blooming for just a few weeks. *Perennial:* Early summer to midsummer

SOWING

Indoors 6–8 weeks before last frost, in peat pots.
Outdoors *Annual:* After last frost. *Perennial:* Early spring, when soil is cool and a light frost is still possible, or in early autumn where winters are mild.
Depth 1/8".

GERMINATING

Time 14–60 days.
Requirements Chip seed or soak in warm water for 24 hours, provide 55°–65°F thereafter.

TRANSPLANTING

Time After last frost or early autumn.
Spacing *Annual:* 12". *Small perennial species:* 12"–18". *Large perennial species:* 24"–36".
Light Full sun to light shade.
Soil Moist, well drained, with a pH level of 5.5–7.0.

CARING FOR PLANTS

Easy. Water and deadhead regularly. Feed with a low-nitrogen, high-phosphorus fertilizer. After flowering, cut down stems to base. Leave plants undisturbed.

PROPAGATING

Divide perennials in early spring, take cuttings in spring or early summer, or grow annuals and perennials from seed. Plants grown from seed will bloom their first year.

COMBINATIONS

Allium, Iris, Leucanthemum, Macleaya, Papaver.

CAUTION

Harmful if eaten.

Lychnis (syn. *Viscaria*)

Bi, HP | Zn 2–10

Campion, Catchfly

p. 408

Clump-forming biennials and perennials, some Lychnis *are rather coarse, displaying clusters of flowers in hot shades of orange, red, or purple; more-refined species have soft green or gray foliage and rose or pale pink blossoms. They range from 12" to 48" tall. Use them in borders or in cottage or wildflower gardens.*

Type Biennial or hardy perennial
Zone 2–10, H 9–1 (see species list, p. 462); most species prefer warm, dry climates
Flowering Season Summer to autumn, depending on species

SOWING

Indoors Prechill seed 8–10 weeks before sowing .
Outdoors Early spring or early autumn.
Depth Surface.

GERMINATING

Time 21–30 days.
Requirements Place seed in a plastic bag together with moist growing medium and refrigerate for 2 weeks. Provide light and 70°F thereafter.

TRANSPLANTING

Time After last frost.
Spacing *Small species:* 8"–10". *Large species:* 12"–15".
Light Full sun or part shade.
Soil Prefers moist, well-drained soil with a pH level of 5.0–7.0, but tolerates dry soil. *L. chalcedonica* is most drought tolerant and can be used in xeriscaping.

CARING FOR PLANTS

Easy. Shearing plants after flowering may result in a second bloom in autumn. Cut back to ground level in autumn and mulch heavily north of Zone 6. Most species are short lived.

PROPAGATING

Divide in spring in the North (in autumn south of Zone 6) or grow from seed. Plant may self-seed. Plants grown from seed will bloom in their first year.

COMBINATIONS

Armeria, Eremurus, Galtonia, Geum, Phlox, Veronica.

Lycoris

HB | Zn 6–10

These late-blooming bulbs bear large clusters of small, lilylike flowers of red, white, pink, or yellow that are held high on thick, leafless, 1'–3' stems. Grow them in borders, massed in front of shrubs, or scattered through light woodland gardens, where their sudden appearance is a wonderful surprise as the rest of the garden is winding down.

Type Hardy bulb
Zone 6–10, H 10–7
Flowering Season Late summer to autumn

SOWING

Indoors Start seed outdoors.
Outdoors *Seed:* As soon as ripe seed is available, usually late summer to autumn. *Bulb:* July to September.
Depth *Seed:* Just cover. *Bulb, small species:* 3"–4". *Large species:* 6"–8".

GERMINATING

Requirements Not often grown from seed, and little literature is available on the subject. Information given here is a general guideline only. Sow seed in shallow containers, plunge in the ground against a north-facing wall, and cover with glass.

TRANSPLANTING

Time Early autumn. Plant seed-grown bulbs shallowly their first year; replant at their proper depth the following autumn.
Spacing *Small species:* 4"–6". *Large species:* 12"–18".
Light Sun or part shade.
Soil Rich, well drained, either acid or neutral. Bulbs require moist-soil during the bloom period, but relatively dry otherwise.

CARING FOR PLANTS

Water regularly while bulbs are in bloom. Feed every other year during the growing season. Do not disturb roots too often.

PROPAGATING

Separate offsets after flowering.

COMBINATIONS

Ferns, *Gentiana, Hosta.* Can be grown successfully through the foliage of any plants past flowering.

Lysichiton

HP | Zn 7–9

Skunk cabbage

p. 408

These primeval-looking bog plants grow 2'–4' tall. Yellowish green or white flowers are borne on short, thick spikes (called a spadix*), surrounded by a white hoodlike spathe. They make an interesting addition to a bog garden or streamside planting.*

Type Hardy perennial
Zone 7–9, H 9–7
Flowering Season Spring

SOWING

Indoors 10–12 weeks before planting out; probably more successful when started outdoors.
Outdoors As soon as ripe seed is available, usually late summer.
Depth 1/4".

GERMINATING

Time 30–60 days.
Requirements 55°–65°F. *Indoors:* Stand flats in a pan of water to keep soil constantly moist. *Outdoors:* Do not allow soil to become dry.

TRANSPLANTING

Time After last frost.
Spacing 36"–48".
Light Prefers full sun but will tolerate part shade.
Soil Deep, rich, wet. Prepare to a depth of 12".

CARING FOR PLANTS

Easy. Keep soil moist at all times; apply mulch if plants are not growing in standing water.

PROPAGATING

Divide in early spring or grow from seed.

COMBINATIONS

Caltha, Gunnera, Hosta, Iris, Ligularia.

Lysimachia

HP | Zn 3–9 | Full sun, Partial shade | Dry soil, Ordinary soil, Moist soil

Lysimachia, Loosestrife

p. 408

Vigorous and mainly upright, these strongly architectural, summer-flowering annuals and perennials have lance-shaped leaves that grow horizontally. Their flowers may be small and white, borne in crooked, pointed clusters, or yellow and star-shaped, growing in terminal whorls. Plants normally grow 1'–3'. Prostrate L. nummularia *reaches only 3" and the tiny-leaved* L. japonica *var.* minutissima *hugs the ground. Both make good rock garden or edging plants. Taller species need plenty of space in a border or bog garden.*

Type Hardy perennial
Zone 3–9, H 8–1 (see species list, p. 462)
Flowering Season Summer

SOWING

Indoors Start seed outdoors.
Outdoors Autumn.
Depth Surface.

GERMINATING

Time 30–90 days.
Requirements Sow seed in flats, sink these into the ground against a north-facing wall, and cover with glass. Moisten soil occasionally, if necessary. Transplant to the garden when seedlings begin to trail.

TRANSPLANTING

Time After last frost.
Spacing 15"–20".
Light Full sun or part shade.
Soil Moist is ideal; will generally tolerate dry if sited in part shade, although plants will not fleurish.

CARING FOR PLANTS

Easy. For best results, keep soil moist. Cut back plants to ground level in autumn. May become invasive.

PROPAGATING

Divide in spring in the North (in autumn south of Zone 6) or grow from seed.

COMBINATIONS

Achillea, Delphinium, Ligularia, Monarda, Tagetes, Veronica.

CAUTION

L. nummularia is invasive in most of the East, South, Midwest, and West Coast. See pp. 494–495 for advice.

Lythrum

HP | Zn 3–9

Loosestrife

These beautiful, highly invasive, summer-blooming perennials were once grown for their 2'–4' spikes of pink or purple blooms. Members of this genus have invaded wetlands throughout North America, and, if grown at all, must be watched carefully and prevented from setting seed. Do not grow if they are listed as invasive in your region.

Type Hardy perennial
Zone 3–9, H 9–1
Flowering Season Summer to early autumn

SOWING

Indoors 6–8 weeks before planting out.
Outdoors Early spring, when soil is cool and a light frost is still possible, or late autumn.
Depth Just cover.

GERMINATING

Time 5–30 days.
Requirements 65°–70°F.

TRANSPLANTING

Time After last frost.
Spacing *Small species:* 18"–24". *Large species:* 24"–36".
Light Full sun or part shade.
Soil Most prefer moist soil with a pH level of 5.0–7.0.

CARING FOR PLANTS

Easy. Deadhead frequently to prevent self-seeding and to encourage abundant flowering. Divide every 3 years.

PROPAGATING

Divide in early spring.

COMBINATIONS

Artemisia, Cosmos, Ligularia, Lysimachia, Persicaria.

CAUTION

L. salicaria is listed as invasive in many areas, including Florida, Indiana, Kentucky, Maryland, Tennessee, and Virginia and much of the rest of the United States from the Midwest to New England and down through Florida—wherever there are wetlands. *L. virgatum* is listed as invasive in many areas, including Virginia. *Lythrum* has been banned in some states; check with your local Cooperative Extension Service before planting or buying seed. See also pp. 494–495 for further advice.

Machaeranthera

A, Bi, TP* | Zn 1–10

Machaeranthera *annuals, biennials, and perennials are native to western North America. Daisylike flowers with blue, purple, or white petals are borne on 2' stems. Use them for borders and cutting.*

Type Annual, biennial, and tender perennial often grown as an annual
Zone 1–10 (see species list, pp. 462); prefers a cool, dry climate but will flower for a short period in a hot, humid location
Flowering season Summer through autumn

SOWING

Indoors Sow prechilled seed 6–8 weeks before planting out.
Outdoors Early spring, when soil is cool and a light frost is still possible, or early autumn.
Depth Surface.

GERMINATING

Time 25–30 days.
Requirements Place seed in a plastic bag together with moist growing medium and refrigerate for 2 weeks. Provide light and 70°F thereafter.

TRANSPLANTING

Time After last frost.
Spacing 9"–12".
Light Full sun or light shade.
Soil Average, well drained, with a pH level of 6.0–7.0.

CARING FOR PLANTS

No special care required. *Machaeranthera* species are short lived in hot, humid climates.

PROPAGATING

Grow from seed only.

Macleaya (syn. Bocconia)

HP | Zn 4–9

Plume poppy

p. 408

These unusual, attractive perennials are highly ornamental, with deeply lobed leaves and tall, airy sprays of tiny pink or white flowers. They are tall, from 5' to 8'. Use them in place of deciduous shrubs or in a very large border.

Type Hardy perennial
Zone 4–9, H 9–1
Flowering season Summer

SOWING

Indoors Start seed outdoors.
Outdoors Early spring, when soil is cool and a light frost is still possible.
Depth Just cover.

GERMINATING

Time 14 days.
Requirements Propagation by division or root cutting is more successful than growing from seed.

TRANSPLANTING

Time After last frost.
Spacing 3'–5' or singly.
Light Sun in cool climates, part shade where summers are hot.
Soil Average, moist, well drained. Plants may spread rampantly in rich soil; their tendency to be invasive is somewhat curtailed in dry soil.

CARING FOR PLANTS

Easy. Water during dry spells, deadhead after blooming, and cut back to the ground in autumn. Divide every 3–4 years.

PROPAGATING

Take root cuttings in winter, carefully divide in early spring, or grow from seed. Plants self-seed.

COMBINATIONS

Hosta, Kniphofia, Lupinus, Phlomis.

CAUTION

All species can be invasive and will spread widely. See pp. 494–495 for advice.

M

Malcolmia

A | Zn 1–9

Malcolm stock

p. 408

Malcolmia is a small genus of fast-growing, quick-to-bloom, erect annuals and perennials, 8"–12" tall. One species, M. maritima, *is the most often grown. Flowers are four-petaled, small and dainty but profuse, in purple, pink, red, or white; some are fragrant. Foliage may have a gray tinge. Grow these in the border or in a cottage garden.*

Type Annual
Zone 1–9, H 9–1 (see species list, p. 462); requires cool temperatures
Flowering season Blooms from spring through mid-autumn with successive sowings

SOWING

Indoors Best started outdoors.
Outdoors For continuous blooming, sow at 3-week intervals from early spring, when a light frost is still possible, through late summer. Where winters are mild, sow in autumn for spring blooms.
Depth Surface.

GERMINATING

Time 10–14 days.
Requirements Light and 55°–60°F.

TRANSPLANTING

Time Set out purchased plants after last frost.
Spacing 3"–4".
Light Sun or part shade.
Soil Will grow in any soil but prefers one that is rich and moist. Add well-rotted manure at planting time.

CARING FOR PLANTS

Easy. Water frequently; *Malcolmia* will die back during prolonged hot spells. Plants may be discarded after flowering, but if self-seeding is desired, allow seed to mature and disperse before uprooting.

PROPAGATING

Grow from seed. Plant may self-seed although colors may not come true.

Malephora

TP* | Zn 9–10

p. 408

Members of this genus are admirably tough little succulents with neat gray-green foliage and brightly colored, daisylike flowers in shades of golden yellow, orange, and orange-red. Blooms continue month after month. Malephora *is tolerant of heat and pollution, making it a good choice for sidewalk plantings. It is also a fine plant for borders, containers, and hanging baskets.*

Type Perennial; often grown as an annual in cooler regions
Zone 9–10, H 12–1 (see species list, p. 462); tolerates considerable heat but not humidity
Flowering season Spring to early autumn

SOWING

Indoors 10–12 weeks before last frost.
Outdoors After last frost.
Depth Just cover.

GERMINATING

Time 15–20 days.
Requirements 65°–75°F.

TRANSPLANTING

Time After last frost.
Spacing 12"–18".
Light Full sun.
Soil Very well drained. Tolerates dry, but supplementary watering is appreciated during very hot, dry weather.

CARING FOR PLANTS

Easy; very tolerant of extreme conditions. When grown as perennials, plants become sparse with age and should be replanted about every 4 years. May be affected by mealybugs.

PROPAGATING

Take stem cuttings in spring or summer or grow from seed.

COMBINATIONS

Coreopsis, Sedum, Sempervivum.

Malope

A | Zn 1–8

Annual mallow

One species in this genus, M. trifida, *is an upright, branching annual that is grown for its attractive lobed foliage and large, open, trumpet-shaped flowers. Blooms, which are held singly, may be deep pink or white; plants grow to 3'. Native to the Mediterranean, use it in the border or cottage garden.*

Type Annual
Zone 1–8, H 8–1; prefers cool temperatures
Flowering season From spring until flowering is stopped by hot weather

SOWING

Indoors Prechilled seed 4–6 weeks before last frost, in peat pots.
Outdoors 2–3 weeks before last frost.
Depth Just cover.

GERMINATING

Time 14–30 days.
Requirements Place seed in a plastic bag together with moist growing medium and refrigerate for 3 weeks. Provide 65°–75°F thereafter.

TRANSPLANTING

Time After last frost.
Spacing *Small species:* 9"–12". *Large species:* 24".
Light Sun or light shade.
Soil Light, well drained. High fertility will result in abundant leaves but few flowers.

CARING FOR PLANTS

Stake young plants individually, being careful not to damage roots. Do not disturb.

PROPAGATING

Grow from seed. Plant may self-seed.

COMBINATIONS

Antirrhinum, Campanula, Delphinium, early-blooming *Salvia.*

Malva

A, Bi, HP | Zn 3–10

Mallow, Musk mallow

p. 408

Bushy, upright annuals, biennials, and perennials of great charm and beauty that grow 2'–4' tall. Plants are covered with 2" cup-shaped blooms of pink, white, or purple. A good choice for the summer border or cottage garden.

Type Annual, biennial, short-lived hardy perennial
Zone 3–7, to Zone 10 in the West, H 8–1 (see species list, p. 462); prefers cool temperatures
Flowering season Summer to early autumn

SOWING

Indoors 6–8 weeks before planting out.
Outdoors Early spring, when soil is cool and a light frost is still possible, or early autumn.
Depth Just cover.

GERMINATING

Time 5–21 days.
Requirements Easy. 70°F.

TRANSPLANTING

Time After last frost.
Spacing *Small species:* 10"–15". *Large species:* 12"–24".
Light Full sun, or part shade where summers are hot.
Soil Prefers dry, well-drained soil; quite tolerant of a wide range of conditions. *M. alcea* and *M. moschata* are useful plants for xeriscaping.

CARING FOR PLANTS

Easy. Feed and water regularly and cut back to ground level in autumn. Plants require more frequent watering during very hot spells.

PROPAGATING

Take cuttings in spring, divide in spring north of Zone 7 (in autumn in the South), or grow from seed. Plant may self-seed. Plants grown from seed will bloom in their first year.

COMBINATIONS

Echinops, annual *Iberis, Limonium.*

CAUTION

Harmful if eaten.

M

Mandevilla (syn. *Dipladenia*)

HP*, TP* | Zn 8–10

p. 409

These popular climbing plants are a favorite choice of gardeners who want to bring a look of the tropics to their back decks, where the 10'–15' woody vines will obligingly twine through railings, flowering tirelessly all summer. The leaves are large, leathery, and somewhat coarse. The real glory of Mandevilla *is its large, showy, trumpet-shaped flowers, which are usually a warm, tropical pink, although white-flowered species are also available.*

Type Perennial or tender perennial; often grown as an annual
Zone 8–10, H 12–2; grow as an annual in cooler zones
Flowering Season From summer until nighttime temperature reaches 40°F

SOWING

Indoors 6–8 weeks before planting out.
Outdoors After last frost, only where plants are perennial.
Depth Just cover.

GERMINATING

Time 14–30 days.
Requirements Sow in a mixture of half peat, half sand at a temperature of 65°–75°F.

TRANSPLANTING

Time 2 weeks after last frost.
Spacing Grow singly or 3'–4' apart.
Light Full sun; plants tolerate light afternoon shade where summers are hot.
Soil Moist, well-drained.

Mandevilla (cont'd)

CARING FOR PLANTS

Pinch young plants to increase branching. Mulch soil, water well, and feed periodically throughout the growing season; reduce watering as flowering begins to diminish in autumn. Where plants are not hardy, bring indoors before the first frost and keep at 60°–65°F, watering sparingly. Prune vines in late winter or early spring, cutting back drastically if necessary. Plants are susceptible to spidermites and whitefly.

PROPAGATING

Cuttings in late spring or summer, or start from seed.

COMBINATIONS

Although mandevillas are most often seen standing alone, they can be grown with many other plants to create exciting combinations. For a romantic look, pair them with other climbers such as *Clematis, Ipomoea alba, Plumbago auriculata,* or *Thunbergia grandiflora.* Or you can create more of a junglelike effect by planting them among other tropicals, such as *Hibiscus, Musa, Phormium,* and *Zantedeschia.* If you grow them in containers, enhance their beauty, and make them look less lonely, by planting a mass of petunias or variegated ivy around the mandevilla vines.

CAUTION

All parts of the plant may be harmful if eaten; contact with sap may cause a rash.

M

Martynia See *Proboscidea*

Matricaria See *Tanacetum*

Matteuccia

HP | Zn 2–9 |  

Ostrich fern

p. 409

One tall, attractive, vase-shaped fern from this small genus is commonly grown: M. struthiopteris. *Its fronds grow neatly from a central core, giving a tropical, almost prehistoric look to an informal garden. These ferns are equally at home in a formal setting, and grown singly in planters they take on a stately appearance that harks back to a more elegant age. Unfortunately, this does not hold true in a hot or dry location.*

Type Hardy perennial
Zone 2–7 in the East or to Zone 9 in the West and Northwest, H 8–1
Flowering season N/A

SOWING

Indoors When spores ripen in late winter.
Outdoors Not recommended.
Depth Surface.

GERMINATING

Time 10–365 days.
Requirements Difficult. Requires 60°–75°F. See pages 24–25 for instructions on starting ferns from spores.

TRANSPLANTING

Time After last frost or early autumn, when plants are 2–3 years old.
Spacing 24".
Light Full to part shade; sun only in really moist soil.
Soil Moist to wet, rich. An ostrich fern grown in dry soil is a sorry sight.

CARING FOR PLANTS

Keep soil moist during dry spells. Mulch annually with organic matter. May be invasive where it is content; keep in check by regularly removing plants that stray beyond their bounds.

PROPAGATING

Divide clumps in autumn or early spring, dig up offsets from underground runners, or grow from spores.

COMBINATIONS

So many plants are enhanced by a few ostrich ferns — *Astilbe, Epimedium, Gallium, Hesperis, Hosta seiboldiana, Rheum, Rhododendron, Rodgersia, Tiarella, Zantedeschia.* Planted with spring flowers that go dormant in summer, these ferns will neatly fill in the gaps but will not overpower the smaller plants while they bloom: *Dicentra, Erythronium, Sanguinaria, Trillium.*

Matthiola

A, Bi, HP* | Zn 2–10

Gillyflower, Stock

p. 409

Erect, bushy plants, 12"–30" tall, Matthiola *bear highly fragrant flowers clustered thickly on long spikes. Blooms are red, purple, pink, blue, or white; lance-shaped leaves have a gray cast. They are stunning in the border.*

Type Annual, biennial, or hardy perennial often grown as an annual
Zone 2–10, H 8–1; performs best where temperatures are cool (below 75°F); must have a night temperature below 60°F
Flowering season Spring

SOWING

Indoors *Annual or perennial:* 6–8 weeks before last frost. *Biennial:* Summer.
Outdoors After last frost. Seed may also be sown in late summer through early autumn in Zones 9–10 for early spring blooms.
Depth Surface.

GERMINATING

Time 3–20 days.
Requirements Light and 55°–65°F. Very susceptible to damping-off; sow in vermiculite and always water from below.

TRANSPLANTING

Time *Annual or perennial:* After last frost in the North, autumn in the South. *Biennial:* Autumn.
Spacing *Dwarf cultivars:* 6"–9". *Large cultivars:* 12"–18".
Light Full sun, except where summers are very hot.
Soil Moist, well drained, very fertile, neutral or alkaline.

CARING FOR PLANTS

Pinch out lateral shoots to produce taller specimens, and keep plants somewhat crowded to induce earlier blooming. Water regularly and fertilize monthly. Watch for aphids and powdery mildew.

PROPAGATING

Take cuttings from perennials in summer or grow all kinds from seed.

COMBINATIONS

Dianthus, Linaria, Stachys, Viola.

Maurandya See *Asarina*

Mazus

HP | Zn 5–8

Mazus

p. 409

These creeping perennials, 2"–4" tall, bear delicate, tubular flowers of blue or white and feature attractive green foliage. Use Mazus *as a ground cover or pathway edging or in woodland or rock gardens; it withstands moderate foot traffic.*

Type Hardy perennial
Zone 5–8, H 8–5 (see species list, p. 463)
Flowering season Spring or summer, depending on species

GERMINATING

Requirements Propagate plants by division.

TRANSPLANTING

Time Set out purchased plants in spring or autumn.
Spacing 8"–10".
Light Part to full shade, or full sun in cool climates.
Soil Cool, moist, peaty.

CARING FOR PLANTS

Mulch in spring to keep soil cool and moist, and again in winter.

PROPAGATING

Divide in spring.

COMBINATIONS

Ferns, *Iris, Sedum.*

Meconopsis

HP | Zn 6–9

M

Asiatic poppy

p. 409

These alpine plants are best known for their enchanting blue, poppylike blooms, although lesser-known species bear yellow, orange, white, red, pink, or purple flowers. Plants grow from 12" to 5' tall, and flowers are held singly on slender stems. Their charm is only enhanced by the brevity of their lives. Use them in borders or rock gardens.

Type Hardy perennial
Zone 6–9, H 9–8 (see species list, p. 463); performs most successfully in the cool, damp climate of the Pacific Northwest
Flowering season Spring to early autumn, depending on species

SOWING

Indoors Best started *in situ.*
Outdoors Early spring to mid-spring.
Depth Just cover.

GERMINATING

Time 21 days.
Requirements 60°–75°F.

TRANSPLANTING

Time Set out purchased plants in spring.
Spacing 8"–12".
Light Sun or part shade.
Soil Moist.

CARING FOR PLANTS

Water during dry spells. Cut back hard in spring.

PROPAGATING

Divide in spring or grow from seed.

COMBINATIONS

Allium, Digitalis, Hosta, Rhododendron, roses.

Megasea See *Bergenia*

Melica

HP | Zn 4–9

Melic grass, Melic

In this large genus of grasses, two are grown ornamentally, M. altissima *and* M. nutans. *Leaves are flat or rolled, 12"–24"; inflorescences are like tight wads of silvery silk. Use these grasses in wildflower gardens or mixed grass plantings.*

Type Hardy perennial
Zone 4–9, H 8–5 (see species list, p. 463)
Flowering season Summer

SOWING

Indoors Best started *in situ.*
Outdoors Early spring to mid-spring.
Depth Just cover.

GERMINATING

Time 21 days.
Requirements 60°–75°F.

TRANSPLANTING

Time Set out purchased plants in spring.
Spacing 8"–12".
Light Sun or part shade.
Soil Average, moist.

CARING FOR PLANTS

Water during dry spells. Cut back hard in spring.

PROPAGATING

Divide in spring or grow from seed.

Melissa

HP | Zn 4–9

Balm

p. 409

The most popular plant in this genus of upright perennials is M. officinalis, *an herb grown for culinary use or ornament. Its leaves are toothed and opposite, and typical of the Mint Family, to which it belongs; one cultivar has golden foliage. Plants grow to 2'. Native to Europe and Asia.*

Type Hardy perennial
Zone 4–9, H 9–1
Flowering season Early summer through autumn

SOWING

Indoors 8–10 weeks before planting out.
Outdoors Late autumn.
Depth Surface.

GERMINATING

Time 14–21 days.
Requirements Light and 70°F.

TRANSPLANTING

Time After last frost.
Spacing 18"–24".
Light Full sun to light shade.
Soil Sandy, dry, with a pH level of 6.5–7.5. Leaves will be more aromatic in poor soil.

CARING FOR PLANTS

Ensure healthy air circulation to avoid powdery mildew. If *M. officinalis* is grown for culinary use, cut back hard periodically to stimulate a fresh supply of new leaves. Cut back to ground level in autumn. Use fresh or dried leaves in cooking. To dry, harvest leaves just prior to or immediately after blooming, dry quickly at 90°F or higher, and store in an airtight container.

PROPAGATING

Divide in early spring, take stem cuttings in spring or summer, or grow from seed. Plants may self-seed.

COMBINATIONS

Campanula, Dianthus, Salvia.

Mentha

HP | Zn 3–10

Mint

p. 409

Spreading perennials, mints are usually grown for culinary use, but variegated leaf forms are also very ornamental. Small pink, white, or purple flowers grow in terminal spikes; plants are 18"–36" tall. Best suited to the herb garden because of their invasiveness.

Type Hardy perennial
Zone 3–10, H 9–1 (see species list, p. 482)
Flowering season Summer

GERMINATING

Requirements Propagation is most successful by division or cuttings.

TRANSPLANTING

Time Spring or autumn.
Spacing *Small species:* 8"–10". *Medium species:* 12"–15". *Large species:* 24".
Light Full sun or part shade.
Soil Moist, well drained, with a pH level of 6.5–8.0. Amend with compost; do not use manure, which may cause rust.

CARING FOR PLANTS

Easy. Pinch back tips of young plants to increase leaf production. Divide and replant to a new location every 3–4 years to maintain vigor. To prevent mint from overtaking your garden, plant roots in a well-drained tub, either above or below ground, cutting back stray growth to prevent rooting. Mint leaves can be dried for use in winter but retain a more appealing flavor if chopped and frozen (wash and dry thoroughly beforehand). Or pot up *M.* × *suaveolens* in early autumn to grow indoors, give plants 5 hours of sunlight a day, feed lightly once a month, do not overwater, and keep leggy growth in check.

PROPAGATING

Take cuttings, divide, or plant runners. In fact, mint's natural urge to overtake the garden is so strong that it can be reproduced by almost any method, except, perversely, by seed.

CAUTION

M. piperata is listed as invasive in some areas, including Kentucky. See pp. 494–495 for advice.

Mentzelia

A, Bi | Zn 3–8

Starflower

Star flower's bushy plants bear golden yellow, cup-shaped blossoms (fragrant in some species) and prominent, hairy stamens; 18"–48". Use these American natives in a sunny border.

Type Annual, biennial
Zone 3–8, H 9–1; prefers cool, dry climates
Flowering season Early summer

SOWING

Indoors Start seed outdoors.
Outdoors After last frost.
Depth Just cover.

GERMINATING

Time 5–21 days.
Requirements 55°–60°F.

TRANSPLANTING

Time Set out purchased plants after last frost, when temperatures remain above 40°F.
Spacing 8"–10".
Light Full sun.
Soil Moist, well drained, fertile, with a pH level of 5.0–8.0; tolerates dry soil.

CARING FOR PLANTS

Easy. Regular feeding and watering are essential if plants are to remain attractive. After first heavy blooming, cut back to 2". Flowers will close on cloudy days. Do not move.

PROPAGATING

Grow from seed. Plant may self-seed in the South.

COMBINATIONS

Bassia, Nigella, Petunia.

Merremia

TP* | Zn 10

p. 410

These climbing vines were, until recently, categorized as Ipomoea; M. tuberosa, *wood rose, is the most popular. Flowers are trumpet-shaped and golden yellow, white, or purple; foliage is lush and attractive.*

Type Tender perennial; usually grown as an annual
Zone 10, H 12–10; grown as an annual in cooler regions
Flowering season Summer, or late winter to spring, depending on species.

SOWING

Indoors 4 weeks before last frost.
Outdoors 3–4 weeks before last frost, only in Zone 10.
Depth ⅛".

GERMINATING

Time 8–35 days.
Requirements Chip seed and soak for 24 hours in warm water, then provide a temperature of 65°–85°F.

TRANSPLANTING

Time After last frost.
Spacing Grow singly.
Light Full sun, or with afternoon shade where summers are very hot.
Soil Prefers deep, fertile, very well-drained soil but will tolerate drought; however, vines may drop leaves during prolonged dry spells.

CARING FOR PLANTS

Provide a trellis and shelter from winds. If growing in containers, allow soil to dry out between waterings. Where plants are perennial, prune in late winter or early spring; these vines can be quite rampant. Spider mites can be a problem.

PROPAGATING

Seed is the most reliable method; propagating by cuttings is possible but difficult.

CAUTION

Seeds are poisonous. *M. tuberosa* is listed as invasive in some areas, including Florida. See pp. 494–495 for advice.

M

Mertensia

HP | Zn 3–9

p. 410

These lovely perennials, some of which are native American wildflowers, are grown for their handsome blue-green foliage and enchanting clusters of small, trumpet-shaped flowers in shades of blue, purple, pink, or white. Plants are 8"–3' tall. Massed and in full bloom, these demure plants are a breathtaking sight, but they are also lovely when grown in small clumps in a mixed woodland planting or rock garden.

Type Hardy perennial
Zone 3–9, H 7–1 (see species list, p. 463)
Flowering season Spring to early summer

SOWING

Indoors Start seed outdoors only.
Outdoors As soon as fresh seed is available, usually in summer.
Depth Just cover.

GERMINATING

Time 30–60 days.
Requirements Sow seed sparsely in flats, sink in the ground against a north-facing wall, and cover with glass. Moisten soil occasionally, if necessary. Transplant seedlings to the garden in autumn after one full growing season.

TRANSPLANTING

Time Set out purchased plants in early spring or autumn.
Spacing 8"–12".
Light Part to full shade; full sun is acceptable only in Northern zones.
Soil Moist, fertile, woods soil, with nearly neutral pH.

Mertensia (cont'd)

CARING FOR PLANTS

Plants grown from seed will take at least 3 years to flower. Mulch to keep soil cool and moist. Water regularly in spring, easing off after blooming and ceasing altogether when plants go dormant in summer; plants will disappear entirely at this point. Do not move.

PROPAGATING

Divide carefully immediately after flowering or grow from seed. Plant may self-seed.

COMBINATIONS

Stunning massed alone, or combine with *Dicentra,* ferns, candelabra *Primula,* or *Tiarella.*

Mesembryanthemum See *Dorotheanthus*

Milium

HP | Zn 6–9

In this small genus of perennial grasses, native to North America, Europe, and Asia, only one is widely grown. Valued for its golden yellow foliage, M. effusum *'Aureum' has narrow and refined leaf blades; its feathery inflorescences are used in dried arrangements. Plants grow to 18". Use it as a foil for contrasting colors and textures.*

Type Hardy perennial
Zone 6–9, H 9–6
Flowering season Late spring to summer

SOWING

Indoors Sow seed outdoors only.
Outdoors Early spring to mid-spring.
Depth Just cover.

GERMINATING

Time 21 days.
Requirements 60°–75°F.

TRANSPLANTING

Time Set out purchased plants in spring.
Spacing 12"–24".
Light Shade.
Soil Moist, fertile.

CARING FOR PLANTS

Water regularly and feed occasionally.

PROPAGATING

Divide in spring in Zone 6 (in autumn in Zones 7–9) or grow from seed. Plant may self-seed.

COMBINATIONS

Aubrieta, Bellis, Erysimum, Myosotis.

Mimulus (syn. *Diplacus*)

A, TP*, HP* | Zn 2–10 

Monkey flower, Musk

p. 410

Grown for their irresistible, tubular, lipped flowers, these charmers come in every shade of red, orange, yellow, and pink. Blooms are often freckled and multicolored. Attractive foliage and neat habit are a bonus. Plants grow from 2" to 36". They are perfect as an edging, in the border, or as a rock garden plant where the climate is right.

Type Annual, tender perennial, hardy perennial
Zone *Annual:* 2–10; *Perennial:* 3–9, H 12–1 (see species list, p. 463); tender perennial species are often grown as annuals in cooler zones; prefers the mild climate of the California coast
Flowering season Spring to autumn, depending on species

SOWING

Indoors Prechilled seed 10–12 weeks before last frost.
Outdoors Late winter.
Depth Surface.

Mimulus (cont'd)

GERMINATING

Time 7–21 days.
Requirements Place seed in a plastic bag together with moist growing medium and refrigerate for 3 weeks. Provide light and 70°–75°F thereafter.

TRANSPLANTING

Time After last frost.
Spacing *Small species:* 6"–9". *Medium species:* 12"–24". *Large species:* 24"–36".
Light Afternoon shade in hot climates, full sun where summers are cool.
Soil Moist, rich, with a pH level of 6.0–7.0.

CARING FOR PLANTS

Easy. Keep soil moist, particularly in hot weather; deadhead regularly. Mulch perennials in winter.

PROPAGATING

Divide perennials, take cuttings in spring, or grow perennials and annuals from seed. Plants grown from seed will bloom in their first year.

COMBINATIONS

Geranium, Hosta, Iris pseudacorus, Lobelia, Primula.

Mina See *Ipomoea*

Minuartia

HP | Zn 4–9

Sandwort

Mossy cushions of minuscule, bright green leaves and tiny white flowers, these charming creeping plants grow happily in the gritty soil of rock gardens, between paving stones, or in dry stone walls. They are also a good choice for oriental-style gardens.

Type Hardy perennial
Zone 4–9, H 9–1
Flowering season Spring to summer, depending on species

SOWING

Indoors 6–8 weeks before last frost.
Outdoors Early spring, when soil is cool and a light frost is still possible, or late autumn.
Depth Surface

GERMINATING

Time 8–30 days.
Requirements Requires light. Sow at 68°F; if germination does not take place within 3–4 weeks, move to 25°–50°F for 2–4 weeks.

TRANSPLANTING

Time After last frost.
Spacing 6"–8".
Light Full sun; part shade where summers are hot.
Soil Moist, well drained and gritty, supplemented with organic matter.

CARING FOR PLANTS

Easy. Feed lightly from time to time; plants sited in full sun will require frequent watering.

PROPAGATING

Take basal cuttings, divide in early to midsummer, or grow from seed.

COMBINATIONS

Anemonella, Prunella, Saxifraga, Shortia, Veronica, Viola.

Mirabilis

A, HP, TP | Zn 3–10

Umbrellawort, Marvel of Peru

p. 410

Mirabilis *species are bushy plants that bear fragrant, trumpet-shaped flowers that open in the evening. Blooms come in white, pink, red, or yellow; plants are 2'–4' tall.* M. jalapa, *four-o'clock, is the most popular species. Plant these near a patio, door, or window to catch their heavenly scent.*

Type Annual, hardy perennial or tender perennial
Zone *Annual:* 3–7. *Perennial:* 5–10, H 12–3 (see species list, p. 463); requires warm temperature, but does not like humid climates
Flowering season Summer to autumn

SOWING

Indoors 6–8 weeks before planting out, in peat pots.
Outdoors 1 week after last frost, or in autumn where winters are mild.
Depth Surface.

GERMINATING

Time 5–21 days.
Requirements Light and 70°F.

TRANSPLANTING

Time After last frost.
Spacing *Small species:* 6"–9". *Medium species:* 12"–18". *Large species:* 24"–36".
Light Full sun to partial shade.
Soil Average, well drained, with a pH level of 6.0–7.0. *M. multiflora* is drought tolerant and suitable for xeriscaping.

CARING FOR PLANTS

Easy. Feed monthly. Blooms more prolifically if watered regularly. Cut back to the ground after flowering. Aphids may be attracted to young plants.

PROPAGATING

Divide tuberous roots in spring or grow from seed. Plant may self-seed in mild climates.

COMBINATIONS

Combine these evening bloomers with silver-leaved plants that reflect the moonlight, such as *Helichrysum, Senecio* or *Stachys,* then add other evening bloomers: *Brugmansia, Ipomoea alba, Lilium* 'Casa Blanca', and *Nicotiana.*

CAUTION

Roots and seeds are toxic if eaten.

Miscanthus

HP | Zn 5–9

Miscanthus, Japanese silver grass

p. 410

The most widely grown ornamental grass, Miscanthus *come in many sizes and colors. Most of these are vigorous and upright, growing from 3' to 9', with handsome, flat leaf blades and very showy, silky inflorescences. They are useful in borders or mixed grass plantings.*

Type Hardy perennial
Zone 5–9, H 9–1
Flowering season Late summer to autumn

SOWING

Indoors Start seed outdoors.
Outdoors After last frost.
Depth Surface.

GERMINATING

Time 14–60 days.
Requirements Start species only from seed. Propagate cultivars by division. Provide light and 60°–75°F.

TRANSPLANTING

Time Set out purchased plants in spring or autumn.
Spacing *Small species and cultivars:* 24"–36". *Large species and cultivars:* Singly, giving 4–6 horizontal feet of growing room.
Light Full sun or light shade.
Soil Average, well drained. *Miscanthus* is drought tolerant but prefers moist soil that is well drained; some species grow well in wet soil. *M. sinensis* 'Variegatus' is suitable for xeriscaping in the southern states.

CARING FOR PLANTS

Little care required; with any encouragement, these grasses will become invasive. Cut back hard in late winter. Many cultivars have a tendency to die back in the center and require dividing every 3–5 years to maintain vigor. Established clumps may require the use of a pick axe.

PROPAGATING

Divide in spring (also in autumn in the South) or grow from seed. Rampant self-seeder.

COMBINATIONS

Coreopsis, Echinacea, Hemerocallis, Sedum; or use to soften and break up shrub plantings.

CAUTION

M. sinensis is listed as invasive in many areas, including Georgia, Indiana, Kentucky, Maryland, and Tennessee. See pp. 494–495 for advice.

Mitchella

HP | Zn 3–9

Partridge berry

p. 410

The Mitchella *genus comprises two prostrate evergreen subshrubs, one of which,* M. repens, *is a native wild-flower grown for its attractive shiny leaves and tiny white flowers. The flowers are followed by showy, bright red berries. An unusual plant for the shady rock garden or as a ground cover.*

Type Hardy perennial
Zone 3–9, H 9–1 (see species list, p. 463); prefers cool climates
Flowering season Early summer

SOWING

Indoors Sow seed *in situ.*
Outdoors As soon as ripe seed is available, usually in October.
Depth 1/4".

GERMINATING

Time Very slow and irregular.
Requirements Sow seed thinly in flats, sink flats in the ground against a north-facing wall, and cover with glass. Moisten soil occasionally, if necessary. Transplant seedlings the following autumn.

TRANSPLANTING

Time Set out purchased plants in spring or autumn.
Spacing 10"–15"
Light Part to full shade.
Soil Rich, moist, acid, with a pH level of 4.0–6.0.

CARING FOR PLANTS

Difficult to establish. Apply a complete fertilizer in spring, mulch to keep soil cool and moist, water regularly, and do not disturb roots.

PROPAGATING

Divide roots in spring in Zones 3–6 (autumn in Zones 7–9), take cuttings in summer, root runners, or grow from seed.

Mitella

HP | Zn 3–8

Bishop's cap, Miterwort

p. 410

These delicate woodland perennials form neat clumps of heart-shaped leaves. Tiny, tubular, greenish white flowers grow along tall, hairy spikes. North American and East Asian natives, miterworts grow to 12". They are just right as a woodland ground cover or in shady rock gardens.

Type Hardy perennial
Zone 3–8 H 7–5 (see species list, p. 463)
Flowering season Spring or summer, depending on species

SOWING

Indoors Sow seed *in situ*.
Outdoors As soon as seed is ripe in summer.
Depth ¼".

GERMINATING

Requirements Because *Mitella* is so easily propagated by runners, plants are rarely started from seed.

TRANSPLANTING

Time Set out new plants in spring or autumn.
Spacing 5"–9".
Light Part to full shade.
Soil Rich, moist, acid.

CARING FOR PLANTS

Water regularly during dry spells. Roots will not tolerate competition or disturbance.

PROPAGATING

Divide carefully in early spring or grow from seed. Plant may self-seed.

Moluccella

A | Zn 2–10  

p. 410

Upright, branching annuals or short-lived perennials, Moluccella *are grown for their densely covered spikes of unusual "flowers," which, in the most popular species,* M. laevis, *bells of Ireland, are in fact green, cone-shaped calyxes encircling the tiny, white, true flowers. Plants grow 18"–36". They make an unusual addition to the border or cottage garden.*

Type Annual
Zone 2–10, H 6–1; happiest in cool climates
Flowering season Mid summer to early autumn

SOWING

Indoors 8–10 weeks before planting out, in peat pots.
Outdoors Early spring, when soil is cool and a light frost is still possible. Where winters are mild, seed may also be sown in late summer for autumn bloom.
Depth Surface.

GERMINATING

Time 8–35 days.
Requirements Place seed in a plastic bag together with moist vermiculite and refrigerate for 5 days; provide light and 50°–60°F thereafter.

TRANSPLANTING

Time After last frost.
Spacing 12".
Light Sun to part shade.
Soil Ordinary.

CARING FOR PLANTS

Easy. Water regularly and fertilize monthly. Stake plants and leave roots undisturbed.

PROPAGATING

Grow from seed. Plant may self-seed.

COMBINATIONS

Campanula, Helenium, Rudbeckia, Salvia.

Momordica

HP* | Zn 8–10

These unusual vines grow 8'–10' long. They have deeply lobed leaves and showy white or yellow flowers, followed by knobbly orange fruit which is edible and said to contain healing properties.

Type Hardy perennial; usually grown as an annual
Zone 8–10; grown as an annual in Zones 3–7; prefers hot, humid climates
Flowering season Summer to frost

SOWING

Indoors 4–6 weeks before planting out, in peat pots.
Outdoors Only where summers are very warm, in early spring.
Depth ⅛".

GERMINATING

Time 14–21 days.
Requirements 65°–75°F.

TRANSPLANTING

Time After last frost.
Spacing 12"–24".
Light Full sun.
Soil Rich and moist.

CARING FOR PLANTS

Water well during dry spells and feed occasionally when plants are in fruit. Provide a trellis or other support.

PROPAGATING

Grow from seed only.

CAUTION

M. charantia (balsam pear) is listed as invasive in some areas, including Florida. See pp. 494–495 for advice.

Monarda

HP | Zn 4–9

Bee balm, Horsemint, Wild bergamot

p. 410

These upright and vigorous summer-blooming perennials are grown for their unique, mop-headed flowers, which appear to have stepped out before brushing their hair. Strong 2'–4' stems hold vibrant red, purple, pink, or white blooms. A joy to behold in the summer border or wildflower garden. Attracts bees, butterflies, and hummingbirds.

Type Hardy perennial
Zone 4–9, H 9–1
Flowering season Mid to late summer

SOWING

Indoors 8–10 weeks before planting out.
Outdoors Early spring, when soil is cool and a light frost is still possible, or early autumn.
Depth Just cover.

GERMINATING

Time 10–40 days.
Requirements 60°–70°F.

TRANSPLANTING

Time Early spring, when soil is cool and a light frost is still possible, or early autumn.
Spacing 18"–24".
Light Part shade; plant in full sun if soil is moist.
Soil Ordinary, with a pH level of 5.5–7.0; most species will grow in either dry or moist. *M. citriodora* and *M. fistulosa* are suitable for xeriscaping.

CARING FOR PLANTS

Easy. Where summers are long and hot, plants will be short lived and prone to mildew. Mulch plants and water frequently, keeping leaves as dry as possible to minimize the risk of disease. Deadhead regularly to prolong blooming. Cut back stems completely in winter. Where they're happy, *Monarda* can become invasive, but this tendency is curtailed in dry soil. Although plants spread widely by rhizomes, they are also inclined to die out of their original place. Dig or divide them every 3 years in spring or autumn.

PROPAGATING

Divide or root basal stem cuttings in spring or grow from seed.

COMBINATIONS

Echinacea, Helenium, Hemerocallis, Ligularia, and *Perovskia.*

Montbretia See *Crocosmia*

Moraea

TB* | Zn 9–10

African lily, Butterfly iris, Natal lily

p. 411

This genus of perennials grows from corms. The flowers strongly resemble the flag iris. They are yellow, purple, red, or white, often multicolored, and are held on tall stems growing 6"–3'. Leaves are short and narrow.

Type Tender bulb
Zone H 12–6. Divided into two categories: summer growers and winter growers. Both summer and winter growers are suitable for Zones 9–10; summer growers can be grown as annuals farther north
Flowering season Spring, summer, or early autumn, depending on species

SOWING

Indoors Start seed outdoors.
Outdoors *Seed:* Sow summer growers in spring, winter growers in autumn. *Corm:* Plant spring bloomers in autumn, summer bloomers in spring.
Depth *Seed:* 1/8". *Large corm:* 3"–4". *Small corm:* 2".

GERMINATING

Time 30–90 days.
Requirements 55°–60°F.

TRANSPLANTING

Spacing *Dwarf species:* 3". *Medium species:* 6"–9". *Large species:* 12"–24".
Light Full sun.
Soil Average, well drained.

CARING FOR PLANTS

Fertilizing is not necessary in average soils. Cut back flower stems partway after blooming. *Summer growers:* Water from spring through autumn, tapering off during winter. *Winter growers:* Water during winter and early spring, keeping quite dry in summer. Where summers are habitually wet, dig and store both winter and spring growers, replanting in early autumn.

PROPAGATING

Plant offsets during the dormant period or grow from seed.

M

Musa

TP* | Zn 9–10

Banana, Manila hemp, Plantain

These are the ultimate in tropical-looking plants for gardens—nontropical and tropical alike. Huge, rippling, oblong leaves form the crown of the treelike structure. "Trunks" are thick and sturdy, 6'–20' tall; fruits may or may not be edible.

Type Tender perennial
Zone 9–10, H 12–5; grown as an annual in cooler zones
Flowering season Mature plants bloom in summer; plants that are cut back hard every year will probably never flower

SOWING

Not all species produce seed.
Indoors Anytime.
Outdoors Not recommended.
Depth 1/4".

GERMINATING

Time 7–180 days.
Requirements Difficult. Soak seed for 24 hours in warm water, then provide darkness and 70°–85°F; fluorescent lights produce the best results.

TRANSPLANTING

Time When temperatures will remain above 60°F.
Spacing *Smaller species:* 3'–4'. *Larger species:* 5'–7'.
Light Sun, with light shade provided from hot afternoon sun.
Soil Moist, well drained, humus-rich, with a pH of 6.1–6.5.

CARING FOR PLANTS

Easy. Shelter from winds to prevent damage to leaves. Water regularly during dry spells; fertilize in the spring and again midseason. The ultimate size of plants grown in containers will be determined by the size of the container. Plants can be overwintered indoors in any of the following ways:

- Before the first frost, bring containers indoors to a warm, bright room; reduce watering and do not feed. Watch for aphids, mealybugs, spider mites, and scale.
- Large species can be cut back to 12" after the first frost and stored in a cool, dark, frost-free place, watering just enough to prevent the soil from becoming completely dry.
- If containers are too large or heavy to bring indoors, or for plants that are grown in the ground, dig up or remove plants from their containers before the first frost and put the entire root system into a large plastic bag; foliage may be cut back or not. Store in a cool, dark, frost-free place for the winter.

PROPAGATING

Divide at any time, take offsets in summer or autumn, or grow from seed. Plants that have flowered and fruited will produce suckers that can be rooted.

COMBINATIONS

Canna, Phormium, Ricinus.

Muscari (syn. *Muscarimia*)

HB | Zn 4–8 | Full sun, Partial shade | Good for xeriscaping, Ordinary soil

Grape hyacinth

p. 411

These small, spring-blooming bulbs have upright, leafless stems that bear dense clusters of tiny, spherical or bell-shaped purple or white flowers. Commonly grown species are 4"–8". Native to the Mediterranean. Plant Muscari *in masses beneath trees or shrubs or in the rock garden.*

Type Hardy bulb
Zone 4–8, H 8–1
Flowering season Spring

SOWING

Indoors Start seed outdoors.
Outdoors *Seed:* As soon as seed is ripe. *Bulb:* Autumn.
Depth *Seed:* Just cover. *Bulb:* 3".

GERMINATING

Time 42–60 days.
Requirements Sow seed in flats, sink in the ground against a north-facing wall, and cover with glass. Moisten soil from time to time. Remove glass when seeds sprout. Transplant young bulbs to the garden in autumn after one full season of growth.

TRANSPLANTING

Spacing 2"–3".
Light Sun or part shade.
Soil Average, well drained, with a pH level of 6.0–7.0. *Muscari* can be used for xeriscaping in areas where there is usually regular rainfall during the spring but might experience drought in summer.

CARING FOR PLANTS

Easy. Water during the growing season if weather is dry. Mulch with well-rotted manure in autumn. Divide crowded plants every 3–4 years.

PROPAGATING

Divide bulblets after foliage has died back in summer or grow from seed. Plant may self-seed.

COMBINATIONS

Bellis, Daphne odora, Galium, Podophyllum. Particularly lovely massed under azaleas or Japanese maples.

Muscarimia See *Muscari*

Myosotidium

HP | Zn 8–9

Chatham Island forget-me-not

*This genus contains a single species—*M. hortensia*—an unusual perennial. At 18" tall, it looks like a cross between* Hosta *and* Bergenia. *Its leaves are large, thick and glossy, heart-shaped, and ribbed; clusters of small blue or white flowers are held on thick stems.*

Type Hardy perennial
Zone 8–9, H 12–1; possibly hardy to Zone 7 with winter protection; requires cool summers
Flowering season Late spring or early summer

SOWING

Indoors Autumn, or as soon as seed is ripe.
Outdoors As soon as seed is ripe, in Zones 8–9 only.
Depth Just cover.

GERMINATING

Time 30–180 days.
Requirements Sow seed and place trays in refrigerator. Remove trays as soon as germination begins, or after 4 weeks. Grow on seedlings at 50°–55°F.

TRANSPLANTING

Time After last frost.
Spacing 18".
Light Part shade; full sun where summers are cool.
Soil Moist, humus-rich, well drained, acid.

CARING FOR PLANTS

Difficult. Site away from winds. Apply an organic mulch in spring, and mulch again in winter where plants are hardy. Water regularly. Do not disturb established plants.

PROPAGATING

Carefully divide after flowering or grow from seed.

Myosotis

A, Bi, HP | Zn 5–8

Forget-me-not, Scorpion grass

p. 411

These ever-popular, clump-forming plants are prized for their masses of tiny, delicate blue flowers. Foliage and habit are neat; plants grow no more than 6"–12". Use them in rock gardens, mixed woodland plantings, or borders; they make a lovely ground cover for a lightly shaded spot.

Type Annual, short-lived hardy perennial, or biennial grown as an annual
Zone 5–8, H 8–1
Flowering season Early spring to summer, depending on species

SOWING

Indoors 8–10 weeks before planting out.
Outdoors *Annual and perennial:* Early spring, when soil is cool and a light frost is still possible. Where winters are mild, sow in early autumn. *Biennial:* Midsummer.
Depth Surface.

GERMINATING

Time 8–30 days.
Requirements Darkness and 65°–70°F. Highly susceptible to damping-off; sow in vermiculite, and water from below only.

TRANSPLANTING

Time Early spring, when soil is cool and a light frost is still possible, or late autumn.
Spacing 6"–8".
Light Part shade, or sun where soil is moist or summers are cool.
Soil Moist, rich, with a pH level of 6.0–7.0. *M. sylvatica* can be grown in either moist or dry soil.

CARING FOR PLANTS

Easy. Water regularly. Remove or cut back plants after flowering to reduce self-seeding. Mildew is a common problem.

PROPAGATING

Divide in early spring or grow from seed. All are inclined to self-seed quite unabashedly.

COMBINATIONS

Dicentra, ferns, *Geranium, Lunaria, Mahonia, Pieris, Primula, Tulipa.*

Myrrhis

HP | Zn 3–9

Sweet Cicely

p. 411

The only species in this genus, M. odorata, *is a perennial with aromatic, fernlike leaves and wiry stalks of 3′–5′ that bear umbels of tiny white flowers. It is best used in mixed plantings for textural contrast.*

Type Hardy perennial
Zone 3–9, H 7–1
Flowering season Summer

SOWING

Indoors 8–10 weeks before planting out.
Outdoors 3 months before last frost.
Depth ⅛″.

GERMINATING

Time 14–42 days.
Requirements Freeze seed for 1 month; provide 55°–65°F thereafter.

TRANSPLANTING

Time Spring or autumn.
Spacing 24″.
Light Sun or part shade.
Soil Fertile, with a pH level of 5.5–6.5. Prepare beds deeply, mixing in plenty of manure.

CARING FOR PLANTS

Prepare beds deeply to accommodate taproot, and do not move once established. Allow flowers to set seed if growing for culinary use; otherwise deadhead to prevent self-seeding.

PROPAGATING

Divide plants in spring or fall or grow from seed. Plant may self-seed.

Narcissus

HB | Zn 3–9

Daffodil

p. 411

A large genus of delightful and hugely popular spring-flowering bulbs, Narcissus *species usually have long, slender leaves. Their flowers are predominantly yellow or white but may have orange or pink cups; many are bicolored. Blooms have a ring of petals framing a cup or trumpet. They range from 3″ to 18″ tall. Incomparable when massed in borders, woodland, or lawn.*

Type Hardy bulb
Zone 3–9, H 9–1; performs most successfully in cool climates
Flowering season Spring

SOWING

Indoors Seed should be started outdoors.
Outdoors *Seed:* As soon as seed is ripe, usually late summer or autumn. *Bulb:* Late autumn in the South, late summer to early autumn farther north.
Depth *Seed:* Just cover. *Small bulb:* 3″–4″. *Large bulb:* 5″–6″.

GERMINATING

Time 28–56 days.
Requirements Sow seed in flats, sink flats in the ground against a north-facing wall, and cover with glass. Moisten soil occasionally, if necessary. Transplant seedlings in the autumn after 2 years of growth.

TRANSPLANTING

Time Autumn.
Spacing *Small species:* 4″. *Large species:* 6″.
Light Full sun in spring but will tolerate part shade after flowering.
Soil Average, with good drainage and a pH level of 6.0–7.5. Add a slow-release, low-nitrogen fertilizer (e.g., bonemeal) to each planting hole. *Narcissus* may be used for xeriscaping in areas that have regular rainfall in spring but may experience drought in summer.

CARING FOR PLANTS

Easy. Feed once in spring and water during dry spells; discontinue after flowering ceases. Cut flowering stems to the ground after blooming but before seed sets to maintain a neat appearance and conserve bulbs' energy. Allow foliage to die back naturally before removing.

PROPAGATING

Divide in spring after foliage has died back (about 6 weeks after flowering) or grow from seed. Plants grown from seed flower in 3–8 years.

COMBINATIONS

Anemone blanda, Myosotis, Primula, Viola. Grow through ground covers such as *Hedera, Pachysandra,* and *Vinca.*

CAUTION

Narcissus are harmful to pets if eaten.

Nelumbo

HP | Zn 4–10 | 

Lotus

p. 411

These water plants are grown for their exquisitely beautiful and fragrant flowers, which resemble delicate artichokes opening to the sun. Blossoms in shades of pink, yellow, or white are followed by handsome seedpods. Showy leaves like dinner plates are 1'–3' across.

Type Hardy perennial
Zone 4–10, H 12–2; will not survive in colder regions in very shallow water if the roots freeze
Flowering season Summer

SOWING

Indoors Any time.
Outdoors Spring.
Depth *Seed:* See Germinating, Requirements. *Rhizome:* 1".

GERMINATING

Time 14–30 days.
Requirements Chip seed and submerge in hot water (75°–85°F); change water twice a day until seeds germinate. To sow *in situ,* roll each seed in a ball of clay and drop onto the bottom of your pond.

TRANSPLANTING

Time After last spring frost, when temperatures remain above 40°F.
Spacing 36"–48".
Light Full sun or very light shade.
Soil Grows in still water, 2'–5' deep, at 60°–70°F.

CARING FOR PLANTS

Easy. Feed monthly during the growing season with commercial aquatic-plant fertilizer. Groom plants by removing faded leaves regularly. In the North, protect from winter freeze by covering pond with boards or canvas, plus a 3" layer of hay; or move container-grown plants to a cool, frost-free location, watering as necessary; or lift clumps of fleshy rhizomes and store over winter in damp sand in a frost-free location. Divide container-grown plants every 2–3 years to maintain vigor.

PROPAGATING

Divide clumps in spring. Although species may be grown from seed, selected forms must be propagated by division.

CAUTION

N. nucifera is listed as invasive in some areas, including the Gulf states. See pp. 494–495 for advice.

Nemesia

A | Zn 2–10

Nemesia

p. 411

These African annuals, perennials, and subshrubs are grown as annuals. Their lovely, two-lipped, tubular flowers are purple, white, yellow, red, or orange with conspicuously blotched throats; 8"–24" tall. Suitable for edging, containers, rock gardens, and borders.

Type Annual
Zone 2–10, H 7–1; prefers a long, cool growing season and will not do well where summers are hot and humid
Flowering season Early spring through early fall; the blooming period will be shortened by heat

SOWING

Indoors 8–10 weeks before last frost where summers are hot; 4–6 weeks before the last frost and every 6 weeks thereafter where summers are cool.
Outdoors After last frost, but only where summers are not too hot; in autumn in western Zones 9–10.
Depth Surface.

GERMINATING

Time 5–21 days.
Requirements 55°–70°F. Seed is very susceptible to damping-off; sow in vermiculite, and water only from below.

TRANSPLANTING

Time After last frost.
Spacing 6"–12".
Light Afternoon shade in hot climates will prolong plants' lives. In full sun, soil must be kept moist.
Soil Rich, moist, well drained.

CARING FOR PLANTS

Easy. Pinch tips of young plants to increase bushiness; feed and water regularly. Plants are susceptible to root rot.

PROPAGATING

Start from seed only.

COMBINATIONS

Limnanthes, Lobelia, Salvia, Viola.

N

Nemophila

A | Zn 2–9

p. 412

These diminutive annuals of neat habit bear delightful cup-shaped flowers with intricate markings. Popular N. maculata *features white petals delicately veined and dotted with blue at the tips, while* N. menziesii *is blue with a white center and prominent anthers with conspicuous dark stamens. These 4"–12" plants exude personality. Use them in rock gardens, containers, or borders, where they make a fine edging.*

Type Annual
Zone 2–9, H 7–1; successful only where summers are cool and nighttime temperatures remain below 65°F
Flowering season Plants sown in autumn in southern states will bloom from winter to spring; in northern climates, *Nemophila* will bloom from July to frost

SOWING

Indoors 6–8 weeks before planting out, in peat pots.
Outdoors Early spring, when soil is cool and a light frost is still possible, or late autumn where winters are mild.
Depth Just cover.

GERMINATING

Time 7–21 days.
Requirements Easy. 55°F.

TRANSPLANTING

Time After last frost.
Spacing *Small selections:* 4"–8". *Large selections:* 12"–15".
Light Full sun or part shade, with afternoon shade where summers are hot.
Soil Cool, moist, light, well drained, with a pH level of 5.0–8.0.

CARING FOR PLANTS

Water regularly and mulch to keep soil cool; watch for aphids on young plants. Plants may be killed by excessive heat or humidity. Do not transplant.

PROPAGATING

Grow from seed. Self-seeds freely in its native habitat.

COMBINATIONS

Centaurea, Lobularia, Phacelia.

Nepeta

HP | Zn 3–9

Catmint

p. 412

Bushy perennials, Nepeta *offer a light, airy appearance and masses of tiny purple, blue, white, or yellow flowers that are very attratcive to bees. Plants are 6"–36" tall. Small species make an excellent edging; taller species add lightness to the border.*

Type Hardy perennial
Zone 3–9, H 9–1 (see species list, pp. 464–465)
Flowering season Late spring to late summer or early autumn, depending on species

SOWING

Indoors 8–10 weeks before planting out.
Outdoors Early spring, when soil is cool and light frost is still possible, or late autumn.
Depth Just cover.

GERMINATING

Time 7–21 days.
Requirements Easy. 60°–70°F.

TRANSPLANTING

Time Early spring, when soil is cool and a light frost is still possible, or late autumn.
Spacing *Small species:* 10"–15". *Large species:* 18"–24".
Light Full sun or part shade.
Soil Light, sandy, with a pH level of 5.5–7.0. Drought tolerant.

CARING FOR PLANTS

Easy. Shear after flowering to encourage a light continuous blooming until frost and to prevent rampant self-seeding. Divide every 3–4 years. If planting *N. cataria,* be prepared for visits from neighborhood cats, who love to roll in this feline narcotic and may inadvertently damage nearby plants. They are not attracted to other species of *Nepeta.* Dry leaves and flowers for several days, store in an airtight container, and surprise your feline friends this winter with an unexpected supply of catnip.

PROPAGATING

Divide in early spring, take cuttings after flowering, or grow from seed. Self-seeds freely. Plants grown from seed will bloom their first year.

COMBINATIONS

Calendula, Coreopsis, Dimorphotheca, Iberis, Platycodon, Stachys, Tanacetum.

Nerine

HB | Zn 8–10

Guernsey lily

p. 412

A bulb from southern Africa grown for its late-season blooms, Nerine *resembles a cluster of small lilies growing on a stiff wand 12"–24" tall. Pink, red, or white flowers usually bloom before leaves appear. Most effective massed behind a low edging that hides their gawky, naked stems.*

Type Hardy bulb
Zone 8–10, H 12–8
Flowering season Summer or autumn, depending on species

SOWING

Indoors Autumn, as soon as seed is ripe.
Outdoors *Seed:* As soon as fresh seed is available. *Bulb:* Early autumn.
Depth *Seed:* Surface. *Bulb:* 4"–6".

GERMINATING

Time 7–21 days.
Requirements 65°–70°F. Be particularly careful not to overwater.

TRANSPLANTING

Time After last frost.
Spacing 5"–8".
Light Full sun or very light shade.
Soil Moist, well drained.

CARING FOR PLANTS

Difficult. Water during early growing period, stopping when plants begin to bloom; resume watering after flowering and continue until leaves die down, tapering off gradually. Flowering is improved when plants are somewhat crowded. Mulch heavily in fall where marginally hardy, or keep in containers year-round and overwinter in a cool, dry place.

PROPAGATING

Divide bulbs in autumn after leaves have died back or grow from seed. Plants grown from seed will flower in 4–5 years.

COMBINATIONS

Aster, Centaurea, ornamental grasses, *Nicotiana.* Probably most successful massed with a contrasting edging, such as *Alyssum* or *Lobelia.*

Nicandra

A | Zn 3–8

Apple of Peru, Shoofly plant

p. 412

This genus contains a single species, N. physalodes, *an upright, branching, herbaceous annual. Plants grow rapidly to 3'–4'. Flowers are violet bells with white throats that bloom for just 1 day, and are followed by papery, everlasting seed cases. Use* Nicandra *in the border or cottage garden.*

Type Annual
Zone 3–8, H 9–1; prefers warm climates
Flowering season Summer to autumn

SOWING

Indoors 6–8 weeks before planting out.
Outdoors Early spring, when soil is cool and a light frost is still possible, or late autumn.
Depth Just cover.

GERMINATING

Time 15–20 days.
Requirements 60°–75°F.

TRANSPLANTING

Time 2–3 weeks before last frost.
Spacing 24"–48".
Light Full sun or part shade.
Soil Rich, well drained.

CARING FOR PLANTS

Feed monthly during the growing season.

PROPAGATING

Grow from seed only.

CAUTION

Harmful if eaten.

Nicotiana

A, TP* | Zn 2–10

Tobacco plant

p. 412

Old-fashioned, erect plants, tobacco plants are prized for their cheerful, brightly colored, trumpet-shaped flowers. Flowers are white, pink, red, green, or yellow. They are seldom as fragrant as described in garden literature. Leaves are rather coarse and vary in size. They are dependable in the border and very much at home in cottage gardens.

Type Annual or short-lived tender perennial; usually grown as an annual
Zone 2–10, H 12–1; prefers warm temperatures
Flowering season Summer

SOWING

Indoors 6–8 weeks before last frost.
Outdoors After last frost.
Depth Surface.

GERMINATING

Time 10–20 days.
Requirements Easy. Light and 70°–75°F.

TRANSPLANTING

Time After last frost.
Spacing *Small species:* 12". *Large species:* 18"–24".
Light Light shade or full sun, with shade from hot afternoon sun.
Soil Tolerant of a wide range of soils but prefers one that is slightly acid.

CARING FOR PLANTS

Easy. Water during hot, dry spells. Deadhead regularly to maintain a neat appearance and encourage further blooming. Stake in windy sites. Aphids can be a problem; plants are susceptible to tobacco mosaic.

PROPAGATING

Grow from seed. Plant may self-seed.

COMBINATIONS

Antirrhinum, Dahlia, Matthiola, Mirabilis, Sedum.

CAUTION

All parts of the plant are toxic if eaten.

Nierembergia

A, TP*, HP* | Zn 2–10

Cup flower

p. 412

These pretty and dainty mat-forming plants are grown for the multitude of open, bell-shaped flowers that blanket them all summer. Leaves are small, oval or feathery, and neat in appearance. Flowers may be white or purple with yellow centers. Plants grow from 2" to 12". They make excellent container, rock garden, or edging plants.

Type Annual, tender perennial, hardy perennial; usually grown as an annual
Zone *Perennial:* 7–10. *Annual:* 2–10; 12–1; refers warm temperatures
Flowering season Summer to early autumn

SOWING

Indoors 8–10 weeks before planting out.
Outdoors Early spring or early autumn.
Depth Just cover.

GERMINATING

Time 15–30 days.
Requirements 70°–75°F.

TRANSPLANTING

Time 2–3 weeks before last frost, or early autumn.
Spacing 6"–8".
Light Full sun; part shade where summers are hot.
Soil Moist, rich, well drained.

CARING FOR PLANTS

Keep soil moist, especially where summers are hot. Top-dress with well-rotted manure in spring. Deadhead regularly for more abundant flowering; cut back in autumn to maintain a tidy appearance.

PROPAGATING

Where hardy, divide perennials in spring, take cuttings in summer, or grow from seed.

COMBINATIONS

Dianthus, Evolvulus, Lithodora.

Nigella

A | Zn 2–10

Devil-in-a-bush, Fennel flower, Love-in-a-mist, Wild fennel

p. 412

These annuals are grown for their feathery foliage and blue, white, or pink flowers. The blooms are like the layered tulle of a ballerina's skirt, and are adorned with very showy stamens. Flowers are often followed by attractive seedpods, which are easily dried for use in arrangements. Plants are 6"–24" and are grown in the border.

Type Annual
Zone 2–10, H 12–1; performs most successfully in cool climates
Flowering season Summer

SOWING

Indoors 6–8 weeks before planting out, in peat pots; however, sowing *in situ* is usually more successful.
Outdoors Early spring, when soil is cool and a light frost is still possible, or autumn where winters are mild. Sow every 4 weeks for the next 3 months for continuous blooms.
Depth Just cover.

GERMINATING

Time 8–15 days.
Requirements 65°–70°F.

TRANSPLANTING

Time After last spring frost, or early autumn.
Spacing 8"–12".
Light Full sun.
Soil Ordinary, well drained, with a pH level of 6.0–7.0; tolerant of dry soil.

CARING FOR PLANTS

Easy. Fertilize and deadhead regularly. Water plants when the soil is dry. Do not disturb. To use seeds of *N. sativa*, black cumin, in cooking, detach brown pods from plants, dry in a shady place, then rub gently to release seeds. Dry completely before storing in an airtight jar.

PROPAGATING

Grow from seed. Plant may self-seed.

COMBINATIONS

Bassia, Coreopsis, Papaver, Santolina.

Nipponanthemum

HP | Zn 5–9

Nippon daisy

Nipponanthemum is a one-genus species that used to be classified as a Chrysanthemum. *These 2' tall plants have bright green, shiny leaves. The flowers are classic daisy-type with white petals and yellow centers, and are very useful for their long bloom late in the season.*

Type Hardy perennial
Zone 5–9, H 9–5
Flowering season Autumn

SOWING

Indoors 6–8 weeks before planting out.
Outdoors Early spring, when soil is cool and a light frost is still possible, or late autumn.
Depth Surface.

GERMINATING

Time 7–28 days.
Requirements 55°–70°F.

TRANSPLANTING

Time After last frost, or autumn.
Spacing 18"–24".
Light Sun, or light shade where summers are hot.
Soil Average, very well drained, on the dry side.

CARING FOR PLANTS

Easy. Cut back to the ground in early spring, pinch out young plants to encourage bushy growth, and/or push twiggy branches into the ground in spring to support floppy plants. Deadhead to prolong blooming. Slugs and aphids can be a problem. Divide every 2–3 years to maintain vigor.

PROPAGATING

Divide in spring or grow from seed.

COMBINATIONS

Nepeta, Physostegia, Sedum.

Nolana

TP* | Zn 9–10

Chilean bellflower

p. 413

Prostrate and heat tolerant, these plants are grown for their ruffle-edged, trumpet-shaped flowers of purple with yellow centers outlined in white. The 3"–10" tall plants are native to Chile and Peru. They are excellent as an edging, in containers, or as rock garden plants.

Type Tender perennial; usually grown as an annual
Zone 9–10, H 12–1; grown as an annual in Zones 2–8
Flowering season Summer

SOWING

Indoors 4–6 weeks before planting out, in peat pots.
Outdoors After last frost.
Depth Just cover.

GERMINATING

Time 7–30 days.
Requirements 60°–70°F.

TRANSPLANTING

Time After last frost.
Spacing 6"–8".
Light Full sun.
Soil Poor, dry, sandy, or gravelly. Plants will become sprawling in moist soil.

CARING FOR PLANTS

Flowers refuse to open on cool, gray days. Prolonged hot weather weakens plants. Difficult to transplant.

PROPAGATING

Grow from seed only.

COMBINATIONS

Salvia, Senecio, Verbena.

N

Nomocharis

HB | Zn 7–9

p. 413

These summer-blooming bulbs display showy, nodding, somewhat flat, lilylike flowers of white, pink, or purple, often spotted and frilled. Flowers are held on slim, erect stalks of 1'–3'. They make an unusual border plant.

Type Hardy bulb
Zone 7–9, H 9–7; prefers the cool damp summers and mild winters of the West Coast
Flowering season Midsummer

SOWING

Indoors 10–12 weeks before planting out, in peat pots.
Outdoors *Seed:* Autumn. *Bulb:* Spring.
Depth *Seed:* Just cover. *Bulb:* 3"–4".

GERMINATING

Time 30–180 days.
Requirements Difficult. *Outdoor sowing:* Sow seed in flats, sink in the ground against a north-facing wall, and cover with glass. Moisten soil occasionally, if necessary. Transplant seedlings to the garden when they reach 3".

TRANSPLANTING

Time After last frost.
Spacing *Small species:* 5"–6". *Large species:* 12"–16".
Light Sun or part shade.
Soil Performs best in soil that is deep, cool, moist, well drained, and acid.

CARING FOR PLANTS

Difficult. Keep soil moist but not wet in summer; mulch in spring. Do not disturb bulbs.

PROPAGATING

Grow from seed only. Division of these fragile bulbs is seldom successful. Plants grown from seed will bloom in 3–4 years.

Ocimum

A | Zn 4–10

Basil

p. 413

Basil is grown both for culinary use and for its ornamental, aromatic foliage. These herbs are upright and branching, 6"–24" tall, with green, purple, maroon, or blue-green leaves. They are useful in the border as well as in the herb garden.

Type Annual
Zone 4–10; prefers warm temperatures
Flowering season Summer

SOWING

Indoors 4–6 weeks before planting out.
Outdoors Start seed outdoors only where summers are long, in early spring and again in midsummer.
Depth Surface.

GERMINATING

Time 5–42 days.
Requirements Easy. Light and 60°–70°F.

TRANSPLANTING

Time In spring, when temperatures remain above 65°F.
Spacing 10"–12".
Light Sun.
Soil Rich, well drained, with a pH level of 5.5–6.5

CARING FOR PLANTS

Easy. Pinch back tips when plants are 5"–6" tall to encourage bushiness. Water regularly. In midsummer, cut plant back by half and apply fertilizer. Harvest leaves for culinary use just before flowering, then either dry leaves in a dark place or freeze immediately. Plants can be lifted in autumn, potted up, and brought inside for winter use. Give plants 5 hours of sunlight daily and a light monthly feeding.

PROPAGATING

Some species can be propagated by cuttings, but growing from seed is the most common method.

Oenothera

A, Bi, HP* | Zn 4–9

Evening primrose, Suncups, Sundrops

p. 413

The annuals, biennials, and perennials in this large genus are grown for their attractive, profuse — although short-lived — flowers. Most blossoms are cup-shaped, pink, yellow, or white; some are night bloomers. Most species are North American natives, growing from 6" to 36" tall. They are effective when massed in the border.

Type Annual, biennial, or hardy perennial sometimes grown as an annual
Zone 4–9, H 8–2; happiest in warm climates
Flowering season Late spring to summer, depending on species

SOWING

Indoors 8–10 weeks before last frost, in peat pots.
Outdoors Early spring; seed also may be sown in autumn where winters are mild.
Depth Just cover.

GERMINATING

Time 5–30 days.
Requirements Darkness and 65°–70°F.

TRANSPLANTING

Time After last frost.
Spacing *Small species:* 5"–9". *Medium species:* 12"–18". *Large species:* 18"–24".
Light Full sun or light shade.
Soil Light, well drained, rather sandy, with a pH level of 5.5–7.0. Tolerates dry soil, and many species can be used successfully for xeriscaping. Excess fertility results in luxuriant foliage but few blooms.

CARING FOR PLANTS

Easy. Top-dress with well-rotted manure in spring, water during dry spells, and prune after flowering to keep plants looking neat. Hot weather may reduce blooming temporarily. Plants are susceptible to powdery mildew.

PROPAGATING

Divide in spring in Zones 4–6 (in autumn in Zones 7–9), take cuttings in spring, or grow from seed. Some species self-seed to the point of invasiveness. Plants grown from seed will bloom their first year.

COMBINATIONS

Iris, Lupinus, Nepeta, Paeonia, Salvia.

Omphalodes

A, HP | Zn 6–9 

Navelseed, Navelwort

p. 413

Omphalodes *includes both annuals and perennials with pretty, delicate, cup-shaped flowers of blue or white. Some, resembling forget-me-nots, are borne on short stalks close to compact foliage; others grow in airy masses along wiry 12" stems. Leaves may be green or grayish. Use them for edgings or in rock gardens.*

Type Annual or hardy perennial
Zone *Annual:* 1–10; *Perennial:* 6–9, H 9–6 (see species list, p. 465); prefers cool temperatures
Flowering season Early spring to summer, depending on species

SOWING

Indoors 10–12 weeks before planting out.
Outdoors Where winters are mild, sow seed in autumn for early-spring blooms; elsewhere, sow after last frost.
Depth 1/8".

GERMINATING

Time 14–42 days.
Requirements 65°–75°F.

TRANSPLANTING

Time After last frost.
Spacing 6"–10".
Light Part to full shade.
Soil Cool, moist, well-drained soil, peaty, and slightly alkaline.

CARING FOR PLANTS

Top-dress with well-rotted manure in spring, mulch to keep soil cool, and water well during dry spells. Where summers are hot, cut back plants hard after blooming.

PROPAGATING

Divide perennials in spring in Zone 6 (in autumn in Zones 7–9) or grow from seed. Both annuals and perennials self-seed.

COMBINATIONS

Begonia, Impatiens, Pulmonaria, Viola.

O

Onosma

HP | Zn 5–9

These unusual plants are grown for their clusters of pendulous, tubular flowers clasped tightly by long green calyxes. Flowers may be pink, white, or yellow; plants grow 6"–18" tall. Use them in borders and rock gardens.

Type Short-lived hardy perennial
Zone 5–9, H 9–7 (see species list, p. 465); not happy where summers are wet
Flowering season Spring to summer

SOWING

Indoors 10–12 weeks before planting out.
Outdoors Autumn.
Depth Just cover.

GERMINATING

Time 30–60 days.
Requirements 50°F.

TRANSPLANTING

Time After last frost.
Spacing *Small species:* 6". *Large species:* 12"–18".
Light Full sun.
Soil Poor, dry, gritty, very well drained, especially in winter.

CARING FOR PLANTS

Apply a topdressing of well-rotted manure in spring. Keep roots cool by mulching lightly with rock chips; mulch again with coarse organic matter after the first hard frost to minimize the chance of winter rot. Plants are short lived and require renewal every few years. Do not move.

PROPAGATING

Take cuttings in summer or grow from seed.

Orchis See *Dactylorhiza*

Ophiopogon

HP | Zn 6–10 | Full sun, Partial shade, Full shade | Dry soil, Ordinary soil, Moist soil

Lilyturf

p. 413

This small genus includes diminutive, grassy, evergreen perennials that grow 6"–12" tall. Leaves are narrow and flat, dark green, deep purple, or striped with white or yellow. Short spikes of tiny blue or white flowers are followed by deep blue–black berries. These grasses are useful as an edging or a ground cover.

Type Hardy perennial
Zone 6–10, H 10–6
Flowering season Midsummer

SOWING

Indoors 6–8 weeks before planting out.
Outdoors Autumn.
Depth ¼".

GERMINATING

Time 30–42 days.
Requirements Soak seed for 24 hours in warm water, then sow and place flats where the temperature will be a constant 65°–70°F.

TRANSPLANTING

Time After last frost.
Spacing *Small species:* 4"–6". *Large species:* 12".
Light Full sun to full shade; at least part shade is desirable where summers are very hot.
Soil Moist, well drained, and rich is ideal, but also tolerates very dry soil.

CARING FOR PLANTS

Easy. Tends to look rather scruffy in winter in the North, but a radical haircut in early spring will greatly improve appearance. Divide every 4–5 years.

PROPAGATING

Divide in early spring (early autumn in the South) or grow from seed.

COMBINATIONS

Adiantum, Anemone, Athyrium, Hosta, Lamium, woodland *Phlox.* The cultivar *O. planiscapus* 'Nigrescens', is stunning in combination with plants that contrast sharply with their almost black leaves.

Origanum

TP*, HP* | Zn 2–9 | Full sun | Dry soil, Ordinary soil

Marjoram, Oregano

p. 413

Some of these herbs are grown for culinary use, others for foliage and flowers. Ornamental species bear masses of pale pink or white tubular flowers surrounded by showy bracts or clouds of tiny tubular flowers of deep pink held on wiry stems; 6"–30" tall. Use them in rock and herb gardens.

Type Tender perennial, hardy perennial; often grown as an annual
Zone 5–9, H 12–5 (see species list, p. 466); often grown as an annual in Zones 2–9
Flowering season Summer

SOWING

Indoors 6–8 weeks before planting out.
Outdoors When spring temperatures remain above 45°F.
Depth Just cover.

GERMINATING

Time 10 days.
Requirements Easy. 55°–65°F.

TRANSPLANTING

Time After last frost.
Spacing *Small species:* 6"–8". *Large species:* 12"–15".
Light Full sun.
Soil Very well drained, with a pH level of 6.0–8.0, tolerant of dry, rocky soil.

CARING FOR PLANTS

Easy. In spring, pinch back young plants to encourage branching and feed with an all-purpose fertilizer. Harvest leaves for culinary use by cutting back stems just before blooming. Drying the leaves (in a warm, dark place) improves their flavor.

PROPAGATING

Divide in spring (early autumn in Zones 8–9), take cuttings in spring, or grow from seed.

COMBINATIONS

Allium, Artemisia, Veronica.

Ornithogalum

HB | Zn 5–10

Star-of-Bethlehem

p. 414

These bulbs bear star-shaped, usually white flowers in terminal spikes on stiff, leafless stalks; 4"–24"tall. Mass them along a path or mix them with other spring-flowering bulbs. The tall species make an unusual addition to the border.

Type Tender bulb or hardy bulb
Zone 5–10, H 12–1 (see species list, p. 466)
Flowering season Spring or summer, depending on species

SOWING

Indoors See Germinating, Requirements.
Outdoors *Seed:* See Germinating, Requirements. *Bulb:* Autumn for spring-flowering species; late spring for summer bloomers.
Depth *Seed:* Just cover. *Bulb:* 3" in warm climates, 6" where winters are cold.

GERMINATING

Time 30–180 days.
Requirements *Autumn sowing:* Sow seed in flats, sink flats in the ground against a north-facing wall, and cover with glass. Moisten soil occasionally, if necessary. Bring flats indoors in spring to 55°–60°F. *Spring sowing:* Sow seed in flats, seal loosely in plastic bags, and refrigerate. After 2–3 weeks, remove flats and sink in the ground in a shady location, covering with glass. Transplant seedlings as they appear.

TRANSPLANTING

Spacing 4"–6".
Light Full sun to light shade.
Soil Prefers rich, well drained. *O. umbellatum* is suitable for xeriscaping

CARING FOR PLANTS

Top-dress with well-rotted manure in April and apply a weak fertilizer periodically throughout the summer. Divide frequently. Some species may be invasive. Tender species may be lifted, stored over winter in a dry, frost-free location, and replanted in spring. Or grow in containers year-round.

PROPAGATING

Plant offsets in autumn or grow from seed. Plant may self-seed. Flowers from seed in 3–4 years.

COMBINATIONS

Lupinus, Muscari, Persicaria, summer *Phlox.*

CAUTION

All parts of the plant are toxic if eaten. Some species are listed as invasive in some regions, including, for instance, *O. nutans* in Maryland and *O. umbellatum* in Indiana, Maryland, and Kentucky. For advice, see pp. 494–495.

Orphanidesia See *Epigaea*

Osmunda

HP | Zn 2–10

Flowering fern

p. 414

This small genus of popular ferns includes fairly large, upright, substantial plants with a traditional ferny look. Stiff fertile fronds emerge from the centers of clumps and mature to a deep rusty brown. They are easy to grow in any moist, shady location.

Type Hardy perennial
Zone 2–10, H 9–1 (see species list, p. 483)
Flowering season N/A

SOWING

Indoors Spores are viable for only a short time; sow as soon as possible after ripening in late spring to early summer.
Outdoors Not recommended.
Depth Surface.

GERMINATING

Time 10–365 days.
Requirements Difficult; 65°–70°F. (See pp. 24–25 for instructions on starting ferns from spores.)

TRANSPLANTING

Time After last frost or early autumn when plants are 2–3 years old.
Spacing 24".
Light Full to part shade. *O. cinnamomea* and *O. regalis* will tolerate sun if the soil remains moist to wet; *O. cinnamomea* will also tolerate deep shade.
Soil Moist to wet; plants will grow considerably taller in wet soil. *O. claytoniana* tolerates fairly dry soil; *O. cinnamomea* must have wet soil.

CARING FOR PLANTS

Mulch with leaf mold in spring to keep soil moist; water regularly. Remove faded fronds periodically to improve appearance. Difficult to transplant. Plants are susceptible to rust.

PROPAGATING

Divide carefully in early spring or autumn or grow from spores.

COMBINATIONS

Hosta, Iris ensata or *I. siberica,* woodland *Phlox, Rheum, Rodgersia.*

Osteospermum

TP* | Zn 9–10 | Full sun | Dry soil, Ordinary soil

Cape daisy, Rain daisy, South African daisy, Star of the Veldt

p. 414

Similar in appearance to Dimorphotheca, *with which they are often confused, these evergreen, tender subshrubs produce an abundance of cheerful, daisylike flowers in irresistible color combinations over a long period. Ray flowers may be either vibrant or pastel shades of red, pink, yellow, or orange, with handsomely contrasting black, dark purple, or rust-colored disks; or they may be white above with purple undersides and blue disks. Even when resting during hot weather, plants are handsome, forming a neat, compact 12"–18" mound. They are attractive in containers, baskets, and borders, and make a fine low, hedge or border.*

Type Tender perennial; often grown as an annual
Zone 9–10, H 10–1. Grown as an annual in cooler zones. Prefers a long growing season and does not perform well where summers are hot and humid.
Flowering Season Most bloom heavily in spring and autumn, but only sporadically throughout hot summers.

SOWING

Indoors 6–8 weeks before planting out.
Outdoors Spring, in Zones 9–10 only. In the West, seeds may also be sown in late summer for autumn and winter bloom.
Depth Just cover.

GERMINATING

Time 7–21 days.
Requirements 60°–85°F. Sow sparsely in vermiculite and water carefully to minimize the risk of fungal disease.

TRANSPLANTING

Time After last frost.
Spacing 12"–18".
Light Full sun.
Soil Soil must be very well drained. Established plants tolerate considerable drought, but look better if soil is moist.

CARING FOR PLANTS

Easy. Pinch back young plants to induce branching. Water often; fertilize and deadhead regularly to prolong blooming. In midseason, cut back plants that have become leggy. To overwinter plants indoors, dig before the first frost and bring indoors to a cool (50°F), sunny location, keeping the soil evenly moist.

PROPAGATING

Take cuttings of nonflowering shoots in spring or summer, or grow from seed.

COMBINATIONS

Agapanthus, Anthemis, Bidens, Nemophila, Verbena, Veronica.

Oxalis

TP*, HP | Zn 6–10

Shamrock, Sorrel

p. 414

Oxalis *is a large genus of plants grown for their neat, attractive foliage and pretty pink or white, cup-shaped flowers that remain tightly furled until opening. They grow 2"–12" tall. Plant them near pathways where their subtlety will not be lost, in rock gardens, or in containers.*

Type Hardy perennial, or tender perennial; often grown as annual in cooler zones
Zone 6–10, H 10–1 (see species list, p. 466); grown as an annual in cooler zones
Flowering season Spring or summer, depending on species

SOWING

Indoors As soon as fresh seed is available.
Outdoors *Seed:* As soon as fresh seed is available, usually late summer to autumn. *Roots:* Autumn.
Depth *Seed:* Just cover. *Roots:* 1"–2".

GERMINATING

Time 14–60 days.
Requirements 55°–70°F.

TRANSPLANTING

Time After last frost, when temperatures remain above 40°F.
Spacing *Small species:* 4"–6". *Large species:* 12"–15".
Light Most species require sun, but *O. acetosella* and *O. violacea* prefer dappled shade.
Soil Average, well drained, with a pH level of 4.0–5.0.

CARING FOR PLANTS

Water only during extremely dry weather. North of Zone 7, lift bulbs or tubers before first frost and store over winter in vermiculite, or keep in pots year-round.

PROPAGATING

Divide tubers in autumn (spring in Zone 6) or grow from seed.

COMBINATIONS

Antirrhinum, Armeria, Bergenia, Hosta, Matthiola.

Oxypetalum

See *Tweedia*

Paeonia

HP | Zn 3–9  

Peony

p. 414

Shrubby perennials of 18"–36" tall, peonies are prized for their large and exquisitely beautiful, fragrant flowers. Blooms are single or extravagantly double in white, yellow, red, purple, and every shade of pink. Their foliage is deeply cut and also very attractive. They are often grown as hedging or in beds of their own, but they are also attractive in mixed borders.

Type Hardy perennial
Zone 3–9, H 8–1 (see species list, p. 466)
Flowering Season Spring to early summer

SOWING

Indoors Prechilled seed 8–10 weeks before planting out.
Outdoors *Seed:* Early spring, when soil is cool and a light frost is still possible. *Roots:* Autumn.
Depth *Seed:* Surface. *Roots:* Plant eyes 1½" below surface.

GERMINATING

Time 30–365 days.
Requirements Place seed in a plastic bag together with moist growing medium and refrigerate for 2–3 weeks. Provide light and 50°–60°F thereafter.

TRANSPLANTING

Time After last frost.
Spacing 24"–36".
Light Full sun or part shade; prefers afternoon shade in Zones 7–9.
Soil Moist, well drained, fertile, with a pH level of 5.5–7.0. Prepare planting holes to a depth of 18" and backfill with compost and good loam.

CARING FOR PLANTS

Fertilize in early spring when new shoots are about 12" high and again lightly after blooming. Do not feed with manure. Water regularly. Deadhead after blooming and cut back plants to ground level in autumn. As growth is retarded for up to 3 years after moving, divide or move plants no more than every 10 years.

PROPAGATING

Carefully divide roots in early spring in Zones 2–6 (in autumn in Zones 7–9); each new root must contain at least two buds. Or, grow from seed.

COMBINATIONS

Digitalis, Geranium, Veronica; there is nothing more sublime that peonies combined with delphiniums and roses (climbing or shrub).

Palafoxia

A | Zn 3–9 | ☼ | dry soil, ordinary soil

Palavox, Spanish needle

These native plants are somewhat ungainly at 2'–3', but their pink, daisylike flowers are pretty and reliable. They are suitable for borders, and they make excellent dried flowers.

Type Annual
Zone 3–9; tolerates hot climates
Flowering Season Summer or autumn, depending on species

SOWING

Indoors 6–8 weeks before last frost.
Outdoors Spring or autumn.
Depth Just cover.

GERMINATING

Time 14–21 days.
Requirements Easy. Needs light and 60°–70°.

TRANSPLANTING

Time 2–3 weeks after last frost.
Spacing *Small species:* 9"–12". *Large species:* 18".
Light Sun.
Soil Well drained, slightly alkaline; tolerant of rocky, dry soil.

CARING FOR PLANTS

Easy. Deadhead to prevent rampant self-seeding. Dried flowers are everlasting: Cut stems just as flowers begin to open, tie stems together, and hang upside down in a cool, airy place, away from direct sunlight.

PROPAGATING

Grow from seed. Self-seeds readily.

CAUTION

Plants are toxic if eaten.

P

Panicum

A, HP | Zn 3–9

Panic grass

p. 414

These ornamental grasses have an erect habit and flat leaves, 8"–24" long. Flower stems are 2'–6', bearing either silken tassels or tiny, airy inflorescences in summer. Use in borders or displays of mixed grasses.

Type Annual or hardy perennial
Zone *Annual:* 3–9; *Perennial:* 4–9, H 12–1 (see species list, p. 466); prefers warm temperatures
Flowering Season Summer

SOWING

Indoors Start seed outdoors only.
Outdoors After last frost.
Depth ⅛".

GERMINATING

Time 21 days.
Requirements Easy. 60°–75°F.

TRANSPLANTING

Time Set out purchased plants in spring or autumn.
Spacing *Small species:* 12". *Large species:* 48".
Light Sun or light shade.
Soil Moist soil if sited in sun; will tolerate dry soil in shade. *P. virgatum* is suitable for xeriscaping.

CARING FOR PLANTS

Easy. Divide perennials every 2–3 years. This is the grass from which brooms are made. To make your own broom, bend stalks about 24" from tips and hang for 2 weeks with tips pointing downward. Cut broom at the bend and fasten securely.

PROPAGATING

Divide perennials in spring in the North (in autumn south of Zone 6) or grow from seed. Plant may self-seed. Propagate annuals by seed.

COMBINATIONS

Asclepias, Echinacea, Solidago.

CAUTION

P. repens is invasive in Florida, Georgia, and Nevada. See pp. 494–495 for advice.

P

Papaver

ANNUAL, BIENNIAL, AND TENDER PERENNIAL

A, Bi, TP* | Zn 1–10

Including P. commutatum, P. glaucum, P. rhoeas, P. somniferum, and P. triniifolium

Poppy

p. 414–415

The annuals, tender perennials, and biennials in this group are grown for their large, delicate, cup-shaped flowers with papery petals in every color but blue. Flowers are held singly on 4"–36" leafless stems; foliage is lobed or toothed. This is a beautiful plant for any sunny location.

Type Annual, biennial, tender perennial
Zone 1–10, H 8–1; flowers most successfully where temperatures are cool
Flowering Season Spring to summer

SOWING

Indoors 6–8 weeks before last frost, in peat pots. Best results come from seed started *in situ.*
Outdoors *Annual:* In Zones 3–7, in early spring, when soil is cool and a light frost is still possible, or late autumn. Where summers are cool, three spring plantings made 6 weeks apart will prolong the blooming season. In Zones 8–10, sow only in autumn. *Biennial:* August.
Depth Just cover.

GERMINATING

Time 20 days.
Requirements Easy. Darkness and 70°–75°F.

TRANSPLANTING

Time After last frost.
Spacing *Small species:* 6"–8". *Large species:* 8"–12".

ANNUAL, BIENNIAL, AND TENDER PERENNIAL *(cont'd)*

Light Full sun; *P. somniferum* will stand shade.
Soil Moist, well drained, not fertile; prefers a pH level of 6.0–7.0. *P. rhoeas* and *P. somniferum* are more tolerant of dry soil.

CARING FOR PLANTS

Easy. Deadhead frequently and remove plants altogether after flowering to reduce self-seeding. Do not move. These delicate plants are quite susceptible to fungal diseases.

PROPAGATING

Grow from seed. Plants self-seed freely.

COMBINATIONS

Anthemis, Centaurea, Chrysanthemum, Iris, Lavandula, Salvia, Santolina.

HARDY PERENNIAL

HP | Zn 3–9

Poppy

p. 414–415

The perennial poppies are among the showiest plants in the spring and summer border. Their crepey, cup-shaped flowers, which can measure up to 8" across, are held singly on stalks ranging from 6" to an impressive 5'. The colors are rich and vibrant: scarlet, salmon, violet, pink, yellow, or white, often with darkly spotted centers. Leaves and stems are usually hairy. They add bright color and dramatic interest to the border, and are excellent for cutting.

Type Hardy perennial
Zone 3–9, H 8–1 (see species list, p. 466). *P. croceum* (syn. *P. nudicaule*) is perennial only where summers are cool; elsewhere, grow as an annual. Most perennial poppies prefer low humidity and cool nighttime temperatures
Flowering Season Mid-spring to summer, depending on species

SOWING

Indoors 6–8 weeks before last frost, in peat pots. Starting plants *in situ* is recommended.
Outdoors Early spring, when soil is cool and a light frost is still possible, or late autumn.
Depth Surface.

GERMINATING

Time 10–30 days.
Requirements 55°F.

TRANSPLANTING

Time After last frost.
Spacing *Small species:* 9"–12". *Large species:* 18"–24".
Light Full sun.
Soil Well drained, rather poor, with a pH level of 5.5–7.0. *P. croceum* tolerates dry soil. Prepare planting hole to 18", adding a layer of gravel and backfilling with half soil and half compost (do not use manure).

CARING FOR PLANTS

Water regularly during dry spells but do not fertilize. Disbud as flowers fade to reduce self-seeding. Stake plants in windy sites. Mulch in winter with compost, digging in carefully in spring. Poppies do not like to be disturbed and should be moved with great care only when dormant.

PROPAGATING

Take root cuttings in autumn or grow from seed. Some may self-seed but often revert to a less desirable color.

COMBINATIONS

Allium, Delphinium, Dianthus, Lupinus, Paeonia, Penstemon, Stachys.

CAUTION

Harmful if eaten.

Paracaryum

Bi | Zn 8–10

Only one species of this genus is commonly available — P. coelestinum. *This charming 2' tall plant features silvery foliage and 1½" flowers of a beautiful sky blue. An easy plant for the border.*

Type Biennial
Zone 8–10
Flowering Season All summer

SOWING

Indoors September to March.
Outdoors July to October.
Depth Surface.

GERMINATING

Time 7–21 days.
Requirements Easy. Requires light and 70°–85°F.

TRANSPLANTING

Time After last frost or autumn.
Spacing 12".
Light Sun to part shade.
Soil Light, well drained.

CARING FOR PLANTS

Easy. Water during dry spells.

PROPAGATING

Grow from seed.

Paradisea

HP | Zn 7–9

Paradise lily, St. Bruno's lily

p. 415

These perennials have gray-green, grassy foliage and slim, 2' tall stems that bear racemes of fragrant white, funnel-shaped flowers. They are lovely in a mixed planting at woodland's edge.

Type Hardy perennial
Zone 7–9
Flowering Season Late spring

SOWING

Indoors See Germinating, Requirements.
Outdoors *Seed:* See Germinating, Requirements. *Roots:* Spring or autumn.
Depth *Seed:* Just cover. *Roots:* 3".

GERMINATING

Time 30–180 days.
Requirements *Autumn sowing:* Sow seed in flats, sink these in the ground against a north-facing wall, and cover with glass. Moisten soil occasionally, if necessary. Bring flats indoors in spring to 50°F. *Spring sowing:* Sow seed in flats, secure in plastic bags, and refrigerate. After 2–3 weeks, remove flats and sink in the ground in a shady location, covering with glass. Transplant seedlings as they appear.

TRANSPLANTING

Time After last frost.
Spacing 12".
Light Sun or part shade.
Soil Prefers deep, rich, well drained.

CARING FOR PLANTS

Easy. Fertilize in spring, mulch well in autumn, and keep well watered. Plants rest without blooming for 1 year after division.

PROPAGATING

Divide in spring or after flowering or grow from seed. Division may lessen blooming for 1 year. Plants grown from seed will flower in 2–3 years.

× Pardancanda

HP | Zn 5–9 | Full sun | Dry soil, Ordinary soil, Moist soil

Candylily

Members of the Iris Family, these cheerful, understated plants have smallish, freckled, saucer-shaped blooms in many colors. Flowers grow on 2'–3' stems above long, sword-shaped leaves. Place candylilies in the border where their unassuming blooms will not be overlooked.

Type Hardy perennial
Zone 5–9, H 9–5; requires hot summer temperatures
Flowering Season Summer

SOWING

Indoors Prechilled seed 8–10 weeks before planting out.
Outdoors Early spring or early autumn.
Depth *Seed:* Just cover. *Roots:* 2"–3".

GERMINATING

Time 15 days.
Requirements Easy. Place seed in a plastic bag together with moist growing medium and refrigerate for 7 days. Place in a warm location (70°–85°F) after chilling.

TRANSPLANTING

Time Early spring, when soil is cool and a light frost is still possible, or late autumn.
Spacing 12".
Light Full sun.
Soil Tolerates most soils but prefers moist conditions.

CARING FOR PLANTS

Easy. Water during dry spells and cut back plants to ground level in autumn. Provide a light winter mulch north of Zone 7.

PROPAGATING

Divide in spring or grow from seed. Plants grown from seed will bloom in their first year.

COMBINATIONS

Coreopsis, Echinacea, Salvia, Veronica.

Parnassia

HP | Zn 3–10 | Full sun, Partial shade | Dry soil, Ordinary soil, Moist soil

Grass of Parnassus, Bog star

Summer-blooming perennials of great charm, Parnassia *have white, saucer-shaped flowers that resemble eager, upturned faces. Flowers are borne singly on sturdy 8"–18" stems; leaves are heart-shaped. Lovely in combination with low-growing foliage plants in a moist garden.*

Type Hardy perennial
Zone 3–10, H 12–1 (see species list, p. 467)
Flowering Season Summer

SOWING

Indoors Start seed outdoors only.
Outdoors As soon as seed is ripe, usually in late summer.
Depth Surface.

GERMINATING

Time 30–180 days.
Requirements Easy. Sow seed in flats, sink flats in the ground against a north-facing wall, and cover with glass. Moisten soil occasionally, if necessary. Transplant seedlings to peat pots when five true leaves have formed. Place pots on trays in light shade and keep constantly moist, watering from below. Transplant to the garden in autumn.

TRANSPLANTING

Time Set out purchased plants in autumn.
Spacing 6"–8".
Light Full sun or light shade.
Soil Rich, swampy, with a pH level of 6.0–7.0. Plants are more tolerant of dry soil when sited in light shade.

CARING FOR PLANTS

Mulch in spring and keep soil constantly moist. Divide every 3 years after flowering.

PROPAGATING

Divide after flowering or grow from seed.

P

Parochetus

TP | Zn 8–10

A genus of low-growing (1"–2"), trailing tender perennials, Parochetus *has bright green, cloverlike foliage and intense blue, pealike flowers. It is useful in rock gardens and containers.*

Type Perennial
Zone 8–10, H 12–8 (see species list, p. 467); can be grown as an annual north of Zone 8 if plants are dug in autumn and overwintered indoors
Flowering Season Summer through autumn

SOWING

Indoors 6–8 weeks before planting out.
Outdoors Start seed indoors.
Depth Just cover.

GERMINATING

Time 30–90 days.
Requirements Soak seed for 24 hours in warm water; provide 50°F thereafter.

TRANSPLANTING

Time Spring or autumn.
Spacing 12"–18".
Light Sun or light shade.
Soil Moist, gritty, poor, well drained; rich soil will produce lush foliage with few flowers.

CARING FOR PLANTS

Water during dry periods.

PROPAGATING

Take cuttings, divide in early spring or autumn, or grow from seed.

Passiflora

TP, HP | Zn 6–10

Granadilla, Passionflower

p. 415

Passiflora *vines are grown for their large, exotic, and intricate flowers, most often in combinations of white and purple, less frequently red. Some plants have ornamental, egg-shaped fruit. Vines grow 15'–30' long.*

Type Hardy perennial or tender perennial
Zone 6–10, H 9–6 (see species list, p. 467)
Flowering Season Spring to autumn, depending on species

SOWING

Indoors 8 weeks before last frost.
Outdoors After last frost.
Depth 1/4".

GERMINATING

Time 30–365 days.
Requirements Difficult. Use only fresh seed. Soak for 12 hours in warm water, sow in flats, and keep at 70°–80°F. If seed has not germinated in 3 months, refrigerate for 3 months.

TRANSPLANTING

Time After last frost, when temperatures remain above 45°F.
Spacing 24"–36".
Light Sun or part shade.
Soil Deep, moist, well drained, moderately rich, with a pH level of 6.0–8.0. Soil that is too rich will produce abundant leaves with few flowers.

CARING FOR PLANTS

Easy. Water regularly and provide a good mulch. Prune 3-year-old vines in autumn or early spring, removing dead branches and cutting back side shoots to 6". A trellis or other support will be necessary.

PROPAGATING

Take cuttings in spring or summer or grow from seed.

COMBINATIONS

Because most vines are very strong growers, they are generally best grown alone, although a less vigorous *Clematis* makes an attractive partner.

Patrinia

HP | Zn 5–8

p. 415

Clump-forming perennials, 8"–36" tall, Patrinia *are grown for the airy clusters of tiny white or golden yellow flowers that cover them in summer. These lacy plants are attractive in the rock garden, border, or cutting bed.*

Type Hardy perennial
Zone 5–8, H 9–5
Flowering Season Early spring to early autumn

SOWING

Indoors 8–10 weeks before planting out.
Outdoors Early spring, when soil is cool and a light frost is still possible, or late autumn.
Depth Just cover.

GERMINATING

Time 10 days.
Requirements 60°–65°F.

TRANSPLANTING

Time Early spring, when soil is cool and a light frost is still possible, or late autumn.
Spacing *Small species:* 6"–12". *Large species:* 12"–18".
Light Full sun to light shade, with afternoon shade where summers are hot.
Soil Light, rich, moist.

CARING FOR PLANTS

Easy. Keep soil moist.

PROPAGATING

Divide in autumn (in spring in Zones 5 and 6) or grow from seed. Plant may self-seed.

COMBINATIONS

Aquilegia, Hosta, Primula.

Pelargonium

TP* | Zn 9–10

Geranium

p. 415

These widely grown plants are prized for their long-blooming, brightly colored flowers, which are borne in umbels on short, sturdy stalks. Blossoms are white, red, orange, or shades of pink. Handsome leaves are usually rounded but may be deeply lobed or cut, and also may be marked with maroon or other colors. Plants grow 6"–36" tall, or much taller in warm climates. Geraniums make excellent container plants, or mass them in a display bed.

Type Tender perennial; usually grown as an annual
Zone 9–10, H 12–1; grown as an annual in Zones 3–8; performs best where days are warm and nights are cool
Flowering Season Mid spring through first frost

SOWING

Indoors 8–10 weeks before last frost.
Outdoors After all danger of frost, in Zones 9–10 only.
Depth Just cover.

GERMINATING

Time 3–21 days.
Requirements 70°–75°F. Provide seedlings with plenty of light as soon as germination has begun. Pinch out young plants to establish a compact form.

TRANSPLANTING

Time 1 week after last frost.
Spacing 12"–18".
Light Full sun; light shade is acceptable where summers are very hot. Variegated species must be shaded from direct sunlight.
Soil Prefers a rich, moist soil with a pH level of 6.0–7.0; performs adequately in average soil with good drainage.

CARING FOR PLANTS

Easy and satisfying, given regular attention. Apply liquid fertilizer monthly, water when soil becomes dry, and deadhead regularly to produce an enviable display. To overwinter indoors, lift plants before the first frost, shake off excess soil, and store in a cool, humid location. In spring, prune back these plants to the main stem before replanting. Or, to grow indoors in the winter, give plants at least 4 hours of sunlight a day and just enough water to keep the soil barely moist, and feed lightly twice a month.

PROPAGATING

In spring or summer, take cuttings with five leaves, remove the bottom three leaves, and plant in a small pot. Cover loosely with a plastic bag and fasten securely. Remove bag when roots have begun to grow, or dry the cuttings for several hours, then dip the ends in rooting powder and root in sharp sand. Or grow from seed.

COMBINATIONS

Alyssum, Campanula, dusty miller, *Helichrysum, Lobelia, Petunia, Verbena.*

Peltiphyllum See *Dormera*

Pennisetum

A, HP* | Zn 1–10

p. 415

These popular ornamental grasses have flat, narrow leaf blades that are sometimes attractively colored, and numerous 2'–4' spikes of soft, fuzzy flowers in late summer. These grasses bring a feel of the wide open spaces to the suburban garden.

Type Annual, hardy perennial
Zone *Annual:* 1–10. *Perennial:* 5–9, H 9–1 (see species list, p. 467). Grows most successfully in warm climates
Flowering Season Mid summer to early autumn

SOWING

Indoors 6–8 weeks before last frost.
Outdoors Early spring to mid-spring.
Depth Just cover.

GERMINATING

Time 15–20 days.
Requirements 70°F.

TRANSPLANTING

Time After last frost.
Spacing 18"–30".
Light Full sun.
Soil Rich, well drained.

CARING FOR PLANTS

For best results, water regularly. Provide winter mulch in colder zones. After last frost, cut back plants to ground level.

PROPAGATING

Divide in spring or grow from seed. *Pennisetum* species, especially *P. alopecuroides* and many of its cultivars, self-seed with complete abandon.

COMBINATIONS

Cosmos, Rudbeckia, Salvia, Sedum.

CAUTION

Pennistenum ssp. are listed as invasive in some areas, including Florida. See pp. 494–495 for advice.

Penstemon

A, TP, HP | Zn 1–10

p. 415–416

These North and Central American natives are exquisite in the summer border or rock garden. Leaves grow sparsely along erect, 12"–36" stems. Some species are rather stiff and twiggy; others are softer, with a more relaxed habit. Stems are topped by loose clusters of tubular, lipped flowers in attractive shades of blue, purple, pink, white, or yellow. Penstemon *are disappointingly short-lived and averse to heat and humidity.*

Type Annual, tender perennial, or hardy perennial
Zone *Annual:* 1–10. *Perennial:* 3–10, H 10–1 (see species list, p. 467); prefer cool temperatures; *P. hirsutus* var. *pygmaeus, P. digitalis* 'Huskar Red',

P. barbatus, and *P.* × *gloxiniodes* are more tolerant of heat and humidity
Flowering Season Late spring to autumn; depending on species

SOWING

Indoors 8–10 weeks before last frost.
Outdoors Spring or autumn.
Depth Surface.

GERMINATING

Time 18–36 days.
Requirements Light and 55°–65°F.

TRANSPLANTING

Time After last frost.
Spacing *Small species:* 12"–18". *Large species:* 20"–30".
Light Sun in cool climates, afternoon shade where summers are hot.
Soil Fertile, well drained, with a pH level of 5.5–7.0. *P. strictus* is tolerant of dry soil and can be used in xeriscaping.

CARING FOR PLANTS

Easy, in ideal conditions. Water regularly in summer and deadhead frequently. Cut plants to ground in autumn and mulch well. Plants will bloom most profusely when grown in full sun but will die out quite quickly, in 1 or 2 years.

PROPAGATING

Take stem cuttings in spring or autumn or grow from seed. Plants grown from seed will bloom in their first year.

COMBINATIONS

Artemisia, Coreopsis, Tradescantia.

Pentas

TP* | Zn 10 | Full sun, Partial shade | Ordinary soil

p. 416

*Only one of this genus of shrubs and tender perennials is commonly grown—*P. lanceolata *and its cultivars. This very heat-tolerant woody plant forms a neat, 1'–3' mini-shrub, with clusters of tiny, brightly colored flowers in all shades of pink, red, white, or violet held above mid-green foliage. It is useful in borders or containers.*

Type Tender perennial; usually grown as annual
Zone 10, H 12–5; grown as an annual farther north
Flowering Season *Perennial:* Almost year-round. *Annual:* Summer to autumn.

SOWING

Indoors 8–10 weeks before last frost.
Outdoors Spring.
Depth Surface.

GERMINATING

Time 7–40 days.
Requirements Easy. Seed needs light and 60°–75°F. Pinch back seedlings to establish a bushy habit.

TRANSPLANTING

Time Several weeks after last frost when soil has warmed to 50°F.
Spacing 12"–18" where summers are cool, 18"–24" in warmer regions.
Light Sun, with light shade from the hot afternoon sun in Zone 10.
Soil Tolerates poor but prefers rich, well drained.

CARING FOR PLANTS

Very easy and carefree. Pinch tips of young plants to encourage branching, water during dry spells, feed periodically, and deadhead regularly to increase blooming. In Zone 10, cut back hard in early spring. As an annual, *Pentas* really comes into its own in mid- to late summer, when it's inclined to smother nearby plants if it hasn't been allowed enough space. Plants can be potted up in autumn and grown indoors in a bright, cool location (55°–60°F), keeping soil on the dry side; prune before replanting in the garden. Plants may attract whiteflies and aphids.

PROPAGATING

Take stem cuttings in late summer or grow from seed.

COMBINATIONS

Aster, Leucanthemum, Petunia.

Perilla

A | Zn 3–10

These bushy annuals grow to 2'. P. frutescens *'Atropurpurea' is grown for its bronze foliage; tiny white tubular flowers are borne on stalks in summer. Use* Perilla *as a foil for plants of contrasting leaf color.*

Type Annual
Zone 3–10, H 12–1; prefers warm temperatures
Flowering Season Summer; flowers are insignificant

SOWING

Indoors 10–12 weeks before last frost, in peat pots.
Outdoors After last frost.
Depth Surface.

GERMINATING

Time 15–30 days.
Requirements Light and 65°–75°F.

TRANSPLANTING

Time After last frost.
Spacing 12"–15".
Light Sun or light shade.
Soil Slightly dry, well drained.

CARING FOR PLANTS

Easy. Pinch out tips when plants reach 6". Move only with great care.

PROPAGATING

Take cuttings or grow from seed. Self-seeds with abandon in warm climates and may become invasive.

COMBINATIONS

Achillea, Artemisia, Galium, Salvia, Santolina, Stachys.

CAUTION

P. frutescens is listed as invasive in many parts of North America. See pp. 494–495 for advice.

Perovskia

HP | Zn 5–9

p. 416

One species in this genus of perennials and subshrubs, P. atriplicifolia, *is grown for its fragrant, lance-shaped or deeply toothed, silver or gray-green foliage. In bloom, plants form a 3'–5' cloud of silver with slender, flowering spikes delicately etched in purple or blue. Adds a light airy texture to the border.*

Type Hardy perennial
Zone 5–9, H 9–4
Flowering Season Mid to late summer

SOWING

Seed is rarely available.

TRANSPLANTING

Time Set out purchased plants in early spring or autumn.
Spacing 24"–36".
Light Full sun.
Soil Ordinary, dry, well drained; must have excellent drainage where winters are wet.

CARING FOR PLANTS

Easy. Cutting plants back to ground level in spring will improve blooming.

PROPAGATING

Take cuttings in spring or summer, plant in flats or individual pots, and cover with glass.

COMBINATIONS

Autumn-blooming *Anemone, Echinacea, Platycodon.*

Persicaria (syn. *Aconogonon, Bistorta, Polygonum, Tovara*) A, HP | Zn 3–10

Fleeceflower, Knotweed, Smartweed

p. 416

Persicaria *is a large genus of annuals and perennials, some of which are evergreen, some trailing or climbing, some aquatic. Most bear small white or red flowers in profusion in racemes or spikes and have handsome foliage. Use in borders, wildflower gardens, and bog or water gardens.*

Type Annual, hardy perennial
Zone *Annual:* 3–10. *Perennial:* 3–9, H 9–1 (see species list, p. 467); prefers warm temperatures
Flowering Season Summer to autumn

SOWING

Indoors 2–3 weeks before last frost.
Outdoors After last frost.
Depth Just cover.

GERMINATING

Time 20–60 days.
Requirements 70°–75°F.

TRANSPLANTING

Time After last frost.
Spacing *Small species:* 8"–12". *Medium species:* 12"–24". *Large species:* 24"–48".
Light Part shade, or full sun where summers are cool.
Soil Moist, well drained, with a pH level of 6.0–7.5.

CARING FOR PLANTS

Water well during the flowering season. Cut back flower stems in autumn. Some species may be invasive.

PROPAGATING

Divide in early spring in Zones 3–6 (in early autumn elsewhere) or grow from seed. Plant may self-seed.

COMBINATIONS

An unassuming plant that becomes quite stunning in combination with others, while simultaneously greatly enhancing its partners. Plant in masses with *Allium, Delphinium, Hosta, Rhododendron, Stachys, Verbena,* or *Veronica.*

Petasites HP | Zn 5–9

Butterbur, Sweet coltsfoot

These invasive perennials are grown for their attractive foliage and ability to form a dense ground cover in difficult sites. Leaves are large (8" to a staggering 6') and heart-shaped or nearly round, similar to Ligularia. *They are held on stiff stems of 1'–3', up to 6' on the largest varieties. Dense cones of prehistoric-looking, greenish white or pink flowers appear before leaves. Not for the small garden or the faint of heart!*

Type Hardy perennial
Zone 5–9, H 9–5 (see species list, p. 467); does not tolerate humid heat
Flowering Season Late winter to early spring, before leaves

SOWING

Indoors Not recommended.
Outdoors Sow seed when fresh in spring, in a cold frame.
Depth Just cover.

GERMINATING

Time Germination is slow and very erratic.
Requirements 41°F.

TRANSPLANTING

Time After last frost.
Spacing *Small species:* 1'–2'. *Large species:* 3'–4'. *Enormous species:* 4'–6'.
Light Part to full shade; sun only where summers are cool.
Soil Moist to wet; will tolerate heavy, rocky, or otherwise difficult conditions.

CARING FOR PLANTS

Easy, requiring only constant moisture. Large leaves are enjoyed by slugs. Grow *Petasites* alone, only where nothing else will flourish, as it can be invasive and difficult to eradicate because of deep roots. Or grow it in containers to restrict growth.

PROPAGATING

Divide in spring or autumn or grow from seed.

CAUTION

See comments regarding invasiveness above under Caring for Plants.

Petrorhagia (syn. *Tunica*)

HP | Zn 5–7

Tunic flower

p. 416

The Petrorhagia *genus contains spreading, low-growing annuals and perennials. The perennial* P. saxifraga *is sometimes used in gardens. This 4" plant bears fine, feathery leaves and a profusion of small, flat, pink, white, or purple flowers. Native to the Mediterranean region, it is a good plant for the rock garden or border's edge.*

Type Hardy perennial
Zone 5–7, H 7–5
Flowering Season Summer

SOWING

Indoors See Germinating, Requirements.
Outdoors See Germinating, Requirements.
Depth Just cover.

GERMINATING

Time 14–60 days.
Requirements Easy. *Autumn sowing:* Sow seed in flats, sink in the ground against a north-facing wall, and cover with glass. Moisten soil occasionally, if necessary. Bring flats indoors in spring to 50°F. *Spring sowing:* Sow seed in flats, place in a plastic bag, and refrigerate for 2–3 weeks. Sink flats in the ground in a shady location, covering with glass. Transplant seedlings as they appear.

TRANSPLANTING

Time Spring or autumn.
Spacing 4"–6".
Light Sun.
Soil Well drained, alkaline.

CARING FOR PLANTS

Easy. No special care is required.

PROPAGATING

Divide in spring or grow from seed. Plant may self-seed.

COMBINATIONS

Cerastium, Dianthus, Leucanthemum.

Petroselinum

Bi | Zn 4–9

Parsley

p. 416

Herbs grown for their strongly flavored leaves, these 6"–18" plants have dark green, deeply toothed, and curly or flat leaves used extensively in cooking. They are most often grown in herb gardens, but may also be used as edgings or in containers.

Type Biennial; usually grown as an annual
Zone 4–9
Flowering Season Parsley will bloom in the early spring of its second year

SOWING

Indoors Late winter, in peat pots.
Outdoors Early spring, when soil is cool and a light frost is still possible, or early autumn.
Depth ¼".

GERMINATING

Time 21–42 days.
Requirements Soak seed in warm water for 24 hours; provide darkness and 70°F thereafter.

TRANSPLANTING

Time Just before last frost.
Spacing 6"–12".
Light Full sun to light shade.
Soil Rich, well drained, with a pH level of 5.5–6.5. Amend with compost or manure at planting time.

CARING FOR PLANTS

Easy. Allow free air circulation around plants. Feed with 5-10-5 when stalks are 4"–6" and again 1 month later; a topdressing of compost will give flagging plants a lift in midseason. Harvest leaves at any time; wash and thoroughly dry before freezing. Start with fresh plants each spring, as older plants lose their flavor and soon go to seed. *To grow indoors in winter:* Carefully dig and pot up plants in late summer, providing at least 5 hours of sunlight a day, a warm situation (70°F), and evenly moist soil. Curly parsley is best for eating raw; flat-leaved parsley is better for cooking.

PROPAGATING

Grow from seed only.

Petunia

A, TP* | Zn 1–10

Petunia

p. 416

One of the most widely grown annuals, petunias are valued for their abundant, brightly colored, trumpet-shaped flowers borne tirelessly over a very long period. Their habit is somewhat procumbent, with stems growing 12"–18". Flowers are white, red, purple, pink, and yellow, and blooms are often bicolored. Provides strong color in containers, borders, or edgings.

Type Annual, tender perennial; usually grown as an annual
Zone 1–10, H 12–3; prefers warm temperature
Flowering Season Late spring to frost

SOWING

Indoors 8–10 weeks before planting out.
Outdoors After last frost. Fancy cultivars and hybrids should be started indoors only.
Depth Surface.

GERMINATING

Time 7–21 days.
Requirements Light and 70°–80°F.

TRANSPLANTING

Time After last frost.
Spacing 7"–10".
Light Full sun or very light shade.
Soil Moist, well drained, with plenty of organic matter added. Prefers a pH level of 6.0–7.5.

CARING FOR PLANTS

Easy. Pinch back young plants to make them bushier. Feed only after plants have become established outdoors, then once again 4 weeks later. Water and deadhead regularly, cutting back any scraggly growth. Plants may be cut back by half at summer's end to encourage new growth. Aphids, as well as beetles, may be a problem.

PROPAGATING

Take cuttings in spring or summer or grow from seed. Plant may self-seed, but resulting plants usually revert to white.

COMBINATIONS

Petunias fit well into almost any planting: *Antirrhinum, Calendula, Cineraria, Convulvulus, Cynoglossum, Helichrysum, Pelargonium, Pentas, Salvia.*

P

Peucedanum See *Anethum*

Phacelia

A | Zn 3–10

Phacelia, Scorpion weed

p. 417

The most popular plants in this genus are bushy annuals, 6"–24" tall. Leaves are often toothed, heart-shaped, and covered in upturned, bell-shaped flowers of deepest blue or lavender. Use them in containers or borders, or as an unusual annual ground cover.

Type Annual
Zone 3–10, H 9–1; grows most successfully where temperatures are cool
Flowering Season Spring or summer

SOWING

Indoors Sow seed of *P. campanularia* in March. All other species should be started *in situ*.
Outdoors Early spring, when soil is cool and a light frost is still possible. Where winters are mild, in late summer or early autumn.
Depth 1/4".

GERMINATING

Time 12–30 days.
Requirements Darkness and 55°–65°F.

Phacelia (cont'd)

TRANSPLANTING

Time After last frost.
Spacing *Small species:* 4"–8". *Large species:* 9"–12".
Light Full sun. *P. campanularia* tolerates part shade.
Soil Ordinary, well drained, with a pH level of 6.5–7.0; tolerates dry soil. *P. campanularia* is suitable for xeriscaping in areas with relatively cool summers.

CARING FOR PLANTS

Pinch back young plants to encourage a bushy habit. Continuous hot weather will cause plants to stop blooming. Do not transplant.

PROPAGATING

Grow from seed. Plant may self-seed.

COMBINATIONS

Centaurea, Echium, ferns, *Linum, Nemophila.*

CAUTION

Contact with skin may cause irritation.

Phalaris

A, HP | Zn 3–10

p. 417

Genus of ornamental grasses, one of which — P. arundinaceae *— is grown for the flat, broad, attractively striped green and white leaves of its cultivars; 18"–36" tall. Flowers are somewhat skimpy, borne on very tall stalks. Use with caution as a ground cover for difficult sites, as plants spread with abandon. It is especially attractive near water.*

Type Annual or hardy perennial
Zone *Annual:* 3–10; *Perennial:* 4–9, H 9–1. Prefers cool temperatures
Flowering Season Summer

SOWING

Indoors Sow seed outdoors only. Propagate variegated forms by division only.
Outdoors Early to mid-spring, or before first frost in autumn.
Depth Just cover.

GERMINATING

Time 21 days.
Requirements 60°–75°F.

TRANSPLANTING

Time Set out purchased plants in spring or autumn.
Spacing 12"–24".
Light Will grow in light shade but flowers best in full sun.
Soil Moist, rich soil produces large, spreading plants; dry soil will produce smaller, less invasive plants. *P. canariensis* and *P. arundinacea* var. *pica* may be used for xeriscaping.

CARING FOR PLANTS

Cut back perennials in spring. Water regularly to encourage more rampant growth; limit water and/or dig up and discard clumps to restrict growth. Divide every 5 years.

PROPAGATING

Divide creeping rootstock of perennials in spring. Grow annuals from seed. Annuals may self-seed.

CAUTION

P. arundinacea is listed as invasive in many areas, including Florida, Indiana, and Maryland. See pp. 494–495 for advice.

Phaneroplebia See *Cyrtomirum*

Pharbitis See *Ipomoea*

Phaseolus (syn. *Vigna*)

A | Zn 1–10

Bean

p. 417

Fast-growing, mainly twining plants, runner beans grow 2'–6' and bear papery blooms of red or white. They are grown both for their attractive flowers and for their long, flat, edible seedpods which follow the flowers.

Type Annual
Zone *Annuals:* 1–10.
Flowering Season Summer to autumn

SOWING

Indoors 4–6 weeks before planting out, in peat pots.
Outdoors 2 weeks after last frost.
Depth 1".

GERMINATING

Time 4–5 days.
Requirements Dust seed with pea or bean inoculant; plant with the eye facing downward. Provide 60°–70°F.

TRANSPLANTING

Time In spring, when temperatures remain above 55°F.
Spacing 6"–8".
Light Sun.
Soil Moist, rich, well drained.

CARING FOR PLANTS

Easy. Provide a trellis for support or they may be grown along a chainlink fence. Water regularly, then sit back and watch them grow. Pick beans for eating when about 4" long, before they become tough.

PROPAGATING

Take cuttings in early spring or grow from seed.

Phlomis

HP | Zn 3–10

p. 417

These eye-catching perennials display an unusual construction, with widely spaced pairs of leaves cushioning dense clusters of flowers along stiff, upright stems of 18"–60". Flowers may be pinkish, purple, yellow, or white. Grow as a specimen or at the back of a spacious border.

Type Hardy perennial
Zone 3–10, H 12–1 (see species list, p. 468); does not do well in hot, humid climates
Flowering Season Spring to summer

SOWING

Indoors 8–10 weeks before planting out.
Outdoors Spring.
Depth Just cover.

GERMINATING

Time 14–42 days.
Requirements 60°F.

TRANSPLANTING

Time After last frost.
Spacing 24".
Light Sun to light shade.
Soil Light, sandy, infertile.

CARING FOR PLANTS

Easy. Water during dry spells. Lightly prune flowering branches in winter. Divide every 3 years to maintain vigor.

PROPAGATING

Take cuttings in summer or autumn, divide in spring in Zones 3–6 (in early autumn in Zones 7–10), or grow from seed.

COMBINATIONS

Allium, Anthemis, Caryopteris, Lavandula, Salvia.

Phlox

ANNUAL Including *P. drummondii*

A | Zn 2–10

Annual phlox, Drummond phlox, Texas pride

p. 417

Upright, fast-growing, cheerful plants, annual phlox bear masses of fragrant, flat red, pink, purple, or white flowers; petals are sometimes fringed. Size ranges from 6"–12" and are useful for containers or edging.

Type Annual
Zone 2–10, H 12–1; prefers cool weather
Flowering Season Late spring to summer

SOWING

Indoors 6–8 weeks before planting out, in peat pots.
Outdoors Early spring, when soil is cool and a light frost is still possible. Where winters are mild, sow between late summer and late autumn.
Depth Just cover.

GERMINATING

Time 10–21 days.
Requirements Darkness and 55°–65°F.

TRANSPLANTING

Time 2–3 weeks before last frost.
Spacing *Dwarf species:* 4"–6". *Large or spreading species:* 12"–18".
Light Full sun or light shade, with shade from hot afternoon sun.
Soil Rich, moist, well drained, with a pH level of 6.5–7.0.

CARING FOR PLANTS

Pinch back young plants to establish a bushy habit. Water regularly and feed once in midsummer. Deadhead frequently to extend the blooming period. Flagging plants may be rejuvenated by cutting back to 2", although excessive heat may weaken them beyond repair. Prone to powdery mildew. Dislike transplanting.

PROPAGATING

Grow from seed only.

COMBINATIONS

Anagallis, Diascia, Gentiana, Helichrysum, Lobelia, Salvia.

P

PERENNIAL

HP | Zn 3–9

Perennial phlox

p. 417

This large group of plants is grown for its showstopping floral display. Spring bloomers are mainly low growing and several are evergreen. Plants bear star-shaped flowers of pink, red, purple, white, or blue. Summer bloomers display substantial clusters of brightly colored flowers on tall, erect stems. Their uses are endless: borders, edging, rock gardens, or ground cover, and in formal, woodland, or wildflower gardens.

Type Hardy perennial
Zone 3–9, H 8–1 (see species list, p. 468)
Flowering Season Spring to early autumn, depending on species

SOWING

Indoors Start seed outdoors only.
Outdoors Autumn.
Depth Just cover.

GERMINATING

Time 25–50 days.
Requirements Sow seed in flats, sink in the ground against a north-facing wall, and cover with glass. Moisten soil occasionally, if necessary. Transplant seedlings in spring or autumn.

TRANSPLANTING

Time Spring or autumn.
Spacing *Small species:* 6"–8". *Medium species:* 10"–15". *Large species:* 24".
Light Full sun, with afternoon shade where summers are hot. *P. adsurgens, P. stolonifera,* and *P. divaricata* prefer part to full shade.
Soil Moist, well drained, fertile, enriched with organic matter (wood ash is ideal). Prefers a pH level between 6.5 and 7.5. *P. bifida* and *P. nana* tolerate poor. *P. subulata* tolerates dry soil and may be used for xeriscaping.

PERENNIAL *(cont'd)*

CARING FOR PLANTS

Deadhead regularly and cut back severely after flowering to keep plants looking neat. Phlox are highly prone to mildew in warm, damp weather. To minimize the risk, site where air circulation is unrestricted (do not plant near walls), thin plants in spring by cutting back all but 3 or 4 stalks per clump, and avoid wetting leaves when watering. Pull up self-seeded plants, as these do not retain the parent flower's color.

PROPAGATING

Divide in spring in the North (in autumn south of Zone 6), take cuttings in early spring, or grow from seed.

COMBINATIONS

Acanthus, Aster, Erigeron, Lunaria, Monarda, Platycodon, Tulipa.

Phormium

HP* | Zn 8–10

Flax lily

p. 417–418

These evergreen perennials resemble yucca with their stiff, sword-shaped, green, maroon, or bronze leaves, often sporting red, yellow, or white stripes. These 3'–10' giants must be positioned with care, but they make a stunning specimen or mass planting; they are also attractive and unusual container plants. Their strongly architectural form should be exploited.

Type Hardy perennial
Zone 8–10, H 10–3; often grown as an annual in Zones 3–7
Flowering Season Summer

SOWING

Indoors 10–12 weeks before planting out.
Outdoors February.
Depth Just cover.

GERMINATING

Time 30–180 days.
Requirements 60°–65°F.

TRANSPLANTING

Time Late spring.
Spacing *Small species:* 12". *Medium species:* 18"–24". *Large species:* 24"–36", or singly.
Light Full sun or part shade.
Soil Sandy, moist, fertile.

CARING FOR PLANTS

Easy. Water well during dry spells and divide every 3–4 years. Where not hardy dig up in fall and over-winter indoors, or grow in containers year-round, moving containers indoors in autumn.

PROPAGATING

Divide in spring or grow from seed.

COMBINATIONS

Euphorbia, ornamental grasses, *Ligularia, Sedum.*

Phuopsis (syn. *Crucianella*)

HP | Zn 4–9

p. 418

This mat-forming perennial (there is only one species in the genus) has narrow leaves that grow in whorls along thin stalks topped with round clusters of tiny pink tubular flowers; 12" tall. Allow plants to cascade over walls, use them in rock gardens, or plant them toward the front of the border.

Type Hardy perennial; sometimes grown as an annual
Zone 4–9, H 8–5; not tolerant of high heat and humidity
Flowering Season Summer

SOWING

Indoors Start seed outdoors.

Outdoors Autumn.
Depth Surface.

GERMINATING

Time 30–40 days.
Requirements Easy. Light and 50°–60°F.

TRANSPLANTING

Time Set out purchased plants in spring or autumn.
Spacing 18"–24".
Light Sun or part shade.
Soil Gritty, moist but very well drained, especially in winter.

CARING FOR PLANTS

Plants spread rapidly, and unwanted plants should be removed regularly.

PROPAGATING

Divide in spring, take cuttings in summer, or grow from seed.

COMBINATIONS

Campanula, Dianthus, Erigeron, Scabiosa.

Phyllitis See *Asplenium*

Phygelius

HP | Zn 7–9

p. 418

South African shrubs or subshrubs, 3'–4' tall, Phygelius *species are grown for their panicles of drooping, trumpet-shaped flowers of white, red, yellow, or pink. Use them in the border, in mixed shrub plantings, or in containers.*

Type Hardy perennial
Zone 7–9, H 9–7 (see species list, p. 468)
Flowering Season Summer to autumn

SOWING

Indoors 6–8 weeks before planting out.
Outdoors Spring or summer.
Depth Just cover.

GERMINATING

Time 10–14 days.
Requirements 70°–75°F.

TRANSPLANTING

Time After last frost.
Spacing 24"–36".
Light Full sun, with afternoon shade where summers are hot and humid.
Soil Light, well drained, with regular moisture during the growing season.

CARING FOR PLANTS

Water when the ground becomes dry. Prune occasionally to maintain a compact size, and cut back to ground level in spring. In colder areas, plant against a south wall and mulch well in autumn. Take cuttings or dig rooted suckers in late summer for overwintering indoors.

PROPAGATING

Divide in autumn (in spring in Zones 5–6), take cuttings in late summer, or grow from seed.

COMBINATIONS

Agapanthus, Verbascum, Veronica.

Physalis

A, HP | Zn 3–9

Ground cherry, Husk tomato

These spreading annuals or perennials bear inconspicuous flowers but the more ornamental perennial species display showy orange seed cases that resemble paper lanterns, and are often used in dried flower arrangements. The less showy annual species include the tomatillo plant. Plants are 1'–4' tall. Grow Physalis *in the border or cutting bed.*

Type Annual or hardy perennial
Zone 3–9, H 8–5 (see species list, p. 468)
Flowering Season Summer to early autumn

SOWING

Indoors Early spring.
Outdoors Spring or summer.
Depth Surface.

GERMINATING

Time 15–30 days.
Requirements Difficult. Light and 70°–75°F.

TRANSPLANTING

Time After last frost.
Spacing 24"–36".
Light Full sun or part shade.
Soil Average, well drained. Plants tend to become weedy in very rich soil.

CARING FOR PLANTS

Easy. Water regularly; cut stems to ground in fall.

PROPAGATING

Divide in early spring or grow from seed.

CAUTION

P. alkekengi is listed as invasive in New England and the Midwest. See pp. 494–495 for advice.

Physostegia (syn. *Dracocephalum*)

HP | Zn 3–9

False dragon head, Obedient plant

p. 418

These stiff, rather coarse perennials bear 1'–4' spikes of tubular pink, white, or purple flowers that generally grow on opposite sides of the stem, giving plants a somewhat flat appearance. Use them in borders and wildflower gardens.

Type Hardy perennial
Zone 3–9, H 8–1
Flowering Season Midsummer to early autumn

SOWING

Indoors 8–10 weeks before planting out.
Outdoors Early spring or early autumn.
Depth Just cover.

GERMINATING

Time 15–30 days.
Requirements 60°–75°F.

TRANSPLANTING

Time Early spring, when soil is cool and a light frost is still possible, or early autumn.
Spacing *Small varieties:* 12"–18". *Large varieties:* 24".
Light Full sun where soil is moist, part shade in drier soil.
Soil Prefers cool, light, moist, slightly acid (pH 5.0–7.0). Grow in dry soil to reduce rampant spreading.

CARING FOR PLANTS

Easy. Mulch plants and water regularly. Stake tall species. Prune roots to control spreading or dig up clumps regularly to contain their spread. Cut back to ground level in autumn.

PROPAGATING

Divide in spring or grow from seed.

COMBINATIONS

Aster, Chrysanthemum, Monarda, Scabiosa.

Phyteuma

HP | Zn 5–8

Horned rampion

Tufted or rosette-forming, these alpine perennials bear white, purple, or blue flowers, either in spikes or on round heads like small barbed Sputniks. They range from 2" to 36" tall, and are useful in rock gardens and dry stone walls.

Type Hardy perennial
Zone 5–8, H 7–5
Flowering Season Summer

SOWING

Indoors See Germinating, Requirements.
Outdoors See Germinating, Requirements.
Depth Just cover.

GERMINATING

Time 30–90 days.
Requirements *Autumn sowing:* Sow seed in flats, sink flats in ground against a north-facing wall, and cover with glass. Moisten soil occasionally. Bring flats indoors in spring to 60°–70°F. *Spring sowing:* Sow seed in flats of moistened medium, secure in a plastic bag, and refrigerate for 2–3 weeks. Sink flats in the ground in a shady location, covering with glass. Transplant seedlings as they appear.

TRANSPLANTING

Time After last frost.
Spacing *Small species:* 8"–12". *Large species:* 18".
Light Sun, or light shade where summers are very hot.
Soil Light, fertile, alkaline, gritty or sandy.

CARING FOR PLANTS

Water only during very dry weather. Do not disturb roots.

PROPAGATING

Divide in spring in Zones 5–6 (in autumn in Zones 7–8) or grow from seed.

COMBINATIONS

Delosperma, Portulaca, Sisyrinchium.

Pimpinella

A, Bi, HP | Zn 4–9

Annual, perennial, and biennial plants, 18"–36" tall, these herbs are grown as ornamentals or for culinary use. Basal foliage is pear-shaped and toothed, while upper leaves are feathery. Tiny white, yellow, or pink flowers are borne in umbels and are similar to those of Queen Anne's lace. They make an unusual and charming addition to the summer border.

Type Annual, biennial, hardy perennial
Zone *Annual:* 4–9; *Perennial:* 5–8 (see species list, p. 468)
Flowering Season Summer to early autumn.

SOWING

Indoors 8–10 weeks before last frost, in peat pots.
Outdoors After last frost.
Depth ¼".

GERMINATING

Time 20–28 days.
Requirements 70°F.

TRANSPLANTING

Time After last frost.
Spacing *Annual:* 4"–12"; plants grown close together will provide support for each other. *Perennial:* 12"–15".
Light *Annual:* Full sun. *Perennial:* Full sun or light shade.
Soil Ordinary, well drained, with a pH level of 5.5–6.5.

CARING FOR PLANTS

Water regularly during dry spells and provide support for lanky growth. Because of their long taproot, plants should not be moved. When seeds of *P. anisum* start turning gray and come away from seed heads easily, they are ready to harvest. Wash and dry seeds thoroughly before storing in an airtight container.

PROPAGATING

Grow from seed only.

COMBINATIONS

Tall campanulas, *Platycodon, Verbena bonariensis.*

Pinguicula

HP | Zn 3–8

Butterwort

Butterworts are small, rosette-forming, carnivorous plants, 5"–8" tall, with sticky, oval basal leaves. Their slender stalks bear lipped, funnel-shaped flowers of purple, white, or yellow. Grow in permanently moist, peaty soil, such as in a bog garden.

Type Hardy perennial
Zone 3–8, H 5–1 (see species list, p. 468); prefers cool temperatures
Flowering Season Spring to summer

SOWING

Indoors 8–10 weeks before planting out.
Outdoors Autumn.
Depth Surface.

GERMINATING

Time 30–130 days.
Requirements Light and 55°–60°F.

TRANSPLANTING

Time When spring temperatures remain above 45°F.
Spacing 2"–4".
Light Full sun.
Soil Prefers moist, neutral, or preferably slightly acid.

CARING FOR PLANTS

Top-dress with leaf mold in early spring. Water well during dry spells to keep soil constantly moist.

PROPAGATING

Plant offsets, root single leaves anchored to moist sand, or grow from seed.

Plagiorhegma See *Jeffersonia*

Platycodon

HP | Zn 3–9

Balloon flower, Chinese bellflower

p. 418

This erect perennial is grown for its purple, white, blue, or pink flowers that grow along arching, 1'–3' stems. New buds are completely round but suddenly open into widemouthed, upturned or outward-facing bells. They are lovely and reliable in the summer border.

Type Hardy perennial
Zone 3–9, H 9–1
Flowering Season Summer

SOWING

Indoors 6–8 weeks before planting out, in peat pots.
Outdoors Spring or summer.
Depth Surface.

GERMINATING

Time 15–30 days.
Requirements Light and 70°F. Seedlings are extremely fragile.

TRANSPLANTING

Time Late spring.
Spacing *Small cultivars:* 9"–12". *Large cultivars:* 12"–18".
Light Full sun or light shade.
Soil Prefers rich, moist, well drained.

CARING FOR PLANTS

Easy. Water and deadhead frequently to prolong the blooming period. Feed lightly from time to time. Stake tall cultivars. *Platycodon* is very fragile and must be handled with care at planting time. Mark locations to avoid damaging before plants emerge in late spring. Plants are slow to recover after division.

PROPAGATING

Take cuttings in summer, divide in spring (in autumn in Zones 7–9) taking care not to damage the taproot, or grow from seed. Plants grown from seed will bloom in their first year.

COMBINATIONS

Hemerocallis, Perovskia, summer *Phlox, Veronica.*

Platystemon

A | Zn 3–9

California poppy, Creamcups

This annual is native to the western United States. Sunny yellow, saucer-shaped flowers are held individually on wiry 12" stems above dull green, lance-shaped leaves. Use it in the border or for edging.

Type Annual
Zone 3–9, H 12–7; prefers temperate western climates
Flowering Season Summer

SOWING

Indoors Sow seed *in situ* only.
Outdoors Early spring, when soil is cool and a light frost is still possible, or late autumn.
Depth Just cover.

GERMINATING

Time 14–30 days.
Requirements 55°–65°F.

TRANSPLANTING

Time Set out purchased plants after last spring frost.
Spacing 4"–8".
Light Full sun.
Soil Well drained. Prefers a sandy loam; will tolerate dry soil.

CARING FOR PLANTS

Top-dress with well-rotted manure in spring. Water regularly for best results.

PROPAGATING

Grow from seed. Plant may self-seed.

COMBINATIONS

Anchusa, Lobelia, Nigella.

Plectranthus

TP* | Zn 10

Plectranthus

p. 418

The trailing and shrubby plants of this very large genus are grown for their attractive foliage. Those most commonly seen usually have silver or variegated leaves, sometimes with purple undersides. The foliage is often highly aromatic and usually thick, with scalloped, sometimes hairy, edges. Those seen in gardens today are seldom more than 2' and are most often used in containers.

Type Tender perennial; usually grown as an annual or houseplant
Zone 10, H 12–1; grown as an annual farther north
Flowering Season Late summer, although flowering rarely occurs where plants are grown as annuals

SOWING

Indoors 8–10 weeks before last frost.
Outdoors Autumn or early spring.
Depth Just cover.

GERMINATING

Time 14–35 days.
Requirements Easy. 65°–75°F. Pinch tips of seedlings twice to induce bushy growth.

TRANSPLANTING

Time Several weeks after last frost, when temperatures will remain above 45°F.
Spacing *Small species:* 1'–2'. *Large species:* 2'–4'.
Light Sun to part shade, with more shade required in Zones 9–10.
Soil Prefers moist, rich, and well drained but will tolerate most.

CARING FOR PLANTS

Pinch back young plants to encourage bushy growth, feed and water regularly throughout the growing season, and deadhead frequently where plants bloom. Mealybugs, spider mites, and leaf spot are possible problems. To overwinter plants indoors, dig before the first frost, pot up, and place in a warm (60°–70°F), bright location. Plants may become leggy after several years, at which point they should be discarded.

PROPAGATING

Take stem cuttings or divide in spring or summer; cuttings root easily in water or soil. Propagating from seed is a less reliable method.

COMBINATIONS

Calibrachoa, Heliotropium, Petunia, Strobilanthes, Verbena.

Podophyllum

HP | Zn 3–9 | ◐ ● | ◒ ●

Mayapple

p. 418

Serene, secretive wildflowers are celebrated for their large, flat, lobed leaves, which grow in pairs above long, slender stems. White, cup-shaped flowers shyly peek out from beneath leaves in spring. They make a beautiful woodland ground cover.

Type Hardy perennial
Zone 3–9, H 8–2 (see species list, p. 468)
Flowering Season Spring

SOWING

Indoors Start seed outdoors.
Outdoors As soon as ripe seed is available, usually July to September.
Depth *Seed:* Just cover. *Rhizome:* 1".

GERMINATING

Time 30–180 days.
Requirements Difficult. Sow seed in flats, plunge these to the rim against a north-facing wall, and cover with glass. Moisten soil, as necessary. Transplant to individual pots after one growing season, to the garden after two growing seasons.

TRANSPLANTING

Time Set out purchased plants in spring or autumn.
Spacing 12"–15".
Light Light to full shade.
Soil Rich, moist, with a pH level of 4.0–7.0.

CARING FOR PLANTS

Easy. Mulch in spring with wood chips and again in autumn with leaf mold; keep the soil constantly moist. Some species die back completely after flowering. Mayapples will quickly fill as much space as they are given.

PROPAGATING

Divide after blooming or grow from seed. Plants may self-seed.

COMBINATIONS

Galium, Impatiens, Muscari, Myosotis, Stylophorum.

CAUTION

All parts of the plant, except for ripe fruit, are toxic if eaten.

Polemonium

HP | Zn 3–8 | ○ ◐ | ◒ ●

Jacob's ladder, Sky pilot

p. 418

These exquisite perennials feature pairs of small, narrow leaves that give plants an airy look. They have pretty, cup-shaped flowers of blue, white, pink, or yellow; use these 6"–36" tall plants in borders and woodland plantings.

Type Hardy perennial
Zone 3–8, H 7–1 (see species list, p. 468); prefer cool climates
Flowering Season Late spring to summer

SOWING

Indoors 8–10 weeks before planting out.
Outdoors Early spring or early autumn.
Depth Just cover.

GERMINATING

Time 20–25 days.
Requirements 70°F.

TRANSPLANTING

Time Early spring, when soil is cool and a light frost is still possible, or early autumn.
Spacing *Small species:* 9"–12". *Large species:* 18"–24".
Light Part shade; full sun only where summers are cool.
Soil Cool, moist, rich, well drained, with a pH level of 5.0–8.0.

CARING FOR PLANTS

Easy. Top-dress with manure or leaf mold in spring. Water plants regularly. Cut back stems to the ground after flowering. Divide with extreme care, as roots are very fragile. Flowering will be inhibited by hot weather.

PROPAGATING

Divide in spring or grow from seed. Plants may self-seed.

COMBINATIONS

Anemone, ferns, *Hosta, Primula, Pulmonaria, Tiarella.*

Polianthes

HP* | Zn 8–10

These tuberous plants of 8"–48" are valued for their grassy foliage and stiff spikes of richly scented, tubular flowers that are usually white. Grow them in borders and containers near walkways and sitting areas where their heavenly fragrance will not be missed.

Type Hardy perennial; often grown as an annual in cooler regions
Zone 8–10, H 11–7; grown as an annual north of Zone 8
Flowering Season Late summer to autumn

SOWING

Requirements Extremely difficult, if not impossible. Trying to grow *Polianthes* from seed can only end in disappointment and is not recommended.
Outdoors *Tuber:* When temperatures remain above 60°F.
Depth *Tuber:* 3".

TRANSPLANTING

Spacing 6"–8".
Light Full sun.
Soil Humus-rich, with a pH level of 6.0–7.5.

CARING FOR PLANTS

Polianthes are not difficult to grow but do require time and attention to grow well. Water regularly in spring and summer and apply liquid fertilizer every 2 weeks during the growing season. Plants may need staking in windy locations. North of Zone 8, lift in autumn and store in a cool, frost-free location, replanting in the spring. Or, keep plants in containers year-round and store dry over winter.

PROPAGATING

Divide tubers in spring.

Polygonatum

HP | Zn 3–9

Solomon's seal

The Polygonatum *genus includes greatly varying perennials, the most widely grown being unassuming but graceful woodland plants with gently arching stems of 2"–48". Small clusters of white tubular flowers hang below paired leaves. They are effective either massed or in mixed woodland plantings.*

Type Hardy perennial
Zone 3–9, H 9–6 (see species list, pp. 468–469)
Flowering Season Spring or early summer

SOWING

Indoors See Germinating, Requirements.
Outdoors See Germinating, Requirements.
Depth *Seed:* Just cover. *Roots:* 2".

GERMINATING

Time 1–18 months.
Requirements *Autumn sowing:* Sow seed in flats, sink flats in the ground against a north-facing wall, and

cover with glass. Moisten soil occasionally, if necessary. Bring indoors in spring to 50°F. *Spring sowing:* Sow seed in flats, secure in plastic bags, and refrigerate for 2–3 weeks. Remove flats and sink in the ground in a shady location, covering with glass. Transplant seedlings as they emerge.

TRANSPLANTING

Time Spring or autumn.
Spacing 18".
Light Part to full shade.
Soil Light, moist, with a pH level of 6.0–7.0; tolerates dry soil if grown in full shade. *P. biflorum* is suitable for xeriscaping.

CARING FOR PLANTS

Easy. Top-dress with manure in early spring and feed periodically all season. Cut to ground level in fall.

PROPAGATING

Divide in early spring in the North (in autumn south of Zone 6) or grow from seed.

COMBINATIONS

Solomon's seals combine well with many plants, including *Alchemilla, Anemone nemerosa, Astilbe, Athyrium, Convallaria, Digitalis, Hakonechloa, Helleborus, Hosta, Myosotis, Rhododendron, Tiarella.*

CAUTION

Harmful if eaten.

Polygonum See *Persicaria*

Polystichum

HP | Zn 3–9 | Full sun, Partial shade, Full shade | Dry soil, Ordinary soil, Moist soil

Holly fern, Sword fern

p. 419

Many of these attractive, useful ferns are evergreen or semievergreen. with very sturdy, tall, stiff fronds, with feathery, deeply cut margins. They look soft but are quite tough, standing up to all but heavy frost or snow.

Type Hardy perennial
Zone 3–9, H 9–1 (see species list, pp. 483–484)
Flowering Season N/A

SOWING

Indoors June to October, when spores are ripe.
Outdoors Not recommended.
Depth Surface.

GERMINATING

Time 10–365 days.
Requirements Difficult. Start at 60°–75°F. (For information on starting ferns from spores, see pp. 24–25.)

TRANSPLANTING

Time After last frost in spring, or autumn, after about 2 years of growth.
Spacing *Small species:* 18". *Large species:* 24"–36".
Light Full to part shade; more tolerant of sun in moist soil. *P. setiferum* tolerates full sun; all others tolerate deep shade.
Soil Moist, acid, well-drained soil enriched with organic matter. All tolerate dry soil. Good drainage is essential, especially in winter. *P. setiferum* thrives in acid to alkaline soil, pH 6.5–8.0.

CARING FOR PLANTS

Very easy. Remove faded fronds to keep plants looking neat. Divide when plants become crowded. Susceptible to crown rot if soil is not well drained.

PROPAGATING

Divide most species in spring or autumn. Some produce bulbils, which can be detached and planted in autumn, or grow from spores.

COMBINATIONS

Bergenia, Corydalis, Dicentra, Hosta, Saxifraga, Thalictrum, Viola odorata.

Porteranchus See *Gillenia*

Portulaca

A | Zn 2–10

Moss rose, Purslane, Rose moss

p. 419

These hardworking annuals bear a profusion of brightly colored flowers, even in extreme heat. Plants are 4"–18" tall with small, succulent leaves and prominent, cup-shaped blooms in every shade of red, pink, yellow, orange. or white. Use them in containers and borders; they also make an interesting, informal ground cover.

Type Annual
Zone 2–10, H 12–3 (see species list, p. 469); thrives where summers are hot
Flowering Season Summer to late autumn

SOWING

Indoors Prechilled seed 6–8 weeks before planting out, in peat pots.
Outdoors After last frost.
Depth Surface.

GERMINATING

Time 7–21 days.
Requirements Place seed in a plastic bag together with moist growing medium and refrigerate for 2 weeks; thereafter provide light and 70°–85°F.

TRANSPLANTING

Time Late spring.
Spacing *Small species:* 5"–8". *Large species:* 12"–24".
Light Full sun.
Soil Poor, sandy, with a pH level of 5.5–7.5. *P. grandiflora, P. oleracea,* and *P. pilosa* are excellent choices for xeriscaping.

CARING FOR PLANTS

Easy, requiring almost no care. Do not water excessively and do not transplant.

PROPAGATING

Grow from seed. Plant self-seeds, especially in warm climates.

COMBINATIONS

Ageratum, Pelargonium, Sedum, Sempervivum.

Potentilla (syn. *Comarum*)

HP | Zn 2–9

P

Cinquefoil, Five-finger

p. 419

These perennials and shrubs can develop a messy habit, but they are grown for their bright yellow, pink, red, or white saucer-shaped flowers, which appear over a long period. Stems are wiry and foliage fine; plants grow 3"–36". Use Potentilla *in rock gardens and borders.*

Type Hardy perennial
Zone 2–9, H 8–1 (see species list, p. 469); prefer cool climates
Flowering Season Mid-spring to autumn, depending on species

SOWING

Indoors 8–10 weeks before planting out.
Outdoors Early spring or early autumn.
Depth Just cover.

GERMINATING

Time 14–30 days.
Requirements 65°–70°F.

TRANSPLANTING

Time Early spring, when soil is cool and a light frost is still possible, or early autumn.
Spacing *Small species:* 8"–12". *Large species:* 12"–18".
Light Full sun, with afternoon shade where summers are hot.
Soil Sandy, well-drained, somewhat poor soil, with a pH level of 5.0–7.0. Excellent winter drainage is important. Many species are suitable for xeriscaping.

CARING FOR PLANTS

Easy, although plants growing in heavy soil or warm climates will develop a scruffy appearance. Apply a light organic dressing in spring and cut back flowering stems in autumn. Plant tall species close together to provide support. Divide every 3 years.

PROPAGATING

Divide in spring in Zones 2–6 (in autumn elsewhere), take cuttings in spring or autumn, or grow from seed.

COMBINATIONS

Achillea, Campanula, Linum, Matthiola, Salvia.

Pratia

HP | Zn 5–9

Creeping evergreen plants, Pratia *feature dense foliage and masses of blue or white star-shaped flowers. Grow them in rock gardens, cascading over walls, or between stepping-stones, where they will withstand light foot traffic.*

Type Hardy perennial
Zone 5–9, H 10–5 (see species list, p. 469)
Flowering Season Spring to late summer, depending on species

SOWING

Indoors 6 weeks before last frost.
Outdoors Autumn.
Depth Just cover.

GERMINATING

Time Germination is erratic and will take several months.
Requirements 41°F.

TRANSPLANTING

Time After last frost.
Spacing 18"–24".
Light Sun to part shade, with increased shade where summers are hot.
Soil Rich and moist, with a pH of 6.1–7.8. Soil must be well drained, especially in winter.

CARING FOR PLANTS

Easy; can become invasive if too happy. Water regularly during dry spells. May attract slugs or aphids. Plants will tolerate light foot traffic.

PROPAGATING

Divide in autumn or grow from seed.

COMBINATIONS

Iris cristata, Lobelia, Lysimachia nummularia, Primula.

Primula

HP* | Zn 3–10

Primula, Primrose

p. 419

These mainly perennial plants have leaves in basal rosettes and tubular, bell-shaped, or flat flowers in a wide array of colors. Plants are usually low-growing (3"–12"), although some reach 30". Variously suited to rock, bog, and woodland gardens, as well as to borders and mass displays.

Type Hardy perennial, sometimes grown as an annual
Zone 3–10, H 10–1 (see species list, p. 469); most primroses are happiest in cool, humid climates
Flowering Season Late winter to summer, depending on species

SOWING

Indoors Prechilled seed 8–10 weeks before last frost.
Outdoors In autumn in Zones 8–10 only.
Depth Surface.

GERMINATING

Time 10–40 days.
Requirements Difficult. Place seed in a plastic bag together with moist growing medium and refrigerate for 3 weeks. Then provide light and 60°–65°F.

TRANSPLANTING

Time After last frost.
Spacing *Small species:* 6"–8". *Large species:* 12"–18".
Light Full sun in cool climates; elsewhere part shade.
Soil Cool, moist, humus-rich, with a pH level of 5.5–7.0. Good winter drainage is essential.

CARING FOR PLANTS

Easy. Feed before flowering (do not use manure). When blooming finishes, top-dress with leaf mold and remove flowering stems. Mulch well where summers are hot. Plants may be attractive to slugs and snails.

PROPAGATING

Divide after flowers fade in the North (in early autumn in the South) or grow from seed.

COMBINATIONS

Alyssum, azaleas, *Daphne odora*, ferns, *Helleborus*, *Hepatica*, *Hosta*, *Rhododendron*, *Tulipa*.

CAUTION

Contact with leaves can cause skin irritation.

Pritzelago (syn. *Hutchinsia*)

HP | Zn 4–8

A small genus of diminutive, tufted alpine plants, members have deep green, lobed leaves; some species have almost no leaves at all. It bears racemes of small white flowers. Grow it in containers and rock gardens.

Type Short-lived hardy perennial
Zone 4–8
Flowering Season Spring to summer

SOWING

Indoors Most successful when started outdoors.
Outdoors When fresh seed is available, in summer.
Depth ¼".

GERMINATING

Time 14–30 days.
Requirements Easy. Mulch to keep soil cool and moist.

TRANSPLANTING

Spacing 3"–6".
Light Full sun where summers are cool, otherwise part to full shade. Flowers are more abundant in sun.
Soil Cool, moist, well drained, with a pH level of 6.0–7.5.

CARING FOR PLANTS

Mulch to keep soil cool and moist, and water regularly during dry spells. These delicate plants are short lived and require regular division.

PROPAGATING

Divide in early spring, take cuttings in summer, or grow from seed.

Proboscidea (syn. *Martynia*)

A | Zn 7–9

Devil's-claw, Elephant-tusk, Proboscis flower, Unicorn plant

Unusual, upright plants, Proboscidea *grows 2'–6' tall with large, rather coarse leaves. These plants are redeemed by their intricately tinted blooms, which resemble miniature orchids. Flowers are followed by strange-looking spiky fruits that are useful in dried arrangements. Grow unicorn plant in borders and containers.*

Type Annual
Zone 7–9, H 12–6; prefers warm temperatures
Flowering Season Summer

SOWING

Indoors 6–8 weeks before last frost.
Outdoors After last frost, but only where summers are long.
Depth ¼".

GERMINATING

Time 20 days.
Requirements 70°–75°F.

TRANSPLANTING

Time After last frost.
Spacing 12".
Light Full sun or part shade.
Soil Rich, well drained; tolerates dry conditions.

CARING FOR PLANTS

Easy. No special care is required.

PROPAGATING

Grow from seed only.

Prunella

HP | Zn 5–8

Heal all, Self heal

p. 419

Self heals are long-blooming, evergreen, mat-forming perennials of 6"–12", some of which are weedy. The tiny flowers, which grow in terminal clusters, are hooded, mainly blue or purple but sometimes pink or white. Grow Prunella *in rock gardens and borders.*

Type Hardy perennial
Zone 5–8, H 8–5
Flowering Season Spring through autumn, depending on species

SOWING

Indoors 8–10 weeks before planting out.
Outdoors Early spring, when soil is cool and a light frost is still possible.
Depth Just cover.

GERMINATING

Time 30–60 days.
Requirements Easy. 55°–65°F.

TRANSPLANTING

Time Spring.
Spacing 12"–18".
Light Full sun in cool climates, part shade where summers are hot.
Soil Fairly tolerant of dry soil when sited in part shade but must be kept moist during hot weather; prefers a pH level of 6.0–7.5.

CARING FOR PLANTS

Easy. Deadhead regularly. Keep soil moist during hot summers. Cut back to ground level after flowering. May be invasive and should not be planted near lawns, where it can become a nuisance.

PROPAGATING

Divide in early spring or grow from seed. Plant may self-seed.

COMBINATIONS

Geranium, Hemerocallis, Phlox, Sedum.

Pseudofumaria See *Corydalis*

Pulmonaria

HP | Zn 3–9

Lungwort

p. 419–420

Woodland plants, Pulmonaria *are grown for their tubular pink, blue, red, purple, or white flowers and attractive foliage, which is often freckled or deeply blotched with white or silver. Excellent edgings or ground covers in shade gardens.*

Type Hardy perennial
Zone 3–9, H 9–1 (see species list, p. 469)
Flowering Season Spring

SOWING

Requirements Seldom grown from seed, as resulting plants are of variable quality. Provide 60°–65°F.
Indoors 7–9 weeks before planting out.
Outdoors Early spring.
Depth Just cover.

GERMINATING

Time 30–42 days.

TRANSPLANTING

Time Autumn.
Spacing *Small species:* 6"–10". *Large species:* 12"–18".
Light Part to full shade.
Soil Moist, cool, rich.

CARING FOR PLANTS

Easy. In early spring, mulch plants well to keep soil moist and apply a balanced fertilizer. Cut back lightly after flowering. Divide plants every 4–5 years. Will survive a certain amount of neglect, but most abundant blooms and attractive foliage will be found on plants that receive ample food and water.

PROPAGATING

Divide in spring north of Zone 7 (in autumn in the South).

COMBINATIONS

Aquilegia, Geranium, Helleborus, Hosta, Omphalodes, Trillium.

Pulsatilla

HP | Zn 4–8

Pasque flower

p. 420

Pulsatilla *is a small genus of perennials, some of which are evergreen, with fine, feathery leaves. Bell- or cup-shaped flowers are borne singly on thick, hairy stalks before foliage emerges; 12". Flowers are red, white, yellow, purple, or bronze. Use in walls or rock gardens.*

Type Hardy perennial
Zone 4–8, H 7–5; prefer cool summers, cold winters
Flowering Season Spring or early summer, depending on species

SOWING

Indoors Sow seed outdoors only.
Outdoors As soon as fresh seed is available, usually in summer.
Depth Just cover.

GERMINATING

Time 30–180 days.
Requirements Difficult. Use only fresh seed; sow seeds in flats, sink flats in ground against a north-facing wall, and cover with glass. Moisten soil occasionally, if needed. Bring indoors in spring to 60°–70°F.

TRANSPLANTING

Time Spring or autumn.
Spacing 8"–12".
Light Full sun; part shade where summers are hot.
Soil Rich, moist, well drained, and slightly alkaline.

CARING FOR PLANTS

Easy. Water regularly during dry spells. Do not disturb established plants.

PROPAGATING

Take cuttings from tips of shoots or grow from seed. Successful division is difficult because of deep roots.

COMBINATIONS

Iris coristata, Stachys, Thymus, dwarf tulips.

CAUTION

Harmful if eaten.

Puschkinia

HB | Zn 4–10

P

p. 420

Plants in this genus of dwarf bulbs have erect, strap-shaped leaves that curve lengthwise and 6" spikes of star-shaped flowers that are pure white or blue-and-white-striped. Use striped squill in rock gardens and borders.

Type Hardy bulb
Zone 4–10, H 9–1; most successful in cool climates
Flowering Season Early to mid spring

SOWING

Indoors Start seed outdoors.
Outdoors *Seed:* Autumn. *Bulb:* Autumn.
Depth *Seed:* ⅛". *Bulb:* 3"–4".

GERMINATING

Time 30+ days.
Requirements Sow seed in flats, sink these in the ground against a north-facing wall, and cover with glass. Moisten soil occasionally, if necessary. Transplant seedlings as they appear.

TRANSPLANTING

Spacing 3"–4".
Light Sun or part shade.
Soil Moist, well drained.

CARING FOR PLANTS

Ample moisture is required for successful flowering. Foliage dies back to ground in summer. Mulch in fall and do not disturb bulbs. Watch for signs of slugs.

PROPAGATING

Divide clumps of bulbs after foliage dies back in autumn and replant offsets. Allow plenty of recuperation time before dividing again. Or grow from seed. Plants grown from seed will bloom in 4 years.

COMBINATIONS

Ajuga, dwarf *Narcissus, Viola.*

Pyrethrum See *Tanacetum*

Ramonda

HP | Zn 5–8

p. 420

These sweet, diminutive (4"), rosette-forming perennials have deeply veined, hairy leaves resembling elephant hide. Short stalks emerge from rosettes and bear delicate, flat, open, purple, pink, or white flowers Plants work well in the rock garden.

Type Hardy perennial
Zone 5–8, H 7–5; best in cool, humid climates
Flowering Season Spring to early summer

SOWING

Indoors Spring
Outdoors Early autumn.
Depth Surface.

GERMINATING

Time 30–60 days.
Requirements Difficult. Diffused light and 55°–60°F.

TRANSPLANTING

Time After last spring frost, 1 year after germinating.
Spacing 4"–6".
Light Part shade.
Soil Sandy, well drained, moist in growing season.

CARING FOR PLANTS

Difficult. Plant against a north-facing wall. Water during dry spells, keeping water off leaves.

PROPAGATING

Take leaf cuttings; plant offsets in summer; grow from seed. If from seed, it takes 3–4 years to flower.

COMBINATIONS

Erythronium, ferns, *Hepatica, Primula.*

Ranunculus

TP*, HP* | Zn 4–9

Buttercup, Crowfoot

p. 420

The cup-shaped flowers of Ranunculus *may be simple or intricately double; colors are rich, intense, and widely assorted. Use this perennial in borders and rock gardens, massed, or mixed casually with other plants.*

Type Hardy perennial or tender perennial often grown as an annual
Zone 4–9, H 12–1 (see species list, p. 470); often grown as annuals in colder regions
Flowering Season Late winter to mid summer, depending on species

SOWING

Indoors See Germinating, Requirements.
Outdoors See Germinating, Requirements.
Depth *Seed:* Just cover. *Roots:* 2".

GERMINATING

Time 15–90 days.
Requirements *Autumn sowing:* Sow seed in flats; sink in ground against north-facing wall; cover with glass. Moisten occasionally, if needed. In spring, bring flats indoors to 50°F. *Spring sowing:* Sow seed in flats; secure in plastic bag; refrigerate 2–3 weeks. Remove flats; sink in ground in shady location, covering with glass. Transplant seedlings as they appear.

TRANSPLANTING

Time After last frost.
Spacing *Small species:* 4"–6". *Medium species:* 8"–12". *Large species:* 24".
Light Full sun if soil is moist, otherwise part shade.
Soil Moist, but very well drained. *R. lingua* prefers boggy soil.

CARING FOR PLANTS

Provide a good summer mulch to keep soil moist; water during dry spells. Where plants can't survive winter, lift those with tubers *(R. asiaticus)* after foliage dies; store in a cool, dry place, replanting in spring, (tubers left in ground all summer may rot).

PROPAGATING

Divide in spring in Zones 4–6 (in fall in Zones 7–9) or grow from seed. If from seed, bloom first year.

COMBINATIONS

Ferns, *Hosta, Iris pseudacorus, Lamium, Lobularia.*

CAUTION

R. repens is invasive. See pp. 494–495 for advice.

Ratibida (syn. *Rudbeckia, Lepachys*)

HB | Zn 3–10

Mexican hat, Prairie coneflower

p. 420

These native North and Central American perennials strongly resemble the Rudbeckia *family from which they were recently separated. Leaves are large and oblong, sometimes an attractive blue-green. They form a low clump from which 2'–5' stems emerge bearing yellow, orange, or puce-colored coneflowers with extraordinarily long "noses." They are wonderful in a wildflower garden, and can add a note of levity to the more formal border.*

Type Hardy perennial
Zone 3–10, H 7–1; very tolerant of heat and humidity
Flowering Season Late spring to autumn, depending on species

SOWING

Indoors Sow prechilled seed 4–6 weeks before planting out.
Outdoors In a cold frame in early spring, or in May–June.
Depth Just cover.

GERMINATING

Time 7–42 days.
Requirements Easy. Prechill seed for 1 week, then provide 68°–75°F.

TRANSPLANTING

Time After last frost, or autumn.
Spacing 1'–2'.
Light Full sun.
Soil Ordinary, well drained; drought tolerant. *R. columnifera* is suitable for xeriscaping.

CARING FOR PLANTS

Easy. Stake tall species. Plants are susceptible to powdery and downy mildew, fungal spots, and leaf smut; site in full sun, mulch plants, and water regularly in the morning during dry spells, keeping leaves as dry as possible, to minimize the risk of fungal diseases.

PROPAGATING

Divide young plants only, in spring or autumn, or grow from seed. Plant may self-seed; plants grown from seed will bloom in their first year.

COMBINATIONS

Aster, Echinacea, Liatris, Monarda.

Rehmannia

HP* | Zn 8–10

p. 420

The clump-forming plants in this small genus bear racemes of tubular, intricately multicolored, two-lipped flowers on 1'–6' stems. They are an interesting addition to the border or to a naturalistic planting.

Type Hardy perennial; often treated as an annual
Zone 8–10, H 10–8; often grown as an annual in colder regions
Flowering Season Late spring to mid summer, depending on species

SOWING

Indoors 6–8 weeks before last frost.
Outdoors Early spring, when soil is cool and a light frost is still possible, or late autumn.
Depth Just cover.

GERMINATING

Time 15–40 days.
Requirements 60°–65°F.

TRANSPLANTING

Time After last frost, when temperatures remain above 40°F.
Spacing *Small species:* 10"–12". *Large species:* 18".
Light Sun, with light shade from hot afternoon sun.
Soil Well drained, fertile.

CARING FOR PLANTS

Mulch with leaf mold in spring. Water well during dry periods throughout the growing season. Where plants are not hardy, uproot and discard after blooming; provide a good winter mulch for plants left in the ground.

PROPAGATING

Take root cuttings in late winter; where hardy, pot up offsets in spring; or grow from seed.

Reseda

A, Bi | Zn 2–10

Mignonette

Mignonettes are upright, branching plants grown for their wonderfully fragrant, white or yellow flowers borne in spikes on stems of 1'–3'. Use them in containers, borders, and cutting beds.

Type Annual or biennial
Zone 2–10, H 6–1; prefers cool temperatures
Flowering Season Early summer until the first frost, if successive sowings are made

SOWING

Indoors 6–8 weeks before last frost, in peat pots.
Outdoors Early spring, when soil is cool and a light frost is still possible, and again every 3 weeks until early summer. Sow seed in late autumn in Zones 9–10.
Depth Surface.

GERMINATING

Time 5–21 days.
Requirements Light and 70°F.

TRANSPLANTING

Time After last frost.
Spacing *Small species:* 6"–8". *Large species:* 10"–12".
Light Part shade, except in very cool regions.
Soil Rich, with a pH level of 6.0–7.0.

CARING FOR PLANTS

Pinch back tips of young plants to encourage branching. Do not move. Blooming will stop in very hot weather.

PROPAGATING

Grow from seed. Plants may self-seed.

Rhazya See *Amsonia*

Rheum

HP | Zn 5–9

Rhubarb

p. 420

Rheum × hybrida *(rhubarb) is the culinary species, but other exotic-looking perennials in this genus are quite ornamental. Many have enormous, toothed, red or bronze leaves and small white flowers on giant (3'–8') stalks. Grow in borders for their color and texture contrast, or mass in a bog or waterside garden.*

Type Hardy perennial
Zone 5–9, H 9–1; prefers cool summer temperatures
Flowering Season Summer

SOWING

Rhubarb grown from seed usually produces plants acceptable for ornamental use, though not desirable for eating. Purchase rootstock for edible rhubarb.
Indoors 8–10 weeks before planting out.
Outdoors 1 month before last frost.
Depth *Seed:* ¼". *Roots:* Plant with buds 1"–2" below surface.

GERMINATING

Time 21–42 days.
Requirements 60°–65°F.

TRANSPLANTING

Time Early spring, when soil is cool and a light frost is still possible, or late autumn.
Spacing *Small species:* 12"–24". *Medium species:* 24"–36". *Large species:* 36"–60".
Light Sun or light shade.
Soil Very rich, deep, moist.

CARING FOR PLANTS

Apply a complete fertilizer in spring, then feed every 2 weeks throughout the growing season with a weak fertilizer solution. Mulch well to keep soil cool and moist; water frequently during dry spells. Cut flower stems to ground after blooming. Do not cut stalks of culinary plants during first year; subsequently, harvest only until late July. Remove flower stems as soon as they appear. Divide when plants begin to decline.

PROPAGATING

Divide in spring or grow from seed.

COMBINATIONS

Ferns, *Hosta, Iris ensata* or *I. siberica, Trollius.*

CAUTION

Leaves are harmful if eaten.

Rhodanthe (syn. *Acroclinium* and *Helipterum*)

A | Zn 3–10

Strawflower

This genus of upright plants contains annuals grown for their papery, many-petaled, daisylike blooms, which are held on wiry stems. Flowers may be red, pink, or white, and are everlasting when dried. Plants grow to 18", and are useful in the border or cutting bed.

Type Annual
Zone 3–10, H 10–1; prefers warm temperatures
Flowering Season Summer

SOWING

Indoors 4–6 weeks before last frost, or 6–8 weeks before last frost where summers are short, in peat pots.
Outdoors 4 weeks after last frost.
Depth Just cover.

GERMINATING

Time 14–20 days.
Requirements 65°–75°F.

TRANSPLANTING

Time After last frost.
Spacing 6"–8".
Light Sun.
Soil Light, somewhat sandy; tolerates dry soil.

CARING FOR PLANTS

Easy. Plants may require staking. To preserve flowers for use in dried arrangements, pull up entire plant when flowering is at its peak and hang upside down in a warm, dry place. Aphids may be a problem on young plants, although mature plants are not generally troubled by them.

PROPAGATING

Grow from seed.

COMBINATIONS

Dianthus, Salvia, Xeranthemum.

Rhodochiton

TP* | Zn 5–10

p. 420

One of the species in this small genus is a vigorous, long-blooming climber with handsome, toothed, heart-shaped leaves. It bears masses of drooping, nearly black tubular flowers, each one under an umbrella-like reddish purple calyx. It grows to 10' long.

Type Tender perennial
Zone 10, H 12–6; often grown as an annual in Zones 5–9; will bloom only where the growing season is very long
Flowering Season Summer through frost

SOWING

Indoors 6–8 weeks before planting out.
Outdoors After last frost, in Zones 9–10 only.
Depth Just cover.

GERMINATING

Time 12–40 days.
Requirements Difficult. 60°–65°F.

TRANSPLANTING

Time 2 weeks after last frost.
Spacing 9"–12".
Light Sun.
Soil Ordinary.

CARING FOR PLANTS

Provide trellis or canes for support. North of Zone 10, container-grown plants can be brought indoors in autumn and overwintered indoors in a cool, bright location.

PROPAGATING

Take cuttings from spring to summer for overwintering indoors or grow from seed.

Rhodohypoxis

HP, TP* | Zn 4–10

p. 421

This small genus of tufted perennials is native to South Africa. Masses of flat, pink, red, or white flowers grow singly on short stems above narrow, lance-shaped leaves. These 2"–4" plants are useful in the rock garden.

Type Hardy perennial or tender perennial grown as annual
Zone 9–10, H 10–9; often grown as an annual in Zones 4–8
Flowering Season Spring to early summer

SOWING

Plants may not come true from seed.
Indoors 8–10 weeks before planting out.
Outdoors Early spring, when soil is cool and a light frost is still possible.
Depth *Seed:* Just cover. *Tuber:* 1"–2".

GERMINATING

Time 30–90 days.
Requirements 50°F.

TRANSPLANTING

Time After last frost.
Spacing 2"–3".
Light Full sun.
Soil Acid, humus-rich, and very well drained, especially in winter.

CARING FOR PLANTS

Feed only occasionally and very lightly. Soil must be fairly dry in winter but moist at all other times. Move only during the growing season.

PROPAGATING

Divide offsets in spring or grow from seed. Plant may self-seed.

Ricinus

A | Zn 3–10

p. 421

A genus of fast-growing, erect plants, Ricinus *are valued for their large, deeply lobed green, bronze, purple, or dark red leaves. Stalks are tipped with clusters of bright red or light green flowers in summer, followed by round, prickly seedpods; 3'–6' tall. Use small groups at the back of the border or mass them in a bed of their own.*

Type Annual
Zone 3–10; prefers hot weather
Flowering Season Midsummer

SOWING

Indoors 6–8 weeks before planting out, in peat pots.
Outdoors Only in Zones 8–10, 1 week after last frost.
Depth ¼".

GERMINATING

Time 15–21 days.
Requirements Soak seed in warm water for 24 hours; provide 70°–75°F thereafter.

TRANSPLANTING

Time 2 weeks after last frost.
Spacing *Small species:* 24"–36". *Large species:* 48"–60".
Light Full sun.
Soil Will grow in almost any soil, but prefers a rich, moist, well-drained loam with a pH level of 6.0–7.0. Rich soil will produce very large plants.

CARING FOR PLANTS

Easy. Feed and water frequently; stake plants if necessary. Likely to become weedy in frost-free climates.

PROPAGATING

Grow from seed only.

COMBINATIONS

Cleome, Cosmos, Musa, Nicotiana.

CAUTION

Seeds are toxic if eaten. *R. communis* is listed as invasive in some areas, including Florida. See pp. 474–475 for advice.

Rodgersia

HP | Zn 4–9

Rodgersia

p. 421

The dramatic perennials in this small genus display very large, compound leaves. Their tall stalks bear clusters of small pink, red, or white flowers that resemble the blooms of enormous astilbes. Plants reach 3'–5' and are most effective massed near water; they also add textural interest to the border.

Type Hardy perennial
Zone 4–7 (4–9 where summers are cool), H 8–5
Flowering Season Summer

SOWING

Indoors 6–8 weeks before last frost.
Outdoors Autumn.
Depth *Seed:* Surface. *Rhizome:* Just below the surface.

GERMINATING

Time 12–60 days.
Requirements Light and 55°–60°F. *Outdoor sowing:* Sow seed in peat pots, sink these in the ground against a north-facing wall, and cover with glass. Moisten soil occasionally, if necessary. Remove glass when germination begins.

TRANSPLANTING

Time Spring or autumn, after 2 years' growth.
Spacing 24"–36".
Light Full sun; shade from intense sun.
Soil Rich, moist or even wet.

CARING FOR PLANTS

Difficult. Mulch in spring to keep soil cool and moist, and water freely during dry spells; maintaining very moist soil is essential to succeed with these striking plants. Feed in spring. Leaves may be damaged by winds or strong sun.

PROPAGATING

Divide in spring or grow from seed.

COMBINATIONS

Camassia, Campanula, Hosta, Iris pseudacorus, Mertensia, Polygonum, Trollius.

Romneya

HP | Zn 7–10

California tree poppy, Matilija poppy, Tree poppy

p. 421

These large, woody-based perennials bear delicately fragrant, white, poppylike flowers with bright yellow eyes and gray foliage. Natives of southern California and Mexico, they grow 3'–8' tall. Use them at the back of the border or in combination with shrubs.

Type Hardy perennial
Zone 7–10, H 8–7; not tolerant of high heat combined with high humidity; prefers the dry California climate
Flowering Season All summer

SOWING

Indoors Prechilled seed 6–8 weeks before last frost, in peat pots.
Outdoors After last frost.
Depth ¼".

GERMINATING

Time 30 days.
Requirements Difficult. 55°–60°F.

TRANSPLANTING

Time After last frost.
Spacing *Small species:* 24"–36". *Large species:* 5'–6'.
Light Full sun.
Soil Average, with very good drainage. Once established, plants are quite drought tolerant.

CARING FOR PLANTS

Difficult. Water only sparingly. Can become invasive; root-prune to curtail spreading, but do not otherwise disturb roots.

PROPAGATING

Root suckers, cutting back to 2"–3" after transplanting, or grow from seed.

COMBINATIONS

Agapanthus or in front of *Clematis* or *Passiflora.*

Roscoea

HP | Zn 6–9

p. 421

Here's a genus of perennials that's rarely grown but has loads of personality. Leaves are erect, broad, and lance-shaped. Flowers are borne on thick stems, 6"–18" tall, just above the foliage. Each outward-facing bloom is hooded with a pair of long lips. A clump of Roscoea *looks remarkably like a gaggle of old men with flowing beards gathered at the corner to reminisce about the old days. Plant in drifts in rock or shade gardens.*

Type Hardy perennial
Zone 6–9, H 9–6 (see species list, p. 470); perform best where summers are cool and humid and winters are mild
Flowering Season Late spring, early to mid summer, or autumn, depending on species

SOWING

Indoors 8–10 weeks before planting out.
Outdoors Autumn or winter.
Depth *Seed:* Surface. *Roots:* 6".

GERMINATING

Time 30–365 days.
Requirements *Indoor sowing:* Place seed in a plastic bag together with moist growing medium and refrigerate for 2–3 weeks. Provide light and 50°–55°F thereafter. *Outdoor sowing:* Sow seed in flats, plunge to the rim in a sheltered position, and cover with glass. Remove glass when seeds sprout. Transplant to the garden when seedlings are large enough to handle.

TRANSPLANTING

Time After last frost.
Spacing 6".
Light Full sun or part shade.
Soil Cool, moist, well drained, with plenty of organic matter added.

CARING FOR PLANTS

Mulch to keep soil cool and moist. Water regularly during the growing season.

PROPAGATING

Divide in spring or early summer or grow from seed.

Rosmarinus

HP, TP | Zn 7–10

Rosemary

p. 421

These shrubby perennials are grown for ornamental appeal as well as for culinary use. Short, narrow, fragrant, oblong leaves cover the woody stems; small blue flowers are scattered over the entire plant. It grows 3'–6' tall, and makes an attractive hedge where plants are hardy. It is also useful in containers or herb beds.

Type Hardy perennial; often grown as a tender perennial
Zone 7–10, H 12–7. Prefers dry, mild winters. Often grown as a tender perennial to be overwintered indoors in cooler regions
Flowering Season Mid spring to summer, depending on species

SOWING

Due to extremely slow germination and early development, rosemary is seldom started from seed.
Indoors Late winter to early spring.
Outdoors After last frost.
Depth 1/4".

GERMINATING

Time Up to 21 days.
Requirements Difficult. Seed requires 70°F to germinate.

TRANSPLANTING

Time After last frost.
Spacing *Small species:* 18"–24". *Large species:* 36"–48".
Light Prefers full sun but will tolerate part shade.
Soil Sandy, somewhat poor, with perfect drainage and a pH level of 6.0–7.5. Plants will not thrive in wet or clay soil. *R. officinalis* is suitable for xeriscaping.

CARING FOR PLANTS

Easy. Do not fertilize or overwater. Cut back any frost-damaged branches in spring and prune periodically throughout the year to keep plants looking well groomed and to restrict their size. Snip leaves for culinary use at any time. Harvest leaves for drying just before flowering; dry leaves in the dark and store in an airtight container. Bring potted plants indoors in winter, either giving a minimum 4 hours of sunlight and keeping soil barely moist in the living room or placing in a cool garage (45°F) with only infrequent watering.

PROPAGATING

Take semi-ripe cuttings in summer, take hardwood cuttings in spring or autumn, or grow from seed.

COMBINATIONS

Dianthus, Iris reticulata, Salvia.

Rudbeckia (syn. *Lepachys, Ratibida*)

A, HP | Zn 2–10

Coneflower

p. 421

These widely grown, carefree North American natives are appreciated for their abundant yellow or orange daisylike flowers with prominent brown eyes. Plants are branched and upright, growing from 1' to 8'. They are attractive in the border or wildflower garden.

Type Hardy perennial or short-lived perennial grown as an annual
Zone *Annual:* 2–10, H 7–1; *Perennial:* 3–9, H 9–1 (see species list, p. 470)
Flowering Season Summer to early autumn

SOWING

Indoors 6–8 weeks before last frost.
Outdoors 2 weeks before last frost.
Depth Surface.

GERMINATING

Time 5–21 days.
Requirements Easy. Provide light and 70°–75°F. *R. fulgida:* Place seed in a plastic bag together with moist growing medium and refrigerate for 2 weeks before sowing.

TRANSPLANTING

Time After last frost.
Spacing *Small species:* 12"–18". *Large species:* 24"–36".
Light Full sun, or part shade where summers are very hot.
Soil Tolerant of a wide range of soils but prefers a well-drained site with a pH level of 6.0–7.0. *R. fulgida* requires heavy soil. All *Rudbeckia* species are useful for xeriscaping once plants are established.

CARING FOR PLANTS

Easy. Apply topdressing of manure annually, water regularly during the summer, and deadhead frequently. Tall species planted in windy locations will require staking. Divide every 3–4 years. Inclined to become invasive.

PROPAGATING

Divide plants grown as perennials in spring north of Zone 7 (in autumn elsewhere), take cuttings in spring, or grow from seed. Plant may self-seed.

COMBINATIONS

Aster, ornamental grasses, *Helenium, Heliotropium, Leucanthemum, Salvia, Sedum.*

Ruellia (syn. *Dipteracanthus*)

TP*, HP | Zn 3–10

p. 421

The showy, fiery red or purple flowers of these woodland perennials are small and delicate or large and exotic. Some have broad ornamental leaves of deep green with white veins; 1' to 5'. Attractive and unusual in containers or shady beds.

Type Hardy perennial or tender perennial; often grown as an annual
Zone 3–10, H 12–10 (see species list, p. 470); grow tender perennials as annuals in cooler zones; prefers hot, humid climates
Flowering Season All summer, some until first frost

SOWING

Indoors 8–10 weeks before planting out.
Outdoors Spring.
Depth Just cover.

GERMINATING

Time 30–60 days.
Requirements 65°–75°F. Seed is rarely available.

TRANSPLANTING

Time Plant out seedlings in spring when the temperatures remain above 60°F.
Spacing 18"–24".
Light Part to full shade.
Soil Moist, well drained, containing plenty of organic matter. Most species are tolerant of a wide range of soils, but require good drainage and plenty of organic matter. *R. malacosperma* thrives in wet or dry soil.

CARING FOR PLANTS

Water regularly; mulch in spring to keep soil moist.

PROPAGATING

Divide in autumn (in spring north of Zone 7), take cuttings in spring or summer, or grow from seed.

CAUTION

R. brittonia is listed as invasive in some areas, including the Gulf states. See pp. 494–495 for advice.

Rumex

HP | Zn 3–9

Dock, Sorrel

p. 422

Perennial herbs, sorrels are grown for culinary or ornamental use. Leaves are deep green and arrow-shaped. Although the culinary plants are invasive and best grown in the vegetable or herb bed, there are several noninvasive ornamental species: R. scutatus *'Silver Shield' has highly ornamental heart-shaped silvery green leaves, and makes an attractive ground cover.*

Type Hardy perennial
Zone 3–9 (see species list, p. 484)
Flowering Season Midsummer

SOWING

Indoors 4 weeks before planting out.
Outdoors Mid-spring to late spring, when soil has warmed.
Depth 1/4".

GERMINATING

Time 7–10 days.
Requirements 65°–70°F.

TRANSPLANTING

Time After last frost.
Spacing *Small species:* 12". *Large species:* Singly.
Light Full sun is preferred but will tolerate part shade.
Soil Rich, moist, with a pH level of 5.5–6.0.

CARING FOR PLANTS

Feed once in spring. Mulch and frequent watering can help to prevent leaves from turning bitter in hot, dry weather; or cut back hard when weather becomes hot. Harvest outer leaves frequently to stimulate new growth. *R. scutatus* has the best flavor for cooking. Replace every 3–4 years. *R. acetosa* spreads quickly and has a tenacious root system, making it difficult to eradicate unwanted plants.

PROPAGATING

Divide in autumn or early spring or grow from seed. Self-seeds with abandon.

CAUTION

R. acetosa and *R. crispus* are listed as invasive in some areas, including Virginia. See pp. 494–495 for advice.

Sagina

HP | Zn 5–9

Pearlwort

p. 422

A cushionlike plant growing just 3"–4", Sagina *has small, handsome, lance-shaped leaves, deep green or lime green in color, and tiny white flowers. It makes a fine ground cover, edging, rock, wall, or paving plant.*

Type Hardy perennial
Zone 5–7 (to Zone 9 on the West Coast), H 9–6; not tolerant of hot, dry weather
Flowering Season Summer

SOWING

Indoors 6–8 weeks before last frost.
Outdoors Early spring, when soil is cool and a light frost is still possible, or late autumn.
Depth Just cover.

GERMINATING

Time 10–25 days.
Requirements Easy. 55°F.

TRANSPLANTING

Time After last frost.
Spacing *Small species:* 2"–4". *Spreading species:* 6"–8".
Light Full sun; part shade where summers are hot.
Soil Light, rather poor, sandy but moist.

CARING FOR PLANTS

Most species are easy to grow but need to be renewed periodically. With regular feeding and watering, plants will spread quite happily. Susceptible to aphids and spider mites.

PROPAGATING

Divide in spring in Zones 5 and 6 (in early autumn in the South) or grow from seed.

COMBINATIONS

Armeria, Campanula, Catananche, Sedum.

Salpiglossis

A | Zn 1–10

Painted tongue

p. 422

A branching annual, 18"–24" tall, painted tongue has lance-shaped leaves and a profusion of trumpet-shaped blooms, often with dark veins and colored throats. Red, orange, pink, purple, and yellow flowers may grow on the same plant. Wonderful for containers, borders, or cut flowers.

Type Annual
Zone 1–10, H 6–1; plants prefer cool temperatures
Flowering Season Summer to frost, where summer heat does not kill plants

SOWING

Indoors 8–10 weeks before planting out, in peat pots.
Outdoors Close to last frost date. Plants need a good start before hot weather sets in.
Depth Surface.

GERMINATING

Time 8–30 days.
Requirements Difficult. Darkness and 70°–75°F. If sown outdoors, cover lightly with straw or cheesecloth to prevent seed from being washed away.

TRANSPLANTING

Time 2 weeks before last frost.
Spacing 12"–15".
Light Full sun or light shade.
Soil Ordinary.

CARING FOR PLANTS

Pinch out young plants to induce branching and support with twiggy branches pushed into the ground. Mulch in spring, water only during dry spells, and feed occasionally with a weak balanced fertilizer. Aphids may be attracted to the stems. Deadhead regularly. Do not transplant.

PROPAGATING

Grow from seed only.

COMBINATIONS

Ageratum, Antirrhinum, Chrysanthemum, Convolvulus, Lobelia, Salvia.

Salvia

A, TP*, HP* | Zn 3–10

Salvia, Sage

p. 422

The plants in this large genus of hardworking annuals and perennials bear stiff spikes of two-lipped, tubular flowers of intense purple, violet, red, or pink or more subdued yellows and whites. Some species have velvety mauve and gray-green leaves. Sizes range from 8" to 6'. All are stunning in masses, containers, and borders.

Type Annual, tender perennial, or hardy perennial; tender perennial are often grown as annuals or biennials
Zone *Annual:* 3–10, H 12–1; *Perennial:* 3–10, H 12–1 (see species list, pp. 470–471). *S. azurea, S. coccinea, S. farinacea,* and *S. guaranitica* are well suited to hot, humid climates. *S. hians, S. jurisicii,* and *S. leucantha* are tolerant of heat, but not combined with high humidity. All species prefer warm climates
Flowering Season Summer to autumn, depending on species

SOWING

Indoors 6–8 weeks before planting out. To grow *S. farinacea* as an annual, start seed 12 weeks before planting out.
Outdoors *Annual and perennial:* 2 weeks after last frost, February or March in Zones 9–10. *Biennial*: Early autumn.
Depth Surface.

GERMINATING

Time 4–21 days.
Requirements Always start with fresh seed, as *Salvia* seeds are short lived. Very susceptible to damping-off; sow in vermiculite, and water from below only. All species require 65°–75°F. *For S. patens* and *S.* × *superba:* Place seeds in a plastic bag together with moist growing medium and refrigerate for 3 weeks.

TRANSPLANTING

Time *Hardy species:* After last frost. *Tender species:* When temperatures remain above 40°F.
Spacing *Small species:* 6"–9". *Medium species:* 12"–18". *Large species:* 20"–30".
Light Full sun, or part shade in very hot climates.
Soil Rich, moist, well drained, with a pH level of 5.5–7.5.

CARING FOR PLANTS

Easy. Pinch back tips when plants are 6" tall. Deadhead often, water regularly during dry spells, and do not overfertilize. Tall plants may need staking in windy sites; leaves may develop powdery mildew. Cut back perennials in autumn to 1"–2". Divide every 3–4 years. *S. patens* can be lifted and stored over winter in sand in a cool, frost-free location and replanted in spring. The leaves of *S. officinalis* can be picked at any time to use in cooking. To dry, cut 6" stalks in late spring and early summer before flowering, hang upside down in the shade for a week, and store in airtight containers.

PROPAGATING

Divide perennials in autumn in Zones 7–10 (in spring in Zones 3–6) or take softwood cuttings in midsummer. Grow annuals and biennials from seed; plants grown from seed will bloom in their first year.

COMBINATIONS

Achillea, Artemisia, Cineraria, Dianthus, Dimorphothica, Geranium.

Sandersonia

TP* | Zn 9–10

p. 422

Climbing plants native to South Africa, Sandersonia *have a sparse scattering of lance-shaped leaves and whimsical orange lanterns nodding on thin stalks; 2' tall. Provide a sheltered site in the border or grow in containers.*

Type Tender perennial
Zone 9–10, H 12–6; often grown as an annual in Zones 5–8
Flowering Season Summer

SOWING

Indoors 8–10 weeks before planting out.
Outdoors After last frost.
Depth *Seed:* ⅛". *Tuber:* 4".

GERMINATING

Time 30–90 days.
Requirements Soak seed for 24 hours in warm water before planting; provide 75°F thereafter.

TRANSPLANTING

Time After last frost.
Spacing 10"–12".
Light Sun.
Soil Well-drained, sandy loam amended with well-rotted manure.

CARING FOR PLANTS

Plants grown from seed will bloom in 3 years. Flowering stems may require staking. Plants die back to the ground after flowering. North of Zone 9, lift tubers in autumn and store in a cool, frost-free location. *Sandersonia* species may survive winters north of Zone 9 if planted deeply against a south-facing wall.

PROPAGATING

Divide in spring or grow from seed. Plants may self-seed.

Sanguinaria

HP | Zn 3–9

Bloodroot, Indian plant, Red poccoon, Tetterwort

p. 422

A single perennial species native to North America belongs to this genus. Plants bear bright white flowers, either flat or double, singly on sturdy stalks above gray-green, deeply lobed leaves. A charming plant for shady borders and woodland plantings whose pure white flowers are curiously refreshing.

Type Hardy perennial
Zone 3–9, H 9–1
Flowering Season Early spring

SOWING

Indoors 8–10 weeks before planting out, in peat pots.
Outdoors Autumn.
Depth Just cover.

GERMINATING

Time 30–90 days.
Requirements 50°–55°F. *Outdoor sowing:* Sow seed sparsely in containers, sink in the ground against a north-facing wall, and cover with glass. Moisten soil occasionally, if necessary. Remove glass when germination begins.

TRANSPLANTING

Time Late August to September.
Spacing 10"–12".
Light Full sun in early spring but will tolerate part shade thereafter. Afternoon shade is beneficial in hot climates.
Soil Not fussy but is happiest in deep, cool, moist soil with a pH level of 5.0–7.0, with plenty of organic matter added.

CARING FOR PLANTS

Easy. Water well during dry spells. Top-dress with well-rotted manure in late winter. Plants die back to the ground after flowering; mark locations to avoid unintentional disturbance. Do not move.

PROPAGATING

Carefully divide in late summer after plants have begun to die down or grow from seed.

COMBINATIONS

Athyrium, Galium, woodland *Phlox, Trillium.*

Sanguisorba (syn. *Poterium*)

HP | Zn 4–9 

Burnet

These perennials are grown for the fuzzy bottlebrushes of tiny white, red, pink, or violet flowers borne on 4'–6' stems in summer. Leaves are light green and lance-shaped. Mass them near water or in the border.

Type Hardy perennial
Zone 4–9, H 9–1 (see species list, p. 471)
Flowering Season Midsummer

SOWING

Indoors 10–12 weeks before planting out.
Outdoors Early spring or late autumn.
Depth Surface.

GERMINATING

Time 30–60 days.
Requirements 55°–55°F.

TRANSPLANTING

Time Plant seedlings in spring of their second year.
Spacing *Small species:* 18"–24". *Large species:* 24"–48".
Light Full sun, with light afternoon shade where summers are hot.
Soil Ordinary, moist but well drained, with a pH level of 6.0–8.0.

CARING FOR PLANTS

Easy. Mulch in spring; keep soil moist in summer; may need staking. In rich soil, will need to be divided yearly. Pick leaves of *S. officinalis* regularly for use cooking and to stimulate growth. *Indoors:* Pot up seedlings; ensure 5 hours of sunlight a day.

PROPAGATING

Divide roots in spring in the North (in autumn south of Zone 6) or grow from seed.

COMBINATIONS

Aconitum, Anemone, Echinacea.

Santolina

HP | Zn 6–9 

p. 422

A low-growing evergreen shrub, Santolina *is often used in the border, in dry stone walls, around paving stones, or for edging. Foliage is very fine, gray-green or mid-green, and aromatic. Buttons of yellow flowers are massed on wiry stems above the foliage. Plants stay a compact 12"–30".*

Type Hardy perennial
Zone 6–9, H 9–5
Flowering Season Late spring to summer

SOWING

Indoors Prechilled seed 8–10 weeks before planting out.
Outdoors Early spring or early autumn.
Depth 1/8".

GERMINATING

Time 15–20 days.
Requirements Place seed in a plastic bag together with moist growing medium and refrigerate for 2–4 weeks; provide 65°–70°F thereafter.

TRANSPLANTING

Time Early spring, when soil is cool and a light frost is still possible, or late autumn.
Spacing 18"–20".
Light Full sun or part shade.
Soil Poor, dry soil; must have very good drainage. *Santolina* species are used very successfully in xeriscaping.

CARING FOR PLANTS

Very easy, requiring little care. Water only during prolonged dry spells and trim plants to 4"–6" after flowering to keep neat and compact. Some people find the yellow flowers of gray-leaved species unattractive and choose to remove these before blooming. If flowers are desired, deadhead or shear as soon as blooming is finished to avoid that depressing, shopworn look. Plants can be potted up and grown indoors with at least 5 hours of sunlight per day.

PROPAGATING

Take cuttings in late summer or autumn or grow from seed.

COMBINATIONS

Buxus, Erigeron, Euphorbia, Nepeta, Salvia.

Sanvitalia

A | Zn 3–10

Creeping zinnia

p. 423

These prostrate annuals are native to North America and Mexico. They have neat, oval leaves and yellow or orange flowers resembling small sunflowers with large, deep brown centers. The 6" plants make an unusual annual ground cover or container plant.

Type Annual
Zone 3–10, H 12–1; particularly well suited to hot, dry locations
Flowering Season Summer to early autumn

SOWING

Indoors 6–8 weeks before planting out, in peat pots.
Outdoors In Zones 3–8, early spring, before the last frost; in Zones 9–10, autumn.
Depth Surface.

GERMINATING

Time 10–21 days.
Requirements Light and 70°F.

TRANSPLANTING

Time Late spring.
Spacing 6"–9".
Light Full sun.
Soil Light, sandy, well drained; tolerant of dry soil. *S. procumbens* is suitable for xeriscaping.

CARING FOR PLANTS

Easy. Apply a weak fertilizer periodically and water well during dry spells. Do not move.

PROPAGATING

Grow from seed only.

COMBINATIONS

Bassia, Salvia, Verbena.

Saponaria

A, HP | Zn 2–10

Soapwort

p. 423

These mat-forming and tufted annuals and perennials have narrow, lance-shaped leaves smothered in small flat pink, white, or red flowers; 6"–36" tall. Grow them in rock gardens and borders.

Type Annual, hardy perennial
Zone *Annual:* 3–10. *Perennial:* 2–9, H 9–1 (see species list, p. 471)
Flowering Season *Annual:* Summer; plants will also bloom in spring from an autumn sowing. *Perennial:* Late spring to early autumn, depending on species

SOWING

Indoors *Annual:* Prechilled seed 4–6 weeks before last frost. *Perennial:* 8–10 weeks before planting out, in peat pots.
Outdoors *Annual:* After last frost. Where winters are mild, seed may be sown again in early autumn for spring blooms. *Perennial:* Early spring or early autumn.
Depth Surface.

GERMINATING

Time 10–21 days.
Requirements Easy. Place seed in a plastic bag together with moist growing medium and refrigerate for 3 weeks; provide light and 70°F thereafter.

TRANSPLANTING

Time *Annual:* After last frost. *Perennial:* Early spring, when soil is cool and a light frost is still possible, or late autumn.
Spacing *Small species:* 4"–8". *Large species:* 10"–15".
Light *Annual:* Sun. *Perennial:* Full sun or light shade.
Soil *Annual:* Ordinary, well drained. *Perennial:* May become invasive in rich, moist soil; performs well in dry, rocky soil where its growth will be curtailed. Compact, rock garden species like *S. caespitosa* need gritty, very well-drained soil. *S. ocymoides* is suitable for xeriscaping.

CARING FOR PLANTS

Easy. *Annual:* Water well during dry spells and feed occasionally throughout the growing season. *Perennial:* Easy. Water only during very dry spells and do not overfeed. Cut back after blooming to keep plants compact and encourage further blooming. Do not move.

PROPAGATING

Divide perennials in early spring in Zones 3–6 (in autumn elsewhere), take softwood cuttings in early summer, or grow perennials and annuals from seed. Plants may self-seed.

COMBINATIONS

Armeria, Dianthus, Heuchera, Gypsophila, Iberis, Veronica.

CAUTION

Harmful if eaten.

Sarracenia

HP | Zn 3–10 | Full sun, Partial shade | Ordinary soil, Moist soil

Pitcher plant, Trumpet leaf

p. 423

This genus of insectivorous plants is native to North America. Flowers may be an eerie green or purple with veined and hooded pitchers growing 6"– 4' long, or complicated structures with drooping yellow petals. Try this curiosity in a damp spot or a bog garden.

Type Hardy perennial
Zone 3–10 (see species list, p. 471)
Flowering Season Late spring

SOWING

Indoors Prechilled seed 8–10 weeks before planting out.
Outdoors Spring, in Zones 9–10 only.
Depth Surface.

GERMINATING

Time 30–90 days.
Requirements Difficult. Place moistened seed in refrigerator (*without* growing medium) for 7 days, then sow on a damp paper towel in a dish, covering with clear plastic. Keep constantly moist at 65°–75°F. Prick out seedlings to individual pots as they germinate.

TRANSPLANTING

Time Spring, when temperatures remain above 40°F.
Spacing 12"–18".
Light Sun or light shade. Plants need constantly wet soil to develop best color if grown in strong sun.
Soil Moist to wet, neutral or acid pH.

CARING FOR PLANTS

Difficult unless precise cultural requirements are met. Plants grown from seed will flower in 3–5 years. Plant high to keep crowns dry, but provide plenty of water in summer. Although it is tempting to put on a mealtime show with these carnivorous plants, feeding them insects or meat is extremely bad for their health and may cause rapid deterioration.

PROPAGATING

Divide in spring north of Zone 7 (in autumn elsewhere) or grow from seed.

CAUTION

It is illegal to dig these wildflowers from their native habitat, and gardeners should be sure to buy only nursery-grown plants from reputable retailers. See p. 11 for further information on purchasing restricted wildflowers.

Satureja

A, HP | Zn 3–10 | Full sun | Dry soil, Ordinary soil

Savory

p. 423

The genus Satureja *includes annual and perennial herbs grown both for the culinary use of their aromatic leaves and for their dainty flowers. Plants are upright, 6"–36" tall, usually bearing narrow, oblong, gray-green leaves. Flowers are small, tubular, two-lipped, purple, white, or pink. Grown in herb and rock gardens.*

Type Annual or hardy perennial
Zone 3–10, H 9–5 (see species list, p. 471). *Annual:* (*S. hortensis,* summer savory): 3–10. *Perennial:* (*S. montana,* winter savory): 5–8, H 9–5.
Flowering Season *Annual:* Midsummer to autumn. *Perennial:* Early summer.

SOWING

Indoors *Annual:* 4 weeks before planting out, in peat pots. *Perennial:* 6–8 weeks before planting out.
Outdoors *Annual:* Early spring, then every 3–4 weeks for a continuous supply of leaves. *Perennial:* Late spring.
Depth Surface.

GERMINATING

Time 10–21 days.
Requirements Light and 60°–70°F.

TRANSPLANTING

Time After last frost.
Spacing *Annual:* 6"–8". *Perennial:* 10"–12". Plants grown close together will provide support for each other.
Light Full sun.
Soil Light, rich, and well drained, with a pH level of 6.5–7.5. *S. hortensis* tolerates dry soil.

CARING FOR PLANTS

Do not move. Pinch back young plants to induce bushy growth. Cut leaves for immediate culinary use at any time. Cut out deadwood of perennials regularly. *For drying:* Harvest in summer before flowering begins and again in autumn, when plants can be cut to the ground; harvest only tender tips of shoots. Hang stalks upside down in a paper bag to dry; remove leaves and store in an airtight container. *To grow indoors in winter:* Cut back plants by half in late summer, dig plants carefully to pot up, and allow to rest outdoors for 2–3 weeks. They require at least 5 hours of sunlight a day, a weak monthly feeding, and soil that is allowed to dry between watering. For perennials left outdoors over winter, mulch after ground freezes. Divide every 2–3 years to maintain vigor.

PROPAGATING

Divide perennials in spring or autumn, take cuttings in spring, or grow perennials and annuals from seed.

Saxifraga

HP | Zn 2–10

Rockfoil, Saxifrage

p. 423

Saxifrage is a very large genus of widely varying plants, though most in common cultivation are low-growing (under 12") and rosette-forming, with small pink, red, or white flowers. Use them in rock gardens and in containers.

Type Hardy perennial
Zone 2–10, H 9–5 (see species list, p. 471); will thrive only in cool climates
Flowering Season Early spring to autumn, depending on species

SOWING

Indoors See Germinating, Requirements.
Outdoors See Germinating, Requirements.
Depth Just cover.

GERMINATING

Time 15–60 days.
Requirements *Autumn sowing:* Sow seed in flats, sink flats in ground against a north-facing wall, and cover with glass. Moisten soil occasionally, if necessary. Bring indoors in spring to 65°–75°F. *Spring sowing:* Sow seed in moistened medium, place in a plastic bag, and refrigerate. After 2–3 weeks, remove containers and sink in the ground in a shady location, covering with glass. Transplant seedlings as they emerge.

TRANSPLANTING

Time After last frost.
Spacing *Small species:* 4"–6". *Medium species:* 8"–12". *Large species:* 12"–18".
Light Most require part shade, with protection from the midday sun, even in mild climates.
Soil Specific needs vary among species, but most require cool, moist, sandy or gritty soil that is neutral to alkaline. It must be very well drained in winter.

CARING FOR PLANTS

Most saxifrages are easy to grow if given the precise conditions they require. Soil must be kept moist in summer; otherwise, little care is required.

PROPAGATING

Separate root runners from the parent plant or grow from seed. Some species self-seed.

COMBINATIONS

Dianthus, ferns, *Gentiana*.

Scabiosa

A, TP*, HP | Zn 1–10 

Pincushion flower, Scabious

p. 423

Most Scabiosa *are grown for their domed, lace-edged flowers of purple, blue, red, white, or yellow, borne singly on long, wiry stems. Plants are often tufted or mat-forming; 6"–48". Use in borders and cutting beds.*

Type Annual, tender perennial, or hardy perennial
Zone 1–10, H 9–1 (see species list, pp. 471–472)
Flowering Season Summer to early autumn, depending on species

SOWING

Indoors *Annual:* 4–5 weeks before last frost. *Perennial:* 8–10 weeks before planting out.
Outdoors *Annual:* After last frost in Zones 3–7; autumn in Zones 8–10. *Perennial:* Early spring; seeds can also be sown in early fall where winters are mild.
Depth Just cover.

GERMINATING

Time 10–15 days.
Requirements 70°–75°F.

TRANSPLANTING

Time *Annual:* After last frost. *Perennial:* Early spring, when soil is cool and a light frost is still possible, or late autumn.
Spacing *Annual:* 8"–12". *Perennial:* 12"–18".
Light Full sun.
Soil Average, humus-rich, well drained, with a pH level of 7.0–8.0.

CARING FOR PLANTS

Easy. Deadhead regularly. In windy locations, support with twiggy branches pushed into the ground when plants are young. Cut back to ground level in autumn. Divide perennials every 3–4 years to maintain vigor. Powdery mildew is common.

PROPAGATING

Annual: Grow from seed only. *Perennial:* Take cuttings in summer, divide in early spring, or grow from seed.

COMBINATIONS

Coreopsis, Dianthus, Geranium, Penstemon.

Scaevola

TP* | Zn 3–10

Fan flower

p. 423

Of the handsome, trailing, tender perennials, scramblers, and shrubs in the genus Scaevola, *one,* S. aemula, *is grown as an annual. Plants have small, rather fleshy, rich green leaves and unusual flowers composed of five petals, all on one side like a fan, in stunning blues and purples. Exquisite in baskets and containers.*

Type Tender perennial
Zone 9–10, H 12–1; often grown as an annual in Zones 3–8; very tolerant of heat and humidity
Flowering Season Spring to frost

SOWING

Indoors 6–8 weeks before last frost.
Outdoors Spring or summer.
Depth Surface.

GERMINATING

Time 21–60 days.
Requirements Light and 65°–75°F.

TRANSPLANTING

Time After last frost.
Spacing *Compact selections:* 18". *Spreading selections:* 24"–36".
Light Sun to part shade.
Soil Average, well drained. Quite drought tolerant.

CARING FOR PLANTS

Very easy, with little care beyond regular watering. Plants overwinter indoors successfully, but produce abundant foliage and sparse blooms the next year.

PROPAGATING

Take softwood cuttings in late spring or summer or grow from seed.

COMBINATIONS

Diascia, Lantana, Petunia, Verbena.

CAUTION

S. sericea is listed as invasive in some areas, including Florida. See pp. 494–495 for advice.

S

Schizanthus

A | Zn 1–10

Butterfly flower, Poor man's orchid

Bushy annuals native to Chile, Schizanthus *has delicately cut foliage and masses of small but showy, orchidlike flowers in white and every shade of red, pink, purple, and yellow, as well as multicolors. Good as an edging, or in borders or containers; 12"–48" tall.*

Type Annual
Zone 1–10, H 8–1 (see species list, p. 472); performs most successfully where summers are cool, with nighttime temperatures below 65°F
Flowering Season In spring from an autumn sowing; summer through autumn from a spring sowing

SOWING

Indoors 8–10 weeks before last frost.
Outdoors Start seed outdoors only in Zones 9–10, where they may be sown in early spring at 2-week intervals for 6 weeks, or in autumn.
Depth 1/8".

GERMINATING

Time 7–20 days.
Requirements Darkness and 60°–75°F.

TRANSPLANTING

Time 2 weeks after last frost, when temperatures remain above 40°F.
Spacing *Small species:* 9"–12". *Medium species:* 12"–18". *Large species:* 24"–36".
Light Sun.
Soil Rich, moist loam with a pH level of 6.0–7.0.

CARING FOR PLANTS

Difficult. Pinch back tips when plants are 3" and again at 6". Provide extra support with twiggy branches pushed into ground when plants are young. Water frequently, keeping flowers and leaves as dry as possible. Young plants may attract aphids.

PROPAGATING

Grow from seed only.

COMBINATIONS

Brachyscome, Dianthus, Myosotis, Viola.

Schizocodon See *Shortia*

Schizostylis

HP* | Zn 7–10

Kaffir lily

p. 423

Grow these southern African natives or their spikes of pink or red cup-shaped flowers. Their foliage is grassy; to 24" tall. Use them in cutting beds and borders.

Type Hardy perennial, sometimes grown as an annual
Zone 8–10, H 9–7; grown as an annual in cool zones; blooms most profusely where summers are damp
Flowering Season Late summer to autumn

SOWING

Indoors 8–10 weeks before planting out.
Outdoors *Seed:* Early spring, when soil is cool and a light frost is still possible. *Rhizome:* Spring.
Depth *Seed:* Just cover. *Rhizome:* 2".

GERMINATING

Time 30–90 days.
Requirements 55°–60°F.

TRANSPLANTING

Time After last frost.
Spacing 9"–12".
Light Full sun or part shade.
Soil Moist, rich, well drained, acid or neutral.

CARING FOR PLANTS

Keep soil cool and moist with spring mulch, water often during dry spells. Feed in spring and once or twice more in growing season. Mulch for first winter to protect newly planted tubers. Divide when plants show signs of decline, once every 2–4 years. Shelter from damaging winds. Where not hardy, keep plants in containers year-round; store in a cool, dry spot.

PROPAGATING

Divide in early spring, leaving three to five eyes per section, or grow from seed.

COMBINATIONS

Aster, Campanula, Dahlia, Dierama.

Scilla (syn. *Endymion, Hyacinthoides*)

HB | Zn 3–10

Scilla, Squill

p. 424

Perennial bulbs with narrow, grasslike leaves, scillas bear spikes of mainly tubular blue, purple, white, or pink flowers. Plants are usually 6"–12" tall (rarely up to 36"). For greatest impact, plant them in masses.

Type Hardy bulb
Zone 3–10, H 9–1 (see species list, p. 472)
Flowering Season Early spring to early summer, depending on species

SOWING

Indoors See Germinating, Requirements.
Outdoors *Seed:* See Germinating, Requirements. *Bulb:* Autumn.
Depth *Seed:* Just cover. *Small bulb:* 3"–4". *Large bulb:* 4"–5".

GERMINATING

Time 30–180 days.
Requirements Easy. *Autumn sowing:* Sow seed in flats, sink in the ground against a north-facing wall, and cover with glass. Moisten soil occasionally, if necessary. Bring flats indoors in spring to 50°F. *Spring sowing:* Sow seed in moistened medium, secure in a plastic bag, and refrigerate for 2–3 weeks. Remove flats and sink in the ground in a shady location, covering with glass. Transplant seedlings as they appear.

TRANSPLANTING

Spacing 3"–5".
Light Most scillas grow well in sun or part shade; *S. peruviana* and *S. litardierei* require full sun and *S. siberica* prefers full shade.
Soil Rich, well-drained loam with a pH level of 6.0–7.0. *S. siberica* tolerates dry soil and can be used for xeriscaping.

CARING FOR PLANTS

Easy. Water regularly until blooming ends, then allow bulbs to dry out. Apply a complete fertilizer in early spring or top-dress with manure in autumn. Scillas spread rapidly and may require division every 3 years. Apart from dividing, do not disturb.

PROPAGATING

Dig clumps and plant offsets in autumn or grow from seed. Plants take 4–5 years to bloom from seed.

COMBINATIONS

Alchemilla, Aubrieta, azaleas, ferns, *Hosta, Ionopsidium, Lunaria, Rhododendron.*

CAUTION

All parts of the plant are toxic.

Scutellaria

HP | Zn 3–8

Helmet flower, Skullcap

p. 424

In this large genus of perennials, the most popular are low and spreading. Their yellow, red, purple, blue, or white tubular flowers are lipped and hooded. Plants are 4"–36" tall, and can be grown in the border or rock garden.

Type Hardy perennial
Zone 3–8, H 9–5 (see species list, p. 472)
Flowering Season Summer

SOWING

Indoors Start seed outdoors only.
Outdoors Autumn, when seed is fresh.
Depth Just cover.

GERMINATING

Time 14–180 days.
Requirements Sow seed in flats, sink these in the ground against a north-facing wall, and cover with glass. Moisten the soil occasionally, if necessary. Transplant to the garden after two full growing seasons.

TRANSPLANTING

Time Autumn.
Spacing *Small species:* 8"–12". *Large species:* 18"–24".
Light Full sun or part shade.
Soil Moist, well drained, with a pH level of 6.0–7.0.

CARING FOR PLANTS

Pinch back tips of young plants to encourage bushiness. Mulch well in spring and do not allow soil to dry out. Divide clumps when plants become overgrown.

PROPAGATING

Divide in early spring, take softwood cuttings in summer, or grow from seed.

COMBINATIONS

Gentiana, Nierembergia, Persicaria, Prunella.

Sedum

HP | Zn 3–9

Sedum, Orpine, Stonecrop

p. 424

This very large genus includes mainly perennial succulents, often trailing, with terminal clusters of small, star-shaped flowers of yellow, pink, or white; 1"–24". Use sedums in containers or dry stone walls, in rock gardens, between paving, as edging, or in the border.

Type Hardy perennial
Zone 3–9, H 12–1 (see species list, p. 472)
Flowering Season Early summer to early autumn, depending on species

SOWING

Indoors See Germinating, Requirements.
Outdoors See Germinating, Requirements.
Depth Surface

GERMINATING

Time 5–30 days.
Requirements *Autumn sowing:* Sow seed in flats, plunge these to the rim against a north-facing wall, and cover with glass. Moisten the soil occasionally, if necessary. Bring indoors in spring to 60°–65°F. *Spring sowing:* Sow seed in containers, place in a plastic bag, and refrigerate for 2–3 weeks. Sink containers in the ground in a shady location, covering with glass. Transplant seedlings as they emerge.

TRANSPLANTING

Time After last frost.
Spacing *Small species:* 6"–8". *Medium species:* 12"–18". *Large species:* 24".
Light Full sun to part shade.
Soil Average, well drained, with a pH level of 6.0–8.0. Many species are suitable choices for xeriscaping.

CARING FOR PLANTS

Easy. Overwatering may cause fungal disease. Cut back to ground level in autumn. Be frugal with fertilizer.

PROPAGATING

Divide in spring in Zones 3–6 (in autumn in Zones 7–9), take cuttings in summer, or grow from seed.

COMBINATIONS

Bergenia, Ceratostigma, Dahlia, ornamental grasses, *Heuchera, Liriope, Lithodora, Solidago.*

CAUTION

Harmful if eaten. Several species of sedum are widely invasive, including *S. acre, S. sarmentosum,* and *S. telephium.* See pp. 494–495 for advice.

Selaginella

HP | Zn 2–10

Little club moss, Spike moss

Many of these odd little evergreen plants look just like arborvitae in a bargain-sized container. Others are low and mosslike, making a useful and attractive ground cover. Most grow no more than 4"–12". A fern ally rather than a true fern, they like the same shady, damp conditions.

Type Hardy perennial
Zone 2–10, H 12–1 (see species list, p. 472)
Flowering Season N/A

SOWING

Indoors As soon as spores are ripe in summer.
Outdoors Not recommended.
Depth Surface.

GERMINATING

Time 10–365 days.
Requirements Difficult. Provide 65°–75°F. (See pp. 24–25 for details of starting plants from spores.)

TRANSPLANTING

Time After last frost, after 2 years' growth.
Spacing 12".
Light Part to full shade; requires shade from hot afternoon sun.
Soil Moist, well drained, very high in organic matter, with a pH of 6.1–7.5.

CARING FOR PLANTS

Remove faded foliage regularly to improve the appearance of plants. Keep soil evenly moist but foliage as dry as possible, particularly in the evening.

PROPAGATING

Root stems at any time, carefully divide in spring, or grow from spores.

Sempervivum

HP | Zn 5–9

Hens and chicks, Houseleek, Live-forever

p. 424

Plants of this genus of mainly low-growing, rosette-forming evergreen succulents grow 4"–12". Plants bear clusters of small, star-shaped flowers of white, yellow, pink, or purple on stalks above the low rosettes. They are useful around paving; in dry stone walls, containers, and rock gardens; and at the front of borders.

Type Hardy perennial
Zone 5–9, H 9–5; does not thrive in humid or rainy climates
Flowering Season Early summer to midsummer

SOWING

Indoors Spring or autumn.
Outdoors Spring.
Depth Surface.

GERMINATING

Time 14–42 days.
Requirements 70°–80°F.

TRANSPLANTING

Time After last frost.
Spacing *Small species:* 6"–8". *Large species:* 12".
Light Full sun.
Soil Poor, dry.

CARING FOR PLANTS

Water and feed only sparingly. Remove flower heads after blooming to improve appearance.

PROPAGATING

Plant detached offsets or grow from seed. Plants cannot be relied on to come true from seed.

COMBINATIONS

Bergenia, Festuca, Saponaria, Sedum, Thymus.

S

Senecio (syn. *Cineraria*)

A, TP*, HP* | Zn 3–9

Cineraria, Groundsel, Ragwort

p. 424

The plants in this immense genus of greatly varying annuals, perennials, and subshrubs have in common their daisylike flowers, which are most often yellow. Many species are grown for their attractive gray foliage. Small species (12") make useful edging and rock garden plants, while taller species (up to 36") are grown in borders and wildflower gardens.

Type Annual, tender perennial, or hardy perennial
Zone *Annual:* 3–8. *Perennial:* 3–9, H 12–1 (see species list, p. 484)
Flowering Season From early spring through late winter, depending on species

SOWING

Indoors 6–8 weeks before planting out, in autumn in Zones 9–10.
Outdoors Early spring, when soil is cool and a light frost is still possible, or late autumn.
Depth Surface.

GERMINATING

Time 10–21 days.
Requirements Light and 65°–75°F. Highly susceptible to damping-off; sow in vermiculite, and water only from below.

TRANSPLANTING

Time After last frost, autumn in Zones 9–10.
Spacing *Small species:* 6". *Medium species:* 10"–12". *Large species:* 18"–24".
Light Most species require full sun, but some will grow in part shade; *S. petasitis* thrives in full shade.
Soil Average, well drained.

CARING FOR PLANTS

Generally easy. Water during very dry spells. Severely cut back perennials in spring. Some people find the yellow flowers of gray-leaved species unattractive and choose to remove these before blooming.

PROPAGATING

Divide perennials in spring. Grow annuals or perennials from seed.

COMBINATIONS

Atriplex, Brachyscome, Dianthus, Heliotropium, Salvia, Viola.

Sesamum

A | Zn 7–10

S

Sesame, Benne

Plants in the genus Sesamum *are erect, annual herbs native to Africa and Asia. One of these,* S. indicum, *is grown for its seed. Plants are 1'–3' tall, with pairs of leaves scattered along stems and pretty tubular flowers of pink, violet, or white. Use is limited to the herb garden.*

Type Annual
Zone 7–10
Flowering Season All summer

SOWING

Indoors 8 weeks before planting out.
Outdoors In Zone 7–10 only, late spring, when nighttime temperatures remain above 60°F. Start seed indoors in cooler zones.
Depth ¼".

GERMINATING

Time 5–7 days.
Requirements 70°–85°F.

TRANSPLANTING

Time In spring, when nighttime temperatures remain above 60°F.
Spacing 8"–12".
Light Full sun.
Soil Any that is well drained.

CARING FOR PLANTS

Do not move plants. To harvest seed, cut stalks to the ground when the uppermost seedpods have turned green and lower seedpods have not yet opened. Dry flower heads in a paper bag, remove seeds, and store in an airtight container.

PROPAGATING

Grow from seed only.

Shortia (syn. *Schizocodon*)

HP | Zn 4–9 | Partial shade, Full shade | Moist soil

Shortia

p. 425

Most of the creeping, evergreen perennials in this genus are native to eastern Asia. One, however, S. galacifolia, *is a North American native.* Shortia *species bear unusual fringed, pink tubular flowers singly on stems above attractive, rounded leaves. Grow them in rock gardens and cool woodlands.*

Type Hardy perennial
Zone 4–9, H 8–5 (see species list, p. 472); performs best in cool climates
Flowering Season Spring

SOWING

Indoors As soon as fresh seed is available.
Outdoors As soon as seed is ripe, in late summer.
Depth Surface.

GERMINATING

Time 30–60 days.
Requirements Difficult; use only fresh seed. Place seed in a plastic bag together with moist growing medium and refrigerate for 3 weeks. Provide a constant 60°–65°F thereafter.

TRANSPLANTING

Time After last frost.
Spacing 10"–12".
Light Part to full shade.
Soil Cool, very moist, acid; amend with leaf mold.

CARING FOR PLANTS

Difficult. Mulch with leaf mold or compost to keep soil cool and moist, and water regularly during dry weather. Do not disturb.

PROPAGATING

Divide in early spring, take cuttings in early summer, or grow from seed.

Sidalcea

HP | Zn 4–9 | Full sun | Dry soil, Ordinary soil

Checker mallow, False mallow, Miniature hollyhock, Prairie mallow

p. 425

These perennials bear pink, purple, or white hollyhock-like flowers along tall (2'–8') erect stems. The leaves are lobed or deeply cut. Native to western and central North America, they are grown in the border.

Type Hardy perennial
Zone 4–9, H 7–5 (see species list, p. 472)
Flowering Season Summer

SOWING

Indoors 6–8 weeks before last frost.
Outdoors Early spring.
Depth ⅛".

GERMINATING

Time 14–42 days.
Requirements Easy. 50°F.

TRANSPLANTING

Time After last frost.
Spacing *Small species:* 9"–12". *Large species:* 18"
Light Full sun.
Soil Ordinary; enrich with manure.

CARING FOR PLANTS

Easy. Water when the weather is dry. Cut back plants severely after flowering to encourage a second bloom and again in late autumn. Stake tall cultivars. Divide every 2–3 years.

PROPAGATING

Divide in autumn (in spring in Zones 5–6) or grow from seed. Plants grown from seed will bloom in their first year.

COMBINATIONS

Artemisia, Eryngium, Gypsophila.

Silene

A, HP | Zn 3–9

Campion, Catchfly

p. 425

These annual and perennial plants, some of which are evergreen, are grown for their masses of small red, pink, or white flowers borne singly or in clusters over a long period. These 2"–24" plants are useful as edging or in the border; some are best as rock garden plants.

Type Annual or hardy perennial
Zone *Annual:* 3–9. *Perennial:* 3–8, H 7–1 (see species list, p. 473). Prefers warm temperatures
Flowering Season Mid spring to early autumn, depending on species and sowing time

SOWING

Indoors 8–10 weeks before planting out.
Outdoors Early spring, when soil is cool and a light frost is still possible. For spring flowering, sow annuals in late autumn.
Depth Just cover.

GERMINATING

Time 5–20 days.
Requirements 70°F.

TRANSPLANTING

Time Early spring, when soil is cool and a light frost is still possible, or early autumn.
Spacing *Small species:* 6"–8". *Medium species:* 12". *Large species:* 18".
Light Full sun or part shade.
Soil Well drained, humus-rich, with a pH level of 5.0–7.0. *S. acaulis* and *S. armeria* tolerates dry soil.

CARING FOR PLANTS

Easy. Water frequently and feed occasionally. Discard annuals after flowering. Do not disturb established plants.

PROPAGATING

Take softwood cuttings of perennials in spring or grow annuals or perennials from seed.

COMBINATIONS

Campanula, Geranium, Leucojum, Stachys, Verbena, Viola tricolor.

Silphium

HP | Zn 3–9

Prairie dock, Rosinweed

p. 425

Tall perennials native to the eastern and central United States, Silphium *have large, coarse leaves and cheerful yellow, sunflower-like blooms. These towering, rapidly spreading 5'–12' plants need plenty of space at the back of the border, near a pond, or among tall shrubs.*

Type Hardy perennial
Zone 3–9, H 9–5 (see species list, p. 473); tolerates hot, humid climates
Flowering Season July to September

SOWING

Indoors Best to start seeds outdoors.
Outdoors As soon as fresh seed is available, in autumn.
Depth ½".

GERMINATING

Time 21 days.
Requirements Chip seed before sowing. Sow seed in flats, sink in the ground against a north-facing wall, and cover with glass. Moisten soil occasionally, if necessary. Bring flats indoors in late winter to a cool location.

TRANSPLANTING

Time Set out purchased plants in spring or autumn.
Spacing 3'–5'.
Light Sun to light shade.
Soil Will grow in most soils but prefers moist, well drained, with a pH level of 6.6–7.8.

CARING FOR PLANTS

Apply low-nitrogen fertilizer in spring. Divide every 2–3 years to keep in bounds. Plants may require staking, especially in soil that is too rich.

PROPAGATING

Divide in spring in the North (in early autumn south of Zone 6) or grow from seed. Plant self-seeds readily, and roots left in the ground when clumps are moved will sprout.

Silybum

Bi* | Zn 6–9

p. 425

Of the two species in this genus, only S. marianum *is grown. It is distinguished by its rosettes of spiny, marbled basal leaves. Plants bear purplish-pink, thistlelike flowers singly on erect stems and reach 4' tall in bloom. Use in naturalistic plantings or for textural contrast in the border.*

Type Biennial; often grown as an annual
Zone 6–9, H 9–6 (see species list, p. 473); grown as an annual in Zones 1–10; prefers cool weather
Flowering Season Summer to early autumn

SOWING

Indoors 8 weeks before planting out.
Outdoors *Annual:* After last frost. *Biennial:* Early summer.
Depth 1/8".

GERMINATING

Time 14–21 days.
Requirements Easy. 55°–60°F.

TRANSPLANTING

Time *Annual:* After last frost. *Biennial:* Late summer to early autumn.
Spacing 24".
Light Full sun or light shade.
Soil Tolerates wet or dry soil; will produce only lush foliage and few flowers in fertile soil.

CARING FOR PLANTS

Easy. To grow as an annual, seed must be started early in the season. To grow as a perennial foliage plant, remove flower buds before they open. Leaves are attractive to slugs.

PROPAGATING

Grow from seed. Self-seeds most efficiently and may become weedy if not deadheaded regularly.

Sisyrinchium

HP | Zn 3–10

These tufted, clump-forming perennials have stiff, grassy leaves and small star-shaped flowers in yellow, white, purple, or blue. The blossoms grow along tall, upright, 12"–36" stems. Native to North and South America, they are grown in both rock gardens and borders.

Type Hardy perennial
Zone 3–10, H 9–6 (see species list, p. 473)
Flowering Season Spring to summer

SOWING

Indoors See Germinating, Requirements.
Outdoors See Germinating, Requirements.
Depth 1/8".

GERMINATING

Time 30–180 days.
Requirements *Autumn sowing:* Sow seed in flats, sink in the ground against a north-facing wall, and cover with glass. Moisten soil occasionally, if necessary. Bring flats indoors in spring to 50°F. *Spring sowing:* Sow seed in containers, place in a plastic bag, and refrigerate for 2–3 weeks. Plunge containers in the ground in a shady location and cover with glass. Transplant seedlings as they appear.

TRANSPLANTING

Time After last spring frost, or in autumn.
Spacing *Small species:* 4"–6". *Large species:* 12"–15".
Light Prefers full sun but will tolerate part shade.
Soil Grows quite well in most situations, but performs best in moist, well-drained, fertile soil with a pH level of 6.6–7.8. *S. atlanticum* prefers a neutral to slightly acid soil.

CARING FOR PLANTS

Do not allow soil to dry out during the growing season. Cut back flowering stems to the ground after blooming. Do not despair if plants disappear in summer; this is normal and they will reappear the following spring. May become invasive if made too comfortable.

PROPAGATING

Divide in spring in Zones 3–6 (in autumn in the South) or grow from seed. Plant may self-seed.

COMBINATIONS

Heuchera, Santolina, Veronica.

Smilacina

HP | Zn 3–9  

Smilacina, False Solomon's seal, Solomon's feathers, Solomon's plume

p. 425

Pairs of handsome, light green leaves grow along arching stems topped with feathery clusters of tiny white or pink flowers, each like a miniature spruce tree; 12"–36" tall. These make excellent woodland plants. Native to North and Central American and Asian woodlands.

Type Hardy perennial
Zone 3–9, H 9–1
Flowering Season Late spring and early summer

SOWING

Indoors Start seed outdoors only.
Outdoors In early fall as soon as ripe seed is available.
Depth Just cover.

GERMINATING

Time 30–180 days.
Requirements Sow seed thinly in flats, sink these in the ground against a north-facing wall, and cover with glass. Moisten soil occasionally, if necessary. Leave one growing season then transplant to garden.

TRANSPLANTING

Time Set out purchased plants in spring or autumn.
Spacing 18"–24".
Light Part to full shade.
Soil Moist, well-drained, rich, acid, with a pH level of 5.0–6.0.

CARING FOR PLANTS

Easy. Mulch with leaf mold and apply a complete fertilizer in early spring. Cut back plants to the ground in late autumn or dig in autumn, leave in a cool, dark location until early spring, then bring into a warm room to force blooms.

PROPAGATING

Divide in spring or autumn or grow from seed. Plant may self-seed.

COMBINATIONS

Astilbe, Brunnera, ferns, *Helleborus, Hosta, Rhododendron, Tiarella.*

Soldanella

HP | Zn 5–8

Snowbell

p. 425

These dainty alpine perennials form clumps of heart-shaped leaves. Their nodding, fringed, bell-shaped flowers of purple, blue, or white are held singly above. Very pretty plants of 3"–15" grown in the rock garden.

Type Hardy perennial
Zone 5–8, H 7–1; likes a cool, humid growing season and dry winters
Flowering Season Early spring to early summer, depending on species

SOWING

Indoors As soon as fresh seed is available.
Outdoors As soon as fresh seed is available.
Depth Surface.

GERMINATING

Time 30–180 days.
Requirements Difficult. *Indoor sowing:* Place seed in a plastic bag with moist growing medium; refrigerate 4 weeks, then provide light and 55°–60°F. *Outdoor sowing:* Sow in flats, sink in ground in sheltered location, cover with glass. Remove glass when seeds sprout. Transplant when large enough to handle.

TRANSPLANTING

Time After last frost.
Spacing 4"–6".
Light Sun, with light shade in hottest part of day.
Soil Very moist, with perfect drainage, especially in winter. Also peaty and slightly acid.

CARING FOR PLANTS

Difficult. Essential to meet cultural needs precisely, particularly soil. Since important to plant where soil won't dry out, frequent watering is seldom necessary. Surround plants with grit to improve winter drainage and discourage slugs. Protect buds from frost by covering crowns with a cloche or straw.

PROPAGATING

Divide after flowering or grow from seed.

COMBINATIONS

Daphne odora, ferns, *Helleborus.*

Solenopsis (syn. *Isotoma, Laurentia*)

TP*, HP | Zn 7–10

These charming, long-blooming plants are native to dry sites in Australia as well as South America. They have slim, 2" long leaves and masses of scented, star-shaped white, blue, or lilac flowers. Use them as ground covers or container plants.

Type Tender perennial, hardy perennial; often grown as an annual
Zone 7–10 (see species list, p. 473); grown as an annual in cooler zones; prefers the dry, moderate California climate
Flowering Season Spring to autumn, depending on sowing time

SOWING

Indoors 8–10 weeks before planting out.
Outdoors In Zones 9–10 only, at any time.
Depth Surface

GERMINATING

Time 10–60 days.
Requirements Requires light and 60°–75°F.

TRANSPLANTING

Time Several weeks after last frost, when temperature will remain above 40°F.
Spacing *Small species:* 6"–8". *Spreading species:* 24".
Light Sun to part shade.
Soil Average to moist, well drained, fertile.

CARING FOR PLANTS

Easy. Deadhead regularly to extend the flowering season. Can be overwintered as a houseplant in a cool, bright location, keeping soil fairly dry.

PROPAGATING

Take stem cuttings in summer, divide, or grow from seed.

COMBINATIONS

Antirrhinum, Dianthus, Lobelia.

CAUTION

Contact may cause skin irritation.

Solenostemon (syn. *Coleus*)

TP* | Zn 10

Coleus

p. 425

Coleus are low-growing, bushy plants valued for their showy, multicolored leaves in unusual colors: black, scarlet, orange, plum, gold, pink, salmon. They grow 1'–3' tall. Plants bear insignificant spikes of tiny, two-lipped blue, white, or purple flowers. Mass coleus in a shady spot for best effect. Spectacular container plants.

Type Tender perennial; often grown as an annual
Zone 10, H 12–1; grown as an annual in Zones 5–9; performs well only where summers are quite warm
Flowering Season Summer, although the flowers are unimportant and are often removed

SOWING

Indoors 8–12 weeks before last frost.
Outdoors Only in Zones 9–10, after last frost.
Depth Surface.

GERMINATING

Time 10–20 days.
Requirements Easy. Light and 65°–75°F.

TRANSPLANTING

Time Several weeks after last frost, when soil is warm and the temperatures remain above 45°F.
Spacing *Dwarf species:* 6"–9". *Tall species:* 12"–20".
Light Part to full shade. Most plants grown in sun will have less-vivid leaf color, but many beautiful cultivars for full sun have been developed.
Soil Moist, rich loam.

CARING FOR PLANTS

Easy. Pinch back young plants to encourage branching. Feed monthly with a high-nitrogen fertilizer and water during dry spells. Plants grown in sun will require frequent watering.

PROPAGATING

Take stem cuttings in summer or autumn for overwintering and root plants in water in a warm location, or grow from seed.

COMBINATIONS

Amaranthus, Fuchsia 'Gartenmeister Bonstedt' and other fuchsias with narrow flowers, *Impatiens, Lobelia.*

Solidago

HP | Zn 3–9

Goldenrod

p. 425

Erect perennials with terminal clusters of tiny yellow flowers, Solidago *species range from 6" to 8' tall, with most growing from 2' to 4'. Use them in borders or in rock or wildflower gardens. Most species are native to North America.*

Type Hardy perennial
Zone 3–9, H 9–1 (see species list, p. 473)
Flowering Season Summer to early autumn

SOWING

Indoors 6–8 weeks before planting out.
Outdoors Early spring, when soil is cool and a light frost is still possible, or late autumn.
Depth Just cover.

GERMINATING

Time 14–42 days.
Requirements Easy. 50°F.

TRANSPLANTING

Time Early spring, when soil is cool and a light frost is still possible, or late autumn.
Spacing *Small species:* 12". *Large species:* 24"–36".
Light Sun or part shade.
Soil Well drained, with a pH level of 5.0–7.0. Tolerates quite dry soil; very rich soil produces lush foliage but few flowers.

CARING FOR PLANTS

Easy. Deadhead after flowering to prevent unwanted self-seeding, and cut back completely in autumn. Staking may be necessary in windy locations. Divide plants every 3–4 years to maintain vigor. Self-seeding and rhizomatous species of goldenrod can be aggressive spreaders, whereas the clump-forming species are more polite members of the borders. These include *S. caesia, S. rigida, S. sphaculata,* and *S. virgaurea.*

PROPAGATING

Divide in spring (in autumn in Zones 7–9) or grow from seed. Plant may self-seed.

COMBINATIONS

Aster, Chrysanthemum, purple-leaved *Heuchera, Salvia.*

Sparaxis

TB* | Zn 9–10

Harlequin flower, Wandflower

p. 426

The perennials in this small genus from South Africa grow from corms. Plants have erect, narrow, lance-shaped leaves and spikes that bear shallow, trumpet-shaped flowers of red, orange, purple, pink, or white, often with yellow centers. Plants are 4"–24" tall. Mass them in the rock garden or under shrubs, or mix with other spring bulbs; they are also pretty in containers.

Type Tender bulb; often grown as an annual
Zone 9–10, H 10–7; grown as an annual in Zones 3–8
Flowering Season Mid-spring to late spring

SOWING

Indoors 8–10 weeks before planting out.
Outdoors *Seed:* Early spring or early autumn. *Corm:* Plant in spring for summer blooms in Zones 3–8. Plant in autumn for spring flowering in Zones 9–10.
Depth *Seed:* Just cover. *Corm:* 3".

GERMINATING

Time 30–90 days.
Requirements 50°–55°F.

TRANSPLANTING

Time *Zones 3–8:* After last frost. *Zones 9–10:* Early autumn.
Spacing 4".
Light Sun.
Soil Somewhat dry, neutral or alkaline. Place a little sand under each bulb at planting. *Sparaxis* spp. are suitable for xeriscaping.

CARING FOR PLANTS

Easy. Top-dress with well-rotted cow manure in spring, then water and feed regularly throughout the growing season. Plants may require staking. North of Zone 9, lift bulbs after the first frost in autumn and store in a cool, frost-free location until spring. *Sparaxis* is short lived in the Southeast.

PROPAGATING

Plant offset, or grow from seed. Plant may self-seed.

COMBINATIONS

Allium, Fritillaria, Thymus.

Sphaeralcea (syn. *Iliama*)

HP | Zn 4–10 | Full sun | Dry soil, Ordinary soil

False mallow, Globe mallow

p. 426

The branching annuals, perennials, and subshrubs of Sphaeralcea *range in height from 18" to 6'. They have lobed leaves and hollyhock-like flowers mainly in shades of red, purple, or orange growing in leaf axils. Use them in the border.*

Type Hardy perennial
Zone 4–9 (to Zone 10 in the West), H 12–8 (see species list, p. 473); prefers warm, dry climates
Flowering Season Summer, sometimes repeating in autumn

SOWING

Indoors Start seed outdoors only.
Outdoors In autumn, as soon as seed is ripe.
Depth ¼".

GERMINATING

Time 14–21 days.
Requirements Easy. 65°–70°F.

TRANSPLANTING

Time Set out purchased plants in spring or autumn.
Spacing *Small species:* 6"–9". *Medium species:* 12"–24". *Large species:* 30"–36".
Light Sun.
Soil Poor, sandy, with a pH level of 5.0–8.0.

CARING FOR PLANTS

Grows admirably in dry soil, but larger plants can be produced by watering regularly. Do not disturb.

PROPAGATING

Divide in autumn, take softwood cuttings in summer, or grow from seed. Plants may self-seed.

S

Spigelia

HP | Zn 5–9 | Full sun, Partial shade | Ordinary soil, Moist soil

Pink root, Worm grass

p. 426

Spigelia *species are North and South American wildflowers, one of which,* S. marilandica, *is grown in the garden. Upright stems are 2' tall with pairs of leaves spaced neatly along their length, ending in a little cluster of erect, bright red, narrow, tubular to funnel-shaped flowers with surprising yellow insides that become visible as the tips of petals reflex outward. Plants are very attractive to hummingbirds. These elegant and unusual plants are most effective when massed.*

Type Hardy perennial
Zone 5–9; tolerates heat and humidity.
Flowering Season Early summer, sometimes repeating in autumn

SOWING

Indoors Autumn.
Outdoors As soon as seed is ripe in summer.
Depth Just cover.

GERMINATING

Time 30–60 days.
Requirements Sow seed in containers, place in a plastic bag, and refrigerate for 3 weeks, then provide 65°–70°F.

TRANSPLANTING

Time After last frost.
Spacing 12".
Light Part shade where summers are hot, sun in cooler areas or where soil is very moist.
Soil Fertile, rich, moist, well drained, with a pH level of 6.1–6.5.

CARING FOR PLANTS

Easy. Keep soil moist and divide every few years.

PROPAGATING

Divide in spring or early autumn, take softwood cuttings, or grow from seed.

CAUTION

All parts of the plant are toxic if eaten.

Sprekelia

TB* | Zn 9–10 

p. 426

This genus contains a single species of Mexican bulb, S. formosissima. *Plants are grown for their exotic, deep red, orchidlike flowers. Leaves are narrow and lance-shaped. These low-growing plants (6"–12") can be massed in a sunny border or grown in containers.*

Type Tender bulb; often grown as an annual
Zone 9–10; grown as an annual in Zones 3–8
Flowering Season Late spring to early summer

SOWING

Indoors Early spring.
Outdoors *Seed:* Start indoors only. *Bulb:* 2–3 weeks after last frost in Zones 3–8; autumn in Zones 9–10.
Depth *Seed:* Just cover. *Bulb:* 4"–6".

GERMINATING

Time 21–120 days.
Requirements Rarely grown from seed and few details are available. Information given here should be used as a general guideline. Provide 65°–70°F. Grow in pots for 1 to 2 years before planting out.

TRANSPLANTING

Time 2–3 weeks after last frost in Zones 3–8, autumn in Zones 9–10.
Spacing 8"–12".
Light Full sun or part shade.
Soil Fertile, well drained.

CARING FOR PLANTS

Easy. Plants grown from seed will not bloom for 7–8 years. Water frequently and apply liquid fertilizer every 2 weeks during the growing season. North of Zone 9, lift bulbs before the first frost and store in vermiculite in a frost-free place over winter.

PROPAGATING

Dig bulbs after flowering, separate offsets, and replant.

S

Stachys (syn. *Betonica*)

TP, HP | Zn 3–10

Betony, Hedge nettle, Woundwort

p. 426

Stachys *is a large genus of mainly spreading perennials and subshrubs, some of which are grown for their fuzzy oblong silver leaves. Others are valued for their dense spikes of small purple, lipped and hooded flowers and crinkled, heart-shaped leaves; 6"–36" tall.* Stachys *species make useful ground covers, edgings, or border plants. Silver species brighten up a humdrum planting.*

Type Hardy perennial, tender perennial
Zone 3–10, H 8–1 (see species list, pp. 473 and 484); dislikes wet winters; *S. byzantina* and *S. coccinea* do not like hot, humid summers
Flowering Season Spring to summer

SOWING

Indoors 8–10 weeks before planting out.
Outdoors Early spring or early autumn.
Depth Just cover.

GERMINATING

Time 15–30 days.
Requirements 70°F.

TRANSPLANTING

Time *Hardy species:* Early spring, when soil is cool and a light frost still possible, or late autumn. *Tender species:* 2–3 weeks after last frost.
Spacing *Small species:* 8"–12". *Medium species:* 12"–18". *Large species:* 18"–24".
Light Full sun to part shade.
Soil Will tolerate dry conditions but performs best in rich, well-drained soil. *S. byzantina* is suitable for xeriscaping.

CARING FOR PLANTS

Easy. Remove flowers after blooming to keep plants looking neat; some people prefer to remove the stems of woolly-leaved species *before* flowering, as the blooms are rather unwieldy and inelegant. Divide every 3–4 years.

PROPAGATING

Divide in spring in the North (in autumn south of Zone 6) or grow from seed.

COMBINATIONS

A useful foil for many plants, especially for those with pink, blue or purple flowers: Purple-leaved *Berberis, Campanula, Delphinium, Dianthus, Perilla, Persicaria, Sedum, Thunbergia.*

Statice See *Limonium*

Stenanthium

HB | Zn 7–10 | Full sun, Partial shade | Moist soil

Plants in this genus of little-known bulbs feature narrow, grasslike leaves 12" long, and 2'–5' spikes bearing feathery panicles of tiny white to purple flowers. Use these North American wildflowers for naturalistic gardens and at edges of ponds.

Type Hardy bulb
Zone 7–10
Flowering Season Late summer

SOWING

Indoors Spring.
Outdoors *Seed:* Autumn. *Bulb:* Early spring.
Depth *Seed:* Just cover. *Bulb:* 3"–5".

GERMINATING

Requirements Seldom grown from seed, and little literature exists. Information given here can be used as a general guideline, but some experimentation may be necessary. *Outdoor sowing:* Sow seed in flats, sink in the ground against a north-facing wall, and cover with glass. Remove when germination begins. *Indoor sowing:* Provide a nighttime temperature of 55°F. Grow for 1 year before potting up, then for 2 years more before planting out.

TRANSPLANTING

Time After last frost.
Spacing 12"–24".
Light Sun or part shade.
Soil Moist, acid, and well drained.

CARING FOR PLANTS

Mulch in spring with compost and keep the soil fairly moist throughout the growing season. Do not disturb.

PROPAGATING

Divide in autumn or grow from seed.

Sternbergia

HB | Zn 6–10

Autumn daffodil

p. 426

Small, crocuslike bulbs with grassy foliage, Sternbergia *species bear sometimes fragrant, bright yellow or white flowers; 4"–8" tall. Use these plants in rock gardens or as an edging.*

Type Hardy bulb
Zone 6–10, H 9–6 (see species list, p. 473)
Flowering Season Spring or autumn, depending on species

SOWING

Indoors Start seed outdoors.
Outdoors *Seed:* Late summer. *Bulb:* Late summer through autumn.
Depth *Seed:* Just cover. *Bulb:* 4".

GERMINATING

Requirements Little data exists on growing this charming bulb from seed, as it is so easily increased by division. Information given here should be used as a general guideline for the adventurous. Seeds usually require 60°–65°F for germination.

TRANSPLANTING

Time Late summer, after one full growing season.
Spacing 4"–6".
Light Sun or light shade.
Soil Fertile, well drained; should be dry in summer when bulbs are resting.

CARING FOR PLANTS

Water regularly during the growing season, tapering off in summer. Allow leaves to wither naturally before removing. Leave plants undisturbed for 3–4 years after planting, then divide only rarely.

PROPAGATING

Dig clumps and separate offsets in autumn (in spring in Zone 6) or grow from seed.

COMBINATIONS

Colchicum, Thymus, Viola.

Stipa (syn. *Achnatherum*)

HP | Zn 5–10

S

Feather grass, Needle grass, Spear grass

p. 426

Ornamental perennial grasses, Stipa *are noticeable for their very showy, feathery flowers on thick, stiff stems of 1'–8'. Small species are grown in borders and mixed grass plantings; tall species make dramatic specimens.*

Type Hardy perennial
Zone 5–10, H 12–1 (see species list, pp. 474 and 484)
Flowering Season Summer

SOWING

Indoors 6–8 weeks before planting out.
Outdoors Early spring to mid-spring.
Depth 1/8".

GERMINATING

Time 21–30 days.
Requirements Easy. 70°F.

TRANSPLANTING

Time 2 weeks after last frost.
Spacing *Small species:* 12"–15". *Medium species:* 18"–24". *Large species:* 36"–48".
Light Full sun.
Soil Fertile, well drained. *Stipa* spp. are suitable for xeriscaping.

CARING FOR PLANTS

Easy. Young plants require plenty of water to become established. Cut back to ground level in early spring. To restrict spreading, divide or remove offsets from sides of clumps periodically.

PROPAGATING

Divide in spring or grow from seed.

COMBINATIONS

Dianthus, Eschscholzia, Leucanthemum, Salvia.

Stokesia

HP | Zn 5–10

Stokes' aster

p. 427

A perennial native to North America, Stokes' aster is grown for its showy, heavily fringed flowers of purple, blue, white, or pink. Use these 1'–2' tall plants near the front of the border.

Type Hardy perennial
Zone 5–10, H 9–5
Flowering Season Summer

SOWING

Indoors 8–10 weeks before planting out.
Outdoors Early spring or early autumn.
Depth Just cover.

GERMINATING

Time 20–30 days.
Requirements 70°F.

TRANSPLANTING

Time Early spring, when soil is cool and a light frost is still possible, or early autumn.
Spacing *Small species:* 10"–12". *Large species:* 18".
Light Full sun or part shade.
Soil Rich, very well drained. Will not survive where the ground is wet.

CARING FOR PLANTS

Easy. Cut back plants to the ground in autumn.

PROPAGATING

Divide in early spring or grow from seed.

COMBINATIONS

Achillea, Aster, Stachys.

Strobilanthes

TP*, HP | Zn 5–10

Mexican petunia

p. 427

Of the genus, Strobilanthes dyerianus *is the only species usually seen in gardens. Its showy, deep purple leaves have a dusky pink sheen. Where perennial, it is 4' tall; it is dramatic in containers at 18". An underused hardy species,* S. atrapurpureus, *has green leaves and tall spikes of tubular violet or blue flowers.*

Type Hardy perennial or tender perennial, often grown as an annual
Zone 5–10, H 9–5 (see species list, pp. 474 and 484); grow tender species as an annual in cooler zones; very tolerant of heat and humidity
Flowering Season Late summer to autumn; plants usually don't bloom until their second year

SOWING

Starting from seed recommended only for hardy species.
Indoors 6–8 weeks before last frost.
Outdoors Spring.
Depth Just cover.

GERMINATING

Requirements Easy. Provide 55°–70°F. Pinch out seedlings once to encourage branching.

TRANSPLANTING

Time Spring, when temperature will remain above 45°F.
Spacing 18"–24".
Light Full sun in cool climates only, with afternoon shade required wherever summers are hot.
Soil Fertile, moist, and well drained.

CARING FOR PLANTS

Easy and trouble-free. Pinch out stem tips on young plants to encourage a bushy habit, and water during dry spells. To overwinter plants indoors, pot up in autumn and bring in to a bright, warm (60°–65°F) location, watering regularly. Prune plants as necessary in spring. Overwintered plants may become woody and foliage may deteriorate, in which case take cuttings and discard the parent plant.

PROPAGATING

Easily started from cuttings taken in spring or early summer, or divide plants in spring. Less frequently, perennials are grown from seed.

COMBINATIONS

Helichrysum, Petunia, Plectranthus, annual *Rudbeckia hirta, Scaevola.*

Stylophorum

HP | Zn 5–8

p. 427

Stylophorum *are woodland plants native to North America and eastern Asia. The most commonly grown,* S. diphyllum, *bears deeply divided leaves and pretty poppylike flowers of yellow or orange. These 18"–24" plants are lovely in a woodland garden.*

Type Hardy perennial
Zone 5–8
Flowering Season Spring to midsummer

SOWING

Indoors Autumn.
Outdoors Spring or autumn.
Depth Just cover.

GERMINATING

Time 20–25 days
Requirements 41°–59°F.

TRANSPLANTING

Time After last frost.
Spacing 12"–18".
Light Part to full shade; flowers are scorched by hot sun.
Soil Average to rich and moist, although established plants are more drought tolerant.

CARING FOR PLANTS

Easy when their cultural requirements are met. Mulch in spring and water during dry spells. Slugs and snails may be a problem.

PROPAGATING

Carefully divide in spring or grow from seed. *S. diphyllum* self-seeds readily and may become a nuisance.

COMBINATIONS

Ferns, *Mertensia, Podophyllum.*

Sutera See *Bacopa*

Symphyandra

HP | Zn 6–9

Ring bellflower

The short-lived perennials in this genus greatly resemble Campanula *species, to which they're closely related. The 1'–2' tall plants have a rather coarse, unkempt appearance, but in bloom they are charming, covered with blue or white tubular bells. They make a very pretty addition to the border.*

Type Short-lived hardy perennial; usually grown as biennial
Zone 6–8, or to Zone 9 in the west; H 9–6; will not tolerate humid heat
Flowering Season Early summer

SOWING

Indoors 5–6 weeks before planting out.
Outdoors Autumn.
Depth Surface.

GERMINATING

Time 10–30 days.
Requirements Easy. Requires light and 60°–70°F.

TRANSPLANTING

Time After last frost, or late summer to autumn.
Spacing 12"–18".
Light Sun, with afternoon shade where summers are hot.
Soil Well drained.

CARING FOR PLANTS

Easy. Plants are short lived. Deadhead frequently to prolong their lives, leaving some seed heads to reproduce. Cut back to ground level after flowering.

PROPAGATING

Grow from seed only. Plants self-seed readily, but not to the point of being a nuisance.

COMBINATIONS

Corydalis, Geranium, Viola.

Symphytum

HP | Zn 3–9

Comfrey

p. 427

Of this small genus of rather coarse perennials, the more attractive species are grown for their handsome variegated foliage and clusters of small, nodding blue, pink, purple, yellow, or white bell-shaped flowers; 1'–4' tall. They are often grown in the wildflower garden but are also useful in borders and in front of dark green shrubs.

Type Hardy perennial
Zone 3–9, H 9–1 (see species list, p. 474)
Flowering Season Late spring through autumn, dependiing on species

SOWING

Growing from seed is not recommended.
Depth *Roots:* 3"–6".

TRANSPLANTING

Time Set out purchased plants in autumn or early spring.
Spacing Allow this giant herb plenty of room, at least 36"–48".
Light Prefers full sun but will grow quite well and remain considerably smaller in shade.
Soil Moist, rich, with a pH level of 6.5–7.5.

CARING FOR PLANTS

Easy, requiring little attention. Water regularly and remove dead leaves in autumn. Divide occasionally to alleviate crowding. Allow plants to grow for 3 years before harvesting leaves, then cut leaves that are 12"–18" tall just before flowering. Cut off flowering stems before blooming to stimulate further foliar production.

PROPAGATING

Divide or take root cuttings in spring or autumn.

COMBINATIONS

Calendula, Lobelia erinus, Lunaria, Myosotis, woodland *Phlox, Scilla.*

CAUTION

Very aggressive and difficult to eradicate once established due to its long taproot. Leaves can be harmful if eaten.

Synthyris

HP | Zn 2–9

Native to Europe and the western United States, these low-growing, spreading perennials are grown in rock gardens. The 3"–12" spikes bear small blue, purple, pink, or white flowers. Heart-shaped leaves have pinked edges.

Type Hardy perennial
Zone 2–9, H 7–9 (see species list, p. 474); at home on the Pacific Coast and will not thrive in hot, dry locations
Flowering Season Early to mid spring, sometimes repeating in autumn

SOWING

Propagate plants by division only.

TRANSPLANTING

Time Set out purchased plants in spring or autumn.
Spacing 4"–6".
Light Part to full shade; shade from the hot afternoon sun is essential.
Soil Rich, gritty, acid, moist or even wet; amend with organic matter.

CARING FOR PLANTS

Difficult. Keep soil moist at all times.

PROPAGATING

Divide after blooming in spring.

S

Tagetes

A | Zn 1–10

Marigold

p. 427

These hardworking, popular annuals of upright habit are grown for their abundant yellow, orange, or rusty red flowers borne singly on sturdy stems. Neat, attractive foliage is bushy and finely toothed; plants are 6"–36" tall. They are suited to containers, edging, borders, or display beds.

Type Annual
Zone 1–10, H 12–1; flowers best in warm climates
Flowering Season Summer through frost

SOWING

Indoors 6–8 weeks before last frost.
Outdoors 2 weeks before last frost.
Depth Just cover.

GERMINATING

Time 4–14 days.
Requirements Easy. 70°–75°F. Seedlings are somewhat susceptible to damping-off; sow in vermiculite, and water only from below as a precaution.

TRANSPLANTING

Time After last frost.
Spacing *Dwarf species:* 6". *Medium species:* 12"–15". *Large species:* 18"–24".
Light Full sun, with afternoon shade where summers are very hot.
Soil Prefers good soil with a pH level of 6.0–7.0, enriched with organic matter, but will tolerate quite dry soil.

CARING FOR PLANTS

Easy. Feed during the early growth period and water regularly. Pinch back tall species once or twice when young to encourage bushy growth, and give plants a more stable framework, avoiding that trampled look in midsummer. If slugs devour young seedlings, replace with more mature plants, which are more resilient. Deadhead to prolong blooming.

PROPAGATING

Grow from seed.

COMBINATIONS

Bassia, Gaillardia, Nasturtium, Salvia, Zinnia.

Talinum

TP*, HP | Zn 5–10

Fameflower

Most of these perennials are low, rosette- or mat-forming succulent plants. Stems of 2"–30" bear five-petaled, cup-shaped flowers in bright pink, violet, or white, with showy yellow anthers. Their foliage is handsome, often blue-green. An attractive plant for a rock garden or dry stone wall.

Type Tender perennial or hardy perennial; often grown as an annual
Zone 5–10, H 8–6 (see species list, p. 474); grow tender species as annuals in cooler zones; does not like high humidity
Flowering Season Spring to autumn, depending on species

SOWING

Indoors 6 weeks before last frost.
Outdoors Autumn.
Depth Surface.

GERMINATING

Time 21–30 days.
Requirements Requires light and 60°–70°F. If seed has not germinated in 4 weeks, give a cold treatment (25°–40°F.) for 4 weeks and return to 60°–70°F.

TRANSPLANTING

Time After last frost.
Spacing 8"–12".
Light Full sun.
Soil Dry, rocky, or sandy, with good drainage; very drought tolerant.

CARING FOR PLANTS

Easy. Allow soil to dry out between waterings. Deadhead to prevent rampant self-seeding.

PROPAGATING

Divide rosette-forming species in spring or grow from seed. Self-seeds freely and may become invasive.

COMBINATIONS

Campanula carpatica, Phyteuma, Portulaca.

Tanacetum (syn. *Balsamita, Pyrethrum*)

A, HP | Zn 3–10

p. 427

A large genus of perennial plants, many of which have finely cut, silvery, or aromatic leaves and white, yellow, pink, or red daisylike flowers. Heights range from 8" to 4'. At times, many members of the genus have been classified as Achillea, Chrysanthemum, *or* Pyrethrum *and are similarly useful in the summer border.*

Type Hardy perennial; the short-lived species are often grown as annuals or biennials
Zone 3–10 H 9–1 (see species list p. 474); prefer cool climates and will burn out quickly where summers are hot
Flowering Season Most bloom in summer; some flower in late spring or autumn

SOWING

Indoors 6–8 weeks before planting out.
Outdoors Early spring (before last frost) or late autumn.
Depth Surface.

GERMINATING

Time 7–30 days.
Requirements Light required for germination. Pre-chill seed for 2–4 weeks, then provide 60°–85°F.

TRANSPLANTING

Time After last frost or autumn.
Spacing *Small species:* 10"–12". *Medium species:* 12"–18". *Large species:* 18"–24".
Light Sun, with afternoon shade where summers are hot.
Soil Neutral to slightly acid, well drained, on the dry side. Good winter drainage is essential. *T. parthenium* prefers moist soil; *T. vulgare* tolerates dry.

CARING FOR PLANTS

Easy. Feed and divide regularly to produce stronger plants. Water during dry periods. Cut back hard immediately after flowering to encourage a second bloom, and to restrict self-seeding if this is not desired. Most are short lived, although self-seeding will keep colonies alive; may be invasive. Can be troubled by spider mites, aphids, leaf miners, or chrysanthemum nematodes.

PROPAGATING

Divide in spring, take basal cuttings in early summer, or grow from seed. Plants grown from seed will bloom in their first year.

COMBINATIONS

Achillea, Ageratum, Limonium, Lupinus, Pennisetum.

Tecophilaea

HB | Zn 7–9

This small genus of diminutive tender perennials that grow from corms is native to Chile. Flowers are funnel-shaped and blue, sometimes with a white throat. Leaves are sparse, erect, and lance-shaped. At 3"–6" tall, they are good rock garden plants.

Type Hardy bulb
Zone 7–9, H 9–7
Flowering Season Early spring

SOWING

Indoors Sow seed outdoors only.
Outdoors *Seed:* Autumn. *Corm:* Late summer through autumn.
Depth *Seed:* Just cover. *Corm:* 3"–5".

GERMINATING

Time 30–365 days.
Requirements Difficult. Sow seed in individual pots, sink these in the ground outdoors in a sheltered position, and cover with glass. Remove glass when germination begins. Do not move seedlings for 2–3 years.

TRANSPLANTING

Time Late summer through autumn.
Spacing 4"–6".
Light Full sun.
Soil Dry, sandy, acid to neutral.

CARING FOR PLANTS

Feed lightly in late winter. Water lightly if necessary in winter and spring, keeping corms on the dry side from early summer through autumn; these plants do not like heavy winter rain. Apply mulch in winter, removing it completely as soon as sprouting begins in spring.

PROPAGATING

Plant offsets in autumn or grow from seed.

T

Tellima

HP | Zn 3–9 

Fringe cups

p. 427

A single unusual perennial native to western North America belongs to this genus. T. grandiflora *plants bear tall, delicate spikes of loosely scattered, bell-shaped white flowers, which turn to pink. The heart-shaped leaves may be green or bronze; 2' tall. Good plants for the wildflower or woodland garden.*

Type Hardy perennial
Zone 3–9, H 8–1
Flowering Season Late spring to early summer

SOWING

Indoors See Germinating, Requirements.
Outdoors See Germinating, Requirements.
Depth Surface.

GERMINATING

Time 30–90 days.
Requirements Always use fresh seed. *Autumn sowing:* Sow seed in flats, sink in the ground against a north-facing wall, and cover with glass. Moisten soil occasionally, if necessary. Bring flats indoors in spring to 55°–60°F. *Spring sowing:* Sow seed in flats, place flats in plastic bags, and refrigerate. After 2–3 weeks, remove and sink in the ground in a shady location. Cover with glass, removing when seeds sprout.

TRANSPLANTING

Time Autumn.
Spacing 18"–24".
Light Part to full shade.
Soil Cool, moist, rich, well drained.

CARING FOR PLANTS

Easy. Mulch in spring and autumn; water during dry spells. *Tellima* spreads rapidly when happy.

PROPAGATING

Divide in spring in Zones 3–6 (in early autumn in Zones 7–9) or grow from seed.

COMBINATIONS

Anemone, ferns, *Hosta, Polygonatum.*

Teucrium

HP | Zn 3–9  

Germander, Wood sage

p. 428

The plants in this large genus of bushy, branched perennials, shrubs, and subshrubs have small but showy flowers in whorled clusters or racemes, colored blue, purple, pink, or yellow. They range in height from 4" to 3'. Use them in rock and wildflower gardens, walls, or borders.

Type Hardy perennial
Zone 3–9, H 9–5 (see species list, p. 474); very tolerant of extreme heat
Flowering Season Summer

SOWING

Indoors 6–8 weeks before last frost.
Outdoors Early spring, when soil is cool and a light frost is still possible, or late autumn.
Depth Surface.

GERMINATING

Time 25–30 days.
Requirements 70°F.

TRANSPLANTING

Time After last frost.
Spacing 12".
Light Full sun or part shade.
Soil Prefers ordinary, well-drained soil but will do quite well even in poor. *T. chamaedrys* is suitable for xeriscaping.

CARING FOR PLANTS

Easy. Fertilize periodically and water during dry spells. Cut back stems by up to one-half in spring to maintain size, shape, and vigor.

PROPAGATING

Take cuttings, divide in spring, or grow from seed.

COMBINATIONS

Berberis atropurpurea, Lavandula, Santolina.

Thalictrum

HP | Zn 3–9

Meadow rue

p. 428

Perennials with attractive lobed or toothed foliage have erect stalks crowned with fluffy heads of purple, yellow, white, or pink flowers; 1′–7′ tall. Grow at the edge of the woodland or near water, in the rock garden, or in the border, where its fine foliage will contrast with large-leaved plants.

Type Hardy perennial
Zone 3–9, H 9–1 (see species list, p. 474); not tolerant of extreme heat and humidity
Flowering Season Summer

SOWING

Indoors Seed should be started outdoors.
Outdoors As soon as seed is ripe, in autumn.
Depth 1/8″.

GERMINATING

Time 15–50 days, or up to 2 years.
Requirements Sow seed in flats, sink in the ground against a north-facing wall, and cover with glass. Moisten soil occasionally, if necessary.

TRANSPLANTING

Time Autumn.
Spacing *Small species:* 6″–8″. *Medium species:* 12″–18″. *Large species:* 24″–36″.
Light Full sun in cool climates; part shade where summers are hot.
Soil Moist, especially where plants are grown in full sun; a pH level of 5.0–6.0 is preferred.

CARING FOR PLANTS

Easy. Feed once in spring with a weak solution—excessive fertilizing will result in weak growth. Mulch in spring and water well during dry spells. Cut back plants to the ground in late autumn. Very tall species require staking. *Thalictrum* species are short lived in hot climates.

PROPAGATING

Divide in early spring or grow from seed.

COMBINATIONS

Cimicifuga, Hosta, Valerian.

CAUTION

Harmful if eaten.

Thelesperma (syn. *Cosmidium*)

A | Zn 3–10

Greenthreads

Eye-catching coreopsis-like plant with sun-ray flowers of deep mahogany with an orange-yellow edge borne on 18–30″ stems. Easy and cheerful in containers or massed in borders.

Type Annual
Zone 3–10
Flowering Season All summer

SOWING

Indoors 6–8 weeks before last frost.
Outdoors After last frost.
Depth Surface.

GERMINATING

Time 7–14 days.
Requirements Light and 60°–70°F.

TRANSPLANTING

Time After last frost.
Spacing 9″–12″.
Light Full sun.
Soil Any that is well drained.

CARING FOR PLANTS

Easy; requires little care.

PROPAGATING

Grow from seed. Plants grown from seed will bloom in 3 months.

COMBINATIONS

Amaranthus, Hemerocallis, Salvia.

Thelypteris

TP, HP | Zn 2–10

Maiden fern

p. 428

A huge genus of nearly 500 deciduous ferns, most Thelypteris *are 1'–4' tall and relatively undistinguished. Deeply toothed fronds tend to arch gracefully and are attractive, but the rampant growth of many species make them really useful only for ground cover, in combination with other plants that can hold their own against them.*

Type Tender perennial, hardy perennial
Zone 2–10, H 8–3 (see species list, p. 484)
Flowering Season N/A

SOWING

Indoors When spores are ripe, in July to September.
Outdoors Not recommended.
Depth Surface.

GERMINATING

Time 10–365 days.
Requirements Difficult. Requires 60°–75°F. (See pp. 24–25 for instructions on starting plants from spores.)

TRANSPLANTING

Time In spring, after 2 years' growth.
Spacing 12".
Light Full sun to full shade.
Soil Neutral to acid; most will grow happily in soil that's either dry or moist. *T. palustris* tolerates wet soil.

CARING FOR PLANTS

Easy, although keeping plants in bounds may require regular attention. Remove faded fronds periodically to improve appearance. Divide plants when clumps become overgrown. May be troubled by rust, scale, or leaf curl.

PROPAGATING

Divide in spring or summer or grow from spores.

COMBINATIONS

Asarum, Aster novae-angliae, Eupatorium, Gunnera, Hosta, Iris, Ligularia, Primula, Rheum.

Thermopsis

HP | Zn 3–9

These handsome perennials of 1'–5' have a relatively short bloom season. They display strongly horizontal leaves and stalks of bright yellow, pealike flowers. The North American native species are most popular. Use them in the shrub or flower border.

Type Hardy perennial
Zone 3–9, H 9–2 (see species list, p. 474); tolerant of heat and humidity
Flowering Season Late spring to summer

SOWING

Indoors 6–8 weeks before last frost, in peat pots.
Outdoors Early spring, when soil is cool and a light frost is still possible, or late autumn.
Depth Just cover.

GERMINATING

Time 15–30 days.
Requirements Chip seed and soak in warm water for 24 hours. Provide 70°F thereafter.

TRANSPLANTING

Time After last frost.
Spacing 18"–24".
Light Full sun; light shade in hot climates.
Soil Prefers well-drained, gritty soil, with a pH level of 5.5–7.0, but will grow almost anywhere.

CARING FOR PLANTS

Easy. A long taproot makes these plants highly drought tolerant but very difficult to move. Staking may be necessary. Removing flower stalks after blooming may prompt a second bloom. Cut plants to ground in late autumn.

PROPAGATING

Divide in spring, being very careful when digging taproot, or grow from seed.

COMBINATIONS

Campanula, Geranium, Veronica.

Thunbergia

A, TP* | Zn 5–10

Thunbergia

p. 428

These climbing plants have attractive foliage. Some are flat, with white, orange, or yellow flowers, sometimes with black centers; others are palest blue or yellow and trumpet-shaped. Grow against a trellis, in baskets, or in pots, or allow them to spill gracefully over a wall.

Type Annual or tender perennial; usually grown as an annual
Zone *Perennial:* 9–10, H 12–6 (see species list, pp. 474–475); grown as an annual in Zones 5–10; most prefer mild summers
Flowering Season Summer to autumn

SOWING

Indoors 6–8 weeks before planting out, in peat pots.
Outdoors Only where winters are very mild, in early spring or late autumn.
Depth Just cover.

GERMINATING

Time 10–21 days.
Requirements 65°–75°F.

TRANSPLANTING

Time When night temperatures remain above 50°F.
Spacing 12"–18".
Light Full sun or light shade.
Soil Moist, fertile, with alot of organic matter added.

CARING FOR PLANTS

Water well throughout the growth period; prune to keep compact. Pot up vines to grow indoors over winter, then plant out after last spring frost. Plants wintered over are much stronger in the second year.

PROPAGATING

Take cuttings in spring or summer; grow from seed.

CAUTION

T. grandiflora is invasive in Florida and Hawaii and possibly in other warm regions. See pp. 494–495.

Thymus

HP | Zn 4–9

Thyme

p. 428

Ground-hugging, strongly aromatic, and evergreen, thyme has neat, tiny leaves and small pink, purple, or white flowers. Grow around paving, dry stone walls, rock gardens, or at the front of borders. They are grown both for culinary stores and for their attractive foliage.

Type Hardy perennial
Zone 4–9, H 9–1 (see species list, p. 475)
Flowering Season Late spring to summer

SOWING

Indoors 6–8 weeks before last frost.
Outdoors 2–3 weeks before last frost, or late autumn.
Depth Surface.

GERMINATING

Time 15–30 days.
Requirements Light and 55°–65°F.

TRANSPLANTING

Time After last frost.
Spacing 8"–12".
Light Sun to part shade.
Soil Prefers light, well drained, dry. *T. serpyllum* is suitable for xeriscaping.

CARING FOR PLANTS

Easy. Cut back by half after bloom for tidiness and strong flavor. Renew every 3–4 years as plants decline. Pick fresh leaves for cooking any time. To dry, cut stems just before flowering and hang upside down in a dark place until completely dry. Strip leaves from stems; store airtight. *Indoors:* Pot plants in late summer using a sandy soil mix. Provide 5 hours minimum sunlight daily; allow soil to dry slightly between waterings.

PROPAGATING

Divide in spring, take cuttings after flowering, or grow from seed.

COMBINATIONS

Use with *Pulsatilla, Sempervivum, or* low-growing *Allium, Aster,* or *Gentiana.*

Tiarella

HP | Zn 3–8

False mitrewort, Foam flower, Sugar scoop

p. 428

Charming little woodland plants, some of which are evergreen in milder climates (roughly south of Zone 6), Tiarella species have dainty spikes of feathery white or pale pink flowers and roughly heart-shaped leaves that form a neat clump. Foliage turns red in autumn and also may be deeply cut and/or marked with maroon. These North American and east Asian natives grow 4"–24" tall and are used in the woodland, wildflower, or rock garden.

Type Hardy perennial
Zone 3–8, H 9–1 (see species list, p. 475)
Flowering Season Mid spring to early summer, depending on species

SOWING

Indoors See Germinating, Requirements.
Outdoors See Germinating, Requirements.
Depth Surface.

GERMINATING

Time 14–90 days.
Requirements *Autumn sowing:* Sow seed in flats, sink these to the rim outdoors against a north-facing wall, and cover with glass. Moisten soil occasionally, if necessary. Bring indoors in spring to 50°F and transplant to the garden after the last spring frost. *Spring sowing:* Sow seed in moistened medium, place in a plastic bag, and refrigerate. After 2–3 weeks, sink containers in the ground in a shady location, covering with glass. Remove glass when seeds sprout. Transplant seedlings to the garden in autumn.

TRANSPLANTING

Time Spring or autumn.
Spacing *Small species:* 6"–8". *Medium species:* 12". *Large species:* 18"–24".
Light Part to full shade.
Soil Prefers cool, rich, moist, well drained, with a pH level of 5.0–6.0, although most will perform surprisingly well in dry soil.

CARING FOR PLANTS

Mulch to keep soil cool and moist, and water often during dry spells. Do not disturb plants.

PROPAGATING

Divide in early spring (in autumn in Zones 7–8) or grow from seed.

COMBINATIONS

Carex, Corydalis, Hosta, woodland *Phlox, Polemonium, Tanacetum.*

Tithonia

A | Zn 3–10

Mexican sunflower

p. 428

Of this genus of annuals, perennials, and shrubs native to Central America, one species, T. rotundifolia, *an annual, is grown for its bright orange, yellow, or red sunflower-like blooms; 2'–6' tall. Grow it in the border.*

Type Annual
Zone 3–10, H 12–1; thrives in warm temperatures
Flowering Season Late summer to autumn

SOWING

Indoors 6–8 weeks before last frost.
Outdoors After last frost, only where winters are mild.
Depth Surface.

GERMINATING

Time 5–14 days.
Requirements 70°F.

TRANSPLANTING

Time After last frost.
Spacing 24".
Light Full sun.
Soil Any light soil; quite drought tolerant.

CARING FOR PLANTS

Easy. Stake plants, and water only during prolonged dry spells.

PROPAGATING

Grow from seed only.

COMBINATIONS

Crocosmia, Dahlia, Rudbeckia, Tagetes.

Torenia

TP* | Zn 3–10

Wishbone flower

p. 428

Torenia *species are grown for their showy, long-blooming, multicolored tubular flowers, which may be any combination of purple, blue, yellow, pink, and white. At 12" tall, they are useful at the front of the border or in containers or hanging baskets.*

Type Tender perennial; often grown as an annual
Zone 9–10, H 6–1; grown as an annual in Zones 3–10; flower most profusely in warm weather
Flowering Season Summer to early autumn.

SOWING

Indoors 6–8 weeks before planting out.
Outdoors 1 week after last frost.
Depth Surface.

GERMINATING

Time 7–30 days.
Requirements Light and 70°–75°F.

TRANSPLANTING

Time 2 weeks after last frost.
Spacing 6"–8".
Light Full sun only where summers are cool. For more intense flower color, give plants afternoon shade.
Soil Moist, rich, well drained, with plenty of organic matter added.

CARING FOR PLANTS

Easy. Pinch back shoots when plants are 3" tall to establish a bushier habit. Water regularly. *Torenia* can be potted up and brought inside for winter blooming.

PROPAGATING

Take cuttings or grow from seed. Self-seeds in very warm climates.

COMBINATIONS

Begonia, Impatiens, Lobelia, Pelargonium.

Tovara See *Persicaria*

Townsendia

HP | Zn 4–8

p. 429

This small genus of very low-growing rock garden perennials includes plants with sparse, narrow leaves and asterlike flowers of pink, purple, or white, sometimes with yellow centers; 4"–8"– tall. They are native to western North America.

Type Short-lived hardy perennial
Zone 4–8, H 7–1 (see species list, p. 475)
Flowering Season Spring to summer

SOWING

Indoors See Germinating, Requirements.
Outdoors See Germinating, Requirements.
Depth Just cover.

GERMINATING

Time 30–90 days.
Requirements *Autumn sowing:* Sow seed in flats, sink these in the ground against a north-facing wall, and cover with glass. Moisten occasionally, if necessary. Bring flats indoors in spring to 60°F. *Spring sowing:* Sow seed in containers, secure in plastic bags, and refrigerate for 2–3 weeks. Sink containers in the ground in a shady location, covering with glass. Remove glass when seeds sprout. Transplant seedlings to the garden when they are large enough to handle.

TRANSPLANTING

Time Spring or autumn.
Spacing 4"–6".
Light Full sun.
Soil Moist, gritty, well drained, especially in winter.

CARING FOR PLANTS

Townsendia species will not tolerate winter wetness; surround plants with fine gravel to ensure rapid drainage. Do not disturb once established. Plants are short lived.

PROPAGATING

Grow from seed only.

T

Trachelium (syn. *Diosphaera*)

TP*, HP* | Zn 3–10

Throatwort

p. 429

A small group of perennials native to the Mediterranean, Trachelium *members are either mat-forming and covered in pale blue pinwheel-shaped flowers or upright, 2′–3′ tall, and bearing heads of tiny, fluffy blue flowers. Use them in rock gardens, borders, and cutting beds.*

Type Hardy perennial, tender perennial; often treated as an annual
Zone *Perennial:* 5–10, H 12–1; tender perennials grown as annuals in Zones 3–7, H 10–1; (see species list, p. 475). *T. caeruleum;* prefers warm weather and dry winters.
Flowering Season Summer

SOWING

Indoors 8–10 weeks before planting out.
Outdoors Start seed outdoors in Zones 9–10 only, in midwinter.
Depth Surface.

GERMINATING

Time 15–21 days.
Requirements Easy. Light and 55°–60°F.

TRANSPLANTING

Time *Zones 9–10:* Early spring or early autumn. *North of Zone 9:* After last frost.
Spacing 12″
Light Full sun to part shade.
Soil Fertile, slightly alkaline, fairly moist, but very well drained.

CARING FOR PLANTS

Easy. Water during dry spells and protect from overhead water in winter.

PROPAGATING

Take cuttings in spring or grow from seed.

COMBINATIONS

Anchusa, Consolida, Globularia, Iris cristata, Pratia, Sisyrinchium.

Trachymene (syn. *Didiscus*)

A | Zn 3–8

Laceflower

p. 429

An upright, branching plant, Trachymene *is native to Australia and the western Pacific. It bears globes of tiny purple flowers on thick, erect stems and closely resembles* Allium. *Use this 6″–24″ tall plant in borders and cutting beds.*

Type Annual
Zone 3–8, H 12–6; prefers cool climates and may not bloom during very hot spells
Flowering Season Summer and autumn

SOWING

Indoors 8–10 weeks before last frost, in peat pots.
Outdoors After last frost.
Depth Just cover.

GERMINATING

Time 15–30 days.
Requirements 70°F and darkness.

TRANSPLANTING

Time After the last spring frost.
Spacing 8″–10″.
Light Full sun, with afternoon shade where summers are hot.
Soil Average, supplemented with organic matter. Happiest in slightly moist soil but will tolerate dry conditions.

CARING FOR PLANTS

Easy. Water only moderately. Pinch tips of young plants to encourage bushiness, and support lanky growth with twiggy branches pushed into the soil. Plants will have more blooms when slightly crowded.

PROPAGATING

Grow from seed only.

Tradescantia

TP, HP | Zn 4–10

Spider-lily, Spiderwort

p. 429

A large genus of perennial plants native to the Americas, some Tradescantia *are grown for their foliage, which may be variegated or an unusual plum color, others are prized for their flat, three-petaled flowers of purple, white, red, or blue, despite a disgracefully messy habit. Low, spreading species (12") make showy ground covers and container plants; upright species (up to 36") are useful in the woodland or naturalistic garden.*

Type Hardy perennial, tender perennial
Zone 4–10, H 12–1 (see species list, p. 475)
Flowering Season Summer, with some repeat blooming in late summer or autumn

SOWING

Indoors 6–8 weeks before planting out.
Outdoors Early spring, when soil is cool and a light frost is still possible, or late autumn.
Depth Just cover.

GERMINATING

Time 10–40 days.
Requirements 70°F. Propagation of tender, trailing species such as *T. fluminesis* and *T. pallida* is most often by cuttings due to the ease and success of this method.

TRANSPLANTING

Time After last frost; move tender species after temperatures remain above 50°F.
Spacing 12"–18".
Light Full sun where summers are cool or soil is moist; does better in part to full shade elsewhere.
Soil Prefers rich, moist, well-drained soil with a pH level of 5.0–6.0, but will tolerate any; to curtail spreading of invasive species, plant in poor soil.

CARING FOR PLANTS

Easy, hardy, and trouble-free. Water regularly where spreading of plants is desirable. Bedraggled plants become an eyesore after blooming; cutting back hard takes care of this problem and stimulates a second bloom in late summer. Divide every 3 years to maintain vigor. Take cuttings of tender species in late summer or early fall to overwinter indoors.

PROPAGATING

Divide in spring in the North (in autumn south of Zone 7) or grow from seed. Plants self-seed, but cultivars will not come true.

COMBINATIONS

Bergenia, ferns, *Heuchera, Hosta, Ligularia.*

CAUTION

T. fluminensis and *T. spathacea* are invasive in some areas, including Florida. See pp. 494–495 for advice.

Tricholaena

TP* | Zn 5–10

This ornamental grass from South Africa is grown for its silky, ruby-colored flowers. Leaves are flat and thin, 8" long.

Type Tender perennial; often grown as an annual
Zone 9–10; grown as an annual in Zones 5–9
Flowering Season Late spring to summer; longer in mild climates

SOWING

Indoors 6–8 weeks before planting out.
Outdoors Very early spring.
Depth Just cover.

GERMINATING

Time 21 days.
Requirements 50°–55°F.

TRANSPLANTING

Time After last frost.
Spacing 12"–18".
Light Full sun.
Soil Will grow in most soils but prefers a soil that is light and well drained.

CARING FOR PLANTS

Easy. Shelter from wind and rain, both of which can easily flatten plants. Keep soil moist. Cut back in autumn, as plants have little winter interest. Flowers are attractive in arrangements but will not keep their color when dried.

PROPAGATING

Grow from seed; division is possible but difficult.

Trichosanthes

A | Zn 3–10 | 

 p. 429

T. cucumeria *is the most commonly grown species of these annual vines. Long, broad leaves, fringed white flowers, and serpentine, 2' long fruits are characteristic of the genus. Vines reach 10'–15'. Grow these as a curiosity on a trellis or arbor.*

Type Annual
Zone 3–10
Flowering Season Late summer to autumn

SOWING

Indoors 6–8 weeks before planting out, in peat pots.
Outdoors After temperature has reached 70°F.
Depth 1".

GERMINATING

Time 14–30 days.
Requirements 65°–75°F.

TRANSPLANTING

Time In spring when temperatures remain above 60°F.
Spacing 48" or singly.
Light Sun, with shade from the afternoon sun where summers are hot.
Soil Moist, humus-rich.

CARING FOR PLANTS

Water frequently during the growing season, tapering off when growth stops. Vines require a trellis or other support.

PROPAGATING

Grow from seed only.

Tricyrtis

HP | Zn 5–9

Toad lily

p. 429

The East Asian perennials in this small genus are grown for their pink, red, purple, yellow, or white, usually freckled blossoms, which appear in summer and autumn. In full bloom, the upturned, bell-shaped flowers of some species look as though they've stood in unison, thrown their hands in the air, and yelled, "Surprise!" Others have the graceful look of a spray of orchids. Plants are 12"–48" tall. Mass along the border's edge.

Type Hardy perennial
Zone 5–9 , H 9–1 (see species list, p. 475)
Flowering Season Midsummer to mid autumn

SOWING

Indoors Begin cold treatment 12–14 weeks before last frost, in peat pots.
Outdoors Early spring, when soil is cool and a light frost is still possible, or late autumn.
Depth 1/8".

GERMINATING

Time 30–90 days.
Requirements Difficult. Sow seed in peat pots, cover, and refrigerate for 6–8 weeks. Provide 65°–70°F thereafter.

TRANSPLANTING

Time After last frost.
Spacing *Small species:* 4"–6". *Large species:* 18"–24".
Light Part shade; full sun where the growing season is short.
Soil Moist, rich, peaty, and slightly acid.

CARING FOR PLANTS

Easy. Mulch in spring and water regularly during hot, dry spells. Leaves may be attractive to slugs.

PROPAGATING

Divide in spring or grow from seed.

COMBINATIONS

Chelone, ferns, *Hosta*, *Pulmonaria*.

Trifolium

A, HP | Zn 3–9 | Full sun, Partial shade | Dry soil, Ordinary soil, Moist soil

Clover, Trefoil

p. 429

This is the clover you know from your lawn, after it's gone to charm school. All have the familiar three- or four-leaved palmate foliage and fluffy flower heads, but they're dressed up now: T. rubens *is 18" tall with elongated flowers of a pretty, dusky pink; the leaves of* T. repens *'Purpurascens' are splashed with chocolate. Use in rock gardens, away from the lawn.*

Type Annual, hardy perennial
Zone 3–9
Flowering Season Summer

SOWING

Remember that the more desirable cultivars will not come true from seed.
Indoors *Annual:* March–April. *Perennial:* February–May.
Outdoors *Annual:* Spring. *Perennial:* Autumn.
Depth *Annual:* Surface. *Perennial:* ¼".

GERMINATING

Time 7–30 days.
Requirements *Annual:* Light and 60°–70°F. *Perennial:* Soak seed for 24 hours, sow in containers, secure in plastic bags, and refrigerate for 3 weeks, then provide 75°F.

TRANSPLANTING

Time After last frost.
Spacing *Small species:* 12". *Large species:* 18"–24".
Light Prefers full sun but will tolerate part shade.
Soil Neutral to slightly alkaline, fertile; prefers moist but will tolerate dry.

CARING FOR PLANTS

Easy. Plants can be invasive where they are happy.

PROPAGATING

Detach rooted stems in spring, divide, or start from seed. Many will self-seed.

Trigonella

A | Zn 6–10 | Full sun | Dry soil

One species in this genus, T. foenum-graecum, *is an annual herb grown for culinary use. Grown only in herb beds, plants are 1'–2' tall, with compound leaves resembling clover. Pealike flowers are small and white.*

Type Annual
Zone 6–10
Flowering Season Midsummer through autumn

SOWING

Indoors Start seed *in situ.*
Outdoors When the soil is very warm — about 60°F.
Depth ¼".

GERMINATING

Time 2–5 days.
Requirements 70°–75°F.

TRANSPLANTING

Time Set out purchased plants after the last frost.
Spacing 4".
Light Full sun.
Soil Rich, well drained, with a pH level of 6.0–7.0.

CARING FOR PLANTS

Snails are attracted to tender seedlings. To harvest seed, cut ripe seedpods and dry in the sun; remove seed and store in an airtight container.

PROPAGATING

Grow from seed only.

Trillium

HP | Zn 3–9

Birthroot, Stinking Benjamin, Trillium, Trinity flower, Wakerobin, Wood lily

p. 429

These stately woodland plants are native to North America as well as Asia. They feature three large, flat, pointed leaves that grow in a horizontal whorl, and large, single, three-petaled flowers of white, pink, yellow, or red. They range in height from 6" to 18". With time, plants form dense colonies and are of unrivaled loveliness in a woodland garden.

Type Hardy perennial
Zone 3–9, H 9–1
Flowering Season Early spring to early summer, depending on species

SOWING

Indoors Any time that fresh seed is available.
Outdoors As soon as fresh seed is available.
Depth *Seed:* Surface. *Roots:* 4"–5".

GERMINATING

Time 18 months–3 years.
Requirements Difficult. Sow seed in a soil-based medium. *Indoors:* Secure flats in plastic bags and refrigerate for 3 months. Remove containers and leave for 3 months at 60°–70°F. Repeat this cycle once more. *Outdoors:* Sow seed ¼" deep in flats and sink these in the ground against a north-facing wall; moisten soil periodically, if necessary. Leave outdoors through two winters. Bring flats indoors to 60°–70°F and surface-sow seed individually in peat pots.

TRANSPLANTING

Time Spring or early autumn.
Spacing *Small species:* 5"–7". *Large species:* 12".
Light Full to part shade.
Soil Cool, rich, moist, well drained, with a pH level of 5.0–6.5.

CARING FOR PLANTS

Difficult. Provide a permanent mulch of leaf mold, and water regularly throughout the year. Do not disturb roots. Slugs may be attracted to young plants.

PROPAGATING

Plants can be divided with care in early spring in Zones 4–6 (in autumn in the South); generally, though, they prefer to be left undisturbed; or grow from seed. Plants grown from seed will bloom in about 5 years.

COMBINATIONS

Anemone, Aquilegia, Erythronium, Pulmonaria, or under azaleas.

T

Tritoma See *Kniphofia*

Tritonia

TB*, HB* | Zn 7–10

Blazing star, Montbretia

p. 430

Tritonia *is a genus of South African plants that grow from corms. Plants have flat, swordlike leaves and arching stems of 6" to 24" that bear spikes of funnel-shaped flowers of red, orange, yellow, pink, or white. Grow them in the border.*

Type Hardy bulb or tender bulb; often grown as an annual
Zone 7–10 (see species list, pp. 475–476); grown as an annual in cooler zones
Flowering Season Midsummer

SOWING

Indoors 6–8 weeks before planting out.
Outdoors *Seed:* In Zones 9–10, sow seed as soon as ripe in autumn; early spring is preferable in Zones 7–8. *Corm:* Autumn in Zones 9–10; spring in Zones 3–8.
Depth *Seed:* Just cover. *Corm:* 3"–4".

GERMINATING

Time 30–90 days.
Requirements Easy. 55°–60°F.

TRANSPLANTING

Time *Zones 3–8:* After last frost. *Zones 9–10:* Spring or autumn.
Spacing 4"–8".
Light Sun.
Soil Rich, sandy, well drained, amended with well-rotted cow manure.

CARING FOR PLANTS

During the growing season, feed once and water frequently, tapering off after flowering. Provide a good winter mulch. Where bulbs are not hardy, lift bulbs in autumn and store in a cool, frost-free place, replanting in spring.

PROPAGATING

Plant offsets at recommended planting time or grow from seed. Plants grown from seed take 3 years to flower.

Trollius

HP | Zn 3–8

Globeflower

p. 430

Perennial plants native to North America, Europe, and Asia, globeflowers have many-petaled orange and yellow flowers held singly high above the foliage. The blossoms resemble large, elegant buttercups, to which they are closely related. The handsome leaves are lobed and deeply cut. Plants grow from 6" to 36". Excellent plants for the rock garden, border, or woodland's edge.

Type Hardy perennial
Zone 3–8, H 7–1 (see species list, p. 476); prefer cool weather
Flowering Season Early spring to late summer, depending on species

SOWING

Indoors Start seed outdoors only.
Outdoors Late summer, as soon as fresh seed is available, in peat pots.
Depth Surface.

GERMINATING

Time 30–365 days.
Requirements Difficult. Due to a very poor germination rate and wide availability of rootstock, *Trollius* species are seldom grown from seed. For the determined: Sow seed in peat pots, stand pots in a pan, and water from below. Transplant to the garden in autumn.

TRANSPLANTING

Spacing 12"–18".
Light Full sun, with afternoon shade in hot climates. Where plants are grown in full sun, keep the soil very moist.
Soil Humus-rich, moist, or even boggy, with a pH level of 5.0–7.0.

CARING FOR PLANTS

Easy to grow if correctly situated. Keep plants well watered, deadhead regularly, and do not disturb once they are established. Carefully divide no more than once every 4 years.

PROPAGATING

Divide in spring (in early autumn in Zones 7–8) or grow from seed.

COMBINATIONS

Hosta, Iris ensata, Ligularia, candelabra *Primula, Rodgersia, Salvia.*

Tropaeolum

A, HP | Zn 1–10

Bitter Indian, Canary-bird vine, Canary-bird flower, Flame flower, Indian cress, Nasturtium

p. 430

Some of the annuals and tender perennials in this genus are climbers. Leaves are rounded, mid-green or gray-green, and often five- or six-lobed. The unusual flowers are trumpet-shaped with long spurs, in yellow, orange, or deep red. Native to Central and South America, they are fine informal plants for containers, edging, or trellises, and are often seen sprawling casually across a garden path. Climbers reach 3'–10'; non-climbers are just 3"–4" tall.

Type Annual, hardy perennial
Zone *Annual:* 1–10, H 12–1. *Perennial:* 8–10 (see species list, p. 476). Most successful where summers are mild and dry and nighttime temperatures remain below 65°F
Flowering Season Summer to autumn

SOWING

Indoors Seed may be started in peat pots 2–4 weeks before last frost, but for *T. majus* especially, sowing *in situ* is usually more successful.
Outdoors *Annual:* 1 week after last frost. *Perennial:* 2 weeks before last frost.
Depth ¼".

GERMINATING

Time *Annual:* 7–12 days. *Perennial:* Up to 2 years
Requirements *Annual:* Darkness and 65°F. *Perennial:* 55°–65°F.

TRANSPLANTING

Time 1–2 weeks after last frost.
Spacing *Small species:* 6"–12". *Medium species:* 12"–20". *Large species:* 24"–36".
Light *Annual:* Full sun, with afternoon shade where summers are hot. *Perennial:* Full sun with shaded roots. Roots may be shaded with a rock or flagstone slab.
Soil *T. majus* prefers poor to average, well drained, slightly acid. Other species prefer moist, acid.

CARING FOR PLANTS

Easy. Water during dry spells and do not fertilize, as this will stimulate lush foliar growth but few flowers. Inspect plants regularly for aphids and treat immediately with insecticidal soap. Provide a trellis or other support for climbing species. *Perennial:* More difficult; keep well watered and do not move established plants. Roots prefer to be shaded and should be lavishly mulched in spring.

PROPAGATING

Take cuttings, divide perennials in spring, or grow from seed.

COMBINATIONS

Non-climbers: *Calendula, Cotoneaster, Dahlia, Hemerocallis, Iris, Lobelia, Pelargonium, Tagetes.* Climbers: *Cobaea,* variegated *Hedera, Quamoclit.*

T

Tulipa

HB | Zn 3–8

Tulip

p. 430–431

Wildly popular and never disappointing, tulips are grown for their lovely, upward-facing, cup- or saucer-shaped flowers, which are held proudly on rigid stems of 4"–24". Blooms come in every imaginable color. There is no place where tulips do not look splendid: massed formally, scattered casually, in containers, rock gardens, and borders.

Type Hardy bulb
Zone 3–8, H 8–1
Flowering Season Spring

SOWING

As plants grown from seed won't flower for 4–6 years, this method of propagation is seldom used.
Indoors See Germinating, Requirements.
Outdoors *Seed:* See Germinating, Requirements. *Bulb:* Autumn.
Depth *Seed:* ⅛". *Bulb:* To prolong the life of bulbs in hot climates, plant 6"–7" deep; elsewhere plant 3"–5".

GERMINATING

Time 60–90 days.
Requirements *Autumn sowing:* Sow seed in flats, sink in the ground against a north-facing wall, and cover with glass. Moisten soil periodically, if necessary.

Bring indoors in spring to 50°F. *Spring sowing:* Place seed in a plastic bag together with moist growing medium and refrigerate for 2–3 weeks. Sow seed in flats, sink in the ground outdoors in a shady location, and cover with glass. Transplant seedlings as they appear.

TRANSPLANTING

Time Autumn.
Spacing *Dwarf species:* 4". *Large species:* 6"–10".
Light Full sun to light shade.
Soil Ordinary, very well drained, with a pH level of 6.0–7.0. The perfect planting hole consists of a layer of very well-rotted manure topped with ½" soil; place the bulb on top of this and backfill with soil mixed with 1 teaspoon bonemeal. However, few of us are that dutiful and for the sake of experience, loosening soil at the bottom of the hole and mixing in bonemeal will suffice.

CARING FOR PLANTS

Store bulbs at no more than 70°F before planting. Water newly planted bulbs immediately, then only during dry spells. Feed lightly in spring. After flowering, do not remove leaves until they are about half dead. Bulbs deteriorate in very hot weather; in the South where summers are very hot (Zones 8–10), bulbs can be lifted and stored in a cool place (40°–45°F), to be replanted in November or December, or start with new bulbs every year.

PROPAGATING

The only really successful way to increase your stock of tulips is to buy new bulbs; offsets seldom produce robust or attractive flowers. Plants grown from seed will flower in 4–6 years.

COMBINATIONS

Alyssum, azaleas, *Bellis, Erysimum, Muscari, Myosotis, Viola.*

CAUTION

Tulips are harmful to pets if eaten.

Tunica See *Petrorhagia*

Tweedia (syn. *Oxypetalum*)

TP* | Zn 2–10 | Full sun, Partial shade | Dry soil, Ordinary soil

*Only one species in this genus of climbing plants is widely grown—*T. caerulea. *It produces a dense curtain of mid-green leaves that provide a pleasing backdrop for sprays of stunning, pale blue, star-shaped flowers. It grows to 3'. Unpleasant-smelling leaves suggest that plants should be situated where they can be appreciated from a distance.*

Type Tender perennial; often grown as an annual
Zone 9–10, H 12–10; grown as an annual in Zones 2–8; prefers cool temperatures
Flowering Season Summer through early autumn

SOWING

Indoors 6–8 weeks before planting out.
Outdoors After last frost.
Depth ¼".

GERMINATING

Time 10–15 days.
Requirements Easy. 70°F.

TRANSPLANTING

Time Transplant seedlings in spring when temperatures remain above 40°F.
Spacing 6"–8".
Light Full sun where summers are cool; part shade in hotter regions.
Soil Prefers a rich, well-drained loam; tolerates poor, dry soil.

CARING FOR PLANTS

Easy. Pinch back young plants to encourage bushy growth. *Tweedia* species are highly susceptible to whiteflies. Delicate flowers require protection from rain, which can disfigure them.

PROPAGATING

Take cuttings in spring or grow from seed.

Ursinia

A | Zn 3–9

These annuals from southern Africa produce narrow, often strongly scented leaves and solitary orange or yellow, daisylike flowers. They grow 1'–2' tall, and make a cheerful addition to the border.

Type Annual
Zone 3–9, H 12–6; performs most successfully where there is a long, mild summer
Flowering Season Midsummer to late summer or early autumn

SOWING

Indoors 6–8 weeks before planting out.
Outdoors After last frost.
Depth Just cover.

GERMINATING

Time 14–30 days.
Requirements 55°–60°F.

TRANSPLANTING

Time In spring, when the temperature remains above 40°F.
Spacing 8"–10".
Light Full sun.
Soil Average or poor, well drained; *Ursinia* species are quite drought tolerant.

CARING FOR PLANTS

Plants may require staking, especially when grown in rich soil. Excessive summer heat may kill them. Plants are attractive to aphids.

PROPAGATING

Grow from seed only.

COMBINATIONS

Caryopteris, Ceanothus, Lavandula, Nepeta.

Uvularia

HP | Zn 3–9

Bellwort, Cowbells, Haybells, Merrybells, Wild oats

p. 431

A genus of perennials native to North America, Uvularia *are grown for their pretty yellow, nodding, bell-shaped flowers. Plants are 12"–30" tall. Although they are invariably described as elegant, some may think that their drooping leaves and flowers give these plants a depressed or thirsty look. Grow in borders and wildflower gardens.*

Type Hardy perennial
Zone 3–9, H 7–1
Flowering Season Spring

SOWING

Indoors It is best to start seed outdoors.
Outdoors As soon as seed is ripe, usually late summer.
Depth Just cover.

GERMINATING

Time 30–180 days.
Requirements Sow seed in flats, plunge in the ground against a north-facing wall, and cover with glass. Moisten soil occasionally, if necessary. Remove glass when seedlings appear. Transplant to the garden in summer.

TRANSPLANTING

Time Summer.
Spacing *Small species:* 6"–8". *Large species:* 12".
Light Part to full shade.
Soil Rich, moist, slightly acid, woodland soil with a pH level of 5.0–6.0.

CARING FOR PLANTS

Easy. Keep soil cool and moist with a permanent mulch of leaf mold. Water regularly during dry spells. Do not disturb roots.

PROPAGATING

Divide in early spring north of Zone 7 (in autumn in the South) or start from seed.

COMBINATIONS

Asarum, Dicentra, Polygonatum, Tiarella.

Valeriana

HP | Zn 4–9

Valerian

p. 431

Most Valeriana *species are grown for their heads of tiny white or pink flowers that are borne on stiff, branched stems of 6"–36". Use them in borders, wildflower plantings, or rock gardens.*

Type Hardy perennial
Zone 4–9, H 9–1; not tolerant of high heat and humidity
Flowering Season Summer

SOWING

Indoors 10–12 weeks before planting out.
Outdoors Early spring.
Depth Just cover.

GERMINATING

Time 21–25 days.
Requirements 70°F.

TRANSPLANTING

Time After last frost.
Spacing *Small species:* 6"–12". *Tall species:* 18"–24".
Light Full sun to part shade.
Soil Prefers rich, moist soil with a pH level of 5.5–7.0, but will grow in almost any.

CARING FOR PLANTS

Easy. Plants may require staking. Remove faded blooms to prevent seed formation, and cut back flowering stems altogether in autumn. Divide every 3–4 years when plants begin to die out.

PROPAGATING

Divide in spring in Zones 4–6 (in autumn in Zones 7–9) or grow from seed.

COMBINATIONS

Campanula, Lavandula, Thalictrum.

Veltheimia

TB* | Zn 9–10

p. 431

These strange but appealing South African tender perennials grow from bulbs. Plants bear dense clusters of long, drooping, red, pink or yellow tubular flowers atop thick, erect stems. Leaves are lance-shaped, often with wavy edges; 12"–18" tall. Veltheimia is guaranteed to enliven a dull border.

Type Tender bulb; sometimes grown indoors as houseplants
Zone 9–10, H 12–10
Flowering Season Early spring

SOWING

Indoors 8–10 weeks before planting out.
Outdoors *Seed:* Autumn. *Bulb:* Autumn.
Depth *Seed:* Just cover. *Bulb:* Plant with top third of bulb above ground.

GERMINATING

Time 30–90 days.
Requirements 55°–65°F.

TRANSPLANTING

Time When spring temperatures remain above 50°F.
Spacing 12".
Light Will grow in light shade, but flowers develop best colors and maintain a neat habit only in full sun.
Soil Acid, well drained.

CARING FOR PLANTS

Easy. Feed with a liquid fertilizer as soon as new growth shows in spring and again every 2 weeks throughout the growth period. Reduce watering and stop feeding in summer. North of Zone 9, grow bulbs in containers year-round. Plant the bulbs in autumn, water very lightly initially, increasing when leaves appear in late winter. Containers may be moved outdoors for the summer.

PROPAGATING

Plant offsets in spring, insert leaves in sandy soil in spring or summer, or grow from seed. Plants grown from seed will bloom in 3 years.

Veratrum

HP | Zn 3–9

p. 431

Genus of North America perennials with very large leaves and stiff, dense spikes of greenish white or brownish purple flowers. At 3'–9', these plants make an extraordinary spectacle in full bloom in a spacious border or near water.

Type Hardy perennial
Zone 3–9, H 9–5; will not perform well where summers are hot and humid
Flowering Season Summer

SOWING

Indoors See Germinating, Requirements.
Outdoors See Germinating, Requirements.
Depth ¼".

GERMINATING

Time 90–365 days.
Requirements Difficult. *Autumn sowing:* Sow seed in flats, sink these in the ground against a north-facing wall, and cover with glass. Moisten soil from time to time, if necessary. Bring indoors in spring to 55°–60°F. *Spring sowing:* Sow seed in containers with moistened medium, place in a plastic bag, and refrigerate. After 2–3 weeks, sink containers in the ground in a shady location, covering with glass. Transplant seedlings as they emerge.

TRANSPLANTING

Time After last frost.
Spacing 24".
Light Part shade, with shade from hot afternoon sun; grow in full sun only in cool climates or very moist soil.
Soil Light, moist, or even wet.

CARING FOR PLANTS

Easy. Mulch heavily in spring to keep soil cool and moist. It may be useful to mark the location of plants before they die back to the ground in summer to avoid inadvertent disturbance. Slugs can do considerable damage to leaves. Division is rarely required.

PROPAGATING

Divide in early spring (in early autumn in Zones 7–9) or grow from seed.

CAUTION

All parts of the plant are poisonous if eaten.

Verbascum (syn. *Celsia*)

Bi, HP | Zn 3–9

Mullein

p. 431

Large genus of erect plants, 1'–5' tall, with rosettes of silvery green, downy leaves and yellow or sometimes white, pink, or purple flowers borne along tall spikes. Some species are coarse and stiff, but many of the newer cultivars have a softer appearance that adds a delicate or romantic touch to the garden. For borders and cottage gardens.

Type Hardy perennial, perennial, or biennial; most are short-lived
Zone 3–9, H 9–1 (see species list, p. 477)
Flowering Season Summer

SOWING

Indoors 6–8 weeks before planting out.
Outdoors Early spring, when soil is cool and a light frost is still possible, or late summer.
Depth Just cover.

GERMINATING

Time 14–30 days.
Requirements 55°–60°F.

TRANSPLANTING

Time After last frost or late summer.
Spacing *Small species:* 12"–18". *Large species:* 24"–36" or singly.
Light *V.* × *hybridum* and *V. phoeniceum* will grow in part shade; plant all other species in full sun.
Soil Ordinary, warm, slightly alkaline; tolerant of dry soil. Plants in rich soil will need staking.

CARING FOR PLANTS

Easy. Cut back flower stalks after blooming and provide a good winter mulch. Take care not to damage the taproot when transplanting. Plants are short lived.

PROPAGATING

Divide plants, take root cuttings in early spring, or grow from seed. Plants will self-seed. Plants grown from seed will bloom in their first year.

COMBINATIONS

Consolida, Leucanthemum, Phygelius, Sedum.

Verbena (syn. *Glandularia*)

TP*, HP* | Zn 3–10

Verbena, Vervain

p. 431

Native from North to South America plus southern Europe, most of these rugged plants produce stiff stems and clusters of small, flat, brightly colored flowers with long bloom time. The dark green foliage is toothed or cut. Usually 4"–24" tall, one species is a towering 5'. Use in containers, borders, rock gardens, or as edging.

Type Hardy perennial or tender perennial; often grown as an annual
Zone 3–10, H 12–1; all species may be grown as annuals north of their hardiness range. (See species list, p. 477.) Prefers warm, dry climates
Flowering Season Summer to frost

SOWING

Indoors 8–10 weeks before planting out.
Outdoors After last frost.
Depth Just cover.

GERMINATING

Time 14–90 days.
Requirements Darkness and 65°–75°F. *V. bonariensis* and *V. rigida:* Place seed in a plastic bag together with moist growing medium and refrigerate for 2 weeks, then sow.

TRANSPLANTING

Time After last frost, when nighttime temperatures remain above 50°F.
Spacing *Small species:* 8"–10". *Medium species:* 12"–18". *Large species:* 24"–36".
Light Full sun; light shade if summers are very hot.
Soil Well-drained, fertile soil with 6.0–7.0 pH. Most tolerate dry; *V. rigida* is suitable for xeriscaping; *V. canadensis* prefers moist but very well drained.

CARING FOR PLANTS

Easy. Feed once or twice in spring. Verbenas can withstand drought but will reward you for regular watering. Pinch out tips of young plants and deadhead frequently to ensure maximum blooming. *V. rigida* and *V. tenuisecta* can be lifted in autumn and stored over winter in a frost-free location; replant in spring or take cuttings.

PROPAGATING

Take cuttings in spring, take cuttings in early autumn to overwinter indoors, or grow from seed. *V. bonariensis* will bloom from seed in its first year.

COMBINATIONS

Asclepias, Coreopsis, Helenium, Kniphofia, Platycodon, Scaevola, Tanacetum.

CAUTION

V. bonariensis self-seeds generously; may be invasive.

Veronica

HP | Zn 3–10

Veronica, Bird's-eye, Speedwell

p. 431

A large genus of mainly upright plants of 4"–48", Veronica *species bear lavish spikes of small, intensely blue, purple, white, or rose flowers. They make lovely plants for the border, container, or rock garden.*

Type Hardy perennial
Zone 3–10, H 8–1 (see species list, p. 477)
Flowering Season Late spring to early autumn, depending on species

SOWING

Indoors 8–10 weeks before planting out.
Outdoors Early spring or early autumn.

Depth Surface.

GERMINATING

Time 15–90 days.
Requirements Light and 60°–70°F.

TRANSPLANTING

Time Early spring, when soil is cool and a light frost is still possible, or late autumn.
Spacing *Small species:* 6"–12". *Spreading species:* 12"–18".
Light Full sun, except *V. prostrata,* which will take sun or part shade.
Soil Moist but well drained, average, with a pH level of 5.5–7.0. Soil that is too rich produces weak plants.

CARING FOR PLANTS

Easy. Water and deadhead regularly but feed only occasionally. Tall species may need some support. Flowering will be reduced in extreme heat. Cut back to ground level in late autumn.

PROPAGATING

Divide after flowering, take cuttings in summer, or grow from seed.

COMBINATIONS

Aster, Bellis, Dimorphotheca, Hypericum, Lychnis, Stachys.

Veronicastrum

HP | Zn 3–8   

Bowman's root, Culver's root

These handsome late-summer bloomers are native to eastern North America. The only species commonly grown in gardens (V. virginicum) *has at times been classified as* Veronica. *Plants are tall and stately—4'–7'—with horizontal whorls of sharply serrated leaves and long, slender racemes of white or pale pink flowers. They are equally at home in a formal or wildflower planting, where they quickly form an elegant stand.*

Type Hardy perennial
Zone 3–8, H 8–1
Flowering Season Late summer and autumn

SOWING

Indoors 8–10 weeks before planting out.
Outdoors Autumn
Depth Surface

GERMINATING

Time 21–40 days.
Requirements Light and 55–68°F. If seeds do not germinate in 4 weeks, move to 25°–40°F for 2–4 weeks, then return to 55°–68°F.

TRANSPLANTING

Time Early spring, when soil is cool and a light frost is still possible, or late autumn.
Spacing 18".
Light Sun to light shade.
Soil Moist but well drained, fertile, slightly acid.

CARING FOR PLANTS

Easy, requiring little care beyond regular watering. Plants grown in part shade may need staking. Divide every 3–4 years if clumps become crowded.

PROPAGATING

Divide in spring or autumn, take softwood cuttings in summer, or grow plants from seed.

COMBINATIONS

Autumn-blooming *Anemone, Artemisia, Aster, Malva, Physostegia.*

Vigna See *Phaseolus*

V

Viola

ANNUAL Including *Viola tricolor, Viola × wittrockiana*

A | Zn 3–10

Pansy, Heartsease, Johnny-jump-up, Pansy, Wild pansy

p. 432

Viola tricolor *are bright little plants with small purple, yellow, and white faces dancing above a 3"–8" mound of narrow, lance-shaped leaves.* Viola × wittrockiana *have very showy, flat 2–4" blooms in rich shades of purple, blue, wine, yellow, orange, or white. Some have characteristic blotches, others are solid. Use both in containers, rock gardens, borders, or edging, remembering that plants are short lived in hot climates.*

Type Annual
Zone 3–10, H 12–1 (see species list, p. 477); will not survive where summers are very hot
Flowering Season These cool season plants will bloom all summer in mild climates, but flag in early summer where temperatures are above 75°F. *V. × wittrockiana* blooms all winter in Zones 7–9.

SOWING

Indoors 10–12 weeks before planting out.
Outdoors Summer in Zones 9–10, elsewhere late summer to early autumn.
Depth ¼".

GERMINATING

Time 14 days.
Requirements Difficult. Darkness and 65°–75°F.

TRANSPLANTING

Time After last frost.
Spacing 6"–9".
Light Part shade, or full sun where summers are cool, or where they are grown for winter blooming.
Soil Cool, rich, moist, well drained, with a pH level of 5.5–6.5.

CARING FOR PLANTS

Easy. Feed once or twice while plants are young. Flowering is diminished in hot weather; mulch in spring to keep soil cool and moist. Remove plants after flowering to prevent self-seeding. These pansies will not survive hot summers and are short lived even in mild climates. In the North, a thick mulch may bring plants through the winter.

PROPAGATING

Grow from seed. Plant may self-seed.

COMBINATIONS

Dianthus, Lychnis, Narcissus, Silene, Tulipa.

PERENNIAL (syn. *Erpetin*)

HP* | Zn 2–10

Horned violet, Pansy, Tufted pansy, Tufted violet, Sweet violet, Violet

Very large genus of perennials, instantly recognizable by their colored markings, or "faces," which give the flowers a strong personality. Solid or multicolored flowers are every shade of red, purple, yellow, orange, blue, pink, black, and white; 2"–12" tall. Always successful in containers, borders, rock gardens, and edging.

Type Hardy perennial; often grown as an annual
Zone 2–10, H 9–1; (see species list, p. 477); *V. odorata* will not perform well where summers are very hot
Flowering Season May bloom at any time of year, depending on the species and the climate

SOWING

Indoors Prechilled seed 8–10 weeks before planting out. *V. odorata:* Sow seed outdoors only.
Outdoors Early spring or early autumn. *V. odorata:* Autumn only.
Depth Just cover.

GERMINATING

Time 10–21 days. *V. odorata:* Up to 50 days.
Requirements Place seed in a plastic bag together with moist growing medium and refrigerate for 2 weeks. Then sow and place in a dark location at 65°–75°F. *V. odorata:* Sow seed in flats, sink in the ground against a north-facing wall, and cover with glass. Moisten soil occasionally, if necessary. Remove glass when seedlings emerge.

PERENNIAL *(cont'd)*

TRANSPLANTING

Time Early spring, when soil is cool and a light frost is still possible, or late autumn. *V. odorata:* After last frost, or autumn where winters are mild.
Spacing 6"–12".
Light Part shade; site violets in full sun only in cool climates.
Soil Rich, moist, well drained, with a pH level of 5.5–7.0. Add well-rotted manure at planting time.

CARING FOR PLANTS

Easy. Mulch to keep soil cool and moist. Feed with liquid seaweed during the early growth stage. Deadhead often to prolong flowering, and cut back drastically after the first heavy bloom to encourage further bud formation. Where summers are hot, plants may be discarded after blooming.

PROPAGATING

Divide in spring or grow from seed. Plants grown from seed will bloom their first year.

COMBINATIONS

Begonia, Camellia, Daphne odora, Dianthus, Heliotropium, Puschkinia, roses, *Tulipa.*

Viscaria See *Lychnis*

Vitaliana (syn. *Douglasia*)

HP | Zn 5–7

These prostrate, rosette-forming perennials bear tight clusters of tiny oblong leaves and masses of yellow or pink tubular flowers. They make good rock garden plants.

Type Hardy perennial
Zone 5–7, H 8–5; requires cool, moist summers
Flowering Season Spring

SOWING

Indoors Late winter to early spring.
Outdoors Autumn.
Depth Surface.

GERMINATING

Time 30 days to 2 years.
Requirements *Outdoor sowing:* Sow seed in flats, sink in the ground against a north-facing wall, and cover with glass. Moisten growing medium occasionally, as necessary. In the spring, bring indoors to 50°–55°F. *Indoor sowing:* Place seed in a plastic bag together with moist growing medium. Refrigerate for 3–5 weeks, then provide 50°–55°F.

TRANSPLANTING

Time Early spring, when soil is cool and a light frost is still possible, or late autumn.
Spacing 8".
Light Full sun or light shade.
Soil Moist, very well drained, neutral or slightly acid.

CARING FOR PLANTS

Difficult. Plants grown from seed will flower in 2 years. Water frequently during dry spells, taking care to keep water off leaves. Protect crowns from heavy rain. Mulch lightly in winter.

PROPAGATING

Divide in autumn, take softwood cuttings in summer, or grow from seed.

Wahlenbergia

A, Bi, HP | Zn 6–10

Wahlenbergia, Rock bell

Members of this genus closely resemble Campanula *species, to which they are related. Flowers are very pretty, star- or bell-shaped, blue or, less often, white. Plants are covered in flowers all summer. They reach a maximum of 1', and are lovely in containers, baskets, or borders.*

Type Annual, biennial, or short-lived hardy perennial
Zone 6–10, H 10–6 (see species list, p. 478); prefers temperate climates
Flowering Season Summer until frost

SOWING

Indoors 6–8 weeks before last frost.
Outdoors After last frost or late summer.
Depth Surface.

GERMINATING

Time 10–28 days.
Requirements Light and 60°–70°F. If seeds have not germinated in 3–4 weeks, refrigerate for 2–4 weeks, then return to 60°–70°F.

TRANSPLANTING

Time After last frost or autumn.
Spacing 8"–10".
Light Sun; part shade where summers are very warm.
Soil Well drained, gritty, neutral to sweet.

CARING FOR PLANTS

Easy, although plants are often short lived. Slugs and snails may be a problem. Plants can be lifted in winter and overwintered indoors.

PROPAGATING

Divide in spring, take stem cuttings in summer, or grow from seed. Plants grown from seed will usually bloom in their first year.

Waldsteinia

HP | Zn 4–8

p. 432

A small genus of creeping, semievergreen perennials, Waldsteinia *species produce three-part leaves and cheerful, yellow, saucer-shaped flowers. These woodland perennials, many of which are North American natives, spread rapidly by runners, making them a useful ground cover for sunny or shady slopes. They are best kept out of the formal garden, however.*

Type Hardy perennial
Zone 4–8, H 7–1
Flowering Season Spring to early summer

SOWING

Because *Waldsteinia* are so easily propagated by rooting runners, they are seldom grown from seed, although this may be done by sowing seed in containers in a cold frame in early spring.

TRANSPLANTING

Time Spring or early autumn.
Spacing 12"–18".
Light Part to full shade, with full sun only where soil is moist.
Soil Prefers moist, slightly acid, very well drained, but is fairly drought tolerant.

CARING FOR PLANTS

Easy. Feed once in spring and water regularly during hot, dry weather. Dig and discard unwanted plants if their spreading becomes invasive. Can be attractive to slugs.

PROPAGATING

Divide in spring or autumn.

COMBINATIONS

Brunnera, ornamental grasses, *Lilium, Salvia.*

Watsonia

TB* | Zn 9–10

p. 432

Watsonia is a South African perennial that grows from corms. Plants bear long, sword-shaped leaves and stiff spikes of bright pink, red, or white trumpet-shaped flowers; 1'–6' tall. Grow them in the border.

Type Tender bulb
Zone 9–10, H 10–9 (see species list, p. 478); grown as an annual north of Zone 9
Flowering Season Late summer

SOWING

Indoors Midwinter.
Outdoors *Seed:* Autumn. *Corm:* Autumn (after last spring frost north of Zone 8).
Depth *Seed:* 1/8". *Corm:* 4" –6".

GERMINATING

Time 30–180 days.
Requirements 55°–65°F.

TRANSPLANTING

Time After last frost.
Spacing 12".
Light Full sun.
Soil Moist, well drained, enriched with manure.

CARING FOR PLANTS

Easy. Feed with liquid manure when buds begin to form, and water regularly throughout the blooming period. Stake when plants reach 6" and tie up new growth periodically to avoid damage to stems. North of Zone 9, lift corms and store over winter in a cool, dry place.

PROPAGATING

Dig clumps and divide cormels in late autumn or grow from seed. Plants grown from seed will bloom in 2–3 years.

COMBINATIONS

Allium, Geranium, Gypsophila, Nigella.

Wisteria

HP | Zn 4–10

Wisteria

p. 432

These much-loved woody vines have handsome compound leaves and an abundance of long, elegant racemes of blue, purple, or white pealike flowers. At 30', they make the perfect climber for any pergola or wall. It should be noted, however, that they require precise and knowledgeable pruning, without which they will spread rampantly and/or fail to bloom. Wisteria *should not be planted where they will not receive this regular attention.*

Type Hardy perennial
Zone 4–9, to Zone 10 in the West, H 9–5 (see species list, p. 478)
Flowering Season Late spring to early summer

SOWING

Indoors 6–8 weeks before last frost.
Outdoors Early spring, when soil is cool and a light frost is still possible, or late autumn.
Depth 1".

GERMINATING

Time 30–35 days.
Requirements Chip seed or soak for 24 hours in warm water; provide 55°–65°F thereafter.

TRANSPLANTING

Time After last frost.
Spacing Singly.
Light Full sun or part shade.
Soil Prefers moist, rich, well-drained soil. *W. sinensis* tolerates dry soil and is suitable for xeriscaping.

CARING FOR PLANTS

Mulch in spring and water well during the growing season. Avoid high-nitrogen fertilizers. Prune after flowering and again in winter, cutting back shoots to two or three buds. Plants that are not pruned regularly will quickly become a tangled mess. *Wisteria* seldom flower their first few years after planting; if vines continue not to bloom, prune during the summer to about six buds. Root-pruning in autumn is a more drastic and potentially harmful measure but often induces flowering when nothing else works. Do not move.

PROPAGATING

Take root and hardwood cuttings in spring or summer, divide in spring, or grow from seed. Plants grown from seed take up to 20 years to flower.

CAUTION

Harmful if eaten. Wisteria is so prevalent in the southern states that it is often assumed to be native. It is, however, a highly invasive exotic and is a listed invasive in many states, including Maryland, Virginia, Tennessee, Georgia, and Florida. See pp. 494–495 for advice.

Xanthisma

A | Zn 3–9

Sleepy daisy

*A single cheerful annual native to Texas belongs in this genus—*X. texana. *It is grown for its wealth of large, bright yellow or orange, daisylike flowers held singly on 2'–3' stems. Plants make a lively display in the border.*

Type Annual
Zone 3–9 (see species list, p. 478); prefers cool weather
Flowering Season Summer

SOWING

Indoors 6–8 weeks before last frost.
Outdoors After last frost.
Depth Just cover.

GERMINATING

Time 25–30 days.
Requirements 70°–75°F.

TRANSPLANTING

Time After last frost.
Spacing 12"–24".
Light Sun.
Soil Light, sandy, well drained, with a pH level of 6.5–7.0; will tolerate poor, dry soil. *Xanathisma* can be used in xeriscaping.

CARING FOR PLANTS

Easy. Plants may require staking.

PROPAGATING

Grow from seed only.

Xeranthemum

A | Zn 2–10

A small genus of annuals native from the Mediterranean to southwestern Asia, Xeranthenum *species produce silvery leaves and tall, wiry stems bearing solitary, everlasting, daisylike flowers of pink or purple. Plants are 24"–36" tall. Grow them in the border or cutting bed.*

Type Annual
Zone 2–10, H 9–1; prefers cool temperatures
Flowering Season Midsummer to late summer

SOWING

Indoors 2–3 weeks before planting out, in peat pots.
Outdoors After last frost, but only where the growing season is long.
Depth Just cover.

GERMINATING

Time 10–15 days.
Requirements 70°F.

TRANSPLANTING

Time After last frost.
Spacing 10"–15".
Light Full sun.
Soil Average; will tolerate dry conditions.

CARING FOR PLANTS

Easy. Support with twiggy branches pushed into the ground when plants are young. To dry for floral arrangements, cut stems when flowers are fully open.

PROPAGATING

Grow from seed.

COMBINATIONS

Heliopsis, Hemerocallis, Veronica.

Xerophyllum

HP | Zn 6–9

p. 432

Genus of two or three species of wildflowers, one of which is native to North America. Its foliage resembles very fine, long pine needles, and its tiny, white star-shaped flowers are borne in terminal clusters on long, wiry stems. It grows 2'–6' tall and makes an elegant plant for the wildflower or woodland garden.

Type Hardy perennial
Zone 6–9, H 10–7 (see species list, p. 478)
Flowering Season Early summer

SOWING

Indoors Start seed outdoors only.
Outdoors Late summer, as soon as fresh seed is available.
Depth ¼".

GERMINATING

Time 30–60 days.
Requirements Sow seeds in flats, sink flats in ground against a north-facing wall, and cover with glass. Moisten soil periodically, if necessary. Allow one full growing season before transplanting seedlings to the garden.

TRANSPLANTING

Time After last spring frost.
Spacing 12"–24".
Light Sun or part shade.
Soil Dry or moist, rich, well drained with a pH level of 6.0–8.0.

CARING FOR PLANTS

Difficult. Water regularly and mulch in spring to keep soil cool. Do not move.

PROPAGATING

Divide in spring in Zone 6 (in autumn in the South), or grow from seed.

Yucca (syn. *Hesperoyucca*)

HP | Zn 3–10

Yucca

p. 432

Evergreen plants with dangerous, sword-shaped leaves and tall, thick stalks bearing small, drooping white flowers; 1'–10' tall. Gardeners often have strong opinions about the imposing flowering stems, judging them to be either wonderfully majestic or remarkably unattractive. Because of their strongly architectural form, they are useful in the border or as specimens; they are also often grown in containers.

Type Hardy perennial
Zone 3–10, H 12–1 (see species list, p. 478)
Flowering Season Midsummer to autumn

SOWING

Indoors Late winter to early spring.
Outdoors Spring.
Depth Just cover.

GERMINATING

Time 30–365 days.
Requirements 65°–75°F. Indoors, grow seedlings for 2–3 years before planting out.

TRANSPLANTING

Time When spring temperatures will remain above 45°F.
Spacing *Small species:* 12"–24". *Medium species:* 24"–36". *Large species:* 48"–60" or singly.
Light Full sun.
Soil Average to poor, dry or very well drained; prefers a pH level of 5.5–7.5. Yucca is useful for xeriscaping.

CARING FOR PLANTS

Easy. Yuccas require no watering. Plants that are not groomed will gradually take on a derelict look. Remove dead leaves regularly (wearing long sleeves and armor-plated gloves). Plants may not bloom every year.

PROPAGATING

Take root cuttings, plant offsets, or grow from seed. Forms with variegated leaves must be propogated by cuttings or division.

COMBINATIONS

Coreopsis, Eupatorium, Gaillardia, ornamental grasses, *Sedum.*

CAUTION

Yucca is harmful to pets if eaten.

Zaluzianskya

A, TP* | Zn 9–10 | Full sun | Dry soil, Ordinary soil, Moist soil

These most unusual, long-blooming plants grow 2' tall. Flat, star-shaped flowers, white with maroon undersides, are carried in spikes. They open in the late evening, filling the air with a strong, delicious fragrance. Grow in containers near patios and decks or in very well-drained beds along walkways.

Type Annual, tender perennial
Zone 9–10, H 10–9; often grown as an annual in cooler regions
Flowering Season Summer

SOWING

Seed is rarely produced from plants grown in the garden.
Indoors 3–4 weeks before last frost.
Outdoors After last frost (or autumn in Zones 9–10).
Depth Just cover.

GERMINATING

Time 7–14 days.
Requirements Easy. 50°–70°F.

TRANSPLANTING

Time After last frost.
Spacing 6"–10".
Light Sun.
Soil Moist; must be very well drained (especially in winter, where plants are hardy). Plants will tolerate dry conditions, but this will cause stems to become woody.

CARING FOR PLANTS

Easy. Water regularly throughout the summer, and deadhead regularly to prolong flowering. Even where perennial, plants are short lived and should be replaced regularly.

PROPAGATING

Take cuttings from tips of nonflowering shoots in summer or grow from seed.

COMBINATIONS

Most attractive when planted in substantial drifts, alone or in combination with other plants such as *Coleus, Sedum, Sempervivum.*

Zantedeschia

HP* | Zn 8–10

Arum lily, Calla lily

p. 432

Exotic plants native to southern and eastern Africa, Zantedeschia *species feature bold, arrow-shaped leaves and large, elegant, funnel-shaped spathes of white, pink, red, or yellow surrounding a white, yellow, or purple spadix. They grow 12"–36" tall and make lovely plants for borders or containers. Some are water plants.*

Type Hardy perennial; often grown as an annual
Zone 8–10, H 7–1 (see species list, p. 478); grown as an annual in Zones 5–8
Flowering Season Spring to early summer, depending on species

SOWING

Indoors Early spring.
Outdoors Autumn, but only where the growing season is long.
Depth *Seed:* Surface. *Rhizome:* 2".

GERMINATING

Time 30–90 days.
Requirements Soak seed in warm water for 24 hours, sow, and place in a light location at 70°–80°F.

TRANSPLANTING

Time In spring, when temperatures remain above 50°F.
Spacing 12"–15".
Light Full sun, or light shade in very hot regions.
Soil Prefers moist, acid, humus rich. Add plenty of manure at planting time. Some species grow in water.

CARING FOR PLANTS

The elegance of these plants belies their easy care; plant a few and your friends will be wildly impressed. Feed regularly using a liquid fertilizer and water frequently. In Zones 7–8, lift plants in autumn before the first frost and store in a frost-free place over winter.

PROPAGATING

Divide tubers in spring or grow from seed.

COMBINATIONS

In front of showy climbers such as *Clematis,* or with *Hosta seiboldiana, Lilium, Matteuca.*

CAUTION

Z. aethiopica is harmful to pets if eaten.

Zauschneria

HP | Zn 8–10 

California fuchsia

A genus of 1'–2' perennials, Zauschneria *includes some species that are woody, bearing small, grayish green, lance-shaped leaves and a tangle of bright red tubular flowers. Grow them in the border or rock garden.*

Type Hardy perennial
Zone 8–10, H 12–8; does not like wet winters and so is seldom successful in Eastern states
Flowering Season Summer to early autumn.

SOWING

Indoors Start seed outdoors only.
Outdoors Spring.
Depth Surface.

GERMINATING

Time 30–60 days.
Requirements Light and 60°–65°F.

TRANSPLANTING

Time Set out purchased plants after last frost.
Spacing 14"–18".
Light Sun or part shade.
Soil Any very well-drained soil with a pH level between 7.0 and 8.0; drought tolerant.

CARING FOR PLANTS

Pinch back tips of young plants to encourage bushy growth, and deadhead frequently to make plants look more attractive. Protect from overhead water. May become invasive.

PROPAGATING

Take stem cuttings in autumn, divide in spring, or grow from seed.

Zephyranthes (syn. *Cooperia*)

TB*, HB* | Zn 8–10

Fairy lily, Rainflower, Rain lily, Zephyr flower, Zephyr lily

p. 432

This genus of small perennials that grow from bulbs produces grassy leaves and delicate, funnel-shaped flowers of pink, red, yellow, or white held singly on erect stems of 2"–12". They are suitable for rock gardens or massed under shrubs, or grow them in containers.

Type Hardy bulb, tender bulb; often grown as an annual
Zone 8–10, H 12–6 (see species list, p. 478); grow as an annual in cooler zones
Flowering Season Spring, summer, or autumn, depending on species

SOWING

Indoors Late winter.
Outdoors *Seed:* Autumn or spring. *Bulb:* October to early November in Zones 9–10, after last spring frost elsewhere.
Depth *Seed:* Just cover. *Bulb:* 3".

GERMINATING

Time 4 months.
Requirements 60°–75°F.

TRANSPLANTING

Time Autumn in Zones 9–10; after last spring frost north of Zone 9.
Spacing 3"–6".
Light Sun or part shade.
Soil Light, rich, moist, well drained, with a pH level of 6.0–7.0.

CARING FOR PLANTS

Easy. Apply a complete fertilizer in spring, and water during dry weather. In colder regions, plant bulbs against a south-facing wall and mulch well in autumn. Where bulbs are grown as annuals, lift in autumn and store in barely moist sand over winter.

PROPAGATING

Divide in early autumn or grow from seed. Plants grown from seed will take 3 years to flower.

Zinnia

A | Zn 2–10

Zinnia

p. 432

Zinnia *is a genus of plants grown for their intensely colored, often extravagantly double, blooms held singly on tall stems of 8"–36". Colors range from light pinks and whites to deep reds and oranges. Plants can be used successfully in carefree summer plantings, formal beds, or containers.*

Type Annual
Zone 2–10, H 12–1; prefers warm temperatures
Flowering Season Summer to frost

SOWING

Indoors 6–8 weeks before planting out; most successful when started *in situ.*
Outdoors After last frost, but only where summers are long.
Depth Just cover.

GERMINATING

Time 5–24 days.
Requirements 70°–80°F.

TRANSPLANTING

Time After last frost.
Spacing *Dwarf species:* 6"–9". *Medium species:* 10"–12". *Large species:* 15"–18".
Light Full sun, with some afternoon shade in very hot climates.
Soil Ordinary, well drained, enriched with manure; prefers a pH level of 6.0–7.0.

CARING FOR PLANTS

Easy. When plants are young, pinch tips to stimulate bushy growth. Feed soon after planting out and again when blooming begins. Water regularly, keeping leaves dry, and deadhead frequently to keep plants looking neat. Avoid transplanting.

PROPAGATING

Grow from seed.

COMBINATIONS

Ageratum, Coreopsis, Pelargonium, Tagetes.

3 A Photo Gallery of Garden Plants

Choosing just the right colors and color combinations is one of the pleasant challenges of gardening. In the section that follows, you will find examples of most of the entries in the A–Z of Garden Plants. Whenever possible, the cultivar name for each plant is included, along with a quick-reference set of information about that species. For information about the plants' AHS Heat Zone, as well as the colors of other plants in the species, see the Garden Planning Charts in Part 4.

A. Botanic name. Genus, species, and, if relevant, cultivar name

B. Type. Plants in this book are divided as follows to describe their life cycle and cold hardiness:

A (Annual)	**HP** (Hardy Perennial)
Bi (Biennial)	**TB** (Tender Bulb)
TP (Tender Perennial)	**HB** (Hardy Bulb)

See page 38 for an explanation of each category.

C. Zone. For information about USDA Hardiness Zones and to identify your zone, see page 499.

D. Bloom season. Ranges have been broken down as follows:

ESp = Early Spring	**ESu** = Early Summer
MSp = Midspring	**MSu** = Midsummer
LSp = Late Spring	**LSu** = Late Summer

EFa = Early Fall
MFa = Mid Fall
LFa = Late Fall

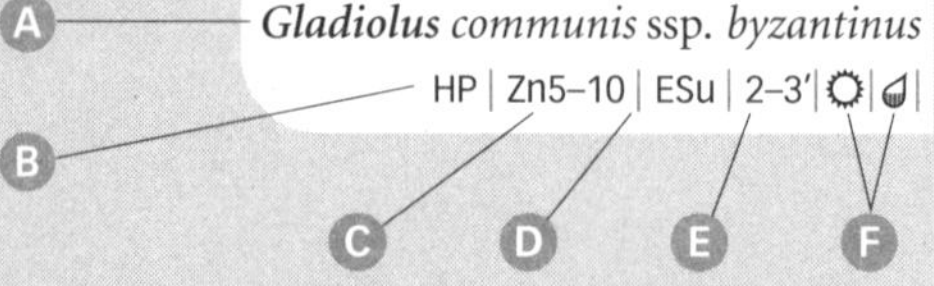

E. Height. Heights given here are more specific than the ranges given in Part 4 and, when appropriate, refer to the height of the cultivar or variety shown, which may differ from that of the species.

F. Light and Soil requirements. See page 434 for an explanation of the following ranges:

= Full sun	= Dry soil
= Partial shade	= Good for xeriscaping
= Full shade	= Average soil
	= Moist soil

***Abutilon** megapotamicum*
HP* | Zn8–10 | LSp–EFa | 3–10′ |

***Acaena** novae-zelandiae*
HP | Zn6–8 | MSu | 4–6″ |

***Acanthus** mollis*
HP | Zn8–10 | ESu–MSu | 4′ |

***Achillea** clavennae*
HP | Zn5–9 | MSu–MFa | 6–8″ |

***Achillea** millefolium* cultivar
HP | Zn3–8 | ESu–LSu | 24″ |

***Aconitum** carmichaelii*
HP | Zn3–8 | EFa | 5–6′ |

***Aconitum** napellus*
HP | Zn3–8 | MSu–LSu | 3–4′ |

***Actinidia** kolomikta*
HP | Zn4–8 | foliage | 15–20′ |

***Actinotus** helianthi*
TP* | Zn9–10 | LSp–ESu | 24″ |

Top row: GBP, JP, JP; Middle row: JP, JP, JDS; Bottom row: JP, JP, GBP

Bloom: ESp = Early Spring; MSp = Midspring; LSp = Late Spring; ESu = Early Summer; MSu = Midsummer; LSu = Late Summer; EFa = Early Fall; MFa = Mid Fall; LFa = Late Fall
Soil: = Dry soil; = Good for xeriscaping; = Ordinary soil; = Moist soil

Adenophora *bulleyana*
HP | Zn4–8 | ESu–LSu | 2–3′| | |

Adiantum *pedatum*
HP | Zn4–8 | foliage | 1–2′| | |

Adiantum *venustum*
HP | Zn4–8 | foliage | 9–12″| | |

Aegopodium *podagraria* 'Variegatum'
HP | Zn3–10 | foliage | 6–12″| | |

Aethionema *grandiflorum*
HP | Zn5–7 | LSp–MSu | 12–18″| | |

Agapanthus *africanus*
HP*|Zn7–10|MSu–LSu|18–36″| | |

Agapanthus *inapertus*
TP*|Zn9–10|LSu–EFa|4–5′| | |

Agastache 'Tutti frutti'
HP | Zn6–10 | MSu–LFa | 2–6′| | |

Ageratum *houstonianum* cultivar
A | Zn1–10 | MSp–LFa | 2′| | |

Top row: MC, JP, GBP; Middle row: JP, JP, GBP; Bottom row: GBP, JP, JP

Type: A = Annual; Bi = Biennial; HP = Hardy Perennial; TP = Tender Perennial; HB = Hardy Bulb; TB = Tender Bulb; * = May be grown as annual in colder regions
Light: = Full sun; = Partial shade; = Full shade

Agrostemma githago

A | Zn1–9 | ESu–LSu | 2–4′ | | |

Ajania pacifica

HP | Zn5–9 | MFa–LFa | 1–2′ | | |

Ajuga reptans

HP | Zn3–10 | LSp | 4–8″ | | |

Alcea rosea

HP | Zn2–9 | MSu–EFa | 5–9′ | | |

Alchemilla alpina

HP | Zn3–8 | MSu | 6–8″ | | |

Alchemilla mollis

HP | Zn3–7 | ESu–MSu | 1–2′ | | |

Allium × *hollandicum*

HB | Zn3–8 | MSu | 3′ | | |

Allium moly

HB | Zn3–9 | ESu | 6–18″ | | |

Allium neapolitanum

HB | Zn5–8 | LSp | 12–18″ | | |

Top row: JP, GBP, JP; Middle row: GBP, JP, JP; Bottom row: IBC, IBC, JP

Bloom: ESp = Early Spring; MSp = Midspring; LSp = Late Spring; ESu = Early Summer; MSu = Midsummer; LSu = Late Summer; EFa = Early Fall; MFa = Mid Fall; LFa = Late Fall

Soil: = Dry soil; = Good for xeriscaping; = Ordinary soil; = Moist soil

***Allium** schoenoprasum*
HB | Zn4–9 | MSu | 12–18″ |

Alstroemeria hybrid cultivar
HP | Zn7–10 | ESu–MSu | 2–3′ |

***Alyssum** montanum* 'Berggold'
HP | Zn3–8 | LSp–LSu | 6″ |

***Alyssum** wulfenianum*
HP | Zn6–9 | ESU–MSu | 4–6″ |

***Amaranthus** caudatus*
A | Zn3–10 | ESu–EFa | 3–5′ |

***Amaryllis** belladonna*
HB* | Zn7–10 | LSu–EFa | 18–30″ |

***Ammobium** alatum*
A | Zn2–10 | ESu–EFa | 3′ |

***Amsonia** hubrechtii*
HP | Zn4–9 | MSu | 2–3′ |

***Anacyclus** pyrethrum* var. *depressus*
HP | Zn6–9 | ESu–MSu | 10–12″ |

Top row: IBC, JP, GBP; Middle row: GBP, JP, GBP; Bottom row: MC, JP, JP

 Type: A = Annual; Bi = Biennial; HP = Hardy Perennial; TP = Tender Perennial; HB = Hardy Bulb; TB = Tender Bulb; * = May be grown as annual in colder regions
Light: ☼ = Full sun; ◐ = Partial shade; ● = Full shade

***Anagallis** monellii* 'Skylover'
HP* | Zn8–10 | ESu–LSu | 12–18" | | |

***Anaphalis** triplinervis*
HP | Zn3–8 | MSu–LSu | 18–24" | | |

***Anchusa** azurea*
HP | Zn3–8 | ESu | 3–5' | | |

***Androsace** chamaejasme*
HP | Zn4–7 | LSp | 1–2" | | |

***Anemone** blanda*
HP | Zn5–10 | ESp | 6–8" | | |

***Anemone** tomentosa*
HP | Zn4–9 | LSu–EFa | 2–4' | | |

***Anemonella** thalictroides*
HP | Zn4–7 | MSp–ESu | 4–8" | | |

***Angelica** gigas*
HP | Zn5–8 | LSu–EFa | 5–6' | | |

***Antennaria** dioica* 'Rubra'
HP | Zn3–8 | LSp–ESu | 2–4" | | |

Top row: JP, JP, JP; Middle row: JP, JP, JP; Bottom row: JP, JP, VB

Bloom: ESp = Early Spring; MSp = Midspring; LSp = Late Spring; ESu = Early Summer; MSu = Midsummer; LSu = Late Summer; EFa = Early Fall; MFa = Mid Fall; LFa = Late Fall
Soil: = Dry soil; = Good for xeriscaping; = Ordinary soil; = Moist soil

***Anthemis** marschalliana*

HP | Zn4–9 | MSu | 6–12"

***Anthemis** tinctoria* 'E.C. Buxton'

HP | Zn4–9 | ESu–EFa | 18–36"

***Anthericum** liliago*

HP | Zn6–9 | ESu | 18–36"

***Anthriscus** sylvestris* 'Ravenswing'

A | Zn3–10 | LSpr–ESu | 30–36"

***Antirrhinum** majus* cultivars

HP* | Zn7–10 | LSp–LFa | 1–3'

***Aquilegia** canadensis*

HP | Zn3–9 | MSp–ESu | 1–2'

***Arabis** blepharophylla* 'Fruhlingszauber'

HP | Zn6–8 | LSP–ESu | 4–10"

***Arabis** caucasica* 'Compinkie'

HP | Zn4–9 | MSp–LSp | 5–6"

Arctotis Harlequin Hybrids

TP* | Zn9–10 | MSu–MFa | 6–12"

Top row: JP, JP, GBP; Middle row: JP, JP, JP; Bottom row: GBP, GBP, JP

 Type: A = Annual; Bi = Biennial; HP = Hardy Perennial; TP = Tender Perennial; HB = Hardy Bulb; TB = Tender Bulb; * = May be grown as annual in colder regions

Light: ○ = Full sun; ◐ = Partial shade; ● = Full shade

***Arenaria** montana*
HP | Zn3–8 | LSp–ESu | 2–4″ | | |

***Argemone** mexicana*
A | Zn3–10 | ESu–LSu | 2–3′ | | |

***Arisaema** triphyllum* 'Black Stem'
HP | Zn3–8 | LSp | 6–24″ | | |

***Armeria** maritima* 'Splendens'
HP | Zn3–8 | LSp–ESu | 6–12″ | | |

***Arnica** cordifolia*
HP | Zn6–9 | MSu | 1–2′ | | |

***Artemisia** schmidtiana* 'Nana'
HP | Zn4–10 | foliage | 3–6″ | | |

***Artemisia** stelleriana* 'Boughton Silver'
HP | Zn4–10 | foliage | 10–12″ | | |

***Arum** italicum* 'Marmoratum'
HP | Zn6–10 | LSpr | 12–18″ | | |

***Aruncus** dioicus*
HP | Zn3–7 | ESu–MSu | 4–7′ | | |

Top row: JP, JP, JP; Middle row: JP, JP, GBP; Bottom row: JP, JP, JP

Bloom: ESp = Early Spring; MSp = Midspring; LSp = Late Spring; ESu = Early Summer; MSu = Midsummer; LSu = Late Summer; EFa = Early Fall; MFa = Mid Fall; LFa = Late Fall
Soil: = Dry soil; = Good for xeriscaping; = Ordinary soil; = Moist soil

Asarina *procumbens*
HP* | Zn7–9 | MSu–EFa | 1–2″ |

Asarum *europaeum*
HP | Zn4–8 | foliage | 5–10″ |

Asarum *shuttleworthii*
HP | Zn7–9 | foliage | 3–8″ |

Asclepias *incarnata*
HP | Zn3–9 | LSu | 4–5′ |

Asclepias *tuberosa*
HP | Zn3–10 | MSu | 1–3′ |

Asperula *orientalis*
A | Zn4–8 | MSu | 9–12″ |

Asphodeline *lutea*
HP | Zn6–8 | LSp–ESu | 3–4′ |

Asplenium *scolopendrium* 'Crispum'
HP | Zn5–9 | foliage | 1–2′ |

Asplenium *trichomanes* ssp. *quadrivalens*
HP | Zn3–9 | foliage | 6–12″ |

Top row: GBP, MC, JP; Middle row: JP, JP, JP; Bottom row: JP, GBP, GBP

Type: A = Annual; Bi = Biennial; HP = Hardy Perennial; TP = Tender Perennial; HB = Hardy Bulb; TB = Tender Bulb; * = May be grown as annual in colder regions
Light: = Full sun; = Partial shade; = Full shade

Aster alpinus
HP | Zn4–9 | ESu | 6–10" | |

Aster × *frikartii*
HP | Zn4–8 | MSu–MFa | 6–12" | |

Aster novae-angliae 'Alma Pötschke'
HP | Zn4–9 | EFa | 3–5' | |

Astilbe × *arendsii* cultivar
HP | Zn4–8 | ESu–LSu | 2–4' | |

Astilbe 'Straussenfeder'
HP | Zn4–8 | MSu | 2' | |

Astrantia major
HP | Zn4–7 | ESu, EFa | 2' | |

Athyrium niponicum var. *pictum*
HP | Zn4–9 | foliage | 12–20" | |

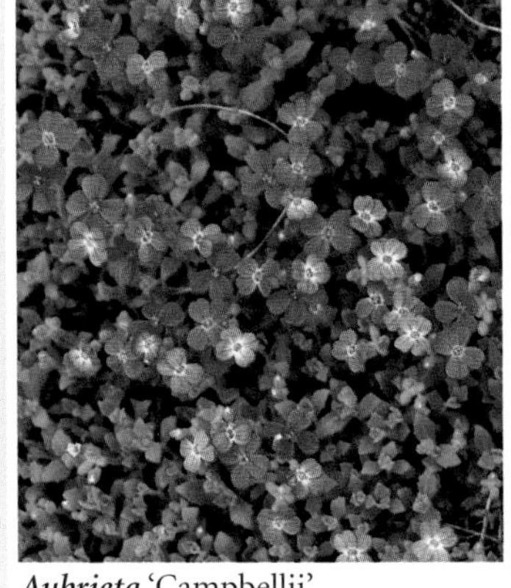

Aubrieta 'Campbellii'
HP | Zn7–10 | MSp | 6–8" | |

Aurinia saxatilis
HP | Zn4–10 | LSp–ESu | 8" | |

Top row: JP, JP, JP; Middle row: JP, JP, JP; Bottom row: JP, GBP, JP

Babiana stricta
HB* | Zn8–10 | ESp–MSp | 4–12″ |

Bacopa 'Snowflake'
TP* | Zn9–10 | MSp–MFa | 3″ |

Baptisia alba
HP | Zn4–9 | ESu | 3′ |

Baptisia australis
HP | Zn4–9 | LSp | 3–6′ |

Bassia scoparia f. trichophylla
A | Zn2–10 | foliage | 30–36″ |

Begonia grandis
HP | Zn6–10 | LSu–MFa | 24–30″ |

Begonia × tuberhybrida 'Pinup Flame'
TP* | Zn10 | ESu–MFa | 10–12″ |

Belamcanda chinensis
HP | Zn5–10 | MSu | 2–3′ |

Bellis perennis cultivar
HP | Zn3–9 | LSp–ESu | 6″ |

Top row: JP, JP, MC; Middle row: MC, JP, JP; Bottom row: JP, JP, JP

 Type: A = Annual; Bi = Biennial; HP = Hardy Perennial; TP = Tender Perennial; HB = Hardy Bulb; TB = Tender Bulb; * = May be grown as annual in colder regions
Light: = Full sun; = Partial shade; = Full shade

Bergenia *cordifolia* 'Purpurea'
HP | Zn4–8 | foliage | 18" |

Bidens *ferulifolia* 'Compact'
HP* | Zn8–10 | MSu–MFa | 1–2' |

Blechnum *penna-marina*
HP | Zn6–9 | foliage | 6–12" |

Bletilla *striata*
HP | Zn5–9 | ESu | 18–24" |

Boltonia *asteroides* 'Pink Beauty'
HP | Zn3–8 | LSu–MFa | 4–5' |

Brachyscome *iberidifolia* 'Mauve Delight'
A | Zn1–10 | ESu–MFa | 12" |

Brimeura *amethystina*
HB | Zn3–8 | LSp | 6–10" |

Briza *media*
HP | Zn4–8 | LSp–ESu | 12–30" |

Browallia *americana*
TP* | Zn9–10 | LSp–EFa | 1–2' |

Top row: JP, JP, JP; Middle row: JP, JP, GBP; Bottom row: IBC, MC, GBP

Bloom: ESp = Early Spring; MSp = Midspring; LSp = Late Spring; ESu = Early Summer; MSu = Midsummer; LSu = Late Summer; EFa = Early Fall; MFa = Mid Fall; LFa = Late Fall
Soil: = Dry soil; = Good for xeriscaping; = Ordinary soil; = Moist soil

Browallia speciosa

TP* | Zn9–10 | LSp–EFa | 1–2′ | | |

Brugmansia × *candida* cultivar

HP* | Zn8–10 | ESu–EFa | 5–10′ | | |

Brunnera macrophylla

HP | Zn3–8 | MSp–LSp | 18″ | | |

Caladium bicolor cultivar

TP* | Zn9–10 | foliage | 2–3′ | | |

Calamagrostis × *acutiflora*

HP | Zn5–9 | MSu–LSu | 3–6′ | | |

Calamintha grandiflora 'Variegata'

HP | Zn5–10 | ESu–MSu | 9–18″ | | |

Calceolaria integrifolia 'Goldbouquet'

TP* | Zn9–10 | ESu–MSu | 18–36″ | | |

Calendula officinalis

A | Zn2–10 | MSp–LSu | 12–30″ | | |

Calibrachoa 'Million Bells Lemon'

TP* | Zn9–10 | ESu–MFa | 3–8″ | | |

Top row: JP, JP, JP; Middle row: MC, JP, JP; Bottom row: GBP, JP, JP

 Type: A = Annual; Bi = Biennial; HP = Hardy Perennial; TP = Tender Perennial; HB = Hardy Bulb; TB = Tender Bulb; * = May be grown as annual in colder regions

Light: ○ = Full sun; ◐ = Partial shade; ● = Full shade

***Callirhoe** involucrata* var. *tenuissima*
HP | Zn3–9 | ESu–LSu | 6–10" | | |

***Callistephus** chinensis*
A | Zn1–10 | ESu–LSu | 1–2' | |

Calochortus 'Golden Orb'
HB | Zn5–10 | LSp–ESu | 10–12" | |

***Caltha** palustris*
HP | Zn4–9 | ESp | 1–2' | |

***Camassia** leichtlinii* 'Alba'
HB | Zn4–9 | MSu | 2–4' | |

***Camassia** quamash*
HB | Zn4–9 | ESu–MSu | 12–30" | |

***Campanula** lactiflora*
HP | Zn4–8 | ESu–LSu | 3–5' | |

***Campanula** persicifolia*
HP | Zn3–8 | ESu–LSu | 2–3' | |

***Campanula** portenschlagiana*
HP | Zn4–8 | ESu–LSu | 6–9" | |

Top row: JP, GBP, IBC; Middle row: JP, JP, JP; Bottom row: JP, JP, JP

Bloom: ESp = Early Spring; MSp = Midspring; LSp = Late Spring; ESu = Early Summer; MSu = Midsummer; LSu = Late Summer; EFa = Early Fall; MFa = Mid Fall; LFa = Late Fall
Soil: = Dry soil; = Good for xeriscaping; = Ordinary soil; = Moist soil

Canna 'Brandywine'

HP* | Zn8–10 | ESu–EFa | 18–24" | | |

Carex elata 'Bowles Golden'

HP | Zn5–9 | foliage | 24–30" | | |

Carex siderosticha 'Variegata'

HP | Zn6–9 | foliage | 12" | | |

Carthamus tinctorius

A | Zn3–9 | MSu | 2–3' | | |

Carum carvi

Bi | Zn3–8 | LSp–ESu | 2–4' | | |

Catananche caerulea

HP | Zn4–9 | MSu–EFa | 2' | | |

Catharanthus roseus

TP* | Zn9–10 | ESu–MFa | 1–2' | | |

Celmisia spectabilis

HP | Zn8–9 | ESu–MSu | 1' | | |

Celosia spicata 'Flamingo Feather'

A | Zn2–10 | ESu–EFa | 2' | | |

Top row: JP, JP, JP; Middle row: GBP, JP, JP; Bottom row: JP, GBP, JP

 Type: A = Annual; Bi = Biennial; HP = Hardy Perennial; TP = Tender Perennial; HB = Hardy Bulb; TB = Tender Bulb; * = May be grown as annual in colder regions

Light: = Full sun; = Partial shade; = Full shade

***Centaurea** montana*

HP | Zn4–8 | ESu–MSu | 1–2′| |

***Centranthus** ruber*

HP | Zn4–9 | LSp–EFa | 18–36″| | |

***Cerastium** tomentosum*

HP | Zn3–9 | MSp–LSp | 6–8″| | |

***Ceratostigma** plumbaginoides*

HP | Zn5–9 | LSu–LFa | 1′| | |

***Cerinthe** major* ‘Purpurascens’

HP | Zn6–9 | ESu–EFa | 18–24″| | |

***Chelidonium** majus* ‘Flore Pleno’

HP | Zn4–8 | MSu | 2′| | |

***Chelone** obliqua*

HP | Zn3–9 | LSu | 3′| | |

***Chenopodium** giganteum*

A | Zn6–10 | foliage | 4–5′| | |

***Chiastophyllum** oppositifolium*

HP | Zn4–8 | LSp–ESu | 6–8″| | |

Top row: JP, JP, JP; Middle row: JP, JP, JP; Bottom row: JP, GBP, GBP

Bloom: ESp = Early Spring; MSp = Midspring; LSp = Late Spring; ESu = Early Summer; MSu = Midsummer; LSu = Late Summer; EFa = Early Fall; MFa = Mid Fall; LFa = Late Fall

Soil: = Dry soil; = Good for xeriscaping; = Ordinary soil; = Moist soil

Chionodoxa luciliae
HB | Zn4–8 | ESp | 3–6″ | |

Chionodoxa sardensis
HB | Zn4–8 | ESp | 4–6″ | |

Chrysanthemum × *morifolium* 'Shelley'
HP | Zn5–9 | LSu–MFa | 12–18″ | |

Chrysanthemum × *morifolium* 'Wild Cherry'
HP | Zn5–9 | LSu–MFa | 12–18″ | |

Chrysogonum virginianum var. *australe*
HP | Zn5–9 | MSp–ESu | 4–8″ | |

Cimicifuga ramosa 'Atropurpurea'
HP | Zn3–9 | EFa | 5–6′ | |

Cimicifuga simplex
HP | Zn3–9 | LSu–MFa | 3–4′ | |

Cirsium japonicum
HP | Zn5–8 | MSu–LSu | 3–4′ | |

Clarkia amoena cultivar
A | Zn2–10 | ESu–LSu | 18–30″ | |

Top row: IBC, IBC, JP; Middle row: MC, JP, JDS; Bottom row: MC, JP, MC

 Type: A = Annual; Bi = Biennial; HP = Hardy Perennial; TP = Tender Perennial; HB = Hardy Bulb; TB = Tender Bulb; * = May be grown as annual in colder regions
Light: = Full sun; = Partial shade; = Full shade

Clarkia hybrids

A | Zn2–10 | ESu–LSu | 18–24" | | |

Claytonia virginica

HP | Zn5–8 | ESp | 4" | | |

Clematis integrifolia

HP | Zn3–9 | ESu–MSu | 2–4′ | | |

Clematis montana var. *rubens* 'Marjorie'

HP | Zn7–9 | LSp | 15–25′ | | |

Clematis tangutica 'Golden Harvest'

HP | Zn7–9 | ESu–EFa | 6–8′ | | |

Cleome hassleriana 'Helen Campbell'

A | Zn2–10 | ESu–MFa | 3–5′ | | |

Clintonia andrewsiana

HP | Zn3–9 | ESu | 18–24" | | |

Clivia miniata

TP* | Zn9–10 | ESp | 18–30" | | |

Cobaea scandens

TP* | Zn9–10 | ESu–MFa | 12–20′ | | |

Top row: JP, JP, MC; Middle row: GBP, MC, JP; Bottom row: JP, JP, JDS

Bloom: ESp = Early Spring; MSp = Midspring; LSp = Late Spring; ESu = Early Summer; MSu = Midsummer; LSu = Late Summer; EFa = Early Fall; MFa = Mid Fall; LFa = Late Fall

Soil: = Dry soil; = Good for xeriscaping; = Ordinary soil; = Moist soil

***Coix** lacryma-jobi*

TP* | Zn9–10 | MSu | 3′ | |

***Colchicum** autumnale*

HB | Zn4–9 | MFa | 4–8″ | |

***Collinsia** bicolor*

A | Zn3–10 | MSp–MSu | 2′ | |

***Colocasia** esculenta* 'Fontanesii'

HP | Zn8–10 | foliage | 3–4′ | |

***Consolida** ajacis*

A | Zn3–9 | ESp–ESu | 1–4′ | |

***Convallaria** majalis*

HP | Zn2–9 | LSp | 8″ | |

***Convolvulus** cneorum*

HP* | Zn8–10 | LSp–EFa | 2–4′ | |

***Convolvulus** tricolor*

A | Zn3–9 | ESu–LSu | 1–2′ | |

***Coreopsis** lanceolata* 'Sterntaler'

HP | Zn4–9 | ESu–LSu | 16″ | |

Top row: GBP, JP, JP; Middle row: JP, JP, JDS; Bottom row: JP, JDS, JP

 Type: A = Annual; Bi = Biennial; HP = Hardy Perennial; TP = Tender Perennial; HB = Hardy Bulb; TB = Tender Bulb; * = May be grown as annual in colder regions

Light: = Full sun; = Partial shade; = Full shade

Coreopsis verticillata 'Moonbeam'
HP | Zn3–10 | LSp–EFa | 1–3′ | |

Coriandrum sativum
A | Zn2–9 | culinary | 2′ | |

Corydalis lutea
HP | Zn5–8 | LSp–EFa | 12–15″ | |

Cosmos bipinnatus cultivar
A | Zn2–10 | ESu–MFa | 30–36″ | |

Cosmos sulfureus 'Ladybird Scarlet'
A | Zn2–10 | ESu–LSu | 2′ | |

Crambe cordifolia
HP | Zn5–9 | ESu | 4–7′ | |

Crocosmia masoniorum
HB | Zn6–10 | ESu–LSu | 30–60″ | |

Crocus chrysanthus
HB | Zn4–9 | MSp | 2–4″ | |

Crocus sieberi
HB | Zn3–8 | MSp | 2–3″ | |

Top row: JP, JP, JP; Middle row: JP, JP, GBP; Bottom row: IBC, IBC, IBC

Bloom: ESp = Early Spring; MSp = Midspring; LSp = Late Spring; ESu = Early Summer; MSu = Midsummer; LSu = Late Summer; EFa = Early Fall; MFa = Mid Fall; LFa = Late Fall
Soil: = Dry soil; = Good for xeriscaping; = Ordinary soil; = Moist soil

***Crocus** tommasinianus* 'Taplow Baby'
HB | Zn4–9 | MSp | 3–4" | | |

***Cuphea** hyssopifolia*
TP | Zn10 | ESp–MFa | 1–2' | | |

***Cuphea** ignea*
TP* | Zn10 | ESu–MFa | 12–30" | | |

***Cyclamen** hederifolium* f. *albiflorum*
HP | Zn5–7 | MFa–LFa | 4–5" | | |

***Cymbalaria** muralis*
HP | Zn4–9 | MSu | 2" | | |

***Cymbopogon** citratus*
TP* | Zn9–10 | culinary | 3–5' | | |

***Cynara** cardunculus*
HP | Zn8–10 | ESu–LSu | 6–8' | | |

***Cyperus** longus*
HP | Zn8–10 | MSu | 5' | | |

***Cypripedium** calceolus*
HP | Zn3–7 | LSp–ESu | 18" | | |

Top row: JP, JP, JP; Middle row: MC, GBP, GBP; Bottom row: JP, GBP, HA

 Type: A = Annual; Bi = Biennial; HP = Hardy Perennial; TP = Tender Perennial; HB = Hardy Bulb; TB = Tender Bulb; * = May be grown as annual in colder regions
Light: = Full sun; = Partial shade; = Full shade

Cypripedium reginae
HP | Zn4–8 | LSp–ESu | 2–3′ | |

Cyrtomium falcatum
HP | Zn7–9 | foliage | 2′ | |

Dactylorhiza foliosa
HP | Zn7–8 | LSp–ESu | 1–2′ | |

Dahlia 'Rebecca Lynn'
TP* | Zn9–10 | MSu–EFa | 1–2′ | |

Dahlia pinnata
TP* | Zn8–10 | MSu–MFa | 5–7′ | |

Darmera peltata
HP | Zn5–9 | foliage | 3–4′ | |

Datura innoxia
TP* | Zn9–10 | ESu–LSu | 3–4′ | |

Datura metel
TP* | Zn9–10 | ESu–LSu | 3–4′ | |

Delosperma cooperi
HP | Zn6–9 | ESu–LSu | 2–5″ | |

Top row: HA, JP, GBP; Middle row: JP, SC, MC; Bottom row: JP, MC, JP

Bloom: ESp = Early Spring; MSp = Midspring; LSp = Late Spring; ESu = Early Summer; MSu = Midsummer; LSu = Late Summer; EFa = Early Fall; MFa = Mid Fall; LFa = Late Fall
Soil: = Dry soil; = Good for xeriscaping; = Ordinary soil; = Moist soil

***Delphinium** grandiflorum* cultivar
HP | Zn3–9 | ESu–LSu | 8–20″ | ○ ◐ |

Delphinium 'Galahad' (Pacific Hybrid)
HP | Zn3–9 | ESu | 5–6′ | ○ ◐ |

***Dennstaedtia** punctiloba*
HP | Zn3–8 | foliage | 2–3′ | ○ ● |

***Dianthus** barbatus*
Bi | Zn2–10 | LSp–ESu | 10–20″ | ○ ◐ |

***Dianthus** chinensis* 'Telstar White'
TP* | Zn9–10 | LSp–ESu | 6–8″ | ○ ◐ |

***Diascia** barberae*
HP | Zn6–8 | ESu–LSu | 10–12″ | ○ ◐ |

***Dicentra** spectabilis*
HP | Zn3–9 | LSp–ESu | 2′ | ○ ● |

***Dictamnus** albus* var. *purpureus*
HP | Zn3–8 | LSp–ESu | 3′ | ○ ◐ |

***Dierama** pulcherrimum*
HB | Zn7–9 | MSu | 3–5′ | ○ |

Top row: JP, JP, GBP; Middle row: JP, JP, JP; Bottom row: JP, JP, GBP

 Type: A = Annual; Bi = Biennial; HP = Hardy Perennial; TP = Tender Perennial; HB = Hardy Bulb; TB = Tender Bulb; * = May be grown as annual in colder regions
Light: ○ = Full sun; ◐ = Partial shade; ● = Full shade

Digitalis laevigata

HP | Zn5–9 | ESu–MSu | 3′ | | |

Digitalis purpurea

HP | Zn4–8 | ESu–MSu | 3–5′ | | |

Dimorphotheca sinuata

TP* | Zn9–10 | ESu–LSu | 12″ | | |

Dodecatheon meadia f. *album*

HP | Zn4–8 | LSp–ESu | 1–2′ | | |

Draba aizoides

HP | Zn5–8 | MSp | 1–4″ | | |

Dryas octopetala

HP | Zn2–6 | LSp–ESu | 2–3″ | | |

Dryopteris marginalis

HP | Zn3–8 | foliage | 2′ | | |

Eccremocarpus scaber

HP* | Zn8–10 | MSu–MFa | 6–12′ | | |

Echinacea purpurea 'Alba'

HP | Zn3–9 | MSu–EFa | 2–4′ | | |

Top row: JP, JDS, JP; Middle row: JP, JP, JP; Bottom row: JP, JP, JP

Bloom: ESp = Early Spring; MSp = Midspring; LSp = Late Spring; ESu = Early Summer; MSu = Midsummer; LSu = Late Summer; EFa = Early Fall; MFa = Mid Fall; LFa = Late Fall

Soil: = Dry soil; = Good for xeriscaping; = Ordinary soil; = Moist soil

***Echinops** ritro*

HP | Zn3–9 | MSu–LSu | 2′–4′ | | |

***Echium** candicans*

Bi | Zn3–8 | MSp–ESu | 5–8′ | | |

***Emilia** coccinea*

A | Zn3–10 | ESu–LSu | 1–2′ | | |

***Epilobium** angustifolium*

HP | Zn3–8 | LSu–EFa | 4–6′ | | |

***Epimedium** grandiflorum*

HP | Zn4–9 | MSp–LSp | 9–12″ | | |

***Epimedium** pinnatum* ssp. *colchicum*

HP | Zn4–9 | MSp–ESu | 12″ | | |

***Epimedium** × versicolor* 'Neosulfureum'

HP | Zn4–8 | ESp–MSp | 12″ | | |

***Eragrostis** trichodes* 'Bend'

HP | Zn4–9 | LSu | 3′ | | |

***Eranthis** hyemalis*

HP | Zn4–9 | ESp | 2–8″ | | |

Top row: JP, JP, JP; Middle row: JP, GBP, GBP; Bottom row: JP, JP, JP

 Type: A = Annual; Bi = Biennial; HP = Hardy Perennial; TP = Tender Perennial; HB = Hardy Bulb; TB = Tender Bulb; * = May be grown as annual in colder regions

Light: = Full sun; = Partial shade; = Full shade

Erigeron karvinskianus
HP | Zn8–9 | ESu–LSu | 6–12″ |

Erinus alpinus
HP | Zn4–9 | LSp–ESu | 2–3″ |

Erodium absinthoides
HP | Zn6–10 | ESu–MSu | 8″ |

Erodium foetidum
HP | Zn7–8 | ESu–MSu | 6–8″ |

Eryngium giganteum
Bi | Zn3–8 | LSu | 3–4′ |

Erysimum cheiri 'Orange Bedder'
HP | Zn3–7 | MSp–LSp | 18–24″ |

Erysimum linifolium
HP* | Zn7–9 | ESu–MSu | 12″ |

Eschscholzia californica
HP* | Zn8–10 | MSp–ESu | 8–18″ |

Eucomis comosa
HB* | Zn8–10 | MSu | 2–3′ |

Top row: JP, JP, GBP; Middle row: GBP, JP, JP; Bottom row: JP, JP, JP

Bloom: ESp = Early Spring; MSp = Midspring; LSp = Late Spring; ESu = Early Summer; MSu = Midsummer; LSu = Late Summer; EFa = Early Fall; MFa = Mid Fall; LFa = Late Fall

Soil: = Dry soil; = Good for xeriscaping; = Ordinary soil; = Moist soil

***Eupatorium** coelestinum*

HP | Zn6–8 | MSu–MFa | 2–3′ |

***Eupatorium** fistulosum* 'Gateway'

HP | Zn4–8 | LSu–EFa | 5′ |

***Eupatorium** rugosum* 'Chocolate'

HP | Zn3–8 | EFa–MFa | 3–4′ |

***Euphorbia** marginata*

A | Zn3–10 | MSu–MFa | 1–3′ |

***Euphorbia** polychroma*

HP | Zn4–9 | MSp–LSp | 18–24″ |

***Evolvulus** pilosus* 'Blue Daze'

HP* | Zn8–10 | LSp–EFa | 12–18″ |

***Farfugium** japonicum* 'Aureomaculata'

HP | Zn7–10 | LSu–EFa | 2′ |

***Festuca** glauca* 'Elijah Blue'

HP | Zn4–9 | foliage | 1′ |

***Filipendula** rubra*

HP | Zn3–9 | MSu | 6–8′ |

Top row: MC, MC, MC; Middle row: JP, JDS, JP; Bottom row: JP, JP, JP

 Type: A = Annual; Bi = Biennial; HP = Hardy Perennial; TP = Tender Perennial; HB = Hardy Bulb; TB = Tender Bulb; * = May be grown as annual in colder regions

Light: ○ = Full sun; ◐ = Partial shade; ● = Full shade

Filipendula ulmaria

HP | Zn3–9 | MSu–LSu | 3–6′ | | |

Foeniculum vulgare

HP | Zn4–10 | foliage | 3–6′ | | |

Francoa sonchifolia

HP | Zn7–10 | MSu | 30″ | | |

Freesia cultivars

TB | Zn9–10 | ESp–MSp | 12–16″ | | |

Fritillaria imperialis 'Rubra Maxima'

HB | Zn5–9 | MSp | 30″ | | |

Fritillaria meleagris

HB | Zn3–8 | MSp | 10–12″ | | |

Fritillaria persica

HB | Zn4–9 | MSp | 2–4′ | | |

Fuchsia 'Gartenmeister Bonstedt'

TP* | Zn9–10 | ESu–MFa | 18–24″ | | |

Gaillardia aristata

HP | Zn3–9 | ESu–LSu | 2–3′ | | |

Top row: JP, JP, GBP; Middle row: IBC, IBC, IBC; Bottom row: IBC, JP, JP

Bloom: ESp = Early Spring; MSp = Midspring; LSp = Late Spring; ESu = Early Summer; MSu = Midsummer; LSu = Late Summer; EFa = Early Fall; MFa = Mid Fall; LFa = Late Fall

Soil: = Dry soil; = Good for xeriscaping; = Ordinary soil; = Moist soil

Gaillardia pulchella
A | Zn1–10 | ESu–EFa | 12–18″ |

Galanthus elwesii
HB | Zn5–9 | ESp | 6–12″ |

Galium odoratum
HP | Zn4–9 | LSp–ESu | 6–12″ |

Galtonia candicans
HB* | Zn6–8 | MSu–EFa | 3–4′ |

Gaura lindheimeri 'Siskiyou Pink'
HP | Zn6–9 | ESu–MFa | 2–3′ |

Gazania rigens
TP* | Zn9–10 | ESu–EFa | 6–18″ |

Gentiana septemfida
HP | Zn3–9 | LSu | 1′ |

Geranium × *magnificum*
HP | Zn4–8 | LSp–ESu | 18–24″ |

Geranium psilostemon
HP | Zn4–8 | ESu–LSu | 30–48″ |

Top row: JP, IBC, JP; Middle row: IBC, JP, JP; Bottom row: JP, JP, JP

 Type: A = Annual; Bi = Biennial; HP = Hardy Perennial; TP = Tender Perennial; HB = Hardy Bulb; TB = Tender Bulb; * = May be grown as annual in colder regions
Light: = Full sun; = Partial shade; = Full shade

Geranium *sanguineum*
HP | Zn4–10 | ESu–MSu | 1′ |

Gerbera *jamesonii* 'Advantage Mix'
TP* | Zn10 | ESu–EFa | 12–18″ |

Geum *chiloense*
HP | Zn5–9 | ESu–LSu | 16–24″ |

Gilia *tricolor*
A | Zn6–10 | ESu–EFa | 12–18″ |

Gillenia *trifoliata*
HP | Zn4–8 | MSu | 2–4′ |

Gladiolus *communis* ssp. *byzantinus*
HB | Zn5–10 | ESu | 2–3′ |

Glaucidium *palmatum*
HP | Zn5–9 | LSp–ESu | 2–4′ |

Glaucium *flavum*
Bi | Zn3–9 | MSu–LSu | 18–24″ |

Globularia *cordifolia*
HP | Zn5–9 | LSp–ESu | 4″ |

Top row: JDS, JP, JDS; Middle row: JP, JP, JP; Bottom row: GBP, GBP, GBP

Bloom: ESp = Early Spring; MSp = Midspring; LSp = Late Spring; ESu = Early Summer; MSu = Midsummer; LSu = Late Summer; EFa = Early Fall; MFa = Mid Fall; LFa = Late Fall
Soil: = Dry soil; = Good for xeriscaping; = Ordinary soil; = Moist soil

Gloriosa *superba*

TP* | Zn9–10 | MSu–EFa | 5–6′ | |

Gomphrena *globosa* 'Gnome Pink'

A | Zn3–10 | ESu–EFa | 8–10″ | |

Gunnera *manicata*

HP | Zn7–10 | foliage | 6–8′ | |

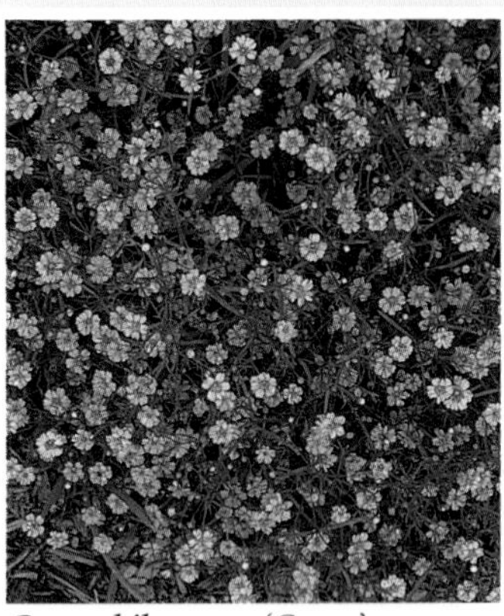

Gypsophila *repens* 'Gypsy'

HP | Zn3–8 | ESu–LSu | 6–12″ | |

Hacquetia *epipactis*

HP | Zn4–9 | ESp | 2–4″ | |

Haemanthus *albiflos*

TB* | Zn10 | MSu | 2–12″ | |

Hakonechloa *macra* 'Aureola'

HP | Zn4–10 | foliage | 12–16″ | |

Hardenbergia *violacea* 'Minihaha'

TP* | Zn9–10 | MSp | 2–3′ | |

Hedychium *coronarium*

HP* | Zn7–10 | LSu–EFa | 4–6′ | |

Top row: JP, JP, JP; Middle row: JP, JP, JP; Bottom row: JP, GBP, JP

 Type: A = Annual; Bi = Biennial; HP = Hardy Perennial; TP = Tender Perennial; HB = Hardy Bulb; TB = Tender Bulb; * = May be grown as annual in colder regions

Light: = Full sun; = Partial shade; = Full shade

Hedyotis caerulea

HP | Zn3–8 | LSp–ESu | 6″ | | |

Helenium autumnale

HP | Zn3–8 | LSu–EFa | 3–5′ | | |

Helianthemum apenninum

HP | Zn6–9 | ESu–MSu | 12–18″ | | |

Helianthemum nummularium 'Buttercup'

HP | Zn6–9 | LSp–ESu | 4–12″ | | |

Helianthus annuus cultivar

A | Zn1–10 | ESu–LSu | 3–12′ | | |

Helianthus maximiliani

HP | Zn4–9 | LSu–EFa | 4–10′ | | |

Helichrysum italicum ssp. serotinum

HP* | Zn7–10 | foliage | 18″ | | |

Helichrysum petiolare 'Limelight'

TP* | Zn9–10 | foliage | 6″ | | |

Helictotrichon sempervirens

HP | Zn4–8 | MSu | 2–4′ | | |

Top row: JP, JP, JP; Middle row: JP, JDS, JP; Bottom row: JP, JP, GBP

Bloom: ESp = Early Spring; MSp = Midspring; LSp = Late Spring; ESu = Early Summer; MSu = Midsummer; LSu = Late Summer; EFa = Early Fall; MFa = Mid Fall; LFa = Late Fall

Soil: = Dry soil; = Good for xeriscaping; = Ordinary soil; = Moist soil

***Heliopsis** helianthoides* 'Light of Loddon'
HP | Zn4–9 | MSu–EFa | 4–5' |

***Heliotropium** arborescens*
TP* | Zn9–10 | MSu–EFa | 18–48" |

***Helleborus** foetidus*
HP | Zn3–9 | ESp | 18" |

***Helleborus** orientalis*
HP | Zn5–9 | ESp | 18–24" |

Hemerocallis 'Elmo Jackson'
HP | Zn3–9 | ESu–MSu | 2–3' |

***Hemerocallis** lilioasphodelus*
HP | Zn3–9 | LSp–ESu | 2–3' |

Hemerocallis 'My Sweet Love'
HP | Zn3–9 | MSu–LSu | 18–24" |

***Hepatica** nobilis*
HP | Zn4–8 | ESp–MSp | 6–9" |

***Hesperis** matronalis*
HP | Zn3–9 | LSp–ESu | 1–3' |

Top row: JP, JP, JP; Middle row: JP, JP, JDS; Bottom row: GBP, JP, JP

 Type: A = Annual; Bi = Biennial; HP = Hardy Perennial; TP = Tender Perennial; HB = Hardy Bulb; TB = Tender Bulb; * = May be grown as annual in colder regions
Light: ○ = Full sun; ◐ = Partial shade; ● = Full shade

***Heuchera** sanguinea* 'Splendens'

HP | Zn3–9 | LSp-MSu | 12–18″ | |

× ***Heucherella** alba* 'Rosalie'

HP | Zn4–9 | LSp–ESu | 18″ | |

***Hibiscus** moscheutos* 'Intense Pink'

HP | Zn4–10 | ESu–LSu | 3–8′ | |

***Hosta** montana* 'Yellow River'

HP | Zn3–9 | MSu | 24–30″ | |

***Hosta** nigrescens*

HP | Zn3–9 | LSu | 2–3′ | |

***Houttuynia** cordata* 'Chameleon'

HP | Zn5–9 | foliage | 6–12″ | |

***Humulus** lupulus*

HP | Zn5–8 | foliage | 15–25′ | |

***Hunnemannia** fumariifolia* 'Sunlight'

TP | Zn9–10 | MSu–EFa | 2′ | |

***Hyacinthoides** italica*

HB | Zn4–9 | MSp | 6–8″ | |

Top row: GBP, GBP, JP; Middle row: GBP, GBP, JP; Bottom row: JP, JP, GBP

Bloom: ESp = Early Spring; MSp = Midspring; LSp = Late Spring; ESu = Early Summer; MSu = Midsummer; LSu = Late Summer; EFa = Early Fall; MFa = Mid Fall; LFa = Late Fall

Soil: = Dry soil; = Good for xeriscaping; = Ordinary soil; = Moist soil

Hyacinthoides non-scripta
HB | Zn4–9 | MSp | 8–12″| | |

Hyacinthus cultivars
HB | Zn5–8 | MSp | 8–12″| | |

Hypericum calycinum
HP | Zn5–9 | MSu–MFa | 12–18″| | |

Hypericum olympicum
HP | Zn7–9 | ESu–LSu | 6–12″| | |

Hypoestes phyllostachya 'White Splash'
TP* | Zn10 | foliage | 1′| | |

Iberis umbellata 'Fantasia'
A | Zn1–10 | ESu–EFa | 9–12″| | |

Impatiens New Guinea Hybrid
TP* | Zn10 | ESu–MFa | 1–2′| | |

Impatiens walleriana
TP* | Zn10 | LSp–MFa | 1–2′| | |

Inula orientalis
HP | Zn3–9 | LSu | 18–24″| | |

Top row: IBC, IBC, GBP; Middle row: GBP, JP, JP; Bottom row: JP, JDS, MC

Type: A = Annual; Bi = Biennial; HP = Hardy Perennial; TP = Tender Perennial; HB = Hardy Bulb; TB = Tender Bulb; * = May be grown as annual in colder regions
Light: = Full sun; = Partial shade; = Full shade

Ipomoea nil
A | Zn3–10 | MSu–EFa | 10–12′ | |

Ipomoea tricolor 'Tie Die'
A | Zn3–10 | MSu–EFa | 10–15′ | |

Iris cristata f. *alba*
HP | Zn6–9 | MSp | 4–6″ | |

Iris fulva
HP | Zn7–10 | MSp | 2–3′ | |

Iris pseudacorus
HP | Zn5–9 | LSp–ESu | 3–6′ | |

Iris sibirica
HP | Zn4–9 | LSp–ESu | 2–4′ | |

Isatis tinctoria
Bi | Zn3–10 | MSu | 3–4′ | |

Ixia maculata
TB* | Zn9–10 | LSp–ESu | 8–20″ | |

Kirengeshoma palmata
HP | Zn5–8 | LSu–EFa | 2–4′ | |

Top row: MC, GBP, JP; Middle row: JP, JP, JDS; Bottom row: JP, JP, JP

Bloom: ESp = Early Spring; MSp = Midspring; LSp = Late Spring; ESu = Early Summer; MSu = Midsummer; LSu = Late Summer; EFa = Early Fall; MFa = Mid Fall; LFa = Late Fall
Soil: = Dry soil; = Good for xeriscaping; = Ordinary soil; = Moist soil

***Kniphofia** uvaria*

HP | Zn5–9 | ESu–EFa | 3–4′ | |

***Lablab** purpureus*

TP* | Zn9–10 | MSu–EFa | 15–30′ | |

***Lamium** galeobdolon* 'Hermann's Pride'

HP | Zn3–9 | LSp–ESu | 1′ | |

***Lamium** maculatum* f. *album*

HP | Zn3–9 | LSP–LSu | 1′ | |

***Lantana** camara*

HP* | Zn8–10 | ESu–MFa | 3–6′ | |

***Lantana** montevidensis*

TP* | Zn8–10 | ESu–MFa | 2–3′ | |

***Lathyrus** latifolius*

HP | Zn6–9 | MSu–EFa | 5–6′ | |

***Lathyrus** odoratus* cultivars

A | Zn1–10 | MSu–EFa | 8–10′ | |

***Lavandula** angustifolia* 'Martha Roderick'

HP | Zn5–9 | MSu | 18″ | |

Top row: JDS, JP, JP; Middle row: JP, JDS, JP; Bottom row: JDS, JP, JP

 Type: A = Annual; Bi = Biennial; HP = Hardy Perennial; TP = Tender Perennial; HB = Hardy Bulb; TB = Tender Bulb; * = May be grown as annual in colder regions

Light: = Full sun; = Partial shade; = Full shade

***Lavandula** stoechas*

HP* | Zn8–9 | LSp–LSu | 1–2′ |

***Lavatera** trimestris* cultivars

A | Zn2–10 | ESu–LSu | 18–24″ |

***Leonotis** leonurus*

TP* | Zn9–10 | LSu–EFa | 3–6′ |

***Leontopodium** alpinum*

HP | Zn4–7 | LSp–ESu | 6–12″ |

***Leucanthemum** × superbum*

HP | Zn5–8 | MSu | 1–4′ |

***Leucojum** vernum* var. *carpathicum*

HB | Zn4–9 | LSp | 6–12″ |

***Levisticum** officinale*

HP | Zn4–8 | foliage | 3–7′ |

***Lewisia** cotyledon*

HP | Zn4–8 | LSp–ESu | 9–12″ |

***Liatris** spicata* 'Callilepsis Purple'

HP | Zn3–10 | LSu–EFa | 2–3′ |

Top row: JP, JP, JP; Middle row: JP, JP, JP; Bottom row: JP, JP, GBP

Bloom: ESp = Early Spring; MSp = Midspring; LSp = Late Spring; ESu = Early Summer; MSu = Midsummer; LSu = Late Summer; EFa = Early Fall; MFa = Mid Fall; LFa = Late Fall

Soil: = Dry soil; = Good for xeriscaping; = Ordinary soil; = Moist soil

***Ligularia** dentata* 'Othello'

HP | Zn4–8 | MSu–LSu | 3–5′| | |

***Lilium** martagon*

HB | Zn4–9 | ESu | 3–6′| | |

***Lilium** regale* 'Album'

HB | Zn4–9 | MSu | 3–4′| | |

***Lilium** speciosum*

HB | Zn5–9 | LSu–EFa | 3–6′| | |

***Limnanthes** douglasii*

A | Zn1–9 | ESu–LSu | 9–12″| | |

***Limonium** latifolium*

HP | Zn4–9 | MSu–LSu | 2′| | |

***Limonium** sinuatum*

HP* | Zn8–9 | LSu–EFa | 18″| | |

***Linaria** maroccana* cultivar

A | Zn2–10 | LSp–ESu | 8–16″| | |

***Linaria** purpurea*

HP | Zn4–9 | ESu | 30–36″| | |

Top row: MC, JP, IBC; Middle row: IBC, JP, JDS; Bottom row: JP, GBP, JP

 Type: A = Annual; Bi = Biennial; HP = Hardy Perennial; TP = Tender Perennial; HB = Hardy Bulb; TB = Tender Bulb; * = May be grown as annual in colder regions

Light: = Full sun; = Partial shade; = Full shade

***Linum** grandiflorum* 'Rubrum'

A | Zn2–10 | ESu–LSu | 18–24" | |

***Liriope** muscari* 'Variegata'

HP | Zn5–9 | LSu–EFa | 8–12" | |

***Lithodora** diffusa* 'Heavenly Blue'

HP | Zn6–9 | ESu | 6–12" | |

***Lobelia** cardinalis*

HP | Zn2–9 | LSu | 3–4' | |

***Lobelia** erinus* 'Crystal Palace'

TP* | Zn9–10 | LSp–MFa | 4–8" | |

***Lobularia** maritima* 'Snow Crystals'

A | Zn3–10 | LSp–MFa | 6–9" | |

***Lunaria** annua*

Bi | Zn3–9 | MSp | 2–3' | |

***Lupinus** arboreus*

P* | Zn8–9 | ESu | 3' | |

***Lupinus** perennis*

HP | Zn4–9 | ESu | 2' | |

Top row: JP, JP, JP; Middle row: JDS, JP, JP; Bottom row: JP, GBP, MC

Lychnis chalcedonica

HP | Zn4–8 | ESu–MSu | 3–4′ |

Lychnis flos-jovis

HP | Zn4–8 | MSu–LSu | 18″ |

Lysichiton americanus

HP | Zn7–9 | MSp | 2–4′ |

Lysimachia clethroides

HP | Zn3–9 | MSu–LSu | 2–3′ |

Lysimachia punctata 'Alexander'

HP | Zn5–9 | MSu | 16–18″ |

Macleaya cordata

HP | Zn4–9 | ESu–LSu | 5–8′ |

Malcolmia maritima

A | Zn1–9 | MSp–MFa | 8″ |

Malephora crocea

TP* | Zn9–10 | LSp–EFa | 8″ |

Malva sylvestris 'Zebrina'

HP | Zn4–8 | ESu–EFa | 2–3′ |

Top row: JDS, JP, JP; Middle row: JP, JP, JP; Bottom row: GBP, GBP, JP

 Type: A = Annual; Bi = Biennial; HP = Hardy Perennial; TP = Tender Perennial; HB = Hardy Bulb; TB = Tender Bulb; * = May be grown as annual in colder regions

Light: ○ = Full sun; ◐ = Partial shade; ● = Full shade

Mandevilla laxa
HP* | Zn8–10 | ESu–EFa | 15′ | | |

Matteuccia struthiopteris
HP | Zn2–9 | foliage | 3–5′ | | |

Matthiola incana
A | Zn2–10 | ESp–LSp | 1–2′ | | |

Mazus reptans
HP | Zn5–8 | LSp–ESu | 2″ | | |

Meconopsis betonicifolia
HP | Zn6–9 | LSp–ESu | 3–4′ | | |

Meconopsis cambrica
HP | Zn6–9 | MSu | 1–2′ | | |

Melissa officinalis
HP | Zn4–9 | MSu–EFa | 2′ | | |

Mentha × piperita 'Black Peppermint'
HP | Zn5–10 | culinary | 1–2′ | | |

Mentha suaveolens 'Variegata'
HP | Zn5–9 | culinary | 12–18″ | | |

Top row: GBP, JP, JP; Middle row: JP, JP, JP; Bottom row: JP, JP, JP

Bloom: ESp = Early Spring; MSp = Midspring; LSp = Late Spring; ESu = Early Summer; MSu = Midsummer; LSu = Late Summer; EFa = Early Fall; MFa = Mid Fall; LFa = Late Fall
Soil: = Dry soil; = Good for xeriscaping; = Ordinary soil; = Moist soil

Merremia tuberosa

TP* | Zn10 | MSu | 20' | ○ ◐ | |

Mertensia pulmonarioides

HP | Zn3–8 | MSp | 1–2' | ○ ● | |

Mimulus × *hybridus* 'Mystic Cream'

HP* | Zn7–9 | ESu–EFa | 1' | ○ ◐ | |

Mirabilis jalapa

A | Zn3–7 | ESu–MFa | 2–4' | ○ ◐ | |

Miscanthus sinensis 'Zebrinus'

HP | Zn5–9 | LSu–EFa | 4–8' | ○ ◐ | |

Mitchella repens

HP | Zn3–9 | ESu | 2" | ◐ ● | |

Mitella breweri

HP | Zn5–7 | ESu | 1' | ◐ ● | |

Moluccella laevis

A | Zn2–10 | MSu–EFa | 2' | ○ ◐ | |

Monarda fistulosa

HP | Zn4–9 | MSu–LSu | 3–4' | ○ ◐ | |

Top row: JP, JDS, MC; Middle row: JDS, JP, JP; Bottom row: GBP, MC, JP

 Type: A = Annual; Bi = Biennial; HP = Hardy Perennial; TP = Tender Perennial; HB = Hardy Bulb; TB = Tender Bulb; * = May be grown as annual in colder regions

Light: ○ = Full sun; ◐ = Partial shade; ● = Full shade

Moraea *spathulata*
TB* | Zn9–10 | MSu | 2–4′ | |

Muscari *armeniacum*
HB | Zn4–8 | MSp | 6–8″ | |

Myosotis *scorpioides*
HP | Zn5–8 | LSp–MSu | 6–12″ | |

Myosotis *sylvatica* 'Blue Basket'
HP | Zn5–8 | LSp–ESu | 6–12″ | |

Myrrhis *odorata*
HP | Zn3–9 | ESu | 3–5′ | |

Narcissus *bulbocodium*
HB | Zn3–9 | MSp | 3–6″ | |

Narcissus 'Dutch Master'
HB | Zn8–9 | ESp | 12–14″ | |

Nelumbo *nucifera*
HP | Zn4–10 | ESu–LSu | 3–5′ | |

Nemesia *strumosa* Carnival Series
A | Zn2–9 | ESp–EFa | 8–12″ | |

Top row: GBP, JP, JDS; Middle row: JP, JP, IBC; Bottom row: JP, JP, JP

Bloom: ESp = Early Spring; MSp = Midspring; LSp = Late Spring; ESu = Early Summer; MSu = Midsummer; LSu = Late Summer; EFa = Early Fall; MFa = Mid Fall; LFa = Late Fall

Soil: = Dry soil; = Good for xeriscaping; = Ordinary soil; = Moist soil

***Nemophila** menziesii*

A | Zn2–9 | ESp–ESu | 4–6″ |

***Nepeta** × faassenii*

HP | Zn4–9 | ESu, LSu | 1–2′ |

***Nepeta** sibirica*

HP | Zn3–9 | MSu | 2–3′ |

***Nerine** bowdenii*

HBu* | Zn8–10 | MFa | 18–24″ |

***Nicandra** physalodes*

A | Zn3–8 | MSu–EFa | 3–4′ |

***Nicotiana** alata* Metro Mix

A | Zn2–10 | LSu | 12–15″ |

***Nicotiana** sylvestris*

A | Zn2–10 | LSu | 3–5′ |

***Nierembergia** caerulea* 'Purple Robe'

A | Zn2–10 | MSu–EFa | 6–8″ |

***Nigella** damascena* cultivar

A | Zn2–10 | MSu | 18–24″ |

Top row: JP, JDS, JP; Middle row: JP, JP, JP; Bottom row: MC, JP, JP

 Type: A = Annual; Bi = Biennial; HP = Hardy Perennial; TP = Tender Perennial; HB = Hardy Bulb; TB = Tender Bulb; * = May be grown as annual in colder regions

Light: ○ = Full sun; ◐ = Partial shade; ● = Full shade

Nolana paradoxa
TP* | Zn9–10 | ESu–LSu | 3″ | | |

Nomocharis pardanthina
HB | Zn7–9 | MSu | 3′ | | |

Ocimum basilicum
A | Zn4–10 | foliage | 2′ | | |

Oenothera macrocarpa
HP | Zn4–9 | MSu | 4–6″ | | |

Oenothera speciosa 'Siskiyou Pink'
HP | Zn5–8 | ESu | 12–18″ | | |

Omphalodes cappadocica 'Starry Eyes'
HP | Zn6–9 | ESp | 6–10″ | | |

Omphalodes verna
HP | Zn6–9 | LSp–ESu | 6–8″ | | |

Ophiopogon planiscapus 'Nigrescens'
HP | Zn6–10 | foliage | 6–10″ | | |

Origanum vulgare 'Aureum'
HP | Zn5–9 | MSu | 18–30″ | | |

Top row: GBP, JP, JP; Middle row: JDS, JP, GBP; Bottom row: JP, JP, JP

Bloom: ESp = Early Spring; MSp = Midspring; LSp = Late Spring; ESu = Early Summer; MSu = Midsummer; LSu = Late Summer; EFa = Early Fall; MFa = Mid Fall; LFa = Late Fall

Soil: = Dry soil; = Good for xeriscaping; = Ordinary soil; = Moist soil

Ornithogalum nutans
HB | Zn5–9 | MSp | 8–18″ | |

Osmunda cinnamomea
HP | Zn3–10 | foliage | 3′ | |

Osmunda regalis
HP | Zn2–10 | foliage | 3–6′ | |

Osteospermum jucundum
TP* | Zn9–10 | MSp–MFa | 6–24″ | |

Oxalis adenophylla
HP | Zn7–9 | MSp | 2″ | |

Paeonia officinalis
HP | Zn3–9 | LSp–ESu | 28–30″ | |

Paeonia suffruticosa cultivar
HP | Zn4–8 | LSp–ESu | 5–7′ | |

Panicum virgatum 'Heavy Metal'
HP | Zn5–9 | LSu | 4′ | |

Papaver croceum cultivars
HP | Zn3–9 | LSp–ESu | 1′ | |

Top row: JP, JP, JP; Middle row: GBP, GBP, JP; Bottom row: JP, JP, JP

 Type: A = Annual; Bi = Biennial; HP = Hardy Perennial; TP = Tender Perennial; HB = Hardy Bulb; TB = Tender Bulb; * = May be grown as annual in colder regions

Light: ○ = Full sun; ◐ = Partial shade; ● = Full shade

Papaver *orientale*

HP | Zn3–9 | ESu | 2–4′ |

Papaver *rhoeas* cultivars

A | Zn1–10 | MSp–LSp | 1–2′ |

Paradisea *liliastrum*

HP | Zn7–9 | LSp | 1–2′ |

Passiflora *caerulea*

HP | Zn7–10 | ESu–EFa | 25–30′ |

Patrinia *scabiosaefolia*

HP | Zn5–8 | MSu–EFa | 3′ |

Pelargonium 'Mabel Grey'

TP* | Zn9–10 | MSp–MFa | 12–14" |

Pelargonium *peltatum* 'Solidor'

TP* | Zn9–10 | MSp–MFa | 12–18" |

Pennisetum *setaceum* 'Purpureum'

HP* | Zn8–10 | MSu–EFa | 2–3′ |

Penstemon *heterophyllus*

HP | Zn7–9 | LSp–ESu | 12–24" |

Top row: JP, JP, GBP; Middle row: GBP, JP, JP; Bottom row: JP, JP, JP

Bloom: ESp = Early Spring; MSp = Midspring; LSp = Late Spring; ESu = Early Summer; MSu = Midsummer; LSu = Late Summer; EFa = Early Fall; MFa = Mid Fall; LFa = Late Fall

Soil: = Dry soil; = Good for xeriscaping; = Ordinary soil; = Moist soil

***Penstemon** strictus*
HP | Zn4–9 | MSu | 20–24" | ○ ◐ | ♉ ◒ |

***Pentas** lanceolata* 'New Look'
TP* | Zn10 | ESu–MFa | 1–3' | ○ | ◒ |

***Perovskia** atriplicifolia*
HP | Zn5–9 | MSu–LSu | 3–5' | ○ | ◒ ◒ |

***Persicaria** bistorta*
HP | Zn3–9 | ESu, LSu | 2–3' | ○ ◐ | ◒ ◒ |

***Persicaria** capitata* 'Afinis'
HP | Zn5–8 | MSu–EFa | 2–6" | ○ ◐ | ◒ ◒ |

***Petrorhagia** saxifraga*
HP | Zn5–7 | MSu | 4–6" | ○ | ◒ ◒ |

***Petroselinum** crispum* cultivar
Bi | Zn4–9 | foliage | 12–18" | ○ ◐ | ◒ |

***Petunia** × hybrida* 'Mirage Red'
A | Zn1–10 | LSp–MFa | 10–12" | ○ | ◒ ◒ |

***Petunia** × hybrida* 'Summer Sun'
A | Zn1–10 | LSp–MFa | 10" | ○ | ◒ ◒ |

Top row: MC, JP, GBP; Middle row: GBP, JP, MC; Bottom row: JP, GBP, GBP

 Type: A = Annual; Bi = Biennial; HP = Hardy Perennial; TP = Tender Perennial; HB = Hardy Bulb; TB = Tender Bulb; * = May be grown as annual in colder regions
Light: ○ = Full sun; ◐ = Partial shade; ● = Full shade

Phacelia campanularia
A | Zn3–10 | MSp–ESu | 6–9″ | | |

Phalaris arundinacea var. *picta*
HP | Zn4–9 | foliage | 24–32″ | | |

Phaseolus coccineus 'Scarlet Emperor'
A | Zn1–10 | ESu–MFa | 5′ | | |

Phlomis russeliana
HP | Zn5–9 | ESu–MSu | 3–4′ | | |

Phlomis tuberosa 'Amazone'
HP | Zn3–9 | MSu | 5′ | | |

Phlox divaricata ssp. *laphamii*
HP | Zn4–9 | MSp | 1′ | | |

Phlox drummondii 'Palona Rose with Eye'
A | Zn2–10 | LSp–ESu | 6–12″ | | |

Phlox subulata 'Marjorie'
HP | Zn3–9 | ESp | 1–2′ | | |

Phormium cookianum 'Jack Spratt'
HP* | Zn8–10 | foliage | 3–6′ | | |

Top row: JP, JP, MC; Middle row: GBP, MC, JP; Bottom row: JP, JP, JP

Bloom: ESp = Early Spring; MSp = Midspring; LSp = Late Spring; ESu = Early Summer; MSu = Midsummer; LSu = Late Summer; EFa = Early Fall; MFa = Mid Fall; LFa = Late Fall
Soil: = Dry soil; = Good for xeriscaping; = Ordinary soil; = Moist soil

Phormium *tenax* 'Purpureum'

HP* | Zn8–10 | foliage | 6–8′ |

Phuopsis *stylosa*

HP | Zn4–9 | MSu | 9–12″ |

Phygelius *aequalis*

HP | Zn7–9 | LSu–EFa | 3′ |

Physostegia *virginiana* 'Variegata'

HP | Zn3–9 | MSu–EFa | 3–4′ |

Platycodon *grandiflorus* 'Sentimental Blue'

HP | Zn3–9 | MSu–LSu | 2–3′ |

Plectranthus *argentatus*

TP* | Zn10 | foliage | 2–3′ |

Podophyllum *peltatum*

HP | Zn3–9 | LSp | 18″ |

Polemonium *caeruleum* var. *lacteum*

HP | Zn3–8 | LSp–ESu | 2′ |

Polemonium *reptans*

HP | Zn3–8 | LSp–ESu | 8–12″ |

Top row: GBP, JP, JP; Middle row: JP, JP, JP; Bottom row: JP, JP, JDS

 Type: A = Annual; Bi = Biennial; HP = Hardy Perennial; TP = Tender Perennial; HB = Hardy Bulb; TB = Tender Bulb; * = May be grown as annual in colder regions

Light: ☼ = Full sun; ◐ = Partial shade; ● = Full shade

***Polystichum** munitum*

HP | Zn5–9 | foliage | 4′

***Portulaca** grandiflora* cultivar

A | Zn2–10 | ESu–EFa | 4–8″

***Potentilla** fruticosa* 'Princess'

HP | Zn3–7 | LSp–LSu | 3′

***Potentilla** neumaniana* 'Nana'

HP | Zn4–8 | LSp–ESu | 4–6″

***Primula** denticulata*

HP | Zn3–8 | ESp | 10–12″

***Primula** japonica*

HP | Zn5–8 | LSp | 1–2′

***Primula** vulgaris*

HP | Zn5–9 | MSp | 6–8″

***Prunella** grandiflora*

HP | Zn5–8 | ESu–LSu | 6–12″

***Pulmonaria** longifolia*

HP | Zn3–9 | MSp | 9–12″

Top row: JP, JDS, GBP; Middle row: GBP, JP, JDS; Bottom row: JP, JP, JDS

Bloom: ESp = Early Spring; MSp = Midspring; LSp = Late Spring; ESu = Early Summer; MSu = Midsummer; LSu = Late Summer; EFa = Early Fall; MFa = Mid Fall; LFa = Late Fall

Soil: = Dry soil; = Good for xeriscaping; = Ordinary soil; = Moist soil

Pulmonaria saccharata 'Sissinghurst White'
HP | Zn4–8 | MSp | 1′ | |

Pulsatilla *vulgaris*
HP | Zn5–7 | MSp | 6–12″ | |

Puschkinia *scilloides*
HB | Zn4–10 | MSp | 6″ | |

Ramonda *myconi*
HP | Zn5–7 | LSp–ESu | 3–4″ | |

Ranunculus *asiaticus* cultivar
HP* | Zn7–9 | ESu | 18–24″ | |

Ratibida *columnifera* 'Buttons and Bows'
HP | Zn3–10 | MSu–EFa | 2–3′ | |

Rehmannia *elata*
HP* | Zn8–10 | ESu–MSu | 2–3′ | |

Rheum *palmatum*
HP | Zn5–9 | ESu | 6–8′ | |

Rhodochiton *atrosanguineus*
TP* | Zn10 | ESu–MFa | 10′ | |

 Type: A = Annual; Bi = Biennial; HP = Hardy Perennial; TP = Tender Perennial; HB = Hardy Bulb; TB = Tender Bulb; * = May be grown as annual in colder regions
Light: = Full sun; = Partial shade; = Full shade

Top row: JP, GBP, JP; Middle row: GBP, JP, MC; Bottom row: JP, JP, JP

***Rhodohypoxis** baurii*
TP* | Zn9–10 | LSp–ESu | 2–4″

***Ricinus** communis* cultivar
A | Zn3–10 | foliage | 5′

***Rodgersia** pinnata* 'Superba'
HP | Zn4–9 | ESu–MSu | 3–4′

***Romneya** coulteri*
HP | Zn7–10 | ESu–LSu | 4–8′

***Roscoea** purpurea*
HP | Zn6–9 | MSu | 8–12″

***Rosmarinus** officinalis* 'Blue Lagoon'
HP* | Zn7–10 | MSp–ESu | 30–36″

***Rudbeckia** hirta* 'Irish Eyes'
A | Zn3–9 | MSu–EFa | 24–30″

***Rudbeckia** laciniata*
HP | Zn3–9 | MSu–EFa | 4–8′

***Ruellia** brittoniana*
TP* | Zn9–10 | MSu–MFa | 3–4′

Top row: JP, JP, JP; Middle row: JP, GBP, GBP; Bottom row: JP, JP, MC

Bloom: ESp = Early Spring; MSp = Midspring; LSp = Late Spring; ESu = Early Summer; MSu = Midsummer; LSu = Late Summer; EFa = Early Fall; MFa = Mid Fall; LFa = Late Fall

Soil: = Dry soil; = Good for xeriscaping; = Ordinary soil; = Moist soil

***Rumex** scutatus* 'Silver Shield'
HP | Zn6–9 | foliage | 1′ |

***Sagina** subulata*
HP | Zn5–9 | MSu | 6″ |

***Salpiglossis** sinuata* Bolero Hybrids
A | Zn1–10 | ESu–EFa | 2′ |

***Salvia** farinacea* 'Victoria'
HP* | Zn8–9 | MSu-MFa | 2′ |

***Salvia** splendens* 'Salsa Rose'
TP* | Zn10 | MSu–EFa | 8–12″ |

***Salvia** verticillata* 'Purple Rain'
HP | Zn5–9 | ESu–LSu | 18″ |

***Sandersonia** aurantiaca*
TP* | Zn9–10 | ESu–MSu | 1–2′ |

***Sanguinaria** canadensis* 'Flore Pleno'
HP | Zn3–9 | ESp | 6–9″ |

***Santolina** chamaecyparissus*
HP | Zn6–9 | foliage | 1–2′ |

Top row: MC, GBP, JP; Middle row: JP, JP, JP; Bottom row: GBP, JP, GBP

 Type: A = Annual; Bi = Biennial; HP = Hardy Perennial; TP = Tender Perennial; HB = Hardy Bulb; TB = Tender Bulb; * = May be grown as annual in colder regions

Light: ○ = Full sun; ◐ = Partial shade; ● = Full shade

***Sanvitalia** procumbens* 'Gold Braid'

A | Zn3–10 | ESu–EFa | 4–8″ | | |

***Saponaria** ocymoides*

HP | Zn2–8 | ESu | 6–9″ | | |

***Sarracenia** purpurea* ssp.*venosa*

HP | Zn3–10 | LSp | 1′ | | |

***Satureja** montana*

HP | Zn5–8 | ESu | 6–12″ | | |

***Saxifraga** oppositifolia*

HP | Zn2–7 | ESp | 2″ | | |

***Scabiosa** atropurpurea* 'Blue Cockade'

A | Zn4–10 | ESu–EFa | 3–4′ | | |

***Scabiosa** caucasica* 'Clive Greaves'

HP | Zn3–9 | ESu–MSu | 18–30″ | | |

***Scaevola** aemula* 'Purple Fanfare'

TP* | Zn9–10 | MSp–MFa | 1′ | | |

***Schizostylis** coccinea*

HP* | Zn7–10 | LSu–EFa | 1–2′ | | |

Top row: JP, JP, GBP; Middle row: GBP, GBP, JDS; Bottom row: GBP, GBP, JP

Bloom: ESp = Early Spring; MSp = Midspring; LSp = Late Spring; ESu = Early Summer; MSu = Midsummer; LSu = Late Summer; EFa = Early Fall; MFa = Mid Fall; LFa = Late Fall

Soil: = Dry soil; = Good for xeriscaping; = Ordinary soil; = Moist soil

Scilla peruviana
HB | Zn8–10 | ESu | 4–10″ |

Scilla siberica 'Alba'
HB | Zn5–8 | ESp | 6″ |

Scutellaria alpina
HP | Zn5–8 | LSu | 6–9″ |

Sedum 'Autumn Joy'
HP | Zn3–9 | ESu–LSu | 1–2′ |

Sedum kamtschaticum
HP | Zn3–9 | MSu–LSu | 6–12″ |

Sedum telephium var. *borderii*
HP | Zn3–9 | LSu–EFa | 1–2′ |

Sempervivum arachnoideum
HP | Zn5–9 | MSu | 2–8″ |

Sempervivum tectorum
HP | Zn5–9 | MSu | 4–6″ |

Senecio cineraria
HP* | Zn8–9 | foliage | 1′ |

Top row: IBC, IBC, JP; Middle row: JP, JP, JP; Bottom row: JP, JP, JP

 Type: A = Annual; Bi = Biennial; HP = Hardy Perennial; TP = Tender Perennial; HB = Hardy Bulb; TB = Tender Bulb; * = May be grown as annual in colder regions
Light: ☼ = Full sun; ◐ = Partial shade; ● = Full shade

***Shortia** solandelloides* var. *ilicifolia*

HP | Zn5–8 | LSp | 6–8″| | |

***Sidalcea** malviflora*

HP | Zn5–9 | ESu–MSu | 2–4′| | |

***Silene** armeria*

A | Zn3–9 | LSu–EFa | 1′| | |

***Silphium** perfoliatum*

HP | Zn5–9 | MSu–EFa | 5–8′| | |

***Silybum** marianum*

Bi | Zn6–9 | MSu–EFa | 4′| | |

***Smilacina** racemosa*

HP | Zn6–9 | LSp–ESu | 30–36″| | |

***Soldanella** alpina*

HP | Zn5–8 | ESp | 3″| | |

***Solenostemon** scutellarioides* cultivar

TP* | Zn10 | foliage | 12–18″| | |

***Solidago** sphacelata* 'Golden Fleece'

HP | Zn5–9 | EFa | 12–18″| | |

Top row: GBP, GBP, JP; Middle row: JP, JP, GBP; Bottom row: JP, JDS, JP

Bloom: ESp = Early Spring; MSp = Midspring; LSp = Late Spring; ESu = Early Summer; MSu = Midsummer; LSu = Late Summer; EFa = Early Fall; MFa = Mid Fall; LFa = Late Fall

Soil: = Dry soil; = Good for xeriscaping; = Ordinary soil; = Moist soil

Sparaxis tricolor
TB* | Zn9–10 | MSp | 4–12″ |

***Sphaeralcea** munroana*
HP | Zn4–10 | ESu–MFa | 18–24″ |

***Spigelia** marilandica*
HP | Zn5–9 | ESu, EFa | 1–2′ |

***Sprekelia** formosissima*
TBu* | Zn9–10 | LSp | 6–12″ |

***Stachys** byzantina* 'Primrose Heron'
HP | Zn4–9 | foliage | 12–18″ |

***Stachys** macrantha*
HP | Zn3–9 | LSp–ESu | 1–2′ |

***Sternbergia** lutea*
HBu | Zn6–10 | EFa | 4–8″ |

***Stipa** gigantea*
HP | Zn7–9 | ESu–LSu | 5–8′ |

***Stipa** tenuissima*
HP | Zn7–10 | MSu–LSu | 1–2′ |

Top row: IBC, JP, JP; Middle row: IBC, JP, JP; Bottom row: IBC, SH, JP

 Type: A = Annual; Bi = Biennial; HP = Hardy Perennial; TP = Tender Perennial; HB = Hardy Bulb; TB = Tender Bulb; * = May be grown as annual in colder regions
Light: ○ = Full sun; ◐ = Partial shade; ● = Full shade

***Stokesia** laevis* 'Blue Danube'
HP | Zn5–10 | ESu–LSu | 1–2′| | |

***Strobilanthes** dyerianus*
TP* | Zn10 | foliage | 2–3′| | |

***Stylophorum** diphyllum*
HP | Zn5–8 | MSp–ESu | 18″| | |

***Symphytum** officinale*
HP | Zn3–9 | LSp–MSu | 3–4′| | |

***Tagetes** patula* (French Group)
A | Zn1–10 | ESu–EFa | 6–12″| | |

Tagetes Gem Series 'Lemon Gem'
A | Zn1–10 | ESu–LSu | 8–12″| | |

***Tanacetum** coccineum*
HP | Zn5–9 | LSp–ESu | 2′| | |

***Tanacetum** parthenium*
A | Zn4–9 | MSu–EFa | 18″| | |

***Tellima** grandiflora*
HP | Zn3–9 | LSp–ESu | 1–2′| | |

Top row: JP, JP, JP; Middle row: JP, JP, JP; Bottom row: JP, JP, JP

Bloom: ESp = Early Spring; MSp = Midspring; LSp = Late Spring; ESu = Early Summer; MSu = Midsummer; LSu = Late Summer; EFa = Early Fall; MFa = Mid Fall; LFa = Late Fall
Soil: = Dry soil; = Good for xeriscaping; = Ordinary soil; = Moist soil

Teucrium hircanicum

HP | Zn7–9 | LSu | 30″| | |

Thalictrum aquilegiifolium

HP | Zn5–8 | LSp–ESu | 3′| | |

Thelypteris noveboracensis

HP | Zn3–8 | foliage | 1–2′| | |

Thunbergia alata

A | Zn5–10 | ESu–EFa | 8–10′| | |

Thymus × citriodorus

HP | Zn5–9 | MSu | 8–12″| | |

Thymus vulgaris 'Silver Rosie'

HP | Zn5–9 | MSu | 10″| | |

Tiarella cordifolia

HP | Zn3–8 | MSp–LSp | 1′| | |

Tithonia rotundifolia 'Torch'

A | Zn3–10 | LSu–MFa | 4–6′| | |

Torenia fournieri

TP*|Zn9–10|ESu–EFa|6–12″| | |

Top row: GBP, JP, JP; Middle row: GBP, JP, JP; Bottom row: MC, GBP, JP

 Type: A = Annual; Bi = Biennial; HP = Hardy Perennial; TP = Tender Perennial; HB = Hardy Bulb; TB = Tender Bulb; * = May be grown as annual in colder regions

Light: = Full sun; = Partial shade; = Full shade

Townsendia parryi
HP | Zn4–7 | LSp | 3–6″ |

Trachelium caeruleum
HP* | Zn8–10 | MSu | 3′ |

Trachymene coerulea 'Madonna Mix'
A | Zn3–8 | MSu–MFa | 1–2′ |

Tradescantia 'Blue and Gold'
HP | Zn4–9 | ESu–LSu | 18″ |

Trichosanthes cucumerina
A | Zn3–10 | fruits | 10–15′ |

Tricyrtis formosana 'Dark Beauty'
HP | Zn5–8 | EFa–MFa | 3–4′ |

Tricyrtis hirta
HP | Zn5–8 | LSu–EFa | 2–3′ |

Trifolium rubens
HP | Zn6–9 | MSu | 18–24″ |

Trillium grandiflorum
HP | Zn4–8 | MSp | 12–18″ |

Top row: GBP, JP, MC; Middle row: GBP, GBP, JP; Bottom row: JP, GBP, JP

Tritonia *crocata* cultivars

HB | Zn7–10 | MSp–LSp | 6–18" | |

Trollius *chinensis* 'Golden Queen'

HP | Zn3–7 | ESu | 3' | |

Trollius *europaeus*

HP | Zn3–8 | LSp–ESu | 1–2' | |

Tropaeolum *majus* Alaska Series

A | Zn1–10 | ESu–EFa | 12–15" | |

Tropaeolum *peregrinum*

A | Zn10 | ESu–MFa | 4–6' | |

Tulipa 'Ile de France' (Triumph)

HB | Zn4–6 | MSp | 14–16" | |

Tulipa *linifolia*

HB | Zn3–8 | ESp | 3–10" | |

Tulipa 'Magier' (Single Late)

HB | Zn3–8 | LSp | 16–20" | |

Tulipa *turkestanica*

HB | Zn3–8 | ESp | 6–10" | |

Top row: IBC, GBP, JP; Middle row: JP, JP, JP; Bottom row: IBC, JP, IBC

 Type: A = Annual; Bi = Biennial; HP = Hardy Perennial; TP = Tender Perennial; HB = Hardy Bulb; TB = Tender Bulb; * = May be grown as annual in colder regions

Light: ○ = Full sun; ◐ = Partial shade; ● = Full shade

Tulipa 'West Point' (Lily Flowered)
HB | Zn4–6 | LSp | 12–16″ | |

***Uvularia** grandiflora*
HP | Zn3–9 | MSp | 18–30″ | |

***Valeriana** officinalis*
HP | Zn4–9 | MSu | 3–4′ | |

***Veltheimia** bracteata*
TB* | Zn9–10 | ESp | 18″ | |

***Veratrum** viride*
HP | Zn3–8 | MSu | 4–6′ | |

***Verbascum** chaixii* f. *album*
HP | Zn5–9 | MSu | 3–4′ | |

***Verbena** canadensis* 'Alba'
HP* | Zn6–10 | ESu–EFa | 6–18″ | |

***Verbena** rigida*
HP | Zn8–10 | MSu–EFa | 18–24″ | |

***Veronica** spicata* 'Sunny Border Blue'
HP | Zn3–8 | MSu | 18–20″ | |

Top row: JP, JP, JP; Middle row: JP, JP, JP; Bottom row: JP, JP, JP

Bloom: ESp = Early Spring; MSp = Midspring; LSp = Late Spring; ESu = Early Summer; MSu = Midsummer; LSu = Late Summer; EFa = Early Fall; MFa = Mid Fall; LFa = Late Fall
Soil: = Dry soil; = Good for xeriscaping; = Ordinary soil; = Moist soil

Viola tricolor
A | Zn3–9 | MSp–LSp | 6–9″ |

Waldsteinia ternata
HP | Zn4–8 | LSp–ESu | 4–6″ |

Watsonia borbonica
TB* | Zn9–10 | LSu | 3–5′ |

Wisteria sinensis
HP | Zn5–10 | LSp | 50–100′ |

Xerophyllum tenax
HP | Zn6–9 | ESu | 2–5′ |

Yucca filamentosa 'Color Guard'
HP | Zn4–10 | MSu–LSu | 4–6′ |

Zantedeschia aethiopica
HP* | Zn8–10 | ESu–MSu | 18–36″ |

Zephyranthes rosea
HB* | Zn8–10 | EFa–MFa | 2–12″ |

Zinnia elegans 'Peter Pan Orange'
A | Zn2–10 | ESu–EFa | 10–12″ |

Top row: JP, GBP, JP; Middle row: JP, JP, JP; Bottom row: JP, IBC, JP

 Type: A = Annual; Bi = Biennial; HP = Hardy Perennial; TP = Tender Perennial; HB = Hardy Bulb; TB = Tender Bulb; * = May be grown as annual in colder regions

Light: ○ = Full sun; ◐ = Partial shade; ● = Full shade

4 Garden Planning Charts by Species

THE MORE YOU GARDEN, the more eager you are to experiment with new plants and interesting plant combinations. The charts in this section have been designed in an at-a-glance format so that you can more quickly get the information you need to create the garden you've always imagined. The first chart includes data about bloom times and flower colors; the second features plants with other desirable characteristics, such as foliage color or interesting seedpods. You'll get the most out of the charts if you are familiar with the characteristics of your site and and have in mind an overall vision of your garden. The letters below refer to the sample chart on p. 434.

A. [camera symbol] The symbol for a camera indicates that there is a photograph of this plant in Part 3.

B. Botanic name. The genus is shown in bold, with species indented and listed below. Where information is provided for only one species, the species name follows on the same line as the genus.

C. Page. This is a cross reference to the main entry for the genus in Part 2.

D. Type. Plants in this book are divided as follows to describe their life cycle and their cold hardiness:

- **A** (Annual): A plant that grows from seed, flowers, produces seed, and dies, all in one year.
- **Bi** (Biennial): A plant with a two-year life span, germinating and producing top growth in the first year, flowering, producing seed, and dying in the second.
- **TP** (Tender Perennial): In this book, "TP" indicates a plant that naturally lives for more than two years, but is cold hardy only south of Zone 8 (see Climate, below). Many TP plants are grown for a season in colder regions and discarded in autum. These plants are starred (*).
- **HP** (Hardy Perennial): Perennials are plants that live for more than two years. In this book, we classify hardy perennials as those plants that can be successfully grown in regions where temperatures regularly fall below freezing, or in Zones 8 or colder (see Climate, below).
- **TB** (Tender Bulb) and **HB** (Hardy Bulb): The designation "tender" or "hardy" is arrived at using the same criteria applied to perennials.

E. Climate. Refer to the maps and explanations on pages 499–501 to determine your USDA Plant Hardiness Zone, AHS Plant Heat Zone, the temperature ranges you can expect to experience where you live, and the average last frost date in your region. (You'll notice that data is not yet available for many

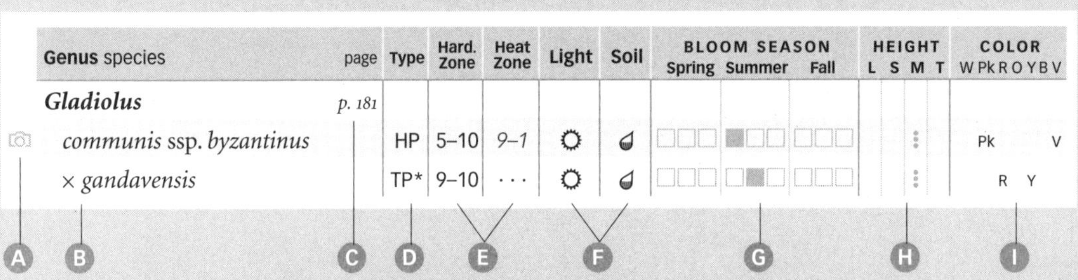

	Genus species	page	Type	Hard. Zone	Heat Zone	Light	Soil	BLOOM SEASON Spring Summer Fall	HEIGHT L S M T	COLOR W Pk R O Y B V
	Gladiolus	*p. 181*								
📷	*communis* ssp. *byzantinus*		HP	5–10	*9–1*	☼	◔	□□□ ■□□ □□□	M	Pk V
	× *gandavensis*		TP*	9–10	· · ·	☼	◔	□□□ □■□ □□□	M	R Y
A	B	C	D	E	F	G	H	I		

plants' heat zones.) It's safest to choose plants that are rated to thrive within your zone, but remember that microclimates created by features such as sheltered spots, windy locations, adjacent bodies of water, or a location at the top or bottom of a hill can mean that areas of your garden may actually experience temperatures more typical of a zone higher or lower than the one indicated on the map. And, conditions can vary greatly from year to year. You'll find that experience is your best guide.

F. Light and soil. The light and soil in your garden are just as important as your hardiness zone when it comes to choosing plants that will succeed. You'll never be happy trying to grow a shade-lover in bright sun or an acid lover in alkaline soil, no matter how much you love them. Here is an explanation of the ranges:

☼ = Full sun: 6 or more hours of sun daily

◐ = Partial shade: 3–4 hours of sun daily or filtered sun

● = Bright reflected light, but little or no direct sun

◯ = Tolerates or actually prefers dry soil.

◯ = Plants that are suitable for xeriscaping. Derived from the Greek word *xeros,* meaning "dry," xeriscaping refers to techniques designed to reduce the water needed to maintain gardens. Xeric plants are especially drought tolerant.

◔ = Ordinary soil is usually termed "average garden soil." This soil drains well, but it holds water long enough for plants to make use of the moisture.

● = Moist soil is damp most of the time.

G. Bloom season. Because the timing for each plant's bloom period varies according to where you live, we refer to seasons (spring, summer, fall), rather than months. Note that each season is further divided into three in order to indicate early-, mid-, and late-season plants.

H. Height. Plant heights refer to these ranges:

L = Low growing (less than 1 foot)
S = Short (1–2 feet)
M = Medium (2–4 feet)
T = Tall (more than 4 feet)

I. Color. Letters in these columns indicate:

W = white; **Pk** = pink; **R** = red; **O** = orange;
Y = yellow; **B** = blue; **V** = violet

Use these charts as an aid in designing a new garden from scratch, or for filling in bare spots in existing beds. Simply determine the most important feature of the plant you're looking for—that it blooms in late summer, for instance—then run your finger down the appropriate column, stopping at every plant that blooms in late summer to see whether it also meets your other aesthetic and cultural requirements. In no time, you'll have a list of possibilities that exactly fit your needs. Some will be old friends, but you will also find many unusual and interesting plants to fuel your imagination.

The list of plants that you develop will meet all your criteria—they survive in your climate, you can provide the light and soil conditions they need, they offer bloom when you want it, and they are the colors you love and heights that you need. And now you are well on the way to designing a garden that not only flourishes but also satisfies your vision of the ideal garden.

Genus species	page	Type	Hard. Zone	Heat Zone	Light	Soil	BLOOM SEASON Spring Summer Fall	HEIGHT L S M T	COLOR W Pk R O Y B V
Abelmoschus *manihot*	p. 40	TP*	9–10	. . .					R Y
Abutilon	p. 40								
megapotamicum		HP*	8–10	12–1					R Y
pictum		HP*	8–10	12–8					O Y
Acaena *(see also p. 479)*	p. 41								
microphylla		HP	6–8	9–6					R
novae-zelandiae		HP	6–8	8–6					W V
Acantholimon	p. 41								
glumaceum		HP	7–9	9–7					Pk
Acanthus	p. 41								
hungaricus		HP	6–10	9–5					W Pk
mollis		HP	8–10	12–7					W V
spinosus		HP	6–10	9–5					W V
Achillea	p. 42								
clavennae		HP	5–9	8–1					W
clypeolata		HP	3–10	9–1					Y
filipendulina		HP	3–10	9–1					Y
millefolium		HP	3–8	8–1					W Pk
ptarmica		HP	3–8	8–1					W
tomentosa		HP	3–10	9–1					Y
Achimenes hybrids	p. 43	TP*	10	12–1					R V
Aconitum	p. 43								
anthora		HP	5–8	8–4					Y
× *cammarum*		HP	5–8	8–4					B
carmichaelii		HP	3–8	8–4					B V
hemsleyanum		HP	3–8	8–4					V
henryi		HP	5–8	8–4					W B V
lycoctonum ssp. *vulparia*		HP	3–8	8–4					Y
napellus		HP	3–8	8–4					B
Actinidia *(see also p. 479)*	p. 44								
deliciosa		HP	7–9	9–7					W Y
Actinotus *helianthi*	p. 45	TP*	9–10	. . .					W
Adenophora	p. 45								
bulleyana		HP	4–8	8–1					B

Height: L = Low (<1′); S = Short (1′–2′); M = Medium (2′–4′); T = Tall (>4′) | **Color**: W = White; Pk = Pink; R = Red; O = Orange; Y = Yellow; B = Blue; V = Violet

Soil: = Dry soil; = Good for xeriscaping; = Ordinary soil; = Moist soil

Genus species	page	Type	Hard. Zone	Heat Zone	Light	Soil	BLOOM SEASON Spring Summer Fall	HEIGHT L S M T	COLOR W Pk R O Y B V
confusa		HP	3–9	*8–1*	○◐				B
Adiantum *(see p. 479)*									
Adlumia *fungosa*	*p. 46*	Bi	5–9	*8–1*	◐●				W
Adonis	*p. 47*								
aestivalis		A	3–9	···	○◐				R
brevistyla		HP	4–9	*9–7*	○◐				W B
vernalis		HP	4–7	*7–1*	○◐				Y
Aegopodium *(see p. 479)*									
Aethionema	*p. 48*								
armenum		HP	7–9	*9–7*	○				Pk
cordifolium		HP	5–9	···	○				Pk
grandiflorum		HP	5–7	*9–7*	○				Pk
schistosum		HP	6–9	···	○				Pk
Agapanthus	*p. 48*								
africanus		HP*	7–10	*12–1*	○◐				B
campanulatus		HP*	7–10	*12–7*	○◐				B
Headbourne Hybrids		TP*	9–10	*12–7*	○◐				B
inapertus		TP*	9–10	*12–7*	○◐				B
Agastache	*p. 49*								
cana		HP	6–9	···	○◐				Pk
foeniculum		HP	6–9	···	○◐				B
mexicana		HP	8–10	*12–7*	○◐				Pk
nepetoides		HP	4–9	···	○◐				Y
Ageratum *houstonianum*	*p. 49*	A	1–10	*12–1*	○◐				Pk B
Agrostemma *githago*	*p. 50*	A	1–9	*9–1*	○				Pk
Agrostis *nebulosa*	*p. 50*	A	3–9	···	○◐				W
Ajania *pacifica (see also p. 479)*	*p. 51*	HP	5–9	*9–1*	○◐				Y
Ajuga	*p. 51*								
pyramidalis		HP	3–10	*9–1*	○●				B
reptans		HP	3–10	*9–1*	○●				B V
Alcea *rosea*	*p. 52*	HP	2–9	*9–1*	○◐				W Pk R Y
Alchemilla	*p. 52*								
alpina		HP	3–8	*7–1*	○◐				Y
mollis		HP	3–7	*7–1*	○◐				Y

Type: A = Annual; Bi = Biennial; HP = Hardy Perennial; TP = Tender Perennial; HB = Hardy Bulb; TB = Tender Bulb; * = May be grown as annual in colder regions

Light: ○ = Full sun; ◐ = Partial shade; ● = Full shade

Genus species	page	Type	Hard. Zone	Heat Zone	Light	Soil	BLOOM SEASON Spring	Summer	Fall	HEIGHT L	S	M	T	COLOR W Pk R O Y B V
Allium	*p. 53*													
caeruleum		HB	3–9	*9–1*	☼◐	Ordinary	□□□	■□□	□□□		•			B
cernuum		HB	4–9	*9–5*	☼●	Dry, Ordinary	□□□	■□□	□□□		•			W Pk
cristophii		HB	4–9	*9–5*	☼◐	Ordinary	□□□	□■□	□□□		•			V
giganteum		HB	4–9	*9–5*	☼◐	Ordinary	□□□	□■□	□□□			•	•	V
× *hollandicum*		HB	3–8	*8–1*	☼◐	Ordinary	□□□	□■□	□□□			•		Pk V
moly		HB	3–9	*9–1*	☼◐	Dry, Ordinary	□□□	■□□	□□□	•	•			Y
neapolitanum		HB	5–8	*9–7*	☼◐	Ordinary	□□■	□□□	□□□	•	•			W
oreophilum		HB	3–9	*9–1*	☼◐	Ordinary	□□□	■□□	□□□	•				Pk V
schoenoprasum		HB	4–9	*9–5*	☼◐	Ordinary	□□□	□■□	□□□		•			V
Alonsoa	*p. 54*													
meridionalis		TP*	9–10	*12–10*	☼◐	Ordinary	□□■	■■■	■■■		•			R
warscewiczii		TP*	9–10	*12–10*	☼	Ordinary	□□■	■■■	■■■		•			R
***Alstroemeria** ligtu*	*p. 54*	HP	7–10	*10–7*	☼◐	Ordinary	□□□	■■■	□□□		•			Pk Y
Alyssum	*p. 55*													
alpestre		HP	3–9	*8–1*	☼	Ordinary	□■■	■□□	□□□	•				Y
montanum		HP	3–8	*8–1*	☼	Ordinary	□□■	■■■	□□□	•				Y
spinosum		HP	7–10	*9–3*	☼	Ordinary	□□■	■□□	□□□		•			W
wulfenianum		HP	6–9	*9–5*	☼	Ordinary	□□□	■■□	□□□	•				Y
Amaranthus *(see also p. 479)*	*p. 55*													
caudatus		A	3–10	*12–5*	☼◐	Ordinary	□□□	■■■	■□□			•	•	R
hypochondriacus		A	3–10	*12–5*	☼◐	Ordinary	□□□	■■■	■□□			•	•	R
***Amaryllis** belladonna*	*p. 56*	HB*	7–10	*12–7*	☼	Ordinary, Moist	□□□	□□■	■□□		•			W Pk
Ammi	*p. 56*													
majus		A	3–9	. . .	☼◐	Ordinary, Moist	□□□	□■■	■□□			•		W
visnaga		A	3–9	. . .	☼◐	Ordinary, Moist	□□□	□□■	■■□			•		W
***Ammobium** alatum*	*p. 57*	A	2–10	. . .	☼	Dry, Ordinary	□□□	■■■	■□□			•		W
Amsonia	*p. 57*													
ciliata		HP	6–8	*8–5*	☼◐	Ordinary, Moist	□□□	□■□	□□□		•	•		B
hubrechtii		HP	4–9	*9–3*	☼◐	Ordinary, Moist	□□□	□■□	□□□			•		B
tabernaemontana		HP	4–8	*8–1*	☼◐	Ordinary, Moist	□□■	■□□	□□□			•		B
Anacyclus	*p. 58*													
pyrethrum var. *depressus*		HP	6–9	*8–6*	☼	Good for xeriscaping, Ordinary	□□□	■■□	□□□	•				W
***Anagallis** monellii*	*p. 58*	HP*	8–10	. . .	☼	Dry, Moist	□□□	■■■	□□□		•			B

Height: L = Low (<1′); S = Short (1′–2′); M = Medium (2′–4′); T = Tall (>4′) | **Color**: W = White; Pk = Pink; R = Red; O = Orange; Y = Yellow; B = Blue; V = Violet

Soil: = Dry soil; = Good for xeriscaping; = Ordinary soil; = Moist soil

Genus species	page	Type	Hard. Zone	Heat Zone	Light	Soil	BLOOM SEASON Spring Summer Fall	HEIGHT L S M T	COLOR W Pk R O Y B V
Anaphalis	*p. 59*								
margaritacea		HP	3–8	*8–1*	○◐				W
triplinervis		HP	3–8	*8–1*	○◐				W
Anchusa	*p. 59*								
azurea		HP	3–8	*8–1*	○◐				B
capensis		A	1–10	· · ·	○				B
cespitosa		HP	5–7	*7–5*	○◐				B
Androsace	*p. 60*								
carnea		HP	5–7	*7–1*	○◐				Pk
chamaejasme		HP	4–7	*7–1*	○◐				W
lanuginosa		HP	4–6	*7–3*	○◐				Pk
sempervivoides		HP	4–7	*7–5*	◐				Pk
Anemone	*p. 60*								
blanda		HP	5–10	*8–1*	○◐				Pk B
coronaria		HP*	7–10	*12–8*	○				W Pk R V
hupehensis		HP	5–10	*7–5*	○◐				W Pk
× hybrida		HP	5–10	*8–5*	○◐				W Pk
narcissiflora		HP	5–9	*8–5*	○◐				W Pk
nemorosa		HP	4–9	*8–1*	○◐				W B
pavonina		HP	7–10	*10–8*	○				R B V
rivularis		HP	6–8	*8–6*	◐				W
sylvestris		HP	3–9	*9–1*	◐				W
tomentosa		HP	4–9	*8–1*	○◐				Pk
***Anemonella** thalictroides*	*p. 61*	HP	4–7	*7–1*	◐				W Pk
***Anethum** graveolens (see p. 479)*									
Angelica	*p. 62*								
archangelica		HP	4–9	*8–2*	○◐				W
atropurpurea		HP	4–9	· · ·	○◐				W
gigas		HP	5–8	*8–2*	○◐				V
***Angelonia** angustifolia*	*p. 63*	TP*	9–10	· · ·	○◐				B V
***Anoda** cristata*	*p. 63*	TP*	9–10	· · ·	○◐				W B
***Anomatheca** laxa*	*p. 64*	HB*	8–10	· · ·	○◐				R
***Anredera** cordifolia*	*p. 64*	TP*	9–10	*12–1*	○				W
***Antennaria** dioica*	*p. 65*	HP	3–8	*9–4*	○				W Pk

 Type: A = Annual; Bi = Biennial; HP = Hardy Perennial; TP = Tender Perennial; HB = Hardy Bulb; TB = Tender Bulb; * = May be grown as annual in colder regions

Light: ○ = Full sun; ◐ = Partial shade; ● = Full shade

Genus species	page	Type	Hard. Zone	Heat Zone	Color (W Pk R O Y B V)
Anthemis	*p. 65*				
marschalliana		HP	4–9	*8–3*	Y
punctata ssp. *cupaniana*		HP	4–9	*9–6*	W
tinctoria		HP	4–9	*9–1*	Y
Anthericum	*p. 66*				
liliago		HP	6–9	*9–7*	W
ramosum		HP	5–8	*8–5*	W
Anthriscus *(see also p. 479)*	*p. 66*				
sylvestris 'Ravenswing'		A	3–10	· · ·	W
Anthyllis montana	*p. 67*	HP	3–8	*8–6*	Pk
Antirrhinum	*p. 67*				
braun-blanquettii		HP	5–10	· · ·	W
hispanicum		HP	5–10	· · ·	W Pk Y
majus		HP*	7–10	*12–1*	W Pk R O Y V
molle		HP	5–10	· · ·	W Pk Y
Aquilegia	*p. 68*				
alpina		HP	3–9	*8–1*	W
caerulea		HP	3–9	*8–1*	B
canadensis		HP	3–9	*8–1*	R Y
flabellata		HP	3–9	*8–1*	B
skinneri		HP	8–9	· · ·	R Y
viridiflora		HP	3–9	*8–1*	Y V
vulgaris		HP	3–9	*8–1*	W Pk R V
Arabis	*p. 68*				
blepharophylla		HP	6–8	*8–5*	Pk
caucasica		HP	4–9	*8–1*	W
ferdinandi-coburgi		HP	6–10	*8–1*	W
procurrens		HP	3–9	*8–1*	W
Arctotis	*p. 69*				
× *hybrida*		TP*	9–10	*12–10*	W Pk R O Y
venusta		TP*	9–10	*12–10*	W B
Arenaria montana	*p. 69*	HP	3–8	*5–1*	W
Argemone	*p. 70*				
grandiflora		A	3–10	*12–7*	W

Height: L = Low (<1'); S = Short (1'–2'); M = Medium (2'–4'); T = Tall (>4') | **Color:** W = White; Pk = Pink; R = Red; O = Orange; Y = Yellow; B = Blue; V = Violet
Soil: = Dry soil; = Good for xeriscaping; = Ordinary soil; = Moist soil

Genus species	page	Type	Hard. Zone	Heat Zone	Light	Soil	BLOOM SEASON Spring	Summer	Fall	HEIGHT L	S	M	T	COLOR W Pk R O Y B V
mexicana		A	3–10	*12–7*	☼	⊗ ◒	□□□	■■■	□□□			•		Y
Arisaema	*p. 70*													
candidissimum		HP	7–9	*9–7*	◐	●	□□□	■□□	□□□		•			W Pk
sikokianum		HP	5–9	*9–3*	◐	●	□□□	■□□	□□□		•			W V
speciosum		HP	4–9	*9–1*	◐	●	□□□	■□□	□□□			•		V
tortuosum		HP	6–9	*9–7*	◐	●	□□□	■□□	□□□			•		V
triphyllum		HP	3–8	*9–1*	◐	●	□□■	□□□	□□□		•			V
Armeria	*p. 71*													
maritima		HP	3–8	*9–1*	☼	⊗ ◒	□□■	■□□	□□□	•				W Pk
pseudarmeria		HP	6–10	*9–4*	☼	○ ◒	□□■	■□□	□□□		•			W Pk
Arnica	*p. 71*													
cordifolia		HP	6–9	*8–5*	☼ ◐	●	□□□	□■□	□□□		•			Y
montana		HP	6–9	*8–5*	☼ ◐	●	□□□	□■□	□□□		•			Y
Artemisia *(see p. 479)*														
Arum *italicum*	*p. 73*	HP	6–10	*9–3*	☼ ◐	◒ ●	□□■	□□□	□□□		•			W
Aruncus	*p. 73*													
aethusifolius		HP	3–7	*9–1*	☼ ◐	●	□□□	■■□	□□□		•			W
dioicus		HP	3–7	*9–1*	☼ ◐	●	□□□	■■□	□□□			•	•	W
Asarina	*p. 74*													
procumbens		HP*	7–9	*9–6*	☼	◒ ●	□□□	□■■	■□□	•				Y
scandens		TP*	9–10	*9–6*	☼ ◐	◒ ●	□□□	□■■	■■□				•	Pk B V
× *wislizensis*		TP*	9–10	*9–6*	☼	◒ ●	□□□	□■■	■□□			•		R
Asarum *(see p. 479)*														
Asclepias *(see also p. 479)*	*p. 75*													
curassavica		HP*	8–10	···	☼ ◐	◒	□□□	□■■	□□□			•		R Y
incarnata		HP	3–9	*9–1*	☼ ◐	●	□□□	□□■	□□□				•	Pk
speciosa		HP	3–9	···	☼ ◐	⊗ ◒	□□□	■■□	□□□			•		V
tuberosa		HP	3–10	*9–2*	☼ ◐	⊗	□□□	□■□	□□□		•	•		O Y
Asperula *orientalis*	*p. 75*	A	4–8	···	☼ ◐	◒ ●	□□□	□■□	□□□	•				W B V
Asphodeline *lutea*	*p. 76*	HP	6–8	*9–6*	☼ ◐	◒	□□■	■□□	□□□			•		Y
Asplenium *(see p. 479)*														
Aster	*p. 77*													
alpinus		HP	4–9	*8–1*	☼	◒	□□□	■□□	□□□	•				W Pk B V
amellus		HP	4–9	*8–1*	☼	◒	□□□	□□■	□□□		•			B

Type: A = Annual; Bi = Biennial; HP = Hardy Perennial; TP = Tender Perennial; HB = Hardy Bulb; TB = Tender Bulb; * = May be grown as annual in colder regions

Light: ☼ = Full sun; ◐ = Partial shade; ● = Full shade

Genus species	page	Type	Hard. Zone	Heat Zone	Light	Soil	BLOOM SEASON Spring Summer Fall	HEIGHT L S M T	COLOR W Pk R O Y B V
divaricatus		HP	3–9	*8–1*					W
ericoides		HP	3–9	*8–1*					W
× *frikartii*		HP	4–8	*8–1*					B V
linosyris		HP	3–9	*8–1*					Y
novae-angliae		HP	4–9	*8–1*					Pk V
novi-belgii		HP	4–9	*8–1*					W Pk B V
puniceus		HP	2–8	*8–1*					V
tataricus		HP	2–8	. . .					Pk B
tongolensis		HP	4–8	*8–1*					B V
Astilbe	*p. 78*								
× *arendsii*		HP	4–8	*8–1*					W Pk R V
chinensis		HP	4–8	*8–1*					W Pk V
chinensis var. *taquetti*		HP	4–8	*8–1*					V
simplicifolia		HP	4–8	*8–1*					W Pk
thunbergii		HP	4–8	*8–1*					W Pk
Astilboides *tabularis*	*p. 78*	HP	4–9	*7–1*					W
Astrantia	*p. 79*								
carniolica		HP	4–8	. . .					Pk
major		HP	4–7	*7–1*					W Pk
maxima		HP	4–8	*8–1*					Pk
minor		HP	5–7	. . .					W
Athyrium *(see p. 479)*									
Atriplex *(see p. 480)*									
Aubrieta *deltoidea*	*p. 80*	HP	4–9	*7–5*					Pk R V
Aurinia *saxatilis*	*p. 81*	HP	4–10	. . .					Y
Azorina *vidalii*	*p. 81*	TP*	10	*12–10*					W Pk
Babiana	*p. 82*								
rubrocyanea		HB*	8–10	*12–10*					V
stricta		HB*	8–10	*12–10*					W Y V
Bacopa sp.	*p. 82*	TP*	9–10	*12–10*					W B
Baptisia	*p. 83*								
alba		HP	4–9	. . .					W
australis		HP	4–9	*9–1*					B
leucophaea		HP	4–9	. . .					W

Height: L = Low (<1′); S = Short (1′–2′); M = Medium (2′–4′); T = Tall (>4′) | **Color:** W = White; Pk = Pink; R = Red; O = Orange; Y = Yellow; B = Blue; V = Violet
Soil: = Dry soil; = Good for xeriscaping; = Ordinary soil; = Moist soil

Genus species	page	Type	Hard. Zone	Heat Zone	Light	Soil	BLOOM SEASON Spring	Summer	Fall	HEIGHT L S M T	COLOR W Pk R O Y B V
pendula		HP	4–9	· · ·	○◐		□□■	□□□	□□□	M	W
perfoliata		HP	6–9	*9–1*	○◐		□□□	■□□	□□□	S	Y
Bassia *(see p. 480)*											
Begonia	*p. 84*										
grandis		HP	6–10	*9–6*	○◐		□□□	□□■	■■□	S	W Pk
semperflorens		TP*	10	*12–1*	○●		□□□	■■■	■■□	S	W Pk R
sutherlandii		HP*	7–10	*12–1*	○◐		□□□	■■■	□□□	S	O
× *tuberhybrida*		TP*	10	*12–1*	◐●		□□□	■■■	■■□	L S	W Pk R O Y
Belamcanda *chinensis*	*p. 84*	HP	5–10	*9–5*	○◐		□□□	□■□	□□□	S M	O Y B V
Bellis	*p. 85*										
perennis		HP	3–9	*9–6*	○◐		□□■	■□□	□□□	L	W Pk R
rotundifolia		HP	6–9	*9–6*	○◐		□□■	■□□	□□□	L	W
Bergenia *ciliata (see also p. 480)*	*p. 85*	HP	5–8	*9–3*	○●		■■□	□□□	□□□	S	W Pk
Bidens *ferulifolia*	*p. 86*	HP*	8–10	*12–8*	○◐		□□□	□■■	■■□	S	Y
Billardiera *(see p. 480)*											
Blechnum *(see p. 480)*											
Bletilla *striata*	*p. 88*	HP	5–9	*9–5*	◐●		□□□	■□□	□□□	L S	W V
Boltonia *asteroides*	*p. 88*	HP	3–8	*9–1*	○◐		□□□	□□■	■■□	T	W Pk V
Brachyscome *iberidifolia*	*p. 89*	A	1–10	*10–1*	○◐		□□□	■■■	■■□	L S	Pk B V
Brimeura *amethystina*	*p. 89*	HB	3–8	*8–4*	○◐		□□■	□□□	□□□	L	B
Briza *(see also p. 480)*	*p. 90*										
maxima		A	5–8	*12–1*	○◐		□□□	■□□	□□□	S	V
media		HP	4–8	*12–1*	○◐		□□■	■□□	□□□	S	V
minor		A	5–8	*12–1*	○◐		□□□	■■■	■□□	L	V
Brodiaea *coronaria*	*p. 90*	HB	6–10	*10–8*	○		□□■	■□□	□□□	L	B V
Browallia	*p. 91*										
americana		TP*	9–10	*8–1*	○◐		□□■	■■■	■□□	S	B V
speciosa		TP*	9–10	*8–1*	○◐		□□■	■■■	■□□	S	B V
Brugmansia	*p. 91*										
× *candida*		HP*	8–10	*12–1*	○◐		□□□	■■■	■□□	T	W Y
sanguinea		HP*	8–10	*12–1*	○◐		□□□	■■■	■□□	T	R O
suaveolens		HP	8–10	*12–1*	○◐		□□□	■■■	■□□	T	W
Brunnera *macrophylla*	*p. 92*	HP	3–8	*7–1*	○◐		□■■	□□□	□□□	S	B
Bulbinella *hookeri*	*p. 92*	HP	7–10	· · ·	○◐		□■■	■■□	□□□	S	Y

 Type: A = Annual; Bi = Biennial; HP = Hardy Perennial; TP = Tender Perennial; HB = Hardy Bulb; TB = Tender Bulb; * = May be grown as annual in colder regions

Light: ○ = Full sun; ◐ = Partial shade; ● = Full shade

Genus species	page	Type	Hard. Zone	Heat Zone	Light	Soil	BLOOM SEASON Spring	Summer	Fall	HEIGHT L	S	M	T	COLOR W Pk R O Y B V
***Bulbocodium** vernum*	p. 93	HB	5–10	*9–7*	☼ ◐	Ordinary, Moist	□■□	□□□	□□□	•				V
***Buphthalmum** salicifolium*	p. 93	HP	5–8	*8–5*	☼ ◐	Ordinary, Moist	□□□	■■■	□□□		•			Y
Bupleurum	p. 94													
falcatum		HP	5–9	· · ·	☼ ◐	Dry, Ordinary	□□□	□■■	□□□			•		Y
ranunculoides		HP	5–9	· · ·	☼ ◐	Dry, Ordinary	□□□	□■□	□□□		•			Y
***Caladium** (see p. 480)*														
***Calamagrostis** (see also p. 480)*	p. 95													
× acutiflora		HP	5–9	*9–6*	☼ ◐	Dry, Moist	□□□	□■■	□□□		•	•	•	V
Calamintha	p. 95													
grandiflora		HP	5–10	· · ·	☼ ◐	Dry, Moist	□□□	■■□	□□□		•			Pk
nepeta		HP	5–10	· · ·	☼ ◐	Dry, Moist	□□□	□□■	■■□		•			B
Calandrinia	p. 96													
discolor		HP*	8–10	· · ·	☼	Dry, Ordinary	□□□	□□■	□□□		•			V
umbellata		HP*	8–10	· · ·	☼	Xeriscaping, Ordinary	□□□	□■■	■■■	•				R
Calceolaria	p. 96													
biflora		HP*	8–9	*6–1*	☼ ◐	Ordinary, Moist	□□□	■■□	□□□		•			Y
darwinii		HP	6–9	*6–1*	☼ ◐	Ordinary, Moist	□□□	■□□	□□□	•				W O
integrifolia		TP*	9–10	*6–1*	☼ ◐	Ordinary, Moist	□□□	■■□	□□□		•	•		Y
***Calendula** officinalis*	p. 97	A	2–10	*6–1*	☼ ◐	Ordinary, Moist	□■■	■■■	□□□		•			O Y
Calibrachoa Million Bells	p. 97	TP*	9–10	· · ·	☼	Dry, Moist	□□■	■■■	■■□	•				W Pk Y V
Callirhoe	p. 98													
involucrata		HP	3–9	*9–1*	☼ ◐	Xeriscaping, Ordinary	□□□	■■■	□□□	•				V
triangulata		HP	5–9	*9–1*	☼ ◐	Dry, Ordinary	□□□	□■■	□□□			•		V
***Callistephus** chinensis*	p. 98	A	1–10	*10–1*	☼ ◐	Ordinary	□□□	■■■	□□□		•			W Pk R V
Calochortus	p. 99													
albus		HB	5–10	*10–6*	☼ ◐	Ordinary	□□■	■□□	□□□		•			W Pk
superbus		HB	5–10	*10–6*	☼ ◐	Ordinary	□□■	■□□	□□□		•			W V
venustus		HB	5–10	*10–6*	☼ ◐	Ordinary	□□■	■□□	□□□	•				W R Y V
***Caltha** palustris*	p. 99	HP	4–9	*7–1*	☼ ●	Moist	■□□	□□□	□□□		•			Y
Camassia	p. 100													
leichtlinii		HB	4–9	*10–1*	☼ ◐	Moist	□□□	□■□	□□□		•	•		W V
quamash		HB	4–9	*10–1*	☼ ◐	Ordinary, Moist	□□□	■■□	□□□		•	•		B V
Campanula	p. 100													
alliariifolia		HP	4–8	*7–1*	☼ ◐	Ordinary	□□□	■■■	□□□			•		W

Height: L = Low (<1′); S = Short (1′–2′); M = Medium (2′–4′); T = Tall (>4′) | **Color:** W = White; Pk = Pink; R = Red; O = Orange; Y = Yellow; B = Blue; V = Violet

Soil: Dry soil; Good for xeriscaping; Ordinary soil; Moist soil

Genus species	page	Type	Hard. Zone	Heat Zone	Light	Soil	Bloom Season: Spring	Summer	Fall	Height: L	S	M	T	Color (W Pk R O Y B V)
barbata		HP	6–8	*8–5*	☼ ◐	◒	□□□	■■■	□□□	•	•			W B
carpatica		HP	3–8	*9–1*	☼ ◐	◒	□□□	■■■	□□□	•				W B
cochleariifolia		HP	4–8	*7–4*	☼ ◐	◒	□□□	■■■	□□□	•				W B V
garganica		HP	4–8	*7–1*	☼ ◐	◒	□□□	■■■	□□□	•				V
glomerata		HP	3–8	*9–1*	☼ ◐	◒	□□□	■■□	□□□		•			V
lactiflora		HP	4–8	*7–5*	☼ ◐	◒	□□□	■■■	□□□			•	•	B
persicifolia		HP	3–8	*9–1*	☼ ◐	◒	□□□	■■■	□□□		•	•		W B
portenschlagiana		HP	4–8	*7–1*	☼ ◐	◒	□□□	■■■	□□□	•				V
poscharskyana		HP	3–8	*9–1*	☼ ◐	○ ◒	□□□	■■■	□□□	•				V
punctata		HP	4–8	*9–1*	☼ ◐	◒	□□□	■■■	□□□		•			W Pk V
pyramidalis		Bi	5–8	*8–6*	☼ ◐	◒	□□□	■■■	□□□			•	•	W B
raineri		HP	5–8	*7–5*	◐	◒	□□□	■■■	□□□	•				V
rotundifolia		HP	3–8	*9–1*	☼ ◐	◒	□□□	■■■	□□□		•			B
sarmatica		HP	3–8	*9–1*	☼	◒	□□□	□■□	□□□		•			B V
takesimana		HP	6–8	···	☼ ◐	◒	□□□	■■■	□□□		•			V
trachelium		HP	5–8	*8–5*	☼ ◐	◒	□□□	■■■	□□□			•		B V
tommasiniana		HP	6–8	···	☼ ◐	◒	□□□	■■■	□□□	•				B
Canna *× generalis*	*p. 101*	HP*	8–10	*12–1*	☼	○ ●	□□□	■■■	■□□		•	•	•	Pk R O Y
Cardamine	*p. 102*													
pratensis		HP	5–8	*8–5*	◐ ●	●	□□■	□□□	□□□		•			W V
trifolia		HP	5–8	*8–5*	◐ ●	●	□□■	■□□	□□□	•				W
Cardiocrinum *giganteum*	*p. 102*	HB	7–9	*9–7*	◐	●	□□□	■■□	□□□				•	W
Cardiospermum *halicacabum*	*p. 103*	TP*	10	*10–5*	☼	◒	□□□	■■■	□□□				•	W
Carex *(see p. 480)*														
Carpanthea *pomeridiana*	*p. 104*	HP*	7–10	···	☼	○ ◒	□■■	■■□	□□□	•				Y
Carthamus *tinctorius*	*p. 104*	A	3–9	*12–1*	☼	○ ◒	□□□	□■□	□□□		•	•		O Y
Carum *carvi*	*p. 105*	Bi	3–8	···	☼	◒	□□■	■□□	□□□			•		W
Cassia *hebecarpa*	*p. 105*	HP	4–9	*12–9*	☼ ◐	○ ◒	□□□	□■□	□□□			•		Y
Catananche *caerulea*	*p. 106*	HP	4–9	*8–1*	☼	○ ◒	□□□	□■■	■□□		•			V
Catharanthus *roseus*	*p. 106*	TP*	9–10	*12–1*	☼ ◐	◒ ●	□□□	■■■	■■□		•			W Pk R
Caulophyllum *(see p. 480)*														
Celmisia	*p. 107*													
semicordata		HP	8–9	···	☼ ◐	◒ ●	□□□	■■□	□□□		•			W
spectabilis		HP	8–9	···	☼ ◐	◒ ●	□□□	■■□	□□□		•			W

Type: A = Annual; Bi = Biennial; HP = Hardy Perennial; TP = Tender Perennial; HB = Hardy Bulb; TB = Tender Bulb; * = May be grown as annual in colder regions

Light: ☼ = Full sun; ◐ = Partial shade; ● = Full shade

Genus species	page	Type	Hard. Zone	Heat Zone	Light	Soil	BLOOM SEASON Spring / Summer / Fall	HEIGHT L S M T	COLOR W Pk R O Y B V
Celosia	*p. 108*								
argentea		A	2–10	*9–2*	☼ ◐	Ordinary, Moist	□□□ ■■■ ■□□	S M	W R O Y
spicata		A	2–10	*9–2*	☼ ◐	Ordinary, Moist	□□□ ■■■ ■□□	S	W Pk
Centaurea *(see also p. 480)*	*p. 109*								
cyanus		A	1–10	*8–1*	☼	Ordinary	□□■ ■■■ □□□	S M	W Pk R B V
dealbata		HP	4–8	*8–1*	☼	Ordinary	□□□ □■□ □□□	M	V
macrocephala		HP	4–8	*8–1*	☼	Xeriscaping, Ordinary	□□□ □■□ □□□	M	Y
montana		HP	4–8	*8–1*	☼	Ordinary	□□□ ■■□ □□□	S	B V
nigra		HP	6–9	· · ·	☼	Ordinary	□□□ □■□ □□□	M T	V
Centaurium *erythraea*	*p. 109*	A	1–9	· · ·	☼ ◐	Xeriscaping, Ordinary	□□□ ■■■ □□□	L	Pk
Centranthus *ruber*	*p. 110*	HP	4–9	*8–5*	☼	Xeriscaping, Ordinary	□□■ ■■■ ■□□	M	Pk
Cephalaphora *aromatica*	*p. 110*	TP*	9–10	· · ·	☼ ◐	Ordinary	□□□ □■■ □□□	S	Y
Cephalaria *gigantea*	*p. 111*	HP	3–9	*8–1*	☼ ◐	Ordinary, Moist	□□□ ■□□ □□□	T	Y
Cephalipterum *drummondii*	*p. 111*	A	1–10	· · ·	☼ ◐	Dry, Moist	□□□ ■■■ □□□	S	W Y
Cerastium *tomentosum*	*p. 112*	HP	3–9	*7–1*	☼ ◐	Xeriscaping, Moist	□■■ □□□ □□□	L	W
Ceratostigma *plumbaginoides*	*p. 112*	HP	5–9	*9–6*	☼ ◐	Xeriscaping, Moist	□□□ □□■ ■■■	L	B
Cerinthe	*p. 113*								
major 'Purpurascens'		HP	6–9	*12–8*	☼ ◐	Ordinary, Moist	□□□ ■■■ ■□□	S	B
Chaenorhinum *glareosum*	*p. 113*	HP*	8–10	· · ·	☼ ◐	Ordinary	□□□ ■□□ □□□	S	B V
Chelidonium *majus*	*p. 114*	HP	4–8	*8–5*	☼ ●	Moist	□□□ □■□ □□□	S	Y
Chelone	*p. 114*								
glabra		HP	3–9	*8–1*	☼ ◐	Moist	□□□ □□■ □□□	T	W
lyonii		HP	3–9	*8–1*	☼ ◐	Moist	□□□ □□■ ■□□	M	Pk
obliqua		HP	3–9	*8–1*	☼ ◐	Moist	□□□ □□■ □□□	M	Pk
Chenopodium *(see p. 480)*									
Chiastophyllum *oppositifolium*	*p. 115*	HP	4–8	*9–6*	☼ ◐	Dry, Ordinary	□□■ ■□□ □□□	L	Y
Chionodoxa	*p. 116*								
luciliae		HB	4–8	*9–1*	☼ ◐	Ordinary, Moist	■□□ □□□ □□□	L	B
forbesii		HB	4–8	*9–1*	☼ ◐	Ordinary, Moist	■□□ □□□ □□□	L	B V
sardensis		HB	4–8	*9–1*	☼ ◐	Ordinary, Moist	■□□ □□□ □□□	L	B
Chlorogalum *pomeridianum*	*p. 116*	TB	8–10	· · ·	☼ ◐	Moist	□□□ □■□ □□□	T	W
Chrysanthemum	*p. 117*								
carinatum		A	3–10	*9–1*	☼	Ordinary	□□■ ■■■ ■□□	M	W
coronarium		A	3–10	*9–1*	☼ ◐	Ordinary	□□■ ■■■ ■□□	M	Y

Height: L = Low (<1'); S = Short (1'–2'); M = Medium (2'–4'); T = Tall (>4') | **Color:** W = White; Pk = Pink; R = Red; O = Orange; Y = Yellow; B = Blue; V = Violet

Soil: (Dry soil icon) = Dry soil; (Xeriscaping icon) = Good for xeriscaping; (Ordinary soil icon) = Ordinary soil; (Moist soil icon) = Moist soil

Genus species	page	Type	Hard. Zone	Heat Zone	Light	Bloom Season: Spring	Summer	Fall	Height	Color
× *morifolium*		HP	5–9	· · ·	○	□□□	□□■	■■□	S M T	W R Y V
***Chrysogonum** virginianum*	p. 118	HP	5–9	9–5	○◐	□■■	■□□	□□□	L	Y
Cimicifuga	p. 118									
racemosa		HP	3–9	8–1	◐●	□□□	□■□	□□□	T	W
ramosa		HP	3–9	8–1	◐●	□□□	□□□	■□□	T	W
simplex		HP	3–9	8–1	◐●	□□□	□□■	■■□	M	W
***Cirsium** japonicum*	p. 119	HP	5–8	· · ·	○◐	□□□	□■■	□□□	M	Pk R
***Cladanthus** arabicus*	p. 120	A	1–9	12–1	○	□□□	■■■	■■□	S	Y
***Clarkia** amoena*	p. 120	A	2–10	7–1	○◐	□□□	■■■	□□□	S	Pk
***Claytonia** virginica*	p. 121	HP	5–8	6–1	●	■□□	□□□	□□□	L	W Pk
Clematis	p. 121									
integrifolia		HP	3–9	9–1	○◐	□□□	■■□	□□□	S M	B
macropetala		HP	6–9	9–3	○◐	□□■	■■□	□□□	T	B V
montana		HP	7–9	9–7	○◐	□□■	□□□	□□□	T	W
tangutica		HP	7–9	9–7	○◐	□□□	■■■	■□□	T	Y
Cleome	p. 122									
hassleriana		A	2–10	12–1	○◐	□□□	■■■	■■□	M	W Pk V
serrulata		A	2–10	12–1	○◐	□□□	■■■	■■□	S	W Pk V
***Clintonia** andrewsiana*	p. 123	HP	3–9	8–1	●	□□□	■□□	□□□	S	Pk
***Clivia** miniata*	p. 123	TP*	9–10	12–1	◐●	■□□	□□□	□□□	S	O
***Cobaea** scandens*	p. 124	TP*	9–10	12–10	○◐	□□□	■■■	■■□	T	W V
***Codonopsis** clemaditea*	p. 124	HP	5–8	9–7	○◐	□□□	□□■	□□□	S	B
***Coix** lacryma-jobi* (see also p. 480)	p. 125	TP*	9–10	12–1	○◐	□□□	□■□	□□□	S M	W V
Colchicum	p. 125									
autumnale		HB	4–9	9–1	○◐	□□□	□□□	□■□	L	W Pk V
speciosum		HB	4–9	9–1	○◐	□□□	□□□	□■□	L	Pk V
Collinsia	p. 126									
bicolor		A	3–10	11–1	○◐	□■■	■■□	□□□	S	W Pk B V
grandiflora		A	3–10	11–1	○◐	□■■	■■□	□□□	L	V
Colocasia (see p. 480)										
Consolida	p. 127									
ajacis		A	3–9	9–1	○	■■■	■□□	□□□	S M	Pk B V
regalis		A	3–9	9–1	○	■■■	■□□	□□□	S	Pk V
***Convallaria** majalis*	p. 128	HP	2–9	8–1	◐●	□□■	□□□	□□□	L	W

 Type: A = Annual; Bi = Biennial; HP = Hardy Perennial; TP = Tender Perennial; HB = Hardy Bulb; TB = Tender Bulb; * = May be grown as annual in colder regions

Light: ○ = Full sun; ◐ = Partial shade; ● = Full shade

Genus species	page	Type	Hard. Zone	Heat Zone	Light	Soil	BLOOM SEASON Spring Summer Fall	HEIGHT L S M T	COLOR W Pk R O Y B V
Convolvulus	p. 128								
cneorum		HP*	8–10	· · ·					W Pk
tricolor		A	3–9	*10–8*					W Y B
Coreopsis	p. 129								
auriculata		HP	4–9	*9–1*					O Y
grandiflora		HP	4–9	*9–1*					Y
lanceolata		HP	4–9	*9–1*					Y
rosea		HP	4–9	*9–1*					Pk
tinctoria		A	2–10	· · ·					R Y
verticillata		HP	3–10	*9–1*					Y
Coriandrum (*see p. 480*)									
Coronilla	p. 130								
orientalis		HP	7–10	· · ·					Y
varia		HP	3–10	· · ·					Pk
Cortaderia (*see also p. 480*).	p. 131								
selloana		HP	8–10	*12–7*					W
selloana 'Pumila'		HP	7–10	*12–7*					W
Corydalis	p. 131								
flexuosa		HP	6–8	*8–6*					B
lutea		HP	5–8	*8–4*					Y
Cosmos	p. 132								
atrosanguineus		HP*	7–10	*12–8*					R
bipinnatus		A	2–10	*12–1*					W Pk R
sulfureus		A	2–10	*12–1*					R O Y
Cotula *coronopifolia*	p. 132	HP	7–10	*9–7*					Y
Crambe *cordifolia*	p. 133	HP	5–9	*9–6*					W
Craspedia	p. 133								
globosa		TP*	9–10	*10–9*					Y
incana		TP*	9–10	*10–9*					Y
Crepis	p. 134								
aurea		HP	4–9	*7–4*					R O
rubra		A	5–7	*7–4*					Pk
Crinum	p. 134								
amoenum		HB	8–10	*12–10*					

Height: L = Low (<1'); S = Short (1'–2'); M = Medium (2'–4'); T = Tall (>4') | **Color:** W = White; Pk = Pink; R = Red; O = Orange; Y = Yellow; B = Blue; V = Violet
Soil: = Dry soil; = Good for xeriscaping; = Ordinary soil; = Moist soil

Genus species	page	Type	Hard. Zone	Heat Zone	Light	Soil	Bloom Season: Spring	Summer	Fall	Height: L	S	M	T	Color: W Pk R O Y B V
macowanii		HB	8–10	*12–10*	○ ◐	◐ ●	□□□	□□□	□■□		•			R
× *powellii*		HB	7–10	*12–8*	○ ◐	◐ ●	□□□	□□■	■□□			•		Pk
***Crocosmia** masoniorum*	*p. 135*	HB	6–10	*9–2*	○ ◐	○ ◐	□□□	■■■	□□□			•	•	O
Crocus	*p. 136*													
biflorus		HB	5–9	*8–1*	○ ◐	○ ◐	■□□	□□□	□□□	•				W V
chrysanthus		HB	4–9	*8–1*	○ ◐	○ ◐	□■□	□□□	□□□	•				W O B
sieberi		HB	3–8	*8–1*	○ ◐	○ ◐	□■□	□□□	□□□	•				W V
speciosus		HB	3–8	*8–1*	○ ◐	○ ◐	□□□	□□□	□■□	•				B V
tommasinianus		HB	4–9	*8–1*	○ ◐	○ ◐	□■□	□□□	□□□	•				V
vernus		HB	4–9	*8–1*	○ ◐	○ ◐	□■□	□□□	□□□	•				W V
Cuminum *(see p. 480)*														
Cuphea	*p. 137*													
hyssopifolia		TP*	10	*12–6*	○ ◐	◐	□□□	■■■	■■□		•			Pk V
ignea		TP*	10	*12–6*	○ ◐	◐	□□□	■■■	■■□		•			R
micropetala		TP*	10	*12–6*	○ ◐	○ ◐	□□□	■■■	■■□			•		R Y
× *purpurea*		TP*	10	*12–6*	○ ◐	◐	□□□	■■■	■■□		•			Pk R
Cyclamen	*p. 137*													
cilicium		HP	5–9	*9–3*	◐	◐	□□□	□□□	□■■	•				W Pk
coum		HP	5–9	*9–5*	◐	◐	■□□	□□□	□□□	•				R
hederifolium		HP	5–7	*9–7*	◐	◐	□□□	□□□	□■■	•				W Pk
purpurascens		HP	5–9	*9–4*	◐	◐	□□□	□□■	■□□	•				Pk R
***Cymbalaria** muralis*	*p. 138*	HP	4–9	*8–1*	○ ◐	●	□□□	□■□	□□□	•				V
Cymbopogon *(see p. 481)*														
***Cynara** cardunculus*	*p. 139*	HP	8–10	*9–7*	○ ◐	●	□□□	■■■	□□□				•	V
***Cynoglossum** amabile*	*p. 139*	Bi	2–10	*8–5*	○ ◐	○ ●	□■■	■■■	■■□		•			B
***Cyperus** longus (see also p. 481)*	*p. 140*	HP	8–10	*12–1*	○ ◐	●	□□□	□■□	□□□				•	V
Cypripedium	*p. 140*													
calceolus		HP	3–7	*7–1*	◐	●	□□■	■□□	□□□		•			Y V
kentuckiense		HP	3–9	. . .	●	●	□□■	□□□	□□□		•			W R
pubescens		HP	3–9	*7–1*	◐	●	□□■	■□□	□□□			•		Y V
reginae		HP	4–8	*7–1*	◐	●	□□■	■□□	□□□			•		W Pk
Cyrtomium *(see p. 481)*														
Dactylorhiza	*p. 142*													
elata		HP	6–8	*8–6*	◐	◐ ●	□□■	■□□	□□□			•		Pk V

 Type: A = Annual; Bi = Biennial; HP = Hardy Perennial; TP = Tender Perennial; HB = Hardy Bulb; TB = Tender Bulb; * = May be grown as annual in colder regions

Light: ○ = Full sun; ◐ = Partial shade; ● = Full shade

Genus species	page	Type	Hard. Zone	Heat Zone	Light	Soil	Bloom Season: Spring / Summer / Fall	Height: L S M T	W	Pk	R	O	Y	B	V
foliosa		HP	7–8	· · ·						Pk					V
Dahlia	*p. 142*														
× *hortensis*		HP	8–10	*12–1*					W	Pk	R	O	Y		V
pinnata		TP*	8–10	*9–3*					W	Pk	R	O	Y		V
Dalechampia *dioscoreifolia*	*p. 143*	TP*	9–10	· · ·						Pk					V
Darmera *peltata* (*see also p. 481*)	*p. 143*	HP	5–9	*9–4*						Pk					
Datura	*p. 144*														
innoxia		TP*	9–10	*12–1*					W	Pk					V
metel		TP*	9–10	*12–1*					W						V
Delosperma	*p. 144*														
cooperi		HP	6–9	*9–6*						Pk					
floribundum		HP	4–9	*9–6*						Pk					
nubigerum		HP	6–9	*9–6*							R	O			
Delphinium	*p. 145*														
Belladonna Group		HP	4–9	*7–1*										B	
Elatum Group		HP	3–9	*7–1*					W					B	V
grandiflorum		HP	3–9	*8–1*										B	
nudicaule		HP	4–9	*9–1*							R				
Pacific Hybrids		HP	3–9	*7–1*					W	Pk				B	V
semibarbatum		HP	8–9	· · ·									Y		
tatsienense		HP	6–9	· · ·										B	
Dennstaedtia (*see p. 481*)															
Dianthus	*p. 146*														
alpinus		HP	5–8	*8–1*						Pk	R				
armeria		Bi	2–10	*9–1*						Pk					
barbatus		Bi	2–10	*9–1*					W	Pk	R				
carthusianorum		HP	5–8	*9–5*						Pk					
chinensis		TP*	9–10	*12–1*					W	Pk	R				
deltoides		HP	5–8	*10–1*					W	Pk	R				V
gratianopolitanus		HP	5–9	*9–1*						Pk					
knappii		HP	2–8	· · ·									Y		
superbus		Bi	2–10	*9–1*						Pk					
Diascia *barberae*	*p. 148*	HP	6–8	*9–8*						Pk					

Height: L = Low (<1′); S = Short (1′–2′); M = Medium (2′–4′); T = Tall (>4′) | **Color:** W = White; Pk = Pink; R = Red; O = Orange; Y = Yellow; B = Blue; V = Violet

Soil: = Dry soil; = Good for xeriscaping; = Ordinary soil; = Moist soil

Genus species	page	Type	Hard. Zone	Heat Zone	Light	Soil	Bloom Season (Spring Summer Fall)	Height (L S M T)	Color (W Pk R O Y B V)
Dicentra	*p. 148*								
cucullaria		HP	3–9	*9–1*	○●				W
'Luxuriant'		HP	3–9	*9–1*	○●				R
spectabilis		HP	3–9	*9–1*	○●				Pk
***Dictamnus** albus*	*p. 149*	HP	3–8	*8–1*	○◑				W Pk
Dierama	*p. 149*								
dracomontanum		HB	7–9	*9–7*	○				Pk V
pulcherrimum		HB	7–9	*9–7*	○				Pk
Digitalis	*p. 150*								
grandiflora		HP	3–8	*8–1*	○◑				Y
laevigata		HP	5–9	. . .	○◑				Y
lutea		HP	3–8	*8–1*	○●				Y
× *mertonensis*		HP	3–8	*8–1*	○◑				Pk
purpurea		HP	4–8	*9–1*	○◑				W Pk R V
Dimorphotheca	*p. 150*								
pluvialis		TP*	9–10	*12–6*	○				W V
sinuata		TP*	9–10	*10–1*	○				W Pk O Y
Dioscorea *(see p. 481)*									
***Disporopsis** fuscopicta*	*p. 152*	HP	7–9	. . .	◑●				W
***Dodecatheon** meadia*	*p. 152*	HP	4–8	*8–1*	◑●				W Pk
Doronicum	*p. 153*								
columnae		HP	4–8	*7–1*	○◑				Y
orientale		HP	4–8	*7–1*	○◑				Y
***Dorotheanthus** bellidiformis*	*p. 153*	TP*	10	*10–1*	○				Pk R O Y V
***Draba** aizoides*	*p. 154*	HP	5–8	*6–1*	○◑				Y
***Dracunculus** vulgaris*	*p. 154*	HP	7–10	*10–8*	◑●				R
***Dryas** octopetala*	*p. 155*	HP	2–6	*6–1*	○◑				W
Dryopteris *(see p. 481)*									
***Eccremocarpus** scaber*	*p. 156*	HP*	8–10	*12–10*	○				R
***Echinacea** purpurea*	*p. 156*	HP	3–9	*8–1*	○◑				Pk
Echinops	*p. 157*								
bannaticus		HP	5–9	*9–5*	○◑				B
exaltatus		HP	3–9	*9–1*	○◑				B
ritro		HP	3–9	*9–1*	○◑				B

 Type: A = Annual; Bi = Biennial; HP = Hardy Perennial; TP = Tender Perennial; HB = Hardy Bulb; TB = Tender Bulb; * = May be grown as annual in colder regions

Light: ○ = Full sun; ◑ = Partial shade; ● = Full shade

Genus species	page	Type	Hard. Zone	Heat Zone	Light	Soil	Bloom Season: Spring	Summer	Fall	Height: L	S	M	T	Color (W Pk R O Y B V)
Echium	*p. 157*													
candicans		Bi	3–8	· · ·	☼	Dry, Moist	□■■	■□□	□□□				•	W B
vulgare		Bi	3–8	· · ·	☼	Dry, Moist	□■■	■□□	□□□		•			W Pk B V
***Emilia** coccinea*	*p. 158*	A	3–10	*9–1*	☼	Dry, Ordinary	□□□	■■■	□□□		•			R O
***Epigaea** repens*	*p. 158*	HP	3–9	*9–1*	◐ ●	Xeriscaping, Ordinary	□■□	□□□	□□□	•				W
Epilobium	*p. 159*													
angustifolium		HP	3–8	*7–1*	☼ ◐	Dry, Ordinary	□□□	□□■	■□□				•	Pk
dodonaei		HP	3–8	· · ·	☼ ◐	Dry, Ordinary	□□□	□■□	□□□			•		Pk
Epimedium	*p. 159*													
grandiflorum		HP	4–9	*8–1*	☼ ●	Dry, Moist	□■■	□□□	□□□	•				W Pk V
perralderianum		HP	5–9	*8–1*	☼ ●	Dry, Moist	■■□	□□□	□□□	•				Y
pinnatum ssp. *colchicum*		HP	4–9	*8–1*	☼ ●	Dry, Moist	□■■	■□□	□□□	•				Y
× *rubrum*		HP	4–9	*8–1*	☼ ●	Dry, Moist	□■■	□□□	□□□	•				Pk R
× *versicolor*		HP	4–8	*8–1*	☼ ●	Dry, Moist	■■□	□□□	□□□	•				Pk R Y
***Eragrostis** trichodes* (see also p. 481)	*p. 160*	HP	4–9	· · ·	☼	Xeriscaping, Ordinary	□□□	□□■	□□□			•		V
***Eranthis** hyemalis*	*p. 160*	HP	4–9	*9–1*	☼ ◐	Ordinary, Moist	■□□	□□□	□□□	•				Y
Eremurus	*p. 161*													
himalaicus		HP	5–9	*8–5*	☼	Ordinary	□□■	■□□	□□□			•	•	W
stenophyllus		HP	6–9	· · ·	☼	Ordinary	□□□	■□□	□□□			•	•	Y
Erigeron	*p. 162*													
aurantiacus		HP	4–8	*8–5*	☼ ◐	Xeriscaping, Ordinary	□□□	■■■	□□□		•			O Y
karvinskianus		HP	8–9	*7–5*	☼ ◐	Xeriscaping, Ordinary	□□□	■■■	□□□	•				W Pk
speciosus		HP	2–9	· · ·	☼ ◐	Xeriscaping, Ordinary	□□□	■■■	□□□		•			V
***Erinus** alpinus*	*p. 162*	HP	4–9	*7–1*	☼ ◐	Dry, Ordinary	□□■	■□□	□□□	•				W Pk R V
***Eriophorum** latifolium*	*p. 163*	HP	4–8	· · ·	☼ ◐	Moist	□□□	□■■	□□□		•			W
Erodium	*p. 163*													
absinthoides		HP	6–10	· · ·	☼ ◐	Dry, Ordinary	□□□	■■□	□□□	•				Pk
foetidum		HP	7–8	*8–6*	☼ ◐	Dry, Ordinary	□□□	■■□	□□□	•				Pk
Eryngium	*p. 164*													
alpinum		HP	5–8	*8–4*	☼	Dry, Ordinary	□□□	□□■	□□□		•			B
amethystinum		HP	3–8	*8–1*	☼	Dry, Ordinary	□□□	□■■	□□□		•			B
bourgatii		HP	5–8	*9–5*	☼	Xeriscaping, Ordinary	□□□	□■■	□□□		•			B
giganteum		Bi	3–8	*8–5*	☼	Dry, Ordinary	□□□	□□■	□□□			•		B
planum		HP	3–8	*9–5*	☼	Dry, Ordinary	□□□	□■■	■□□			•		B

Height: L = Low (<1′); S = Short (1′–2′); M = Medium (2′–4′); T = Tall (>4′) | **Color**: W = White; Pk = Pink; R = Red; O = Orange; Y = Yellow; B = Blue; V = Violet
Soil: Dry soil; Good for xeriscaping; Ordinary soil; Moist soil

Genus species	page	Type	Hard. Zone	Heat Zone	Light	Soil	Bloom Season: Spring	Summer	Fall	Height (L S M T)	Color (W Pk R O Y B V)
× zabelii		HP	5–8	*8–5*	○	✕◇ ◒	□□□	□■■	□□□	S	B
Erysimum	*p. 164*										
cheiri		HP	3–7	*7–1*	○◐	◇ ◒	□■■	□□□	□□□	S	W Pk R O Y
linifolium		HP*	7–9	*9–7*	○◐	✕◇ ◒	□□□	■■□	□□□	S	V
Erythronium	*p. 165*										
dens-canis		HP	4–9	*9–1*	◐●	◆	□■□	□□□	□□□	L	W Pk V
revolutum		HP	4–9	*8–5*	◐●	◆	□■□	□□□	□□□	L	Pk
Eschscholzia	*p. 166*										
caespitosa		HP*	8–10	*9–1*	○	◇ ◒	□□□	□■■	■□□	L	Y
californica		HP*	8–10	*9–1*	○	✕◇ ◒	□■■	■□□	□□□	L	O Y
Eucomis	*p. 166*										
bicolor		HB*	8–10	*10–1*	○	◒	□□□	□■□	□□□	S	W
comosa		HB*	8–10	*10–1*	○	◒	□□□	□■□	□□□	S M	W Pk
Eupatorium	*p. 167*										
coelestinum		HP	6–8	· · ·	○◐	◇ ◆	□□□	□■■	■■□	S M	V
fistulosum		HP	4–8	· · ·	○◐	◇ ◆	□□□	□□■	■□□	T	Pk
maculatum		HP	4–10	*9–1*	○◐	◇ ◆	□□□	□□■	■□□	T	R
purpureum		HP	3–8	*9–1*	○◐	◇ ◆	□□□	□□■	■□□	T	Pk V
rugosum		HP	3–8	*9–1*	○◐	◇ ◆	□□□	□□□	■■□	M	W
Euphorbia	*p. 167*										
amygdaloides		HP	7–9	*9–6*	○●	◇ ◒	■■□	□□□	□□□	S	Y
cyparissias		HP	3–9	*8–1*	○	◇ ◒	□□□	■■□	□□□	S	Y
griffithii		HP	5–9	*9–1*	○◐	◒ ◆	□□■	□□□	□□□	M	R O
marginata		A	3–10	*12–1*	○	✕◇ ◒	□□□	□■■	■■□	S M	W
myrsinites		HP	5–9	*8–5*	○	◇ ◒	□■■	■□□	□□□	L	Y
nicaeensis		HP	6–10	*8–5*	○	◇ ◒	□□□	□■■	■□□	S	Y
polychroma		HP	4–9	*9–1*	○◐	◒	□■■	□□□	□□□	S	Y
***Eustoma** grandiflorum*	*p. 168*	TP*	9–10	*12–1*	○	◒ ◆	□□■	■■■	□□□	S	W Pk B V
***Evolvulus** pilosus*	*p. 169*	HP*	8–10	· · ·	○◐	◒ ◆	□□■	■■■	■□□	S	B
***Farfugium** japonicum*	*p. 169*	HP	7–10	*9–7*	◐●	◆	□□□	□□■	■□□	S	Y
***Felicia** amelloides*	*p. 170*	TP*	9–10	*12–1*	○	✕◇ ◒	□□□	■■■	□□□	S	B
Festuca *(see p. 481)*											
Filipendula	*p. 171*										
rubra		HP	3–9	*9–1*	○◐	◒ ◆	□□□	□■□	□□□	T	Pk

 Type: A = Annual; Bi = Biennial; HP = Hardy Perennial; TP = Tender Perennial; HB = Hardy Bulb; TB = Tender Bulb; * = May be grown as annual in colder regions

Light: ○ = Full sun; ◐ = Partial shade; ● = Full shade

Genus species	page	Type	Hard. Zone	Heat Zone	Light	Soil	BLOOM SEASON Spring	Summer	Fall	HEIGHT L	S	M	T	COLOR W Pk R O Y B V
ulmaria		HP	3–9	*9–1*	◐	◒ ●	□□□	□■■	□□□			•	•	W
vulgaris		HP	3–9	*9–1*	☼ ◐	◌ ◒	□□□	□■□	□□□		•			Y
Foeniculum *(see p. 481)*														
Francoa *sonchifolia*	*p. 172*	HP	7–10	*9–7*	☼ ◐	◒ ●	□□□	□■□	□□□			•		Pk
Freesia *lactea*	*p. 172*	TB	9–10	*12–6*	☼	◌ ◒	■■□	□□□	□□□	•				W
Fritillaria	*p. 173*													
imperialis		HB	5–9	*9–4*	☼ ◐	◒	□■□	□□□	□□□			•		O
meleagris		HB	3–8	*7–1*	☼ ◐	●	□■□	□□□	□□□	•				W V
persica		HB	4–9	*8–6*	☼ ◐	◒	□■□	□□□	□□□		•	•		V
Fuchsia	*p. 173*													
'Gartenmeister Bonstedt'		TP*	9–10	*12–9*	☼ ◐	●	□□□	■■■	■■□		•			R
× *hybrida*		TP*	9–10	*12–9*	☼ ◐	●	□□□	■■■	■■□		•			W Pk R V
magellanica		HP*	7–9	. . .	☼ ◐	●	□□□	■■■	■■□			•		R
Gaillardia	*p. 174*													
aristata		HP	3–9	. . .	☼	◒ ●	□□□	■■■	□□□			•		R O Y
× *grandiflora*		HP	3–9	*8–1*	☼	◒ ●	□□□	■■■	■□□			•		R Y
pulchella		A	1–10	*12–1*	☼	◒	□□□	■■■	■□□		•			R Y
Galanthus	*p. 175*													
elwesii		HB	5–9	*9–1*	☼ ◐	◒ ●	■□□	□□□	□□□	•				W
ikariae		HB	3–9	*9–1*	☼ ◐	◒ ●	■□□	□□□	□□□	•				W
nivalis		HB	2–8	*9–1*	☼ ◐	◒ ●	■□□	□□□	□□□	•				W
Galega *officinalis*	*p. 175*	HP	3–9	*8–5*	☼ ◐	◒	□□□	□■□	□□□			•	•	B
Galium *odoratum*	*p. 176*	HP	4–9	*8–5*	◐ ☀	◌ ●	□□■	■□□	□□□	•				W
Galtonia	*p. 176*													
candicans		HB*	6–8	*10–8*	☼	◒ ●	□□□	□■■	■□□			•		W
viridiflora		HB*	8–10	*10–8*	☼	◒ ●	□□□	□■■	■□□			•		W
Gaura *lindheimeri*	*p. 177*	HP	6–9	*9–6*	☼	♉ ◒	□□□	■■■	■■□		•	•		W Pk
Gazania *rigens*	*p. 177*	TP*	9–10	*12–3*	☼	♉ ◒	□□□	■■■	■□□	•	•			Y
Gentiana	*p. 178*													
acaulis		HP	3–9	*8–5*	☼ ◐	◒ ●	□■□	□□□	■□□	•				B
asclepiadea		HP	3–9	*9–6*	☼ ◐	●	□□□	□■■	■□□			•		B V
lutea		HP	3–9	*8–7*	☼	●	□□□	□■□	□□□			•		Y
septemfida		HP	3–9	*8–6*	☼ ◐	●	□□□	□□■	□□□		•			B V
verna		HP	3–9	*8–5*	☼ ◐	◒ ●	□□■	■□□	□□□	•				B

Height: L = Low (<1'); S = Short (1'–2'); M = Medium (2'–4'); T = Tall (>4') | **Color:** W = White; Pk = Pink; R = Red; O = Orange; Y = Yellow; B = Blue; V = Violet
Soil: ◌ = Dry soil; ♉ = Good for xeriscaping; ◒ = Ordinary soil; ● = Moist soil

Genus species	page	Type	Hard. Zone	Heat Zone	Light	Soil	Bloom Season: Spring	Summer	Fall	Height: L	S	M	T	Color: W Pk R O Y B V
Geranium	*p. 178*													
cinereum		HP	4–9	*9–5*	○		□□■	■■□	□□□	•				W Pk
incanum		TP	9–10	*8–5*	○		□□□	□■□	□□□		•			Pk
macrorrhizum		HP	5–9	*8–1*	○◐		□□■	■□■	□■□		•			Pk
× magnificum		HP	4–8	*8–1*	○◐		□□■	■□□	□□□		•			B V
× oxonianum		HP	4–8	*8–1*	○◐		□□□	■■■	■□□		•			Pk
phaeum		HP	4–9	*8–1*	◐●		□□■	■■□	□□□		•			W Pk V
pratense		HP	4–8	*8–1*	○◐		□□□	■□□	□□□		•			W B V
psilostemon		HP	4–8	*8–5*	○◐		□□□	■■■	□□□			•		Pk
sanguineum		HP	4–10	*8–1*	○		□□□	■■□	□□□		•			W Pk
sylvaticum		HP	4–8	*8–1*	◐●		□■■	□□□	□□□		•			B
***Gerbera** jamesonii*	*p. 179*	TP*	10	*12–6*	○◐		□□□	■■■	■□□		•			W Pk R O Y
Geum	*p. 180*													
chiloense		HP	5–9	*8–1*	○◐		□□□	■■■	□□□		•			R
montanum		HP	4–8	*8–3*	○◐		□□□	■□□	□□□	•				Y
Gilia	*p. 180*													
capitata		A	6–10	*12–1*	○		□□□	■■■	■□□		•			B V
tricolor		A	6–10	*12–1*	○		□□□	■■■	■□□		•			B V
***Gillenia** trifoliata*	*p. 181*	HP	4–8	*9–5*	○◐		□□□	□■□	□□□			•		W
Gladiolus	*p. 181*													
communis ssp. *byzantinus*		HP	5–10	*9–1*	○		□□□	■□□	□□□			•		Pk V
× gandavensis		TP*	9–10	· · ·	○		□□□	□■□	□□□			•		R Y
***Glaucidium** palmatum*	*p. 182*	HP	5–9	*9–6*	◐●		□□■	■□□	□□□		•			V
***Glaucium** flavum*	*p. 182*	Bi	3–9	*9–6*	○		□□□	□■■	□□□		•			O Y
***Globba** winitii*	*p. 183*	TP*	9–10	*9–6*	◐●		□□□	□□■	□□□			•		V
Globularia	*p. 183*													
cordifolia		HP	5–9	*7–5*	○◐		□□■	■□□	□□□	•				B V
meridionalis		HP	5–9	*7–5*	○◐		□□□	■□□	□□□	•				B V
***Gloriosa** superba*	*p. 184*	TP*	9–10	*12–7*	○		□□□	□■■	■□□				•	R Y
Gomphrena	*p. 184*													
globosa		A	3–10	*12–1*	○		□□□	■■■	■□□	•	•			W Pk V
haageana		A	3–10	*12–1*	○		□□□	■■■	■□□		•			R O
Gunnera *(see p. 481)*														

 Type: A = Annual; Bi = Biennial; HP = Hardy Perennial; TP = Tender Perennial; HB = Hardy Bulb; TB = Tender Bulb; * = May be grown as annual in colder regions

Light: ○ = Full sun; ◐ = Partial shade; ● = Full shade

Genus species	page	Type	Hard. Zone	Heat Zone	Light	Soil	BLOOM SEASON Spring Summer Fall	HEIGHT L S M T	COLOR W Pk R O Y B V
Gypsophila	*p. 185*								
cerastioides		HP	6–9	*8–5*					W
elegans		A	2–10	*9–1*					W Pk
paniculata		HP	4–8	*9–4*					W
repens		HP	3–8	*9–1*					W V
***Hacquetia** epipactis*	*p. 186*	HP	4–9	*7–5*					Y
Haemanthus	*p. 186*								
albiflos		TB*	10	*12–10*					W
multiflorus		TP*	10	*12–10*					R
***Hakonechloa** (see p. 481)*									
***Hardenbergia** violacea*	*p. 188*	TP*	9–10	*12–6*					V
***Hedychium** coronarium*	*p. 188*	HP*	7–10	*12–6*					W
***Hedyotis** caerulea*	*p. 189*	HP	3–8	*8–1*					B
***Hedysarum** coronarium*	*p. 189*	HP	4–9	*9–1*					R
Helenium	*p. 190*								
autumnale		HP	3–8	*8–1*					Y
hoopesii		HP	3–8	*8–1*					O Y
Helianthemum	*p. 190*								
apenninum		HP	6–9	. . .					W
nummularium		HP	6–9	*8–6*					O Y
Helianthus	*p. 191*								
annuus		A	1–10	*12–1*					R Y
maximiliani		HP	4–9	*8–1*					Y
× multiflorus		HP	3–10	*9–5*					Y
salicifolius		HP	4–9	*9–6*					Y
strumosus		HP	4–9	. . .					Y
***Helichrysum** (see also p. 481)*	*p. 191*								
'Sulphur Light'		TP*	9–10	*10–9*					Y
Helictotrichon	*p. 192*								
sempervirens (see also p. 481)		HP	4–8	*9–1*					W
***Heliophila** longifolia*	*p. 192*	A	3–9	. . .					B
Heliopsis	*p. 193*								
helianthoides		HP	4–9	*9–1*					Y
helianthoides ssp. *scabra*		HP	4–9	*9–1*					Y

Height: L = Low (<1′); S = Short (1′–2′); M = Medium (2′–4′); T = Tall (>4′) | **Color:** W = White; Pk = Pink; R = Red; O = Orange; Y = Yellow; B = Blue; V = Violet
Soil: = Dry soil; = Good for xeriscaping; = Ordinary soil; = Moist soil

Genus species	page	Type	Hard. Zone	Heat Zone	Light	Soil	BLOOM SEASON Spring Summer Fall	HEIGHT L S M T	COLOR W Pk R O Y B V
***Heliotropium** arborescens*	*p. 193*	TP*	9–10	*12–1*	○◐				V
Helleborus	*p. 194*								
argutifolius		HP	6–8	*9–6*	○◐				W
foetidus		HP	3–9	*9–6*	◐●				V
× hybridus		HP	5–9	*9–6*	◐				W Pk
lividus		HP	7–9	*9–8*	◐●				Pk
niger		HP	3–9	*8–1*	◐●				W
orientalis		HP	5–9	*9–1*	◐●				W Pk V
purpurascens		HP	5–8	*8–5*	◐				V
× sternii		HP	6–9	*9–6*	◐				Pk
viridis		HP	6–8	*8–1*	◐				W
Hemerocallis	*p. 195*								
citrina		HP	3–9	*9–1*	○◐				Y
lilioasphodelus		HP	3–9	*9–1*	○◐				Y
middendorffii		HP	3–9	*9–1*	○◐				O Y
'Stella de Oro'		HP	3–9	*9–1*	○◐				O Y
***Hepatica** nobilis*	*p. 196*	HP	4–8	*8–4*	◐●				B
***Heracleum** mantegazzianum*	*p. 196*	HP	3–9	*9–1*	○◐				W
Herniaria *(see p. 481)*									
***Hesperis** matronalis*	*p. 197*	HP	3–9	*9–1*	○●				W V
Heuchera	*p. 198*								
americana		HP	3–9	*8–1*	◐				W
× brizoides		HP	3–9	*8–1*	○◐				W Pk R
micrantha		HP	3–9	*8–1*	○◐				W
sanguinea		HP	3–9	*8–1*	○◐				R
× Heucherella	*p. 198*								
alba		HP	4–9	*8–5*	○◐				Pk
tiarelloides		HP	4–9	*8–5*	○◐				Pk
Hibiscus	*p. 199*								
acetosella		TP*	10	. . .	○◐				R V
moscheutos		HP	4–10	. . .	○◐				W Pk R
rosa-sinensis		A	3–10	*12–1*	○◐				R
trionum		TP*	10	*12–10*	○◐				W V
***Hordeum** jubatum*	*p. 199*	HP	3–10	*8–1*	○				Pk V

 Type: A = Annual; Bi = Biennial; HP = Hardy Perennial; TP = Tender Perennial; HB = Hardy Bulb; TB = Tender Bulb; * = May be grown as annual in colder regions

Light: ○ = Full sun; ◐ = Partial shade; ● = Full shade

Genus species	page	Type	Hard. Zone	Heat Zone	Light	Soil	BLOOM SEASON Spring Summer Fall	HEIGHT L S M T	COLOR W Pk R O Y B V
Hosta *(see also p. 481)*	*p. 200*								
fluctuans		HP	3–9	*9–1*					W
'Fortunei'		HP	3–9	*9–1*					V
montana		HP	3–9	*9–1*					V
nigrescens		HP	3–9	*9–1*					V
plantaginea		HP	3–9	*9–1*					W
sieboldiana		HP	3–9	*9–1*					V
sieboldii		HP	3–9	*9–1*					V
'Tokudama'		HP	3–9	*9–1*					W
'Undulata'		HP	3–9	*9–1*					V
ventricosa		HP	3–9	*9–1*					V
Houttuynia *(see p. 482)*									
Humulus *(see p. 482)*									
Hunnemannia fumariifolia	*p. 201*	TP*	9–10	*12–9*					Y
Hyacinthoides	*p. 202*								
hispanica		HB	4–9	*9–1*					W Pk B
italica		HB	4–9	*9–1*					B
non-scripta		HB	4–9	*9–1*					W B
Hyacinthus orientalis	*p. 202*	HB	5–8	*9–5*					W Pk R Y B V
Hylomecon japonica	*p. 203*	HP	5–8	*8–5*					Y
Hymenocallis	*p. 204*								
× festalis		HB*	8–10	*10–8*					W
narcissiflora		TB*	9–10	*10–8*					W
Hypericum	*p. 204*								
calycinum		HP	5–9	*9–4*					Y
olympicum		HP	7–9	*9–7*					Y
patulum		HP	7–9	*9–7*					Y
Hypoestes *(see p. 482)*									
Hyssopus officinalis	*p. 205*	HP	3–10	*9–6*					B
Iberis	*p. 206*								
amara		A	1–10	*12–1*					W V
saxatilis		HP	3–9	*9–7*					W
sempervirens		HP	3–9	*9–4*					W
umbellata		A	1–10	*12–1*					W Pk R V

Height: L = Low (<1'); S = Short (1'–2'); M = Medium (2'–4'); T = Tall (>4') | **Color:** W = White; Pk = Pink; R = Red; O = Orange; Y = Yellow; B = Blue; V = Violet

Soil: ◌ = Dry soil; ◌ = Good for xeriscaping; ◌ = Ordinary soil; ◌ = Moist soil

Genus species	page	Type	Hard. Zone	Heat Zone	Light	Soil	BLOOM SEASON Spring	Summer	Fall	HEIGHT L	S	M	T	COLOR W Pk R O Y B V
Impatiens	*p. 207*													
balfourii		TP*	10	*12–1*	◐ ●	●	□□■	■■■	□□□			•••	••••	Pk
balsamina		A	3–10	*12–1*	☼ ◐	◒ ●	□□■	■■■	■□□		••			W Pk
New Guinea Hybrids		TP*	10	*12–1*	☼ ◐	●	□□■	■■■	■■□		••			W Pk R O V
walleriana		TP*	10	*12–1*	◐ ●	●	□□■	■■■	■■□		••			W Pk R O V
***Incarvillea** mairei*	*p. 207*	HP	4–9	*8–1*	☼ ◐	◒ ●	□□■	■□□	□□□	•				Pk Y
Inula	*p. 208*													
ensifolia		HP	3–9	*8–1*	☼ ◐	◒ ●	□□□	□■□	□□□		••			Y
orientalis		HP	3–9	*8–1*	☼	◒ ●	□□□	□□■	□□□		••			O Y
royleana		HP	3–7	*8–1*	☼	◒ ●	□□□	□■□	□□□		••			O Y
***Ionopsidium** acaule*	*p. 208*	A	1–10	. . .	☼ ◐	○ ●	□□□	■■■	■□□	•				W B V
Ipomoea	*p. 209*													
alba		A	3–10	*12–10*	☼	○ ●	□□□	□□■	□□□				••••	W
hederacea		A	3–10	*12–10*	☼	○ ●	□□□	□■■	■□□				••••	Pk R B V
nil		A	3–10	*12–1*	☼	○ ●	□□□	□■■	■□□				••••	W B V
purpurea		A	3–10	*12–10*	☼	○ ●	□□□	□■■	■□□				••••	R B V
quamoclit		A	3–10	*12–6*	☼	○ ●	□□□	□■■	■■□				••••	R O
tricolor		A	3–10	*12–1*	☼	○ ●	□□□	□■■	■□□				••••	W B V
Iris	*p. 209*													
chrysographes		HP	5–9	*9–1*	☼ ◐	◒	□□□	□■□	□□□		••			V
cristata		HP	6–9	*10–1*	☼ ◐	◒	□■□	□□□	□□□	•				W V
ensata		HP	5–9	*8–4*	☼ ◐	●	□□□	■■□	□□□			•••		W B V
foetidissima		HP	7–9	*9–2*	◐	●	□□■	■□□	□□□			•••		Y
fulva		HP	7–10	*9–3*	☼ ◐	●	□■□	□□□	□□□			•••		R O
germanica		HP	4–9	*9–1*	☼	○ˣ ◒	□□■	■□□	□□□			•••		Y B V
histriodes		HB	5–9	*8–4*	☼	◒	■□□	□□□	□□□	•				B V
latifolia		HB	6–9	*9–5*	◐	◒ ●	□□■	■□□	□□□			•••		Y B V
pallida		HP	6–9	*9–1*	☼	○ ◒	□□■	■□□	□□□			•••		Y B V
pseudacorus		HP	5–9	*8–3*	◐	●	□□■	■□□	□□□			•••	••••	Y
pumila		HP	4–9	*9–1*	☼	◒	□■□	□□□	□□□	•				Y B V
reticulata		HB	5–9	*8–4*	☼	◒	■□□	□□□	□□□	•				Y B V
sibirica		HP	4–9	*9–1*	☼ ◐	●	□□■	■□□	□□□		••	•••		B V
spuria		HP	6–9	*9–5*	☼	◒	□□□	■□□	□□□		••	•••		W Y B V
versicolor		HP	3–9	*9–1*	☼ ◐	○ ●	□□■	■□□	□□□		••	•••		B V

 Type: A = Annual; Bi = Biennial; HP = Hardy Perennial; TP = Tender Perennial; HB = Hardy Bulb; TB = Tender Bulb; * = May be grown as annual in colder regions

Light: ☼ = Full sun; ◐ = Partial shade; ● = Full shade

Genus species	page	Type	Hard. Zone	Heat Zone	Light	Soil	Bloom Season (Spring, Summer, Fall)	Height (L S M T)	Color (W Pk R O Y B V)
xiphium		HB	5–9	*9–5*					B V
***Isatis** tinctoria*	*p. 211*	Bi	3–10	*8–1*					Y
Ixia	*p. 211*								
maculata		HB*	8–10	*12–10*					Pk O Y
viridiflora		HB*	8–10	*12–7*					W
***Ixiolirion** tataricum*	*p. 212*	HB	7–10	*12–7*					B
***Jasione** laevis*	*p. 212*	HP	6–9	*8–6*					B
Jeffersonia	*p. 213*								
diphylla		HP	5–8	*8–5*					W Y
dubia		HP	5–8	*8–5*					B V
***Justicia** carnea*	*p. 213*	HP*	10	12–9					Pk V
Kalimeris	*p. 214*								
pinnatifida 'Hortensia'		HP	5–8	*8–1*					W Y
***Kirengeshoma** palmata*	*p. 214*	HP	5–8	*8–5*					Y
***Knautia** macedonica*	*p. 214*	HP	5–9	*9–5*					R
Kniphofia	*p. 215*								
rooperi		HP	6–9	*9–4*					R O Y
uvaria		HP	5–9	*9–1*					R O
Koeleria *(see p. 482)*									
***Lablab** purpureus*	*p. 216*	TP*	9–10	*12–7*					V
Lagerstroemia × 'Chickasaw'	*p. 217*	HP	7–10	*9–7*					V
***Lagurus** ovatus*	*p. 217*	A	3–10	*12–1*					W V
Lamium *(see also p. 482)*	*p. 218*								
galeobdolon		HP	3–9	···					Y
maculatum		HP	3–9	···					W Pk
***Lampranthus** spectabilis*	*p. 218*	TP*	9–10	*12–1*					Pk
Lantana	*p. 219*								
camara		HP	8–10	*12–1*					R Y
montevidensis		TP*	8–10	*12–1*					Pk
***Lapageria** rosea*	*p. 219*	HP*	8–10	*12–9*					R
Lathyrus	*p. 220*								
grandiflorus		HP	6–9	*9–6*					Pk R V
latifolius		HP	6–9	*9–5*					Pk V
odoratus		A	1–10	*8–1*					W Pk B V

Height: L = Low (<1'); S = Short (1'–2'); M = Medium (2'–4'); T = Tall (>4') | **Color**: W = White; Pk = Pink; R = Red; O = Orange; Y = Yellow; B = Blue; V = Violet

Soil: = Dry soil; = Good for xeriscaping; = Ordinary soil; = Moist soil

Genus species	page	Type	Hard. Zone	Heat Zone	COLOR W Pk R O Y B V
Lavandula	*p. 221*				
angustifolia		HP	5–9	*9–3*	V
× intermedia		HP	5–9	*9–3*	B V
stoechas		HP*	8–9	*9–8*	Pk V
Lavatera	*p. 222*				
cachemiriana		HP	4–10	*9–1*	Pk
trimestris		A	2–10	*12–1*	Pk
***Layia** platyglossa*	*p. 222*	A	3–10	*12–6*	W Y
***Leonotis** leonurus*	*p. 223*	TP*	9–10	*12–6*	O
***Leontopodium** alpinum*	*p. 223*	HP	4–7	*6–1*	W
***Leucanthemella** serotina*	*p. 224*	HP	4–9	*9–1*	W
Leucanthemum	*p. 224*				
× superbum		HP	5–8	*9–1*	W
vulgare		HP	4–8	*9–1*	W
Leucojum	*p. 225*				
aestivum		HB	4–9	*9–1*	W
vernum		HB	4–9	*9–1*	W
***Levisticum** (see p. 482)*					
Lewisia	*p. 226*				
cotyledon		HP	4–8	*8–3*	Pk
nevadensis		HP	4–7	*7–1*	W
Liatris	*p. 227*				
pycnostachya		HP	3–9	*9–1*	V
spicata		HP	3–10	*9–1*	V
***Libertia** grandiflora*	*p. 227*	HP*	8–10	*12–8*	W
Ligularia	*p. 228*				
dentata		HP	4–8	*8–1*	O Y
przewalskii		HP	4–8	*8–1*	Y
Lilium	*p. 228*				
auratum		HB	5–9	*8–1*	W
candidum		HB	4–9	*9–6*	W
davidii		HB	3–8	*8–1*	R O
formosanum		HB	6–9	*8–4*	W V
longiflorum		HB	7–9	*9–1*	W

 Type: A = Annual; Bi = Biennial; HP = Hardy Perennial; TP = Tender Perennial; HB = Hardy Bulb; TB = Tender Bulb; * = May be grown as annual in colder regions

Light: ☼ = Full sun; ◐ = Partial shade; ● = Full shade

Genus species	page	Type	Hard. Zone	Heat Zone	Light	Soil	Bloom Season: Spring	Summer	Fall	Height: L	S	M	T	Color (W Pk R O Y B V)
martagon		HB	4–9	*7–1*	part shade	ordinary	□□□	■□□	□□□			•	•	Pk V
monadelphum		HB	4–9	*8–5*	sun	ordinary	□□□	■□□	□□□		•	•	•	Y
pyrenaicum		HB	5–9	*7–1*	sun	ordinary	□□■	■□□	□□□		•	•		Y
regale		HB	4–9	*7–1*	sun, part shade	ordinary	□□□	□■□	□□□			•	•	W V
speciosum		HB	5–9	*8–1*	sun, part shade	ordinary	□□□	□□■	■□□			•	•	W Pk
***Limnanthes** douglasii*	*p. 229*	A	1–9	*9–1*	sun, part shade	moist	□□□	■■■	□□□	•				W Y
Limonium	*p. 230*													
latifolium		HP	4–9	· · ·	sun	dry, ordinary	□□□	□■■	□□□		•			B
perezii		TP*	9–10	*12–1*	sun	dry, ordinary	□□■	■□□	□□□			•		V
sinuatum		HP*	8–9	*9–3*	sun	dry, ordinary	□□□	□□■	■□□		•			W Pk Y B
Linaria	*p. 230*													
maroccana		A	2–10	*9–1*	sun	dry, moist	□□■	■□□	□□□	•	•			W Pk O Y V
purpurea		HP	4–9	*8–5*	sun	dry, moist	□□□	■□□	□□□			•		V
***Linnaea** borealis*	*p. 231*	HP	1–5	*6–1*	part shade, shade	moist	□□□	■□□	□□□	•				W Pk
Linum	*p. 231*													
flavum		HP	5–9	*9–3*	sun	dry, ordinary	□□■	■□□	□□□		•			Y
grandiflorum 'Rubrum'		A	2–10	*8–1*	sun, part shade	dry, moist	□□□	■■■	□□□		•			Pk R
narbonense		HP	5–9	*9–3*	sun	dry, ordinary	□□■	■□□	□□□		•			B
perenne		HP	5–9	*9–3*	sun	xeriscaping, ordinary	□□■	■■□	□□□		•			B
***Liriope** (see also p. 482)*	*p. 232*													
muscari		HP	5–9	*12–1*	part shade, shade	dry, moist	□□□	□□■	■□□	•	•			V
spicata		HP	4–9	*12–1*	part shade, shade	xeriscaping, moist	□□□	□□■	■□□		•			V
***Lithodora** diffusa*	*p. 233*	HP	6–9	*8–6*	sun, part shade	dry, moist	□□■	■□□	□□□	•				B
Lobelia	*p. 233*													
cardinalis		HP	2–9	*8–1*	sun, shade	moist	□□□	□□■	□□□			•		R
erinus		TP*	9–10	*9–1*	part shade, shade	moist	□□■	■■■	■■□	•				B V
× *gerardii*		HP	6–8	*9–8*	sun, shade	dry, moist	□□□	□□■	■□□			•		V
siphilitica		HP	4–8	*8–4*	part shade, shade	moist	□□□	□□■	□□□			•		B
× *speciosa*		HP	3–9	· · ·	sun, part shade	moist	□□□	□■□	□□□		•	•	•	R
tupa		HP*	8–10	*10–8*	sun, part shade	moist	□□□	□□■	□□□				•	R
***Lobularia** maritima*	*p. 234*	A	3–10	*12–1*	sun, part shade	xeriscaping, moist	□□■	■■■	■■□	•				W
***Lonas** annua*	*p. 235*	A	3–9	· · ·	sun	dry, ordinary	□□□	■■■	■□□	•				Y
***Lopezia** (see also p. 482)*	*p. 235*													
racemosa		A	3–10	· · ·	sun, part shade	ordinary	□■■	■■■	■□□	•				W Pk R V

Height: L = Low (<1'); S = Short (1'–2'); M = Medium (2'–4'); T = Tall (>4') | **Color**: W = White; Pk = Pink; R = Red; O = Orange; Y = Yellow; B = Blue; V = Violet

Soil: Dry soil; Good for xeriscaping; Ordinary soil; Moist soil

Genus species	page	Type	Hard. Zone	Heat Zone	Light	Soil	BLOOM SEASON Spring Summer Fall	HEIGHT L S M T	COLOR W Pk R O Y B V
***Lunaria** annua*	p. 236	Bi	3–9	*9–1*					V
Lupinus	p. 237								
arboreus		HP*	8–9	*9–8*					Y
hartwegii		A	1–9	*9–1*					V
perennis		HP	4–9	· · ·					W Pk V
polyphyllus		HP	4–9	*9–7*					V
Lychnis	p. 237								
× arkwrightii		HP	4–8	· · ·					R O
chalcedonica		HP	4–8	· · ·					R
flos-jovis		HP	4–8	· · ·					Pk
viscaria		HP	3–9	· · ·					Pk
Lycoris	p. 238								
radiata		HB	7–10	*10–7*					R
squamigera		HB	6–10	*12–6*					Pk
***Lysichiton** americanus*	p. 238	HP	7–9	*9–7*					Y
Lysimachia	p. 239								
ciliata		HP	3–9	*8–1*					Y
clethroides		HP	3–9	*8–1*					W
ephemerum		HP	6–9	· · ·					W
nummularia		HP	3–9	*8–1*					Y
punctata		HP	5–9	*8–1*					Y
***Machaeranthera** tanacetifolia*	p. 240	A	1–10	· · ·					V
***Macleaya** cordata*	p. 241	HP	4–9	*9–1*					W
***Malcolmia** maritima*	p. 241	A	1–9	*9–1*					W Pk R
***Malephora** crocea*	p. 242	TP*	9–10	· · ·					Y
***Malope** trifida*	p. 242	A	1–8	*8–1*					Pk
Malva	p. 243								
alcea		HP	4–10	*9–1*					Pk V
moschata		HP	3–10	*9–1*					Pk
sylvestris		HP	4–10	*9–1*					Pk
Mandevilla	p. 243								
laxa		HP*	8–10	· · ·					W
sanderi		HP*	8–10	· · ·					Pk
***Matteuccia** (see p. 482)*									

 Type: A = Annual; Bi = Biennial; HP = Hardy Perennial; TP = Tender Perennial; HB = Hardy Bulb; TB = Tender Bulb; * = May be grown as annual in colder regions

Light: ☼ = Full sun; ◐ = Partial shade; ● = Full shade

Genus species	page	Type	Hard. Zone	Heat Zone	Light	Soil	Bloom Season: Spring	Summer	Fall	Height (L S M T)	Color (W Pk R O Y B V)
Matthiola	p. 245										
incana		A	2–10	···	☼ ◐	Ordinary	■■■	□□□	□□□	S	W V
longipetala ssp. *bicornis*		A	2–10	···	☼ ◐	Ordinary	■■■	□□□	□□□	S	V
***Mazus** reptans*	p. 246	HP	5–8	8–5	☼ ●	Ordinary, Moist	□□■	■□□	□□□	L	V
Meconopsis	p. 246										
betonicifolia		HP	6–9	8–6	☼ ◐	Moist	□□■	■□□	□□□	M	B
cambrica		HP	6–9	8–6	☼ ◐	Moist	□□□	□■□	□□□	S	Y
grandis		HP	6–9	8–6	☼ ◐	Moist	□□□	■□□	□□□	M	W B V
***Melica** altissima*	p. 247	HP	5–9	8–5	☼ ◐	Ordinary	□□□	■■□	□□□	S	W
***Melissa** officinalis*	p. 247	HP	4–9	9–1	☼ ◐	Dry	□□□	□■■	■□□	S	W
Mentha *(see p. 482)*											
***Mentzelia** lindleyi*	p. 248	A	3–8	9–1	☼	Dry, Ordinary	□□□	■□□	□□□	S	Y
***Merremia** tuberosa*	p. 249	TP*	10	12–10	☼ ◐	Dry, Ordinary	□□□	□■□	□□□	T	Y
***Mertensia** pulmonarioides*	p. 249	HP	3–8	7–1	☼ ●	Ordinary, Moist	□■□	□□□	□□□	S	B
Milium	p. 250										
effusum 'Aureum' *(see also p. 482)*		HP	6–9	9–6	●	Moist	□□■	■□□	□□□	S	W
Mimulus	p. 250										
× *hybridus*		HP*	7–9	6–1	☼ ◐	Moist	□□□	■■■	■□□	S	W Pk R O Y
lewisii		HP	5–9	8–5	☼ ◐	Moist	□□□	■■■	□□□	M	Pk
luteus		HP	6–9	9–7	☼ ◐	Moist	□□□	■■■	□□□	L	Y
***Minuartia** verna* *(see also p. 482)*	p. 251	HP	4–9	9–1	☼ ◐	Ordinary, Moist	□■■	□□□	□□□	L	W
Mirabilis	p. 252										
jalapa		A	3–7	12–3	☼ ◐	Ordinary	□□□	■■■	■■□	M	W Pk R Y
multiflora		HP	7–10	···	☼ ◐	Xeriscaping, Ordinary	□□□	■■■	□□□	S M	Pk
Miscanthus *(see also p. 482)*	p. 252										
floridulus		HP	5–9	···	☼ ◐	Dry, Moist	□□□	□□□	■■□	T	W
sinensis		HP	5–9	9–1	☼ ◐	Xeriscaping, Moist	□□□	□□■	■□□	T	W
***Mitchella** repens*	p. 253	HP	3–9	9–1	◐ ●	Ordinary, Moist	□□□	■□□	□□□	L	W R
Mitella	p. 253										
breweri		HP	5–7	7–5	◐ ●	Moist	□□□	■□□	□□□	L	W
diphylla		HP	3–8	···	◐ ●	Moist	□□■	■□□	□□□	L	W
***Moluccella** laevis*	p. 254	A	2–10	6–1	☼ ◐	Ordinary	□□□	□■■	■□□	S	W Pk
***Momordica** balsamina*	p. 254	HP*	8–10	···	☼	Ordinary, Moist	□□□	■■■	■■□	T	W Y

Height: L = Low (<1'); S = Short (1'–2'); M = Medium (2'–4'); T = Tall (>4') | **Color**: W = White; Pk = Pink; R = Red; O = Orange; Y = Yellow; B = Blue; V = Violet

Soil: Dry soil; Good for xeriscaping; Ordinary soil; Moist soil

Genus species	page	Type	Hard. Zone	Heat Zone	Light	Soil	BLOOM SEASON Spring	Summer	Fall	HEIGHT L	S	M	T	COLOR W Pk R O Y B V
Monarda	*p. 255*													
didyma		HP	4–9	*9–1*	○ ◐	◈	□□□	□■■	□□□			⋮		R
fistulosa		HP	4–9	*9–1*	○ ◐	✗◇ ◈	□□□	□■■	□□□			⋮		Pk
Moraea	*p. 256*													
huttonii		TB*	9–10	*10–9*	○	◈	□□□	□■□	□□□			⋮		Y
spathulata		TB*	9–10	*10–8*	○	◈	□□□	□■□	□□□			⋮	⋮	Y
Musa *(see p. 483)*														
Muscari	*p. 257*													
armeniacum		HB	4–8	*8–1*	○ ◐	✗◇ ◈	□■□	□□□	□□□	.				B
botryoides f. *album*		HB	2–8	*8–1*	○ ◐	✗◇ ◈	□■□	□□□	□□□	.				W
comosum		HB	4–8	*8–1*	○ ◐	✗◇ ◈	□□■	□□□	□□□	.				Y B
latifolium		HB	4–8	*8–1*	○ ◐	✗◇ ◈	□■□	□□□	□□□	.				V
Myosotidium *hortensia*	*p. 258*	HP	8–9	*12–1*	○ ◐	◆	□□■	■□□	□□□		⋮			B
Myosotis	*p. 258*													
alpestris		HP	5–8	*8–1*	○ ◐	◆	□□■	■□□	□□□	.				B
scorpioides		HP	5–8	*8–5*	○ ◐	◆	□□■	■■□	□□□	.				B
sylvatica		HP	5–8	*7–1*	○ ◐	◇ ◆	□□■	■□□	□□□	.				B
Myrrhis odorata	*p. 259*	HP	3–9	*7–1*	○ ◐	◈	□□□	■□□	□□□			⋮	⋮	W
Narcissus	*p. 259*													
asturiensis		HB	3–9	*9–1*	○	◈	■□□	□□□	□□□	.				Y
bulbocodium		HB	3–9	*9–1*	○	◆	□■□	□□□	□□□	.				Y
cyclamineus		HB	3–9	*9–1*	○ ◐	◇ ◈	■□□	□□□	□□□	.				Y
jonquilla		HB	5–9	*9–1*	○ ◐	◇ ◈	□■□	□□□	□□□	.				Y
obvallaris		HB	3–9	*9–1*	○ ◐	◇ ◈	■□□	□□□	□□□	.				Y
× *odorus*		HB	4–9	. . .	○ ◐	◇ ◈	□■□	□□□	□□□	.				Y
poeticus		HB	3–7	. . .	○ ◐	◇ ◈	□□■	□□□	□□□		⋮			Y
tazetta		HB	5–9	*9–1*	○ ◐	◇ ◈	■■□	□□□	□□□	.				Y
Nelumbo nucifera	*p. 260*	HP	4–10	*10–2*	○	◆	□□□	■■■	□□□			⋮	⋮	Pk
Nemesia *strumosa*	*p. 261*	A	2–9	*7–1*	○ ◐	◆	■■■	□■■	■□□	.	⋮			W R O Y V
Nemophila	*p. 261*													
maculata		A	2–9	*7–1*	○ ◐	◈ ◆	■■■	■□□	□□□	.				W V
menziesii		A	2–9	*7–1*	○ ◐	◈ ◆	■■■	■□□	□□□	.				W B
Nepeta	*p. 262*													
cataria		HP	3–7	. . .	○ ◐	◇ ◈	□□□	□■■	■□□			⋮		W V

 Type: A = Annual; Bi = Biennial; HP = Hardy Perennial; TP = Tender Perennial; HB = Hardy Bulb; TB = Tender Bulb; * = May be grown as annual in colder regions

Light: ○ = Full sun; ◐ = Partial shade; ● = Full shade

Genus species	page	Type	Hard. Zone	Heat Zone	Light	Soil	BLOOM SEASON Spring	Summer	Fall	HEIGHT L	S	M	T	COLOR W Pk R O Y B V
× *faassenii*		HP	4–9	*8–1*	Sun, Part shade	Dry, Ordinary	□□□	■□■	□□□		•			B V
nervosa		HP	4–9	*9–1*	Sun, Part shade	Dry, Ordinary	□□□	■■□	□□□		•			B
sibirica		HP	3–9	*8–1*	Sun, Part shade	Dry, Ordinary	□□□	□■□	□□□			•		B
subsessilis		HP	5–9	*9–1*	Sun, Part shade	Dry, Ordinary	□□□	□■■	■□□		•			B V
Nerine	*p. 262*													
bowdenii		HB	8–10	*12–8*	Sun, Part shade	Ordinary, Moist	□□□	□□□	□■□		•			Pk
filifolia		HB	8–10	*10–8*	Sun, Part shade	Ordinary, Moist	□□□	□□□	□■□	•				Pk
***Nicandra** physalodes*	*p. 263*	A	3–8	*9–1*	Sun, Part shade	Ordinary	□□□	□■■	■□□			•		B V
Nicotiana	*p. 263*													
alata		A	2–10	*12–1*	Sun, Part shade	Dry, Moist	□□□	□□■	□□□		•	•		W Pk
langsdorffii		A	2–10	*12–1*	Sun, Part shade	Dry, Moist	□□□	□■□	□□□			•	•	Y
× *sanderae*		A	2–10	*12–1*	Sun, Part shade	Dry, Moist	□□□	■■■	■□□		•			R
sylvestris		A	2–10	*12–1*	Sun, Part shade	Dry, Moist	□□□	□□■	□□□			•	•	W
Nierembergia	*p. 264*													
caerulea		A	2–10	*12–1*	Sun, Part shade	Moist	□□□	□■■	■□□	•				V
repens		HP*	7–10	*12–7*	Sun, Part shade	Moist	□■■	■□□	□□□	•				W
Nigella	*p. 265*													
damascena		A	2–10	*12–1*	Sun	Dry, Ordinary	□□□	□■□	□□□		•			W B
hispanica		A	2–10	*12–1*	Sun	Dry, Ordinary	□□□	□■□	□□□		•			B
Nipponanthemum	*p. 265*													
nipponicum		HP	5–9	*9–5*	Sun, Part shade	Dry, Ordinary	□□□	□□□	■□□	•	•			W Y
***Nolana** paradoxa*	*p. 266*	TP*	9–10	*12–1*	Sun	Dry, Ordinary	□□□	■■■	□□□	•				Y V
***Nomocharis** pardanthina*	*p. 266*	HB	7–9	*9–7*	Sun, Part shade	Ordinary, Moist	□□□	□■□	□□□			•		W Pk
Ocimum *(see p. 483)*														
Oenothera	*p. 267*													
fruticosa		HP	4–8	· · ·	Sun, Part shade	Dry, Ordinary	□□■	■■□	□□□		•	•		Y
macrocarpa		HP	4–9	*8–2*	Sun, Part shade	Xeriscaping, Ordinary	□□□	□■□	□□□	•				Y
odorata		HP	5–8	*8–1*	Sun, Part shade	Dry, Ordinary	□□□	□■□	□□□			•		Y
speciosa		HP	5–8	*8–1*	Sun, Part shade	Dry, Ordinary	□□□	■□□	□□□	•	•			Pk
Omphalodes	*p. 268*													
cappadocica		HP	6–9	*9–6*	Part shade, Shade	Moist	■□□	□□□	□□□	•				B
verna		HP	6–9	*9–6*	Part shade, Shade	Moist	□□■	■□□	□□□	•				B
***Onosma** echioides*	*p. 268*	HP	5–9	*9–7*	Sun	Dry	□■■	■■□	□□□		•			Y
Ophiopogon *(see p. 483)*														

Height: L = Low (<1′); S = Short (1′–2′); M = Medium (2′–4′); T = Tall (>4′) | **Color:** W = White; Pk = Pink; R = Red; O = Orange; Y = Yellow; B = Blue; V = Violet
Soil: Dry soil; Good for xeriscaping; Ordinary soil; Moist soil

Genus species	page	Type	Hard. Zone	Heat Zone	Light	Soil	Bloom Season: Spring	Summer	Fall	Height	Color (W Pk R O Y B V)
Origanum	*p. 269*										
laevigatum		HP	5–9	*9–5*	☼	○ ◒	□□□	□■□	□□□	L	V
rotundifolium		HP	5–9	*9–5*	☼	○ ◒	□□□	■■■	□□□	L	Y
vulgare		HP	5–9	*9–5*	☼	○ ◒	□□□	□■□	□□□	S	V
Ornithogalum	*p. 270*										
balansae		HB	7–10	*10–7*	☼ ◐	◒	□■□	□□□	□□□	L	W
nutans		HB	5–9	*9–5*	◐	◒	□■□	□□□	□□□	L S	W
thyrsoides		HB	7–10	*10–7*	☼ ◐	◒	□□□	□■□	□□□	S	W
umbellatum		HB	6–10	*10–1*	☼ ◐	⊗ ◒	□■□	□□□	□□□	L	W
Osmunda *(see p. 483)*											
Osteospermum	*p. 271*										
hybrida		TP*	10–11	*10–1*	☼	○ ◒	□□■	■■■	■■□	L	Pk O V
hyoseroides		TP*	10	*10–1*	☼	○ ◒	□□□	■■■	■□□	S	O Y
jucundum		TP*	9–10	*10–1*	☼	○ ◒	□■■	■■■	■■□	L	Pk V
Oxalis *adenophylla*	*p. 272*	HP	7–9	*8–6*	☼	○ ◒	□■□	□□□	□□□	L	Pk
Paeonia	*p. 272*										
delavayi		HP	3–8	*8–1*	☼	◒ ●	□□■	■□□	□□□	T	R
lactiflora		HP	4–8	*8–1*	☼ ◐	◒ ●	□□■	■□□	□□□	S M	W Pk
lutea		HP	3–8	*8–1*	☼ ◐	◒ ●	□□■	■□□	□□□	T	Y
mlokosewitschii		HP	5–8	*8–1*	☼ ◐	◒ ●	□■□	□□□	□□□	M	Y
officinalis		HP	3–9	*8–1*	☼ ◐	◒ ●	□□■	■□□	□□□	M	Pk R
suffruticosa		HP	4–8	*8–1*	☼ ◐	◒ ●	□□■	■□□	□□□	T	W Pk
Palafoxia *texana*	*p. 273*	A	3–9	· · ·	☼	○ ◒	□□□	■■■	□□□	S	Pk
Panicum *virgatum* (see also p. 483)	*p. 274*	HP	5–9	*12–1*	☼ ◐	⊗ ●	□□□	□□■	□□□	M T	Pk
Papaver	*p. 274*										
bracteatum		HP	5–8	· · ·	☼	◒	□■■	□□□	□□□	M T	R
croceum		HP	3–9	*9–2*	☼	○ ◒	□□■	■□□	□□□	L	W Pk R O Y
orientale		HP	3–9	*8–1*	☼	◒	□□□	■□□	□□□	S M	R
rhoeas		A	1–10	*8–1*	☼	○ ◒	□■■	□□□	□□□	S	R
rupifragum		HP	6–9	· · ·	☼	◒	□□■	■■□	□□□	S	O
somniferum		A	1–10	*8–1*	☼ ●	○ ◒	□□■	□□□	□□□	S	W Pk R V
Paracaryum *coelestinum*	*p. 276*	HB*	8–10	· · ·	☼ ◐	○ ◒	□□□	■■■	□□□	S	B
Paradisea *liliastrum*	*p. 276*	HP	7–9	*9–7*	☼ ◐	◒ ●	□□■	□□□	□□□	S	W
× ***Pardancanda*** *norrisii*	*p. 277*	HP	5–9	*9–5*	☼	○ ●	□□□	□■□	□□□	M	R O Y B V

 Type: A = Annual; Bi = Biennial; HP = Hardy Perennial; TP = Tender Perennial; HB = Hardy Bulb; TB = Tender Bulb; * = May be grown as annual in colder regions

Light: ☼ = Full sun; ◐ = Partial shade; ● = Full shade

Genus species	page	Type	Hard. Zone	Heat Zone	Light	Soil	BLOOM SEASON Spring Summer Fall	HEIGHT L S M T	COLOR W Pk R O Y B V
***Parnassia** palustris*	*p. 277*	HP	3–9	*12–1*					W
***Parochetus** communis*	*p. 278*	HP*	8–10	*12–8*					B
Passiflora	*p. 278*								
caerulea		HP	7–10	*9–6*					W B
vitifolia		TP*	10	*12–10*					W Pk R Y
***Patrinia** scabiosaefolia*	*p. 279*	HP	5–8	*9–5*					Y
Pelargonium	*p. 279*								
× hortorum		TP*	9–10	*12–1*					W Pk R O
peltatum		TP*	9–10	*12–1*					W Pk R O V
***Pennisetum** (see also p. 483)*	*p. 280*								
alopecuroides		HP	5–9	*9–1*					W
setaceum		HP*	8–10	*9–1*					Pk V
Penstemon	*p. 280*								
barbatus		HP	3–9	*9–1*					R
digitalis		HP	3–9	*9–1*					W Pk
hartwegii		HP	4–9	*9–1*					R
heterophyllus		HP	7–10	*10–7*					B
strictus		HP	4–9	. . .					B V
***Pentas** lanceolata*	*p. 281*	TP*	10	*12–5*					W Pk R V
***Perilla** (see p. 483)*									
***Perovskia** atriplicifolia (see also p. 483)*	*p. 282*	HP	5–9	*9–4*					V
Persicaria	*p. 283*								
affinis		HP	3–9	*8–1*					Pk
bistorta		HP	3–9	*8–1*					Pk
capitata		HP	5–8	*8–5*					W Pk
***Petasites** japonicus*	*p. 283*	HP	5–9	*9–5*					W
***Petrorhagia** saxifraga*	*p. 284*	HP	5–7	*7–5*					W Pk
***Petroselinum** (see p. 483)*									
***Petunia** × hybrida*	*p. 285*	A	1–10	*12–3*					W Pk R Y V
Phacelia	*p. 285*								
campanularia		A	3–10	*9–1*					B
tanacetifolia		A	3–10	*9–1*					B V
***Phalaris** (see p. 483)*									
***Phaseolus** coccineus*	*p. 287*	A	1–10	. . .					R

Height: L = Low (<1′); S = Short (1′–2′); M = Medium (2′–4′); T = Tall (>4′) | **Color:** W = White; Pk = Pink; R = Red; O = Orange; Y = Yellow; B = Blue; V = Violet

Soil: = Dry soil; = Good for xeriscaping; = Ordinary soil; = Moist soil

Genus species	page	Type	Hard. Zone	Heat Zone	Light	Soil	Bloom Season: Spring	Summer	Fall	Height: L	S	M	T	Color (W Pk R O Y B V)
Phlomis	*p. 287*													
russeliana		HP	5–9	*9–3*	○◐	◈	□□□	■■□	□□□			•		Y
tuberosa		HP	3–9	*8–3*	○◐	◈	□□□	□■□	□□□				•	V
Phlox	*p. 288*													
carolina		HP	4–9	. . .	○◐	◆	□□□	■□□	□□□			•		Pk V
divaricata		HP	4–9	*8–1*	◐●	◈◆	□■□	□□□	□□□	•				B
drummondii		A	2–10	*12–1*	○◐	◆	□□■	■□□	□□□	•				W Pk R Y B V
maculata		HP	4–8	*8–4*	○◐	◈◆	□□□	■□□	□□□			•		Pk V
paniculata		HP	3–9	*8–1*	○◐	◈◆	□□□	□■■	□□□			•		W Pk R V
pilosa		HP	4–9	. . .	○◐	◆	□□■	■□□	□□□		•			Pk
stolonifera		HP	3–9	*8–1*	◐●	◆	□■□	□□□	□□□	•				B V
subulata		HP	3–9	*8–1*	○	◇◈	■□□	□□□	□□□	•				W Pk V
Phormium *(see p. 483)*														
Phuopsis *stylosa*	*p. 289*	HP	4–9	*8–5*	○◐	◇◈	□□□	□■□	□□□	•				Pk
Phygelius	*p. 290*													
aequalis		HP	7–9	*9–7*	○◐	◈◆	□□□	□□■	■□□			•		Pk R Y
capensis		HP	7–9	*9–7*	○◐	◈◆	□□□	□□■	■□□			•		R O
Physalis *alkekengi*	*p. 291*	HP	3–9	*8–5*	○◐	◈	□□□	□□□	■■□		•			O
Physostegia *virginiana*	*p. 291*	HP	3–9	*8–1*	○◐	◇◆	□□□	□■■	■□□			•		Pk V
Phyteuma *orbiculare*	*p. 292*	HP	5–8	*7–5*	○◐	◇◈	□□□	■□□	□□□	•				B
Pimpinella *major*	*p. 292*	HP	5–8	. . .	○◐	◈	□□□	□■■	■□□			•		Pk
Pinguicula *grandiflora*	*p. 293*	HP	3–8	*5–1*	○	◆	□□□	■■□	□□□	•				V
Platycodon *grandiflorus*	*p. 293*	HP	3–9	*9–1*	○◐	◈◆	□□□	□■■	□□□		•	•		V
Platystemon *californicus*	*p. 294*	A	3–9	*12–7*	○	◇◈	□□□	■■□	□□□	•				Y
Plectranthus *(see p. 483)*														
Podophyllum *peltatum*	*p. 295*	HP	3–9	*8–2*	◐●	◈◆	□□■	□□□	□□□		•			W
Polemonium	*p. 295*													
caeruleum		HP	3–8	*7–1*	○◐	◆	□□■	■□□	□□□		•			B
carneum		HP	5–8	*7–1*	○◐	◆	□□□	■□□	□□□		•			Pk
reptans		HP	3–8	*7–1*	○◐	◆	□□■	■□□	□□□	•				B
Polianthes *tuberosa*	*p. 296*	HP*	8–10	*11–7*	○	◈◆	□□□	□■□	□□□			•		W
Polygonatum	*p. 296*													
biflorum		HP	3–9	*9–1*	◐●	◇◆	□□■	□□□	□□□		•	•		W
falcatum		HP	4–9	. . .	◐●	◇◆	□■□	□□□	□□□	•				W

Type: A = Annual; Bi = Biennial; HP = Hardy Perennial; TP = Tender Perennial; HB = Hardy Bulb; TB = Tender Bulb; * = May be grown as annual in colder regions

Light: ○ = Full sun; ◐ = Partial shade; ● = Full shade

Genus species	page	Type	Hard. Zone	Heat Zone	Light	Soil	BLOOM SEASON Spring Summer Fall	HEIGHT L S M T	COLOR W Pk R O Y B V
multiflorum		HP	4–8	*8–1*					W
Polystichum *(see p. 483)*									
Portulaca *grandiflora*	*p. 298*	A	2–10	*12–3*					W Pk R O Y
Potentilla	*p. 298*								
alba		HP	5–8	*8–3*					W
fruticosa		HP	3–7	*7–1*					Pk Y
nepalensis		HP	5–8	*9–4*					Pk
neumaniana		HP	4–8	. . .					Y
Pratia *pedunculata*	*p. 299*	HP	5–7	*7–5*					B
Primula	*p. 299*								
auricula		HP	3–9	*8–1*					Y
denticulata		HP	3–8	*8–1*					W Pk Y
florindae		HP	5–9	*8–1*					Y
japonica		HP	5–8	*8–1*					W Pk R V
obconica		HP	8–10	*6–1*					W V
Polyanthus Group		HP	3–9	*8–1*					W Pk R O Y B V
veris		HP	4–9	*8–1*					Y
vialii		HP	5–9	*8–3*					R V
vulgaris		HP	5–9	*8–1*					Y
Pritzelago *alpina*	*p. 300*	HP	4–8	. . .					W
Proboscidea *louisianica*	*p. 300*	A	7–9	*9–7*					R V
Prunella *grandiflora*	*p. 301*	HP	5–8	*8–5*					V
Pulmonaria	*p. 201*								
longifolia		HP	3–9	*9–1*					B
officinalis		HP	4–8	*8–6*					Pk V
rubra		HP	5–8	*8–4*					R
saccharata		HP	4–8	*8–1*					B
Pulsatilla	*p. 302*								
alpina		HP	4–8	*7–5*					W
halleri		HP	5–7	*7–5*					V
vernalis		HP	4–7	*7–1*					W
vulgaris		HP	5–7	*7–5*					V
Puschkinia	*p. 302*								
scilloides var. *libanotica*		HB	4–10	*9–1*					B

Height: L = Low (<1′); S = Short (1′–2′); M = Medium (2′–4′); T = Tall (>4′) | **Color:** W = White; Pk = Pink; R = Red; O = Orange; Y = Yellow; B = Blue; V = Violet

Soil: = Dry soil; = Good for xeriscaping; = Ordinary soil; = Moist soil

Genus species	page	Type	Hard. Zone	Heat Zone	Light	Soil	BLOOM SEASON Spring	Summer	Fall	HEIGHT L	S	M	T	COLOR W Pk R O Y B V
Ramonda *myconi*	*p. 303*	HP	5–7	*7–5*	◐	●	□□■	■□□	□□□	•				V
Ranunculus	*p. 303*													
asiaticus		HP*	7–9	*12–7*	○◐	●	□□□	■□□	□□□		•			W R O Y
lingua		HP	4–9	*9–1*	○◐	●	□□□	□■□	□□□			•		Y
repens		HP	4–8	· · ·	○◐	●	□□■	■■□	□□□		•			Y
Ratibida *columnifera*	*p. 304*	HP	3–10	*7–1*	○	✕◌ ◒	□□□	□■■	■□□			•		R Y
Rehmannia *elata*	*p. 304*	HP*	8–10	*10–8*	○◐	◒	□□□	■■□	□□□		•	•		Pk
Reseda *odorata*	*p. 305*	A	2–10	*6–1*	◐	◒	□□□	■■■	■□□		•			W
Rheum *palmatum* (*see also p. 484*)	*p. 305*	HP	5–9	*9–1*	○◐	●	□□□	■□□	□□□				•	R
Rhodanthe	*p. 306*													
chlorocephala ssp. *rosea*		A	3–10	*10–1*	○	◌ ◒	□□□	■■■	□□□		•			W Pk
Rhodochiton *atrosanguineus*	*p. 306*	TP*	10	*12–6*	○	◒	□□□	■■■	■■□				•	R V
Rhodohypoxis *baurii*	*p. 307*	TP*	9–10	*10–9*	○	◌ ◒	□□■	■□□	□□□	•				W Pk R
Ricinus (*see p. 484*)														
Rodgersia	*p. 308*													
aesculifolia		HP	4–9	*8–5*	○◐	●	□□□	□■□	□□□			•	•	W Pk
pinnata		HP	4–9	*8–5*	○◐	●	□□□	■■□	□□□			•		R
Romneya *coulteri*	*p. 308*	HP	7–10	*8–7*	○	◌ ◒	□□□	■■■	□□□				•	W
Roscoea *purpurea*	*p. 309*	HP	6–9	· · ·	○◐	◒ ●	□□□	□■□	□□□	•				V
Rosmarinus *officinalis*	*p. 309*	HP*	7–10	*12–7*	○◐	✕◌ ◒	□■■	■□□	□□□			•	•	B V
Rudbeckia	*p. 310*													
fulgida		HP	3–9	*9–1*	○◐	✕◌ ●	□□□	□■■	■□□			•		O Y
hirta		A	3–9	*7–1*	○◐	✕◌ ●	□□□	□■■	■□□		•	•		Y
laciniata		HP	3–9	*9–1*	○◐	✕◌ ●	□□□	□■■	■□□				•	Y
maxima		HP	4–9	· · ·	○◐	✕◌ ●	□□□	□■■	□□□				•	Y
nitida		HP	6–9	· · ·	○◐	✕◌ ●	□□□	□■■	□□□			•		Y
Ruellia	*p. 311*													
brittoniana		TP*	9–10	· · ·	○◐	◌ ●	□□□	□■■	■■□			•		B
humilis		HP	3–9	· · ·	○◐	◌ ◒	□□□	■■■	□□□		•			B V
Rumex (*see p. 484*)														
Sagina *subulata* (*see also p. 484*)	*p. 312*	HP	5–9	*9–6*	○◐	◒ ●	□□□	□■□	□□□	•				W
Salpiglossis *sinuata*	*p. 312*	A	1–10	*6–1*	○◐	◒	□□□	■■■	■□□		•			R O Y V
Salvia	*p. 313*													
coccinea		A	3–10	*12–1*	○	◒ ●	□□■	■■■	■□□		•			R

 Type: A = Annual; Bi = Biennial; HP = Hardy Perennial; TP = Tender Perennial; HB = Hardy Bulb; TB = Tender Bulb; * = May be grown as annual in colder regions

Light: ○ = Full sun; ◐ = Partial shade; ● = Full shade

Genus species	page	Type	Hard. Zone	Heat Zone	Light	Soil	Bloom Season: Spring	Summer	Fall	Height: L	S	M	T	Color: W	Pk	R	O	Y	B	V
farinacea		HP*	8–9	*12–1*	☼	Ordinary, Moist	□□□	■■■	■■□		•								B	
greggii		TP*	9–10	*8–1*	☼ ◐	Dry, Ordinary	□□□	□■■	■□□		•					R				
nemerosa		HP	5–9	*9–5*	☼ ◐	Ordinary, Moist	□□□	□■■	□□□			•								V
patens		HP*	8–9	*9–1*	☼ ◐	Ordinary, Moist	□□□	■■■	■■□		•								B	
splendens		TP*	10	*12–1*	☼ ◐	Ordinary, Moist	□□□	□■■	■□□	•						R				
× *superba*		HP	5–9	*9–5*	☼	Ordinary, Moist	□□■	■■■	□□□		•	•								V
× *sylvestris*		HP	5–9	. . .	☼ ◐	Ordinary, Moist	□□□	■■□	□□□			•			Pk					V
uliginosa		HP*	8–10	*12–8*	☼ ◐	Moist	□□□	□□□	■■□				•						B	
verticillata		HP	5–9	*8–1*	☼ ◐	Ordinary, Moist	□□□	■■■	□□□		•									V
viridis		A	3–10	*9–1*	☼	Ordinary, Moist	□□□	□■■	■□□		•			W	Pk					V
Sandersonia *aurantiaca*	*p. 313*	TP*	9–10	*12–6*	☼	Dry, Ordinary	□□□	■■□	□□□		•						O			
Sanguinaria *canadensis*	*p. 314*	HP	3–9	*9–1*	☼ ◐	Ordinary, Moist	■□□	□□□	□□□	•				W						
Sanguisorba	*p. 315*																			
officinalis		HP	4–9	*9–1*	☼ ◐	Ordinary, Moist	□□□	□□■	□□□			•								V
tenuifolia		HP	4–9	*9–1*	☼ ◐	Ordinary, Moist	□□□	□■□	□□□			•				R				
Santolina *(see p. 484)*																				
Sanvitalia *procumbens*	*p. 316*	A	3–10	*12–1*	☼	Xeriscaping, Ordinary	□□□	■■■	■□□	•								Y		
Saponaria	*p. 316*																			
× *lempergii*		HP	6–8	*8–1*	☼ ◐	Dry, Ordinary	□□□	□■■	■□□		•				Pk					
ocymoides		HP	2–8	*8–1*	☼ ◐	Xeriscaping, Ordinary	□□□	■□□	□□□	•					Pk					
Sarracenia *purpurea*	*p. 317*	HP	3–10	*9–1*	☼ ◐	Moist	□□■	□□□	□□□	•						R				V
Satureja *(see also p. 484)*	*p. 317*																			
hortensis		A	3–10	*9–5*	☼	Dry	□□□	□■■	■□□	•				W	Pk					
montana		HP	5–8	*9–5*	☼	Ordinary	□□□	■□□	□□□	•										V
Saxifraga	*p. 318*																			
cotyledon		HP	4–6	*6–1*	◐	Ordinary, Moist	□□■	■□□	□□□	•				W						
fortunei		HP	6–8	*8–6*	◐	Ordinary, Moist	□□□	□□□	■□□	•				W						
oppositifolia		HP	2–7	*7–1*	◐	Ordinary, Moist	■□□	□□□	□□□	•					Pk					V
× *urbium*		HP	6–9	*7–5*	◐	Ordinary, Moist	□□■	■□□	□□□	•				W						
Scabiosa	*p. 319*																			
atropurpurea		A	4–10	*8–3*	☼	Ordinary	□□□	■■■	■□□			•							B	V
caucasica		HP	3–9	*9–1*	☼	Ordinary	□□□	■■□	□□□		•								B	
columbaria		HP	3–9	*9–1*	☼	Ordinary	□□□	■■■	□□□	•									B	
ochroleuca		HP	5–9	*9–1*	☼	Ordinary	□□□	□□■	□□□		•							Y		

Height: L = Low (<1'); S = Short (1'–2'); M = Medium (2'–4'); T = Tall (>4') | **Color:** W = White; Pk = Pink; R = Red; O = Orange; Y = Yellow; B = Blue; V = Violet

Soil: Dry soil; Good for xeriscaping; Ordinary soil; Moist soil

Genus species	page	Type	Hard. Zone	Heat Zone	Light	Soil	Bloom Season Spring Summer Fall	Height L	S	M	T	Color W Pk R O Y B V
stellata		A	1–10	· · ·					•			W Pk B
***Scaevola** aemula*	p. 319	TP*	9–10	*12–1*					•			B V
***Schizanthus** pinnatus*	p. 320	A	1–10	*8–1*					•			W Pk Y V
***Schizostylis** coccinea*	p. 320	HP*	7–10	*9–7*					•			R
Scilla	p. 321											
bifolia		HB	3–8	*8–1*				•				W Pk B V
litardierei		HB	5–8	*9–6*				•				V
mischtschenkoana		HB	5–8	*9–6*				•				B
peruviana		HB	8–10	*9–8*				•				B V
siberica		HB	5–8	*8–5*				•				B
Scutellaria	p. 321											
alpina		HP	5–8	*9–5*				•				Y V
baicalensis		HP	6–8	· · ·				•				B V
Sedum	p. 322											
acre		HP	3–9	*12–3*				•				Y
album		HP	3–9	*12–3*				•				W
'Autumn Joy'		HP	3–9	*10–1*					•			Pk
cauticola		HP	5–9	*12–3*				•				Pk V
kamtschaticum		HP	3–9	*9–5*				•				Y
rupestre		HP	6–9	*9–6*				•				Y
sieboldii		HP	6–9	*12–3*				•				Pk
spathulifolium		HP	5–9	*9–5*				•				Y
spectabile		HP	4–9	*9–1*					•			Pk
spurium		HP	3–9	*9–1*	· · ·			•				Pk
telephium		HP	3–9	*9–1*					•			R V
Selaginella *(see p. 484)*												
Sempervivum *(see also p. 484)*	p. 323											
arachnoideum		HP	5–9	*9–5*				•				Pk R
giuseppii		HP	7–9	*9–7*				•				Pk R
tectorum		HP	5–9	*9–5*				•				Pk V
Senecio *(see p. 484)*												
Sesamum *(see p. 484)*												
***Shortia** solandelloides*	p. 325	HP	5–8	*8–5*				•				W Pk
***Sidalcea** malviflora*	p. 325	HP	5–9	· · ·						•		Pk

Type: A = Annual; Bi = Biennial; HP = Hardy Perennial; TP = Tender Perennial; HB = Hardy Bulb; TB = Tender Bulb; * = May be grown as annual in colder regions

Light: ○ = Full sun; ◐ = Partial shade; ● = Full shade

Genus species	page	Type	Hard. Zone	Heat Zone	Light	Soil	BLOOM SEASON Spring	Summer	Fall	HEIGHT L S M T	COLOR W Pk R O Y B V
Silene	*p. 326*										
acaulis		HP	3–5	*5–1*	Sun, Part shade	Dry, Ordinary	□■□	□□□	□□□	L	Pk
alpestris		HP	4–7	*7–1*	Sun, Part shade	Ordinary	□□■	□□□	□□□	L	W
armeria		A	3–9	*8–1*	Sun, Part shade	Dry, Ordinary	□□□	□□■	■□□	L	Pk
caroliniana		HP	5–8	. . .	Sun, Part shade	Ordinary	□□□	■□□	□□□	L	Pk
hookeri		HP	4–6	*8–5*	Sun, Part shade	Ordinary	□□□	□□■	□□□	L	Pk O
pendula		A	3–9	. . .	Sun, Part shade	Ordinary	□□□	□□■	■□□	L	Pk
schafta		HP	4–8	*7–4*	Sun, Part shade	Ordinary	□□□	□■■	□□□	L	Pk
***Silphium** perfoliatum*	*p. 326*	HP	5–9	*9–5*	Sun, Part shade	Ordinary, Moist	□□□	□■■	■□□	T	Y
***Silybum** marianum*	*p. 327*	Bi	6–9	*9–6*	Sun, Part shade	Dry, Moist	□□□	□■■	■□□	M	Pk
***Sisyrinchium** graminoides*	*p. 327*	HP	4–9	*9–6*	Sun, Part shade	Ordinary, Moist	□□■	■□□	□□□	L	B
***Smilacina** racemosa*	*p. 328*	HP	3–9	*9–1*	Part shade, Shade	Ordinary, Moist	□□■	■□□	□□□	M	W
***Soldanella** alpina*	*p. 328*	HP	5–8	*7–1*	Sun, Part shade	Moist	■□□	□□□	□□□	L	V
***Solenopsis** axillaris*	*p. 329*	TP*	9–10	. . .	Sun, Part shade	Ordinary, Moist	□□□	■■■	■□□	L	V
***Solenostemon** (see p. 484)*											
Solidago	*p. 330*										
canadensis		HP	3–9	. . .	Sun, Part shade	Dry, Ordinary	□□□	□□■	□□□	M T	Y
rugosa		HP	3–9	. . .	Sun, Part shade	Dry, Ordinary	□□□	□□■	■□□	T	Y
sphacelata		HP	5–9	. . .	Sun, Part shade	Dry, Ordinary	□□□	□□□	■□□	S	Y
***Sparaxis** tricolor*	*p. 330*	TB*	9–10	*10–7*	Sun	Xeriscaping, Ordinary	□■□	□□□	□□□	L	W Pk R O V
Sphaeralcea	*p. 331*										
ambigua		HP	6–10	*12–8*	Sun	Dry, Ordinary	□□□	□■■	■□□	M	O
munroana		HP	4–10	*12–8*	Sun	Dry, Ordinary	□□□	■■■	■■□	S	Pk
***Spigelia** marilandica*	*p. 331*	HP	5–9	. . .	Sun, Part shade	Ordinary, Moist	□□□	■□□	■□□	M	R Y
***Sprekelia** formosissima*	*p. 332*	TB*	9–10	*12–10*	Sun, Part shade	Ordinary	□□■	□□□	□□□	L	R
***Stachys** (see also p. 484)*	*p. 332*										
coccinea		HP	7–10	*8–1*	Sun, Part shade	Dry, Ordinary	□□□	■■■	□□□	S	R V
macrantha		HP	3–9	*8–1*	Sun, Part shade	Dry, Ordinary	□□■	■□□	□□□	S	Pk
officinalis		HP	4–9	*8–1*	Sun, Part shade	Dry, Ordinary	□□□	■■□	□□□	S	W Pk V
***Stenanthium** gramineum*	*p. 333*	HB	7–10	*9–7*	Sun, Part shade	Moist	□□□	□■□	□□□	T	W
Sternbergia	*p. 334*										
candida		HB	8–10	*10–8*	Sun, Part shade	Dry, Ordinary	□■□	□□□	□□□	L	W
lutea		HB	6–10	*9–6*	Sun, Part shade	Dry, Ordinary	□□□	□□□	■□□	L	Y

Height: L = Low (<1′); S = Short (1′–2′); M = Medium (2′–4′); T = Tall (>4′) | **Color:** W = White; Pk = Pink; R = Red; O = Orange; Y = Yellow; B = Blue; V = Violet

Soil: Dry = Dry soil; Xeriscaping = Good for xeriscaping; Ordinary = Ordinary soil; Moist = Moist soil

Genus species	page	Type	Hard. Zone	Heat Zone	Light	Soil	Bloom Season (Spring Summer Fall)	Height (L S M T)	Color (W Pk R O Y B V)
Stipa *(see also p. 484)*	*p. 334*								
arundinacea		HP	5–8	*12–1*	○		□□□ □■■ □□□	T	V
gigantea		HP	7–8	*12–1*	○		□□□ ■■■ □□□	T	Y
tenuissima		HP	7–10	. . .	○		□□□ □■■ □□□	S	W
Stokesia *laevis*	*p. 335*	HP	5–10	*9–5*	○◐		□□□ ■■■ □□□	S	V
Strobilanthes *(see also p. 484)*	*p. 335*								
atropurpureus		HP	5–9	*9–5*	○◐		□□□ □□■ ■□□	M	V
Stylophorum *diphyllum*	*p. 336*	HP	5–8	*8–1*	◐●		□■■ ■□□ □□□	S	Y
Symphyandra *armena*	*p. 336*	HP	6–9	*9–6*	○◐		□□□ ■□□ □□□	S	W B
Symphytum *officinale*	*p. 337*	HP	3–9	. . .	○◐		□□■ ■■□ □□□	M	Pk Y V
Synthyris *stellata*	*p. 337*	HP	7–9	*9–7*	◐●		□■□ □□□ □□□	L	V
Tagetes	*p. 338*								
erecta		A	1–10	*12–1*	○◐		□□□ ■■■ ■□□	S M	Y
patula		A	1–10	*12–1*	○◐		□□□ ■■■ ■■□	L	R O Y
tenuifolia		A	1–10	*12–1*	○◐		□□□ ■■■ □□□	L	O Y
Talinum *calycinum*	*p. 338*	HP	5–9	*8–6*	○		□□■ ■■■ ■■□	S	Pk
Tanacetum	*p. 339*								
coccineum		HP	5–9	. . .	○◐		□□■ ■□□ □□□	S	W Pk R Y
parthenium		A	4–9	*9–1*	○◐		□□□ □■■ ■□□	S	W Y
Tecophilaea *cyanocrocus*	*p. 339*	HB	7–9	*9–7*	○		■□□ □□□ □□□	L	B
Tellima *grandiflora*	*p. 340*	HP	3–9	*8–1*	◐●		□□■ ■□□ □□□	S	W
Teucrium	*p. 340*								
chamaedrys		HP	4–9	*9–5*	○◐		□□□ □■■ □□□	L S	V
hircanicum		HP	7–9	*10–7*	○◐		□□□ □□■ □□□	S	V
Thalictrum	*p. 341*								
aquilegiifolium		HP	5–8	*8–5*	○◐		□□■ ■□□ □□□	M	V
delavayi		HP	5–8	*9–4*	○◐		□□□ □■□ □□□	T	V
diffusiflorum		HP	5–8	*9–5*	○◐		□□□ □■□ □□□	M	V
kiusianum		HP	5–7	*8–5*	◐		□□□ □■□ □□□	L	V
Thelesperma *burridgeanum*	*p. 341*	A	3–10	. . .	○		□□□ ■■■ □□□	S M	R Y
Thelypteris *(see p. 484)*									
Thermopsis *villosa*	*p. 342*	HP	3–9	*9–1*	○◐		□□■ ■□□ □□□	M	Y
Thunbergia	*p. 343*								
alata		A	5–10	*12–6*	○◐		□□□ ■■■ ■□□	T	O Y

 Type: A = Annual; Bi = Biennial; HP = Hardy Perennial; TP = Tender Perennial; HB = Hardy Bulb; TB = Tender Bulb; * = May be grown as annual in colder regions

Light: ○ = Full sun; ◐ = Partial shade; ● = Full shade

Genus species	page	Type	Hard. Zone	Heat Zone	Light	Soil	BLOOM SEASON Spring Summer Fall	HEIGHT L S M T	COLOR W Pk R O Y B V
grandiflora		TP*	9–10	*12–6*					B V
Thymus	*p. 343*								
× citriodorus		HP	5–9	*9–6*					Pk Y
serpyllum		HP	4–9	*9–1*					V
vulgaris		HP	5–9	· · ·					Pk
Tiarella	*p. 344*								
cordifolia		HP	3–8	*7–1*					W
wherryi		HP	3–8	*9–1*					W
***Tithonia** rotundifolia*	*p. 344*	A	3–10	*12–1*					R O Y
Torenia	*p. 345*								
flava		TP*	9–10	*6–1*					Y
fournieri		TP*	9–10	*6–1*					V
***Townsendia** parryi*	*p. 345*	HP	4–7	*7–1*					B V
***Trachelium** caeruleum*	*p. 346*	HP*	8–10	*10–1*					B V
***Trachymene** coerulea*	*p. 346*	A	3–8	*12–6*					B V
***Tradescantia** (see also p. 484)*	*p. 347*								
Andersoniana Group		HP	4–9	*9–5*					R B V
virginiana		HP	4–9	· · ·					B V
***Tricholaena** rosea*	*p. 347*	TP*	9–10	· · ·					R
***Trichosanthes** (see p. 484)*									
Tricyrtis	*p. 348*								
formosana		HP	5–8	*9–6*					Pk V
hirta		HP	5–8	*6–1*					V
latifolia		HP	6–9	*8–1*					Y V
Trifolium	*p. 349*								
incarnatum		A	3–9	· · ·					R
rubens		HP	6–9	· · ·					Pk
***Trigonella** (see p. 484)*									
Trillium	*p. 350*								
erectum		HP	3–9	*9–1*					V
grandiflorum		HP	4–8	*7–3*					W
nivale		HP	5–8	*8–5*					W
Tritonia	*p. 350*								
crocata		HB	7–10	*10–8*					W Pk O

Height: L = Low (<1′); S = Short (1′–2′); M = Medium (2′–4′); T = Tall (>4′) | **Color:** W = White; Pk = Pink; R = Red; O = Orange; Y = Yellow; B = Blue; V = Violet
Soil: = Dry soil; = Good for xeriscaping; = Ordinary soil; = Moist soil

Genus species	page	Type	Hard. Zone	Heat Zone	Light	Soil	BLOOM SEASON Spring Summer Fall	HEIGHT L S M T	COLOR W Pk R O Y B V
disticha ssp. *rubrolucens*		TB*	9–10	*10–9*	○				Pk
Trollius	*p. 351*								
chinensis		HP	3–7	*7–1*	○●				O
europaeus		HP	3–8	*7–1*	○●				Y
pumilus		HP	5–7	*6–1*	○●				Y
yunnanensis		HP	5–7	*7–1*	○●				O Y
Tropaeolum	*p. 352*								
majus		A	1–10	*12–1*	○◑				R O Y
peregrinum		A	1–10	*12–1*	○◑				Y
Tulipa	*p. 352*								
batalinii		HB	3–8	*8–1*	○◑				Y
biflora		HB	3–8	*8–1*	○◑				W Y
clusiana		HB	3–8	*8–1*	○◑				W Pk
fosteriana		HB	3–8	*8–1*	○◑				R Y
greigii		HB	3–8	*8–1*	○◑				R Y
hageri		HB	3–8	*8–1*	○◑				R
humilis		HB	3–8	*8–1*	○◑				Pk
kaufmanniana		HB	3–8	*8–1*	○◑				W Y
linifolia		HB	3–8	*8–1*	○◑				R
marjolletti		HB	3–8	*8–1*	○◑				W Pk
orphanidea		HB	3–8	*8–1*	○◑				O
praestans		HB	3–8	*8–1*	○◑				R
saxatilis		HB	3–8	*8–1*	○◑				Pk V
tarda		HB	3–8	*8–1*	○◑				W
turkestanica		HB	3–8	*8–1*	○◑				W
Tweedia	*p. 353*								
caerulea		TP*	9–10	*12–10*	○◑				B V
Ursinia	*p. 354*								
anthemoides		A	3–9	*12–6*	○				O
sericea		A	3–9	*12–10*	○				Y
Uvularia *grandiflora*	*p. 354*	HP	3–9	*7–1*	◑●				Y
Valeriana	*p. 355*								
officinalis		HP	4–9	*9–1*	○◑				W Pk
supina		HP	4–9	*9–1*	○◑				W Pk

 Type: A = Annual; Bi = Biennial; HP = Hardy Perennial; TP = Tender Perennial; HB = Hardy Bulb; TB = Tender Bulb; * = May be grown as annual in colder regions

Light: ○ = Full sun; ◑ = Partial shade; ● = Full shade

Genus species	page	Type	Hard. Zone	Heat Zone	Light	Soil	Bloom Season: Spring	Summer	Fall	Height: L	S	M	T	Color (W Pk R O Y B V)
***Veltheimia** bracteata*	*p.355*	TB*	9–10	*12–10*	sun, part shade	ordinary	■□□	□□□	□□□		•			Pk Y V
Veratrum	*p.356*													
nigrum		HP	4–9	*9–6*	sun, shade	moist	□□□	□■□	□□□				•	V
viride		HP	3–8	· · ·	sun, shade	moist	□□□	□■□	□□□				•	Y
Verbascum	*p.356*													
bombyciferum		Bi	5–9	*8–1*	sun	dry, ordinary	□□□	□■□	□□□				•	Y
chaixii		HP	5–9	*9–5*	sun	dry, ordinary	□□□	□■□	□□□			•		Y
× hybridum		HP	6–9	· · ·	sun, part shade	dry, moist	□□□	■■□	□□□			•	•	W Pk O Y V
olympicum		HP	6–9	*9–5*	sun	dry, ordinary	□□□	□■□	□□□				•	Y
phoeniceum		HP	6–9	· · ·	sun, part shade	dry, ordinary	□□□	■□□	□□□			•		W Pk R V
Verbena	*p.357*													
bonariensis		HP*	7–10	*10–1*	sun, part shade	dry, ordinary	□□□	■■■	■□□			•	•	V
canadensis		HP*	6–10	· · ·	sun, part shade	ordinary	□□□	■■■	■□□	•	•			W Pk
× hybrida		TP*	9–10	*12–1*	sun, part shade	dry, ordinary	□□□	■■■	■□□	•	•			W Pk R V
peruviana		TP*	9–10	*12–1*	sun, part shade	dry, ordinary	□□□	■■■	■□□	•				R
rigida		HP*	8–10	*12–1*	sun, part shade	xeric, ordinary	□□□	□■■	■□□		•			V
tenuisecta		HP*	8–10	· · ·	sun, part shade	dry, ordinary	□□□	■■■	■■□	•				V
Veronica	*p.357*													
alpina		HP	4–8	*8–1*	sun	ordinary, moist	□□■	□□□	□□□	•				B
austriaca ssp. *teucrium*		HP	4–8	*8–1*	sun	ordinary, moist	□□■	■□□	□□□	•				B
gentianoides		HP	4–9	*7–1*	sun	ordinary, moist	□□□	■□□	□□□		•			W B
longifolia		HP	4–10	*8–1*	sun	ordinary, moist	□□□	■□□	□□□		•			B
peduncularis		HP	6–8	*8–6*	sun	ordinary, moist	□■■	■■□	□□□	•				B
prostrata		HP	4–7	*8–4*	sun, part shade	ordinary, moist	□□□	■■□	□□□	•				B
spicata		HP	3–8	*8–1*	sun	ordinary, moist	□□□	□■□	□□□		•			B
spicata ssp. *incana*		HP	3–8	*8–1*	sun	ordinary, moist	□□□	□■□	□□□	•				B V
***Veronicastrum** virginicum*	*p.358*	HP	3–8	*8–1*	sun, part shade	ordinary, moist	□□□	□□■	■□□			•	•	Pk B
Viola	*p.359*													
cornuta		HP	6–9	*9–1*	sun, part shade	ordinary, moist	□■■	■■□	□□□	•				V
labradorica		HP	2–5	· · ·	sun, part shade	ordinary, moist	□■■	■□□	□□□	•				V
odorata		HP	6–8	*8–6*	sun, part shade	ordinary, moist	■■□	□□□	□□□	•				V
sororia		HP	4–8	· · ·	sun, part shade	ordinary, moist	□■■	■■□	□□□	•				W V
tricolor		A	3–9	*12–1*	sun, part shade	ordinary, moist	□■■	□□□	□□□	•				Y V
× wittrockiana		A	3–10	*9–1*	sun, part shade	ordinary, moist	■■■	■■■	■■■	•				W Pk R O Y B V

Height: L = Low (<1′); S = Short (1′–2′); M = Medium (2′–4′); T = Tall (>4′) | **Color**: W = White; Pk = Pink; R = Red; O = Orange; Y = Yellow; B = Blue; V = Violet

Soil: (dry) = Dry soil; (xeric) = Good for xeriscaping; (ordinary) = Ordinary soil; (moist) = Moist soil

Genus species	page	Type	Hard. Zone	Heat Zone	Light	Soil	BLOOM SEASON Spring	Summer	Fall	HEIGHT L	S	M	T	COLOR W Pk R O Y B V
Vitaliana *primuliflora*	*p.360*	HP	5–7	*8–5*	☼ ◐	◒ ●	□■□	□□□	□□□	•				Y
Wahlenbergia	*p.361*													
albomarginata		HP	6–7	*7–6*	☼ ◐	◒	□□□	■■■	□□□	•				W B
congesta		HP	8–10	*10–8*	☼ ◐	◒	□□□	■■■	■□□	•				W B V
Waldsteinia *ternata*	*p.361*	HP	4–8	*7–1*	☼ ●	○ ●	□□■	■□□	□□□	•				Y
Watsonia	*p.362*													
borbonica		TB*	9–10	*12–6*	☼	◒ ●	□□□	□□■	□□□			•	•	Pk
pillansii		TB*	9–10	*12–6*	☼	◒ ●	□□□	□□■	□□□			•		R O
Wisteria	*p.362*													
floribunda		HP	4–10	···	☼ ◐	◒ ●	□□■	□□□	□□□				•	V
frutescens		HP	6–9	···	☼ ◐	◒ ●	□■□	■□■	□□□				•	B
sinensis		HP	5–10	···	☼ ◐	✗○ ●	□□■	□□□	□□□				•	B V
Xanthisma *texana*	*p.363*	A	3–9	···	☼	✗○ ◒	□□□	■■■	□□□		•			O
Xeranthemum	*p.363*													
annuum		A	2–10	*9–1*	☼	○ ◒	□□□	□■■	□□□		•			V
cylindraceum		A	2–10	*9–1*	☼	○ ◒	□□□	□■■	□□□		•			V
Xerophyllum *tenax*	*p.364*	HP	6–9	*10–7*	☼ ◐	○ ●	□□□	■□□	□□□		•	•	•	W
Yucca filamentosa	*p.364*	HP	4–10	*10–1*	☼	✗○ ◒	□□□	□■■	□□□				•	W
Zaluzianskya *capensis*	*p.365*	TP*	9–10	*10–9*	☼	○ ●	□□□	■■■	□□□		•			W
Zantedeschia	*p.366*													
aethiopica		HP*	8–10	*7–1*	☼ ◐	◒ ●	□□□	■■□	□□□		•	•		W
albomaculata		TP*	10	*12–7*	☼ ◐	◒ ●	□□□	□■□	□□□		•			W
elliottiana		HP*	8–10	*10–4*	☼ ◐	◒ ●	□□□	□■□	□□□		•			Y
Zauschneria californica	*p.366*	HP	8–10	*12–8*	☼ ◐	○ ◒	□□□	□□■	■□□		•			R
Zephyranthes	*p.367*													
candida		HB*	8–10	*9–6*	☼ ◐	◒ ●	□□□	□■■	■□□	•				W
citrina		HB*	8–10	*10–7*	☼ ◐	◒ ●	□□□	□□■	■□□	•				Y
rosea		HB*	8–10	*12–1*	☼ ◐	◒ ●	□□□	□□□	■■□	•				Pk
Zinnia	*p.367*													
angustifolia		A	2–10	*12–1*	☼ ◐	◒	□□□	■■■	■□□		•			O Y
elegans		A	2–10	*12–1*	☼ ◐	◒	□□□	■■■	■□□		•			W Pk R O Y
haageana		A	2–10	*12–1*	☼ ◐	○ ◒	□□□	■■■	□□□		•			O

 Type: A = Annual; Bi = Biennial; HP = Hardy Perennial; TP = Tender Perennial; HB = Hardy Bulb; TB = Tender Bulb; * = May be grown as annual in colder regions

Light: ☼ = Full sun; ◐ = Partial shade; ● = Full shade

Plants with Special Features

Genus species	page	Type	Hard. Zone	Heat Zone	Light	Soil	HEIGHT L	S	M	T	Foliage notes
Acaena *(see also p. 435)*	*p. 41*										
caesiiglauca		HP	6–8	*9–6*	○◐	Dry, Ordinary	•				*blue foliage*
Actinidia *(see also p. 435)*	*p. 44*										
kolomikta		HP	4–8	*9–7*	○●	Moist				•	*pink, white & green foliage*
Adiantum	*p. 46*										
capillus-junonis		HP	6–9	*9–3*	◐	Ordinary, Moist		•			*light green foliage*
pedatum		HP	4–8	*8–1*	◐	Ordinary, Moist		•			*mid-green foliage*
venustum		HP	4–8	*8–5*	◐	Ordinary, Moist	•				*light green foliage*
Aegopodium	*p. 47*										
podagraria 'Variegatum'		HP	3–10	*12–1*	○◐	Xeric, Moist	•				*cream-edged green foliage*
Ajania *pacifica (see also p. 436)*	*p. 51*	HP	5–9	*9–1*	○◐	Dry, Moist		•			*silver-edged foliage & fall flowers*
Amaranthus *(see also p. 437)*	*p. 55*										
tricolor		A	3–10	*12–5*	○◐	Ordinary		•	•		*green, purple & red foliage*
Anethum graveolens	*p. 61*	A	3–10	…	○	Ordinary			•		*culinary use of leaves*
Anthriscus *(see also p. 439)*	*p. 66*										
sylvestris 'Ravenswing'		A	3–10	…	◐	Moist			•		*purple foliage*
Artemisia	*p. 72*										
absinthium		HP	4–10	*12–5*	○◐	Xeric, Ordinary			•		*silver foliage*
ludoviciana		HP	5–10	*12–8*	○◐	Xeric, Ordinary			•		*silver foliage*
schmidtiana		HP	4–10	*8–5*	○◐	Xeric, Ordinary	•	•			*silver foliage*
stelleriana		HP	4–10	*7–1*	○◐	Xeric, Ordinary		•			*silver foliage*
Asarum	*p. 74*										
canadense		HP	2–9	…	◐●	Ordinary, Moist	•				*green foliage*
europaeum		HP	4–8	*8–1*	◐●	Ordinary, Moist	•				*glossy evergreen foliage*
shuttleworthii		HP	7–9	*9–1*	◐●	Ordinary, Moist	•				*evergreen, silver & green foliage*
Asclepias *physocarpa (see also p. 440)*	*p. 75*	HP*	8–10	…	○◐	Ordinary				•	*large, spiky seedpods*
Asplenium	*p. 76*										
scolopendrium		HP	5–9	*8–6*	○◐	Ordinary, Moist		•			*frilled evergreen foliage*
trichomanes		HP	3–9	*8–3*	○◐	Ordinary, Moist	•				*dark green foliage*
Athyrium	*p. 79*										
filix-femina		HP	4–9	*9–1*	○●	Ordinary, Moist			•		*light green foliage*
niponicum		HP	4–9	*8–1*	◐●	Dry, Ordinary		•			*light green foliage*

Height: L = Low (<1'); S = Short (1'–2'); M = Medium (2'–4'); T = Tall (>4') | **Color:** W = White; Pk = Pink; R = Red; O = Orange; Y = Yellow; B = Blue; V = Violet

Soil: Dry = Dry soil; Xeric = Good for xeriscaping; Ordinary = Ordinary soil; Moist = Moist soil

Genus species	page	Type	Hard. Zone	Heat Zone	Light	Soil	HEIGHT L	S	M	T	Foliage notes
Atriplex *hortensis* var. *rubra*	p. 80	A	5–9	9–7	○	◇ ▲			•		*deep red foliage*
Bassia	p. 83										
scoparia f. *trichophylla*		A	2–10	9–2	○	◇ ◭			•		*green foliage & red fall color*
Bergenia (*see also p. 442*)	p. 85										
cordifolia		HP	4–8	8–1	○ ●	◇ ▲		•			*bronze winter foliage*
crassifolia		HP	2–8	8–1	○ ●	◇ ▲		•			*mahogany winter foliage*
purpurascens		HP	5–8	8–1	○ ●	△ ▲		•			*crimson winter foliage*
Billardiera *longifolia*	p. 87	HP	8–9	9–8	○ ◐	▲				•	*showy purple fruit in autumn*
Blechnum	p. 87										
penna-marina		HP	6–9	···	◐ ●	△ ▲	•				*dark green foliage*
spicant		HP	6–8	···	◐ ●	◭ ▲		•			*evergreen dark green foliage*
Briza (*see also p. 442*)	p. 90										
maxima		A	5–8	12–1	○ ◐	◇ ◭		•			*mid-green grass*
media		HP	4–8	12–1	○ ◐	◇ ◭		•			*evergreen grass*
minor		A	5–8	12–1	○ ◐	◭	•				*mid-green grass*
Caladium *bicolor*	p. 94	TP*	9–10	12–4	○ ◐	◭ ▲			•		*varieg. white, pink, or red foliage*
Calamagrostis (*see also p. 443*)	p. 95										
× *acutiflora*		HP	5–9	9–6	○ ◐	△ ▲		•	•	•	*mid-green grass*
Carex	p. 103										
buchananii		HP	6–9	···	○ ◐	▲		•			*evergreen, copper, grasslike*
elata		HP	5–9	9–3	○ ◐	▲			•		*evergreen, yellow-green, grasslike*
morrowii		HP	5–9	···	○ ◐	▲		•			*evergreen, deep green, grasslike*
muskingumensis		HP	3–8	···	○ ◐	▲		•			*mid-green, grasslike*
siderosticha		HP	6–9	···	○ ◐	▲		•			*mid-green, grasslike*
Caulophyllum *thalictroides*	p. 107	HP	4–7	···	◐ ●	▲		•	•		*foliage & berries*
Centaurea (*see also p. 445*)	p. 109										
cineraria		HP*	7–8	···	○	◭			•		*silver foliage*
Chenopodium *giganteum*	p. 115	A	6–10	···	○ ◐	△			•	•	*purple & green foliage*
Coix *lacryma-jobi* (*see also p. 446*)	p. 125	TP*	9–10	12–1	○ ◐	◭		•	•		*mid-green grass*
Colocasia *esculenta*	p. 126	HP	8–10	12–8	◐ ●	▲			•		*enormous green leaves*
Coriandrum *sativum*	p. 130	A	2–9	···	○ ◐	◭		•			*culinary use of leaves*
Cortaderia *selloana* (*see also p. 447*)	p. 131	HP	8–10	12–7	○	◇ ◭				•	*gray-green grass*
Cuminum *cyminum*	p. 136	A	5–10	···	○	◭	•				*culinary use of seeds*

 Type: A = Annual; Bi = Biennial; HP = Hardy Perennial; TP = Tender Perennial; HB = Hardy Bulb; TB = Tender Bulb; * = May be grown as annual in colder regions

Light: ○ = Full sun; ◐ = Partial shade; ● = Full shade

Genus species	page	Type	Hard. Zone	Heat Zone	Light	Soil	HEIGHT L	S	M	T	Foliage notes
***Cymbopogon** citratus*	p. 138	TP*	9–10	· · ·	Sun	Ordinary, Moist		•	•	•	*culinary use of foliage*
***Cyperus** longus* (see also p. 448)	p. 140	HP	8–10	12–1	Sun, Part shade	Moist				•	*green grassy "umbrellas"*
Cyrtomium	p. 141										
falcatum		HP	7–9	8–1	Part shade, Shade	Moist		•			*glossy evergreen foliage*
fortunei		HP	7–9	8–1	Part shade, Shade	Moist		•			*evergreen foliage*
***Darmera** peltata* (see also p. 449)	p. 143	HP	5–9	9–4	Sun, Part shade	Ordinary, Moist			•		*huge foliage, red in autumn*
***Dennstaedtia** punctiloba*	p. 145	HP	3–8	· · ·	Sun, Shade	Dry, Moist			•		*pale green foliage*
Dioscorea	p. 151										
batatas		HP	6–10	· · ·	Sun, Part shade	Ordinary				•	*purple-green foliage*
discolor		TP*	9–10	12–10	Sun, Part shade	Ordinary				•	*variegated foliage*
Dryopteris	p. 155										
cycadina		HP	5–8	9–6	Part shade, Shade	Moist		•			*bright green foliage*
erythrosora		HP	5–8	9–1	Part shade, Shade	Moist		•			*red spring foliage*
filix-mas		HP	4–8	8–1	Sun, Shade	Xeriscaping, Moist			•		*leathery green foliage*
goldieana		HP	3–8	8–5	Part shade, Shade	Moist			•		*leathery green foliage*
marginalis		HP	3–8	8–1	Part shade, Shade	Dry, Moist		•			*evergreen blue-green foliage*
remota		HP	4–8	· · ·	Part shade, Shade	Moist			•		*dark green foliage*
***Eragrostis** trichodes* (see also p. 451)	p. 160	HP	4–9	· · ·	Sun	Xeriscaping, Ordinary			•		*dark green grass*
***Festuca** glauca*	p. 170	HP	4–9	9–5	Sun, Part shade	Xeriscaping, Ordinary	•				*light blue foliage*
Foeniculum	p. 171										
vulgare 'Purpureum'		HP	4–10	9–6	Sun, Part shade	Dry, Ordinary			•	•	*purple-bronze foliage*
Gunnera	p. 185										
magellanica		HP	8–9	9–8	Sun, Part shade	Moist	•				*unusual foliage*
manicata		HP	7–10	12–7	Sun, Part shade	Moist				•	*enormous leaves*
Hakonechloa	p. 187										
macra		HP	4–10	9–5	Sun, Part shade	Moist		•			*grassy foliage, bronze autumn color*
Helichrysum (see also p. 455)	p. 191										
italicum ssp. *serotinum*		HP*	7–10	10–7	Sun	Dry, Ordinary		•			*silver foliage*
petiolare		TP*	9–10	12–10	Sun	Dry, Ordinary	•				*silver foliage*
Helictotrichon	p. 192										
sempervirens (see also p. 455)		HP	4–8	9–1	Sun	Dry, Ordinary			•		*grey-green grass*
***Herniaria** glabra*	p. 197	HP	3–9	· · ·	Sun, Part shade	Dry, Ordinary	•				*fine evergreen foliage*
Hosta (see also p. 457)	p. 200										
fluctuans		HP	3–9	9–1	Part shade, Shade	Ordinary, Moist			•		*large cream-edged leaves*

Height: L = Low (<1'); S = Short (1'–2'); M = Medium (2'–4'); T = Tall (>4') | **Color:** W = White; Pk = Pink; R = Red; O = Orange; Y = Yellow; B = Blue; V = Violet

Soil: Dry soil; Good for xeriscaping; Ordinary soil; Moist soil

Genus species	page	Type	Hard. Zone	Heat Zone	Light	Soil	HEIGHT L	S	M	T	Foliage notes
'Fortunei'		HP	3–9	*9–1*	◐●	◒⬤		•			*long gray-green leaves*
montana		HP	3–9	*9–1*	◐●	◒⬤		•	•		*large dark green leaves*
nigrescens		HP	3–9	*9–1*	◐●	◒⬤		•	•		*large gray-green leaves*
plantaginea		HP	3–9	*9–1*	○◐	◒⬤		•			*large pale-green leaves*
sieboldiana		HP	3–9	*9–1*	◐●	◒⬤			•		*large, puckered, blue-gray leaves*
sieboldii		HP	3–9	*9–1*	◐●	◒⬤		•			*long white-edged leaves*
'Tokudama'		HP	3–9	*9–1*	◐●	◒⬤		•			*large, puckered blue leaves*
'Undulata'		HP	3–9	*9–1*	◐●	◒⬤		•			*green- & cream-striped leaves*
ventricosa		HP	3–9	*9–1*	◐●	◒⬤			•		*large dark green leaves*
***Houttuynia** cordata*	*p. 200*	HP	5–9	*8–1*	○●	◌⬤	•	•			*green & red foliage*
Humulus	*p. 201*										
japonicus 'Variegatus'		HP	3–9	*8–3*	○◐	◌⬤				•	*varieg. foliage & decorative fruit*
lupulus		HP	5–8	*8–1*	○◐	◌⬤				•	*foliage & decorative fruit*
***Hypoestes** phyllostachya*	*p. 205*	TP*	10	*12–1*	○◐	◒	•				*freckled pink foliage*
***Koeleria** glauca*	*p. 216*	HP	6–9	. . .	○	⊗◒		•			*grassy blue foliage*
***Lamium** (see also p. 459)*	*p. 218*										
galeobdolon		HP	3–9	. . .	◐●	⊗◒	•				*silver & green foliage*
maculatum		HP	3–9	. . .	◐●	◌◒	•				*silver, white, green, or varieg. foliage*
***Levisticum** officinale*	*p. 226*	HP	4–8	. . .	○◐	⬤			•	•	*culinary and medicinal use*
***Liriope** (see also p. 461)*	*p. 232*										
muscari		HP	5–9	*12–1*	◐●	◌⬤		•			*grasslike evergreen foliage*
spicata		HP	4–9	*12–1*	◐●	⊗⬤		•			*grasslike evergreen foliage*
***Lopezia** racemosa (see also p. 461)*	*p. 235*	A	3–10	. . .	○◐	◒	•				*interesting fruit*
***Luffa** aegyptiaca*	*p. 236*	A	5–10	. . .	○	◒				•	*spongelike fruit*
***Matteuccia** struthiopteris*	*p. 244*	HP	2–9	*8–1*	◐●	⬤			•	•	*erect green foliage*
Mentha	*p. 248*										
× *gracilis*		HP	6–9	*9–6*	○◐	◒⬤		•			*culinary use of leaves*
× *piperita*		HP	5–10	. . .	○◐	◒⬤		•			*culinary use of leaves*
spicata		HP	5–10	. . .	○◐	◒⬤		•			*culinary use of leaves*
suaveolens		HP	5–9	*9–5*	○◐	◒⬤		•			*culinary use of leaves*
Milium	*p. 250*										
effusum 'Aureum' *(see also p. 463)*		HP	6–9	*9–6*	●	⬤		•			*golden yellow foliage*
***Minuartia** verna (see also p. 463)*	*p. 251*	HP	4–9	*9–1*	○◐	◒⬤	•				*mossy, evergreen cushions*
***Miscanthus** (see also p. 463)*	*p. 252*										

 Type: A = Annual; Bi = Biennial; HP = Hardy Perennial; TP = Tender Perennial; HB = Hardy Bulb; TB = Tender Bulb; * = May be grown as annual in colder regions

Light: ○ = Full sun; ◐ = Partial shade; ● = Full shade

Genus species	page	Type	Hard. Zone	Heat Zone	Light	Soil	HEIGHT L	S	M	T	Foliage notes
floridulus		HP	5–9	···	○ ◐	dry, moist				•	*silvery green foliage*
sinensis		HP	5–9	*9–1*	○ ◐	xeriscaping, moist				•	*green, wine, yellow, or silver foliage*
Musa	*p. 256*										
acuminata 'Zebrina'		TP*	10	···	○ ◐	moist				•	*huge red-striped leaves*
coccinea		TP*	9–10	*10–5*	○ ◐	ordinary, moist			•		*tropical foliage*
sikkimensis		TP*	8–10	···	○ ◐	ordinary, moist				•	*huge red-tinged leaves*
***Ocimum** basilicum*	*p. 267*	A	4–10	···	○	ordinary		•			*ornamental red leaves; culinary*
Ophiopogon	*p. 269*										
japonicus		HP	6–10	*10–6*	○ ●	dry, moist	•				*dark green, grassy, evergreen foliage*
planiscapus 'Nigrescens'		HP	6–10	*10–6*	○ ●	dry, moist	•				*dk. purple, grassy, evergreen foliage*
Osmunda	*p. 270*										
cinnamomea		HP	3–10	*9–1*	○ ●	moist			•		*pale green foliage*
claytoniana		HP	2–10	*9–1*	◐ ●	dry, moist			•		*pale green foliage*
regalis		HP	2–10	*9–1*	○ ●	ordinary, moist			•	•	*bright green foliage*
***Panicum** virgatum* (*see also p. 466*)	*p. 274*	HP	5–9	*12–1*	○ ◐	xeriscaping, moist			•	•	*green, grassy foliage*
Pennisetum (*see also p. 467*)	*p. 280*										
alopecuroides		HP	5–9	*9–1*	○	ordinary			•		*bright green, grassy foliage*
setaceum		HP*	8–10	*9–1*	○	ordinary		•	•		*green or purple grassy foliage*
***Perilla** frutescens* 'Atropurpurea'	*p. 282*	A	3–10	*12–1*	○ ◐	dry, ordinary		•			*purple with metallic sheen*
Perovskia	*p. 282*										
atriplicifolia (*see also p. 467*)		HP	5–9	*9–4*	○	dry, ordinary			•	•	*silver foliage*
***Petroselinum** crispum*	*p. 284*	HB	4–9	···	○ ◐	ordinary	•	•			*culinary use of leaves*
Phalaris	*p. 286*										
arundinacea var. *picta*		HP	4–9	*9–1*	○ ◐	xeriscaping, moist		•	•		*grassy green- & white-striped foliage*
Phormium	*p. 289*										
cookianum		HP*	8–10	*10–3*	○ ◐	dry, moist			•	•	*evergreen architectural form*
tenax		HP*	8–10	*10–3*	○ ◐	ordinary, moist				•	*dramatic sword-shaped leaves*
Plectranthus	*p. 294*										
amboinicus		TP*	10	*12–1*	○	ordinary, moist		•			*variegated foliage*
argentatus		TP*	10	*12–1*	○	ordinary, moist			•		*silver foliage*
Polystichum	*p. 297*										
acrostichoides		HP	3–9	*8–1*	◐ ●	ordinary, moist		•			*evergreen, dark green foliage*
munitum		HP	5–9	*8–1*	◐ ●	dry, moist			•		*leathery evergreen foliage*
polyblepharum		HP	5–9	*8–5*	◐ ●	dry, moist			•		*shiny, dark green foliage*

Height: L = Low (<1'); S = Short (1'–2'); M = Medium (2'–4'); T = Tall (>4') | **Color:** W = White; Pk = Pink; R = Red; O = Orange; Y = Yellow; B = Blue; V = Violet
Soil: dry = Dry soil; xeriscaping = Good for xeriscaping; ordinary = Ordinary soil; moist = Moist soil

Genus species	page	Type	Hard. Zone	Heat Zone	Light	Soil	HEIGHT L	S	M	T	Foliage notes
tsus-simense		HP	6–9	*9–5*	◐●	open drop, solid drop		•			*leathery green foliage*
***Rheum** palmatum (see also p. 470)*	*p. 305*	HP	5–9	*9–1*	○◐	solid drop				•	*huge lobed leaves*
***Ricinus** communis*	*p. 307*	A	3–10	*12–1*	○	open drop, solid drop				•	*striking foliage*
Rumex	*p. 311*										
acetosa		HP	3–9	· · ·	○◐	solid drop		•			*culinary use of leaves*
scutatus 'Silver Shield'		HP	6–9	· · ·	○◐	solid drop	•				*silvery green foliage*
***Sagina** subulata (see also p. 470)*	*p. 312*	HP	5–9	*9–6*	○◐	half drop, solid drop	•				*mosslike evergreen cushions*
***Santolina** chamaecyparissus*	*p. 315*	HP	6–9	*9–5*	○◐	crossed drop		•			*gray foliage*
Selaginella	*p. 323*										
involvens		HP	5–10	· · ·	◐●	solid drop	•				*evergreen fernlike foliage*
moellendorfii		HP	6–10	· · ·	◐●	solid drop	•				*amber-tipped green foliage*
uncinata		HP	6–10	· · ·	◐●	solid drop	•				*blue-green foliage*
***Sempervivum** (see also p. 472)*	*p. 323*										
arachnoideum		HP	5–9	*9–5*	○	open drop	•				*succulent evergreen rosettes*
giuseppii		HP	7–9	*9–7*	○	open drop	•				*succulent evergreen rosettes*
tectorum		HP	5–9	*9–5*	○	open drop	•				*succulent evergreen rosettes*
***Senecio** cineraria*	*p. 324*	HP*	8–9	*12–1*	○	half drop	•				*silver foliage*
***Sesamum** indicum*	*p. 324*	A	7–10	· · ·	○	open drop, half drop			•		*culinary use of seeds*
***Solenostemon** scutellarioides*	*p. 329*	TP*	10	*12–1*	○●	solid drop		•			*multicolored leaves*
***Stachys** byzantina (see also p. 473)*	*p. 332*	HP	4–9	*8–1*	○◐	crossed drop, half drop		•			*fuzzy silver foliage*
***Stipa** (see also p. 474)*	*p. 334*										
arundinacea		HP	5–8	*12–1*	○	crossed drop, half drop				•	*bronze-tinged evergreen grass*
gigantea		HP	7–8	*12–1*	○	crossed drop, half drop				•	*gray-green grass*
tenuissima		HP	7–10	· · ·	○	crossed drop, half drop		•			*mid-green grass*
***Strobilanthes** (see also p. 474)*	*p. 335*										
dyerianus		TP*	10	· · ·	○◐	solid drop			•		*iridescent purple and silver foliage*
Thelypteris	*p. 342*										
noveboracensis		HP	3–8	· · ·	○●	open drop, solid drop		•			*yellow-green foliage*
palustris		HP	3–8	*8–3*	○●	solid drop			•		*light green foliage*
***Tradescantia** (see also p. 475)*	*p. 347*										
pallida 'Purpurea'		TP*	9–10	*12–1*	○●	half drop, solid drop		•			*dark purple foliage*
***Trichosanthes** cucumerina*	*p. 348*	A	3–10	· · ·	○◐	solid drop				•	*long, whimsical fruits*
***Trigonella** foenum-graecum*	*p. 349*	A	6–10	· · ·	○	half drop	•				*culinary use of seeds*

 Type: A = Annual; Bi = Biennial; HP = Hardy Perennial; TP = Tender Perennial; HB = Hardy Bulb; TB = Tender Bulb; * = May be grown as annual in colder regions

Light: ○ = Full sun; ◐ = Partial shade; ● = Full shade

Appendixes

Bulb, Plant, and Seed Mail-Order Suppliers

When purchasing plants by mail it is a good idea to buy from nurseries in your geographic region whenever possible. Their stock will be best suited to your climate and soil type, and consequently more likely to thrive in your own garden.

There are several useful websites where customers provide feedback on their experiences with specific mail-order nurseries. The Garden Watchdog *(www.gardenwatchdog.com)* is an impressively comprehensive site that includes the former Plants by Mail FAQ. Checking this site before making a purchase through the mail could save you time, money, and aggravation. If you have a positive experience with a nursery, do take a minute to add your comments as a thank-you to the nursery and to help your fellow gardeners.

Imported Plants

Restrictions on imported plant materials may make it necessary to obtain a permit before ordering any plants from foreign nurseries; there are seldom restrictions on the import of seeds. To obtain further information on restrictions and permits, Canadian gardeners should contact Agriculture Canada's Animal and Plant Health Directorate at *www.utoronto.ca/forest/eso/agrcan.htm* or by phone at 613-998-9320, before ordering plants from the United States. Americans ordering plants from Canada or other countries should contact the USDA Plant Protection and Quarantine Permit Unit at *www.APHIS.USDA.gov/ppq/permits* or by phone at 877-770-5990.

Buying Wildflowers

Before purchasing live wildflower plants, always check to be sure that they are nursery propagated and not wild-collected. It is illegal to dig many native plants in the wild, but this does not stop all the growers in this increasingly large market from selling plants that have been illegally dug. To further complicate the matter, not all nurseries that claim to propagate their own plants actually do so. Always take the time to research a nursery to determine whether their plants are nursery propagated. Your local native plant society can provide you with a directory of sanctioned nurseries; a list of native plant and wildflower societies begins on page 495.

ARKANSAS

Holland Wildflower Farm S, W
P. O. Box 328, Elkins, AR 72727
800-684-3734 | *www.hwildflower.com*

CALIFORNIA

Bay View Gardens Iris
1201 Bay Street, Santa Cruz, CA 95060
831-423-3656

California Flora Nursery California natives
P. O. Box 3, Fulton, CA 95439
707-528-8813

Canyon Creek Nursery
Unusual California natives, Mediterranean plants
3527 Dry Creek Road, Oroville, CA 95965
530-533-2166 | *www.canyoncreeknursery.com*

Clyde Robin Seed Company S, W
P. O. Box 2366, Castro Valley, CA 94546-0366
800-647-6475 | *www.clyderobin.com*

Cornflower Farms California natives
Box 896, Elk Grove, CA 95759-0896
www.cornflowerfarms.com

J.L. Hudson, Seedsman H, S, W
Star Route 2, Box 337, La Horda, CA 94020
www.jhudsonseeds.net

King's Mums Chrysanthemums
P. O. Box 368, Clements, CA 95227
209-759-3571 | *www.kingsmums.com*

Larner Seeds S, W
P. O. Box 407, Bolinas, CA 94924
415-868-9407 | *www.larnerseeds.com*

Las Pilitas Nursery California natives
3232 Las Pilitas Road, Santa Margarita, CA 93453
805-438-5992 | *www.laspilitas.com*

Moon Mountain Wildflowers S, W
P. O. Box 725, Carpinteria, CA 93014-0725
805-684-2565

Redwood City Seed S
P. O. Box 361, Redwood City, CA 94064
650-325-7333 | *www.batnet.com/rwc-seed*

World Seed H, S
300 Morning Drive, Bakersfield, CA 93306-6620
661-366-6291 | *www.worldseed.com*

COLORADO

Applewood Seed Company S, W
5380 Vivian Street, Arvada, CO 80002-1921
303-431-7333 | *www.applewoodseed.com*

D.V. Burrell Seed Growers Company H, S
P. O. Box 150, Rocky Ford, CO 81067
719-254-3318

Smith & Hawken B, P
P. O. Box 8690, Pueblo, CO 81008-9998
800-940-1170 | *www.smithandhawken.com*

CONNECTICUT

Caprilands Herb Farm H, P, S
P. O. Box 190, Coventry, CT 06238
800-568-7132 | *www.caprilands.com*

Catnip Acres Herb Nursery H, P, S
67 Christian Street, Oxford, CT 06478
203-888-5649

Comstock, Ferre, and Company H, S, W
263 Main Street, Wethersfield, CT 06109
800-733-3773 | *www.comstockferre.com*

John Scheepers, Inc. B
23 Tulip Drive, Bantam, CT 06750
860-567-0838 | *www.johnscheepers.com*

Logee's Greenhouses H, Rare P
141 North Street, Danielson, CT 06239-1939
888-330-8038 | *www.logees.com*

Van Engelen Inc. B
23 Tulip Drive, Bantam, CT 06750
860-567-8734 | *www.vanengelen.com*

White Flower Farm B, P
P. O. Box 50, Route 63, Litchfield, CT 06759
800-503-9624 | *www.whiteflowerfarm.com*

FLORIDA

Caladium World Caladiums
P. O. Drawer 629, Sebring, FL 33871
863-385-7661 | *www.caladiumworld.com*

IDAHO

High Altitude Gardens H, S, W
308 So. River, P. O. Box 1048, Hailey, ID 83333
208-788-4363

Seeds Blum Heirloom S
Idaho City Stage, Boise, ID 83706-9725
208-342-0858

 B = Bulbs; H = Herb seeds and/or plants; P = Live Plants; S = Seeds; W = Wildflower seeds and/or plants

ILLINOIS

Burgess Seed and Plant Company H, P
905 Four Seasons Road, Bloomington, IL 61701
309-663-9551 | *www.directgardening.com*

The Natural Garden P, W
38W443 Hwy. 64, St. Charles, IL 60175
630-584-0150

The Wildflower Source P, W
The Propagator's Private Stock
8805 Kenman Road, Hebron, IL 60034
815-648-4397

IOWA

Earl May Seed and Nursery Company S
208 N. Elm Street, Shenandoah, IA 51603
800-831-4193 | *www.earlmay.com*

KENTUCKY

Ferry-Morse H, S, W
P. O. Box 488, Fulton, KY 42041-0488
www.ferry-morse.com

MAINE

Daystar Alpines
Route 2, Box 250, Litchfield, ME 04350
207-724-3369

Johnny's Selected Seeds H, S
184 Foss Hill Road, RR1 Box 2580
Albion, ME 04910-9731
207-437-4301 | *www.johnnyseeds.com*

Merry Spring Park P
P. O. 893, Camden, ME 04843
207-236-2239 | *www.merryspring.org*

Pinetree Garden Seeds S
P. O. Box 300, New Gloucester, ME 04260
207-926-3400, *www.superseeds.com*

MARYLAND

The Crownsville Nursery P, W
P. O. Box 797, Crownsville, MD 21032
410-849-3143 | *www.crownsvillenursery.com*

Environmental Concern, Inc.
Northeastern wetland natives
P. O. Box P, St. Michaels, MD 21663
410-745-9620 | *www.wetland.org*

Kurt Bluemel, Inc. Ornamental grasses, P
2740 Greene Lane, Baldwin, MD 21013-9523
410-557-7229

MASSACHUSETTS

Peter de Jaeger Bulb Company B
P. O. Box 2010, 1888 Asbury Street
So. Hamilton, MA 01982
508-468-4707

Tranquil Lake Nursery Daylilies, irises
45 River Street, Rehoboth, MA 02769-1395
508-252-4002 | *www.tranquil-lake.com*

MICHIGAN

Arrowhead Alpines Rare plants
P. O. Box 857, Fowlerville, MI 48836
517-223-3581 | *www.arrowhead-alpines.com*

Englerth Gardens Perennials
Daylilies, Hostas, Irises
2461 22nd Street, Hopkins, MI 49328-9639
616-793-7196

Far North Gardens Unusual S, W
59400 Pontiac Trail, New Hudson , MI 48165
248-486-4203

Fox Hill Farm H, P
444 W. Michigan Avenue, Box 9, Parma, MI 49269
517-531-3179

H & H Botanicals H, P, W
P. O. Box 291, Bancroft, MI 48414
989-634-9016 | *www.handhbotanicals.com*

MINNESOTA

Ambergate Gardens B, P
8730 Country Road 43, Chaska, MN 55318-9358
877-211-9769 | *www.ambergategardens.com*

Borbeleta Gardens, Inc. Daylilies, Irises, Lilies, Peonies
15980 Canby Avenue, Faribault, MN 55021
507-334-2807 | *http://1rl.com/borbeleta.htm*

Busse Gardens P
17160 245th Avenue, Big Lake, MN 55309
800-544-3192 | *www.bussegardens.com*

Orchid Gardens Midwestern P, W
2232 139th Avenue N.W., Andover, MN 55304-3908
763-755-0205

Prairie Moon Nursery P, S, W
Rt. 3, Box 163, Winona, MN 55987-9515
507-452-1362 | *www.prairie-nursery.com*

Savory's Gardens, Inc. Hostas
5300 Whiting Avenue, Edina, MN 55439-1249
952-941-8755

Shady Oaks Nursery Shade-loving P
P. O. Box 708, Waseca, MN 56093
800-504-8006 | *www.shadyoaks.com*

MISSOURI

Gilbert H. Wild & Son B, P
3044 State Highway 37, Sarcoxie, MO 64862
888-449-4537 | *http://gilbertwild.com*

Herb Gathering, Inc. H, S
5742 Kenwood Avenue, Kansas City, MO 64110
816-523-2653

Missouri Wildflowers Nursery P, S, W
9814 Pleasant Hill Road
Jefferson City, MO 65109
573-496-3492 | *www.mowildflowers.net*

Sharp Brothers Seed Company Native S, W
396 S.W. Davis St.-Ladue, Clinton, MO 64735
800-451-3779 | *www.sharpbro.com*

NEBRASKA

De Giorgi Seed Company S, W
6011 N Street, Omaha, NE 68117-1634
402-731-3901

Stock Seed Farms, Inc. S, W
28008 Mill Road, Murdock, NE 68407-2350
800-759-1520 | *www.stockseed.com*

NEW JERSEY

Fairweather Gardens P
P. O. Box 330, Greenwich, NJ 08323
856-451-6261 | *www.fairweathergardens.com*

Mary Mattison Van Schaik Imported Dutch Bulbs B
P. O. Box 188, Temple, NJ 03084
603-878-2592

Thompson & Morgan Seedsmen, Inc. P, S
P. O. Box 1308, Jackson, NJ 08527-0308
800-274-7333 | *www.thompson-morgan.com*

Well-Sweep Herb Farm H, P
205 Mount Bethel Road, Port Murray, NJ 07865
908-852-5390 | *www.wellsweep.com*

NEW MEXICO

Bernardo Beach Native Plant Farm
P, W native to the Southwest
Star Route 7, Box 145, Veguita, NM 86062
505-345-6248

High Country Gardens H, P, W
2902 Rufina Street, Santa Fe, NM 87505-2929
800-925-9387 | *www.highcountrygardens.com*

Plants of the Southwest
P, S, W suited to the Southwest
3095 Aqua Fria Road, Santa Fe, NM 87501
800-788-7333 | *www.plantsofthesouthwest.com*

Seeds of Change H, P, S, W
P. O. Box 15700, Santa Fe, NM 87506-5700
888-762-7333 | *www.seedsofchange.com*

NEW YORK

D.S. George Nurseries Clematis
2491 Penfield Road, Fairport, NY 14450
585-377-0731

Harris Seeds B, P, S
355 Paul Road, Rochester, NY 14624- 0966
800-514-4441 | *www.harrisseeds.com*

Roslyn Nursery P
211 Burrs Lane, Dix Hills, NY 11746
631-643-9347 | *www.roslynnursery.com*

Stokes Seeds, Inc. S, W
P. O. Box 548, Buffalo, NY 14240-0548
800-396-9238 | *www.stokeseeds.com*

Van Bourgondien Dutch Bulbs B, P
245 Farmingdale Road, P. O. Box 1000
Babylon, NY 11702-0597
800-622-9997 | *www.dutchbulbs.com*

Van Dyck's Flower Farms, Inc. B
P. O. Box 430, Brightwaters, NY 11718-0430
800-248-2852 | *www.vandycks.com*

Wildginger Woodlands P, W
P. O. Box 1091, Webster, NY 14580-9550
585-872-4033

NORTH CAROLINA

Gardens of the Blue Ridge B, P, W
P. O. Box 10, Pineola, NC 28662
828-733-2417 | *www.gardensoftheblueridge.com*

Holbrook Farm and Nursery P, W
Route 2, Box 223B, Fletcher, NC 28732
704-891-7790

Meadowbrook Nursery/We-Du Natives P, W
2055 Polly Spout Road, Marion, NC 28752
828-738-8300 | *www.we-du.com*

Niche Gardens B, P, W
1111 Dawson Road, Chapel Hill, NC 27516
919-967-0078 | *www.nichegdn.com*

Plant Delights H, P, W
9241 Sauls Road, Raleigh, NC 27603
919-772-4794 | *www.plantdelights.com*

Powell's Gardens P
9468 U.S. Highway 70 E., Princeton, NC 27569
919-936-4421

Sandy Mush Herb Nursery H, P, W
316 Surrett Cove Road, Leicester, NC 28748
828-683-2014 | *www.brwm.org/sandymushherbs*

Terra Ceia Farms B
3810 Terra Ceia Road, Pantego, NC 27860-9312
800-858-2852 | *www.terraceiafarms.com*

OHIO

Bluestone Perennials, Inc. H, P
7211 Middle Ridge Road, Madison, OH 44057
800-852-5243 | *www.bluestoneperennials.com*

Homestead Division of Sunnybrook Farms P, S
9448 Mayfield Road, Chesterland, OH 44026
440-729-9838 | *www.hostahomestead.com*

Mellinger's Inc. B, P, S
P. O. Box 157, North Lima, OH 44452
800-321-7444 | *www.mellingers.com*

Spring Hill Nurseries P
P. O. Box 330, Harrison, OH 45030-0330
513-354-1509 | *www.springhillnursery.com*

OREGON

Cooley's Gardens Irises
P. O. Box 126-PG, Silverton, OR 97381
503-873-5463 | *www.cooleysgardens.com*

Forest Farm H, P, W
990 Tetherow Road, Williams, OR 97544-9599
541-846-7269 | *www.forestfarm.com*

Goodwin Creek Gardens H, P, S, W
P. O. Box 83, Williams, OR 97544
800-846-7359 | *www.goodwincreekgardens.com*

Grant E. Mitsch Novelty Daffodils B
P. O. Box 218, Hubbard, OR 97032
503-651-2742 | *www.web-ster.com/havensr/mitsch*

Greer Gardens P
1280 Goodpasture Island Road
Eugene, OR 97401-1794
800-548-0111 | *www.greergardens.com*

Jackson & Perkins B, P
2518 S. Pacific Highway, Medford, OR 97501
800-292-4769 | *www.jackson-perkins.com*

Joy Creek Nursery H, P, W
20300 N.W. Watson Road, Scappoose, OR 97056
503-543-7474 | *www.joycreek.com*

The Lily Garden B
36752 S.E. Bluff Road, Boring, OR 97009
503-668-5291

Nichols Garden Nursery Unusual H, P, S, W
1190 Old Salem Road, NE, Albany, OR 97321
800-422-3985 | *www.gardennursery.com*

Oregon Bulb and Perennial Farms B, P
39391 S.E. Lusted Road, Sandy, OR 97055
503-663-3133 | *www.oregonbulb.com*

Russell Graham P, W
4030 Eagle Crest Road, N.W., Salem, OR 97304
503-362-1135

Schreiner's Iris Gardens Irises
3625 Quinaby Road, N.E., Salem, OR 97303
800-525-2367 | *www.schreinergardens.com*

Siskiyou Rare Plant Nursery P, W
2825 Cummings Road, Medford, OR 97501
541-772-6846 | *www.srpn.net*

Swan Island Dahlias B
P. O. Box 700, Canby, OR 97013
800-410-6540

Territorial Seed Company P, S, W
P. O. Box 158, Cottage Grove, OR 97424-0061
541-942-9547 | *www.territorial-seed.com*

PENNSYLVANIA

Appalachian Wildflower Nursery P, W, Alpines
723 Honey Creek Road, Reedsville, PA 17084
717-667-6998

Heirloom Seeds S, H
P. O. Box 245, West Elizabeth, PA 15088-0245
412-384-0852 | *www.heirloomseeds.com*

The Primrose Path P
921 Scottsdale-Dawson Road, Scottsdale, PA 15683
724-887-6759 | *www.theprimrosepath.com*

The Rosemary House and Gardens, Inc. H, S
120 S. Market Street, Mechanicsburg, PA 17055
717-697-5111 | *www.therosemaryhouse.com*

W. Atlee Burpee Seed Company B, H, P, S, W
300 Park Avenue, Warminster, PA 18974
800-333-5808 | *www.burpee.com*

SOUTH CAROLINA

Park Seed Co. B, H, P, S
1 Parkton Avenue, Greenwood, SC 29649-0001
800-213-0076 | *www.parkseed.com*

Twilley Seed Company, Inc. S
121 Gary Road, Hodges, SC 29653
800-622-7333 | *www.twilleyseed.com*

Wayside Gardens H, P
1 Garden Lane, Hodges, SC 29695-0001
800-213-0379 | *www.waysidegardens.com*

Woodlander's, Inc. P, Southern natives
1128 Colleton Avenue, Aiken, SC 29801
803-648-7522 | *www.woodlanders.net*

TENNESSEE

Native Gardens P, W
5737 Fisher Lane, Greenback, TN 37742
423-856-0220 | *www.native-gardens.com*

Sunlight Gardens P, W
174 Golden Lane, Andersonville, TN 37705
800-272-7396 | *www.sunlightgardens.com*

TEXAS

Green Horizons S, W
218 Quinlan 571, Kerrville, TX 78028
512-257-5141

Hilltop Herb Farm H, P
Box 1734, Cleveland, TX 77327
281-592-5859

Wildseed Farms, Inc. S, W
P. O. Box 3000, Fredericksburg, TX 78624
800-848-0078 | *www.wildseedfarms.com*

VERMONT

American Meadows W
P. O. Box 5, Route 7, Charlotte, VT 05445-0005
802-425-3931 | *www.americanmeadows.com*

Dutch Gardens Holland Bulbs B
144 Intervale Road, Burlington, VT 05401
800-944-2250 | *www.dutchgardens.com*

VIRGINIA

Andre Viette Farm and Nursery P
P. O. Box 1109, Fishersville, VA 22939
800-975-5538 | *www.viette.com*

Brent and Becky's Bulbs B
7900 Daffodil Lane, Gloucester, VA 23061
804-693-3966 | *www.brentandbeckysbulbs.com*

Seymours Selected Seeds S, W
P. O. Box 1346, Sussex, VA 23884-0346
803-663-3084 | *www.seymourseeduk.com*

Southern Exposure Seed Exchange S
P. O. Box 460, Mineral, VA 23117
540-894-9480 | *www.southernexposure.com*

WASHINGTON

Abundant Life Seed Foundation H, S, W
P. O. Box 930, Port Townsend, WA 98368
360-385-5660 | *www.abundantlifeseed.org*

B & D Lilies B
P. O. Box 2007, Port Townsend, WA 98368
360-765-4341

Collectors Nursery Rare and unusual plants
16804 N.E. 102nd Avenue
Battleground, WA 98604-6162
360-574-3832 | *www.collectorsnursery.com*

Connell's Dahlias Dahlias
10616 Waller Road East, Tacoma, WA 98446-2231
253-531-0292 | *www.connells-dahlias.com*

Fancy Fronds Nursery Ferns
P. O. Box 1090, Gold Bar, WA 98251
360-793-1471 | *www.fancyfronds.com*

Foliage Gardens Ferns
2003 128th Avenue, SE, Bellevue, WA 98005
425-747-2998 | *www.foliagegardens.com*

Frosty Hollow Ecological Restoration S, W
P. O. Box 53, Langley, WA 98260
360-579-2332

Heronswood Nursery P
7530 N.E. 288th Street, Kingston, WA 98346
360-297-4172 | *www.heronswood.com*

Plants of the Wild P
P. O. Box 866, Tekoa, WA 99033
509-284-2848

Robyn's Nest Nursery P
14324 S.E. 206th Street, Snohomish, WA 98296
425-486-6919 | *www.robynsnestnursery.com*

WEST VIRGINIA

Wrenwood H, P
Rt. 4, Box 361, Berkeley Springs, WV 25411
304-258-3071

WISCONSIN

American Natives P, W, Ornamental grasses
P. O. Box 306, Westfield, WI 53964
800-476-9453 | *www.american-natives.com*

Country Wetlands Nursery and Consulting P, S, W
P. O. Box 126, Muskego, WI 53150
262-679-8003

Hauser's Superior View Farm P
Route 1, Box 199, Bayfield, WI 54814
715-779-5404 | *http://superiorviewfarm.com*

J.W. Jung Seed Company B, P, S
335 S. High Street, Randolph, WI 53957
414-326-3121

Klehm's Song Sparrow Perennial Farm P
13101 E. Rye Road, Avalon, WI 53505
800-553-3715 | *www.klehm.com*

McClure & Zimmerman B
108 W. Winnebago Street, P. O. Box 368
Friesland, WI 53935
800-883-6998 | *www.mzbulb.com*

Milaeger's Gardens H, P, W
4838 Douglas Avenue, Racine, WI 53402-2498
800-669-9956 | *www.milaegers.com*

Prairie Nursery, Inc. P, S, W
P. O. Box 306, Westfield, WI 53964
800-476-9453 | *www.prairienursery.com*

Prairie Ridge Nursery P, S, W
9738 Overland Road, Mount Horeb, WI 53572
608-437-5245 | *www.prairieridgenursery.com*

Prairie Seed Source S, W
P. O. Box 83, North Lake, WI 53064
262-673-7166
www.ameritech.net/users/rasillon/Seed.html

CANADA

ALBERTA

Alberta Nurseries & Seeds, Ltd. B, P, S
P. O. Box 20, Bowden, AB T0M 0K0
403-224-3544

Parkland Perennials B, Daylilies, Irises, Lilies, Peonies
P. O. Box 506, Bruderheim, AB T0B 0S0
780-796-2382 | *www.parklandperennials.com*

Valley K Greenhouses P, Lilies, Roses
RR 1, Edberg, AB T0B 1J0
780-877-2547 | *www.valleyk.com*

BRITISH COLUMBIA

Beachwood Daylily & Perennial P, Daylilies
7075 264th Street, Aldergrove, BC V4W 1M6
604-856-8806 | *www.beachwooddaylily.com*

Botanus, Inc. B, P, Ferns, Hostas, Ornamental grasses, Peonies, Roses
2489 Wayburne Crescent, Langley, BC V2Y 1B6
800-672-3413 | *www.botanus.com*

Brentwood Bay Nurseries P
1395 Benvenuto Avenue
Brentwood Bay, BC V8M 1J5
250-652-1507 | *www.brentwoodbaynurseries.com*

The Butchart Gardens Ltd. S
Box 4010, Victoria, BC V8X 3X4
www.butchartgardens.com

Ferncliff Gardens B, P
8394 McTaggart Street, Mission, BC V2V 6S6
604-826-2447 | *www.ferncliffgardens.com*

Florabunda Seeds S
641 Rainbow Road
Salt Spring Island, BC V8K 2M7

Lindel Lilies B
5510 239th Street, Langley, BC V3A 7N6
604-534-4729

Perennial Gardens B, P
13139 224th Street, Maple Ridge, BC V4R 2P6
604-467-4218 | *www.perennialgardener.com*

West Coast Seeds S, W
3925 64th Street, Delta, BC, V4K 3N2
604-952-8820 | *https://secure.westcoastseeds.com*

MANITOBA

Boughen Nurseries Valley River Ltd. P
Box 12, Valley River, MB R0L 2B0
204-638-7618

 B = Bulbs; H = Herb seeds and/or plants; P = Live Plants; S = Seeds; W = Wildflower seeds and/or plants

The Lily Nook Lilies
Box 846, Neepawa, MB R0J 1H0
www.lilynook.mb.ca

Lindenberg Seeds Ltd. B, P, S
803 Princess Avenue, Brandon, MB R7A 0P5
204-727-0575 | *www.lindenbergseeds.mb.ca*

McFayden Seeds B, P, S
30 Ninth Street, P. O. Box 1800
Brandon, MB R7A 6E1
204-725-7300 | *www.mcfayden.com*

T & T Seeds Ltd. H, P, S, W
Box 1710, Winnipeg, MB R3C 3P6
204-895-9964 | *www.ttseeds.mb.ca*

NOVA SCOTIA

Old Heirloom Roses Roses
P. O. Box 9106, Stn. A, Halifax, NS B3K 5M7
902-471-3364 | *www.oldheirloomroses.com*

ONTARIO

Aimers Seed S, W
126 Catherine Street North, Hamilton, ON L84 1JA
905-529-2601

Borghese Gardens S
Ottawa, ON, Canada
www.BorgheseGardens.com

Crescent Nursery P
8540 Highway #7, Rockwood, ON, N0B 2K0
519-856-1000 | *http://home.ican.net/~rdcrwfrd/*

Cruickshank's Ltd. Native B, P
1015 Mount Pleasant Road, Toronto, ON M4P 2M1
800-665-5605

Dominion Seed House B, S, W
Box 2500, Georgetown, ON L7G 5L6
800-784-3037 | *www.dominion-seed-house.com*

Garden Import Inc. B, P
P. O. Box 760, 135 West Beaver Creek Road
Richmond Hill, ON L4B 1C6
800-881-3499 | *www.gardenimport.com*

Gardens North S, W
RR #3, North Gower, ON K0A 2T0
613-489-0065

Hortico, Inc. B, H, P, W
723 Robson Road, R.R. 1, Waterdown, ON L0R 2H1
905-689-9323 | *www.hortico.com*

JDS Gardens P
RR #4, 2277 County Road 20, Harrow, ON N0R 1G0
www.jdsgardens.com

McMillen's Iris Gardens B, Iris, Daylilies
R.R. 1, Norwich, ON N0J 1P0
519-468-6508 | *www.execulink.com/~iris*

Pickering Nurseries P
670 Kingston Road, Pickering, ON L1V 1A6
905-839-2111 | *www.pickeringnurseries.com*

Richter's Herb Specialist H, S, W
357 Highway 47, Goodwood, ON L0C 1A0
905-640-6677 | *www.richters.com*

William Dam Seeds B, S, W
P. O. Box 8400, Dundas, ON L9H 6M1
905-628-6641 | *www.damseeds.com*

PRINCE EDWARD ISLAND

Vesey's Seeds Ltd. H, P, S
P. O. Box 9000, Charlottetown, PEI C1A 8K6
800-363-6333 | *www.veseys.com*

QUEBEC

Guru Garden (Patrick Studio Inc.) P, S, W
18 Haendel Street, Kirkland, PQ H9H 4Y9
866-695-8399 | *www.thegurugarden.com*

La Pivoinerie D'Aoust Peonies
Box 220, Hudson Heights, Quebec, PQ J0P 1J0
450-458-2759

SASKATCHEWAN

Honeywood Lilies B, P
P. O. Box 68, Parkside, SK S0J 2A0
306-747-3296

Native Plant Societies

One of the great joys of gardening is discovering a wonderful new plant, finding the perfect home for it in your garden, and seeing it flourish, perhaps even spread so lavishly that you can divide it and share its beauty with your friends. But in the last few years we've learned that we can no longer be so carefree with our garden purchases — we now have to worry about "invasive exotics," those plants that have been introduced to an area far from their native habitat, either accidentally or intentionally; plants that flourished so well, and spread so lavishly, that they threaten the survival of native species.

Most gardeners are aware of the devastating effects of kudzu, "the vine that ate the South." Frightening in its assiduity and unattractive to boot, kudzu is clearly a bad plant. But what about that other well-known invasive, purple loosestrife? Far from unattractive, it is lovely in a flowerbed and positively stunning en masse. If purple loosestrife is so beautiful, why are we not thrilled to have it spread? Unfortunately, it has been at the expense of less aggressive native plants, growing so rampantly that many less vigorous native plants can't survive.

Again, you might wonder why we need so many different plants. The reasons are sometimes subtle. Aesthetically, of course, variety is desirable. More practically, plants, as well as animals and microorganisms, keep our planet alive and healthy, running like an efficient business. They purify our water, feed the animals we eat, and provide us with key ingredients for nearly 80% of our medications. And an enormous variety of plants are required to accomplish this extraordinary feat.

Purple loosestrife and cheatgrass, two of the most aggressive non-native plants in North America, provide excellent examples of the exotic plants' threat to the delicate balance of our natural environment. Purple loosestrife spreads and multiplies aggressively, each plant producing at least 200,000 seeds, each seed viable for up to 10 years, even under 2 feet of water. It has no natural predators in North America. With little chance against this efficient propagating machine, other plants are quickly overwhelmed. An example of a plant that has suffered is the cattail. Muskrats use cattails as both building material and food. Muskrats in turn are eaten by mink, owls, and hawks. Muskrats also contribute to their watery environment by clearing openings in the marshes, so that submerged aquatic plants can grow. A variety of insects feed on this submerged vegetation, and these insects are an important food source for wildfowl. Efficiently, these wildfowl use the abandoned muskrat lodges to build their nests. The muskrat is not able to survive in wetlands that have been choked with purple loosestrife, and so the chain is broken at the first link.

Highly flammable, non-native cheatgrass is another troublesome invasive weed. Over the last hundred years it has aggressively devoured grassland overgrazed by cattle. Where established, serious fires occur every three to five years, rather than the usual 60 to 110 years. At this frequency, native sagebrush is unable to regenerate, leaving the indigenous sage grouse without their primary source of food — the insects that live in the sagebrush. Not only have sage grouse populations been devastated, but jackrabbit populations, which depend on sage for cover, are severely diminished. And these jackrabbits are the primary food source for eagles. Consider these facts:

- Every day 4,600 acres of public natural areas are lost to invasive exotics.
- Purple loosestrife infests wetlands in 48 states, overwhelming at least 44 native plants species. It now covers about 400,000 acres of Federal land.
- Cheatgrass covers over 101 million acres in the U.S. and is now the dominant plant in the Intermountain West.

❧ Almost as much land is consumed each year by non-natives as is consumed by fire.

❧ Invasives cover an estimated 100 million acres in the U.S., an area about the size of California, and spread at the rate of about 14 million acres per year.

What does this mean for the responsible home gardener? Although most non-native plants are *not* invasive and are themselves easily overwhelmed by native species, periodically contact local Native Plant societies, Cooperative Extension Services, or a national environmental organization for new advice about invasives. If you know which plants are invasive or about to join the list, don't plant them. If any new plants are spreading aggressively in your garden, curtail their spread or remove them altogether, and don't share them with your friends. Note that plants that are not considered invasive in one area may be a serious problem in another because of differences in such natural features as climate or soil.

If the following list does not contain a contact in your state or province, seek advice from the society in a neighboring region, as their information generally covers a very broad area.

ALABAMA

Wildflowers of Alabama
www.auburn.edu/~deancar

ALASKA

Alaska Native Plant Society
P. O. Box 141613, Anchorage, AK 99514-1613
907-333-8212
www.alaskarafts.com/pages/anps.htm

ARIZONA

Arizona Native Plant Society
P. O. Box 41206, Sun Station, Tucson, AZ 85717
www.aznps.org

ARKANSAS

Arkansas Native Plant Society
P. O. Box 250250, Little Rock, AR 72225
501-279-4705 | *www.anps.org*

CALIFORNIA

California Native Plant Society
1722 J Street, Suite 17, Sacramento, CA 95814
916-447-2677 | *www.cnps.org*

COLORADO

Colorado Native Plant Society
P. O. Box 200, Fort Collins, CO 80522-0200
http://carbon.cudenver.edu/~shill/conps.html

CONNECTICUT

Connecticut Botanical Society
55 Harvest Lane, Glastonbury, CT 06033
860-633-7557 | *www.vfr.com/cbs*

Connecticut Chapter
New England Wild Flower Society
www.newfs.org/chapters.html

DELAWARE

Delaware Native Plant Society
P. O. Box 369, Dover, DE 19903
www.delawarenativeplants.org

DISTRICT OF COLUMBIA

Botanical Society of Washington
Botany Department, MRC 166
Smithsonian Institution,
Washington, DC 20560-0166
www.fred.net/kathy/bsw.html

FLORIDA

Florida Native Plant Society
P. O. Box 278, Melbourne, FL 32902
772-462-0000 | *www.fnps.org*

GEORGIA

Georgia Native Plant Society
P. O. Box 422085, Atlanta, GA 30342-2085
770-343-6000 | *www.gnps.org*

HAWAII

Native Hawaiian Plant Society
www.angelfire.com/hi4/nhps

IDAHO

Idaho Native Plant Society
P. O. Box 9451, Boise, ID 83707-3451
www.idahonativeplants.org

ILLINOIS

Illinois Native Plant Society
Forest Glen Preserve
20301 E. 900 North Road, Westville, IL 61883
217-662-2142 | *www.inhs.uiuc.edu/inps*

INDIANA

Indiana Native Plant & Wildflower Society
www.inpaws.org

IOWA

Iowa Prairie Network
www.iowaprairienetwork.org

KANSAS

Kansas Wildflower Society
R.L. McGregor Herbarium
University of Kansas
2045 Constant Avenue, Lawrence, KS 66047

KENTUCKY

Kentucky Native Plant Society
www.knps.org

LOUISIANA

Louisiana Native Plant Society
www.lnps.org

MAINE

Maine Chapter
New England Wild Flower Society
www.newfs.org/chapters.html

MARYLAND

Maryland Native Plant Society
P. O. Box 4877, Silver Spring, MD 20914
www.mdflora.org

MASSACHUSETTS

New England Wild Flower Society
180 Hemenway Road, Framingham, MA 01701
508-877-7630 | *www.newfs.org*

MICHIGAN

Michigan Botanical Club
University of Michigan Herbarium
North University Building
1205 N. University, Ann Arbor, MI 48109-1057
www.michbotclub.org

Wildflower Association of Michigan
www.wildflowersmich.org

MINNESOTA

Minnesota Native Plant Society
University of Minnesota
220 Biological Science Center
1445 Gortner Avenue, St. Paul, MN 55108-1020
www.stolaf.edu/depts/biology/mnps

MISSISSIPPI

Mississippi Native Plant Society
Crosby Arboretum
P. O. Box 1639, Picayune, MS 39466
601-799-2311
www.msstate.edu/dept/crec/camnps.html

Mississippi Native Plant Society
Coastal Plains Chapter
www.mnpscp.gulfcoast-gardening.com

MISSOURI

Missouri Native Plant Society
P.O Box 20073, St. Louis, MO 63144-0073
314-577-9522
www.missouri.edu/~umo_herb/monps

MONTANA

Montana Native Plant Society
P. O. Box 8783, Missoula, MT 59807-8783
www.umt.edu/mnps

NEVADA

State of Nevada
Department of Conservation & Natural Resources
1550 East College Parkway, Suite 137
Carson City, NV 89706-7921
775-687-4245 | *http://heritage.nv.gov*

NEW HAMPSHIRE

New Hampshire Chapter
New England Wild Flower Society
www.newfs.com/chapters.html

NEW JERSEY

The Native Plant Society of New Jersey
Cook College
102 Ryders Lane, New Brunswick, NJ 08901
www.npsnj.org

NEW MEXICO

Native Plant Society of New Mexico
http://npsnm.unm.edu

NEW YORK

New York Flora Association
New York State Museum
3140 CEC, Albany, NY 12230
www.nyflora.org

Niagara Frontier Botanical Society
Buffalo Museum of Science
1020 Humboldt Parkway, Buffalo, NY 14211
www.acsu.buffalo.edu/~insrisg/botany

NORTH CAROLINA

North Carolina Wildflower Preservation Society
North Carolina Botanical Garden
P. O. Box 3375 Totten Center
University of North Carolina
Chapel Hill, NC 27599-3375
www.ncwildflower.org

OHIO

Ohio Native Plant Society
6 Louise Drive, Chagrin Falls, Ohio 44022
440-338-6622
http://dir.gardenweb.com/directory/onps1

Native Plant Society of Northeastern Ohio
640 Cherry Park Oval, Aurora, OH 44202
330-562-4053
http://groups.msn.com/NativePlantSocietyofNortheastOhio

OKLAHOMA

Oklahoma Native Plant Society
Tulsa Garden Center
2435 S. Peoria, Tulsa, OK 74114
918-747-0735 | *www.usao.edu/~onps*

OREGON

Native Plant Society of Oregon
P. O. Box 902, Eugene, OR 97440-0902
www.npsoregon.org

PENNSYLVANIA

Pennsylvania Native Plant Society
Box 281, State College, PA 16801
www.pawildflower.org

RHODE ISLAND

Rhode Island Wild Plant Society
PO Box 114, Peacedale, RI 02883-0114
401-783-5895 | *www.riwps.org*

Rhode Island Chapter
New England Wild Flower Society
www.newfs.com/chapters.html

SOUTH CAROLINA

South Carolina Native Plant Society
P. O. Box 759, Pickens, SC 29671
864-868-7798 | *www.scnps.org*

SOUTH DAKOTA

Great Plains Native Plant Society
P. O. Box 461, Hot Springs, SD 57747-0461
cascade@gwtc.net

TENNESSEE

The Wildflower Society
Goldsmith Civic Garden Center
750 Cherry Road, Memphis, TN 38119-4699
901-685-1566

TEXAS

Lady Bird Johnson Wildflower Center
4801 La Crosse Avenue, Austin, TX 78739-1702
512-292-4200 | *www.wildflower.org*

Native Plant Society of Texas
P. O. Box 891, Georgetown, TX 78627-0891
512-868-8799 | *www.npsot.org*

UTAH

Utah Native Plant Society
P. O. Box 520041, Salt Lake City, UT 84152-0041
801-272-3275 | *www.unps.org*

VERMONT

Vermont Botanical and Bird Clubs
959 Warren Road, Eden, VT 05652
802-635-7794

Vermont Chapter
New England Wild Flower Society
www.newfs.org/chapters.html

VIRGINIA

Virginia Native Plant Society
Blandy Experimental Farm
400 Blandy Farm Lane, Unit 2
Boyce, VA 22620
540-837-1600 | *www.vnps.org*

WASHINGTON

Washington Native Plant Society
6310 N.E. 74th Street, Suite 215E
Seattle, WA 98115
206-527-3210 | *www.wnps.org*

WEST VIRGINIA

West Virginia Native Plant Society
P. O. Box 75403, Charleston, WV 25443
www.wvnps.org

Eastern Panhandle Native Plant Society
P. O. Box 1268, Shepherdstown, WV 25443
www.epnps.org

WISCONSIN

Botanical Club of Wisconsin
Wisconsin Academy of Arts, Sciences, and Letters
1922 University Avenue, Madison, WI 53705
www.botany.wisc.edu/herbarium/BCWindex.html

WYOMING

Wyoming Native Plant Society
P. O. Box 3452, Laramie, WY 82070
www.uwadmnweb.uwyo.edu/wyndd/wnps_home.htm

CANADA

North American Native Plant Society
P. O. Box 84, Station D
Etobicoke, ON M9A 4X1
416-680-6280 | *www.nanps.org*

ALBERTA

Alberta Native Plant Council
Box 52099, Garneau Postal Outlet
Edmonton, AB T6G 2T5
www.anpc.ab.ca

BRITISH COLUMBIA

Native Plant Society of British Columbia
2012 William Street, Vancouver BC V5L 2X6
604-255-5719 | *www.npsbc.org*

MANITOBA

Native Orchid Conservation, Inc.
117 Morier Avenue, Winnipeg, MB R2M 0C8
204-231-1160 | *www.nativeorchid.com*

NEWFOUNDLAND

The Wildflower Society of Newfoundland and Labrador
MUN Botanical Garden
Memorial University of Newfoundland
St. John's, NF A1C 5S7
www.chem.mun.ca/~hclase/wf

NOVA SCOTIA

Nova Scotia Wild Flora Society
Nova Scotia Museum of Natural History
1747 Summer Street, Halifax, NS B3H 3A6
www.chebucto.ns.ca/~nswfs

ONTARIO

Waterloo-Wellington Wildflower Society
Department of Botany
University of Guelph, Guelph, ON N1G 2W1
www.uoguelph.ca/~botcal

QUEBEC

Flora Quebeca
83 rue Chenier, Saint-Eustache, PQ J7R 1W9
www.floraquebeca.qc.ca

SASKATCHEWAN

Native Plant Society of Saskatchewan
P. O. Box 21099, Saskatchewan, SK S7H 5N9
306-668-3940 | *www.npss.sk.ca*

USDA Plant Hardiness Zone Map

The United States Department of Agriculture (USDA) created this map to give gardeners a helpful tool for selecting and cultivating plants. The map divides North America into 11 zones based on each area's average minimum winter temperature. Zone 1 is the coldest, and Zone 11, the warmest. Once you determine your zone, you can use that information to select plants that are most likely to thrive in your climate.

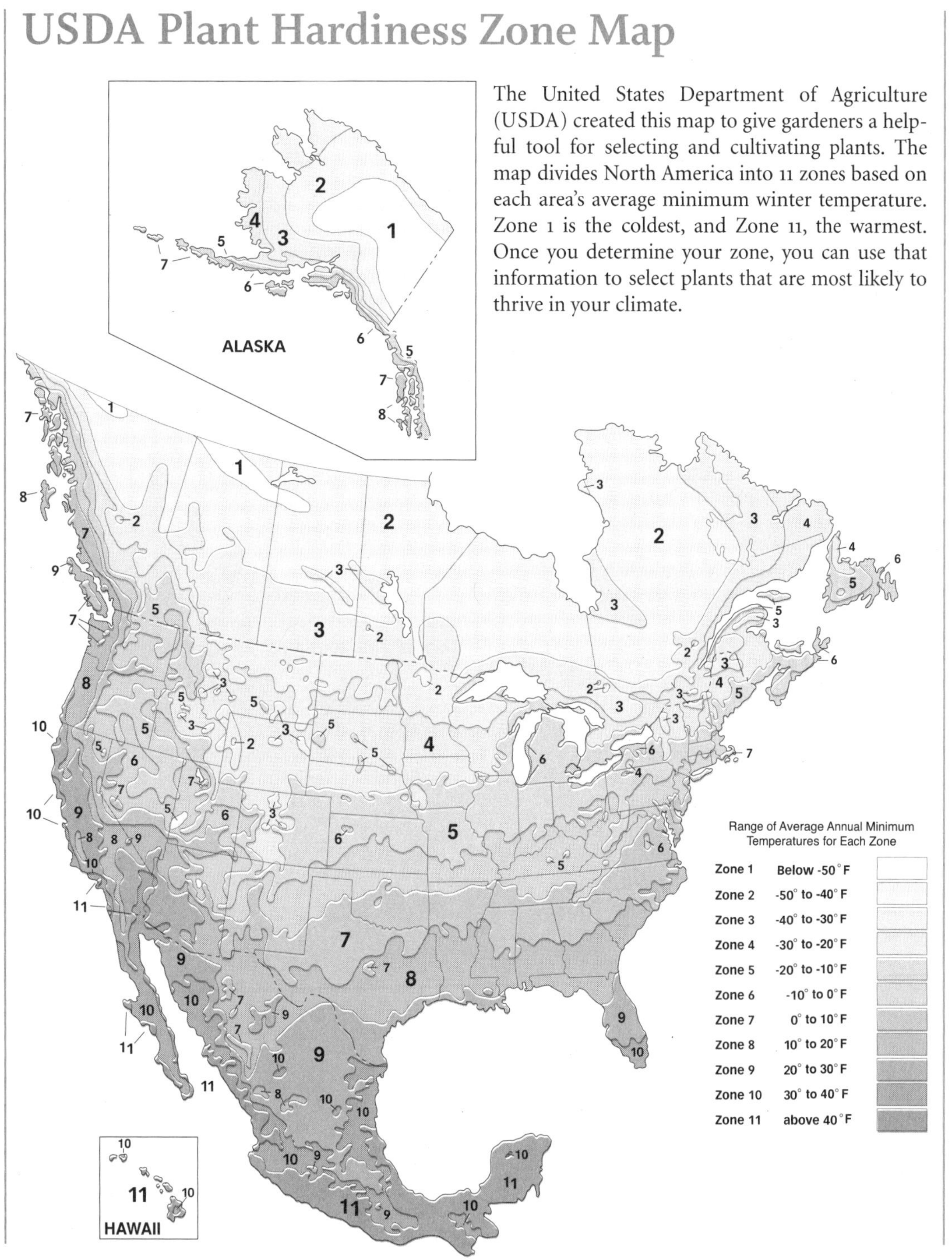

AHS Plant Heat Zones

The following information is adapted with permission from the American Horticultural Society's website (www.ahs.org). Refer to this website for more information and a color-coded map to locate your heat zone. To order a map, go to their website or call (800) 777-7931 ext. 110. A color version of the map also appears in Lewis and Nancy Hill's *The Flower Gardener's Bible* (Storey Publishing, 2003).

Use the AHS Plant Heat-Zone Map in the same way that you do the USDA Hardiness Zone Map. Start by finding your town or city on the map. The 12 zones of the map indicate the average number of days each year that a given region experiences "heat days"—that is, temperatures over 86°F (30°C). That is the point at which plants begin suffering physiological damage from heat. The zones range from Zone 1 (less than one heat day) to Zone 12 (more than 210 heat days).

In this book, most plants have received both USDA Hardiness Zone and AHS Heat Zone designations. For example, a tulip may be listed as 3–8, H 8–1. If you live in USDA Zone 7 and AHS Zone 7, you will know that you can leave tulips outdoors in your garden year-round. An ageratum may be 10–11, H 12–1, indicating that it can withstand summer heat throughout the United States, but will overwinter only in our warmest zones. An English wallflower may be 5–8, H 6–1. It is relatively cold hardy, but can't tolerate extreme summer heat.

It will take several years for a majority of our garden plants to receive heat-zone ratings. After almost 40 years, the American Horticultural Society is still perfecting the zone ratings for the Hardiness Map. Plants vary in their ability to withstand heat, not only from genus to genus but even among individual plants of the same genus. Unusual seasons—with fewer or more hot days than normal, for example—invariably affect results in your garden. And even more than with the hardiness zones, gardeners may find that many plants survive outside their designated heat zone, because so many other factors complicate a plant's reaction to heat.

Most important, the AHS Plant Heat-Zone ratings assume that adequate water is supplied to the roots of the plant at all times. The accuracy of the zone coding can be substantially distorted by a lack of water, even for a brief period in the life of the plant. Although some plants are naturally more drought tolerant than others, horticulture by definition means growing plants in a protected, artificial environment where stresses are different from those in nature. No plant can survive becoming completely dessicated. Heat damage is always linked to an insufficient amount of water being available to the plant. Herbaceous plants are 80 to 90 percent water, and woody plants are about 50 percent water. Plant tissues must contain enough water to keep their cells turgid and to sustain the plant's processes of chemical and energy transport. Watering directly at the roots of a plant (through drip irrigation for instance) conserves water that would be lost to evaporation or runoff during overhead watering. In addition, plants take in water more efficiently when it is applied to their roots rather than to their leaves. Mulching also helps conserve water. Other environmental and cultural factors, such as soil aeration, light, day length, air movement, surrounding structures, and soil pH, can affect the health of plants and skew the heat-zone rating. For this reason, it is always important to select plants appropriate to the conditions of the site.

Average Last Frost Dates

United States

Canada (selected cities)

BRITISH COLUMBIA

Chilliwack	Apr. 6
Dawson Creek	June 5
Kamloops	May 1
Kelowna	May 19
Nanaimo	Apr. 28
Port Alberni	May 8
Prince George	June 4
Terrace	May 5
Vancouver	Mar. 28
Vernon	Apr. 29
Victoria	Apr. 19

NORTHWEST TERRITORY & YUKON

Whitehorse	June 11
Yellowknife	May 27

ALBERTA

Athabaska	June 1
Calgary	May 23
Edmonton	May 7
Grande Prairie	May 18
Lethbridge	May 17
Medicine Hat	May 16
Red Deer	May 25

SASKATCHEWAN

Moose Jaw	May 20
Prince Albert	June 2
Regina	May 21
Saskatoon	May 21
Weyburn	May 22

MANITOBA

Brandon	May 27
The Pas	May 27
Thompson	June 15
Winnipeg	May 25

ONTARIO

Barrie	May 26
Hamilton	Apr. 29
Kingston	May 2
London	May 9
Ottawa	May 6
Owen Sound	May 12
Parry Sound	May 17
Peterborough	May 18
St. Catharines	May 2
Sudbury	May 17
Thunder Bay	June 1
Timmins	June 8
Toronto	May 9
Windsor	Apr. 25

QUEBEC

Baie Comeau	May 28
Chicoutimi	May 17
Montreal	May 3
Quebec	May 13
Rimouski	May 13
Sherbrooke	June 1
Trois-Rivieres	May 19
Thetford Mines	May 28

NEW BRUNSWICK

Bathurst	May 19
Edmundston	May 28
Fredericton	May 20
Grand Falls	May 24
Moncton	May 24
Saint John	May 18

PRINCE EDWARD ISLAND

Charlottetown	May 17
Summerside	May 9
Tignish	May 23

NOVA SCOTIA

Halifax	May 6
Kentville	May 16
Shelburne	May 14
Sydney	May 24
Yarmouth	May 1

NEWFOUNDLAND

Corner Brook	May 22
Grand Falls	June 2
St. John's	June 2

Glossary

Acid soil Having a pH level below 7.0.

Alkaline soil Having a pH level above 7.0.

Annual A plant that grows from seed, flowers, produces seed, and dies, all in one year.

Axil The angle between a leaf stalk or flower stalk, and the stem or branch from which it is growing.

Basal cutting A cutting taken from the base of a plant.

Biennial A plant with a two-year life span, germinating and producing top growth in the first year, flowering, producing seed, and dying in the second.

Bract A leaflike part, most often located at the base of a flower or inflorescence.

Bulb A bud that contains food stores and grows underground, producing leaves and flowers that appear above ground.

Bulbil A miniature bulblike bud or bulblet that forms in the leaf axil of some bulbous plants, and can develop into a new plant if planted.

Bulblet A miniature bulblike bud that forms below ground on the parent bulb, and can develop into a new plant if planted.

Calyx A group of small, leaflike or petallike parts surrounding the true petals of a flower.

Compost Organic matter that has decomposed over time to form a crumbly substance with which soil is enriched and plants are fed.

Corm A fleshy underground stem, similar to a bulb.

Cormel A miniature corm that is produced from the base of a parent corm.

Cormlet Another name for a cormel.

Cotyledon Commonly called a seed leaf, the first leaves to appear on a seedling, containing enough nutrients to nourish the new seedling for a short period until it develops true leaves.

Damping-off A potentially lethal fungal disease most often affecting young seedlings.

Deadhead The removal of flower heads after blooming.

Eye A bud from which new growth will sprout.

Heaving The process of a plant being pushed out of the soil that occurs when the ground alternately freezes and thaws in winter.

Humus Decomposed organic matter.

Inflorescence A flower cluster.

In situ This Latin term is usually used to mean sowing a seed outdoors where the plant will flower.

Limy soil Alkaline soil, or soil having a pH level above 7.0.

Mulch Organic or inorganic material that is laid over the soil in order to reduce moisture evaporation, to keep the soil cool in summer or to warm it in early spring, to restrict growth of weeds, protect delicate roots—the uses and benefits of mulch are many and varied.

Neutral soil Having a pH level of 7.0.

Overwinter The process of bringing frost-tender plants through the winter by moving them indoors—the horticultural equivalent of Canadians spending the winter in Florida.

Panicle A loose flower cluster that begins blooming at the bottom, with uppermost flowers blooming later. The cluster does not end in a terminal flower.

Perennial A plant that lives for more than two years, generally referring to herbaceous plants.

pH The scale used for measuring the degree of acidity or alkalinity of soil.

Pinching out The removal of growth at the tips of a plant.

Pricking out Transplanting seedlings, usually from a communal growing situation, such as a flat, to individual pots.

Raceme A long, slender flower cluster with one main stem to which individual flowers are attached by short stalks. There is no terminal flower.

Rhizome An underground or rootlike stem that stores food, produces roots below ground, and leaves and flowers above.

Rosette A radiating formation of foliage, often grown at the end of a short stem.

Self-seed The process of a plant naturally releasing its seed, which readily germinates and produces new plants.

Sidedressing See Topdressing.

Spadix A dense, upright flowering spike resembling an exclamation mark, usually surrounded by a spathe.

Spathe One or more large, hoodlike bracts partially surrounding a spadix or other inflorescence.

Spike A long flower cluster whose individual blooms are attached to the main stem without a stalk.

Stake Support by the means of upright props to which stems can be tied.

Topdressing The application of fertilizer or organic matter around a plant, the material being left on the soil surface rather than being dug in. Also known as sidedressing.

Tuber A short, swollen underground stem in which food is stored and from which roots and leaves grow.

Umbel A usually flat-topped cluster of flowers whose individual stems grow from a central point at the main stem, like the spokes of an umbrella.

Metric Conversion Chart

WHEN THE GIVEN MEASUREMENT IS	TO CONVERT TO	MULTIPLY BY
inches	centimeters	2.54
feet	meters	0.305
mils	millimeters	0.254
square feet	square meters	0.093
ounces	grams	31.1
pounds	kilograms	0.373
tons	metric tons	0.907
gallons	liters	3.785
°F	°C	°F – 32 × 5/9

Common to Botanic Names

Common names are on the left; botanic names, on the right.

Aaron's beard	*Hypericum calycinum*
Aaron's rod bush pea	*Thermopsis villosa*
Aconite	*Aconitum*
Adam-and-Eve	*Erythronium americanum*
Adam's needle	*Yucca filamentosa* *Yucca smalliana*
Adder's tongue	*Erythronium*
African blood lily	*Haemanthus*
African blue lily	*Agapanthus*
African corn lily	*Ixia*
African daisy	*Arctotis* *Calendula officinalis* *Dimorphotheca* *Gerbera jamesonii* *Lonas* *Osteospermum fruitcosum*
African hairbell	*Dierama*
African lily	*Agapanthus africanus* *Moraea*
African marigold	*Tagetes* African Group
Aleutian maidenhair fern	*Adiantum aleuticum*
Alfilaria	*Erodium cicutarium*
Alkanet	*Anchusa*
Allegheny vine	*Adlumia fungosa*
Allgood	*Chenopodium bonus-henricus*
Alpine anemone	*Pulsatilla alpina*
Alpine snowbell	*Soldanella alpina*
Alpine violet	*Cyclamen*
Alpine wallflower	*Erysimum linifolium*
Alum root	*Heuchera*
American cow parsley	*Heracleum sphondylium* ssp. *montanum*
American cowslip	*Dodecatheon*
American ipecac	*Gillenia ipecacuanha* *Gillenia stipulata*
American lotus	*Nelumbo lutea*
American marigold	*Tagetes erecta*
Amethyst violet	*Browallia*
Amole	*Chlörogalum*
Amur silver grass	*Miscanthus floridulus*
Anderson's holly fern	*Polystichum andersonii*
Angel's fishing rod	*Dierama*
Angel's trumpet	*Datura innoxia*
Angels' trumpets	*Brugmansia, B. arborea*
Angel wings	*Caladium, C. bicolor*
Anise	*Myrrhis odorata* *Pimpinella anisum*
Anise fern	*Myrrhis odorata*
Annual aster	*Callistephus*
Annual carnation	*Dianthus chinensis*
Annual delphinium	*Consolida ajacis*
Annual mallow	*Lavatera trimestris* *Malope*
Annual phlox	*Phlox drummondii*
Annual pink	*Dianthus chinensis*
Annual poinsettia	*Euphorbia cyathophora*
Annual vinca	*Catharanthus*
Annunciation lily	*Lilium candidum*
Apple of Peru	*Nicandra, N. physalodes*
Arborvitae fern	*Selaginella braunii*
Archangel	*Angelica archangelica*
Arctic poppy	*Papaver alpinum* *Papaver croceum*
Argemony	*Argemone*
Arguta	*Actinidia arguta*
Artichoke	*Cynara scolymus*
Arum lily	*Zantedeschia*
Asarabacca	*Asarum*
Asiatic poppy	*Meconopsis*
Atamasco lily	*Zephyranthes atamasca*
Atlantic camassia	*Camassia scilloides*
Aubretia	*Aubrieta*
Australian everlasting	*Rhodanthe manglesii*
Australian sarsaparilla	*Hardenbergia violacea*
Autumn crocus	*Colchicum*
Autumn daffodil	*Sternbergia*
Autumn fern	*Dryopteris erythrosora*
Avalanche lily	*Erythronium grandiflorum* *Erythronium montanum*
Avens	*Geum*
Aztec lily	*Sprekelia formosissima*
Aztec marigold	*Tagetes erecta*
Azure sage	*Perovskia atriplicifolia*
Baboon flower	*Babiana*

Baboon root	*Babiana*
Baby-blue-eyes	*Nemophila menziesii*
Baby's breath	*Gypsophila elegans* *Gypsophila paniculata*
Baby snapdragon	*Linaria*
Bachelor's button	*Centaurea cyanus* *Craspedia*
Bachelor's buttons	*Ranunculus aconitifolius*
Balloon flower	*Platycodon, P. grandiflorus*
Balloon vine	*Cardiospermum halicacabum*
Balm	*Melissa*
Balsam	*Impatiens*
Balsam apple	*Momordica balsamina*
Balsam pear	*Momordica charantia*
Bamboo lily	*Lilium japonicum*
Banana	*Musa*
Barberton daisy	*Gerbera, G. jamesonii*
Barley	*Hordeum*
Barren strawberry	*Waldsteinia fragariodes*
Barrenwort	*Epimedium*
Basil	*Ocimum basilicum*
Basket flower	*Centaurea americana* *Hymenocallis, H. narcissiflora*
Basket of gold	*Aurinia saxatilis*
Bath asparagus	*Ornithogalum pyrenaicum*
Bean	*Phaseolus*
Beard-tongue	*Clintonia uniflora* *Penstemon eriantherus* *Penstemon gracilis* *Penstemon grandiflorus* *Penstemon rostriflorus* *Penstemon strictus*
Bear grass	*Xerophyllum tenax*
Bear's breeches	*Acanthus, A. montanus*
Beauty-of-the-night	*Mirabilis jalapa*
Bedstraw	*Galium*
Bee balm	*Monarda, M. didyma*
Beefsteak plant	*Perilla frutescens* 'Atropurpurea'
Beggars tick	*Bidens*
Belladonna lily	*Amaryllis belladonna*
Bellflower	*Campanula*
Bells of Ireland	*Moluccella laevis*
Bellwort	*Uvularia*
Belvedere	*Bassia scoparia*
Bengal lily	*Crinum bulbispermum*
Benne	*Sesamum indicum*
Bent grass	*Agrostis*
Bergamot	*Monarda didyma*
Bethlehem sage	*Pulmonaria saccharata*
Betony	*Stachys*
Beverly bells	*Rehmannia elata*
Bidi-bidi	*Acaena*
Billy buttons	*Craspedia*
Bindweed	*Convolvulus*
Bird's-eye	*Veronica*
Bird's eyes	*Gilia tricolor*
Bird's-foot trefoil	*Trigonella ornithopodioides*
Bird's-nest fern	*Asplenium nidus*
Birthroot	*Trillium*
Bishop's cap	*Mitella*
Bishop's hat	*Epimedium, E. grandiflorum*
Bishops' mitre	*Epimedium*
Bishop's weed	*Aegopodium* *Ammi*
Bishop's wort	*Stachys officinalis*
Bistort	*Persicaria amplexicaulis* *Persicaria bistorta*
Bittercress	*Cardamine*
Bitter Indian	*Tropaeolum*
Bitterroot	*Lewisia rediviva*
Blackberry lily	*Belamcanda chinensis*
Black cohosh	*Cimicifuga racemosa*
Black cumin	*Nigella sativa*
Black-eyed Susan	*Rudbeckia fulgida* *Rudbeckia hirta*
Black-eyed Susan vine	*Thunbergia alata*
Blackroot	*Veronicastrum virginicum*
Black snakeroot	*Cimicifuga racemosa*
Blackwort	*Symphytum officinale*
Bladder vetch	*Anthyllis*
Blanket flower	*Gaillardia, G. pulchella*
Blazing star	*Liatris, L. spicata* *Mentzelia lindleyi* *Tritonia*
Bleeding heart	*Dicentra, D. spectabilis*
Blister cress	*Erysimum perofskianum*
Blood lily	*Haemanthus*
Bloodroot	*Sanguinaria*
Bluebead	*Clintonia uniflora*

Bluebell	*Campanula rotundifolia* *Eustoma grandiflorum* *Hyacinthoides* *Nicandra pysalodes* *Scilla campanulata* *Wahlenbergia albomarginata*
Bluebells	*Aquilegia vulgaris* *Mertensia macdougalii* *Mertensia virginica* *Polemonium reptans* *Tradescantia virginiana*
Bluebonnet	*Lupinus subcarnosus* *Lupinus texensis*
Bluebottle	*Centaurea cyanus*
Blue buttons	*Knautia arvensis*
Blue cohosh	*Caulophyllum thalictroides*
Blue cupidone	*Catananche*
Blue daisy	*Felicia, F. amelloides*
Blue-dicks	*Dichlostemma pulchellum*
Blue-eyed grass	*Sisyrinchium graminoides*
Blue-eyed Mary	*Collinsia verna* *Omphalodes verna*
Blue false indigo	*Baptisia australis*
Blue hair grass	*Koeleria glauca*
Blue June grass	*Koeleria macrantha*
Blue lace flower	*Trachymene coerulea*
Bluelips	*Collinsia grandiflora*
Blue marguerite	*Felicia, F. bergeriana*
Blue oat grass	*Helictotrichon sempervirens*
Blue poppy	*Meconopsis betonicifolia*
Blue squill	*Hyacinthoides hispanica* *Scilla natalensis*
Blue star	*Amsonia, A. ciliata*
Blue star creeper	*Solenopsis axillaris*
Blue succory	*Catananche caerulea*
Blue thimble flower	*Gilia capitata*
Blue throatwort	*Trachelium caeruleum*
Bluets	*Hedyotis, H. caerulea*
Blue wax flower	*Cerinthe major purpurescens*
Bluewings	*Torenia fournieri*
Bog star	*Parnassia*
Bonavist	*Lablab purpureus*
Boneset	*Eupatorium perfoliatum*
Bonnet bellflower	*Codonopsis*
Bouncing Bet	*Saponaria officinalis*
Bowles' golden grass	*Milium effusum* 'Aureum'
Bowman's root	*Gillenia trifoliata*
Brass buttons	*Cotula, C. coronopifolia*
Braun's holly fern	*Polystichum braunii*
Brazilian jasmine	*Mandevilla sanderi*
Brazilian plume	*Justicia carnea*
Bridal wreath	*Francoa*
Bride's bonnet	*Clintonia uniflora*
Broad buckler fern	*Dryopteris dilatata*
Brompton stock	*Matthiola incana*
Brooklime	*Veronica*
Broom corn millet	*Panicum miliaceum*
Buckler fern	*Dryopteris*
Bugbane	*Cimicifuga*
Bugle lily	*Watsonia borbonica*
Bugleweed	*Ajuga, A. reptans*
Bugloss	*Anchusa arvensis* *Brunnera macrophylla* *Echium pininana* *Echium vulgare* *Mertensia maritima* *Pulmonaria officinalis*
Bulrush	*Cyperus papyrus*
Bur marigold	*Bidens*
Burnet	*Sanguisorba*
Burnet saxifrage	*Pimpinella saxifraga*
Burning bush	*Bassia scoparia* f. *trichophylla* *Dictamnus, D. albus*
Bush violet	*Browallia, B. speciosa*
Busy Lizzie	*Impatiens, I. walleriana*
Butter and eggs	*Linaria vulgaris*
Butterbur	*Petasites*
Buttercup	*Ranunculus*
Butterfly flower	*Schizanthus*
Butterfly iris	*Moraea*
Butterfly lily	*Hedychium coronarium*
Butterfly tulip	*Calochortus*
Butterfly weed	*Asclepias tuberosa*
Butterwort	*Pinguicula*
Button snakeroot	*Liatris*
Calamint	*Calamintha*
California bluebell	*Phacelia campanularia*
California fuchsia	*Zauschneria*
California poppy	*Eschscholzia, E. californica* *Platystemon*
California tree poppy	*Romneya*
Calla lily	*Zantedeschia*
Calliopsis	*Coreopsis tinctoria*

Camass	*Camassia, C. cusickii*
Camosh	*Camassia*
Campion	*Lychnis*
	Silene
Canary-bird flower	*Tropaeolum*
Canary-bird vine	*Tropaeolum*
Canary creeper	*Tropaeolum peregrinum*
Canary grass	*Phalaris arundinaceae*
Canchalagua	*Centaurium*
Candylily	*Pardancanda norissi*
Candytuft	*Iberis*
Canterbury bells	*Campanula medium*
Cape daisy	*Arctotis fastuosa*
	Felicia amelloides
	Osteospermum
Cape forget-me-not	*Anchusa capensis*
Cape fuchsia	*Phygelius capensis*
Cape gooseberry	*Physalis peruviana*
Cape lily	*Crinum bulbispermum*
	Crinum × powellii
Cape marigold	*Dimorphotheca*
Cape stock	*Heliophila*
Caraway	*Carum, C. carvi*
Cardinal climber	*Ipomoea quamoclit*
	Ipomoea × multifida
Cardinal flower	*Lobelia cardinalis*
Cardoon	*Cynara cardunculus*
Carnation	*Dianthus*
Carolina lupine	*Thermopsis villosa*
Cartwheel flower	*Heracleum mantegazzianum*
Castor bean	*Ricinus communis*
Castor-oil plant	*Ricinus communis*
Catchfly	*Lychnis*
	Silene
Cathedral bells	*Cobaea scandens*
Catherine wheel	*Haemanthus coccineus*
Catmint	*Nepeta*
Catnip	*Nepeta cataria*
Cat's ear	*Calochortus*
	Antennaria
Celandine	*Chelidonium majus*
	Macleaya cordata
	Stylophorum diphyllum
Celandine poppy	*Chelidonium majus*
	Macleaya cordata
	Stylophorum diphyllum
Centaury	*Centaurium, C. erythraea*

Chameleon plant	*Houttuynia cordata* 'Chameleon'
Chamise lily	*Erythronium grandilforum*
Chatham Island forget-me-not	*Myosotidium, M. hortensia*
Checkerbloom	*Sidalcea malviflora*
Checkered lily	*Fritillaria meleagris*
Checker mallow	*Sidalciea*
Cheddar pink	*Dianthus gratianopolitanus*
Cherry pie	*Heliotropium arborescens*
Chervil	*Ammi visnaga*
	Anthriscus cerefolium
	Anthriscus sylvestris
	Myrrhis odorata
Chickabiddy	*Maurandya scandens*
Chilean bell flower	*Lapageria*
Chilean bellflower	*Lapageria rosea*
	Nolana
Chilean crocus	*Tecophilaea cyanocrocus*
Chilean glory flower	*Eccremocarpus, E. scaber*
Chilean jasmine	*Mandevilla laxa*
Chile bells	*Lapageria*
Chiming bells	*Mertensia virginica*
China aster	*Callistephus*
China fleece vine	*Persicaria aubertii*
China pink	*Dianthus chinensis*
Chincherinchee	*Ornithogalum thyrsoides*
Chinese bellflower	*Platycodon*
Chinese forget-me-not	*Cynoglossum amabile*
Chinese foxglove	*Rehmannia elata*
Chinese gooseberry	*Actinidia deliciosa*
Chinese kidney bean	*Wisteria sinensis*
Chinese lantern	*Abutilon*
	Physalis alkekengi
Chinese-lantern lily	*Sandersonia aurantiaca*
Chinese parsley	*Coriandrum sativum*
Chinese rhubarb	*Rheum palmatum*
Chinese trumpet flower	*Incarvillea delavayi*
Chinese yam	*Dioscorea batatas*
Chives	*Allium schoenoprasum*
Christmas bells	*Sandersonia aurantiaca*
Christmas candlestick	*Leonotis nepetifolia*
Christmas fern	*Polystichum acrostichoides*
Christmas rose	*Helleborus niger*
Chufa	*Cyperus esculentus*
Cigar flower	*Cuphea ignea*
Cilantro	*Coriandrum*
Cineraria	*Senecio*

Common name	Botanic name
Cinnamon fern	*Osmunda cinnamomea*
Cinnamon vine	*Dioscorea batatas*
Cinquefoil	*Potentilla*
Cleavers	*Galium*
Climbing fumitory	*Adlumia fungosa*
Climbing lily	*Gloriosa*
Climbing nasturtium	*Tropaeolum majus*
Climbing snapdragon	*Asarina antirrhinifolia*
Clock vine	*Thunbergia grandiflora*
Cloud grass	*Agrostis nebulosa*
Clover	*Trifolium*
Coastal wallflower	*Erysimum capitatum*
Coat flower	*Petrorhagia saxifraga*
Cockscomb	*Celosia*
Cocoyam	*Colocasia, C. esculenta*
Cohosh	*Cimicifuga*
Coleus	*Solenostemon*
Colewort	*Crambe cordifolia*
Columbine	*Aquilegia*
Comfrey	*Symphytum*
Common stock	*Matthiola incana*
Compass plant	*Silphium laciniatum*
Coneflower	*Echinacea* *Rudbeckia, R. laciniata*
Copihue	*Lapageria*
Copper tip	*Crocosmia aurea ambig.*
Coral bells	*Heuchera, H. sanguinea*
Coral flower	*Heuchera*
Coral pea	*Hardenbergia*
Coriander	*Coriandrum*
Corn cockle	*Agrostemma*
Corn flag	*Gladiolus italicus*
Cornflower	*Centaurea cyanus*
Corn lily	*Clintonia borealis* *Ixia*
Corn marigold	*Chrysanthemum segetum*
Corn poppy	*Papaver rhoeas*
Cosmea	*Cosmos*
Costa Rica butterfly vine	*Dalechampia dioscoreifolia*
Cottage pink	*Dianthus plumarius*
Cotton grass	*Eriophorum,* *E. angustifolium*
Cowbells	*Digitalis purpurea* *Uvularia*
Cow herb	*Saponaria vaccaria*
Cow parsley	*Anthriscus sylvestris*
Cow-parsnip	*Heracleum*
Cowslip	*Dodecatheon meadia* *Primula auricula* *Primula florindae* *Primula veris* *Pulmonaria officinalis* *Caltha palustris*
Cranesbill	*Geranium*
Crape myrtle	*Lagerstroemia indica*
Crape myrtlette	*Lagerstroemia Hybrids*
Creamcups	*Platystemon*
Creeping buttercup	*Ranunculus repens*
Creeping Charlie	*Lysimachia nummularia* *Sedum acre*
Creeping forget-me-not	*Omphalodes verna*
Creeping Jenny	*Lysimachia nummularia*
Creeping lily	*Gloriosa*
Creeping zinnia	*Sanvitalia, S. procumbens*
Crested hair grass	*Koeleria macrantha*
Crimson clover	*Trifolium incarnatum*
Crimson flag	*Schizostylis coccinea*
Crinum lily	*Crinum*
Crosswort	*Phuopsis stylosa*
Crowfoot	*Ranunculus*
Crown daisy	*Chrysanthemum coronarium*
Crown imperial	*Fritillaria imperialis*
Crown of thorns	*Euphorbia milii*
Crown vetch	*Coronilla, C. varia*
Cuban lily	*Scilla peruviana*
Cuban oregano	*Plectranthus* 'Cuban Oregano'
Cuckoo flower	*Cardamine pratensis* *Lychnis flos-cuculi*
Cuckoo-pint	*Arum maculatum*
Culver's root	*Veronicastrum virginicum*
Cumin	*Cuminum cyminum*
Cup and saucer vine	*Cobaea scandens*
Cup fern	*Dennstaedtia*
Cup flower	*Nierembergia*
Cupid's bower	*Achimenes*
Cupid's dart	*Catananche, C. caerulea*
Cup plant	*Silphium perfoliatum*
Curled mallow	*Malva verticillata*
Curry plant	*Helichrysum italicum*
Cypress vine	*Ipomoea quamoclit*
Daffodil	*Narcissus*

Common name	Botanic name
Daisy	*Bellis* *Leucanthemum vulgare* *Leucanthemum × superbum*
Dame's violet	*Hesperis matronalis*
Dancing girl ginger	*Globba racemosa*
Dandelion	*Crepis incana* *Crepis rubra*
Dasheen	*Colocasia, C. esculenta*
Daylily	*Hemerocallis*
Deadnettle	*Lamium*
Deer fern	*Blechnum spicant*
Desert candle	*Eremurus*
Desert evening primrose	*Oenothera deltoides*
Desert hollyhock	*Sphaeralcea ambigua* var. *rosacea*
Desert mallow	*Sphaeralcea ambigua*
Devil-in-a-bush	*Nigella, N. damascena*
Devil's-claw	*Proboscidea*
Devil's paintbrush	*Emilia coccinea*
Diamond flower	*Ionopsidium acaule*
Dill	*Anethum, A. graveolens*
Dishcloth gourd	*Luffa*
Dittany	*Dictamnus*
Dock	*Rumex*
Dog fennel	*Anthemis*
Dog's-tooth violet	*Erythronium*
Dolichos bean	*Lablab purpureus*
Dragon arum	*Dracunculus, D. vulgaris*
Dragon plant	*Arisaema dracontium* *Dracunculus vulgaris* *Physostegia virginiana*
Dragonroot	*Arisaema dracontium*
Dropwort	*Filipendula, F. vulgaris*
Drummond phlox	*Phlox drummondii*
Drumsticks	*Craspedia globosa*
Dusty miller	*Centaurea cineraria* *Senecio cineraria*
Dutchman's breeches	*Dicentra cucullaria*
Dwarf marigold	*Tagetes tenuifolia*
Dwarf snapdragon	*Chaenorhinum*
Dwarf snowbell	*Soldanella pusilla*
Dyer's woad	*Isatis tinctoria*
Eastern camassia	*Camassia scilloides*
Edelweiss	*Leontopodium, L. alpinum*
Edging lobelia	*Lobelia erinus*
Egyptian star cluster	*Pentas lanceolata*
Elecampane	*Inula helenium*
Elephant ears	*Colocasia esculenta*
Elephant's ears	*Caladium, C. bicolor*
Elephant-tusk	*Proboscidea*
Eleven o'clock	*Portulaca grandiflora*
English daisy	*Bellis perennis*
English marigold	*Calendula officinalis*
English painted fern	*Athyrium otophorum*
English primrose	*Primula vulgaris*
Epazote	*Chenopodium ambrosioides*
Eryngo	*Eryngium*
Estragon	*Artemisia dracunculus*
Eulalia grass	*Miscanthus sinensis*
Evening primrose	*Oenothera, O. biennis*
Evening stock	*Matthiola longipetala*
Evergreen Solomon's seal	*Disporopsis*
Everlasting	*Ammobiumm alatum* *Anaphalis margaritacea* *Antennaria* *Lathyrus grandiflorus* *Sedum telephium*
Everlasting flower	*Helichrysum*
Everlasting pea	*Lathyrus grandiflorus* *Lathyrus latifolius*
Eygptian bean	*Lablab purpureus*
Fairy fan-flower	*Scaevola aemula*
Fairy foxglove	*Erinus*
Fairy lantern	*Calochortus, C. albus*
Fairy lily	*Zephyranthes*
Fairy primrose	*Primula malacoides*
Fairy wallflower	*Erysimum perofskianum*
Fall crocus	*Colchicum*
False alumroot	*Tellima grandiflora*
False aster	*Kalimeris pinnatifida*
False baby's breath	*Galium mollugo*
False chamomile	*Boltonia, B. asteroides*
False coleus	*Perilla frutescens*
False dragon head	*Physostegia, P. virginiana*
False goatsbeard	*Astilbe biternata*
False hellebore	*Veratrum album*
False indigo	*Baptisia*
False lupine	*Thermopsis macrophylla*
False mallow	*Sidalcea* *Sphaeralcea*
False mitrewort	*Tiarella*
False Queen Anne's lace	*Ammi majus* *Anthriscus sylvestris*
False rock cress	*Aubrieta*
False saffron	*Carthamus tinctorius*

Common name	Botanic name
False Solomon's seal	*Smilacina, S. racemosa*
False spikenard	*Smilacina racemosa*
False spiraea	*Astilbe*
False starwort	*Boltonia asteroides* var. *decurrens*
False sunflower	*Helenium autumnale* *Heliopsis, H. helianthoides*
Fameflower	*Talinum*
Fan flower	*Scaevola*
Farewell-to-spring	*Clarkia*
Fathen	*Chenopodium bonus-henricus*
Fawn lily	*Erythronium, E. californicum*
Feather bells	*Stenanthium gramineum*
Feathered columbine	*Thalictrum aquilegifolium*
Feather-fleece	*Stenanthium gramineum* var. *robustum*
Feather grass	*Stipa*
Feather reed grass	*Calamagrostis × acutiflora*
Feathertop	*Pennisetum villosum*
Fennel	*Foeniculum*
Fennel flower	*Nigella*
Fenugreek	*Trigonella foenum-graecum*
Fescue	*Festuca*
Feverfew	*Tanacetum parthenium*
Field poppy	*Papaver rhoeas*
Filaree	*Erodium cicutarium* *Erodium moschatum*
Firebush	*Bassia scoparia*
Fire-cracker flower	*Brodiaea* *Cuphea ignea* *Penstemon barbatus*
Firecracker plant	*Cuphea ignea*
Fire-on-the-mountain	*Euphorbia cyathophora*
Fire pink	*Silene virginica*
Fireweed	*Epilobium angustifolium*
Fire wheels	*Gaillardia pulchella*
Fishtail fern	*Cyrtomium falcatum*
Five-finger	*Potentilla*
Five-fingered maidenhair fern	*Adiantum pedatum*
Five-spot	*Nemophila maculata*
Flame flower	*Tropaeolum*
Flame nettle	*Solenostemon scutellarioides*
Flaming fountain	*Amaranthus tricolor*
Flanders poppy	*Papaver rhoeas*
Flannel flower	*Actinotus, A. helianthi*

Common name	Botanic name
Flax	*Linum*
Flax lily	*Phormium*
Fleabane	*Erigeron*
Fleece flower	*Persicaria*
Flora's paintbrush	*Emilia coccinea*
Florida marigold	*Bidens mitis*
Florist mum	*Chrysanthemum morifolium*
Floss flower	*Ageratum*
Flowering fern	*Osmunda, O. regalis*
Flowering maple	*Abutilon*
Flowering spurge	*Euphorbia corollata*
Flowering tobacco	*Nicotiana alata*
Flower-of-an-hour	*Hibiscus trionum*
Flower of Jove	*Lychnis flos-jovis*
Flower of the Western wind	*Zephyranthes candida*
Foam flower	*Tiarella*
Foamy bells	*× Heucherella*
Forget-me-not	*Myosotis*
Forget-me-not anchusa	*Anchusa capensis* *Brunnera macrophylla*
Fortnight lily	*Moraea bicolor*
Fountain grass	*Pennisetum alopecuroides* *Pennisetum setaceum*
Fountain plant	*Amaranthus tricolor* var. *salicifolius*
Four o'clocks	*Mirabilis jalapa*
Foxglove	*Digitalis, D. purpurea*
Fox's brush	*Centranthus ruber*
Fox-tail barley	*Hordeum jubatum*
Foxtail lily	*Eremurus*
Fraxinella	*Dictamnus, D. albus*
Freckle face	*Hypoestes phyllostachya*
French honeysuckle	*Hedysarum coronarium*
French marigold	*Tagetes French Group*
French parsley	*Anthriscus cerefolium*
French spinach	*Atriplex hortensis*
French willow	*Epilobium angustifolium*
Fried eggs	*Limnanthes douglasii*
Fringe bell	*Shortia soldanelloides*
Fringe cups	*Tellima*
Fringed galax	*Shortia soldanelloides*
Fringe flower	*Mitella diphylla* *Schizanthus solanceae*
Fritillary	*Fritillaria*
Frostweed	*Helianthemum canadense*
Fuki	*Petasites japonicus*

Common name	Botanic name
Fumewort	*Corydalis cava* *Corydalis solida*
Fumitory	*Corydalis*
Funkia	*Hosta*
Galingale	*Cyperus longus*
Gardener's garters	*Phalaris arundinaceae*
Garden heliotrope	*Valeriana officinalis*
Garden myrrh	*Myrrhis odorata*
Garden rocket	*Hesperis matronalis*
Garland lily	*Hedychium*
Gas plant	*Dictamnus albus*
Gayfeather	*Liatris, L. spicata*
Gentian	*Gentiana*
Geranium	*Pelargonium*
Gerber daisy	*Gerbera*
Germander	*Teucrium*
German primrose	*Primula obconica*
Ghostplant	*Artemisia lactiflora*
Ghost weed	*Euphorbia marginata*
Giant butterbur	*Petasites japonicus*
Giant cup	*Darmera peltata*
Giant Himalayan lily	*Cardiocrinum giganteum*
Giant hogweed	*Heracleum mantegazzianum*
Giant holly fern	*Polystichum munitum*
Giant hyacinth-flowered candytuft	*Iberis umbellata*
Giant hyssop	*Agastache*
Giant lily	*Cardiocrinum*
Giant mallow	*Hibiscus*
Giant rhubarb	*Gunnera manicata*
Giant wood fern	*Dryopteris goldieana*
Gilly flower	*Dianthus caryophyllus*
Gillyflower	*Erysimum cheiri* *Matthiola*
Ginger lily	*Hedychium*
Glade fern	*Athyrium pycnocarpon*
Gland bellflower	*Adenophora*
Globe amaranth	*Gomphrena globosa*
Globe artichoke	*Cynara scolymus*
Globe candytuft	*Iberis umbellata*
Globe daisy	*Globularia*
Globeflower	*Trollius*
Globe lily	*Allium tanguticum* *Calochortus albus* *Doryanthes excelsa*
Globe mallow	*Sphaeralcea*
Globe thistle	*Echinops*
Globe tulip	*Calochortus*
Gloriosa daisy	*Rudbeckia hirta*
Gloriosa lily	*Gloriosa superba*
Glory flower	*Eccremocarpus*
Glory lily	*Gloriosa*
Glory of the snow	*Chionodoxa*
Goat's beard	*Aruncus, A. dioicus*
Goat's rue	*Galega*
Godetia	*Clarkia*
Gold-and-silver chrysanthemum	*Ajania pacifica*
Gold dust	*Aurinia saxatilis* *Sedum acre*
Golden ageratum	*Lonas*
Golden cup	*Hunnemannia*
Golden drop	*Onosma taurica*
Golden fleece	*Bidens mitis*
Golden garlic	*Allium moly*
Golden glow	*Rudbeckia hirta* *Rudbeckia laciniata* 'Hortensia'
Golden knee	*Chrysogonum*
Golden male fern	*Dryopteris affinis*
Golden marguerite	*Anthemis tinctoria*
Golden moss	*Sedum acre*
Golden-rayed lily	*Lilium auratum*
Goldenrod	*Solidago*
Goldenstar	*Chrysogonum virginianum*
Goldie's fern	*Dryopteris goldieana*
Good King Henry	*Chenopodium bonus-henricus*
Goodnight-at-noon	*Hibiscus trionum*
Goosefoot	*Chenopodium*
Goutweed	*Aegopodium*
Granadilla	*Passiflora*
Granny's bonnet	*Aquilegia*
Grape hyacinth	*Muscari*
Grass flower	*Claytonia virginica* *Echium vulgare*
Grassnut	*Triteleia laxa*
Grass of Parnassus	*Parnassia, P. palustris*
Greater celandine	*Chelidonium majus*
Greater spearwort	*Ranunculus lingua*
Grecian stock	*Matthiola longipetala*
Greek hay	*Trigonella foenum-graecum*
Green-and-gold	*Chrysogonum*
Greenthreads	*Thelesperma*
Gromwell	*Lithodora*

Common name	Botanic name
Ground cherry	*Physalis*
Ground laurel	*Epigaea repens*
Groundsel	*Senecio*
Guernsey lily	*Nerine sarniensis*
Guinea-hen flower	*Fritillaria meleagris*
Hair grass	*Briza media* *Koeleria, K. vallesiana*
Hakone grass	*Hakonechloa*
Hard fern	*Blechnum, B. spicant*
Hardheads	*Centaurea*
Hard shield fern	*Polystichum aculeatum*
Hardy ageratum	*Eupatorium coelestinum*
Hardy amaryllis	*Lycoris squamigera*
Hardy geranium	*Geranium*
Hardy gloxinia	*Incarvillea delavayi*
Hardy mum	*Chrysanthemum morifolium*
Hardy orchid	*Bletilla striata*
Harebell	*Campanula rotundifolia*
Harebell poppy	*Meconopsis quintuplinervia*
Hare's ear	*Bupleurum falcatum* *Bupleurum fruticosum* *Bupleurum rotundifolium*
Hare's tail	*Lagurus ovatus*
Hare's tail grass	*Lagurus*
Harlequin flower	*Sparaxis*
Hart's tongue fern	*Asplenium scolopendrium*
Hattie's pincushion	*Astranita*
Hawk's beard	*Crepis*
Haybells	*Uvularia*
Hay-scented fern	*Dennstaedtia punctiloba*
Heal all	*Prunella*
Heart pea	*Cardiospermum halicacabum*
Heartsease	*Viola tricolor*
Heart seed	*Cardiospermum halicacabum*
Hedge nettle	*Stachys*
Heliotrope	*Heliotropium, H. arborescens*
Hellebore	*Helleborus*
Helmet flower	*Scutellaria*
Hemp agrimony	*Euaptorium*
Hen-and-chicken fern	*Asplenium bulbiferum*
Hens and chicks	*Sempervivum, S. tectorum*
Heron's bill	*Erodium*
Himalaya fairy grass	*Miscanthus nepalensis*
Himalayan blue poppy	*Meconopsis betonicifolia, M. grandis*
Himalayan fleece flower	*Persicaria affinis*
Himalayan mayapple	*Podophyllum hexandrum*
Holly fern	*Cyrtomium falcatum* *Polystichum, P. munitum*
Hollyhock	*Alcea, A. rosea*
Hollyhock mallow	*Malva alcea*
Holy flax	*Santolina rosmarinifolia*
Holy thistle	*Silybum marianum*
Honesty	*Lunaria, L. annua*
Honeywort	*Cerinthe major*
Hoop petticoat	*Narcissus bulbocodium*
Hops	*Humulus*
Horned poppy	*Glaucium*
Horned rampion	*Phyteuma*
Horned violet	*Viola cornuta*
Horseheal	*Inula helenium*
Horsemint	*Monarda*
Hottentot fig	*Dorotheanthus bellidiformis*
Hot water plant	*Achimenes*
Hound's tongue	*Cynoglossum, C. nervosum, C. officinale*
Houseleek	*Sempervivum*
Hummingbird's mint	*Agastache cana*
Hungarian clover	*Trifolium pannonicum*
Huntsman's cup	*Sarracenia purpurea*
Husk tomato	*Physalis*
Hyacinth	*Hyacinthus*
Hyacinth bean	*Lablab purpureus*
Hyacinth-of-Peru	*Scilla peruviana*
Hyssop	*Hyssopus*
Iceland poppy	*Papaver croceum*
Ice plant	*Delosperma* *Dorotheanthus* *Sedum spectabile*
Iceplant	*Malephora crocea*
Immortelle	*Helichrysum orientale* *Xeranthemum annuum*
Indian bean	*Lablab purpureus*
Indian blanket	*Gaillardia pulchella*
Indian borage	*Plectranthus amboinicus*
Indian cress	*Tropaeolum, T. majus*
Indian cup	*Darmera peltata* *Sarracenia purpurea* *Silphium perfoliatum*
Indian mint	*Plectranthus amboinicus*
Indian paint	*Lithodora* *Sanguinaria canadensis*

Indian physic	*Gillenia trifoliata*
Indian pink	*Dianthus chinensis*
	Spigelia marilandica
Indian plant	*Anethum gravelolens*
	Chlorogalum pomeridianum
	Darmera peltata
	Dodecatheon meadia
	Drancunculus vulgaris
	Monarda didyma
	Sanguinaria, S. purpurea
	Silphium perfoliatum
Indian poke	*Veratrum viride*
Indian rhubarb	*Darmera peltata*
Indian shot	*Canna*
Indian turnip	*Arisaema triphyllum*
Indigo squill	*Camassia scilloides*
Innocence	*Collinsia bicolor*
	Hedyotis caerulea
Interrupted fern	*Osmunda claytoniana*
Irish moss	*Euphorbia cyparissias*
	Minuartia verna
	Sagina subulata
Isotoma	*Solenopsis axillaris*
Italian clover	*Trifolium incarnatum*
Ithuriels' spear	*Triteleia laxa*
Jaburan lily	*Ophiopogon jaburan*
Jack-in-the-pulpit	*Arisaema triphyllum*
Jacobean lily	*Sprekelia formosissima*
Jacob's ladder	*Polemonium, P. caeruleum*
Jacob's rod	*Asphodeline*
Japanese anemone	*Anemone hupehensis* var. *japonica*
	Anemone × hybrida
Japanese aster	*Kalimeris pinnatifida*
Japanese beech wood fern	*Thelypteris decursive-pinnata*
Japanese butterbur	*Petasites japonicus*
Japanese forest grass	*Hakonechloa macra*
Japanese holly fern	*Cyrtomium falcatum*
Japanese hops	*Humulus japonicus*
Japanese iris	*Iris ensata*
Japanese lily	*Lilium callosum*
	Lilium concolor
	Lilium hansonii
	Lilium japonicum
	Trillium hirta
Japanese painted fern	*Athyrium niponicum*
Japanese primrose	*Primula japonica*

Japanese silver grass	*Miscanthus, M. sinensis*
Japanese thistle	*Cirsium japonicum*
Japanese water iris	*Iris laevigata*
Japanese wood fern	*Dryopteris sieboldii*
Jersey lily	*Amaryllis belladonna*
Jerusalem cross	*Lychnis chalcedonica*
Jerusalem sage	*Phlomis fruticosa*
Jewels of Opar	*Talinum paniculatum*
Job's tears	*Coix lacryma-jobi*
Joe Pye weed	*Eupatorium fistulosum*
	Eupatorium maculatum
	Eupatorium purpureum
Johnny-jump-up	*Viola tricolor*
Jonquil	*Narcissus jonquilla*
Joseph's coat	*Amaranthus tricolor*
June grass	*Koeleria macrantha*
Jupiter's beard	*Centranthus ruber*
	Anthyllis, A. barba-jovis
Kaffir lily	*Clivia*
	Schizostylis
Kenilworth ivy	*Cymbalaria muralis*
Keys of heaven	*Centranthus ruber*
Kidney vetch	*Anthyllis, A. vulneraria*
Kingcup	*Caltha*
Kingfisher daisy	*Felicia*
King's crown	*Justicia carnea*
King's spear	*Asphodeline lutea*
	Eremurus
Kiss-me-over-the-garden-gate	*Persicaria orientale*
Kiwi vine (hardy)	*Actinidia arguta*
Knapweed	*Centaurea*
Knit bone	*Symphytum officinale*
Knotweed	*Persicaria*
Kolomikta vine	*Actinidia kolomikta*
Korean rock fern	*Polystichum tsus-simense*
Laceflower	*Gypsophila paniculata*
	Trachymene
Lace grass	*Achillea millefolium*
	Eragrostis capillaris
Ladies-tobacco	*Antennaria*
Ladybells	*Adenophora, A. confusa*
Lady fern	*Athyrium filix-femina*
Lady-in-the-bath	*Dicentra spectabilis*
Lady's bedstraw	*Galium verum*
Lady's finger	*Anthyllis*
Lady's mantle	*Alchemilla*
Lady's slipper	*Impatiens balsamina*

Lady's slipper orchid	*Cypripedium*
Lady's smock	*Cardamine pratensis*
Lady's thistle	*Silybum marianum*
Lamb's ears	*Stachys byzantina*
Lamb's quarters	*Chenopodium album* *Trillium erectum*
Lamb's tongue	*Stachys byzantina*
Languid ladies	*Mertensia ciliata*
Larkspur	*Consolida, C. ajacis*
Lavender	*Lavandula*
Lavender cotton	*Santolina chamaecyparissus*
Leadwort	*Ceratostigma plumbaginoides*
Leather flower	*Clematis*
Leather wood fern	*Dryopteris marginalis*
Lemon balm	*Melissa officinalis*
Lemon grass	*Cymbopogon citratus*
Lemon lily	*Lilium parryi*
Lenten rose	*Helleborus orientalis*
Lent lily	*Narcissus pseudonarcissus*
Leopard flower	*Belamcanda chinensis*
Leopard lily	*Lilium catesbaei* *Lilium pardalinum*
Leopard plant	*Ligularia*
Leopard's bane	*Doronicum*
Lesser celandine	*Ranunculus ficaria*
Licorice plant	*Helichrysum petiolare*
Lily	*Lilium*
Lily leek	*Allium moly*
Lily of Peru	*Alstroemeria*
Lily-of-the-Altai	*Ixiolirion*
Lily-of-the-Incas	*Alstroemeria*
Lily-of-the-Nile	*Agapanthus africanus* *Zantedeschia aethiopica*
Lily-of-the-valley	*Convallaria*
Lilyturf	*Liriope* *Ophiopogon*
Lion's ear	*Leonotis, L. leonurus*
Lion's tail	*Leonotis*
Little club moss	*Selaginella*
Little hard fern	*Blechnum penna-marina*
Live-forever	*Sempervivum*
Liverleaf	*Hepatica acutiloba* *Hepatica nobilis*
Liverwort	*Hepatica americana*
Livingstone daisy	*Dorotheanthus, D. bellidiformis*
Loddon lily	*Leucojum aestivum*
Log fern	*Dryopteris celsa*
London pride	*Saxifraga* × *urbium*
Long-head coneflower	*Ratibida columnifera*
Loofah	*Luffa*
Loosestrife	*Lysimachia* *Lythrum*
Lord Anson's blue pea	*Lathyrus nervosus*
Lords and ladies	*Arum*
Lotus	*Nelumbo*
Lovage	*Levisticum officinale*
Love grass	*Eragrostis*
Love-in-a-mist	*Nigella, N. damascena*
Love-in-a-puff	*Cardiospermum halicacabum*
Love-lies-bleeding	*Amaranthus caudatus*
Lungwort	*Pulmonaria*
Lupin	*Lupinus*
Lupine	*Lupinus*
Madagascar periwinkle	*Catharanthus, C. roseus*
Madeira vine	*Anredera cordifolia*
Madonna lily	*Lilium candidum*
Madwort	*Alyssum*
Magic lily	*Lycoris squamigera*
Maiden fern	*Thelypteris*
Maiden grass	*Miscanthus sinensis* 'Gracillimus'
Maidenhair fern	*Adiantum*
Maiden pink	*Dianthus deltoides*
Maiden's tears	*Silene vulgaris*
Maiden's wreath	*Francoa sonchifolia*
Malcolm stock	*Malcolmia*
Male fern	*Dryopteris, D. filix-mas*
Mallow	*Hibiscus* *Lavatera* *Malva*
Mallow-wort	*Malope trifida*
Maltese cross	*Lychnis chalcedonica*
Mangles everlasting	*Rhodanthe manglesii*
Manila hemp	*Musa*
Marginal wood fern	*Dryopteris marginalis*
Marigold	*Tagetes*
Mariposa tulip	*Calochortus*
Marjoram	*Origanum*
Marsh fern	*Thelypteris palustris*
Marsh marigold	*Caltha, C. palustris*
Marsh orchid	*Dactylorhiza*
Marsh rosemary	*Limonium*
Martagon lily	*Lilium martagon*

Marvel of Peru	*Mirabilis, M. jalapa*
Mary's thistle	*Silybum marianum*
Mask flower	*Alonsoa*
Masterwort	*Angelica atropurpurea* *Astrantia, A. major* *Heracleum sphondylium*
Matilija poppy	*Romneya*
Mayapple	*Podophyllum, P. peltatum*
May-blob	*Caltha palustris*
Mayflower	*Epigaea repens*
Maypops	*Passiflora incarnata*
Meadow bright	*Caltha palustris*
Meadow clary	*Salvia pratensis*
Meadow cress	*Cardamine pratensis*
Meadow foam	*Limnanthes, L. douglasii*
Meadow hyacinth	*Camassia scilloides*
Meadow lily	*Lilium canadense*
Meadow rue	*Thalictrum*
Meadow saffron	*Colchicum, C. autumnale*
Meadowsweet	*Filipendula*
Melic grass	*Melica*
Melick	*Melica*
Mercury	*Chenopodium bonus-henricus*
Merrybells	*Uvularia*
Mexican cigar plant	*Cuphea ignea*
Mexican firebush	*Bassia scoparia*
Mexican fire lily	*Sprekelia formosissima*
Mexican fire plant	*Euphorbia cyathophora*
Mexican hat	*Ratibida*
Mexican heather	*Cuphea hyssopifolia*
Mexican hyssop	*Agastache*
Mexican ivy	*Cobaea scandens*
Mexican marigold	*Tagetes minuta*
Mexican mint	*Plectranthus amboinicus* *Tagetes lucida*
Mexican petunia	*Strobilanthes*
Mexican poppy	*Argemone mexicana*
Mexican sunflower	*Tithonia, T. rotundifolia*
Mexican tea	*Chenopodium ambrosioides*
Mexican tulip poppy	*Hunnemannia, H. fumariifolia*
Mexican zinnia	*Zinnia haageana*
Michaelmas daisy	*Aster novae-belgii*
Mignonette	*Reseda*
Mignonette vine	*Anredera cordifolia*
Mile-a-minute plant	*Persicaria aubertii*
Milk-and-wine lily	*Crinum, C. zeylanicum*
Milk thistle	*Silybum marianum*
Milkweed	*Asclepias, A. syriaca*
Millefoil	*Achillea*
Million bells	*Calibrachoa* Million Bells
Miniature hollyhock	*Sidalcea*
Mint	*Mentha*
Mintleaf	*Plectranthus madagascariensis*
Missouri evening primrose	*Oenothera macrocarpa*
Mistflower	*Eupatorium coelestinum*
Miterwort	*Mitella, M. breweri*
Moccasin flower	*Cypripedium*
Mole plant	*Euphorbia lathyris*
Molten fire	*Amaranthus tricolor*
Molucca balm	*Moluccella laevis*
Monarch of the veldt	*Arctotis fastuosa*
Mondo grass	*Ophiopogon japonicus*
Money plant	*Lunaria annua*
Moneywort	*Lysimachia nummularia*
Monkey flower	*Mimulus*
Monkey musk	*Mimulus luteus*
Monkeyroot	*Babiana*
Monkshood	*Aconitum, A. napellus*
Montbretia	*Crocosmia, C. × crocosmiiflora* *Tritonia*
Moonflower	*Ipomoea alba*
Moonwort	*Lunaria*
Morning glory	*Convolvulus* *Ipomoea, I. purpurea, I. tricolor*
Mosquito flower	*Lopezia racemosa*
Moss campion	*Silene acaulis*
Moss pink	*Phlox subulata*
Moss rose	*Portulaca*
Mother-in-law plant	*Caladium bicolor*
Mother of thyme	*Thymus pulegioides*
Mother spleenwort	*Asplenium bulbiferum*
Mountain asphodel	*Xerophyllum asphodeloides*
Mountain avens	*Dryas, D. octopetala*
Mountain bluebell	*Mertensia ciliata*
Mountain bluet	*Centaurea montana*
Mountain daisy	*Celmisia*
Mountain flax	*Phormium cookianum*
Mountain fringe	*Adlumia fungosa*
Mountain pink	*Centaurium*
Mountain snuff	*Arnica montana*

Mountain spinach	*Atriplex hortensis*
Mountain tassel	*Soldanella montana*
Mountain tobacco	*Arnica montana*
Mount Atlas daisy	*Anacyclus, A.pyrethrum* var. *depressus*
Mourning-bride	*Scabiosa atropurpurea*
Mourning widow	*Geranium phaeum*
Mouse-ear chickweed	*Cerastium*
Mugwort	*Artemisia*
Mugwort (white)	*Artemisia lactiflora*
Mullein	*Verbascum*
Mullein pink	*Lychnis coronaria*
Mum	*Chrysanthemum morifolium*
Musk	*Mimulus*
Musk mallow	*Abelmoschus moschatus* *Malva, M. moschata*
Naked boys	*Colchicum autumnale*
Naked ladies	*Amaryllis belladonna* *Colchicum*
Namaquāland daisy	*Dimorphotheca sinuata*
Narrow buckler fern	*Dryopteris carthusiana*
Nasturtium	*Tropaeolum, T. majus*
Natal grass	*Tricholaena rosea*
Natal lily	*Moraea*
Navelseed	*Omphalodes*
Navelwort	*Omphalodes*
Needle grass	*Stipa*
New England aster	*Aster novae-belgii*
New York fern	*Thelypteris noveboracensis*
New Zealand bluebell	*Wahlenbergia albomarginata*
New Zealand burr	*Acaena*
New Zealand daisy	*Celmisia*
New Zealand flax	*Phormium tenax*
Night phlox	*Zaluzianskya capensis*
Night-scented stock	*Matthiola longipetala* ssp. *bicornis*
Nippon bells	*Shortia uniflora* 'Grandiflora'
Nippon daisy	*Nipponanthemum*
None-so-pretty	*Silene armeria*
Northern bedstraw	*Galium boreale*
Northern maidenhair fern	*Adiantum aleuticum*
Northern sea oats	*Chasmanthium latifolium*
Northern shorewort	*Mertensia maritima*
Nut orchid	*Achimenes*
Oat grass	*Helictotrichon*
Obedient plant	*Physostegia, P. virginiana*
Oconee bells	*Shortia galacifolia*
October daphne	*Sedum sieboldii*
Okra	*Abelmoschus*
Old man's beard	*Clematis*
Onion	*Allium*
Opium poppy	*Papaver somniferum*
Orach	*Atriplex, A. hortensis*
Orange clock vine	*Thunbergia gregorii*
Orange milkweed	*Asclepias tuberosa*
Orange sunflower	*Heliopsis helianthoides*
Orchid	*Bletilla*
Oregano	*Origanum*
Oriental poppy	*Papaver orientale*
Ornamental rhubarb	*Rheum palmatum*
Orpine	*Sedum, S. telephium*
Ostrich fern	*Matteuccia, M. struthiopteris*
Oswego tea	*Monarda didyma*
Our Lady's bedstraw	*Galium verum*
Our Lady's milk thistle	*Silybum marianum*
Ox eye	*Buphthalmum* *Heliopsis*
Ox-eye daisy	*Leucanthemum vulgare*
Oxlip	*Primula elatior*
Oyster plant	*Mertensia maritima*
Ozark sundrops	*Oenothera macrocarpa*
Paintbrush lily	*Haemanthus coccineus*
Painted daisy	*Tanacetum coccineum*
Painted leaf	*Euphorbia cyathophora*
Painted nettle	*Solenostemon scutellarioides*
Painted tongue	*Salpiglossis*
Palma christi	*Ricinus communis*
Palm Springs daisy	*Cladanthus arabicus*
Pampas grass	*Cortaderia, C. selloana*
Panic grass	*Panicum*
Pansy	*Viola × wittrockiana*
Paper plant	*Cyperus papyrus*
Papoose root	*Caulophyllum thalictrioides*
Papyrus	*Cyperus papyrus*
Paradise lily	*Paradisea*
Parlor maple	*Abutilon*
Parsley	*Petroselinum*
Partridge berry	*Mitchella, M. repens*
Partridge pea	*Cassia fasciculata*
Pasque flower	*Pulsatilla, P. vulgaris*
Passionflower	*Passiflora*

Patience plant	*Impatiens, I. walleriana*
Patient Lucy	*Impatiens wallerana*
Peach bells	*Campanula persicifolia*
Pearl grass	*Melica ciliata*
Pearlwort	*Sagina*
Pearly everlasting	*Anaphalis*
Penny flower	*Lunaria annua*
Pennyroyal	*Mentha pulegium*
Peony	*Paeonia*
Perennial candytuft	*Iberis saxatilis*
Perennial honesty	*Lunaria rediva*
Perennial pea	*Lathyrus grandiflorus, L. latifolius*
Perennial pea	*Lathyrus sylvestris*
Persian shield	*Strobilanthes dyerianus*
Persian violet	*Cyclamen*
Peruvian daffodil	*Hymenocallis narcissiflora*
Peruvian lily	*Alstroemeria*
Pheasant's eye	*Adonis vernalis*
Pigsqueak	*Bergenia*
Pigweed	*Chenopodium*
Pilikai	*Ipomoea tuberosa*
Pilot plant	*Silphium laciniatum*
Pimpernel	*Anagallis*
Pin clover	*Erodium cicutarium*
Pincushion flower	*Scabiosa, S. atropurpurea*
Pincushion plant	*Consolida ambigua*
Pineapple flower	*Eucomis*
Pineapple lily	*Eucomis*
Pink root	*Spigelia*
Pinks	*Dianthus*
Pitcher plant	*Sarracenia*
Pitchforks	*Bidens*
Plantain	*Musa*
Plantain lily	*Hosta*
Pleurisy root	*Asclepias tuberosa*
Plumbago	*Ceratostigma*
Plume poppy	*Macleaya, M. cordata*
Plume thistle	*Cirsium*
Poached-egg plant	*Limnanthes, L. douglasii*
Pocketbook flower	*Calceolaria*
Polecat geranium	*Lantana montevidensis*
Polka dot plant	*Hypoestes, H. phyllostachya*
Polyanthus	*Primula Polyanthus Group*
Poor man's orchid	*Schizanthus, S. pinnatus*
Poor man's weatherglass	*Anagallis arvensis*
Poppy	*Papaver*
Poppy mallow	*Callirhoe*
Pot marigold	*Calendula officinalis*
Pot marjoram	*Origanum onites*
Pouch flower	*Calceolaria*
Prairie coneflower	*Ratibida*
Prairie dock	*Silphium*
Prairie gentian	*Eustoma grandiflorum*
Prairie June grass	*Koeleria macrantha*
Prairie mallow	*Sidalcea* *Sphaeralcea coccinea*
Prairie pine	*Liatris spicata*
Prairie pointer	*Dodecatheon meadia*
Pretty Betsy	*Centranthus macrosiphon*
Prickly poppy	*Argemone, A. mexicana*
Prickly rhubarb	*Gunnera manicata*
Prickly thrift	*Acantholimon*
Pride of Madeira	*Echium candicans*
Primrose	*Primula*
Prince's feather	*Amaranthus cruentus* *Persicaria orientale*
Proboscis flower	*Proboscidea*
Puccoon	*Lithodora*
Pudding grass	*Mentha pulegium*
Purple amaranth	*Amaranthus cruentus*
Purple bell vine	*Rhodochiton atrosanguineus*
Purple coneflower	*Echinacea, E. purpurea*
Purple globe ginger	*Globba globulifera*
Purple loosestrife	*Lythrum salicaria*
Purple rock cress	*Aubrieta*
Purple willow herb	*Lythrum salicaria*
Purslane	*Claytonia* *Portulaca*
Pussley	*Portulaca oleracea*
Pussy-toes	*Antennaria*
Quaker-ladies	*Hedyotis caerulea*
Quaking grass	*Briza, B. media*
Quamash	*Camassia*
Queen Anne's thimble	*Gilia capitata*
Queencup	*Clintonia uniflora*
Queen of the meadow	*Filipendula ulmaria*
Queen of the prairie	*Filipendula rubra*
Quinoa	*Chenopodium quinoa*
Rabbit-tail grass	*Lagurus*
Ragged robin	*Centaurea cyanus* *Lychnis flos-cuculi*
Ragged sailor	*Centaurea cyanus*
Rag gourd	*Luffa*
Ragwort	*Senecio*
Rainbow moss	*Selaginella uncinata*

Rain daisy	*Dimorphotheca pluvialis*
	Osteospermum
Rainflower	*Zephyranthes*
Rain lily	*Zephyranthes*
Rattletop	*Cimicifuga*
Rattle-weed	*Baptisia tinctoria*
Red amaranth	*Amaranthus cruentus*
Red-hot-poker	*Kniphofia*
Redmaids	*Calandrinia ciliata*
Red Morocco	*Adonis annua*
Red puccoon	*Sanguinaria*
Red sage	*Lantana camara*
Red Sally	*Lythrum salicaria*
Reed grass	*Calamagrostis*
Regal lily	*Lilium regale*
Remote wood fern	*Dryopteris* × *remota*
Resurrection plant	*Selaginella lepidophylla*
Rheumatism root	*Jeffersonia diphylla*
Rhubarb	*Rheum*
Ribbon grass	*Phalaris arundinaceae*
Ring bellflower	*Symphyandra*
River fern	*Thelypteris kunthii*
Rock bell	*Wahlenbergia*
Rock cress	*Arabis*
Rocket candytuft	*Iberis amara*
Rockfoil	*Saxifraga*
Rock jasmine	*Androsace*
Rock pink	*Talinum calycinum*
Rock purslane	*Calandrinia umbellata*
Rock rose	*Helianthemum*
Rock soapwort	*Saponaria ocymoides*
Rocky Mountain garland	*Clarkia*
Rodger's flower	*Rodgersia aesculifolia*
Roof iris	*Iris tectorum*
Rose balsam	*Impatiens balsamina*
Rosebay willowherb	*Epilobium angustifolium*
Rose campion	*Lychnis coronaria*
Rose mallow	*Hibiscus, H. moscheutos*
Rosemary	*Rosmarinus*
Rose moss	*Portulaca, P. grandiflora*
Rose-of-heaven	*Lychnis coeli-rosa*
	Silene coeli-rosa
Rose of Jericho	*Selaginella lepidophylla*
Rose of Sharon	*Hypericum calycinum*
Rosinweed	*Silphium*
Royal fern	*Osmunda regalis*
Royal lily	*Lilium regale*
Royal sweet-sultan	*Amberboa moschata*
Ruby grass	*Tricholaena rosea*
Rue anemone	*Anemonella thalictroides*
Running box	*Mitchella repens*
Rupture-wort	*Herniaria*
Russian sage	*Perovskia atriplicifolia*
Russian vine	*Persicaria baldschuanica*
Safflower	*Carthamus, C. tinctorius*
Saffron	*Crocus sativus*
Saffron thistle	*Carthamus lanatus*
Sage	*Salvia*
Sagebrush	*Artemisia*
Salt bush	*Atriplex*
Sand pink	*Dianthus arenarius*
Sandwort	*Arenaria*
	Minuartia
Sarawak bean	*Lablab hosei*
Satin flower	*Clarkia amoena*
	Lunaria
Savory	*Satureja*
Saxifrage	*Saxifraga*
Saxifrage pink	*Petrorhagia saxifraga*
Scabious	*Cephalaria*
	Scabiosa
Scarlet lightning	*Lychnis chaledonica*
Scarlet plume	*Euphorbia fulgens*
Scarlet runner bean	*Phaseolus coccineus*
Scarlet star-glory	*Ipomoea quamoclit*
Scorpion grass	*Myosotis*
Scorpion weed	*Phacelia*
Scotch moss	*Sagina subulata*
Scottish flame flower	*Tropaeolum speciosum*
Sea fig	*Dorotheanthus bellidiformis*
Sea holly	*Eryngium*
Sea hollyhock	*Hibiscus moscheutos*
Seakale	*Crambe maritima*
Sea lavender	*Limonium, L. latifolium*
Sea marigold	*Dorotheanthus bellidiformis*
Sea pink	*Armeria*
	Limonium scabrum
Sea poppy	*Glaucium*
Sea purslane	*Atriplex hortensis*
Sedge	*Carex*
Sego lily	*Calochortus*
Self heal	*Prunella*
Senna	*Cassia*
Serpent cucumber	*Trichosanthes cucumerina*
Serpent gourd	*Trichosanthes anguina*
Sesame	*Sesamum indicum*

Shaggy shield fern	*Dryopteris cycadina*
Shamrock	*Oxalis* *Trifolium repens*
Shamrock pea	*Parochetus africana*
Shasta daisy	*Leucanthemum × superbum*
Sheep's bit	*Jasione*
Sheep's scabious	*Jasione laevis*
Shellflower	*Chelone*
Shell flower	*Moluccella laevis*
Shepherd's clock	*Anagallis arvensis*
Shepherd's scabious	*Jasione laevis*
Shield fern	*Dryopteris* *Polystichum braunii*
Shirley poppy	*Papaver rhoeas*
Shoofly plant	*Nicandra, N. physalodes*
Shooting star	*Dodecatheon*
Shrimp plant	*Justicia brandegeeana*
Shrubby hare's ear	*Bupleurum fruticosum*
Shrub verbena	*Lantana*
Shuttlecock fern	*Matteuccia struthiopteris*
Siberian bugloss	*Brunnera macrophylla*
Siberian forget-me-not	*Brunnera macrophylla*
Siberian lily	*Ixiolirion tataricum*
Siberian tea	*Bergenia crassifolia*
Siberian wallflower	*Erysimum × allionii*
Side-saddle flower	*Sarracenia purpurea*
Signet marigold	*Tagetes Signet Group*
Silk flower	*Abelmoschus*
Silver banner grass	*Miscanthus sacchariflorus*
Silverbush	*Convolvulus cneorum*
Silver crown	*Chiastophyllum oppositifolium*
Silver dollar	*Lunaria annua*
Silver fleece vine	*Persicaria aubertii*
Silver-flowered everlasting	*Cephalipterum*
Silver lace vine	*Persicaria aubertii*
Silvermound	*Artemisia schmidtiana*
Silver vine	*Actinidia polygama*
Skullcap	*Scutellaria*
Skunk cabbage	*Lysichiton*
Skyflower	*Thunbergia grandiflora*
Sky pilot	*Polemonium*
Sky vine	*Thunbergia grandiflora*
Sleepy daisy	*Xanthisma, X. texana*
Slipper flower	*Calceolaria*
Slipper orchid	*Cypripedium*
Slipperwort	*Calceolaria*
Smallweed	*Calamagrostis*
Smartweed	*Persicaria*
Snake gourd	*Trichosanthes cucumerina*
Snakeroot	*Cimicifuga* *Liatris*
Snakesbeard	*Ophiopogon jaburan*
Snakeshead	*Chelone glabra*
Snake's-head fritillary	*Fritillaria meleagris*
Snakeweed	*Persicaria bistorta*
Snapdragon	*Antirrhinum*
Sneezeweed	*Helenium, H. autumnale*
Sneezewort	*Achillea ptarmica*
Snowbell	*Soldanella*
Snowcup	*Anoda cristata*
Snowdrop	*Galanthus*
Snowdrop windflower	*Anemone sylvestris*
Snowflake	*Leucojum*
Snow-in-summer	*Cerastium tomentosum*
Snow on the mountain	*Euphorbia marginata*
Soap plant	*Chlorogalum*
Soapweed	*Yucca elata*
Soapwort	*Saponaria, S. officinalis*
Soft shield fern	*Polystichum setiferum*
Solomon's feather	*Smilacina*
Solomon's plume	*Smilacina*
Solomon's seal	*Polygonatum*
Sorrel	*Oxalis* *Rumex*
South African daisy	*Dimorphotheca sinuata* *Osteospermum*
Southern maidenhair fern	*Adiantum capillus-veneris*
Southern star	*Tweedia* 'Heavenborn'
Southernwood	*Artemisia abrotanum*
Southern wood fern	*Dryopteris ludoviciana*
Sow bread	*Cyclamen*
Spanish bayonet	*Yucca aloifolia*
Spanish bluebell	*Hyacinthoides hispanica*
Spanish dagger	*Yucca gloriosa*
Spanish flag	*Ipomoea lobata*
Spanish needle	*Palafoxia arida*
Spanish needles	*Bidens*
Spanish thyme	*Plectranthus amboinicus*
Spear grass	*Stipa*
Speedwell	*Veronica*
Spider flower	*Cleome, C. hassleriana*

Common name	Botanic name
Spider lily	*Crinum* *Hymenocallis* *Lycoris radiata* *Tradescantia*
Spiderwort	*Tradescantia,* *T.* Andersoniana Group
Spike moss	*Selaginella*
Spinulose wood fern	*Dryopteris carthusiana*
Spiraea	*Aruncus dioicus* *Astilbe*
Spleenwort	*Asplenium*
Sponge gourd	*Luffa*
Spotted orchid	*Dactylorhiza*
Spring beauty	*Claytonia, C. virginica*
Spring crocus	*Crocus*
Spring meadow saffron	*Bulbocodium vernum*
Spring vetch	*Lathyrus vernus*
Spring vetchling	*Lathyrus vernus*
Spurge	*Euphorbia*
Spurred snapdragon	*Linaria*
Squawberry	*Mitchella repens*
Squaw grass	*Xerophyllum tenax*
Squaw root	*Caulophyllum thalictrioides*
Squill	*Scilla*
Squirreltail barley	*Hordeum jubatum*
Squirrel-tail grass	*Hordeum jubatum*
St. Bernard's lily	*Anthericum liliago*
St. Bruno's lily	*Paradisea, P. liliastrum*
St. James' lily	*Sprekelia formosissima*
St. John's wort	*Hypericum*
St. Patrick's cabbage	*Saxifraga spathularis* *Sempervivum tectorum*
Standing cypress	*Gilia rubra*
Star cluster	*Pentas lanceolata*
Starflower	*Mentzelia*
Star flower	*Pentas lanceolata*
Star ipomoea	*Ipomoea coccinea*
Star-of-Bethlehem	*Ornithogalum,* *O. umbellatum*
Star of Texas	*Xanthisma texana*
Star of the Veldt	*Dimorphotheca sinuata* *Osteospermum*
Star thistle	*Centaurea*
Star tulip	*Calochortus*
Statice	*Limonium, L. sinuatum*
Stinking Benjamin	*Trillium*
Stock	*Matthiola, M. incana*
Stokes' aster	*Stokesia*
Stone cress	*Aethionema*
Stonecrop	*Sedum*
Stork's bill	*Erodium*
Strainer vine	*Luffa*
Strawbell	*Uvularia sessifolia*
Strawberry geranium	*Saxifraga stolonifera*
Strawflower	*Helichrysum bracteatum* *Rhodanthe*
Striped squill	*Puschkinia scilloides*
Sugar scoop	*Tiarella*
Sulla clover	*Hedysarum coronarium*
Sultana	*Impatiens*
Summer cypress	*Bassia scoparia* f. *trichophylla*
Summer fir	*Artemisia sacrorum* var. *viridis*
Summer forget-me-not	*Anchusa capensis*
Summer hyacinth	*Galtonia candicans*
Summer poinsettia	*Amaranthus tricolor*
Summer snapdragon	*Angelonia angustifolia*
Summer snowflake	*Leucojum aestivum*
Suncups	*Oenothera*
Sundrops	*Oenothera, O. fruticosa*
Sunflower	*Helianthus*
Sun lovers	*Heliophila longifolia*
Sun marigold	*Dimorphotheca*
Sun moss	*Portulaca grandiflora*
Sun plant	*Portulaca grandiflora*
Sun rose	*Helianthemum*
Swamp lily	*Crinum americanum*
Swamp rose mallow	*Hibiscus moscheutos*
Swamp water fern	*Blechnum indicum*
Swan River daisy	*Brachyscome, B. iberidifolia*
Swan River everlasting	*Rhodanthe manglesii*
Swedish ivy	*Plectranthus australis*
Sweet alyssum	*Lobularia, L. maritima*
Sweet balm	*Melissa officinalis*
Sweet chervil	*Myrrhis odorata*
Sweet Cicely	*Myrrhis, M. odorata*
Sweet coltsfoot	*Petasites*
Sweet marjoram	*Origanum majorana*
Sweet pea	*Lathyrus odoratus*
Sweet rocket	*Hesperis matronalis*
Sweet scabious	*Scabiosa atropurpurea*
Sweet-sultan	*Amberboa moschata*
Sweet violet	*Viola odorata*

Common name	Botanic name
Sweet William	*Dianthus armeria* *Dianthus barbatus* *Dianthus superbus*
Sweet William catchfly	*Silene armeria*
Sweet woodruff	*Gallium odoratum*
Switch grass	*Panicum virgatum*
Sword fern	*Polystichum*
Sword lily	*Gladiolus*
Tahoka daisy	*Machaeranthera tanacetifolia*
Tampala	*Amaranthus tricolor*
Tangier pea	*Lathyrus tingitanus*
Tansy	*Tanacetum vulgare*
Tara vine	*Actinidia arguta*
Taro	*Colocasia*
Tarragon	*Artemisia dracunculus*
Tartar lily	*Ixiolirion tataricum*
Tassel fern	*Polystichum polyblepharum*
Tassel flower	*Amaranthus caudatus* *Emilia*
Tassel hyacinth	*Muscari comosum*
Ten-weeks stock	*Matthiola annua*
Tetterwort	*Sanguinaria*
Texas bluebonnet	*Lupinus texensis*
Texas pride	*Phlox drummondii*
Thorn apple	*Datura*
Thoroughwort	*Eupatorium perfoliatum*
Thorow-wax	*Bupleurum*
Three-birds-flying	*Linaria tiornithophora*
Thrift	*Armeria*
Throatwort	*Trachelium*
Thyme	*Thymus*
Tickseed	*Coreopsis*
Tickseed sunflower	*Bidens*
Tidy tips	*Layia platyglossa*
Toadflax	*Linaria, L. vulgaris*
Toad lily	*Fritillaria meleagris* *Tricyrtis*
Tobacco plant	*Nicotiana*
Toothwort	*Cardamine diphylla*
Toper's plant	*Sanguisorba minor*
Torch lily	*Kniphofia*
Touch-me-not	*Impatiens balsamina*
Trailing arbutus	*Epigaea repens*
Trailing lantana	*Lantana montevidensis*
Trailing petunia	*Calibrachoa* Million Bells
Transvaal daisy	*Gerbera, G. jamesonii*
Traveler's joy	*Clematis*
Treasure flower	*Gazania*
Tree mallow	*Lavatera, L. arborea, L. thuringiaca*
Tree poppy	*Romneya*
Trefoil	*Trifolium*
Tricolor chrysanthemum	*Chrysanthemum carinatum*
Trinity flower	*Tradescantia ohiensis* *Tradescantia* Andersoniana Group *Trillium*
Trout lily	*Erythronium*
Trumpet leaf	*Sarracenia*
Tuberose	*Polianthes tuberosa*
Tufted pansy	*Viola cornuta*
Tufted violet	*Viola cornuta*
Tulip	*Tulipa*
Tulip poppy	*Papaver glaucum*
Tunic flower	*Petrorhagia, P. saxifraga*
Turkeybeard	*Xerophyllum asphodeloides*
Turk's-cap lily	*Lilium martagon*
Turnsole	*Heliotropium*
Turtlehead	*Chelone, C. glabra*
Tussock grass	*Cortaderia*
Twinflower	*Linnaea*
Twining snapdragon	*Asarina*
Twinleaf	*Jeffersonia, J. diphylla*
Twinspur	*Diascia barberae*
Umbrella grass	*Cyperus involucratus*
Umbrella plant	*Darmera peltata*
Umbrella sedge	*Cyperus alternifolius*
Umbrellawort	*Mirabilis*
Unicorn plant	*Proboscidea*
Urahagusa	*Hakonechloa*
Valerian	*Centranthus* *Valeriana*
Vase vine	*Clematis*
Vegetable sponge	*Luffa cylindrica*
Venus maidenhair fern	*Adiantum capillus-veneris*
Vervain	*Verbena, V. rigida*
Vinca	*Catharanthus*
Vine lilac	*Hardenbergia violacea*
Violet cress	*Ionopsidium acaule*
Viper's bugloss	*Echium vulgare*
Virginia bluebells	*Mertensia pulmonarioides*
Virginia cowslip	*Mertensia pulmonarioides*
Virginia stock	*Malcolmia maritima*
Virgin's bower	*Clematis*
Wakerobin	*Trillium, T. sessile*

Walking fern	*Asplenium rhizophyllum*
Wall cress	*Arabis*
Wallflower	*Erysimum, E. cheiri*
Wallich's wood fern	*Dryopteris wallichiana*
Wall pepper	*Sedum acre*
Wandering Jew	*Tradescantia fluminensis* *Tradescantia zebrina*
Wand flower	*Dierama*
Wandflower	*Sparaxis*
Water hyssop	*Bacopa*
Wax pink	*Portulaca grandiflora*
Weeping lantana	*Lantana montevidensis*
Welsh poppy	*Meconopsis cambrica*
Western maidenhair fern	*Adiantum aleuticum*
Western sword fern	*Polystichum munitum*
White cup	*Nierembergia repens*
White dill	*Ammi majus*
White Dutch runner	*Phaseolus coccineus*
White hellebore	*Veratrum album*
White lace flower	*Ammi, A. majus*
White snakeroot	*Eupatorium rugosum*
Whitlow grass	*Draba aizoides*
Wild bergamot	*Monarda*
Wild fennel	*Nigella*
Wild ginger	*Asarum*
Wild heliotrope	*Phacelia crenulata* *Phacelia distans*
Wild hyacinth	*Camassia scilloides*
Wild indigo	*Baptisia*
Wild mandrake	*Podophyllum peltatum*
Wild oats	*Uvularia sessifolia*
Wild onion	*Allium cernuum*
Wild pansy	*Viola tricolor*
Wild parsnip	*Angelica archangelica*
Wild petunia	*Ruellia carolinensis* *Ruellia humilis*
Wild pink	*Silene caroliniana*
Wild senna	*Cassia marilandica*
Wild spinach	*Chenopodium bonus-henricus*
Willow herb	*Epilobium*
Windflower	*Anemone*
Winecups	*Babiana rubrocyanea*
Wine cups	*Callirhoe involucrata*
Winged everlasting	*Ammobium, A. alatum*
Winter aconite	*Eranthis, E. hyemalis*
Winter cherry	*Cardiospermum halicacabum* *Physalis alkekengi*
Winter daffodil	*Sternbergia lutea*
Winter heliotrope	*Petasites fragrans*
Wishbone flower	*Torenia, T. fournieri*
Woad	*Isatis, I. tinctoria*
Wolfsbane	*Aconitum lycoctonum*
Wood daffodil	*Uvularia grandiflora*
Wood-fern	*Dryopteris*
Wood lily	*Trillium*
Wood millet	*Milium effusum*
Wood poppy	*Hylomecon japonica* *Stylophorum diphyllum*
Wood rose	*Merremia tuberosa*
Woodruff	*Asperula, A. nitida*
Wood sage	*Teucrium*
Wood spurge	*Euphorbia amygdaloides*
Woolflower	*Celosia*
Worm grass	*Sedum album* *Spigelia, S. marilandica*
Wormwood	*Artemisia, A. absinthium*
Woundwort	*Stachys*
Yang-tao	*Actinidia arguta*
Yarrow	*Achillea*
Yellow ageratum	*Lonas*
Yellow archangel	*Lamium galeobdolon*
Yellow autumn crocus	*Sternbergia lutea*
Yellow morning glory	*Merremia tuberosa*
Yellow rock jasmine	*Vitaliana primulifolia*
Yellow sage	*Lantana camara*
Yellow wax-bells	*Kirengeshoma palmata*
Youth-and-old-age	*Zinnia elegans*
Zebra grass	*Miscanthus sinensis* 'Zebrinus'
Zephyr flower	*Zephyranthes*
Zephyr lily	*Zephyranthes*

Botanic Synonyms

The former botanic name is on the left and current name on the right.

Former name	Current name
Acaena caerulea	*Acaena caesiiglauca*
Acanthus balcanicus	*Acanthus hungaricus*
Achnatherum	*Stipa*
Acidanthera	*Gladiolus*
Aconitum volubile	*Aconitum hemsleyanum*
Aconogonon	*Persicaria*
Acroclinium	*Rhodanthe*
Actinidia chinensis	*Actinidia deliciosa*
Adlumia cirrhosa	*Adlumia fungosa*
Aethionema pulchellum	*Aethionema grandiflorum*
Allium aflatunense	*Allium* × *hollandicum*
Allium albopilosum	*Allium christophii*
Allium azureum	*Allium caeruleum*
Allium cowanii	*Allium neapolitanum*
Allium ostrowskianum	*Allium oreophilum*
Alstroemeria aurantiaca	*Alstroemeria aurea*
Althaea	*Alcea*
Althaea rosea	*Alcea rosea*
Alyssum maritimum	*Lobularia maritima*
Alyssum saxatile	*Aurinia saxatilis*
Amphicome	*Incarvillea*
Anacyclus depressus	*Anacyclus pyrethrum* var. *depressus*
Anchusa caespitosa	*Anchusa cespitosa*
Anchusa italica	*Anchusa azurea*
Anchusa myosotidiflora	*Brunnera macrophylla*
Anemone hepatica	*Hepatica nobilis*
Anemone vitifolia	*Anemone tomentosa*
Angelica officinalis	*Angelica archangelica*
Antholyza	*Crocosmia*
Arctotis stoechadifolia	*Arctotis venusta*
Arisaema atrorubens	*Arisaema triphyllum*
Arum dracunculus	*Dracunculus vulgaris*
Aruncus sylvester	*Aruncus dioicus*
Asperula	*Galium*
Asperula azurea	*Asperula orientalis*
Aster amelloides	*Felicia amelloides*
Aster capensis	*Felicia amelloides*
Aster coelestis	*Felicia amelloides*
Aster tanacetifolius	*Machaeranthera tanacetifolia*
Athyrium goeringianum	*Athyrium niponicum*
Atragene	*Clematis*
Avena candida	*Helictotrichon sempervirens*
Avena sempervirens	*Helictotrichon sempervirens*

Former name	Current name
Azorina	*Campanula*
Balsamita	*Tanacetum*
Bartonia aurea	*Mentzelia lindleyi*
Betonica	*Stachys*
Betonica officinalis	*Stachys officinalis*
Bistorta	*Persicaria*
Bletilla hyacinthina	*Bletilla striata*
Bocconia	*Macleaya*
Boussingaultia	*Anredera*
Boussingaultia baselloides	*Anredera cordifolia*
Brachychilum	*Hedychium*
Brachycome	*Brachyscome*
Brittonastrum	*Agastache*
Brodiaea grandiflora	*Brodiaea coronaria*
Cacalia	*Emilia*
Caladium × *hortulanum*	*Caladium bicolor*
Calliopsis	*Coreopsis*
Calonyction aculeatum	*Ipomoea alba*
Campanula vidalii	*Azorina vidalii*
Camptosorus rhizophyllus	*Asplenium rhizophyllum*
Campula pusilla	*Campanula cochleariifolia*
Carex morrowii	*Carex oshimensis*
Carex stricta	*Carex elata*
Celmisia coriacea	*Celmisia semicordata*
Ceterach	*Asplenium*
Chamaenerion	*Epilobium*
Charieis	*Felicia*
Cheiranthus	*Erysimum*
Cheiranthus cheiri	*Erysimum cheiri*
Chelone barbata	*Penstemon barbatus*
Chelone obliqua var. *alba*	*Chelone glabra*
Chionodoxa gigantea	*Chionodoxa luciliae*
Chrysanthemum coccineum	*Tanacetum coccineum*
Chrysanthemum leucanthemum	*Leucanthemum vulgare*
Chrysanthemum maximum	*Leucanthemum* × *superbum*
Chrysanthemum nipponicum	*Nipponanthemum nipponicum*
Chrysanthemum parthenium	*Tanacetum parthenium*
Chrysanthemum tricolor	*Chrysanthemum carinatum*
Chrysanthemum × *superbum*	*Leucanthemum* × *superbum*

Cineraria	*Senecio*
Clarkia	*Godetia*
Cleome spinosa	*Cleome hassleriana*
Coleostephus	*Chrysanthemum*
Coleus	*Solenostemon*
Coleus blumei var. *verschaffeltii*	*Solenostemon scutellarioides*
Collinsia heterophylla	*Collinsia bicolor*
Colocasia antiquorum	*Colocasia esculenta*
Comarum	*Potentilla*
Conoclinium coelestinum	*Eupatorium coelestinum*
Consolida ambigua	*Consolida ajacis*
Convolvulus minor	*Convolvulus tricolor*
Convolvulus purpureus	*Ipomoea purpurea*
Cooperia	*Zephyranthes*
Coronilla cappadocica	*Coronilla orientalis*
Cortaderia argentea	*Cortaderia selloana*
Cosmidium	*Thelesperma*
Crucianella	*Phuopsis*
Cuphea platycentra	*Cuphea ignea*
Curtonus	*Crocosmia*
Dactylorhiza maderensis	*Dactylorhiza foliosa*
Dahlia variabilis	*Dahlia pinnata*
Datura wrightii	*Datura metel*
Datura × *candida*	*Brugmansia* × *candida*
Delphinium consolida	*Consolida ajacis*
Delphinium zalil	*Delphinium semibarbatum*
Dentaria	*Cardamine*
Dianthus caesius	*Dianthus gratianopolitanus*
Didiscus	*Trachymene*
Didiscus coeruleus	*Trachymene coerulea*
Digitalis ambigua	*Digitalis grandiflora*
Dimorphotheca annua	*Dimorphotheca pluvialis*
Dimorphotheca aurantiaca	*Dimorphotheca sinuata*
Diosphaera	*Trachelium*
Diplacus	*Mimulus*
Dipteracanthus	*Ruellia*
Dolichos	*Lablab*
Dolichos lablab	*Lablab purpureus*
Dolichos niger	*Lablab purpureus*
Dolichos purpureus	*Lablab purpureus*
Dondia	*Hacquetia*
Doronicum caucasicum	*Doronicum orientale*
Doronicum cordatum	*Doronicum columnae*
Dorotheanthus littlewoodii	*Dorotheanthus bellidiformis*
Douglasia	*Androsace*
Douglasia	*Vitaliana*
Douglasia vitaliana	*Vitaliana primulifolia*
Dracocephlum	*Physostegia*
Echium fastuosum	*Echium candicans*
Emilia javanica	*Emilia coccinea*
Endymion	*Hyacinthoides*
Ensete ventricosum	*Musa ensete*
Erigeron mucronatus	*Erigeron karvinskianus*
Erodium petraeum	*Erodium foetidum*
Erpetion	*Viola*
Erythraea	*Centaurium*
Eucharidium	*Clarkia*
Eunomia	*Aethionema*
Eupatorium urticifolium	*Eupatorium rugosum*
Euphorbia variegata	*Euphorbia marginata*
Eustoma russellianum	*Eustoma grandiflorum*
Evolvulus nuttallianus	*Evolvulus pilosus*
Filipendula hexapetala	*Filipendula vulgaris*
Freesia alba	*Freesia lactea*
Galeobdolon	*Lamium*
Gentiana excisa	*Gentiana acaulis*
Geranium armenun	*Geranium psilostemon*
Geum coccineum	*Geum chiloense*
Geum quellyon	*Geum chiloense*
Gladiolus byzantinus	*Gladiolus communis* ssp. *byzantinus*
Glandularia	*Verbena*
Godetia	*Clarkia*
Gunnera brasiliensis	*Gunnera manicata*
Hardenbergia monophylla	*Hardenbergia violacea*
Helianthus orgyalis	*Helianthus salicifolius*
Helichrysum angustifolium	*Helichrysum italicum* ssp. *serotinum*
Helichrysum bracteatum	*Bracteantha bracteata*
Helichrysum petiolatum	*Helichrysum petiolare*
Heliosperma alpestris	*Silene alpestris*
Heliotropium peruvianum	*Heliotopium arborescens*
Heliperum manglesii	*Rhodanthe manglesii*
Helipterum	*Rhodanthe*
Helleborus corsicus	*Helleborus argutifolius*
Hemerocallis flava	*Hemerocallis lilioasphodelus*
Hesperoyucca	*Yucca*
Heterotropa	*Asarum*
Hexastylis	*Asarum*
Hibiscus	*Abelmoschus*
Hibiscus eetveldeanus	*Hibiscus acetosella*
Homoglossum	*Gladiolus*
Hosta albomarginata	*Hosta sieboldii*
Houstonia	*Hedyotis*
Houstonia caerulea	*Hedyotis caerulea*

Hutchinsia	*Pritzelago*
Hutchinsia alpina	*Pritzelago alpina*
Hymenocallis calathina	*Hymenocallis narcissiflora*
Iliamna	*Sphaeralcea*
Ipomoea bona-nox	*Ipomoea alba*
Ipomoea imperialis	*Ipomoea nil*
Ipomoea tuberosa	*Merremia tuberosa*
Iris cuprea	*Iris fulva*
Iris kaempferi	*Iris ensata*
Ismene	*Hymenocallis*
Isotoma	*Solenopsis*
Ixiolirion montanum	*Ixiolirion tataricum*
Ixiolirion pallasii	*Ixiolirion tataricum*
Jasione perennis	*Jasione laevis*
Kochia	*Bassia*
Kochia trichophylla	*Bassia scoparia f. trichophylla*
Lamiastrum	*Lamium*
Lamiastrum galeobdolon	*Lamium galeobdolon*
Lantana delicatissima	*Lantana montividensis*
Lapeirousia	*Anomatheca*
Laurentia	*Solenopsis*
Laurentia axillaris	*Solenopsis axillaris*
Lavatera cachemirica	*Lavatera cachemiriana*
Layia elegans	*Layia platyglossa*
Leopolida comosa	*Muscari comosum*
Lepachys	*Ratibida*
Leucanthemum lacustre × L. maximum	*Leucanthemum × superbum*
Liatris callilepis	*Liatris spicata*
Ligularia clivorum	*Ligularia dentata*
Ligularia tussilaginea	*Farfugium japonicum*
Lilium szovitsianum	*Lilium monadelphum*
Liriope platyphylla	*Liriope muscari*
Lisianthus	*Eustoma*
Lisianthus russellianus	*Eustoma grandiflorum*
Lithospermum	*Lithodora*
Lithospermum diffusum	*Lithodora diffusa*
Lobelia × vedrariensis	*Lobelia × gerardii*
Lonas inodora	*Lonas annua*
Luffa cylindrica	*Luffa aegyptiaca*
Lunaria biennis	*Lunaria annua*
Maianthemum racemosum	*Smilacina racemosa*
Majorana onites	*Origanum onites*
Malvastrum coccineum	*Sphaeralcea coccinea*
Mandevilla suaveolens	*Mandevilla laxa*
Martynia	*Proboscidea*
Matricaria parthenium	*Tanacetum parthenium*
Matteuccia pennsylvanica	*Matteuccia struthiopteris*
Matthiola bicornis	*Matthiola longipetala ssp. bicornis*
Maurandya	*Asarina*
Megasea	*Bergenia*
Mentha rotundifolia	*Mentha suaveolens*
Mertensia virginica	*Mertensia pulmonarioides*
Mesembryanthemum	*Dorotheanthus*
Mesembryanthemum criniflorum	*Dorotheanthus bellidiformis*
Mina	*Ipomoea*
Montbretia	*Crocosmia*
Moraea spathacea	*Moraea spathulata*
Musa uranoscopus	*Musa coccinea*
Muscarimia	*Muscari*
Myosotidium nobile	*Myosotidium hortensia*
Myosotis palustris	*Myosotis scorpiodes*
Myosotis rupicola	*Myosotis alpestris*
Narcissus campernelli	*Narcissus × odorus*
Narcissus minimus	*Narcissus asturiensis*
Narcissus pseudonarcissus	*Narcissus obvallaris*
Nemophila insignis	*Nemophila menziesii*
Nepeta macrantha	*Nepeta sibirica*
Nicotiana affinis	*Nicotiana alata*
Nierembergia hippomanica	*Nierembergia caerulea*
Nierembergia rivularis	*Nierembergia repens*
Nolana grandiflora	*Nolana paradoxa*
Nomocharis mairei	*Nomocharis pardanthina*
Oenothera linearis	*Oenothera fruticosa*
Oenothera missouriensis	*Oenothera macrocarpa*
Operculina tuberosa	*Merremia tuberosa*
Orchis	*Dactylorhiza*
Orchis elata	*Dactylorhiza elata*
Orchis maderensis	*Dactylorhiza foliosa*
Ornithogalum oligophyllum	*Ornithogalum balansae*
Orphanidesia	*Epigaea*
Oxypetalum	*Tweedia*
Papaver nudicaule	*Papaver croceum*
Passiflora sanguinea	*Passiflora vitifolia*
Peltiphyllum	*Darmera*
Pennisetum compressum	*Pennisetum alopecuroides*
Pennisetum rueppellii	*Pennisetum setaceum*
Pentas carnea	*Pentas lanceolata*
Petunia	*Calibrachoa*
Peucedanum	*Anethum*
Peucedanum graveolens	*Anethum graveolens*
Phanerophlebia	*Cyrtomium*
Pharbitis	*Ipomoea*

Pharbitis purpurea	*Ipomoea purpurea*
Phormium colensoi	*Phormium cookianum*
Phyllitis	*Asplenium*
Phyllitis scolopendrium	*Asplenium scolopendrium*
Plagiorhegma	*Jeffersonia*
Plagiorhegma dubia	*Jeffersonia dubia*
Polyanthus × *polyantha*	*Primula Polyanthus Group*
Polygonatum canaliculatum	*Polygonatum biflorum*
Polygonum	*Persicaria*
Polygonum affine	*Persicaria affinis*
Polygonum bistorta	*Persicaria bistorta*
Polygonum campanulatum	*Persicaria capitata*
Polygonum orientale	*Persicaria bistorta*
Porteranthus	*Gillenia*
Potentilla verna	*Potentilla neumaniana*
Poterium	*Sanguisorba*
Prunella × *webbiana*	*Prunella grandiflora*
Pseudofumaria	*Corydalis*
Pyrethrum	*Tanacetum*
Pyrethrum coccineum	*Tanacetum coccineum*
Pyrethrum parthenium	*Tanacetum parthenium*
Pyrethrum roseum	*Tanacetum coccineum*
Quamoclit pennata	*Ipomoea quamoclit*
Ramonda pyrenaica	*Ramonda myconi*
Rehmannia angulata	*Rehmannia elata*
Rhazya	*Amsonia*
Rhodochiton volubilis	*Rhodochiton astrosanguineus*
Roscoea procera	*Roscoea purpurea*
Rudbeckia	*Ratibida*
Rudbeckia gloriosa	*Rudbeckia hirta*
Salvia horminum	*Salvia viridis*
Santolina incana	*Santolina chamaecyparissus*
Saxifraga spathularis × *S. umbrosa*	*Saxifraga* × *urbium*
Scabiosa rumelica	*Knautia macedonica*
Scadoxus multiflorus	*Haemanthus multiflorus*
Schizocodon	*Shortia*
Scilla	*Hyacinthoides*
Scilla hispanica	*Hyacinthoides hispanica*
Scilla italica	*Hyacinthoides italica*
Scilla non-scripta	*Hyacinthoides non-scripta*
Scilla pratensis	*Scilla litardierei*
Scilla tubergeniana	*Scilla mischtschenkoana*
Scolopendrium vulgare	*Asplenium scolopendrium*
Setcreasea purpurea	*Tradescantia pallida* 'Purpurea'
Sedum 'Herbstfreude'	*Sedum* × 'Autumn Joy'
Sedum reflexum	*Sedum rupestre*
Senecio maritimus	*Senecio cineraria*
Senecio przewalskii	*Ligularis przewalskii*
Sisyrinchium angustifolium	*Sisyrinchium graminoides*
Sisyrinchium bermudiana	*Sisyrinchium graminoides*
Sisyrinchium birameum	*Sisyrinchium graminoides*
Spiraea aruncus	*Aruncus dioicus*
Spiraea ulmaria	*Filipendula ulmaria*
Stachys betonica	*Stachys officinalis*
Stachys grandiflora	*Stachys macrantha*
Stachys lanata	*Stachys byzantina*
Stachys olympica	*Stachys byzantina*
Statice	*Limonium*
Sutera cordata	*Bacopa*
Thermopsis caroliniana	*Thermopsis villosa*
Tovara	*Persicaria*
Tradescantia × *andersoniana*	*Tradescantia* Andersoniana Group
Tricyrtis stolonifera	*Tricyrtis formosana*
Tritoma	*Kniphofia*
Tritonia hyalina	*Tritonia crocata*
Tritonia rosea	*Tritonia disticha* ssp. *rubroluscens*
Trollius ledebourii	*Trollius chinensis*
Tropaeolum aduncum	*Tropaeolum peregrinum*
Tropaeolum canariense	*Tropaeolum peregrinum*
Tulipa aitchisonii	*Tulipa clusiana*
Tulipa bakeri	*Tulipa saxatilis*
Tulipa dasystemon	*Tulipa tarda*
Tulipa polychroma	*Tulipa biflora*
Tunica	*Petrorhagia*
Tunica saxifraga	*Petrorhagia saxifraga*
Veltheimia capensis	*Veltheimia bracteata*
Venidium	*Arctotis*
Verbena chamaedrifolia	*Verbena peruviana*
Verbena patagonica	*Verbena bonariensis*
Verbena venosa	*Verbena rigida*
Veronica teucrium	*Veronica austriaca* ssp. *teucrium*
Veronica virginica	*Veronicastrum virginicum*
Vigna	*Phaseolus*
Viscaria	*Lychnis*
Wahlenbergia saxicola	*Wahlenbergia congesta*
Waldsteinia trifolia	*Waldsteinia ternata*
Watsonia beatricis	*Watsonia pillansii*
Watsonia pyramidata	*Watsonia borbonica*
× *Venidioarctotis*	*Arctotis*

Index to Part One

For specific plants, see alphabetical listing by botanic name in Parts 2–4. *For common names,* see Common to Botanic Names, pp. 504–522. *For botanic synonyms,* see pp. 523–526.

2 1982 01500 1914

MAR 17 2004

Acknowledgements

I WOULD LIKE TO EXPRESS my sincere gratitude to Storey Publishing for giving me their total support and encouragement from start to finish. In all our dealings they have demonstrated an extraordinary level of personal caring and integrity.

Within their organization I owe the biggest thanks to Gwen Steege, my editor, friend, sounding-board, and cheerleader. This book has really been a collaborative effort between the two of us, with her enthusiasm and creativity fueling my ideas and interests. Having her on my team has been a real blessing. Special thanks, too, go to Deborah Balmuth, for the support she's given me in the past, and for making it possible for so many of the staff to devote so much of their time to this project. I am also deeply grateful to Barbara Ellis for her meticulous scrutiny of the manuscript for inaccuracies and omissions, as well as for sharing her impressive knowledge and love of plants; and to the book's designer, Kent Lew, whose intelligent planning and creative problem solving have resulted in such a beautiful and user-friendly book.

I'd also like to thank those people with whom I had less personal contact, but whose hard work I appreciate no less: Publisher Janet Harris, for all of her support and creative input; Cindy McFarland, for art direction and achieving the difficult task of keeping the production on schedule; Jennifer Jepson Smith, for the countless hours she spent laying out the pages and making what must have seemed like a never-ending stream of changes; Elayne Sears for her helpful illustrations; Andrea Dodge and Sarah Guare for editorial assistance; Mark Raymaker for helping me with my frustrating computer struggles; Chris Meyer for her extraordinary skill and good humor in typing the manuscript and setting up the charts; and last but not least, Doris Troy for the heroic task of copyediting and proofreading.

Enormous thanks also go to Jerry Pavia, Global Book Publishing, Henry W. Art, the International Bloembollen Centrum, Joseph DeSciose, Stacey Cyrus, Saxon Holt, and Valleybrook International Ventures for the many beautiful color photographs that so enrich the book; Elizabeth Stell for her expertise in selecting and reviewing the photographs; Ilona Sherratt for her help with both the illustrations and locating photographs; Laurie Figary for keeping all the photo details straight; and Greg Van Houten for his superb color work.